CLASSIFICATION OF DEVELOPMENTAL LANGUAGE DISORDERS

Theoretical Issues and Clinical Implications

CLASSIFICATION OF DEVELOPMENTAL LANGUAGE DISORDERS

Theoretical Issues and Clinical Implications

Edited by

Ludo Verhoeven
Hans van Balkom
University of Nijmegen

LEA   LAWRENCE ERLBAUM ASSOCIATES, PUBLISHERS
2004   Mahwah, New Jersey   London

MW

Lawrence Erlbaum Associates, Inc., Publishers
10 Industrial Avenue
Mahwah, New Jersey 07430

Library of Congress Cataloging-in-Publication Data

Classification of developmental language disorders : theoretical issues and clinical
implications / edited by Ludo Verhoeven, Hans van Balkom.
    p. cm.
  Includes bibliographical references and index.
  ISBN 0-8058-4122-9 (alk. paper) — ISBN 0-8058-4123-7 (pbk. : alk. paper)
  1. Language disorders in children. 2. Child development deviations. 3. Classification.
4. Psycholinguistics. 5. Child psychopathology. I. Verhoeven, Ludo Th. II. Balkom,
Hans van.

RJ496.L35 C56 2004
618.92'855—dc21   2002032529
                                                                        CIP

Books published by Lawrence Erlbaum Associates are printed on acid-free paper,
and their bindings are chosen for strength and durability.

Printed in the United States of America
10 9 8 7 6 5 4 3 2 1

09/22/03

Contents

Preface

The present volume was meticulously prepared. It all began with a workshop organized by the present editors, which had the purpose of clarifying the notion of developmental language disorder. Much depends on transparent, broadly supported classification in this field. At issue is not only the decision making in individual cases of intervention, but also the allocation of educational and remedial funds as well as political decision making at large in matters of human health care. Still the editors eschewed fast, shortcut solutions. The ultimate, firm base for classification of developmental language impairment, they argued, should be theoretical. To mark this intention, they organized the workshop at the Max Planck Institute for Psycholinguistics, an institution entirely dedicated to the study of language processing in normal adults and children. This indeed set the tone for deep, theoretical discussions among the galaxy of participants. In their turn, these discussions provided the springboard for the joint production of the present volume.

What is it that the theoretical modeling of language use may have to contribute? In my opinion, it is threefold at least. The first thing experimental psycholinguists provide is ever-refined componential models of language processing. They partition the processes underlying speech understanding and production in components that are supposedly functioning in relative autonomy. This notion is, of course, as old as the work of Wernicke and the diagram makers, but there has been substantial progress since then. We have gained substantial insight into the linguistic representations that are computed in going from a communicative intention via grammatical and phonological encoding down to planning and executing syllabic gestures—or inversely up from the auditory signal via acoustic-phonetic processing, phonological, syntactic, and semantic parsing to the pragmatic interpretation of a perceived utterance. We have a reasonable understanding now of the linguistic entities computed by the various processing components involved. We have also observed substantial progress in the computational modeling of these processes. Sophisticated computational accounts are now available for a range of core components in the processing architecture. Probably most advanced are the computational models of word perception and word production. They concern the lexical aspects of processing components. Increasingly, the integration of lexical processing in the larger context of grammatical encoding and decoding are being modeled. This computational modeling could not have become so successful without the crucial expansion of the empirical base that has emerged over the last three decades or so. The traditional diagrams were almost exclusively based on the symptomatology of language disorders and spontaneous derailments in slips of the tongue, misperceptions, and tip-of-the-tongue states. Current modeling, however, is largely based on chronometric studies of normal speech production and perception. Chronometry has become a refined experimental art with two major branches: the reaction time paradigm and the electrophysiological event-related response paradigm.

The second contribution experimental psycholinguistics is beginning to provide is insight in the neural architecture that subserves the componential processing. Increasingly, current processing models are being used to define the experimental and control tasks in linguistic brain imaging experiments. It is not acceptable anymore to be psycholinguistically naive in designing one's brain imaging experiments. One should *not* study the locus of semantic encoding by means of a verb generation task or the locus of phonological encoding by means of a rhyming task. Rather, experimental and control tasks used in neuroimaging should be based on natural computations performed by the theoretically distinguished processing components. Applying current processing models to brain imaging research is beginning to provide us with subtle insights that are of direct relevance to the issue of classification. For instance, there is increasing evidence now that the retrieval of lexical/phonological codes for speech production involves Wernicke's area, but that the use of these codes in the rapid syllabification of a word involves the left posterior inferior frontal lobe. Current processing models require that crucial distinction to be made (i.e., between retrieving and implementing a phonological code). Hence, one should wonder which of these two mechanisms is involved in different kinds of developmental speech pathology. More generally, the combined use of modeling and brain imaging can help focus the search for underlying causes of language and speech pathology.

The third contribution that is in the offing concerns plasticity or, if you want, adaptability. The occasion for my optimism here is one outcome of the now completed aphasiology project jointly carried out by the Max Planck Institute and Nijmegen University. It is the so-called *adaptation theory* developed by Kolk and Heeschen. Its basic claim is that the aphasiological phenotype you observe combines symptoms of disorder with symptoms of adaptation. One critical phenomenon studied was the *telegraphic speech* of Broca's patients. Numerous theories have tried to explain this phenomenon in terms of particular disorders, such as loss of syntax, loss of access to function words, disordered phonological encoding, and so on. However, the project revealed that elliptical speech is a register that the patient can or cannot use dependent on the requirements of the communicative situation. The elliptical register is one that we all utilize occasionally. It is syntactically as rule governed as our full register, but it capitalizes heavily on shared knowledge and contextual informality. The real disorder in Broca's aphasia is not the elliptical register. In fact that is precisely what is least disturbed in the speech of these patients. The disorder is rather the patient's inability to keep retrieved word syntax and semantics active long enough to integrate it successfully in the incrementally developing sentence context. Using the preexisting elliptical register is just one way to cope with this problem. There are fewer words to be retrieved and less syntax to be kept in abeyance when generating an elliptic utterance. This can indeed be an efficient way to adapt to the ever-threatening speech need. Not all patients adapt this way, and no patient adapts this way all the time.

From the perspective of current theoretical modeling, a first step in accounting for the adaptability of the system is the multiple route idea. The normal, undisturbed system often has multiple ways to realize the same linguistic goal. We have both a full and an elliptical register at hand for the grammatical encoding of our communicative intentions; both can be and have been modeled computationally. It depends on the context of discourse which register we are going to use. If the production system gets lesioned, the resulting pragmatic pressure may shift the balance of functionality between registers. Another well-known multiple-route system is reading. Experienced readers can go straight to lexical semantics and syntax from recognizing the visual word, but they can also take an alternative, phonological route by running grapheme-to-phoneme conversion on individual letters. I believe the present consensus is that usually both routes are run in parallel, but that the direct route tends to win out because it is the faster one. Again, in pathology, the relative functionality may shift between these routes, and there will be adaptation. A more re-

cent contribution to the multiple-route approach is Baayen and Schreuder's modeling of morphological parsing. Understanding a morphologically complex word such as *nationalize* probably involves both a direct,
whole-word route and a morpheme-by-morpheme parsing route. The balance between them depends on word frequency, and learning is shifting
the balance more and more toward the direct whole-word route. In pathology, one or the other route may become less functional dependent on
the type of pathology. The multiple-route perspective may become quite
useful in developing a well-founded classification system for language
pathologies.

However, multiple-route explanations are probably not enough to account for all adaptation in language pathology. Especially for developmental disorders, one must consider the possibility that partially or entirely new systems develop for coping with the initial disorder. An
apparent negative example is the behavioral pathology that can emerge
from the overstressed parent–child interaction as a consequence of even
relatively mild developmental language disorders. Here the adaptation is
worse than the pathology. On the positive side, there is increasing evidence that new brain regions are going to be involved in language processing in response to early brain injury. It is of great theoretical significance to find out to what extent these alternative regions process linguistic
information in the same way as the regions they replace. It is also of great
practical significance: How should an alternative brain region be trained
to approximately compute the relevant linguistic representation?

Any useful and theoretically sophisticated classification of developmental language disorders has to include, on the one hand, symptoms of
disorder that relate to affected processing components and their cerebral
implementation. On the other hand, it includes symptoms of adaptation
that relate to preexisting multiple processing routes or to more far-going
behavioral and neural reorganizations. There is still a long way to go here,
but the present volume provides important and diverse theoretical en-
lightenment for clinical practice in the classification of developmental language impairment.

—*Willem J. M. Levelt,*
Nijmegen, Max Planck Institute for Psycholinguistics

INTRODUCTION

Developmental Language Disorders: Classification, Assessment, and Intervention

Ludo Verhoeven
Hans van Balkom
University of Nijmegen

Language development is characterized by a great deal of variation. For a substantial group of children, there is such a delay in the development of speech and language that we speak of developmental language disorders (DLDs). Exclusionary conditions are often used to identify this population for which a broad variety of labels has been used in the past, including developmental dysphasia/aphasia and more recently specific language impairment (SLI; see Leonard, 1987; Stark & Tallal, 1981). Children with SLIs are diagnosed as exhibiting a significant deficit in the production and/or comprehension of language that cannot be explained by general cognitive impairment, sensorimotor deficits, frank neurological disorder, psychiatric diagnosis, or a general lack of exposure to language (cf. Leonard, 1998). The prevalence of SLI in children varies between 5% and 10% of the population (see Law et al., 1998). The heterogeneity of the language profiles of the children is considerable. To successfully prevent and/or remediate DLDs in children, a better understanding of its underlying nature is mandatory. Within the framework of the International Classification of Impairment, Disabilities, and Handicaps (ICIDH), the assessment of DLDs does not yet involve indication criteria for differentiating requests for help within a certain type of intervention, but concerns primarily the decision of whether special care is needed and, if so, which type is most appropriate (cf. Rispens & Van Yperen, 1997). Its selective function relates to either the decision of whether special education is required or extra facilities in an integrated care setting. It should be noted that an observed impairment is in itself not sufficient as a criterion; educational constraints should also be present. The procedure usually comprises four phases. The first phase involves the intake by means of questionnaires, an educational report, available dossiers, and screening instruments. In the next phase, an independent and multidisciplinary referrals board formulates a hypothesis on the basis of the available information. The third phase may include an assessment that, insofar as possible, is made on the basis of previously determined standardized measuring instruments. In the assessment, the notion of educational constraint is also worked out in more detail by looking for disabilities related to information acquisition, information processing, independent functioning, or social functioning in regular education. In the last phase, the assessment board formulates and issues a decision regarding a child's eligibility for special care.

Previous surveys of the indication criteria for DLD brought to light that the procedures were standardized to a rather limited degree (Rapin, 1996; Rapin & Allen, 1983, 1988). Furthermore, there was much doubt as to the validity of placement decisions (Aram, Morris, & Hall, 1993; Dunn, Flax, Sliwinsky, & Aram, 1996). This raises the question as to how a more standardized DLD assessment can be realized. The focus of this book is thus on the classification of subtypes of DLDs. An attempt is made to clarify the vague and often inconsistent definitions used to characterize DLDs from the perspective of assessment and (early) intervention. The child's development of language and communication is defined as a result of the interaction between his or her biological potential, the health conditions of the child, and the support available from the environment, family, therapeutic setting, and educational facilities. A wide range of theoretical stances on DLDs is reviewed. Moreover, competing hypotheses regarding the nature of SLI are tested in the domains of auditory perception, speech output, lexicon, morphology, syntax, and pragmatics. In addition to the issue of classification, the present volume addresses the prevention and remediation efforts relevant to DLDs. The question is how children's linguistic environment can be restructured in such a way that children at risk will not have years of failure and can develop important adaptive skills in the domains of self-care, social interaction, learning, and problem solving.

COMMUNICATION PROBLEMS AND SCHOOLING

DLDs often lead to communication problems at an early age. In the interaction with parents and peer groups, these problems manifest themselves as a limited functioning of preverbal and prelinguistic behavioral aspects such as eye contact, listening attitude, imitation, and symbol development. van Balkom (1991), for example, found that communication patterns in families with DLD children and in families with 3-year-old children with normal language acquisition differed with regard to a number of characteristic aspects. Whereas parents normally determine the course of conversation in such a way that there is a balance between verbal and nonverbal acts, DLD children proved to determine the course of conversation through nonverbal acts. Moreover, it turned out that the verbal capacity of DLD children, as well as the quality and quantity of motherese, decreased sharply over a period of 18 months. The fact that the first years in the life of the child are considered a critical period for language acquisition stresses the importance of early diagnosis and intervention (cf. Paul, 2000). In many cases, young children whose language development is at risk require ambulatory guidance or care in an institutional environment. In addition to programs aimed at strengthening the communication between parent and child and the language supply in the child's environment, specific language training programs may be implemented at an early age (see Ellis-Weismer, 2000).

For the majority of children with severe DLDs, regular education is virtually inaccessible (cf. Haynes & Naidoo, 1991). These children have difficulties understanding class instruction. In complex listening situations in and outside class characterized by much background noise, poor acoustics, and competitive speech at a normal language level, these children often prove unable to understand the linguistic and educational content. In addition, children with language problems prove to have great difficulty with learning to communicate efficiently in a classroom situation. The additional planning time that these children need in the communication process and the limited possibilities for monitoring their own speech place considerable constraints on their linguistic functioning in regular education. Their speech and language problems threaten these children's development already at a preschool age. Generally, their problems are diagnosed late or too late, and the time lapse between diagnosis and intervention is therefore relatively large.

An adapted environment with facilities for supportive communication for children with severe DLDs is therefore urgently required at an early stage (cf. Conti-Ramsden & Botting, 2000; Whitehurst & Fischel, 1996). The communicative situation needs to be adapted by regulating the volume of the speech signal and speed of speech input; providing support in the form of written text, manual signs, or graphic symbols; regulating the allocation of turns in dialogues and group discussions; adjusting the language level; providing feedback during communication; and allowing children to experience effective communication. In addition, training programs that stimulate specific aspects of the communicative competence of children may be implemented. In this respect, one may think of programs for verbal communication in conversations (Camarata, 1993), auditory training programs to improve discrimination skills and encoding/decoding skills (cf. Almost & Rosenbaum, 1998; Tallal et al., 1996), and programs to promote the understanding and production of sentence patterns (cf. Fey, Cleave, Long, & Hughes, 1993) and monologues (Warren, 1999). Furthermore, the children may be taught compensatory strategies so they can learn to cope with permanent communicative limitations. Intervention programs can be implemented directly, for example, by a speech therapist or remedial educationalist or indirectly through parents or teachers. On the basis of an extensive review, Law, Boyle, Harris, Harkness, and Nye (1998, 2000) came to the conclusion that a direct approach is particularly effective in the remediation of speech problems, whereas an indirect approach proves particularly effective in interventions aimed at lexical and language comprehension problems. A combination of the two approaches proved most suitable for monitoring expressive language problems. It should also be mentioned that severe DLDs can impede the transfer of knowledge and skills in other school subjects such as reading, spelling, counting, arithmetic, and factual subjects (cf. Beitchman et al., 1996a; Tallal, Allard, Miller, & Curtis, 1997). In secondary education, the children often have great difficulties learning foreign languages. All this requires a special instructional approach in class aimed at strengthening receptive and productive textual skills, developing language–thought relations, increasing school vocabulary, and teaching meta-cognitive and/or compensatory strategies.

Finally, it is of great importance that children with severe DLDs receive intensive socioemotional guidance when learning to communicate with people in their environment (see Rice, Sell, & Halley, 1991). In practice, the occurrence of DLDs often proves to coincide with withdrawal behavior and problematic social functioning in class. Contacts with the peer group become more difficult, which may lead to aggression and frustration (Beitchman et al., 1996b). As a result, children with speech and/or language problems run the risk of becoming socially isolated. They no longer have an open, uninhibited attitude toward the environment, and they develop a fear of failure with regard to school learning. This impedes both their functioning in groups and their processing of the information on offer.

COMPETITIVE HYPOTHESES ABOUT DLD

Regarding the cause of severe DLDs, various hypotheses have been formulated in the literature. In describing DLD, distinctions can be made among etiological, neurobiological, psychological, and behavioral aspects. At the etiological level, diverse factors may play a role such as missing genes, chromosomal aberrations, toxemia of pregnancy, congenital brain damage, and sensory impairments possibly accompanied by a limited language supply. Comparing the prevalence of DLD among identical and fraternal twins, Bishop (1994) concluded that hereditary factors play a role here: The degree of correspondence of DLD was 48% among fraternal twins and 89% among identical twins. Gilger's (1995) findings also show that 20% to 50% of the people with DLD have a first-degree relative with a similar diagnosis. At the neurobiological level, a distinction can be made between dysfunctions as a result of insufficient development of neurons, abnormal migration of neurons, partial brain damage, abnormal regulation of neural conduction, and weak links between nerve cells (see Fitch, Miller, & Tallal, 1997). By means of techniques such as event-related potentials (ERPs; see Leppänen et al., chap. 4, this volume, for further information), it has been established that the language function is located in specific parts of the brain and impairments as such can be localized to some extent (cf. Obrzut & Hynd, 1991). At the psychological level, problems can be described in terms of different aspects of speech and language processing (cf. Gillam, Cowan, & Marler, 1998). At the behavioral level, such matters as intelligibility and language production problems can be described.

Even when etiological and neurobiological factors are left out of consideration, there are still large differences in the interpretative possibilities as far as DLD is concerned. In this connection, it is important to regard language development and language learning problems as dynamic processes and the individual as a self-organizing cognitive system that is constantly interacting with its environment (cf. Van Geert, chap. 12, this volume). On the basis of this dynamic system theory, it may be stated that language can be regarded as a complex system in which stable situations relieve each other. An important point of departure here is that cognitive processes are time- and context-bound. The time-bound aspect of language impairment plays a role, for example, in explaining complex syndromes such as the Landau–Kleffner syndrome, a language impairment in which, after an initial normal development, a deterioration of language skills occurs accompanied by latent or manifest epileptic symptoms (cf. Deonna, 2000; van Dongen, 1988).

An important question is to what extent language proficiency can be regarded as a monolithic phenomenon. The procedure of selective diagnostics worked out within the framework of assessment for financing individual pupils does not do justice to the nature of the impairment of children with severe DLDs. The purpose of the desired diagnostic research into this target group is to confirm the formulated hypothesis that pupil X will benefit from DLD education. This may involve an assessment on the basis of that pupil's score on a previously specified test for DLDs below the two standard deviations of the average. This procedure is based on the assumption that language proficiency is unidimensional. However, there is little evidence that supports this assumption (see Karmiloff-Smith, 1997). Current language-user models are based on a modular structure in which each separate module is regarded as an independently operating specialistic mechanism (see Levy, 1996). Processing language is supposed to be staged and feedforward (Levelt, 1989; Levelt, Roelofs, & Meyer, 1999). Language production starts with conceptual preparation processes during which thoughts and intentions are being ordered. Thoughts and intentions are transformed into sentences through syntactic encoding, lexical selection, morphological and phonological encoding, phonetic encoding, and articulation. In a similar vein, the following processes are involved in language comprehension: recognition of speech sounds, sentence parsing, word recognition, and sentence interpretation. There is empirical evidence that these staged language processes play a role in language problems and that the functions of certain processes are interdependent (Bishop, 1997; Leonard, 1998).

However, in the light of this modular conception of language, one should also take account of the explanatory potential of connectionist models based on neural networks that use input to generate a language system that does not necessarily have a modular structure (Elman et al., 1996; Harley, 1993). The traditional approach to language development assumes that two explanatory mechanisms are required: a memory bank for both frequent and irregular components of language, and a rule-governed system that allocates the correct allomorphs of those components (cf. Pinker & Prince, 1988). Here overgeneralizations are regarded as interference between two mechanisms. In contrast, connectionist models are based on just one mechanism in the shape of a single-layer neural network that uses input to produce associations between components of language. As Plunkett (1995) pointed out, the two approaches are not at variance with each other; the language system may be regarded as a symbolic processing system that elaborates on a connectionist implementation of the neurological system.

On the basis of an exhaustive review, Bishop (1992) concluded that, with regard to SLI, at least six different hypotheses can be formulated: (a) impairment in the processes that are involved in converting underlying linguistic knowledge into a speech signal, (b) impairment of auditory perception that influences the course of language acquisition, (c) impairment of the specialized linguistic mechanisms that have evolved to handle language processing, (d) generalized deficit in conceptual development affecting language development, (e) abnormal language learning strategies including hypothesis-testing procedures, and (f) limitations in the speed and capacity of the information-processing system. As Bishop pointed out, research on the underlying nature of language impairment is still in its infancy. An extensive program of fundamental research is therefore required to test the hypotheses just mentioned.

The question of whether language learning problems are specifically language based or more generically related to information processing can be seen as highly relevant. Information processing involves subaspects such as selective and nonselective attention, discrimination, memory, encoding/decoding of information, and temporal processing. One possible hypothesis is that language learning problems have their origins in problems with information processing—more particularly, in problems with processing sequential information (cf. Kushnir & Blake, 1996; Tallal, 1990). In the light of this hypothesis, a recent pilot study of children with DLD examined the relationship between simultaneous and sequential processing abilities in two modalities: verbal and nonverbal (Verhoeven, van Daal, & van Weerdenburg, 1999). The results represented next reveal that there are indeed significant relations between simultaneous and sequential abilities in children with DLD.

	Nonverbal	
	Simultaneous	*Sequential*
Verbal		
Simultaneous	.44**	.31
Sequential	.30	.42**

All this shows that there are several competitive hypotheses that try to explain the occurrence of serious speech/language problems.

In clinical practice, some people have tried to get a grip on the classification of DLD. A classic categorization is the one advanced by Rapin and Allen (1983, 1988; Rapin, 1996), which is based on a classification into three main categories: mixed receptive/expressive impairments, expressive impairments, and higher order processing disorders. In the first category, a distinction is made between verbal auditory agnosia (central auditory processing problems) and phonological-syntactic deficits. In both cases, the impairment leads to problems with both language comprehension and language production. The second category includes verbal dyspraxia, which usually involves problems with fluency, and speech-motor deficits, which make the organizational aspects of speech problematic. The third category includes lexical deficits, especially those accompanied by word-finding problems and semantic-pragmatic deficits, which limit conversation skills in particular.

A number of psychometric studies have been conducted with regard to the empirical foundations of current classifications of serious speech and language problems. Korkman and Hakkinen-Rihu (1994) performed a wide range of tests involving 42 children with DLD. Factor analysis resulted in empirical evidence for four subgroups: global comprehension/ production problems, verbal dyspraxia, specific language comprehension problems, and word-finding deficits. In addition to congruence, Aram, Morris, and Hall (1993) found differences in the classification of DLD-based clinical and psychometric criteria. They mentioned divergent clinical perspectives and a limited availability of measuring instruments as the main causes of the difference in interpretations. Conti-Ramsden, Crutchley, and Botting (1997) studied the psychometric and clinical classifications of 242 seven-year-old children with DLD. They identified six subgroups: (a) problems with morphology and syntax, (b) phonological problems in combination with expressive deficits, (c) problems with articulation, phonology, and language expression, (d) the same problems as mentioned under c, but now with a greater spread over other measured skills, (e) problems with articulation, phonology, morphology, and syntax, and (f) semantic-pragmatic problems. According to the researchers in question, these clusters approximate the categorization proposed by Rapin and Allen.

Current developments in connectionist modeling and the extension of principles of dynamical systems have resulted in a new perspective on language development labeled *emergentism* (see Evans, 2001; van Geert, chap. 14, this volume). According to such perspective, language is seen as a dynamic system that can be represented as a distribution of probabilistic information. Language development is then defined as a result of an integration of multiple acoustic, linguistic, social, and communicative cues within the context of communicative interaction. DLDs are then taken to be the result of the interaction between the intrinsic properties of the child's processing system and the distributional properties of the language input. Instability of language skills is taken to be an important characteristic of children with DLD.

DEMARCATION PROBLEMS

Severe DLDs can be of a monofactorial or multifactorial nature (for a discussion on this topic, see Leonard, 1998). A distinction can be made between more central impairments characterized by a loss on several components and peripheral impairments such as defective articulation. Furthermore, DLDs may be limited to verbal language use or accompanied by related disabilities in written language use (cf. Stockhouse, 2000). All this may have far-reaching consequences for the nature of the associated educational constraints.

After DLD has been hypothesized, audiological, logopaedic, and neurological examinations may be performed to ascertain whether a child has a speech and/or language deficit (see e.g., Paul, 1992). Usually a number of tests along with samples of natural speech are performed to examine the possible loss on the speech/language components that need to be differentiated. However, the multifactorial organization of speech and language problems makes it impossible to use simple selective diagnostics for the demarcation of DLD. A broad range of diagnostic techniques is needed to trace language problems in natural and (semi)structured situations. These should cover the following linguistic aspects: speech production, speech perception, morpho-syntactic knowledge, lexical/semantic knowledge, and pragmatic skills. In addition, to test exclusionary conditions, the (non)verbal learning capacity, hearing skills, and psychopathology of the children should also be examined. In practice, language problems are usually of a complex nature. This means that losses on several aspects are often found. As a result, demarcation of DLD is not simply a question of calculating the standard deviations from the average. Clinical judgments are needed to validate the test outcomes.

Demarcation of language learning problems of immigrant children is even more problematic. The obvious choice is to assess these children's language skills in the second language *and* the mother tongue. One important question involves the role of cognition in learning a second language compared with learning the mother tongue. A recent study examined to what extent basic cognitive mechanisms in learning rules and making verbal associations correspond with the developmental levels of first- and second-language learners at age 4 (Verhoeven & Vermeer, 1999). The results show a high correlation between language proficiency and learning rules for first-language learners and between language proficiency and associative learning for second-language learners. All this may have implications for the interpretation of the language development level of immigrant children.

Special attention should also be given to the demarcation of language problems of children with multiple handicaps. Complex interaction between various development domains, such as cognitive impairment behavioral and personality impairments, psychiatric problems (e.g., autistic children), and somatic disorders, makes the demarcation of language learning problems quite controversial. In this respect, one should first think of children with borderline intelligence and mentally retarded children. Research in the field of intelligence measurement brought to light that there is considerable correlation between verbal and nonverbal intelligence (Sternberg, 1990). It is generally assumed that skills underlying the development of cognition in the broad sense also play a role in the acquisition of verbal and written language proficiency. Here two aspects are important: the children's learning capacity (cf. Rosenberg & Abbeduto, 1993; Warren & Abbeduto, 1992) and their memory capacity (Kushnir & Blake, 1996). However, such a relation does not necessarily imply that the structure of the language acquisition process differs in children with divergent intelligence profiles (see Cole, Dale, & Mills, 1992). Generally speaking, the diagnosis of SLI involves children with normal intelligence and extremely weak language skills. Particularly the tenability of the discrepancy hypothesis is at issue here. It is often maintained that it is merely a question of specific language learning problems when a child's verbal skills remain one standard deviation below its nonverbal skills. However, contrary to the assumption underlying this hypothesis, the scaling of children's learning capacities and learning speeds proves to be more continuous than discrete (see Aram, Morris, & Hall, 1992; Fletcher, 1992).

BOTTLENECKS IN THE ASSESSMENT

To arrive at a valid identification of developmental language disorders, the goal of assessment must be explicitly focused on classification. The standards of expectations for comparing language performance and determining differences must also be clear. In local practice, professionals rely on the expertise they have acquired through the years to come to a well-founded diagnosis of DLDs. Observation and registration procedures play an important role here. A problem is that descriptive diagnostics are often lacking, which makes an objective comparison of assessments in peer reviews difficult (see e.g., Hux, Morris-Friehe, & Sanger, 1993). Little research data are available that might guide an assessment of children with DLD based on a wide range of instruments measuring distinctive aspects of DLDs. In other words, there is limited systematic research to indicate how divergent profiles of DLDs across various age groups should be interpreted (see Bishop, chap. 13, this volume). The nonavailability of instruments is another specific problem. It is true that there are quite a number of diagnostic instruments available to establish a child's eligibility for special care. However, the problem is that test analyses show that the reliability and validity of instruments leave much to be desired. Such analyses make clear that reliable and valid instruments are certainly not available for all aspects and age groups (Cole, Schwartz, Notari, Dale, & Mills, 1995; Conti-Ramsden, Crutchley, & Botting, 1997).

DLD in young children is extremely difficult to diagnose in practice (cf. Paul, 2000). To determine the extent to which the language development has been retarded or disturbed, a longitudinal screening is required, in which the child's language data are compared with those of normal children in its peer group (see e.g., Conti-Ramsden & Botting, 1999). However, the available tests provide only limited, cross-sectional reference data (Plante & Vance, 1994).

The care provisions for and guidance of older children with DLD have so far received relatively little attention (see Norris, 1995). Specific instruments for measuring the language proficiency of children over 12 are rarely available if at all. The decision that a child should receive special care in advanced education is primarily based on case history data gathered during the previous stages of the child's development.

The assessment of immigrant children is another bottleneck. The fact that only a limited number of diagnostic instruments are available for minority languages makes a valid assessment of this target group extremely difficult. In addition, the demarcation between language problems and cognitive capacities of immigrant children demands necessary attention.

THE PRESENT VOLUME

The chapters in this volume address the classification of DLDs from a variety of perspectives. A multidisciplinary view is presented, combining insights from linguistics, cognitive science, neuropsychology, early intervention, and education. Moreover, an attempt is made to show how theoretical claims about the origin and prevalence of language impairment can be translated into practical implications as regards assessment techniques and interventions. The present volume is organized into three parts.

Part I focuses on the etiological background of SLI. The chapters in this part go into questions regarding the underlying nature of SLI. The parallels and differences between acquired and developmental language disorders, on the one hand, and between oral versus written language disorders, on the other, are extensively discussed. Moreover, research into neuropsychological, information-processing, and environmental factors in SLI are reviewed. Botting and Conti-Ramsden's chapter (chap. 1, this volume) reveals what language profiles of children with SLI may look like, and the chapters that follow describe how such profiles fit into a theoretical explanatory framework that can be seen as a starting point for typological questions.

Part II focuses on the nature of SLI. Starting from a modular conception of language processing, a distinction is made between subclasses of SLI: speech output disorders, central auditory processing disorders, problems with lexical access, morphological-syntactic disorders, and pragmatic impairment. For each of these prototypes, an attempt is made to specify its underlying nature and show how problems can be divided into component parts. In many cases, the possible interrelatedness of SLI subtypes in clinical practice is also highlighted.

Part III steps back to present more explicitly clinical perspectives on SLI. Diagnostic dilemmas are extensively discussed. On the basis of research and clinical evidence so far, Bishop proposes four clinical subtypes of SLI—verbal dyspraxia, auditory agnosia, phonological-syntactic impairment, and pragmatic impairment—which may be taken as a starting point for diagnostic screening. In this part, the dynamics of language disorders in the course of time is also discussed. Furthermore, early assessment and intervention are highlighted, whereas the teachability of SLI is also reviewed from a meta-analytic perspective.

PART I: ETIOLOGY

Part I focuses on the etiology of SLI. In the opening chapter, Botting and Conti-Ramsden (chap. 1) present the basic characteristics of children with SLI. They describe the extent to which SLI subclasses can be distinguished on the basis of both clinical observation and empirical research. In the next chapter, children with focal brain injury and children with SLI are compared by Reilly, Weckerly, and Wulfeck (chap. 2). They empirically explore issues of plasticity and development in complementary studies of morphology and syntax with the two groups of children. They then discuss the degree to which early brain localization for various aspects of language function appears to exist and the extent to which the brain can flexibly respond to early injury. In chapter 3, Been and Zwarts present language disorders across modalities. They show how the behavioral level of language disorders in the spoken and written domain can be related to the neurophysiological level in models of interacting neuronal populations. For this purpose, a model of discrimination during speech perception is used and tested in the context of developmental dyslexia. In chapter 4, Leppänen, Lyytinen, Choudhury, and Benasich review the neuropsychological aspects of language impairment. They describe how neurophysiological measures may increase the validity of language assessment procedures. The authors demonstrate how ERPs can reveal electrocortical differences for the subtypes of language disorders. In addition, they demonstrate the relevance of hemodynamic imaging tools measuring bloodflow and metabolism to localize functions and identify hemispheric differences in children with language disorders. With the assessment of ERPs, they provide evidence of pathological changes in the time course of language processing and possible compensatory routes under conditions of SLI. In chapter 5, Gillam and Hoffman provide an information-processing account of DLDs. The authors argue that attention, perception, memory, reasoning, and language learning in children with SLI are all affected by general limitations in activation rates, decay rates, and/or organization of various sorts of mental representations. In chapter 6, Goorhuis-Brouwer, Coster, Nakken, and Spelberg highlight the importance of environmental factors in the assessment of language disorders. On the basis of empirical studies, they show that children with language disorders are at risk for behavioral problems. There is also considerable variation in the degree of uncertainty among parents on how to raise children with SLI. Uncertainty among caregivers may lead to more demanding and less spontaneous communication with the child, which may then lead to greater internalizing behavior. Early assessment of parental attitudes and behavior may be necessary to prevent behavioral problems in children with SLI.

PART II: TYPOLOGY

Part II focuses on a typology of SLI. Six alternative hypotheses with respect to the underlying nature of SLI are subsequently addressed. To start with, Maassen (chap. 7) provides evidence of speech output disorders in children with SLI. He shows how phonological encoding and speech motor processes can be the cause of developmental apraxia of speech. Data are presented to compare this type of disorder with speech delay and dysarthria. The extent to which phonological processes, phonetic encoding, and motor deficits contribute to a particular speech output disorder is also shown to be decisive for not only classification, but also remediation. Katz and Tillery (chap. 8) discuss the occurrence of auditory processing problems in SLI. They show that such problems can occur in many ways and are often associated with other disorders. To clarify the nature of central auditory processing disorders, they present a category system that helps differentiate the various subtypes of central auditory processing disorders. Leonard and Deevy (chap. 9) consider the lexical abilities of children with DLDs. The authors show that children with SLI are late to acquire early words and slow to add new words (verbs in particular). The lexical networks in children with SLI turn out to be relatively sparse: The default activation levels and links among entries are weak. The children's lexical difficulties with verbs appear to be accompanied by syntactic problems with verbs. Ravid, Levie, and Ben-Zvi (chap. 10) examine the role of morphological factors in the language of Hebrew-speaking children with language disorders. By demonstrating differences between children with and without language problems in their knowledge of the structure and semantics of Hebrew morphology, they argue that SLI involves a deviant linguistic system. de Jong (chap. 11) shows that children with SLI not only have problems with inflectional morphology, but also such syntactic phenomena as word order, argument structure, and verb agreement. He then provides an overview of those linguistic theories that appear to explain such syntactic impairment. Alternative hypotheses regarding the syntactic nature of SLI are then tested with empirical data from young children. Finally, van Balkom and Verhoeven (chap. 12) provide evidence for pragmatic disorders in children with SLI. *Pragmatic impairment* is defined as problems making connections among linguistic forms, context, and discourse. In an analysis of the communicative behavior of children with SLI, the problems that children have with the identification of contingencies and cohesive relationships among utterances, speech acts, and propositional knowledge are illustrated.

PART III: ASSESSMENT AND INTERVENTION

Part III focuses on the clinical implications of recent research results. The question here is how new insights into the nature of DLDs can be translated into guidelines for assessment and remediation. Bishop (chap. 13) opens this part of the book with a discussion of the diagnostic dilemmas associated with SLI. According to Bishop, there is little agreement on the question of how to subclassify SLI. In general, the classifications tend to be based on a linguistic characterization of the language impairment, as shown in Part II of the present volume. On the basis of clinical and empirical studies, at least four subclasses can be distinguished: severe impairment of auditory comprehension, receptive-expressive impairments affecting phonology and syntax, severe expressive speech impairment, and pragmatic impairment. Although paradigmatic cases of each subtype can be identified, the boundaries among the different subtypes are not always clear-cut. It is therefore argued that the classificatory systems should be improved with the inclusion of information on etiology and behavioral data. van Geert (chap. 14) presents a dynamic view of DLDs and explores the possibility of SLI being the result of self-organizing processes combining conditions in a nonlinear manner. He also discusses the possibility of a dynamic approach to diagnostic categorization. de Ridder and van der Stege (chap. 15) show how early assessment of DLDs can be enabled. They describe the results of a large-scale empirical study to validate a screening instrument for young children at risk for DLDs in The Netherlands. The screening involved 10 moments of reported communicative competence among more than 10,000 children ages 0 to 3 years. The final three chapters address the remediation of language disorders. Warren and Yoder (chap. 16) examine what is known about the precursors to language disorders and opportunities for early intervention. They then present a developmental model of early communication and language intervention. They also raise some critical issues to be addressed to minimize the long-term effects of early impairment. Verhoeven and Segers (chap. 17) summarize research on the benefits of speech manipulation in intervention programs for children with SLI. This idea starts with the underlying hypothesis that many children with DLDs have difficulty discriminating rapidly successive phonetic elements and nonspeech sound stimuli. In the literature, it is claimed that the slowing of the speech signal and amplification of fast transitional elements may possibly help children overcome early auditory problems. In this chapter, a review of such adaptive auditory training studies is presented. Finally, Law (chap. 18) discusses the teachability of language-impaired children. He presents the results of a meta-analysis of intervention studies carried out over the past two decades. The results show relatively high mean effect sizes for the treatment of expressive and receptive language disorders. The effects of intervention for speech deficits appear to be lower, although this may be due to considerable variation in the use of direct versus indirect treatment. The more far-reaching practical implications of these findings are discussed in closing.

REFERENCES

Almost, D., & Rosenbaum, P. (1998). Effectiveness of speech intervention for phonological disorders: A randomized controlled trial. *Developmental Medical Child Neurology, 40,* 319–352.

Aram, D. M., Morris, R., & Hall, N. E. (1992). The validity of discrepancy criteria for identifying children with developmental language disorders. *Journal of Learning Disabilities, 25,* 549–554.

Aram, D. M., Morris, R., & Hall, N. E. (1993). Clinical and research congruence in identifying children with specific language impairment. *Journal of Speech and Hearing Research, 36,* 580–591.

Beitchman, J. H., Wilson, B., Browlie, E. B., Walters, H., Inglis, A., & Lancee, W. (1996a). Long-term consistency in speech/language profiles: I. Developmental and academic outcomes. *Journal of the American Academy of Child and Adolescent Psychiatry, 35,* 804–814.

Beitchman, J. H., Wilson, B., Browlie, E. B., Walters, H., Inglis, A., & Lancee, W. (1996b). Long-term consistency in speech/language profiles: II. Behavioural, emotional and social outcomes. *Journal of the American Academy of Child and Adolescent Psychiatry, 35,* 815–825.

Bishop, D. (1992). The underlying nature of specific language impairment. *Journal of Child Language Psychology & Psychiatry, 33,* 3–66.

Bishop, D. (1994). Is specific language impairment a valid diagnostic category? Genetic and psycholinguistic evidence. *Phil. Trans. R. Soc. London Bulletin, 346,* 105–111.

Bishop, D. V. (1997). *Uncommon understanding: Development and disorders of language comprehension in children.* Cambridge, England: Psychology Press.

Camarata, S. (1993). The application of naturalistic conversation training to speech production in children with speech disabilities. *Journal of Applied Behavioral Analysis, 26,* 173–182.

Cole, K. N., Dale, P. S., & Mills, P. E. (1992). Stability of the intelligence quotient relation: Is discrepancy modeling based on a myth? *American Journal on Mental Retardation, 97,* 131–145.

Cole, K. N., Schwartz, I. S., Notari, A. R., Dale, Ph. S., & Mills, P. E. (1995). Examination of the stability of two methods of defining specific language impairment. *Applied Psycholinguistics, 16*, 103–123.

Conti-Ramsden, G., & Botting, N. (1999). Classification of children with specific language impairment: Longitudinal considerations. *Journal of Speech, Language and Hearing Research, 42*, 1195–1204.

Conti-Ramsden, G., & Botting, N. (2000). Educational placements for children with specific language impairment. In D. V. M. Bishop & L. B. Leonard (Eds.), *Speech and language impairment in children: Causes, characteristics, interventions and outcome* (pp. 211–226). Hove, England: Psychology Press.

Conti-Ramsden, G., Crutchley, A., & Botting, N. (1997). The extent to which psychometric tests differentiate subgroups of children with specific language impairment. *Journal of Speech, Language and Hearing Research, 40*, 765–777.

Deonna, Th. (2000). Acquired epileptic aphasia of Landau-Kleffner syndrome: From childhood to adulthood. In D. V. M. Bishop & L. B. Leonard (Eds.), *Speech and language impairment in children: Causes, characteristics, interventions and outcome* (pp. 261–272). Hove, England: Psychology Press.

Dunn, M., Flax, J., Sliwinsky, M., & Aram, D. (1996). The use of spontaneous language measures of criteria for identifying children with specific language impairment: An attempt to reconcile clinical and research incongruence. *Journal of Speech and Hearing Disorders, 39*, 643–654.

Ellis-Weismer, S. (2000). Intervention for children with developmental language delay. In D. V. M. Bishop & L. B. Leonard (Eds.), *Speech and language impairment in children: Causes, characteristics, interventions and outcome* (pp. 157–176). Hove, England: Psychology Press.

Elman, J. L., Bates, E., Johnson, M., Karmiloff-Smith, A., Parisi, D., & Plunkett, K. (1996). *Rethinking innateness: A connectionist perspective on development.* Cambridge, MA: MIT Press.

Evans, J. L. (2001). An emergent account of language impairments in children with specific language impairment: Implications for assessment and intervention. *Journal of Communication Disorders, 34*, 39–54.

Fey, M. E., Cleave, P. L., Long, S. H., & Hughes, D. L. (1993). Two approaches to the facilitation of grammar in children with language impairment: An experimental evaluation. *Journal of Speech and Hearing Research, 36*, 141–157.

Fitch, R. H., Miller, S., & Tallal, P. (1997). Neurobiology of speech perception. *Annual Review Neuroscience, 20*, 331–353.

Fletcher, J. M. (1992). The validity of distinguishing children with language and learning disabilities according to discrepancies with IQ. *Journal of Learning Disabilities, 25*(9), 546–548.

Gilger, J. W. (1995). Behavioral genetics: Concepts for research and practice in language development. *Journal of Speech, Language and Hearing Research, 38*, 1126–1142.

Gillam, R. B., Cowan, N., & Marler, J. A. (1998). Information processing by school-age children with specific language impairment: Evidence from a modality effect paradigm. *Journal of Speech, Language and Hearing Research, 41*, 913–926.

Harley, T. A. (1993). Connectionist approaches to language disorders. *Aphasiology, 7*, 221–249.

Haynes, C., & Naidoo, S. (1991). *Children with specific speech and language impairment.* Oxford: Blackwell Scientific Publications.

Hux, K., Morris-Friehe, M., & Sanger, D. D. (1993). Language sample practices: A survey of nine states. *Language, Speech and Hearing Services in Schools, 24*, 84–91.

Karmiloff-Smith, A. (1997). *Beyond modularity: A developmental perspective on cognitive science.* Cambridge, MA: MIT Press.

Korkman, M., & Hakkinen-Rihu, P. (1994). A new classification of developmental language disorders. *Brain and Language, 47*, 96–116.

Kushnir, C. C., & Blake, J. (1996). The nature of the cognitive deficit in specific language impairment. *First Language, 16*, 21–40.

Law, J., Boyle, J., Harris, F., Harkness, A., & Nye, C. (1998). *Screening for speech and language delay: A systematic review of the literature.* Southampton: NCCHTA.

Law, J., Boyle, J., Harris, F., Harkness, A., & Nye, C. (2000). The relationship between the natural history and prevalence of primary speech and language delays: Findings from a systematic review of the literature. *International Journal of Language and Communication Disorders, 35*(2), 165–188.

Leonard, L. B. (1987). Is specific language impairment a useful construct? In S. Rosenberg (Ed.), *Advances in applied psycholinguistics: Disorders of first language development* (Vol. I, pp. 1–39). Cambridge, NY: Cambridge University Press.

Leonard, L. B. (1998). *Children with specific language impairment.* Cambridge, MA: MIT Press.

Levelt, W. J. M. (1989). *Speaking: From intention to articulation.* London: Bradford.

Levelt, W. J. M., Roelofs, A., & Meyer, A. S. (1999). A theory of lexical access in speech production. *Behavioral and Brain Sciences, 22,* 1–75.

Levy, Y. (1996). Modularity of language reconsidered. *Brain and Language, 55,* 240–263.

Norris, J. (1995). Expanding language norms for school-age children and adolescents: Is it pragmatic? *Language, Speech and Hearing Services in Schools, 26,* 342–352.

Obrzut, J. E., & Hynd, G. W. (1991). *Neuropsychological foundations of learning disabilities.* New York: Academic Press.

Paul, R. (1992). Language and speech disorders. In S. R. Hooper, G. W. Hynd, & R. E. Mattison (Eds.), *Developmental disorders: Diagnostic criteria and clinical assessment* (pp. 209–238). Hillsdale, NJ: Lawrence Erlbaum Associates.

Paul, R. (2000). Predicting outcomes of early expressive language delay: Ethical implications. In D. V. M. Bishop & L. B. Leonard (Eds.), *Speech and language impairment in children: Causes, characteristics, interventions and outcome* (pp. 195–210). Hove, England: Psychology Press.

Pinker, S., & Prince, A. (1988). On language and connectionism: Analysis of a parallel distributed processing model of language acquisition. *Cognition, 28,* 73–193.

Plante, E., & Vance, R. (1994). Selection of preschool language tests: A data-based approach. *Language, Speech and Hearing Services in Schools, 25,* 15–24.

Plunkett, K. (1995). Connectionist approaches to language acquisition. In P. Fletcher & B. MacWinney (Eds.), *The handbook of child language* (pp. 36–72). London: Basil Blackwell.

Rapin, I. (1996). Practitioner review. Developmental language disorders: A clinical update. *Journal of Child Psychology & Psychiatry, 37,* 643–655.

Rapin, I., & Allen, D. A. (1983). Developmental language disorders: Nosologic considerations. In U. Kirk (Ed.), *Neuropsychology of language, reading, and spelling* (pp. 155–184). New York: Academic Press.

Rapin, I., & Allen, D. A. (1988). Syndromes in developmental dysphasia and adult dysphasia. In F. Plum (Ed.), *Language, communication, and the brain* (pp. 57–75). New York: Raven.

Rice, M. L., Sell, M. A., & Hadley, P. A. (1991). Social interactions of speech- and language-impaired children. *Journal of Speech and Hearing Research, 34,* 1299–1307.

Rispens, J., & Van Yperen, T. A. (1997). How specific are specific developmental disorders? The relevance of the concept of specific developmental disorders for the classification of childhood developmental disorders. *Journal of Child Psychology and Psychiatry, 38,* 351–363.

Rosenberg, S., & Abbeduto, L. (1993). *Language and communication in mental retardation.* Hillsdale, NJ: Lawrence Erlbaum Associates.

Stark, R. E., & Tallal, P. (1981). Selection of children with specific language deficits. *Journal of Speech and Hearing Disorders, 46,* 114–122.

Sternberg, R. (1990). *Metaphors of mind: Conceptions of the nature of intelligence.* New York: Cambridge University Press.

Stockhouse, J. (2000). Barriers to literacy development in children with speech and language difficulties. In D. V. M. Bishop & L. B. Leonard (Eds.), *Speech and language impairment in children: Causes, characteristics, interventions and outcome* (pp. 73–98). Hove, England: Psychology Press.

Tallal, P. (1990). Fine-grained discrimination deficits in language learning impaired children are specific neither to the auditory modality nor to speech perception. *Journal of Speech, Language and Hearing Research, 33,* 616–617.

Tallal, P., Allard, L., Miller, S., & Curtis, S. (1997). Academic outcomes of language impaired children. In C. Hulme & M. Snowling (Eds.), *Dyslexia: Biology, cognition, and intervention* (pp. 167–181). London: Whurr.

Tallal, P., Miller, A. L., Bedi, G., Byma, G., Wang, X., Nagarajan, S., Schreiner, C., Jenkins, W., & Merzenich, M. (1996). Language comprehension in language learning impaired children improved with acoustically modified speech. *Science, 271,* 81–84.

van Balkom, H. (1991). *The communication of language impaired children.* Amsterdam: Swets & Zeitlinger.

van Dongen, H. R. (1988). *Clinical aspects of acquired aphasia and dysarthria in childhood.* Doctoral dissertation, Erasmus Universiteit, Rotterdam.

Verhoeven, L., van Daal, J., & van Weerdenburg, M. (1999, March 21–25). *In search of (sub)classification of developmental language disorders: Cognitive factors and language impairment.* Poster presented at the Third International Aphasic Conference, York.

Verhoeven, L., & Vermeer, A. (1999). Cognitive factors in early first and second language proficiency. *AILA Review, 16,* 97–110.

Warren, S. (1999, January 5–6). *Early intervention for children with SLI: Promises and pitfalls.* Paper presented at the International Workshop on Classification of Language Disorders, Max Planck Instituut Nijmegen.

Warren, S., & Abbeduto, L. (1992). The relation of communication and language disorders to mental retardation. *American Journal on Mental Retardation, 97,* 125–130.

Whitehurst, G. J., & Fischel, J. E. (1996). Practitioner review: Early developmental language delay: What, if anything, should the clinician do about it? *Journal of Child Psychology and Psychiatry, 35,* 613–648.

I

ETIOLOGY

Characteristics of Children With Specific Language Impairment

Nicola Botting
Gina Conti-Ramsden
University of Manchester

The identification and classification of a clinical population such as children with specific language impairment (SLI) is universally recognized as a continuing challenge for clinicians and researchers alike (Bishop, 1997; Leonard, 1998). SLI is not a homogeneous disorder, but a term currently used to describe children with a range of profiles, all of which include marked language difficulties in the context of normal cognitive abilities. It represents a pattern of impairment where no other identifiable cause for communication difficulties is present. Thus, SLI works on an exclusionary basis, in which children with autism, general learning disability, physical or neurological damage (such as cleft palate, cerebral palsy, or head injury) are not included in the categorization. Despite that SLI has been studied and treated in some form or another for over 100 years, positive definitions have been hard to agree on (Aram, 1991; Bishop, 1994; Johnston, 1991; Leonard, 1987, 1991). This is due in part to the wide spectrum of different impairments often made up of combinations of deficits in particular areas of communication (phonology, morphology, syntax, semantics, pragmatics). The profiles of children with SLI are also dynamic over time. That is, children who are identified as having a certain pattern of difficulties may improve in some areas and not in others, giving a different profile from year to year.

In England, since the 1960s, the education system has allowed special status to children with SLI who have persistent problems. A wide range of models of intervention is current, from full-time special school placement to the provision of part-time support in mainstream schools. Language units located in mainstream schools and catering specifically for children with SLI are of particular interest as they appear to be the most common provision made for children with SLI.

Language units or language resource units are language-based classrooms for children with SLI. To be placed in a language unit, children generally have to fulfill a number of criteria. Most units in England require children to have statements of special educational needs (or to be undergoing assessment for one), which detail their difficulties and the professional input they require, including intensive speech and language treatment. Across England, specific criteria for entry vary from educational authority to educational authority. Unit criteria generally require that the child's language disorder be the child's primary problem. Unit criteria also usually specify that the child would find it difficult to cope in mainstream education even with support and thus needs placement in a structured small-group setting. There are currently about 250 units in England.

Much of this chapter refers to a nationwide study based at Manchester (led by the second author) and funded by the Nuffield Foundation. The project recognized the need at this stage in the development of specialist education for children with SLI to map out the characteristics of children attending language units and examine different profiles of difficulties presented by these children. Using a randomly selected sample, half of the Year 2 (7-year-old) children then attending language units in England were recruited into the study. Two hundred and forty-two children were seen at 7 years of age and again at 8 years of age. The socioeconomic backgrounds of the children participating in the study resembled the distribution found in the general population as indicated by the income per household (Office of National Statistics, 1998).

CHARACTERISTICS OF CHILDREN WITH SLI

Nonverbal Abilities

Two hundred and thirty-three children were able to complete the nonverbal assessment: 206 children scored above the 15.9 percentile (above minus one standard deviation), 24 children performed between 2.5 and 15.9 percentiles (between minus 1 and minus 2 standard deviations below the mean), and only 3 children performed below the 2.5 percentile suggesting these 3 children had more global delays. Table 1.1 presents the overall mean, standard deviations, and 95% confidence intervals for all the tests, including the Raven's Matrices nonverbal scores. Overall, the sample had a mean Raven's score of 61.9 percentiles.

TABLE 1.1
Assessment Means, Standard Deviations,
and 95% Confidence Intervals for the Entire Sample

	Test for Reception of Grammar	BAS Naming Vocabulary	Goldman–Fristoe Test of Articulation	Renfrew Bus Story	Raven's Matrices
Mean (SD)	20.0 (19.9)	32.1 (25.6)	41.9 (33.6)	18.5 (19.1)	61.9 (29.5)
95% CI	17.8 to 23.4	30.2 to 37.2	37.3 to 46.3	16.5 to 21.8	58.0 to 66.0

Note. SD = standard deviation; CI = confidence interval.

Discrepancy Between Verbal and Nonverbal Ability

Traditional discrepancy criteria for SLI suggest that there should be a discrepancy between language age and both chronological age and mental age in children with SLI (Aram, Morris, & Hall, 1992; Stark & Tallal, 1981; Tallal, 1988). Data from our cohort study were available for 233 children (9 children had missing Raven's scores as described in the prior section). Fifty-eight children (25%) had both nonverbal abilities and all language test scores within the normal range (above one standard deviation below the mean or 15.9 percentiles). Of these 58 children, 83% (48 children) had nonverbal-language scores at least 40 percentiles above language scores, thus fitting the traditional discrepancy criteria for SLI. Ten children (17%) did not meet the 40 percentile discrepancy criteria between verbal and nonverbal scores. We followed 9 of those 10 children the year after and found that 5 had fully integrated into regular mainstream education, suggesting that this small group of children recovered after intervention.

This left 175 children who had at least one test of language below 15.9 percentiles. Of these 175 children, 85% (n = 148) had nonverbal cognitive scores within one standard deviation of the mean (above 15.9 percentiles), thus these 148 children met the traditional discrepancy criteria for SLI. Fourteen percent of the children (n = 24) had nonverbal cognitive abilities between one and two standard deviations below the mean (between 15.9 and 2.6 percentiles) making it difficult to apply the discrepancy criteria. Both IQ and language test scores were between one and two standard deviations below the mean for these children. Finally, only three children scored below two standard deviations below the mean (2.5 percentiles or less) in the nonverbal test and also did poorly in the language tests. It was thought that these children were more globally delayed.

In summary, most of the children attending language units (196 out of 233 or 84%) met the traditional discrepancy criteria for SLI (for further details, see Conti-Ramsden & Botting, 1999). The results of the present investigation clarify that language units in England cater for children with SLI who have normal cognitive abilities. The percentage of children with global delays in language units was extremely small (1%).

In Search of Language Impairment Profiles

The data used to establish subgroups of children came from two sources: results from standardized tests and information from a teacher/speech-language pathologist interview. We thought it would be particularly useful to see how much information could be obtained from a single assessment session, such as would be feasible in a clinical setting. This ruled out lengthy procedures involving a number of sessions with each child or the collection of spontaneous language samples. We chose breadth rather than depth of assessment and selected the following test battery:

1. Test for Reception of Grammar (TROG; Bishop, 1982). This oral comprehension test presents children with four pictures while the examiner reads a sentence. Each child is asked to pick the picture that illustrates the sentence. These items begin very simply, with four distinct objects and one word read out, and progress to complex grammar structures (e.g., "The cat the cow chases is black"). Items are organized into blocks of four grammatically related sentences. The child must answer all four correctly to pass the block. After five consecutive blocks have been failed, the test is discontinued. The number of blocks passed is then noted and transformed into age-adjusted percentile ranges (e.g., 5th–10th percentile). For ease of statistical comparison, in the present study, these ranges have been transformed further into midpoint percentiles for that range (e.g., 5th–10th percentile becomes 7.5th percentile).

2. Three Subtests of the British Ability Scales (BAS; Elliot, 1983).

Number skills. Children are presented with picture cues and asked to perform calculations. These range in complexity and include counting, finding similarities, simple addition, subtraction, multiplication and division, matching figures to groups of objects, and tests of concepts. Responses are scored as correct or incorrect, and the test is discontinued once the child has answered five questions incorrectly. The number of correct answers is summed and a percentile for age recorded.

Naming vocabulary. Children are asked to name a series of pictures of everyday objects. Responses are scored as correct or incorrect, and testing is discontinued after the child has named five items incorrectly. The number of correct answers is summed and a percentile for age recorded.

Word reading. Children are presented with a list of single words and asked to read them out loud. This assessment measures only single-word sight reading and is not designed to assess reading comprehension or fluency. Testing is discontinued after 10 incorrect attempts. The total number of correctly read words is summed and transformed into a percentile for age.

3. *Goldman–Fristoe Test of Articulation* (Goldman & Fristoe, 1986). Again children are asked to name a series of pictures of everyday items. Children

may be given clues about the object's name, but not about pronunciation. Responses are scored as correctly or incorrectly pronounced. The number of errors is totaled and a percentile score for age and gender recorded. In this study, three allowances were made for all children to account for regional variation. These were the use of /v/ in "feather" (Plate 20), and of /f/ in "bath" (Plate 23) and "thumb" (Plate 24).

4. *The Bus Story Expressive Language Test* (Renfrew, 1991). In this assessment, the examiner tells the child a short story about a bus while the child looks through a book of pictures illustrating the story. The child must then retell the story as accurately as possible using only the pictures as cues. Stories are audiotaped, transcribed, and scored for the amount of correct information given. Two points are given for information central to the story and one point for peripheral details. The total information score is then compared to age-relevant population norms, and a centile range is assigned. In this study, ranges were transformed into midpoint percentiles as for the TROG assessment.

In addition, the following test was administered to allow for comparison of nonverbal abilities across subgroups (once established):

5. *Raven's Matrices* (Raven, 1986). This nonverbal cognition test presents the child with a series of patterns from which a piece is missing. The child is instructed to look very hard at the pattern and select (from six alternative pieces printed below the pattern) the one and only piece that can complete the pattern. The test is split into three sets of 12 patterns each. Each set begins with more simple and progresses to more complex patterns. The child's responses are noted and afterward scored as correct or incorrect. The total score is then compared to age-relevant population norms and a percentile range is assigned. These ranges were again transformed into midpoint percentiles as for the TROG assessment.

As detailed earlier, some tests provide exact percentiles for age (British Ability Scale subtests and Goldman Fristoe Test of Articulation), whereas others provide only a percentile range for age (TROG, Bus Story, and Raven's Matrices).

Six Profiles of Difficulties

Initial visual, qualitative inspection of combinations of test results suggest six natural groups in the data. A cluster analysis procedure was used to identify six robust clusters, and this number was also found to produce the best statistical results (see Anderberg, 1973, for more details about

cluster analysis). In this context, *robust* was defined as the presence of significant differences between clusters on all included variables. The same
procedure was repeated at Time 2 when the children were 8 years of age.
Figure 1.1 presents the details of Time 1 and Time 2 clusters. Tables 1.2
and 1.3 show the mean percentiles and 95% confidence intervals for Time
1 and Time 2 clusters.

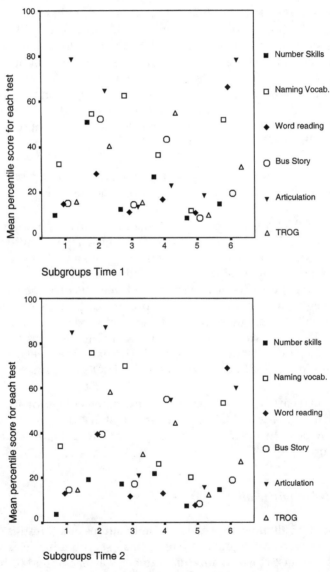

FIG. 1.1.   Description of the tests used in the assessment battery.

TABLE 1.2
Cluster Percentile Means and 95% Confidence Intervals for Time 1

Cluster Group	Test for Reception of Grammar	BAS Number Skills	BAS Naming Vocabulary	BAS Word Reading	Goldman–Fristoe Test of Articulation	Renfrew Bus Story
1 (n = 52)	15.6	9.9	32.4	14.8	78.9	15.2
	11.8 to 19.5	7.3 to 12.6	25.8 to 39.0	11.3 to 18.3	74.2 to 83.6	11.7 to 18.7
2 (n = 16)	40.0	50.9	54.7	28.2	64.9	52.3
	27.8 to 52.2	36.9 to 65.0	45.7 to 63.6	20.2 to 36.2	52.8 to 77.0	41.2 to 63.4
3 (n = 29)	15.1	12.7	62.7	11.3	14.1	14.6
	10.3 to 19.9	7.4 to 18.1	57.5 to 67.8	6.3 to 16.3	8.9 to 19.2	8.2 to 20.9
4 (n = 23)	54.7	26.8	36.6	16.8	23.1	43.3
	47.0 to 62.3	18.0 to 34.5	27.3 to 45.8	9.9 to 23.8	15.1 to 31.1	34.8 to 51.7
5 (n = 84)	9.4	8.6	11.7	11.2	19.0	8.7
	7.2 to 11.5	6.2 to 10.9	9.6 to 13.8	8.3 to 14.2	15.7 to 22.3	6.9 to 10.5
6 (n = 25)	30.8	14.9	52.0	66.3	78.4	19.4
	22.7 to 38.8	10.3 to 19.5	42.5 to 61.5	60.0 to 72.6	68.1 to 88.7	13.1 to 25.7

Note. All tests showed a significant variation of mean scores across clusters at $p < .001$.

TABLE 1.3
Cluster Percentile Means and 95% Confidence Intervals
for Time 2 New Cluster Analysis (n = 207 Children)

Cluster Group	Test for Reception of Grammar	BAS Number Skills	BAS Naming Vocabulary	BAS Word Reading	Goldman–Fristoe Test of Articulation	Renfrew Bus Story
1 (n = 30)	13.7	3.5	33.8	12.9	84.0	14.3
	9.2 to 18.2	2.0 to 5.0	26.6 to 41.0	8.0 to 17.9	77.8 to 90.3	8.7 to 19.8
2 (n = 25)	58.0	19.3	75.8	39.4	87.5	39.4
	48.9 to 67.1	12.5 to 26.1	69.3 to 82.5	29.1 to 35.3	79.5 to 95.6	30.5 to 48.3
3 (n = 38)	30.7	17.4	69.7	12.0	21.5	17.7
	15.3 to 32.2	10.5 to 24.4	65.1 to 74.3	8.2 to 15.8	16.4 to 26.6	11.3 to 24.2
4 (n = 19)	44.2	21.8	26.0	12.9	54.8	55.1
	33.4 to 54.8	13.8 to 29.7	18.4 to 33.6	8.2 to 17.5	41.0 to 68.7	45.7 to 64.6
5 (n = 77)	11.7	7.2	20.2	7.7	16.0	8.3
	8.6 to 14.9	5.0 to 9.6	16.6 to 23.8	5.5 to 9.8	12.9 to 19.0	6.4 to 10.3
6 (n = 18)	26.8	14.7	53.2	68.7	60.3	18.8
	16.5 to 37.0	8.6 to 20.9	39.8 to 66.5	60.2 to 77.3	46.0 to 74.6	10.8 to 26.0

Note. All tests were significantly different from each other across clusters at $p < .001$.

Results of this analysis were visually compared to previous classifications of SLI. We found that the characteristics of children in our clusters and those of children described in Rapin and Allen (1987) were quite similar. It was found that five of our six clusters closely matched the subgroups proposed by Rapin and Allen, and a full description of the comparisons are available in Conti-Ramsden, Cruthley, and Botting (1997).

One of the clusters, Cluster 2, had no match with Rapin and Allen's categories and was composed of children who appeared to be performing within the normal range (the children's test scores for language measures were above the 40th percentile and for word reading above the 28th percentile). In addition, Rapin and Allen (1987) had a further subgroup in their categorization system (i.e., children with verbal auditory agnosia). No such children were found in our cohort. Auditory agnosia clinically is no longer considered to fall within SLI (e.g., it is usual for auditory agnosia to be prevalent with seizure disorders). Thus, it is not surprising that we found no such individuals in our cohort of children attending language units. Consequently, there were five common subgroups of children (the terminology in parentheses is that of Rapin and Allen): Cluster 1 (lexical-syntactic deficit syndrome), Cluster 3 (verbal dyspraxia), Cluster 4 (phonologic programming deficit syndrome), Cluster 5 (phonological-syntactic deficit syndrome), and Cluster 6 (semantic-pragmatic deficit syndrome). It is also important to point out that we are not in agreement with Rapin and Allen's labeling of Cluster 3 as verbal dyspraxia. Verbal dyspraxia is considered a motor speech disorder rather than a language disorder, although expressive language scores may well be affected. Our Cluster 3 children had good naming vocabulary, but were poor at all other tests used in the study. Furthermore, we find the labeling of different profiles of SLI as *deficit syndromes* problematic and prefer to describe the subgroups as different profiles of SLI. We now describe the clusters we found in more detail in terms of the profiles of difficulties they presented.

Cluster 1 children have difficulties with comprehension of grammar, word reading, and retelling a story in the context of good phonology and adequate expressive vocabulary. Cluster 3 children have problems with comprehension of grammar, word reading, phonology, and retelling a story in the context of good expressive vocabulary. Cluster 4 children were similar to Cluster 3 children except their scores were better across the tests used, and their expressive vocabulary was not as good as that of Cluster 3 children. Cluster 5 children performed poorly on all the tests used and appeared to have difficulties across all areas of language. Finally, Cluster 6 children had difficulties retelling a story in the context of good phonology, good expressive vocabulary, good word reading, and adequate comprehension of grammar. These children's difficulties were mainly evident at the discourse level when they were required to retell a story.

Stability of Children's Classification

Two types of stability were examined with respect to the clusters. First, do patterns of impairment look the same over time? Second, do children stay with a similar profile or do they move to different profiles over time?

TABLE 1.4
Movement of Children Across Clusters
From Time 1 to Time 2 (n = 201 Children)

Time 1 Clusters	Time 2 Clusters					
	Cluster 1	Cluster 2	Cluster 3	Cluster 4	Cluster 5	Cluster 6
Cluster 1	<u>18</u>	3	4	5	8	3
Cluster 2	—	<u>8</u>	3	4	—	1
Cluster 3	1	—	<u>15</u>	—	10	—
Cluster 4	1	6	4	<u>8</u>	2	1
Cluster 5	9	—	11	2	<u>51</u>	2
Cluster 6	1	8	—	—	1	<u>11</u>

Note. Underlined numbers indicate the Ss that remained in the same cluster (111/201) or 55%.

To examine the stability of the six subgroups across time, the degree of match between the two independent cluster analyses was investigated. There appeared to be a good match between Time 1 and Time 2 clusters for Subgroups 1, 3, 4, 5, and 6 and not a good match for Cluster 2 (see Fig. 1.1). An examination of the means and 95% confidence intervals for Time 1 and Time 2 clusters revealed no statistically significant differences between 5/6 test means for Clusters 1 and 6, 4/6 test means for Cluster 5, and 3/6 test means for Clusters 3 and 4. For Cluster 2, there were significant differences in all the means examined.

The movement of children between clusters is shown in Table 1.4. Cluster data for Time 1 and Time 2 were available for 201 children. Fifty-five percent (111/201) of the children remained in the same clusters, and this proportion is reflected in each cluster considered separately (kappa = 0.43, 95% confidence intervals = 0.34 to 0.51). Consequently, 45% of children moved clusters from Time 1 to Time 2, suggesting relative instability in the children's cluster membership across time.

Movement of Children Across Clusters: Addressing Test–Retest Reliability

As emphasized previously, cluster profiles remained stable across time (i.e., the means of tests for each cluster at Time 2 were not significantly different from Time 1), whereas a substantial number of children moved cluster membership due to individual change in test scores. It is important to address the question of whether this fluidity of cluster membership might be the result of poor test–retest reliability in the measures used. Therefore, we examined the major shifts of group (those moves made by eight or more children) to determine the degree of test score change.

TABLE 1.5
Change of Test Score in Movement Groups

Movement Group (n)	Test of Interest	Minimum Change	Maximum Change	Mean Change (SD)
1 to 5 (8)	GF-Articulation*	–22 percentiles	–66 percentiles	–41 (13) percentiles
3 to 5 (10)	BAS Naming V*	–6 percentiles	–37 percentiles	–24 (12) percentiles
5 to 1 (9)	GF-Articulation*	+23 percentiles	+91 percentiles	+55 (28) percentiles
	BAS Naming V	–2 percentiles	+57 percentiles	+20 (19) percentiles
5 to 3 (11)	BAS Naming V*	+14 percentiles	+67 percentiles	+45 (18) percentiles
6 to 2 (8)	GF-Articulation*	+0 percentiles	+59 percentiles	+9 (21) percentiles
	BAS Naming V	–3 percentiles	+46 percentiles	+18 (19) percentiles
	Bus Story	–20 percentiles	+62 percentiles	+27 (26) percentiles
	TROG	–13 percentiles	+65 percentiles	+20 (24) percentiles

Note.   All children moved in same direction.

Moves in cluster membership are not usually caused by a change in performance on all measures, but rather a significant clinical shift in one or two areas of language skill and secondarily by lesser changes in other assessment scores. Thus, we identified the tests in each movement group that appeared to represent the most change. Table 1.5 lists the mean, minimum, and maximum changes in score on the test(s) identified as the major cause of movement for each cluster. These can be compared with the overall cohort changes presented in Table 1.6.

As can be seen, the moves are substantial and represent real clinical changes in profile, especially compared with whole-cohort changes. In most groups, even the most conservative changes in score are quite large and are all in one direction. This is not so clear for the children moving from Cluster 6 (semantic-pragmatic deficit syndrome) to Cluster 2 (normal group). These data support the argument made previously that Cluster 2 children are difficult to include in a classification of language impairment because their profiles appear normal, on average, on the measures used in this study.

TABLE 1.6
Whole-Cohort Changes on Tests

Test	Minimum Change	Maximum Change	Mean Change (SD)
GF–Articulation	–66 percentiles	+92 percentiles	+3 (26) percentiles
BAS Naming Vocabulary	–60 percentiles	+81 percentiles	+9 (24) percentiles
BAS Word Reading	–41 percentiles	+95 percentiles	–0.5 (12) percentiles
BAS Number Skills	–48 percentiles	+70 percentiles	–2 (12) percentiles
Bus Story	–58 percentiles	+63 percentiles	+3 (17) percentiles
TROG	–40 percentiles	+65 percentiles	+5 (18) percentiles

It is also important to note that the changes that result in cluster membership shifts are not in the same direction for each movement group. For example, those moving from Cluster 1 (lexical-syntactic deficit syndrome) to Cluster 5 (phonological-syntactic deficit syndrome) all show a marked decrease in articulation skill for age, whereas those moving from Cluster 6 (semantic-pragmatic deficit syndrome) to Cluster 2 (normal group) all show an increase in articulation score. First, if score changes were due simply to test–retest reliability difficulties, we would expect to see a random pattern of change (in both directions for each subgroup). If the test showed a systematic positive bias for scores to, say, improve on second testing, one might expect that systematic rise in scores to be reflected across all subgroups in the same increasing direction. As already mentioned, neither of these patterns were the case in data obtained from this study. Instead, strong directional shifts were seen in different subgroups, some all increasing, others all decreasing. Second, the magnitude of the changes observed should be relatively small, assuming that these tests are reliable to some extent, which clinical experience and in some cases reported reliability coefficients suggest they are. In contrast, the changes observed in this study were large. Third, each movement group showed at least one test where all children moved uniformly in a given direction (see Table 1.6)—a pattern not predicted by measurement error.

Unfortunately, not all the tests used report adequate test–retest information (means and *SD* at both time points), making it difficult to determine their reliability boundaries. In addition, numbers of children moving clusters were too small to allow statistical analysis (which may have confirmed that the moves across subgroups were unlikely to be caused by random measurement error). However, it is highly unlikely that any standardized test would have such poor reliability that *all* scores at Time 2 would show these patterns of change from Time 1 by chance or through measurement error. Reported test–retest reliability was available for the BAS number skills test at 0.95. In addition, the Goldman–Fristoe test and the BAS word reading test, which appear to be two major factors in cluster movement at this age, report a 0.95 median agreement for +/- errors in production of words and a 0.97 test–retest reliability coefficient, respectively. It has been pointed out (Wilcox & Morris, 1995) that at certain ages relatively small changes in performance on tests such as the Goldman–Fristoe may lead to large changes in percentile score (i.e., improvement on four or five items may result in 30 to 40 percentile changes). However, this is the nature of standardized tests. The percentile score represents age-related information for the reason that raw scores can be misleading. It may be that, at a certain age, a 4-item change represents a significant clinical improvement, whereas at another age, the same increase in raw performance leads to little change in normalized scores. Consequently, it is possible that relatively small changes in articulation may have shifted children from Cluster 1 (lexical-syntactic deficit syndrome) to Cluster 5 (phonological-syntactic deficit syndrome) and from Cluster 6 (semantic-pragmatic deficit syndrome) to Cluster 2 (normal group). Nonetheless, it needs to be pointed out that cluster analysis compares scores on all the tests used for clustering of which articulation is one, albeit important, factor.

Thus, taking all the prior evidence into consideration, it appears that the majority of movements of children across clusters were due to genuine clinical change in language profile.

CONCLUSIONS AND DISCUSSION

This chapter has found a number of interesting points concerning children with SLI. Most children attending language units in England have normal nonverbal abilities and fit broad discrepancy criteria for SLI. Children with SLI attending language units in England have a variety of difficulties and can be classified into six subgroups of SLI. The picture that emerges around classification is both interesting and complex: Profiles of difficulties in language impairment are stable, although individual children may be moving across subgroups. Why may this be the case?

SLI is not a unitary, static condition, but a dynamic difficulty that evolves with developmental time (Conti-Ramsden & Adams, 1995; Miller, 1996). Thus, it is possible that as signs of SLI change with time for individual children, the relations among those signs retain some predictability, resulting in those signs covarying in a limited number of ways. In the investigations discussed here, a clustering technique was used. The clustering technique assigns children to subgroups taking into consideration the performance of the children on all six measures used in the study. Having said this, two signs or areas of difficulty appeared to be particularly involved in individuals changing across subgroups from one year to the next (i.e., phonology and vocabulary; see Table 1.5). When changes occurred and children moved to a different subgroup, the profiles of such children became similar to the profiles of those children belonging to another subgroup. Consequently, although children moved across subgroups, patterns of difficulties remained stable. For example, children who moved from Cluster 5 (all areas of language affected) to Cluster 3 (good naming vocabulary, but poor on all other tests used) were children who improved significantly in their expressive vocabulary. These children no longer had problems across all areas of language like other children in Cluster 5. Now these children had problems across all language areas except for expressive vocabulary. Interestingly, there was already a cluster of children who had exactly those characteristics (i.e., Cluster 3).

To reiterate, what is interesting about these findings is that changes in children's linguistic profiles did not produce a whole new set of subgroups. Instead, children's profiles of difficulties continued to fall into a limited number of patterns already observed at Time 1.

The exception to this finding was Cluster 2 (i.e., children who appeared to be performing within the normal range and arguably should not be included in the classification of children with SLI). Nonetheless, Cluster 2 children may well be a group of children whose language difficulties have resolved by the time they participated in the study (age 7 at Time 1). This interpretation is supported by the work of Bishop and Edmundson (1987). These investigators found that approximately 37% of children who were found to have SLI at the preschool age of 4 years no longer presented with SLI at 5;6 years; that is, they appeared to have recovered. Following this line of argument, it is expected that a proportion of children with SLI may no longer present with SLI profiles at later ages. In the present investigation, the percentage of children with SLI who appeared to have recovered (Cluster 2 children) was 7% at Time 1 (7 years) and 12% at Time 2 (8 years).

Thus, patterns of language strengths and weaknesses change with developmental time and no doubt with the influence of other important factors such as intervention. However, despite these unknown influences, it appears that there are still only a limited number of profiles of language strengths and weaknesses in children with SLI. Five such patterns of strengths and weaknesses have been identified in children with SLI who are 7 to 8 years of age (excluding Cluster 2, normal group children, as discussed earlier). Recall the characteristics of the clusters found. Cluster 1 children had difficulties with comprehension of grammar, word reading, and retelling a story in the context of good phonology and adequate expressive vocabulary. Cluster 3 children had problems with comprehension of grammar, word reading, phonology, and retelling a story in the context of good expressive vocabulary. Cluster 4 were similar to Cluster 3 children except that their scores were better across the tests used and their expressive vocabulary was not as good as that of children in Cluster 3. Cluster 5 children performed poorly on all the tests used and appeared to have difficulties across all areas of language. Finally, Cluster 6 children had difficulties retelling a story in the context of good phonology, good expressive vocabulary, good word reading, and adequate comprehension of grammar. These children's difficulties were mainly evident at the discourse level when they were required to retell a story.

In any classification exercise, the resulting subgroups are necessarily dependent on the measures used in the investigation and the psychometric properties of the measurement instruments used. This is particularly relevant in two ways. One is the specificity of measurement within certain language construct domains (e.g., it is hard to measure pragmatics, and current tests may collapse across many dimensions of syntax), which necessarily restrict our ability to test discrete constructs such as *semantics, syntax,* or *pragmatics.* Another way is that detection of stability may be obscured by psychometric properties of measurement (e.g., the test–retest and raw-score/percentile score issues discussed earlier). Nonetheless, it is also important to emphasize that the five patterns or subgroups of SLI identified are based on studies that have a number of strengths (Conti-Ramsden, Crutchley, & Botting, 1997; Conti-Ramsden & Botting, 1999). The present investigations involved a large sample of children (n = 242) representing a random sample of 50% of all 7-year-olds attending language units in England. Although there are advantages to studies with methodologies that specify a priori and in detail the criteria used for selecting subjects as belonging (or not) to SLI, the reverse also has its own advantages. In this investigation, a large cohort of children receiving speech-language services in language units were identified and then the question, "What sorts of problems do these children have?" was asked. In addition, the study was uniform in terms of age (7 years at Time 1 and 8 years at Time 2). This is a major methodological advantage as developmental effects and changes are not confounded in the classification system. Most previous studies (Miller, 1996; Rapin & Allen, 1987; Wilson & Risucci, 1986) have had mixed age groups, therefore developmental and age-related changes are confounded.

Findings presented here lend further weight to the argument that children with SLI fall into distinct subgroups. The present investigations also add an important caveat to the argument: Although profiles of language strengths and weaknesses in the form of distinct subgroups appear to be stable over time, individual children's language strengths and weaknesses change with time. Consequently, a large proportion of children move to different subgroups, resulting in poor membership stability from one year to the next (for children ages 7 and 8 years). Thus, it appears that SLI is a dynamic condition that changes with developmental time and likely with the influence of other important factors such as intervention. At present, we are in the process of seeing these children again at the age of 11 years. With this longer time scale, it may be possible for future research to begin to provide some information on predicting the developmental course of different subgroups of children with SLI.

ACKNOWLEDGMENTS

The authors gratefully acknowledge the support of the Nuffield Foundation for grant number AT251 [OD], Educational Transitions of Language-Impaired Children. We would also like to thank Alison Crutchley for help with data collection, Dr. Brian Faragher for statistical advice, and the schools and language units who gave their time and facilities for our assessments.

REFERENCES

Anderberg, M. R. (1973). *Cluster analysis for applications*. New York: Academic Press.

Aram, D. M. (1991). Comments on specific language impairment as a clinical category. *Language, Speech, and Hearing Services in Schools, 22,* 84–88.

Aram, D. M., Morris, R., & Hall, N. E. (1992). The validity of discrepancy criteria for identifying children with developmental language disorders. *Journal of Learning Disabilities, 25,* 549–554.

Bishop, D. V. M. (1982). *Test for reception of grammar*. Published by the author: Age and Cognitive Performance Research Centre, Department of Psychology, University of Manchester, Oxford Road, Manchester M13 9PL.

Bishop, D. V. M. (1994). Is specific language impairment a valid diagnostic category? Genetic and psycholinguistic evidence. *Philosophical Transactions of the Royal Society Lond. B., 346,* 105–111.

Bishop, D. V. M. (1997). *Uncommon understanding*. Hove, England: Psychology Press.

Bishop, D. V. M., & Edmundson, A. (1987). Language-impaired four-year-olds: Distinguishing transient from persistent impairment. *Journal of Speech and Hearing Disorders, 52,* 156–173.

Conti-Ramsden, G., & Adams, C. (1995). Transitions from the clinic to school: The changing picture of specific language impaired children from pre-school to school age. *Journal of Clinical Speech and Language Studies, 5,* 1–11.

Conti-Ramsden, G., & Botting, N. (1999). Classification of children with specific language impairment: Longitudinal considerations. *Journal of Speech, Language and Hearing Research, 42*(5), 1205–1219.

Conti-Ramsden, G., Crutchley, A., & Botting, N. (1997). The extent to which psychometric tests differentiate subgroups of children with SLI. *Journal of Speech, Language, and Hearing Research, 40,* 765–777.

Elliot, C. D. (1983). *British ability scales*. Windsor: NFER-Nelson.

Goldman, R., & Fristoe, M. (1986). *Goldman–Fristoe test of articulation*. Minnesota: American Guidance Association.

Johnston, J. R. (1991). The continuing relevance of cause: A reply to Leonard's specific language impairment as a clinical category. *Language, Speech, and Hearing Services in Schools, 22,* 75–80.

Kirk, S. A., McCarthy, J. J., & Kirk, W. D. (1968). *Illinois test of psycholinguistic abilities*. Illinois: University of Illinois Press.

Leonard, L. B. (1987). Is specific language impairment a useful construct? In S. Rosenberg (Ed.), *Advances in applied psycholinguistics: Volume 1. Disorders of first-language development* (pp. 1–39). New York: Cambridge University Press.

Leonard, L. B. (1991). Specific language impairment as a clinical category. *Language, Speech, and Hearing Services in Schools, 22,* 66–69.

Leonard, L. B. (1998). *Children with specific language impairment*. Cambridge, MA: MIT Press.

Miller, J. F. (1996). The search for the phenotype of disordered language performance. In M. Rice (Ed.), *Toward a genetics of language* (pp. 297–314). Mahwah, NJ: Lawrence Erlbaum Associates.

Office for National Statistics. (1998). *Family spending 1996/1997*. London: The Stationery Office.

Rapin, I., & Allen, D. A. (1987). Developmental dysphasia and autism in preschool children: Characteristics and subtypes. In J. Martin, P. Fletcher, P. Grunwell, & D. Hall (Eds.), *Proceedings of the first international symposium on specific speech and language disorders in children* (pp. 20–35). London: AFASIC.

Raven, J. C. (1986). *Coloured progressive matrices.* London: H. K. Lewis & Co.

Renfrew, C. (1991). *The bus story: A test of continuous speech.* C. E. Renfrew, 2a North Place, Old Headington, Oxford, England.

Stark, R. E., & Tallal, P. (1981). Selection of children with specific language deficits. *Journal of Speech and Hearing Disorders, 46,* 114–180.

Tallal, P. (1988). Developmental language disorders. In J. F. Kavanagh & T. J. Truss, Jr. (Eds.), *Learning disabilities: Proceedings of the national conference* (pp. 181–272). Parkton, MD: York.

Wilcox, K. A., & Morris, S. R. (1995). Speech outcomes of the language-focused curriculum. In M. L. Rice & K. A. Wilcox (Eds.), *Building a language-focused curriculum for the pre-school classroom* (pp. 171–180). Baltimore, MD: Paul Brookes.

Wilson, B., & Risucci, D. (1986). A model for clinical-quantitative classification: Generation 1. Application to language-disordered pre-school children. *Brain and Language, 27,* 281–309.

Neuroplasticity and Development: The Acquisition of Morphosyntax in Children With Early Focal Lesions and Children With Specific Language Impairment

Judy Reilly
Jill Weckerly
Beverly Wulfeck
San Diego State University

In the 1960s, both Lenneberg (1967) and Basser (1962) noted that children with brain damage did not suffer to the same extent as adults with comparable damage. These observations provoked much interest in the issue of brain plasticity, especially with respect to language, and much attention has been devoted to how neuroanatomical regions become specialized for specific language functions. One fruitful means to address such issues is to chart the course of language development in groups of children in special circumstances. In this chapter, we draw from two complementary studies (Reilly, Losh, Bellugi, & Wulfeck, in press; Weckerly, Reilly, & Wulfeck, in press) to consider fundamental issues in hemispheric specialization and plasticity by examining the language abilities of two clinical groups of children purported to demonstrate atypical language behavior: children with early unilateral focal brain lesions (FL) and children with specific language impairment (SLI). Although children with SLI have no overt anatomical abnormalities or specific lesions that might be linked to their impairments, they exhibit a number of language deficits quite similar to patterns seen among adult aphasics who have suffered a clear neurological insult. In contrast, children who have sustained focal brain damage early in infancy have clear and localizable anatomical abnormalities, yet their language difficulties are more subtle, if nonexistent, on many measures. The contrastive neurobehavioral profiles of these two groups, along with typically developing controls, present a unique opportunity to address basic issues in brain–language relationships, including: (a) localization of function, (b) neuroplasticity, and (c) nature of the language acquisition process. In this chapter, we first present a brief overview of the adult model for brain–language relations, and then introduce the two experimental groups of children. We then discuss the two morphosyntactic tasks and their results, which bear on our original questions.

THE ADULT MODEL

From the extensive work on both normal adults and those who have suffered unilateral strokes (Goodglass, 1993), 150 years of research have consistently confirmed Broca's original findings that the left hemisphere mediates core aspects of language (i.e., phonology, morphology, and syntax) for more than 90% of the population. Even in the case of native deaf signers, adults with left frontal damage show problems in production, but their comprehension remains relatively intact, and those with left temporal damage show basically the reverse profile—fluent, but empty production, and problems with comprehension (Poizner, Klima, & Bellugi, 1987). These findings hold true across a broad range of spoken and signed languages.

Grammatical morphology, sometimes called *morphosyntax*, is said to be one of the most linguistic and left hemisphere-mediated aspects of language. Despite the limited repertoire of grammatical morphemes in English, studies of typical and atypical language behavior have regarded grammatical morphemes as an index of language (dys)function as well as a window into the functional components of language behavior. In the literatures of both the hemispheric specialization for language and the nature of language impairment, the acquisition and mastery of grammatical morphology has been a focus of inquiry. This chapter examines the acquisition of morphology in two distinct contexts: a narrative task that offers a sample of behavior in a more or less naturalistic setting, and a sentence production task in which language elements occur in a tightly constrained form. Each of these different tasks involves a gradual acquisition that depends on not only the mastery of specific morphological markers, but also simultaneously coordinating these and other linguistic tasks amid heavy processing demands.

More recent research has injected some fuzzy boundaries on the initial truisms of the left hemisphere being not only dominant for language, but so uniquely suited to this task that development or use of the right hemisphere for language is assumed to be inherently limited. Over the last 25 years, increasing evidence suggests that the right hemisphere plays a role in language as well: Adult patients with right hemisphere damage (RHD) often do poorly with nonliteral language (e.g., sarcasm, irony, metaphor, idioms, and jokes; Brownell, Michel, Powelson, & Gardner, 1983; Van Lancker & Kempler, 1986). With respect to discourse, studies have shown that patients with RHD also struggle with reference, discourse cohesion, and coherence (Gardner, Brownell, Wapner, & Michelow, 1983; Hough, 1990; Joanette, Goulet, & Hannequin, 1990; Kaplan, Brownell, Jacobs, & Gardner, 1990). Given that both hemispheres play a significant role in adult language behavior, a primary question at the intersection of plasticity and localization of function is, how does language develop when one hemisphere is damaged or otherwise not available in the usual way at the outset of language acquisition?

ATYPICALLY DEVELOPING CHILDREN

In the current report, all the children were participants in a large neuro-developmental study at the Project in Cognitive and Neural Development in San Diego. The children with unilateral focal brain damage represent a rare group: They have suffered a single unilateral cerebral insult before 6 months of age prior to the normal language acquisition process. Charting their language development permits us to address the issues of neuro-plasticity and localization of function by looking to see whether there are specific behavioral profiles—in this case, patterns of language acquisition—associated with the site of the child's lesion and how flexibly the developing brain can respond to an early insult. These strokes are structurally similar to those suffered by adults later in life; according to the adult model, we would expect a child with early left hemisphere damage (LHD) to have problems with morphology and syntax, whereas those aspects of language would be spared in children with RHD. In contrast, those with early RHD would be expected to make fewer inferences and show problems with discourse coherence, but have few problems with morphology or syntax per se. Our previous studies with these children have demonstrated initial delay at the onset of language with some early site-specific profiles. For example, Bates et al. (1997) found that, within the overall group delay, infants with RHD were below the LHD group on early lexical comprehension. They also reported that the toddlers and preschoolers with left temporal damage performed lower on lexical production and had shorter MLUs than the rest of the FL group, again in the context of an overall delay for the FL group compared with controls. A complementary finding comes from the narratives of children with early left temporal damage. They too performed below the rest of the FL group on morphology up to the age of about 5 years; after age 5, there were no site-specific differences, although the group as a whole continued to fall behind typically developing controls. However, by age 8 or so, the children with focal brain damage were performing in the low normal range on all the narrative measures (Reilly, Marchman, & Bates, 1998). In summary, the children with focal brain damage have clear and specified neurological impairments, but their behavioral development with respect to language, although initially delayed, shows remarkable development (Bates et al., 1997; Reilly et al., 1998).

In contrast, the language deficits of children with SLI are extensive and well documented, but as yet there are no clear structural patterns of significant neurological dysfunction to account for these behavioral profiles (Trauner, Wulfeck, Tallal, & Hesselink, 2000). Overall, their language performance is poor and behaviorally these children's language often resembles that of aphasic adults (Bishop, 1997; Leonard, 1998; Rice, 1996). Although this group of children's performance IQs are within the normal range, their scores on an expressive standardized language test are at least one standard deviation below the mean for their age. Explanations for such profiles have proposed a range of mechanisms, knowledge deficits, missing or malfunctioning components of grammar, or reduced processing capabilities as the source of this devclopmental difficulty. Accounts of SLI also differ as to whether the primary deficits of this disorder are attributable to specific knowledge-based deficits in grammatical morphology. In some accounts of SLI (Gopnik, 1990), these deficits are considered hardwired and conceptualized as feature blindness for particular morphological markers such as agreement or auxiliary selection. Studies of children with SLI have consistently shown that these children have deficits relative to their normally developing peers on measures of morphology, which target such features as the use of auxiliary verbs (Cleave & Rice, 1997; Rice & Wexler, 1996) and agreement marking on verbs (Bishop, 1994; Rice & Oetting, 1993). The protracted delay of language development in children with SLI stands in striking contrast to the remarkable developmental trajectory evidenced in the performance of the children with early brain damage. As such, the language profile of children with SLI represents a challenge to the notion of developmental neuroplasticity.

Reviewing the literature on language development, numerous studies have demonstrated that, by age 5, children have mastered the majority of the morphosyntactic structures of their language (Brown, 1973; Slobin, 1985, 1992, 1997a, 1997b). Nonetheless, the conversations of a 5-year-old still differ significantly from those of a 12-year-old. Language development after 5 includes learning how and when to use this repertoire of structures fluently and flexibly for diverse linguistic functions. By examining a specific aspect of language behavior, grammatical morphology during the school years, across two different tasks, we hope to achieve a broad-based sampling of a domain of language behavior that can be used to address some of the fundamental questions in the development of brain–behavior relationships. By contrasting the development in these two etiologically distinct populations across tasks, we provide additional insight into the nature and constraints of neuroplasticity, as well as into the process of language acquisition by identifying those aspects of language that are vulnerable in different conditions as opposed to those that are more resilient.

MORPHOSYNTAX IN THE WILD: TELLING A STORY

Because stories are common in children's lives, in contrast to standardized tests, they provide an ecologically valid measure of a child's linguistic performance. In part due to their pervasiveness, narratives, as a discourse form, are accessible to even the youngest in society: Children have a clear notion of what a story is by age 3 (Appleby, 1978). Given their high frequency in children's lives and their everyday nature, narratives provide an excellent quasinaturalistic measure of children's spontaneous language, reflecting distinctive structural and linguistic changes through childhood and adolescence. Narratives provide a rich context to evaluate multiple aspects of linguistic development in school-age children. As such, narratives have been a popular topic in both typically developing children (Bamberg, 1987; Bamberg & Reilly, 1994; Berman & Slobin, 1994; Peterson & McCabe, 1983; Reilly, 1992) and atypical populations (Bamberg & Damrad-Frye, 1991; Capps, Kehres, & Sigman, 1998; Capps, Losh, & Thurber, 2000; Dennis, Jacennik, & Barnes, 1992; Liles, 1993; Losh, Bellugi, Reilly, & Anderson, 2001; Loveland, McEvoy, & Tunali, 1990; Reilly, Klima, & Bellugi, 1991; Reilly, Bates, & Marchman, 1998; Tager-Flusberg & Sullivan, 1995). In their classic article on narratives, Labov and Waletzky (1967) characterized a narrative as a sequence of temporally related clauses. They also identified the referential and evaluative functions of narrative. Building on their conceptual framework, we understand the referential to include information about the characters and events of the story. These constitute the plot or story line, whereas the evaluative aspects of narrative provide the narrator's perspective on those events and also serve to engage the listener.

To tell a good story, a child must draw on linguistic, cognitive, and affective/social skills. Linguistically, she must lexically encode information about the characters and events of the story in a temporally coherent and logically organized manner. By exploiting the appropriate morphosyntactic devices, the sequence of events and their temporal relations are made explicit. This represents the plot of the story or referential information. Cognitively, she must also make numerous inferences, including characters' motivations for their actions and behaviors, the logical relations between events, and the extraction and articulation of the theme or point of the story. Ultimately, the storyteller makes a choice in how story information is conveyed. That is, there are a variety of syntactic forms that serve to arrange and deliver information. Therefore, using complex sentences may be an especially efficient way to tell a story. However, it is also grammatical, but perhaps less economical, to use a series of simple sentences that allow the listener to infer the relations between the clauses. Given the range of skills/abilities required to produce a good narrative, analyzing children's stories permits us to address questions regarding not only complex language development and its use in school-age children, but also the relationship of language development to other cognitive and affective abilities. Here we focus on linguistic proficiency and use, specifically, the development of morphology and syntax.

For this task, 169 English-speaking children, ages 3;11 to 12;11 years, from three populations participated: 73 typically developing control children (CTL), 44 children with SLI, and 52 children with focal brain lesions (FL; 33 with early LHD and 19 with early damage to the right hemisphere). Subjects were participants in a large neurodevelopmental study of language and cognition, and all groups were within the normal range on Performance IQ. Children with early focal lesions and typically developing children were also within normal limits on Verbal IQ, whereas children with SLI were below the other groups on Verbal IQ. Expressive language as measured by the Clinical Evaluation of Language Fundamentals–Revised (CELF; Semel, Wiig, & Secord, 1987) was within the normal range for typically developing children ($M = 100$), and children with early focal lesions and SLI scored about 1 to 2 SDs below the mean, respectively.

In the narrative task, children looked through a 24-page wordless picture book, *Frog, Where Are You?* (Mayer, 1969) and then were asked to tell the story to the experimenter. This story is about a boy and his dog and their search for their missing pet frog. The children's narratives were both audiotaped and videotaped, and the CHAT format from the CHILDES system was used for transcription (MacWhinney, 1991). Stories were first coded for length as measured by number of propositions; because our focus in this chapter is on morphosyntax, they were then coded for the frequency of morphological errors as well as types of complex sentences (see Reilly et al., 1998, for a fuller description).

Our first measure reflects story length and, indirectly, quantity of a child's talk. We found that children with SLI told shorter stories compared with normally developing children and children with focal lesions. Moreover, there were no differences in story length between children with early LHD versus RHD. Because children's narratives vary significantly in length, to compare morphosyntactic performance (e.g., the number or frequency of morphological errors), we used story length to create proportional scores to neutralize differences. Specifically, measures of story length were used to construct proportions of morphological errors and frequency of complex sentences.

As can be seen in Fig. 2.1, typically developing children make few morphological errors by age 5 to 6; they make about one error every 12 clauses or propositions. By ages 7 to 9, they are only committing an error about every 20 propositions. Interestingly, children with either RHD or LHD do equally poorly at the youngest age, but improve significantly and perform within the normal range by ages 7 to 8. In the younger ages, children with SLI commit as many errors as children with early focal lesions. They do show improvement over time. However, their rate of improvement is significantly slower than the children with brain damage. Even by ages 9 to 10, the children with SLI still commit significantly more errors than normally developing children as well as more than the children with early focal brain damage.

In general, omission errors in tense and number agreement for verbs and agreement for pronouns were most common. Interestingly, in all three populations, the type and quality of the errors were similar to those of normal children. Specifically, the errors found in the stories of children with SLI and those with FL are the same types of errors found in the stories of younger typically developing children. Thus, the difference is in quantity, but not in quality of errors, as shown in Table 2.1.

In measures of syntactic complexity, as typically developing children get older, they use complex sentences more frequently and increasingly use different types of complex sentences in their stories. In fact, there is a decrease in the number of coordinate sentences and an increase in subordination. Children with early LHD follow the normal trajectory, but at a slower rate (Fig. 2.2); in the older group, their performance is within the normal range. For children with early RHD, the rate at which they recruit complex sentences appears to be relatively flat from the first to the second data point as can be seen in Fig. 2.2. Because complex sentences, especially adverbial clauses, are one mechanism to tie episodes of the story together, we speculate that this plateau on the part of the children with early RHD may reflect a broader integrative deficit as seen in their performance on visuospatial tasks (Stiles et al., 1997). Children with SLI use complex sentences with increasing frequency, but are still below their typically developing peers, at least in this age range. These profiles are depicted in Fig. 2.2.

In summary, all groups make fewer morphological errors and use more complex syntax with age, although the developmental slopes are signifi-

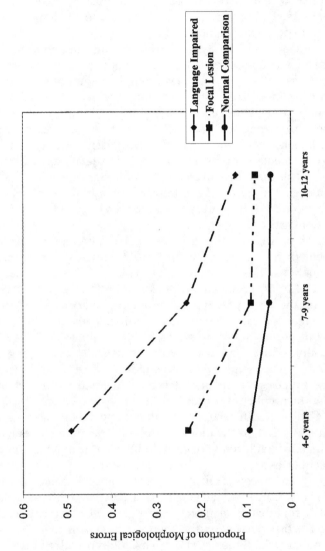

FIG. 2.1. Proportion of morphological errors in narratives (Reilly et al., in press).

46

TABLE 2.1
A Sample of Morphological Errors

Group	Age	Example
FL	4;9	then the boy **look** in his hat
	5;0	the dog jumped and **falled** down
	6;0	he **get** out **0** his bowl
	6;8	the boy called **to** a hole
SLI	4;3	**0** frog **0** going to sleep with the dog
	4;4	he **growl**
	7;6	then when they **woked** up in the morning they saw the frog was gone
	9;3	the frog is jumping out of the jar and the dog and the boy **is sleep**
NC	4;1	an' their dog was going to **broke** *the* glass while he was falling
	4;5	the boy **0** going for the frog
	5;0	an' the little boy **felled** down
	5;4	an' then the dog **look** over an' the boy looked over

cantly different for each group. Both clinical groups show some delay compared with their same-age peers, and errors committed by both clinical groups are similar to those of younger normally developing children. With increasing age, children with early focal lesions perform better than children with SLI. More important, there are no significant differences in the profile of children with early LHD compared with those with early RHD with respect to morphological errors; both groups perform similarly to their normally developing peers by middle childhood. As such, in this narrative task, and consonant with our earlier findings, the patterns of children with early LHD do not map onto those predicted by the adult model. However, there is a hint that children with early RHD are showing similarities to adults with damage to the right hemisphere, although much more subtly. Their lag in the use of complex syntax may reflect a problem integrating different aspects of the story.

Overall in the narratives, with respect to morphology, we saw that children with RHD perform similarly to those with LHD, and as a group they do significantly better—that is, they master English morphology at a significantly faster rate than the SLI group, which has no frank neurological damage. Although as a discourse genre narratives have some formal constraints, and in this case the content is also constrained, the linguistic structures that the storyteller uses reflect a rhetorical choice. As such, this developmental profile of morphological acquisition reflects the child's functional everyday use of language. To acquire another perspective, we next describe how our study populations perform on a structured morphosyntactic task, the Tags Question Task.

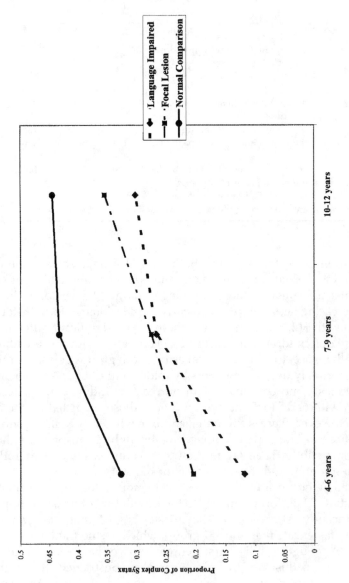

FIG. 2.2.   Proportion of complex sentences in narratives (Reilly et al., in press).

MORPHOSYNTAX IN THE LAB:
PRODUCING TAG QUESTIONS

English speakers often append a tag question at the end of a declarative statement, which is used to solicit confirmation from the listener (i.e., He wants chocolate ice cream, doesn't he?). The Tags Question Task (Dennis, Sugar, & Whitaker, 1982) consists of 48 declarative statements; in each of these, the child is required to repeat the main clause statement followed by a tag question. This measure offers a number of unanticipated advantages in the study of the acquisition of morphosyntax. First, it is a conceptually simple task. Children are familiar with the pragmatic function that tag questions serve, and they have at least receptive familiarity with their use. Second, although producing a tag question also places relatively few demands on the speaker in terms of motor output (two words), it nevertheless involves the analysis of a number of components of the stimulus clause, perhaps holding some of this information in working memory and then synthesizing and transforming these features into the tag question. Children must either repeat or correctly pronominalize the main clause subject in the tag question, select the appropriate auxiliary verb (equal instances of the auxiliary verbs *do*, *be*, or *can*), supply agreement marking where needed, and invert the polarity of the main clause sentence.

Taken together, the analysis of component processes in tag question production measures performance on some of the fundamental elements of English morphology, such as agreement marking and auxiliary selection, along with measures of subject selection and polarity. In addition, the correct production of a tag question not only requires mastery of each of these morphological features, but also involves the simultaneous processing and coordination of multiple components. The number of correctly produced tag questions can be considered a measure of how well the various tag features were synthesized and coordinated in the response. In this sense, the production of tag questions offers tests of both linguistic knowledge and language processing. Given these multiple demands, we would predict differential performance in our clinical groups: In terms of questions relating to the localization of language functions, using the adult aphasia model as a starting point, we might expect that children with LHD will perform below children with RHD on aspects of grammatical morphology. Because early RHD is associated with greater delays on tasks that require integration of multiple sources of information (Stiles, Stern, Trauner, & Nass, 1996; Stiles & Thal, 1993; Stiles, Trauner, Engel, & Nass, 1997; Zamora & Reilly, 2001), we might also predict that children with early RHD will perform worse than children with LHD on aspects of these tasks that require more global linguistic analysis, such as performance on features such as polarity in tag questions.

It is of particular interest to gauge SLI children's performance on vary-ing tasks that target grammatical morphology. If the deficits of children with SLI are primarily attributable to deficits in morphological knowl-edge, such as agreement or auxiliary selection, we might hypothesize that SLI children will demonstrate deficits compared with normally develop-ing children on auxiliary and agreement across tasks. That is, they will make more morphological errors on agreement and auxiliary in the pro-duction of tag questions. Because tag questions involve multiple features, the pattern of performance across features can be compared, in addition to the direct comparisons to performances of normally developing children on individual tag features. With four primary tag features (auxiliary, agreement, polarity, and subject), there is the potential for distinct pat-terns of strengths and weaknesses in SLI versus FL versus normally devel-oping groups of children. In the evaluation of within-group performance, we hypothesize that SLI children will perform disproportionally worse on agreement and auxiliary than their performance on features such as polar-ity and subject when compared with the profiles of normally developing children.

In this second study, 69 children (ages 4–16 years) participated: 24 typi-cally developing control children (CTL), 24 children with SLI, and 21 chil-dren with FL. The children were divided into three age groups: 4 to 7 years, 8 to 11 years, and 12 to 14 years, and all but the oldest were in Study 1. Performance was measured by scoring both the individual tag features (auxiliary, polarity, subject, and agreement) and the overall number cor-rect. Hence, for each response, a child may have been able to generate a correct response in terms of the choice of auxiliary and local agreement, but incorrect in terms of polarity and subject. Examples of errors and scor-ing are shown in the following box.

He takes the morning train, don't he?
   (correct auxiliary, subject, polarity;
   incorrect agreement)

He takes the morning train, doesn't
   she?
   (correct auxiliary, agreement, polarity;
   incorrect subject)

He takes the morning train, isn't he?
   (correct agreement, subject, polarity;
   incorrect auxiliary)

He takes the morning train, does he?
   (correct auxiliary, agreement, subject;
   incorrect polarity)

Overall, we found children with RHD and LHD performed compara-bly on all aspects of the Tags Question Task. In addition, there were no group differences on overall correct in the youngest age group as is shown in Fig. 2.3. However, at ages 8 to 11, normally developing children and children with early focal lesions scored higher on overall total correct than

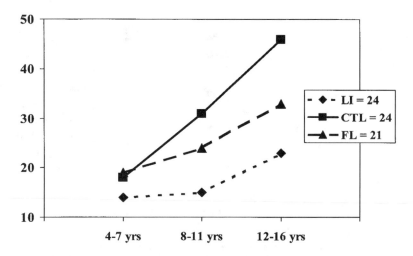

FIG. 2.3. Overall correct for tags (Weckerly et al., in press).

children with SLI, and in the oldest age group (ages 12–16), typically developing children outscored both clinical groups, with FL children outscoring children with SLI.

When we considered performance on the individual tag features, we found no differences in performance of normally developing children compared with children with FL. Although their scores were somewhat lower, children with SLI generally scored within the same range as normally developing children on the tag features of auxiliary, agreement, and subject, whereas children with SLI and children with brain damage in the older age groups scored lower than their normally developing peers on polarity (see Fig. 2.4).

We found that children with both SLI and FL scored worse on polarity than they did on the other three tag features at all ages, whereas only the younger normally developing children showed this same pattern. That is, neither children with SLI nor FL showed a profile of disproportionally poorer performance on agreement and auxiliary compared with subject and polarity. In examining the profiles of strengths and weaknesses on tag components, we found that all three groups demonstrated the same ranked order of difficulty across tag features, scoring lowest on correct polarity responses and highest on responses on agreement, with performance on auxiliary and subject falling in between. All children across all ages almost always scored highest on agreement. At every age and group by age comparison, children scored worst on polarity (see Fig. 2.5).

In summary, the results of the Tag Questions Task are: (a) All groups improve with age; (b) children with early RHD and LHD perform similarly; (c) children with FL cluster with typically developing children until

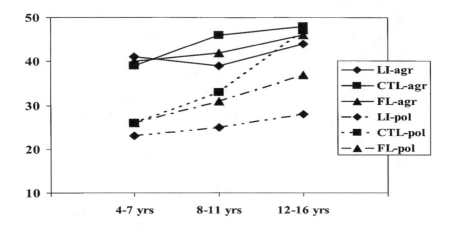

FIG. 2.4.   Acquisition of agreement and polarity across age for SLI, FL, and normally developing children (Weckerly et al., in press).

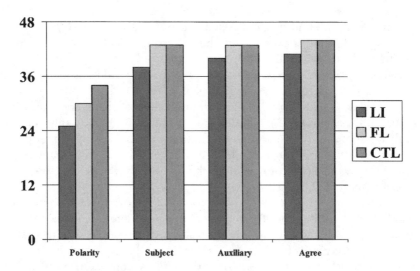

FIG. 2.5.   Ranked order of difficulty of tag features by group (Weckerly et al., in press).

adolescence, and both groups outperform children with SLI; and (d) individual parameters are of the same ranked difficulty across groups, suggesting all the children are approaching the task in a similar manner. Performance profiles for the tag question data depict similar developmental patterns to the data from the narrative task: Children with SLI are no better than and, in fact, are slower to acquire this aspect of language than children with large or small cerebral infarcts.

DISCUSSION

The Tags Question Task proved to be an informative way to track the acquisition of a number of morphosyntactic processes in the context of gradual mastery of tag questions. Linguistically based accounts of SLI most often attribute language difficulties to some form of knowledge deficit of a particular morphological feature (Clahsen, 1989; Gopnik, 1990). Based on these accounts, we hypothesized that both the narrative task and the Tags Question Task are linguistically demanding contexts in which underlying deficits in a particular aspect of grammatical development would be most apparent. Our findings led us to some surprising responses to our original questions.

Localization of Function

We hypothesized that not only are there many patterns and dissociations possible in the Tags Questions Task, but a profile of performance within tag features that somehow reflected a disproportional difficulty with agreement marking would support the notion of specific deficits in grammatical morphology. We hypothesized that children with SLI and early LHD would show a profile of disproportionally poorer performance on agreement and auxiliary compared with subject and polarity. We found the opposite pattern. Features such as agreement and auxiliary selection were most robust to the challenges of multiple-feature coordination, whereas performance on polarity suffered to a greater degree than the other tag features. This pattern was observed in both clinical groups and the younger normally developing children. These results confirm earlier reports (Bates et al., 2001; Bishop, 1993; Reilly et al., 1998) suggesting that the language profiles of the children with focal brain damage do not map onto those of adults with comparable damage. Although perhaps not optimally suited for language, our data demonstrate that multiple areas of the brain can subserve language functions. That we see initial delay with later catch-up in children with early focal brain damage, regardless of their lesion site, suggests that the brain areas to acquire language may be more broadly distributed than those necessary to maintain language functioning.

Neuroplasticity

Studies of language development in children with early FL have found both a pattern of early deficits that gradually disappear, as well as a pattern of deficits observed at older ages on more complex language tasks. In the narrative task, we saw evidence of the first pattern: By the end of the elementary school years, children in the FL group, irrespective of damage site, were performing within the normal range on morphosyntactic measures, although the acquisition of these milestones was delayed with respect to their typically developing peers. On the Tags task, given its multiple dimensions, we hypothesized that both patterns might be observed, and we predicted that children with early FL would perform lower than normally developing children on overall correct at every age. Children with early FL generally started off similarly to their same-age peers, but they improved more slowly than normally developing children. In the 12 to 16 age group, they scored significantly lower than normally developing children on correctly produced tags, but still better than their peers with SLI. Because performance on polarity tended to drive scores on overall total correct for all groups, there was also a trend for older children with early FL to perform below the level of age-matched controls on number of correct polarity responses. Although children with early FL scored comparably to controls on many tag features, performance on polarity and overall correct provides some evidence of the presence of deficits on more complex operations of language. This latter pattern also suggests that this task begins to reveal some limits to neuroplasticity.

If we look at morphology findings of the FL group on both the narrative and Tag, they present an overall picture of fairly rapid acquisition of the morphosyntax of English, and their performance on both tasks provides strong evidence of the flexibility of the developing brain in the acquisition of morphological structures. In contrast, children with SLI show significantly protracted development; they do not achieve typical performance levels on either task in this age range. What biological or neurodevelopmental factors prohibit their acquisition of these same structures? Although the children with early FL have frank brain damage, and we do not yet know how such an early stroke might affect the intra- or interhemispheric connectivity, the remaining brain tissue of these children is putatively normal and appears to assume language learning functions. In contrast, over the last 15 years, several neuroimaging studies have demonstrated subtle neuroanatomical anomalies in children with SLI. Generally, in typical brains, the planum temporale and perisylvian regions are larger in the left hemisphere than in the right. Plante and her colleagues (Plante, Swisher, Vance, & Rapcsak, 1991) looked at eight boys with SLI and found several atypical symmetries: The right perisylvian area was as large or larger than that of the left. These anomalies were hypothesized to stem from a failure of subtractive events in the course of early brain development. They are also consistent with early findings of Galaburda and colleagues (Galaburda, Sherman, Rosen, Aboitiz, & Geschwind, 1985) who also found a lack of asymmetry in the planum temporale in four dyslexic adults, three of whom were reported to have had delayed onset of language as well as speech problems as children. In a study by Jernigan et al. (1991), findings in groups of children with SLI included anomalous asymmetries in the prefrontal regions with right exceeding left and in the parietal areas with left exceeding right. Finally, in a large group of children, Trauner et al. (2000) found a higher proportion of neurological soft signs in the SLI group than in controls as well as structural abnormalities on one third of the MRI scans of the SLI group; these included ventricular enlargement, areas of white matter intensities, and periventricular leukomalacia. This small and growing body of literature demonstrates subtle and possibly distributed neurological abnormalities. Thus, rather than circumscribed structural lesions, as we see in the FL group, we might characterize the children with SLI as suffering functional or systemic lesions. The resultant subtle and diffuse damage does not permit language acquisition as quickly or efficiently as the putatively normal, nonaffected cerebral tissue of the FL children.

The Nature of the Language Acquisition Process

In the narrative data, we saw that the types of morphological errors were similar for all groups. That is, errors of omission and commission found in the stories of children with SLI or FL were of the same categories as those found in the stories of younger typically developing children. Moreover, with respect to complex sentences, the types of complex sentences, as well as the frequency of recruiting such structures, increased with age for each of the groups. In addition, younger children in all of the groups tended to favor coordinate sentences over complex sentences with subordinate clauses. In the middle and older groups, however, the proportion of subordinate structures outstripped coordinates for children with SLI, FL, and the control group as well. Thus, even internal developmental patterns were consistent across groups. Looking at the Tags results, we see a similar pattern: The morphological errors of all the groups of children are of the same types, and the different parameters of the Tags Questions Task present the same ranked order of difficulty for all groups. If performance on any one Tag feature is suggestive of particular difficulty across groups, it is polarity. There were a number of potential patterns of performance among the individual features that could have been observed among our groups. Yet more than anything, the overall pattern across groups was strikingly similar. All groups scored lowest on polarity and highest on local agreement, with remaining features showing basically the same ranked order of difficulty. In terms of the analysis of other errors (i.e., tense, inversion), we found that all children make all types of errors. This suggests that all children experienced the same difficulties in analyzing and synthesizing tag features.

In summary, these complementary findings from the Narrative and Tag Question Tasks suggest that the process of acquiring English morphosyntax is robust and fairly rigid in nature, and that developmental differences are best characterized as one of timing rather than of kind. Perhaps most striking is that the brain structures and brain organization from the two clinical groups of children are quite different, yet the acquisition of the morphology and syntax of English persists in following the same constrained path. Despite the apparent rigidity of the process, the differences in our groups suggest that language learning can be mediated by a variety of neural substrates.

CONCLUSIONS

In these studies, we have looked at how the performance of children with early focal brain damage and children with SLI compare to that of typically developing children of the same age on two different language production tasks: a narrative task that represents a quasinaturalistic discourse task and a more constrained task of morphosyntax, the production of Tag questions. Although both clinical groups show initial delay, by middle childhood, the FL group performs within the normal range (although there appears to be some slowing with complex tasks in adolescence). Interestingly, children with LHD generally perform comparably to those with RHD, unlike adults with comparable strokes. In contrast to the striking plasticity demonstrated by the FL group, children with SLI fall consistently behind both controls and the children with early brain damage, suggesting limits to plasticity. Comparing the performance of these three groups of children with contrastive neurobehavioral profiles has provided another lens on the nature of the language acquisition process, the extent of neuroplasticity, as well as its boundaries and limitations.

ACKNOWLEDGMENTS

The research reported here was supported in part by funding from NIH-NINDS Grant P50 NS22343 and NIH-NIDCD DC01289. We would like to thank the children and parents who participated in this study. Thanks also to research staff at the San Diego Project in Cognitive and Neural Development/Language Research Center for assistance with recruiting, screening, and testing subjects.

REFERENCES

Appleby, A. (1978). *The child's concept of story.* Chicago: University of Chicago Press.

Bamberg, M. (1987). *The acquisition of narratives.* Berlin: Mouton de Gruyter.

Bamberg, M., & Damrad-Frye, R. (1991). On the ability to provide evaluative comments: Further explorations of children's narrative competencies. *Journal of Child Language, 8*(3), 689–710.

Bamberg, M., & Reilly, J. S. (1994). Emotion, narrative and affect. In D. I. Slobin, J. Gerhardt, A. Kyratzis, & J. Guo (Eds.), *Social interaction, social context and language. Essays in honor of Susan Ervin-Tripp.* Hillsdale, NJ: Lawrence Erlbaum Associates.

Basser, L. S. (1962). Hemiplegia of early onset and the faculty of speech with special reference to the effects of hemispherectomy. *Brain, 85,* 427–460.

Bates, E., Thal, D., Trauner, D., Fenson, J., Aram, D., Eisele, J., & Nass, R. (1997). From first words to grammar in children with focal brain injury. *Developmental Neuropsychology, 13*(3), 275–343.

Bates, E. A., Reilly, J., Wulfeck, B., Dronkers, N., Opie, M., Fenson, J., Kriz, S., Jeffries, R., Miller, L., & Herbst, K. (2001). Differential effects of unilateral lesions on language production by children and adults. *Brain & Language, 7,* 223–265.

Berman, R., & Slobin, D. I. (1994). *Relating events in narrative: A crosslinguistic developmental study.* Hillsdale, NJ: Lawrence Erlbaum Associates.

Bishop, D. V. M. (1993). Language development after focal brain damage. In D. Bishop & K. Mogford (Eds.), *Language development in exceptional circumstances* (pp. 203–219). Hillsdale, NJ: Lawrence Erlbaum Associates.

Bishop, D. V. M. (1994). Grammatical errors in specific language impairment—Competence or performance limitations. *Applied Psycholinguistics, 15*(4), 507–550.

Bishop, D. V. M. (1997). *Uncommon understanding: Development and understanding of language comprehension in children.* East Sussex: Psychology Press.

Brown, R. (1973). *A first language.* Cambridge, MA: Harvard University Press.

Brownell, H., Michel, D., Powelson, J., & Gardner, H. (1983). Surprise but not coherence: Sensitivity to verbal humor in right-hemisphere patients. *Brain & Language, 18,* 20–27.

Capps, L., Kehres, J., & Sigman, M. (1998). Conversational abilities among children with autism and developmental delay. *Autism, 2,* 325–344.

Capps, L., Losh, M., & Thurber, C. (2000). "The frog ate a bug and made his mouth sad": Narrative competence in children with autism. *Journal of Abnormal Child Psychology, 28*(2), 193–204.

Clahsen, H. (1989). The grammatical characterization of developmental dysphasia. *Linguistics, 27*(5), 897–920.

Cleave, P. L., & Rice, M. L. (1997). An examination of the morpheme BE in children with specific language impairment: The role of contractibility and grammatical form class. *Journal of Speech & Hearing Research, 40*(3), 480–492.

Dennis, M., Jacennik, B., & Barnes, M. (1992). The content of narrative and discourse in children and adolescents after early-onset hydrocephalus and in normally-developing age peers. *Brain and Language, 46*(1), 129–165.

Dennis, M., Sugar, J., & Whitaker, H. A. (1982). The acquisition of tag questions. *Child Development, 53*(5), 1254–1257.

Galaburda, A. M., Sherman, G. F., Rosen, G. D., Aboitiz, F., & Geschwind, N. (1985). Developmental dyslexia: Four consecutive patients with cortical anomalies. *Annals of Neurology, 18*(2), 222–233.

Gardner, H., Brownell, H., Wapner, W., & Michelow, D. (1983). Missing the point: The role of the right hemisphere in the processing of complex linguistic materials. In E. Perceman (Ed.), *Cognitive processing in the right hemisphere.* New York: Academic Press.

Goodglass, H. (1993). *Understanding aphasia*. San Diego: Academic Press.

Gopnik, M. (1990). Feature-blind grammar and dysphasia. *Nature*, 344(6268), 715.

Hough, M. (1990). Narrative comprehension in adults with right and left-hemisphere brain damage: Theme organization. *Brain & Language, 38,* 253–277.

Jernigan, T. L., Hesselink, J. R., Sowell, E., & Tallal, P. A. (1991). Cerebral structure on magnetic resonance imaging in language- and learning-impaired children. *Archives of Neurology, 48*(5), 539–545.

Joanette, Y., Goulet, P., & Hannequin, D. (1990). *Right hemisphere and verbal communication.* New York: Springer-Verlag.

Kaplan, J., Brownell, H., Jacobs, J., & Gardner, H. (1990). The effects of right hemisphere damage on the pragmatic interpretation of conversational remarks. *Brain and Language, 38,* 315–333.

Kohn, B., & Dennis, M. (1974). Selective impairments of visuospatial abilities in infantile hemiplegics after right cerebral hemidecortication. *Neuropsychologia, 12,* 505–512.

Labov, W., & Waletzky, J. (1967). Narrative analysis: Oral versions of personal experience. In J. Helm (Ed.), *Essays on the verbal and visual arts* (pp. 12–44). Seattle: University of Washington Press.

Lenneberg, E. H. (1967). *Biological foundations of language*. New York: Wiley.

Leonard, L. (1998). *Children with specific language impairment*. Cambridge, MA: MIT Press.

Liles, B. (1993). Narrative discourse in children with language disorders and children with normal language: A critical review of the literature. *Journal of Speech and Hearing Research, 36,* 868–882.

Losh, M., Bellugi, U., Reilly, J., & Anderson, D. (2001). The integrity and independence of evaluation in narratives: Evidence from children with Williams Syndrome. *Narrative Inquiry, 10*(2), 265–290.

Loveland, K., McEvoy, R., & Tunali, B. (1990). Narrative story-telling in autism and Down syndrome. *British Journal of Developmental Psychology, 8,* 9–23.

MacWhinney, B. (1991). *The CHILDES Project: Tools for analyzing talk*. Hillsdale, NJ: Lawrence Erlbaum Associates.

Mayer, M. (1969). *Frog, where are you?* New York: Dial Press.

Peterson, C., & McCabe, E. (1983). *Developmental psycholinguistics: Three ways of looking at a child's narrative.* New York: Plenum.

Plante, E., Swisher, L., Vance, R., & Rapcsak, S. (1991). MRI findings in boys with specific language impairment. *Brain & Language, 41*(1), 52–66.

Poizner, H., Klima, E., & Bellugi, U. (1987). *What the hands reveal about the brain.* Cambridge, MA: MIT/Bradford Books.

Reilly, J., Klima, E., & Bellugi, U. (1991). Once more with feeling: Affect and language in atypical populations. *Development and Psychopathology, 2*(4), 367–391.

Reilly, J., Losh, M., Bellugi, U., & Wulfeck, B. (in press). "Frog, where are you?" Narratives in children with specific language impairment, early focal brain injury and Williams Syndrome. In B. Wulfeck & J. Reilly (Eds.), *Plasticity and development: Language in atypical children.*

Reilly, J. S. (1992). How to tell a good story: The intersection of language and affect in children's narratives. *Journal of Narrative and Life History, 2*(4), 355–377.

Reilly, J. S., Marchman, V. A., & Bates, E. A. (1998). Narrative discourse in children with early focal brain injury. *Brain & Language, 61*(3), 335–375.

Rice, M. (1996). *Toward a genetics of language*. Mahwah, NJ: Lawrence Erlbaum Associates.

Rice, M. L., & Oetting, J. B. (1993). Morphological deficits of children with SLI: Evaluation of number marking and agreement. *Journal of Speech & Hearing Research, 36*(6), 1249–1257.

Rice, M. L., & Wexler, K. (1996). Toward tense as a clinical marker of specific language impairment in English-speaking children. *Journal of Speech & Hearing Research, 39*(6), 1239–1257.

Semel, E., Wiig, E. H., & Secord, W. (1987). *Clinical evaluation of language fundamentals-revised.* San Antonio, TX: Psychological Corporation.

Slobin, D. I. (1985). *The cross-linguistic study of language acquisition: Volume 1. The data.* Hillsdale, NJ: Lawrence Erlbaum Associates.

Slobin, D. I. (1992). *The crosslinguistic study of language acquisition* (Vol. 3). Hillsdale, NJ: Lawrence Erlbaum Associates.

Slobin, D. I. (1997a). *The crosslinguistic study of language acquisition* (Vol. 4). Mahwah, NJ: Lawrence Erlbaum Associates.

Slobin, D. I. (1997b). *The crosslinguistic study of language acquisition: Vol. 5. Expanding the contexts.* Mahwah, NJ: Lawrence Erlbaum Associates.

Stiles, J., Stern, C., Trauner, D., & Nass, R. (1996). Developmental change in spatial grouping activity among children with early focal brain injury: Evidence from a modeling task. *Brain & Cognition, 31*(1), 46–62.

Stiles, J., & Thal, D. (1993). Linguistic and spatial cognitive development following early focal brain injury: Patterns of deficit and recovery. In M. H. Johnson (Ed.), *Brain development and cognition: A reader* (pp. 643–664). New York: Blackwell.

Stiles, J., Trauner, D., Engel, M., & Nass, R. (1997). The development of drawing in children with congenital focal brain injury: Evidence for limited functional recovery. *Neuropsychologia, 35*(3), 299–312.

Tager-Flusberg, H., & Sullivan, K. (1995). Attributing mental states to story characters: A comparison on narratives produced by autistic and mentally retarded individuals. *Applied Psycholinguistics, 16*(3), 241–256.

Thal, D. J., Marchman, V. A., Stiles, J., & Aram, D. (1991). Early lexical development in children with focal brain injury. *Brain & Language, 40*(4), 491–527.

Tomblin, J. B., & Pandich, J. (1999). Lessons from children with specific language impairment. *Trends in Cognitive Sciences, 3*(8), 283–285.

Trauner, D., Wulfeck, B., Tallal, P., & Hesselink, J. (2000). Neurological and MRI profiles of children with developmental language impairment. *Developmental Medicine & Child Neurology, 42,* 470–475.

Van Lancker, D., & Kempler, D. (1986). Comprehension of familiar phrases by left- but not by right-hemisphere-damaged patients. *Brain & Language, 32,* 265–277.

Weckerly, J., Reilly, J., & Wulfeck, B. (in press). In B. Wulfeck & J. Reilly (Eds.), *Plasticity and development: Language in atypical children.*

Zamora, A., & Reilly, J. S. (2001, June). *Frogs: A longitudinal study of narratives in children with early brain damage.* Poster presented at the meeting for the Society for Research in Child Language Disorders, Madison, WI.

3

Language Disorders Across Modalities: The Case of Developmental Dyslexia

Pieter H. Been
Frans Zwarts
University of Groningen

Developmental language impairment is a risk factor for other developmental disorders. Prospective studies following children with early developmental language impairment have shown a striking link with subsequent learning disabilities, especially developmental dyslexia (Bishop & Adams, 1990; Catts, 1993). In studies comparing dyslexic children with language-impaired children, both groups are specifically characterized by deficits in phonological analysis (Liberman et al., 1974; Wagner & Torgerson, 1987).

Indeed, converging evidence indicates that developmental dyslexia is a language disorder that often critically affects the phonological domain of language, although disturbances in the visual system also have been identified (Cornelissen et al., 1995; Eden et al., 1996; Lovegrove, Garzia, & Nicholson, 1990). The findings regarding visual problems are consistent with the processing of rapid information by the magnocellular pathway of the visual system. It has also been proposed that a slowed processing rate of acoustic cues may account for disturbances in phonological processing (Tallal, Miller, & Fitch, 1993). Increasing evidence indicates that rapid processing in general, across at least the auditory and visual modalities, is impaired in dyslexics. As far as the auditory modality is involved, a rapid temporal processing deficit may lead to problems with that part of language sounds (e.g., transients in some consonants, which require rapid processing). This may lead, in turn, to ambiguous entries in the phonological lexicon ultimately resulting in reading problems. As a matter of fact, about half a dozen studies have demonstrated speech-perception deficits in the reading-impaired showing up in deviant patterns of identification and discrimination among poor readers using synthetic continua between consonant vowel pairs (e.g., /ba/-/da/).

Both the auditory and visual systems mature during the first year of life. The cortical processing of the phonetical features of speech in adults is mainly handled by the left hemisphere, gravitating around Broca's area (Zatorre, Evans, Meyer, & Gjedde, 1992). Left-hemisphere cortical processing is tuned to the mother language. Listening to an unknown other language activates both hemispheres (Mazoyer et al., 1993). This hemisphere specialization develops soon after birth. Four-day-old babies can differentiate the mother language from an unknown language and two unknown languages from each other. At the age of 2 months, the language specialization of the left hemisphere seems to be established. The mother language can be differentiated from an unknown language, but the ability to differentiate two unknown languages from each other has vanished (Mehler, Dupoux, Pallier, & Dehaene-Lambertz, 1995). For adults, it is difficult to discriminate between vowels and consonants of other languages that are alien to the own language. Yet very young children are able to make these discriminations of alien vowels and consonants. The ability to discriminate alien consonants vanishes between the age of 8 and 12 months (Werker & Tees, 1984) and the ability to discriminate alien vowels at about the age of 6 months (Kuhl et al., 1992). The different ages at which specialization for vowels and consonants materialize fit within two-stage processing theories of speech perception (Berent & Perfetti, 1995). For the visual system, Johnson (1992, 1995) provided a detailed analysis of its maturation, which can be inferred from developmental patterns in eye movements. The connectivity between the cortical and subcortical structures of the parvocellular pathway is completed at the age of 3 months, that of the magnocellular pathway at 2 months.

Regarding the early maturation of the processes related to reading problems, delayed or deviant maturational processes could be used for the early diagnosis of risk at dyslexia. Moreover, when these processes are causal to reading problems, preventive intervention becomes feasible. Indeed discrimination in speech perception by very young infants as a predictor of later language skills is a target variable in recent prospective studies (Leppänen & Lyytinen, 1997; Molfese & Molfese, 1997; Richardson, 1998). Recently, it has been claimed that brain potentials evoked by consonant vowel pairs obtained within 36 hours after birth predict dyslexia at the age of 8 years with 81% accuracy (Molfese, 2000).

Dyslexics not only differ at the behavioral level when compared with normal readers; the dyslexic brain may also be different. Anomalies have been claimed at the level of neurons (thalamus and cortex) and global architecture. Among others, autopsies have revealed cortical ectopies in dyslexics (e.g., a reduced number of neurons in the upper layers of the cortex and an increased number in the lower ones; Galaburda, 1994). The fundamental cause is suspected to be genetic in origin.

The aim of this study is to relate the dyslexic brain to dyslexic behavior in auditory discrimination by means of dynamic modeling at the aggregated level of neuronal populations. Of course such a model is a simplification of reality. Yet such a model of interacting brain structures can provide better intuition than simple reasoning, especially in the case of nonlinearity and feedback loops. Comparison of model predictions with experimental results can lead to new insights, and predictions can be generated for new paradigms and interventions.

Here a model tailored to discrimination in speech perception (Grossberg, Boardman, & Cohen, 1997) is used for this purpose, which we extended with a layer for the detection of transients (linear sweeps) in the auditory signal. Dependent variables in the equations represent evoked potentials, which can be related to the behavioral level by assuming a detection threshold. The model incorporates equations for neurotransmitter dynamics. Assuming a lowered neuronal density in the case of dyslexia, reflecting ectopies, it may be postulated that less neuronal surface is available for synaptic connections resulting in a lowered synaptic density and thus a lowered amount of available neurotransmitter. A lowered synaptic density also implies a reduced amount of membrane surface available for neurotransmitter metabolism. By assuming both a reduced upper bound of neurotransmitter and a reduced metabolic transmitter rate in the dyslexic variety of the model, discrimination in speech perception can be modeled for the dyslexic and the normal case.

The first focus of this study are the results of a Finnish experiment assessing geminate stop perception in 6-month-old children. Perception was assessed by head turning employing an oddball paradigm (Richardson, 1998) and assessed in a subgroup of the same children by evoked potentials (Leppänen & Lyytinen, 1997). Stimuli were sampled from a synthetic continuum between /ata/ and /atta/. Two subgroups participated: a subgroup with genetic risk for dyslexia and a subgroup of controls.

The second focus of this study are the results of a Dutch experiment (Schwippert, 1998) assessing discrimination along a /bak/-/dak/ stimuli continuum by adult dyslexics and controls in a forced-choice paradigm. Starting from the /bak/ stimulus, spoken by a female native speaker, a synthetic continuum of 10 stimuli was derived by manipulating a 100-ms transient in the second formant. These stimuli were developed for the purpose of assessing the development of auditory discrimination of infants in the Dutch prospective study on dyslexia (National Steering Group Dyslexia, 1999).

Before we go into more detail of the dynamic model relating the neuronal level to the behavioral level, we discuss auditory discrimination in relation to dyslexia. In addition, we take a closer look at the neuroanatomical factors involved in dyslexia and its familial transmission. Finally, the results of the model simulations of stop perception and second formant transition perception are discussed—in relation to the experimental data, but also related to model predictions for intervention.

DEVELOPMENTAL DYSLEXIA: PHONOLOGY, NEUROANATOMY, AND FAMILIAL TRANSMISSION

We turn to a more in-depth treatment of some aspects of dyslexia that are of importance in this context. These aspects relate to phonology (especially phonological discrimination), neuroanatomical factors as revealed by autopsies, and familial risk.

Phonology

Phonological processing entails the segmental analysis of words for ordinary speaking and listening, as well as the metaphonological skills required for analyzing the sound structure of speech into the phonemic components represented by the alphabet. Many studies have shown dyslexic children to be inferior to same-age normal readers in their perceptual discrimination of phonemes, phonological awareness measured by tasks requiring the isolation and manipulation of phonemes within words, speed and accuracy in lexical access for picture names, verbal short-term and working memory, syntactic awareness, and semantic processing in tasks such as listening comprehension (Olson, 1994). Many of these weaknesses may arise from a subtle, but ramifying deficit in speech perception. Recent studies have provided ample evidence that differences in spoken language skills—especially awareness of phonemic segments—lead to difficulties in the phonological coding of written language, which is a key prerequisite for word recognition and spelling ability. The processing problems manifested by dyslexics give rise to the most diagnostic symptom of reading impairment: difficulty in pronouncing pseudowords (Bruck, 1988, 1990, 1992; Felton & Wood, 1992; Liberman & Shankweiler, 1985; Mann, 1984; Siegel & Ryan, 1988; Snowling, 1981, 1991; Stanovich, 1986). Although reading skills contribute reciprocally to the development of phonological skills as well (Wagner & Torgesen, 1987), indications are that a phonological deficit is causal to reading disability (Bradley & Bryant, 1978, 1983; Stanovich, 1988; Wagner, 1986).

The precursor to the phonological coding difficulty appears to be an impairment of segmental language skills sometimes termed *phonological awareness* or *phonological sensitivity* (Vellutino & Scanlon, 1987). Becoming aware of the segmental structure of language is thought to be a prerequisite to rapid reading acquisition in an alphabetic orthography because reduced phonological awareness inhibits the learning of the alphabetic coding patterns that underlie fluent word recognition (Goswami & Bryant, 1990; Stanovich, Cunningham, & Cramer, 1984). The intimate connection between phonological processing and reading skills began to be a focus of direct investigation about 30 years ago, when Liberman, Shankweiler, Fischer, and Carter (1974) provided the first experimental evidence of children's difficulty in explicitly identifying individual segments as compared with syllables. Following Mattingly (1972), they argued that this metalinguistic ability may be the major hurdle to be overcome in learning to read an alphabetic script. A number of other studies confirmed the general inability of many preliterate children to demonstrate awareness of phonemes in various tasks and began to show a relationship between phonemic awareness and learning to read (Fox & Routh, 1976; Lundberg, Olofsson, & Wall, 1980; Stanovich, Cunningham, & Cramer, 1984; Tunmer, Herriman, & Nesdale, 1988). The literature demonstrating the details of this relationship has become substantial, and research continues unabated today (see Perfetti, 1985; Vihman, 1996, for book-length surveys).

Perhaps the most impressive body of work concerning speech-perception deficits in the reading impaired are the half a dozen studies reporting deviant patterns of identification and discrimination among poor readers. Godfrey, Syrdal-Lasky, Millay, and Knox (1981), comparing performances on two synthetic continua, [ba]-[da] and [da]-[ga], found that dyslexic children were significantly less consistent in identification even at the extremes of the continua. Other studies have reported similar results for [ba]-[da] (Reed, 1989; Werker & Tees, 1987) and for [sa]-[sta] (Steffens, Eilers, Gross-Glen, & Jallad, 1992). In several of these studies, inconsistent identification also gave rise to deviant patterns of discrimination along synthetic continua. Impaired readers performed significantly worse than normal controls between phoneme categories but not within, indicating that they could not easily exploit the phonological contrast that normally enhances discrimination across a phoneme boundary (De Weirdt, 1988; Godfrey, Syrdal-Lasky, Millay, & Knox, 1981; Pallay, 1986; Werker & Tees, 1987). Their difficulties were primarily in identifying and discriminating phonetically similar, although phonologically contrastive, synthetic syllables. Such results suggest that speech categories may be broader and less sharply separated in reading-disabled than in normal children (Mody, Studdert-Kennedy, & Brady, 1996; Reed, 1989; Studdert-Kennedy & Mody, 1995).

Although the connection between phonology and reading is no longer in doubt, the directionality and nature of the postulated interaction remains controversial (see reviews by Bowey & Francis, 1991; Perfetti, 1994; Wagner & Torgesen, 1987).

Recent evidence (Torgesen, Wagner, & Rashotte, 1994; Wagner & Torgesen, 1987; Wagner, Torgesen, & Rashotte, 1994) shows that phonological awareness is a multivariate construct containing a number of partly independent variables, none of which represents a unitary core feature. Many dyslexic individuals, although aware of the segmental structure of language (Van Bon, Schreuder, Duighuisen, & Kerstholt, 1994), are less sensitive to phonemic elements of speech and less able to manipulate them, but the results demonstrate that this may be related either to the poorer quality of the acquired phonological representations (Elbro, Nielsen, & Petersen, 1994) or a poorly organized phonological lexicon (Aaron, 1989).

Neuroanatomical Factors

Although the pathophysiology of developmental dyslexia below the level of behavior is less well understood, postmortem studies and, more recently, in vivo observations by means of magnetic resonance imaging (MRI), event-related potentials (ERP), and positron emission tomography (PET) indicate that dyslexia is accompanied by fundamental changes in the anatomy and physiology of the brain, which can be attributed to an anomalous balance in cerebral hemisphere development. The reported anomalies are largely restricted to the left hemisphere, extend to areas known to be critical to the support of normal linguistic capacity, and involve several stages in the processing stream. In fact, Galaburda and his colleagues (Humphreys, Kaufmann, & Galaburda, 1990) found alterations in the pattern of cortical asymmetry that may point to left-hemisphere brain dysfunction. Specifically, the ordinary pattern of leftward asymmetry of the planum temporale is absent, and the perisylvian cortex displays minor cytoarchitectonic malformations, including foci of ectopic neurons in the molecular layer and focal microgyria (Galaburda, 1994; Galaburda, Rosen, & Sherman, 1989) and an excessive number of neurons in the deeper layers of the neocortex, but relatively few in the upper layers (Galaburda, 1983; Galaburda & Kemper, 1979; Kemper, 1984). In addition, anomalies in the anterior callosal pathways connecting the right and left temporal planes have been found (Hynd, Marshall, & Gonzalez, 1991; Hynd, Marshall, & Semrud-Clikeman, 1991; Semrud-Clikeman, Hynd, Novey, & Eliopulos, 1991).

A second set of observations involves subcortical structures and relates to the human dyslexic thalamus. Galaburda and Livingstone (1993), Livingstone, Rosen, Drislane, and Galaburda (1991), and Galaburda, Menard, and Rosen (1994) found that neurons in the magnocellular layers of the lateral geniculate nucleus and in the left medial geniculate nucleus are smaller than expected. The former is associated with slowness in the early segments of the magnocellular pathway of the visual system, as assessed by evoked response techniques measuring both magnocellular and parvocellular function. The latter may relate to the temporal processing abnormalities described in the auditory system of language-impaired children (Tallal & Piercy, 1973), which have long been suspected to underlie deficits of aphasic patients as well (Efron, 1963). As Galaburda (1994) noted, the relationship between the lack of asymmetry and the cortical malformations found in dyslexic brains, on the one hand, and the anomaly in rapid temporal processing associated with thalamic changes, on the other, is an important research question.

Familial Transmission

The observation that common forms of dyslexia are hereditary has recently been the focus of renewed interest. Familial transmission of dyslexia and the significant genetic risk to first-degree relatives have both been known for almost a century (Pennington, 1990). It was reported in a number of case studies that dyslexic children often had an affected relative (e.g., Thomas, 1905).

The magnitude of familial risk for dyslexia has not been measured in a representative population sample until recently. In a selected sample of Stockholm families, Hallgren (1950) found the risk to first-degree relatives to be 41%, which is considerably higher than the population risk (5%-10%).

Hallgren's diagnoses of affected family members were not based on testing, however, and ascertainment biases may have led to the selection of families with higher than normal proportions of affected relatives. Recent evidence from large data sets, such as the Iowa Family Study of Reading Disabilities (Gilger, Pennington, & DeFries, 1991), indicates that both dyslexic boys and girls often have an affected parent. The odds are five- to sevenfold increased for boys and ten- to twelvefold for girls. Bayesian estimates of the posterior probability that a child will be dyslexic given a dyslexic parent vary from 0.38 to 0.53 (median rate: 0.43) for male offspring of dyslexic men (Gilger, Pennington, & DeFries, 1991).

Another question to consider is whether familiality indicates genetic transmission. To provide an answer to this question, research has concentrated almost exclusively on twins. Several well-designed twin studies have recently been conducted. They have shown a substantial genetic component to the disorder, with heritable variation estimated at 50% to 70% (DeFries, Fulker, & LaBuda, 1987).

Modeling Phonological Discrimination
Within the Context of Reading

The role of phonology in reading can be exemplified by the global dynamic model of reading in Fig. 3.1 (e.g., Coltheart, Curtis, Atkins, & Haller, 1993; Seidenberg & McClelland, 1989), which can be related functionally to (sub)cortical regions for auditory and speech processing.

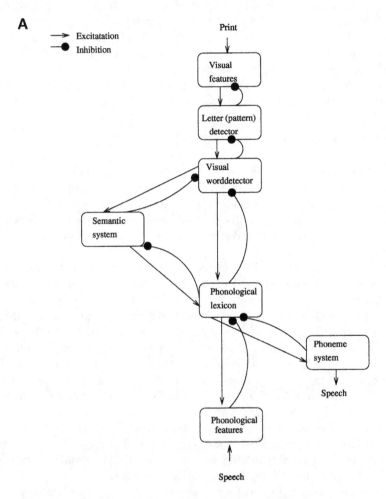

FIG. 3.1. (A) Reading model. Relationship to cortical structures (Petersen et al., 1988). Visual features: striate cortex. Letter pattern and word detector: extrastriate cortex. Semantic system: Broca's area. Phonological lexicon: temperoparietal cortex. Phoneme system: inferior premotor sylvian areas, supplementary motor cortex, lateral premotor cortex. Phonological features: primary auditory cortex.

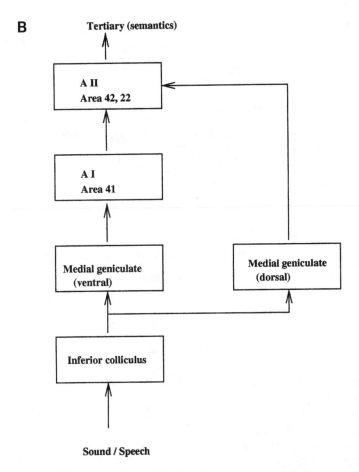

FIG. 3.1. (B) More detailed model of auditory perception including cortical level (primary auditory cortex: A I, secondary auditory cortex: A II) and thalamic part (medial geniculate ventral: parvo part, dorsal: magno part). The ventral medial geniculate–A I–A II route is involved in e.g., frequency and intensity mapping of sounds. The dorsal medial geniculate–A II route is probably involved in processing vocalizations and sensitive to transients in the formants of speech signals.

As can be derived from the global reading model in Fig. 3.1A, the conjecture is that, at the cortical level, phonological features in interaction with a phonological lexicon are responsible for speech processing. It can be hypothesized that disturbed auditory processing results in a deficient phonological lexicon. Because the phonological lexicon is also involved in speech recognition and speech production, impairment in these processes is predicted by the hypothesis. Ultimately, at the reading age, a deficient phonological lexicon can cause disturbances in grapheme to phoneme

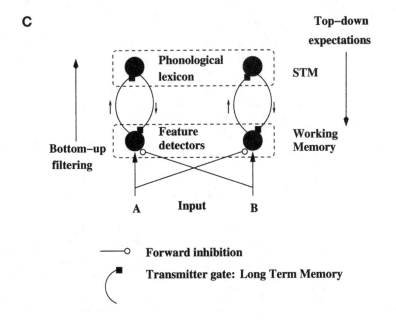

FIG. 3.1.   (C) Basic architecture of ARTPHONE.

conversion by the interaction between the module for visual word detection and the phonological lexicon module.

A global sketch of the cortical and subcortical structures involved in sound and speech processing is depicted in Fig. 3.1B. Before sound is processed in the cortex, the signal transmitted by the cochlea has passed a number of subcortical structures in the brain, of which in this context the thalamus and inferior colliculus are the most important (Kolb & Wishaw, 1995). Cortical structures for auditory processing feed back to the thalamus and inferior colliculus. In the primary auditory cortex, there are cortical maps, among others, for pitch and frequency, which project to the secondary auditory cortex (Schreiner, 1995). Studies in primates show that groups of neurons in secondary auditory cortical areas (e.g., the superior temporal gyrus) are sensitive to vocals with communicative meaning independent of variations in the spectral makeup of the vocalization. The same cortical area also contains a large proportion of neurons that are sensitive to frequency changes in auditory stimuli (Rauschecker, Tian, & Hauser, 1995). Groups of neurons in higher auditory cortex tuned to frequency modulation and vocal perception could play a role in human speech perception (King, 1995). Indeed, PET studies show that, in humans, the posterior region of the superior temporal gyrus, which is part of the secondary auditory cortex surrounding the primary auditory cortex, is involved in phoneme identification (Zotorre et al., 1996).

Although the auditory system does not have a distinct magnocellular pathway for processing transients like the visual system, there is an auditory subsystem characterized by large neurons that is responsible for processing acoustic transients (Stein & Walsh, 1997). In terms of Fig. 3.1B, this means that the (magno) dorsal route via the medial geniculate in the thalamus to the secondary auditory cortex plays an important role in speech and frequency modulation processing. Again in terms of Fig. 3.1B, the (parvo) ventral route via the medial geniculate in the thalamus and the primary auditory cortex to the secondary auditory cortex provides for processing of frequency and intensity. This arrangement is reminiscent of separate channels in the visual system for processing transient input (dorsal stream) and sustained input (ventral stream).

Boardman, Grossberg, Myers, and Cohen (1999) hypothesized that the parallel dorsal stream for detecting transients (e.g., frequency modulations and formant transitions) and ventral stream for detecting steady state features (e.g., frequencies) serve to separate coarticulated consonants and vowels in an early stage of auditory filtering. Based on animal studies and in line with the diagram in Fig. 3.1B, the inferior colliculus is a good candidate for such a separation process (Fuzzessary & Hall, 1996).

Dynamic Model

As we have seen, converging evidence indicates that developmental dyslexia is a language disorder that often critically affects the phonological domain of language. Heritable differences in spoken language skills—especially awareness of phonemic segments—lead to difficulties in the phonological coding of written language, which is a key prerequisite for word recognition and spelling ability. These weaknesses may arise from a subtle deficit in speech perception. About half a dozen studies have demonstrated speech-perception deficits in the reading impaired showing up in deviant patterns of identification and discrimination among poor readers using synthetic continua between consonant vowel pairs (e.g., /ba/-/da/). Discrimination in speech perception by very young infants as a predictor of later language skills and reading problems is a target variable in recent prospective studies (Leppänen & Lyytinen, 1997; Molfese, 2000; Molfese & Molfese, 1997; Richardson, 1998). In such prospective studies, one can take advantage of the genetic risk of dyslexia (Scarborough, 1989, 1990, 1991). By sampling at-risk infants with at least one affected parent and preferably an affected first-degree relative, the odds that a child in the sample ultimately becomes dyslexic are raised to the 40% range compared with a 5% to 10%

population risk. Such a sample suffices to compare ultimately affected and unaffected children on a number of measurements obtained in the prospective study. Intermediate results can be obtained by adding a sample of children without genetic risk. The presumed oversampling of ultimate dyslexics in the at-risk group biases the results in the direction of the results ultimately obtained when comparing at risks and controls. Therefore, comparing at-risk children and controls during the prospective study reflects the final results of group comparisons, be it less pronounced. Such a sampling strategy has been adopted in a Finnish prospective study (Leppänen & Lyytinen, 1997; Richardson, 1998) and recently in a Dutch prospective study (National Steering Group Dyslexia, 1999).

We have also seen that the dyslexic brain may be different. Anomalies have been claimed at the level of neurons (thalamus and cortex) and global architecture. Among others, autopsies have revealed cortical ectopies in dyslexics (e.g., a reduced number of neurons in the upper layers of the cortex and an increased number in the lower ones).

In dynamic models of phonological perception, the behavioral level can be related to the neurophysiological level at different levels of detail and neural plausibility. These model levels range from large-scale networks of individual neurons to connectionist networks of abstract type, emphasizing functionality rather than neuronal plausibility. At the detailed level of individual neurons, Buonomano and Merzenich (1995) demonstrated that a network of 400 neurons in two neocortical layers, with proportions excitatory and inhibitory connections derived from neurophysiological studies, is able to learn /ba/-/pa/ discriminations. At the more abstract level of connectionist models, it has been demonstrated that disturbed phonological processing produces problems in pseudoword reading as seen in developmental dyslexics (Brown, 1997) and impairment in inflectional morphology resembling those of developmental dysphasia (Hoeffner & McClelland, 1993). Although the output of both detailed networks of neurons and connectionist models can be interpreted unequivocally, the intermediate processes are less transparent. Intermediate types of dynamic models at the aggregated level of groups of neurons (Cowan & Ermentrout, 1978) offer the advantage that potentials evoked at intermediate levels of processing can be studied. Here ARTPHONE, an aggregated model tailored to discrimination in speech perception (Grossberg, Boardman, & Cohen, 1997), is used for this purpose. Dependent variables in the equations represent evoked potentials, which can be related to the behavioral level by assuming a detection threshold. The model incorporates equations for neurotransmitter dynamics. Assuming a lowered neuronal density in the case of dyslexia, reflecting ectopies, it may be postulated that less neuronal surface is available for synaptic connections resulting in a lowered synaptic density and thus a lowered amount of available neurotransmitter. A lowered synaptic density also implies a reduced amount of membrane surface available for neurotransmitter metabolism. By assuming both a reduced upper bound of neurotransmitter and a reduced metabolic transmitter rate in the model, discrimination in speech perception can be modeled for the dyslexic and the normal case.

ARTPHONE

The ARTPHONE model was developed by Grossberg, Boardman, and Cohen (1997) as a neuronal model to quantitatively simulate experimental data on stop consonant perception in /ib/-/ga/ and /ib/-/ba/ stimuli as reported by Repp (1980). Dependent on the silent interval between /ib/ and /ga/ or /ib/ and /ba/, fusion can occur resulting in the percepts /iga/ and /iba/.

The basic architecture of ARTPHONE is depicted in Fig. 3.1C. It consists of neuronal ensembles with dedicated functions, which can be thought of as groups of neurons represented by the black circles. There is a layer of two ensembles representing the phonological lexicon and a layer of two auditory feature detectors denoted by black circles. This minimal configuration suffices to sketch the principles involved in the working of the model.

The dynamics of each ensemble is described by one first-order differential equation and generates a model potential. An input delivered activates the left-feature detector and inhibits the right-feature detector by means of forward inhibition. The activation is passed to the left ensemble in the phonological lexicon along the pathway with the upward arrow. The activation is multiplied by a transmitter gate (black box), which can be thought of as a connection of aggregated synapses. Also the dynamics of a transmitter gate is described by a first-order differential equation describing exponential inactivation and resupply of transmitter when the activation is passed to the left ensemble in the lexicon. When the activation passed to the ensemble in the lexicon exceeds a predefined activation threshold, resonance in the lexical ensemble sets in, sweeping the activation level above perceptual threshold.

Resonance can only occur when the transmitter supply at the transmitter gate, representing long-term memory by the strength of synaptic connections, is sufficient. In this case, the transmitter gate acts as a bottom–up filter.

The activation of the lexical detector is fed back to the feature detector along the pathway with the top–down arrow. Again activation is multiplied by a transmitter gate. This feedback loop represents the top–down expectation. When the synaptic connection is strong enough, transmitter supply is sufficient for the transmitter gate to keep the resonance going— hence the acronym ART, which stands for adaptive resonance theory.

Transmitter levels at the bottom–up and top–down relays become exponentially inactivated at sufficiently high activation levels: a habituation process. This leads to a subsequent decrease of the activations levels of the ensembles at the feature level and the lexicon.

For the differential equations and a detailed explanation of the workings of ARTPHONE, as far as needed for our model study, the reader is referred to Been and Zwarts (2000).

For the purpose of illustration, suppose that the /b/ part of the /ib/-/ga/ stimulus is delivered at A and the /g/ part at B with a short interval. In that case, the loop connected to the A input is quenched off by the feed forward inhibition delivered by the /g/ part at B before resonance can set in. Activation in the loop connected to A does not exceed perceptual threshold, and the resulting percept is [iga]. Perceptual fusion has occurred. With an interval of sufficient length between delivery of /b/ and /g/, both loops exceed perceptual threshold by resonance and [ibga] is perceived.

In the case of the /ib/-/ba/ stimulus, stop consonant gemination, which refers to the percept of a double consonant arising from a single closure production, can occur in the model. In this case, only one loop in the model (e.g., the loop above input A) is needed. When the second /b/ is delivered at A with a sufficiently long silent interval after the first /b/, activation in the lexical ensemble above A can rise above perceptual threshold and fall down below it before activated by the second /b/. A double stop [ibba] is perceived. Taking a short interval between delivery of the first and second /b/ at A does not allow the activation at the lexical ensemble to fall below perceptual threshold before it is activated by the second /b/. As a result, the percept is [iba].

The ARTPHONE model is tailored to stop perception and consequently is well suited to simulate the results of the Finnish experiment assessing geminate stop perception in 6-month-old infants as assessed by head turning employing an oddball paradigm (Richardson, 1998) and as assessed in a subgroup of the same children by evoked potentials (Leppänen & Lyytinen, 1997). However, the ARTPHONE model is not suited for the simulation of the processing of frequency changes at different rates. For that reason, we added a SWEEP model to ARTPHONE consisting of a layer of groups of neurons that exhibit sensitivity to rate of change of frequency.

SWEEP

For the simulation of frequency change processing, the transient detector (SWEEP) depicted in Fig. 3.2 was designed. The global architecture of the model is in line with the cortical structures involved in auditory processing in Fig. 3.2. The path via the transient detector resembles the dorsal pathway of the medial geniculate and the path via the sustained signal the ventral pathway.

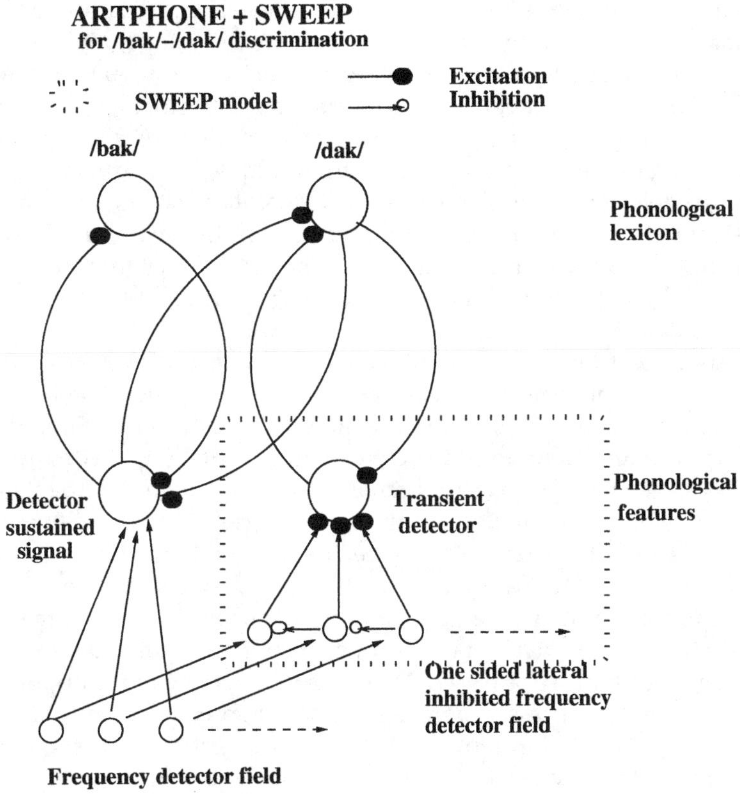

ARTPHONE + SWEEP
for /bak/–/dak/ discrimination

FIG. 3.2. Combined ARTPHONE and SWEEP model for /bak/-/dak/ discrimination. Input is received at the cortical level by groups of neurons that are sensitive to specific frequencies. Groups of neurons arranged along an isofrequency gradient are found in the primary auditory cortex. Such groups of neurons can feed a field with one-sided lateral inhibition suited for the detection of sweeps in a (non) preferred direction as shows up in electrophysiological studies of neurons in the posterior auditory field of the cat (Heil & Dexter, 1998). Such arrangements have been proposed for a synaptic movement detection mechanism in the visual cortex (Torre & Poggio, 1978). Alternatively, in line with arrangements found in the visual system, the information streams to the transient and sustained system may already be separated below the cortical level. In that case, the information stream is not passed from the frequency detector field to the one-sided lateral inhibited frequency detector field, but receive both fields separated input. However, the results of the simulations would be the same in both cases. Equations and parameter values in Been and Zwarts (2000).

The basic idea of SWEEP is that a layer of a neuronal groups, in which each group is sensitive to a narrow frequency range, feed forward to a similar layer in which the neuronal groups inhibit laterally in one direction: There is a one-to-one correspondence between a frequency detector field and a one-sided lateral inhibited frequency detector field. The output of the lateral inhibited frequency detector field converges to a transient detector. Transients in the speech signal or frequency modulated sounds excite the detectors in fast succession. These excitations are summed at the transient detector by the converging input from the lateral inhibited detector field. Because of the rise and fall times of the excitations in the frequency detectors and the transient detector, the summed excitation at the transient detector is sensitive to the rate of change of frequency. Inputs delivered at short intervals at the transient detector accumulate to higher levels than inputs at longer intervals. However, at short intervals, the short rise times also restrict the possible level of accumulation. Hence, there is a nonlinear relationship between the stimulation rate of the inhibited frequency field and the accumulated excitation in the transient detector. Moreover, the summation at the transient detector is sensitive to the direction of the transient in the speech signal or frequency modulated sound. When excitations traverse the field in the one-sided lateral inhibited direction, excited detectors are simultaneously inhibited that suppresses the level of excitation. As a consequence, the summed input at the transient detector is suppressed. Excitations traversing in the opposite direction are not suppressed because inhibition spreads behind.

The input to the transient detector has to reflect the variable rates of change of frequency (RCFs) as occur in transients in the speech signal. Electrophysiological data of the activity of neurons in the auditory cortex elicited by auditory signals with different RCFs can provide information to estimate the amplitude of the input into the transient detector dependent on the RCF. Such data, obtained in the posterior auditory field of the cat, are provided by Heil and Dexter (1998). On average, there is a curvilinear relationship between the RCF of the auditory signal and response of neurons as measured by the number of spikes generated (cf. Heil et al., 1998). There is a different sensitivity to RCFs in the upward and downward directions.

In principle, these data can be used to estimate the amplitude of the input into the transient detector in the model, assuming there is a linear relationship between number of spikes generated and (model) evoked potential at the transient detector. However, a difference in stimulus characteristics used in the Heil et al. study and transients in speech signals is prohibitive for this straightforward application. In the Heil et al. study, stimuli RCFs were of fixed extent and variable duration. However, transients in speech stimuli often have fixed duration and variable extent.

Therefore, we specified a dynamic model (SWEEP) for RCF detection, with one-sided lateral inhibition to arrange for different sensitivity to the direction of RCF as show up in the Heil et al. data. The arrangement we used has been proposed for a synaptic movement-detection mechanism in the visual cortex (Torre & Poggio, 1978). The SWEEP model, as used here, consists of a field of 20 one-sided lateral inhibited frequency detectors, which are all connected to the transient detector (cf. Fig. 3.2). For the implementation, we used the same first-order differential equations as in ARTPHONE (Been & Zwarts, 2000). In SWEEP, there are only lateral and bottom–up connections, which are gated by transmitter dynamics.

First, the SWEEP model was calibrated to the Heil et al. data using input of variable duration and fixed extent. Next, simulations were run to determine the response to input of fixed duration and variable extent as in speech stimuli. The model output in the nonpreferred direction for both input conditions is different. For the input condition with fixed extent and variable duration (Heil), the model output increases exponentially with RCF in the relevant RCF range. For the fixed duration and variable extent input condition (speech), model output decreases exponentially with RCF in the same range. For humans, downward changes of rate of frequency seem to be the nonpreferred direction (Collins, 1984). So in the simulations, downward RCFs are processed in the inhibited direction of the detector field.

Model Simulations and Experimental Results

The next step is to test the capability of the ARTPHONE and SWEEP models to reproduce experimental data obtained from controls and dyslexics or infants at risk for dyslexia.

Stop Perception: AT(T)A

First we turn to the capability of the ARTPHONE model to simulate double- versus single-stop perceptions, dependent on the silent interval, in simulating the experimental results obtained with a Finnish pseudoword: the /at/-/ta/ stimulus.

In the Finnish prospective study on dyslexia, the pseudoword stimulus AT(T)A was used to investigate the role of duration in categorization of speech sounds by at-risk infants and control infants at the age of 6 months. Finnish is a quantitative language: Nearly all vowels and consonants can be long or short and make a difference in the meaning of a word. So the ability to differentiate double stops from single stops is an important one in Finnish language acquisition. The choice for the AT(T)A stimulus reflects this importance of duration in the Finnish language. The AT(T)A stimulus was constructed from the utterance /ata/ of a female native speaker pronouncing the pseudoword in the context of meaningful text.

The duration of the silent closure stage after the dental stop /t/ was 95 ms in the original utterance. Starting from the original utterance, a synthetic continuum of eight stimuli (ATTA1 to ATTA8) was constructed by incrementing the duration of the silent closure with 20 ms steps until ATTA7 with a 215 ms closure. For the final ATTA8, an extra 20 ms was added resulting in a 255 ms silent closure interval. Along this synthetic continuum, perception gradually shifts from a single-stop consonant [ata] to a double-stop consonant [atta] (Richardson, 1998). Discrimination experiments were run in a behavioral and an evoked potential variety, in both cases employing an oddball paradigm, using repeated delivery of the standard ATTA1 stimulus (silent interval 95 ms) interspersed with an occasional deviant ATTA2 to ATTA8 (silent intervals 115 to 255 ms).

Behavioral Head Turning Experiment

In the behavioral experiment, the technique of head turning was used. The infant is trained to turn its head to a rewarding device when the deviant is perceived. About half of the 6-month-old children did not pass the training procedure. The comparison between the at-risk group and the control group is based on the results of 43 at-risk infants and 46 control infants (Richardson, 1998). The results are depicted in Fig. 3.3. The caption is relatively self-contained, so we summarize the conclusion that the perceptual boundary for the at-risk infants is shifted to the right in comparison with the control infants. A longer silent interval is needed to shift perception from ATA to ATTA.

For the simulation of the behavioral AT(T)A experiment, an ART-PHONE model was used as exemplified by the /ib/-/ba/ example. As in the case of the /ib/-/ba/ stimulus, in the /at/-/ta/ stimulus, stop consonant gemination can occur in the model. Only one loop of the model is needed. When the second part of the stimulus after the closure interval is delivered at the input side with a sufficiently long silent interval after the the stimulus part before the closure interval, activation in the lexical ensemble can rise above perceptual threshold and fall down below it before activated by the second part. A double stop [atta] is perceived. Taking a short interval between delivery of the first and second parts of the stimulus does not allow the activation at the lexical ensemble to fall below perceptual threshold before it is activated by the second part. As a result, the percept is [ata].

In the model simulation, the same silent intervals were used as in the experiment. In the simulation, white noise was added to the threshold (Grossberg et al., 1997), which may be considered equivalent to a constant threshold and a noisy ongoing brain activity (Anderson, 1983).

A Model simulation controls

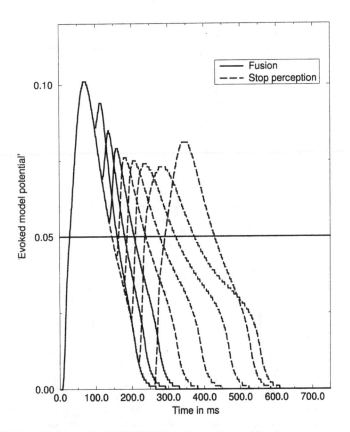

FIG. 3.3. Model results (ARTPHONE) and experimental head turning results (Richardson, 1998) for the at-risk and control infants with the AT(T)A
stimuli. The amount of neurotransmitter is reduced by 10% in the model of
the at risks and the exponential parameter determining metabolic rate is set
to a lower value. See also Been and Zwarts (2000). All other parameters
were the same for the control and at-risk models. The lower upper bound
and the lower metabolic rate of neurotransmitter reflect the ectopy hypothesis based on autopsies of the dyslexic brain. (A) Output of the neuronal ensemble at the level of the phonological lexicon for the controls. When the
model potential does not fall below threshold level before the stimulus part
after the silent interval is processed (solid lines), fusion occurs and the percept is /ATA/. When the model potential falls below threshold level, the
geminate stop is perceived (dashed lines) and the percept is /ATTA/.

B   Model simulation at risks

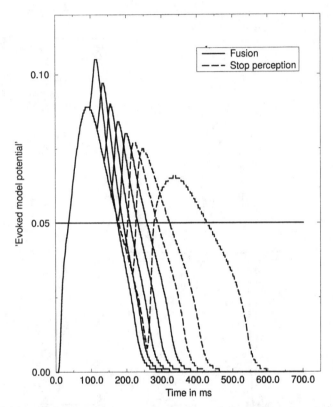

FIG. 3.3.   (B) Output of the neuronal ensemble at the level of the phonological lexicon for the infants at risk for dyslexia. Compared to the model results of the control infants, (a) the latency onto peak amplitude is longer, (b)
the peak amplitude is lower, and (c) the decay rate of the first and second
waves is slowed down. Consequently, the same observations are predicted
for evoked potential studies.

   The ectopy hypothesis was incorporated in the simulations by assuming that less neurons are available at the feature level and the lexical level
in the at-risk infants. So there is less neuronal surface available for synaptic connections and there are less synapses. This results in a lower amount
of neurotransmitter and less synaptic surface for release and reuptake of
transmitter. This was reflected in the model simulations by a lower upper
bound of transmitter and slowed down release and reuptake parameter
(Been & Zwarts, 2000).
   As can be seen in Fig. 3.3A, the activity at the lexical level falls below
threshold between ATTA3 and ATTA4 for the simulation of the control

C   Head turning controls

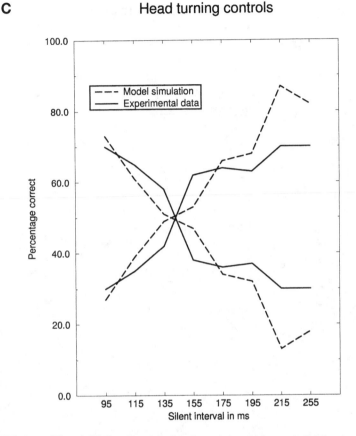

FIG. 3.3.   (C) and (D) Results of the head turning experiment (solid lines) and the model simulation (dotted lines): (C) control infants, and (D) at-risk infants. Ascending curves represent the percentages perceived deviants (y axis) with an increased silent interval (x axis). Descending curves represent the complement: the odds that the difference is not perceived. The crossing of perceived percentages and its complements at chance level (50%) is considered the perceptual boundary. The perceptual boundary for the at-risk infants is shifted to the right in comparison to the control infants. A longer silent interval is needed to shift perception from ATA to ATTA.

infants and about ATTA5 for the at-risk infants (Fig. 3.3B). As to be expected by the parameter settings, there is a slowed down inactivation and recuperation of transmitter. By running 500 simulations with white noise added to the perceptual threshold, the behavioral data can be approximated to a considerable degree (dashed lines of the model compared to the solid lines obtained in the experiment; Fig. 3.3A left: controls, Fig. 3.3B right: at risks).

D   Head turning at risks

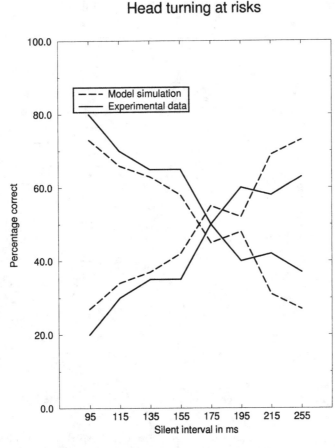

FIG. 3.3.   *(Continued)*

The upper bound of neurotransmitter and the release and reuptake parameter were varied in these simulations to fit the data. In the remaining simulations, comparing at risks (dyslexics) and controls, they were fixed to the values as obtained in this simulation. All other parameters were also kept fixed.

Evoked Potential Study

Part of the infants participating in the head turning study (Richardson, 1998) also took part in the evoked potential study. The same oddball paradigm was used for the delivery of stimuli as in the behavioral study without eliciting a response. A preliminary analysis of the data obtained from

18 at-risk infants and 17 controls was provided by Leppänen and Lyytinen (1997). The difference between the potential evoked by the deviant ATTA8 stimulus and the standard ATTA1 stimulus revealed a significant difference between the control group and the at-risk group at electrode position C3 (Fig. 3.4). The amplitude of the difference wave was lower for the at risks compared with the controls.

In the simulation of the evoked potential study, the same equations and parameter values were used as in the behavioral model study. The model potential (activity) at the lexical node for the ATTA8 condition was simply subtracted from the model potential in the ATTA1 condition. As in the evoked potential data, the difference wave of the model potentials shows a diminished amplitude of the difference wave for the at-risk simulation (Fig. 3.4).

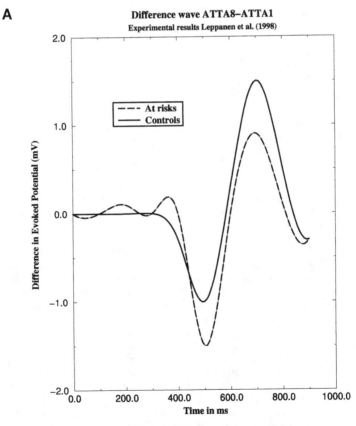

FIG. 3.4.   (Continued)

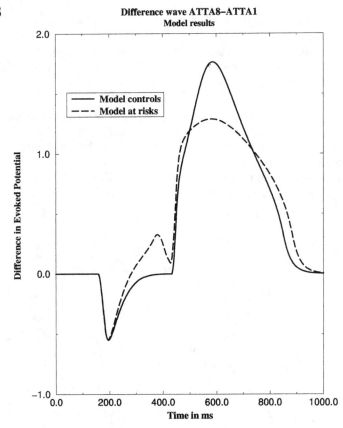

Difference wave ATTA8–ATTA1
Model results

FIG. 3.4. Model results (ARTPHONE) and experimental results of the evoked potential study with the AT(T)A stimuli (Leppänen et al., 1998). Part of infants participating in the head turning study (Richardson, 1998) also took part in the evoked potential study. In the simulation of the evoked potential study, the same parameter values were used as in the simulation of the head turning study. The head turning study and the evoked potential study employed the same oddball paradigm. Left part: The difference of the average potential evoked by the ATTA8 and ATTA1 stimulus revealed a significant difference between at-risk infants and controls at electrode C3. The difference waves of the at-risk and control infants were reproduced from Leppänen et al. (1998). The amplitude of the difference wave in the 600 ms to 1,000 ms interval is reduced for the at-risk infants compared with the difference wave of the control infants. Right part: Difference wave between ATTA8 and ATTA1 derived from the simulation with the ARTPHONE equations. The simulation also produces a difference wave of diminished amplitude for the at-risk infants. Again as in the simulation study of the head turning data, only the parameters for the upper bound of neurotransmitter and the metabolic rate of neurotransmitter were set to (the same) lower values for the at-risk infants.

Second Formant Transitions: /bak/-/dak/

The next subject of our model study concerns the results of two experiments assessing the perceptions of transients in the second formant with Dutch /bak/-/dak/ stimuli comparing adult dyslexics and controls (Schwippert, 1998; ter Beek & Klooster, 2000). The synthetic /bak/-/dak/ continuum was developed by Schwippert (1998). Taking a /bak/ stimulus uttered by a Dutch native female speaker, in a 100 ms interval in the second formant, the initial frequency of 1100 Hz was raised in 9 equal steps of 78 Hz to 1800 Hz, which produces rates of change of frequencies ranging from .78 Hz/ms to 7 Hz/ms. This resulted in 10 stimuli along a synthetic continuum, of which the percept gradually changes from /bak/ to /dak/.

In the discrimination experiments of Schwippert (1998) and ter Beek et al. (2000), using the Schwippert stimuli, a paired comparison paradigm was used. From the synthetic continuum of 10 stimuli, three point-equidistant pairs along the continuum were presented: 1–4, 2–5, to 7–10. All stimuli were of 600 ms duration. In the Schwippert study, interstimulus intervals (ISIs) of 25 and 400 ms were used. In the ter Beek et al. study, 1,000 ms intervals were used. In the Schwippert study, participants were 12 adult dyslexics and 12 adult controls; in the ter Beek study, eight dyslexics and eight controls participated. The results for the Schwippert 25 ms ISIs and the ter Beek 1,000 ms ISIs for the 2–5 to 7–10 comparisons can be found in Fig. 3.5A.

Discrimination is best for the 2–5 to 4–7 stimuli contrasts, with a peak for the 3–5 comparison in both studies and for both groups. In both studies, discrimination is worse for the dyslexic adults, the difference in both studies yielding statistical significance. On the average, the discriminated proportions for the 2–5 to 4–7 stimuli contrasts are somewhat higher in the ter Beek et al. study.

For the simulation, the combined ARTPHONE–SWEEP model depicted in Fig. 3.2 was used. The ARTPHONE part consists of two detectors at the level of the phonological lexicon: one for /bak/ and one for /dak/. In the simulation, the fixed part of the stimulus determines the sustained input and the synthetic part the input to the transient detector. The input to the sustained detector was fixed and of the same amplitude and type— a square input function, as in the simulations of stop perception. The input to the transient detector was delivered by the SWEEP model. The SWEEP model, as used here, consisted of a field of 20 one-sided lateral inhibited frequency detectors, which all feed to the transient detector where the input is summed. Transients transferred the detector field in the nonpreferred direction (e.g., in the direction of the lateral inhibitory connections) because for humans downward changes of rate of frequency seem to be the nonpreferred direction (Collins, 1984).

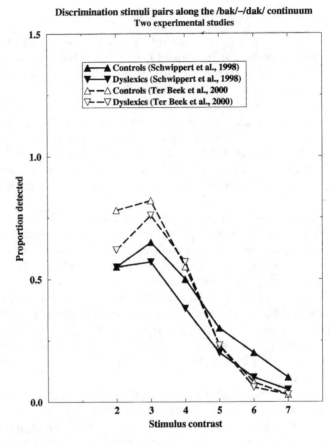

A

Discrimination stimuli pairs along the /bak/–/dak/ continuum
Two experimental studies

FIG. 3.5.   *(Continued)*

Simulation and Experimental Data

To simulate the /bak/-/dak/ experiments, we used four varieties of the combined ARTPHONE and SWEEP model. A variety with transmitter parameters as for the controls in the stop perception simulation, both for the ARTPHONE and SWEEP part; and three varieties in which the transmitter parameters were set to the dyslexic values of the stop perception simulation. In the latter case, either SWEEP or ARTPHONE transmitter parameters were set to dyslexic values or both. The results can be found in Fig. 3.5B (right upper part). As in the experiments, discrimination is best for the 2–5 and 3–6 contrasts. The control model performs best. Model performance is gradually decreasing for the ARTPHONE dyslexic condition, the SWEEP dyslexic condition, and the both parts dyslexic condition, in that order. As a next step, the control model output was fitted by regres-

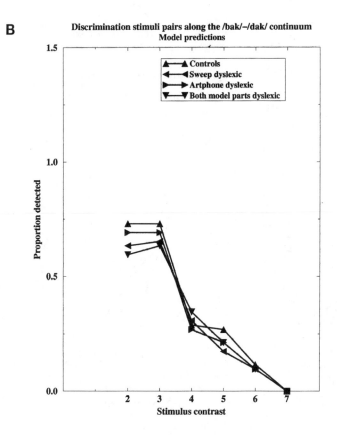

FIG. 3.5. *(Continued)*

sion to the combined scores of the Schwippert and the ter Beek data (Fig. 3.5C, lower left). The regression weights were used to calibrate the model results for the dyslexic varieties. Experimental data for the dyslexics and model outputs are depicted in Fig. 3.5D (right lower part). By the eye, the ARTPHONE dyslexic model output fits best to the Schwippert data of the dyslexics and SWEEP dyslexic model output best to the ter Beek data. However, the differences are too slight to be decisive.

DISCUSSION

Somewhat amazing, but not unexpected, is that functional principles of the visual system, as implemented in SWEEP, can perform auditory functions by different labeling (e.g., auditory frequency detector instead of spatial location detector). Other authors have already pointed in this direction (Shamma, Fleshman, Wiser, & Versnel, 1993; Rauschecker, Tian, &

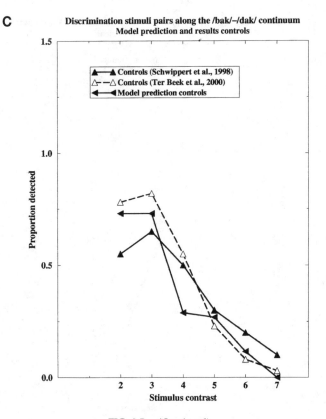

C   **Discrimination stimuli pairs along the /bak/–/dak/ continuum**
Model prediction and results controls

FIG. 3.5.   *(Continued)*

Hauser, 1995). It has been argued that the development of the auditory and visual cortical maps may diverge largely because of the different nature of their inputs, rather than of their underlying principles (Shamma et al., 1993). Illustrative is an animal study that shows that auditory cortical neurons show a visually driven response with feature processing typical of the visual cortex when retinal cells are induced to project to the auditory thalamus and cortex (Sur, Garraghty, & Roe, 1988). Moreover, auditory processing has been shown in visual brain areas of early blind humans (Alho, Kujala, Paavilainen, Summala, & Näätänen, 1993).

Also in the visual system, transient and sustained parts of the input are handled by segregated processing streams corresponding to the magnocellular and parvocellular pathway (Mishkin, Ungerleider, & Macko, 1983). Often dyslexics with a phonological deficit also show signs of disturbances in the transient part of the visual system (e.g., motion detection; Eden et al., 1996). Autopsies have revealed anomalies in both the auditory and visual magnocellular nuclei of the thalamus of dyslexic brains, which

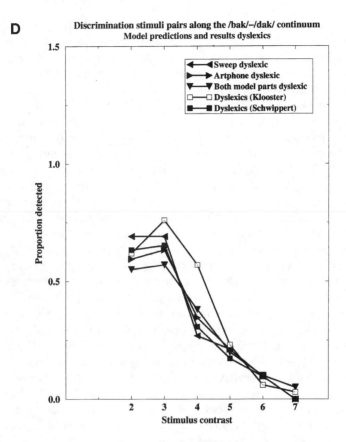

FIG. 3.5. Experimental results and model results of discriminating /bak/-/dak/ stimuli along a synthetic continuum. Upper left: results of experiments conducted by Schwippert (1998) and ter Beek et al. (2000) with dyslexics and controls. Upper right: model predictions by the combined ARTPHONE and SWEEP model. Four varieties were simulated: control, dyslexic ARTPHONE/normal SWEEP, normal ARTPHONE/dyslexic SWEEP, dyslexic ARTPHONE/dyslexic SWEEP. Lower left: model prediction and experimental results controls. Lower right: model predictions and experimental results dyslexics.

may result from a lack of cortical innervation (Galaburda, Menard, & Rosen, 1994). Thus, a general magnocellular processing deficit might be associated with developmental dyslexia, which may be related to deficits in the perception of short and fast-changing stimuli (Tallal, Miller, & Fitch, 1993) or fast changes within stimuli, be it visual or auditory.

The general auditory account of phonological deficits in both language- and reading-impaired children claims that the basic deficit is in temporal processing and that the deficit is general rather than specific to speech

(Tallal et al., 1993). A recent study by Mody, Studdert-Kennedy, and Brady (1996) lends no support to either of these claims for dyslexic children. They concluded that deficits in speech perception among reading-impaired children are domain specific and phonological rather than general and auditory in origin.

The architecture of the combined ARTPHONE and SWEEP model may reconcile these opposing views. It shows that a reduced cellular density in the magnocellular (transient) processing stream (equivalent to dyslexic SWEEP) may produce impairment in auditory discrimination as found in dyslexics. The transient detector in SWEEP is not language specific. The same symptoms, however, can be produced by assuming a reduced cellular density at the level of the phonological lexicon (dyslexic ARTPHONE), which is language specific. This shows that both general and domain-specific deficits can produce the same symptoms.

Apparently the dynamics of auditory perception of specific stimuli can be approximated to a considerable degree by applying a few neurophysiological principles in a dynamic model of auditory processing at the level of the auditory cortex, when the model at hand is carefully tuned to the stimulus characteristics and the processes involved. This opens the way for generating model-based predictions, both for other experimental paradigms (Been, 1998) and stimuli designed for intervention studies (Been, 1994). Because the model contains global equations for neurotransmitter dynamics in principle, predictions for pharmaceutical interventions can be generated.

It is claimed that speech perception can be trained in language-learning impaired children with acoustically modified consonant vowel (CV) stimuli in which the duration of the consonant is prolonged by a maximum of 50% and the transients are enhanced by a maximum of 20 dB. The total duration of the CV pair is kept constant. The training task is to discriminate between two CV pairs by forced choice with feedback. Task parameters are the consonant duration, amplification of the consonant elements, and interstimulus intervals. Children are driven to age-appropriate performance levels (Merzenich et al., 1996).

There seems to be transfer to a number of language-related tasks, such as speech discrimination, language comprehension as assessed by a Token Test, and grammatical comprehension (Tallal et al., 1996). In addition to speech stimuli, nonverbal stimuli consisting of frequency-modulated sounds are trained. The training procedure consists of presenting initially frequency-modulated sounds and CV stimuli with consonant transitions of prolonged duration. The consonant transition in CV pairs is amplified with a maximum of 20 dB. Durations are altered adaptively during training aiming for age-appropriate performance levels. Children receive feedback of correct performances during training and are rewarded for progress (Merzenich et al., 1996).

Simulation with the ARTPHONE model shows that in the stop perception model for the AT(T)A stimulus, the perceptual boundary of the at-risk model shifts to the boundary of the controls when the amplitude of the input signal is increased by 25%. Raising the amplitude of the input to the detector field of SWEEP with the same percentage gives similar results for the /bak/-/dak/ simulation. Discrimination levels of the model in the range above chance level reach the levels of the empirical data of controls.

According to the simulation results, normal discrimination levels can be obtained in infants at risk for dyslexia and adult dyslexics by part of the acoustic modifications used in the training program of Tallal, Merzenich, and colleagues. The results of the training procedure can be underpinned by neural network theory adopting the hypothesis of reduced neural density in the magnocellular subdivision of the auditory system and plasticity in these parts.

In the auditory system, most specific thalamic projection is from a ventral subdivision of the medial geniculate body to the primary auditory cortex (AI). By contrast, the magnocellular subdivision projects not only to the primary auditory cortex, but to a number of surrounding cortical areas as well (Shepherd, 1994). In AI, limited overlap between receptive fields does not allow for territorial competition in the high-frequency ranges (3–5 kHz and above) in the ventral part of the thalamus and AI. However, there are no such barriers to territorial competition in the lower frequency sectors of these representations (Merzenich, Jenkins, & Middlebrooks, 1984). Probably the same principles apply to the secondary auditory cortex and the dorsal part of the thalamus. Speech signals are typically in the range below 5 kHz. In that case, neural plasticity for receptive fields in the speech range seems warranted.

A basic result from neural network theory is that the number of neurons and synaptic relays place an upper limit to the storage capacity of a neural net. This storage capacity depends on the learning mode: supervised (feedback) or unsupervised (no feedback). In the unsupervised condition, the storage capacity is equivalent to 15 or perhaps 40% of the number of neurons in the net (Okada, 1996). The storage capacity improves by a factor 10 or more when supervised learning is used (Gardner, 1988). Auditory perception in infants seems to develop in an environment providing little direct feedback. The implication is that, in the case of reduced neural nets (e.g., ectopies), learning and language disorders can develop in the natural unsupervised environment, but perhaps can be remediated in supervised learning conditions when plasticity remains. In that case, the network can be retrained by providing explicit feedback.

In addition to positive feedback and rewarding, negative feedback should be considered because it weakens faulty representations, whereas positive feedback strengthens the adequate ones (Anderson, 1983).

In summary, our model study and neural network theory support the approach from Merzenich and Tallal pointing to enhanced discriminability by amplification of transients and feedback as effective parameters. However, because the model is tightly focused on two synthetic continua, one should hesitate to make too broad generalizations. Furthermore, the basic assumption of the model is a reduced local neural density. This claim is supported by autopsies of dyslexic brains. As far as we know, no such data are available for the language-impaired brain. Consequently, the assumption has to be accepted on face value when applying the results of our model study to this group.

REFERENCES

Aaron, P. G. (1989). Orthographic systems and developmental dyslexia: A reformulation of the syndrome. In P. G. Aaron & R. M. Joshi (Eds.), *Reading and writing disorders in different orthographic systems* (pp. 379–400). Dordrecht: Kluwer.

Alho, K., Kujala, T., Paavilainen, P., Summala, H., & Näätänen, R. (1993). Auditory processing in visual brain areas of the early blind: Evidence from event-related potentials. *Electroencephalography and Clinical Neurophysiology, 86,* 418–427.

Anderson, J. R. (1983). *The architecture of cognition.* Cambridge, MA: Harvard University Press.

Been, P. H. (1994). Dyslexia and irregular dynamics of the visual system. In K. P. van den Bos, L. S. Siegel, D. J. Bakker, & D. L. Share (Eds.), *Current directions in dyslexia research* (pp. 93–116). Lisse: Swets & Zeitlinger.

Been, P. H. (1998). Nonlinear dynamics of brain regions and the design of neuronal growth-cycle-based cognitive tasks. In K. Newell & P. C. M. Molenaar (Eds.), *Applications of nonlinear dynamics to developmental process modeling* (pp. 179–198). Mahwah, NJ: Lawrence Erlbaum Associates.

Been, P. H., & Zwarts, F. (2000, September). *Developmental dyslexia and speech perception: A model study.* Paper presented at the symposium "The reading brain," Amsterdam, Holland.

Berent, I., & Perfetti, C. A. (1995). A rose is a REEZ: The two-cycles model of phonology assembly in reading English. *Psychological Review, 102*(1), 146–184.

Bishop, D. V., & Adams, C. (1990). A prospective study of the relationship between specific language impairment, phonological disorders and reading retardation. *Journal of Speech and Hearing Disorders, 51,* 339–357.

Boardman, I., Grossberg, S., Myers, C., & Cohen, M. (1999). Neural dynamics of perceptual order and context effects for variable-rate speech perception. *Perception and Psychophysics, 61*(8), 1477–1500.

Bowey, J. A., & Francis, J. (1991). Phonological analysis as a function of age and exposure to reading instruction. *Applied Psycholinguistics, 12,* 91–121.

Bradley, L., & Bryant, P. E. (1978). Difficulties in auditory organization as a possible cause of reading backwardness. *Nature, 271,* 746–747.

Bradley, L., & Bryant, P. E. (1983). Categorizing sounds and learning to read—a causal connection. *Nature, 301,* 419–421.

Brown, G. D. (1997). Connectionism, phonology, reading and regularity of developmental dyslexia. *Brain and Language, 59,* 207–235.

Bruck, M. (1988). The word recognition and spelling of dyslexic children. *Reading Research Quarterly, 23,* 51–69.

Bruck, M. (1990). Word-recognition skills of adults with childhood diagnoses of dyslexia. *Developmental Psychology, 26,* 439–454.

Bruck, M. (1992). Persistence of dyslexics' phonological awareness deficits. *Developmental Psychology, 28,* 874–886.

Buonomano, D. V., & Merzenich, M. M. (1995). Temporal information transformed into a spatial code by a neural network with realistic properties. *Science, 267,* 1028–1030.

Catts, H. W. (1993). The relationship between speech-language impairments and reading disabilities. *Journal of Speech and Hearing Research, 40,* 948–958.

Collins, M. J. (1984). Tone-glide discrimination: Normal and hearing-impaired listeners. *Journal of Speech and Hearing Research, 27,* 403–412.

Coltheart, M., Curtis, B., Atkins, P., & Haller, M. (1993). Models of reading aloud: Dual route and parallel distributed processing approaches. *Psychological Review, 100*(4), 589–608.

Cornelissen, P., Richardson, A., Mason, A., Fowler, S., & Stein, J. (1995). Contrast sensitivity and coherent motion detection measured at photopic luminance levels in dyslexics and controls. *Vision Research, 2,* 1483–1495.

Cowan, J. D., & Ermentrout, G. B. (1978). Some aspects of the "eigenbehavior" of neural nets. In S. A. Levin (Ed.), *Studies in mathematical biology: Part I. Cellular behavior and the development of pattern* (pp. 67–116). Washington, DC: Mathematical Association of America.

DeFries, J. C., Fulker, D. W., & LaBuda, M. C. (1987). Evidence for a genetic etiology in reading disability of twins. *Nature, 329,* 537–539.

De Weirdt, W. (1988). Speech perception and frequency discrimination in good and poor readers. *Applied Psycholinguistics, 16,* 163–183.

Eden, G. F., Vanmeter, J. M., Rumsey, J. M., Maisgog, J. M., Woods, R. P., & Zeffiro, T. A. (1996). Abnormal processing of visual motion in dyslexia revealed by functional brain imaging. *Nature, 382,* 66–69.

Efron, R. (1963). Temporal perception, aphasia, and déja vu. *Brain, 36,* 403–424.

Elbro, C., Nielsen, I., & Petersen, D. (1994). Dyslexia in adults: Evidence for deficits in nonword reading and in the phonological representation of lexical items. *Annals of Dyslexia, 44,* 205–226.

Felton, R. H., & Wood, F. R. (1992). A reading level match study of nonword reading skills in poor readers with varying IQs. *Journal of Learning Disabilities, 25,* 318–326.

Fox, B., & Routh, D. K. (1976). Phonemic analysis and synthesis as word-attack skills. *Journal of Educational Psychology, 68,* 70–74.

Fuzessary, Z. M., & Hall, J. C. (1996). Role of GABA in shaping frequency tuning and creating FM sweep selectivity in the inferior colliculus. *Journal of Neurophysiology, 76,* 1059–1073.

Galaburda, A. (1983). Developmental dyslexia: Current anatomical research. *Annals of Dyslexia, 33,* 41–53.

Galaburda, A. M. (1994). Developmental dyslexia and animal studies: At the interface between cognition and neurology. *Cognition, 50,* 133–149.

Galaburda, A. M., & Kemper, T. L. (1979). Cytoarchitectonic abnormalities in developmental dyslexia: A case study. *Annals of Neurology, 6,* 94–100.

Galaburda, A. M., & Livingstone, M. (1993). Evidence for a magnocellular defect in developmental dyslexia. In P. Tallal, A. M. Galaburda, R. R. Llins, & C. von Euler (Eds.), *Temporal information processing in the nervous system: Special reference to dyslexia and dysphasia* (*Annals of the New York Academy of Sciences, 682,* 70–82). New York: New York Academy of Sciences.

Galaburda, A. M., Menard, M. T., & Rosen, G. D. (1994). Evidence for aberrant auditory anatomy in developmental dyslexia. *Proceedings of the National Academy of Sciences USA, 91,* 8010–8013.

Galaburda, A. M., Rosen, G. D., & Sherman, G. F. (1989). The neural origin of developmental dyslexia: Implications for medicine, neurology, and cognition. In A. M. Galaburda (Ed.), *From reading to neurons* (pp. 377–388). Cambridge, MA: MIT Press.

Gardner, E. (1988). The space of interactions in neural network models. *Journal of Physics A: Mathematical and General, 21,* 257–270.

Gilger, J. W., Pennington, B. F., & DeFries, J. C. (1991). Risk for reading disability as a function of parental history in three family studies. *Reading and Writing: An Interdisciplinary Journal, 3,* 205–217.

Godfrey, J. J., Syrdal-Lasky, A. K., Millay, K. K., & Knox, C. M. (1981). Performance of dyslexic children on speech perception tests. *Journal of Experimental Child Psychology, 32,* 401–424.

Goswami, U., & Bryant, P. (1990). *Phonological skills and learning to read.* Hove, England: Lawrence Erlbaum Associates.

Grossberg, S., Boardman, I., & Cohen, M. (1997). Neural dynamics of variable rate speech categorization. *Journal of Experimental Psychology: Human Perception and Performance, 23,* 418–503.

Hallgren, B. (1950). Specific dyslexia (congenital word-blindness): A clinical and genetic study. *Acta Psychiatrica et Neurologica (Suppl. 65),* 1–287.

Heil, P., & Dexter, R. F. I. (1998). Functional specialization in auditory cortex: Response to frequency modulated stimuli in the cat's posterior auditory field. *Journal of Neurophysiology, 79*(6), 3041–3059.

Hoffner, J. A., & McClelland, J. L. (1993). Can a perceptual processing deficit explain the impairment of inflectional morphology in developmental dysphasia? A computational investigation. *Child Language Research Forum, 25,* 38–49.

Humphreys, P., Kaufmann, W. E., & Galaburda, A. M. (1990). Developmental dyslexia in women: Neuropathological findings in three cases. *Annals of Neurology, 28,* 727–738.

Hynd, G. S., Marshall, R., & Gonzalez, J. (1991). Learning disabilities and presumed central nervous system dysfunction. *Learning Disability Quarterly, 14,* 283–296.

Hynd, G. S., Marshall, R., & Semrud-Clikeman, M. (1991). Developmental dyslexia, neurolinguistic theory and deviations in brain morphology. *Reading and Writing: An Interdisciplinary Journal, 3,* 345–362.

Johnson, M. H. (1993). Cortical maturation and the development of visual attention in early infancy. In M. H. Johnson (Ed.), *Brain development and cognition* (pp. 167–194). Oxford: Blackwell.

Johnson, M. H. (1995, April). Brain and cognitive development in infancy. *Current Opinion in Neurobiology: Cognitive Neuroscience,* pp. 218–225.

Kemper, T. L. (1984). Asymmetrical lesions in dyslexia. In N. Geschwind & A. M. Galaburda (Eds.), *Cerebral dominance: The biological foundations* (pp. 75–89). Cambridge, MA: Harvard University Press.

King, A. J. (1995). Asking the auditory cortex the right question. *Current Biology, 5*(10), 1110–1113.

Kolb, B., & Wishaw, I. Q. (1995). *Human neuropsychology.* New York: Freeman.

Kuhl, P. K., Williams, K. A., Lacerda, F., Stevens, K., & Lindblom, B. (1992). Linguistic experience alters phonetic perception in infants by 6 months of age. *Science, 255,* 606–608.

Leppänen, P. H. T., & Lyytinen, H. (1997). Auditory event related potentials in the study of developmental language-related disorders. *Audiology Neuro-Otology, 2,* 308–340.

Liberman, I. Y., & Shankweiler, D. (1985). Phonology and the problems of learning to read and to write. *Remedial & Special Education, 6,* 8–17.

Liberman, I. Y., Shankweiler, D. P., Fischer, F. W., & Carter, B. (1974). Explicit syllable and phoneme segmentation in the young child. *Journal of Experimental Child Psychology, 18,* 201–212.

Livingstone, M. S., Rosen, G. D., Drislane, F. W., & Galaburda, A. M. (1991). Physiological and anatomical evidence for a magnocellular defect in developmental dyslexia. *Proceedings of the National Academy of Sciences USA, 88,* 7493–7947.

Lovegrove, W., Garzia, L., & Nicholson, S. (1990). Experimental evidence for a transient system deficit is specific reading disability. *Journal of the American Optometric Association, 2,* 137–146.

Lundberg, I., Olofsson, A., & Wall, S. (1980). Reading and spelling skills in the first school years predicted from phonemic awareness skills in kindergarten. *Scandinavian Journal of Psychology, 21*(3), 159–173.

Mann, V. A. (1984). Longitudinal prediction and prevention of early reading difficulty. *Annals of Dyslexia, 34,* 117–136.

Mattingly, I. G. (1972). Reading, the linguistic process, and linguistic awareness. In J. F. Kavanagh & I. G. Mattingly (Eds.), *Language by ear and by eye: The relationships between speech and reading* (pp. 133–147). Cambridge, MA: MIT Press.

Mazoyer, B. M., Dehaene, S., Tzourio, N., Frak, G., Murayama, N., Cohen, L., Levrier, O., Raynaud, L., Salamon, G., Syroto, A., & Mehler, J. (1993). The cortical representation of continuous speech. *Journal of Cerebral Blood Flow and Metabolism, 13*(Suppl. 1), S261.

Mehler, J., Dupoux, E., Pallier, C., & Dehaene-Lambertz, S. (1995, April). Cross-linguistic approaches to speech processing. *Current Opinion in Neurobiology: Cognitive Neuroscience,* pp. 171–176.

Merzenich, M. M., Jenkins, W. M., Johnston, P., Schreiner, C., Miller, S. L., & Tallal, P. (1996). Temporal processing deficits of language-learning impaired children ameliorated by training. *Science, 271,* 77–80.

Merzenich, M. M., Jenkins, M., & Middlebrooks, J. C. (1984). Observations and hypotheses on special organizational features of the central auditory nervous system. In G. M. Edelman, W. E. Gall, & W. M. Cowan (Eds.), *Dynamic aspects of neocortical function* (pp. 397–424). New York: Wiley.

Mishkin, M., Ungerleider, L. G., & Macko, K. A. (1983). Object vision and spatial vision: Two cortical pathways. *Trends in Neuroscience, 6,* 414–417.

Mody, M., Studdert-Kennedy, M., & Brady, S. (1996). Speech perception deficits in poor readers: Auditory processing or phonological coding? *Journal of Experimental Child Psychology, 64,* 199–231.

Molfese, D. (2000). Predicting dyslexia at 8 years of age using neonatal brain responses. *Brain and Language, 72,* 238–245.

Molfese, D. L., & Molfese, V. J. (1997). Discrimination of language skills at five years of age using event-related potentials recorded at birth. *Developmental Neuropsychology, 13,* 135–156.

National Steering Group Dyslexia, Netherlands Organization for Scientific Research. (1999). *Early precursors of familial dyslexia: A prospective longitudinal study.*

Okada, M. (1996). Notions of associative memory and sparse coding. *Neural Networks, 9*(2), 1429–1458.

Olson, R. K. (1994). Language deficits in "specific" reading disability. In M. A. Gernsbacher (Ed.), *Handbook of psycholinguistics* (pp. 895–916). San Diego: Academic Press.

Pallay, S. L. (1986). *Speech perception in dyslexic children.* Unpublished doctoral dissertation, City University of New York.

Perfetti, C. A. (1985). *Reading ability.* New York: Oxford University Press.

Perfetti, C. A. (1994). Psycholinguistics and reading ability. In M. A. Gernsbacher (Ed.), *Handbook of psycholinguistics* (pp. 849–894). San Diego: Academic Press.

Rauschecker, J. P., Tian, B., & Hauser, M. (1995). Processing of complex sounds in the macaque nonprimary auditory cortex. *Science, 268*, 111–114.

Reed, M. A. (1989). Speech perception and the discrimination of brief auditory cues in reading disabled children. *Journal of Experimental Child Psychology, 48*, 270–292.

Repp, B. H. (1980). *A range frequency effect on perception of silence in speech* (Status report on speech research SR-61, 151-165). New Haven, CT: Haskins Laboratories.

Richardson, U. (1998). *Familial dyslexia and sound duration in the quantity distinctions of Finnish infants and adults.* Doctoral dissertation. Jyväskyla: Jyväskyla University Printing House.

Scarborough, H. S. (1989). Prediction of reading disability from familial and individual differences. *Journal of Educational Psychology, 27*, 723–737.

Scarborough, H. S. (1990). Very early language deficits in dyslexic children. *Child Development, 61*, 1728–1743.

Scarborough, H. S. (1991). Early syntactic development of dyslexic children. *Annals of Dyslexia, 41*, 207–220.

Schreiner, C. E. (1995, August). Order and disorder in auditory cortical maps. *Current Opinion in Neurobiology: Sensory Systems*, pp. 489–496.

Schwippert, C. E. (1998). *Categorical perception in dyslexic and normal-reading adults: Discrimination and classification of three phoneme contrasts.* Unpublished master's thesis, University of Amsterdam (IFA-report nr. 135).

Seidenberg, M. S., & McClelland, J. L. (1989). A distributed developmental model of word recognition and naming. *Psychological Review, 96*, 523–568.

Semrud-Clikeman, M., Hynd, G. S., Novey, E., & Eliopulos, D. (1991). Dyslexia and brain morphology: Relationships between neuroanatomical variation and neurolinguistic tasks. *Learning and Individual Differences, 3*, 225–242.

Shamma, S. A., Fleshman, J. W., Wiser, P. R., & Versnel, H. (1993). Organization of response areas in ferret primary auditory cortex. *Journal of Neurophysiology, 69*(2), 376–383.

Shepherd, G. M. (1994). *Neurobiology.* Oxford: Oxford University Press.

Siegel, L. S., & Ryan, E. B. (1988). Development of grammatical-sensitivity, phonological, and short-term memory skills in normally achieving and learning disabled children. *Developmental Psychology, 24*, 28–37.

Snowling, M. (1981). Phonemic deficits in developmental dyslexia. *Psychological Research, 43*, 219–234.

Snowling, M. (1991). Developmental reading disorders. *Journal of Child Psychology and Psychiatry, 32*, 49–77.

Stanovich, K. E. (1986). Cognitive processes and the reading problems of learning-disabled children: Evaluating the assumption of specificity. In J. Torgesen & B. Wong (Eds.), *Psychological and educational perspectives on learning disabilities* (pp. 87–131). New York: Academic Press.

Stanovich, K. E. (1988). Explaining the differences between the dyslexic and the garden-variety poor reader: The phonological-core variable-difference model. *Journal of Learning Disabilities, 21*, 590–604.

Stanovich, K. E., Cunningham, A. E., & Cramer, B. B. (1984). Assessing phonological awareness in kindergarten children: Issues of task comparability. *Journal of Experimental Child Phonology, 38*, 175–190.

Steffens, M. L., Eilers, R. E., Gross-Glenn, K., & Jallad, B. (1992). Speech perception in adult subjects with familial dyslexia. *Journal of Speech and Hearing Research, 35*(1), 192–200.

Stein, J., & Walsh, V. (1997). Temporal processing and dyslexia. *Trends in Neurocience, 20*(4), 147–152.

Studdert-Kennedy, M., & Mody, M. (1995). Auditory temporal perception deficits in the reading-impaired: A critical review of the evidence. *Psychonomic Bulletin and Review, 2*, 508–514.

Sur, M., Garraghty, P. E., & Roe, A. W. (1988). Experimentally induced visual projections into auditory thalamus and cortex. *Science, 242,* 1437–1441.

Tallal, P., Miller, S. L., Bedi, G., Byma, G., Wang, X., Nagarajan, S. S., Schreiner, C., Jenkins, W. M., & Merzenich, M. M. (1996). Language comprehension in language-learning impaired children improved with acoustically modified speech. *Science, 271,* 81–84.

Tallal, P., Miller, S., & Fitch, R. H. (1993). Neurobiological basis of speech: A case for the preeminence of temporal processing. In P. Tallal, A. M. Galaburda, R. R. Llins, & C. von Euler (Eds.), *Temporal information processing in the nervous system: Special reference to dyslexia and dysphasia (Annals of the New York Academy of Sciences, 682,* 27–47). New York: New York Academy of Sciences.

Tallal, P., & Piercy, M. (1973). Developmental aphasia: Impaired rate of non-verbal processing as a function of sensory modality. *Neuropsychologia, 11,* 389–398.

ter Beek, J., & Klooster, K. (2000). *The phonological lexicon: Dyslexic versus normal readers.* Unpublished report, Department of Dutch, University of Groningen.

Thomas, C. (1905). Congenital word-blindness and its treatment. *Ophthalmoscope, 3,* 380–385.

Torgesen, J. K., Wagner, R. K., & Rashotte, C. A. (1994). Longitudinal studies of phonological processing and reading. *Journal of Learning Disabilities, 27,* 276–286.

Torre, V., & Poggio, V. (1978). A synaptic mechanism possibly underlying directional sensitivity to motion. *Proceedings of the Royal Society London B, 202,* 409–416.

Tunmer, W. E., Herriman, M. L., & Nesdale, A. R. (1985). Metalinguistic awareness abilities and beginning reading. *Reading Research Quarterly, 23,* 134–158.

Van Bon, W. H. J., Schreuder, R., Duighuisen, H. C. M, & Kerstholt, M. T. (1994). Phonemic segmentation: Testing and training. In K. P. van den Bos, L. S. Siegel, D. J. Bakker, & D. L. Share (Eds.), *Current directions in dyslexia research* (pp. 169–181). Lisse: Swets & Zeitlinger.

Vellutino, F. R., & Scanlon, D. M. (1987). Phonological coding, phonological awareness, and reading ability: Evidence from a longitudinal and experimental study. *Merrill-Palmer Quarterly, 33,* 321–363.

Vihman, M. M. (1996). *Phonological development: The origins of language in the child.* Oxford, England: Blackwell.

Wagner, R. K. (1986). Phonological processing abilities and reading: Implications for disabled readers. *Journal of Learning Disabilities, 19,* 623–630.

Wagner, R. K., & Torgesen, J. K. (1987). The nature of phonological processing and its causal role in the acquisition of reading skills. *Psychological Bulletin, 101,* 192–212.

Wagner, R. K., Torgesen, J. K., & Rashotte, C. A. (1994). Development of reading-related phonological processing abilities: New evidence of bidirectional causality from a latent variable longitudinal study. *Developmental Psychology, 30,* 73–87.

Werker, R. F., & Tees, R. C. (1984). Cross-language speech perception: Evidence for perceptual reorganization during the first year of life. *Infant Behavior Development, 7,* 49–63.

Werker, J., & Tees, R. C. (1987). Speech perception in severely disabled and average reading children. *Canadian Journal of Psychology, 41,* 48–61.

Zatorre, R. J., Evans, A. C., Meyer, E., & Gjedde, A. (1992). Lateralization of phonetic and pitch discrimination in speech processing. *Science, 256,* 864–869.

Zatorre, R. J., Myer, E., Gjedde, A., & Evans, A. C. (1996). PET studies of phonetic processes in speech perception: Review, replication and re-analysis. *Cerebral Cortex, 6,* 21–30.

4

Neuroimaging Measures in the Study of Specific Language Impairment

Paavo H. T. Leppänen
Heikki Lyytinen
University of Jyväskylä, Finland

Naseem Choudhury
April A. Benasich
Rutgers University

Specific language impairment (SLI) is a complex syndrome whose etiology remains elusive. Although several hypotheses exist to account for its development (see van Balkom & Verhoeven, chap. 12, this volume), there is some consensus that SLI is associated with subtle structural and functional cortical deviations that may be developmental in origin. Advances in modern brain research have increased interest in the search for potential neural substrates of this disorder, but as yet the number of neuroimaging studies with children with SLI is surprisingly small. In this chapter, we review neurobiological correlates of SLI at three different levels: neuroanatomical, hemodynamic, and electrocortical.

Neuroanatomical measures can reveal subtle structural changes of the brain that are associated with cognitive disorders. Studies showing anatomical differences in SLI populations have used magnetic resonance imaging (MRI)—a technique that has provided an unprecedented opportunity to visualize human brain structure with clarity comparable to autopsy evaluation. Differences in brain function have been studied with hemodynamic and event-related potential (ERP) techniques. Hemodynamic techniques (e.g., positron emission tomography [PET], related single photon emission computerized tomography [SPECT], and functional magnetic resonance imaging [fMRI]) rely on detecting small changes in blood flow and measure oxygen consumption in active brain areas. Hemodynamic techniques are well suited to imaging brain activation during relatively long periods of ongoing cognitive processing. The ERP technique and related magnetoencephalography (MEG) assess event (stimulus)-related processing in the time frame of tens of milliseconds, thus allowing measurement of fast stimulus-driven changes in neural networks.

NEUROANATOMICAL FINDINGS

Currently, magnetic resonance imaging (MRI) is the primary technique used to measure anatomical brain structures, such as structural landmarks, relative volumes, and differences in white and gray matter (for the method, see Banich, 1997; Damasio & Damasio, 1989; for a review of the method for developmental neuroimaging, see Courchesne & Plante, 1996; Filipek & Kennedy, 1991). For a diagrammatic representation of the brain areas appearing in this review, see Fig. 4.1.

MRI relies on magnetic fields that distort the behavior of atoms. Based on the information of how long the atoms take to recover from this distortion, one can create an image of the anatomy of the brain. Magnetic fields make particles of various substances (e.g., of water and fat) behave differently. MRIs can be tuned to these substances. When tuned to water, images reveal a picture of tissue density, and these images can be used to detect brain atrophy and increases in cerebrospinal fluid. When tuned to fat, they are often applied for measuring myelination and detection of demyelinating diseases, such as multiple sclerosis.

The search for neuroanatomical correlates for SLI has been largely motivated by the findings of Galaburda and colleagues with dyslexics (Galaburda, Sherman, Rosen, Aboitiz, & Geschwind, 1985). For example, in the majority (> 70%) of normal readers, the left planum temporale (PT) is relatively larger than the right planum, whereas in a number of dyslexics, the left planum has been reported to be smaller or of equal size in both autopsy (e.g., Galaburda, 1991; Geschwind & Levitsky, 1968; Humphreys, Kaufmann, & Galaburda, 1990; Rosen, Sherman, & Galaburda, 1993) and MRI studies (Hynd & Hiemenz, 1997; Hynd, Marshall, & Semrud-Clikeman, 1991; Hynd, Semrud-Clikeman, Lorys, Novey, & Eliopulos, 1990; Jancke, Schlaug, Huang, & Steinmetz, 1994; Larsen, Höien, Lundberg, & Ödegaard, 1990; Leonard et al., 1993; Schultz et al., 1994; for a review, see Morgan & Hynd, 1998; for similar results on the temporal lobe subcortical areas lateral to insula, see Dalby, Elbro, & Stödkilde-Jörgensen, 1998). The PT is a bilateral structure in the perisylvian region at the temporal lobes (forming their superior posterior surface). In the left hemisphere, this region is part of Wernicke's area and is thought to be involved in receptive language and phonological processing (Pennington, 1991). This may, at least partly, explain the reported

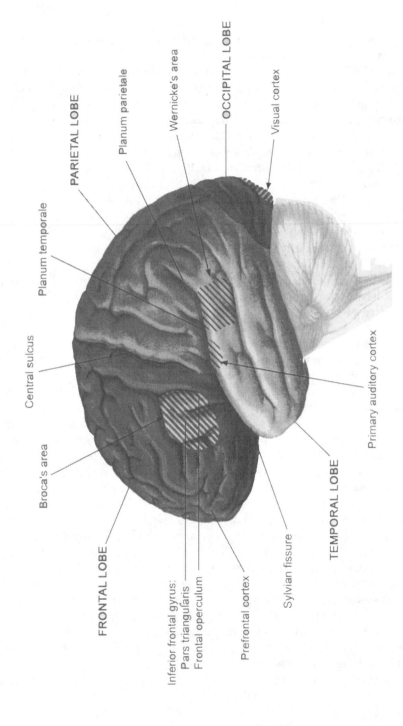

FIG. 4.1. The lateral view of the left cerebral hemisphere: A diagrammatic representation of the four major lobes and brain regions referred to in this review.

association between altered planum temporale asymmetry and the phonological coding deficits found in dyslexics.

Several MRI studies have been conducted in individuals with SLI in an attempt to identify corresponding cortical structural changes, especially in hemispheric asymmetry. Abnormal asymmetries could result from left-hemispheric structures being smaller than in normal populations, from right-hemispheric structures being larger, or from a combination of both. Plante and colleagues have carried out a number of anatomical studies with children with SLI (for a review, see Plante, 1996). Using a volumetric MRI measure of structures surrounding the sylvian fissure—or lateral sulcus—including portions of the frontal operculum anteriorly and the planum temporale posteriorly, they found that six of eight boys with SLI ages 4 to 9 years had an atypical pattern of asymmetry of the perisylvian structures, with the right area usually larger than in the controls (Plante, Swisher, Vance, & Rapcsak, 1991). These data are in line with previous findings of PT differences in dyslexics and add the frontal area above the sylvian fissure to regions implicated in SLI. Similar atypical perisylvian asymmetries were also found in most of the parents from four of the same families of boys with SLI studied (Plante, 1991). Parents who reported a history of communication difficulty (i.e., difficulty with speech, language, or academic skills as children) had a greater probability of having an atypical pattern than parents without such a history. This atypical symmetric pattern was also found in many siblings of the studied children.

Likewise in posterior perisylvian regions, especially in the left hemisphere, reduced volume was found by Jernigan and colleagues (1991) in twenty 8- to 20-year-old language- and learning-impaired children as compared with 12 matched controls. Asymmetry differences between groups, comparable to those reported by Plante and colleagues (1991), were not found in this region. However, a significantly larger variance in the R > L asymmetries of these regions was seen in the SLI participants (in 10 out of 20 language-impaired participants, the right structure was larger than the left one, whereas only 1 of 7 controls had the same pattern). The results by Jernigan and colleagues (1991) should not be regarded as contrary to Plante and colleagues (1991) because the size of the PT was not addressed, although it fell within the larger posterior perisylvian area measured. Therefore, the authors suggest that their results provide supportive evidence of more frequent hemispheric reversals in the posterior perisylvian area in children with SLI comparable to earlier findings in dyslexics. More recently, Gauger and colleagues (1997), using a high-resolution volumetric MRI scan, reported converging evidence for asymmetries in the posterior perisylvian region in eleven 9-year-old children with SLI as compared with 19 age-matched control children. The clinical group showed a greater rightward asymmetry of the total size of the planum area.

Asymmetry findings are not limited to posterior perisylvian regions. In the study by Jernigan and colleagues (1991), atypical asymmetries were found in SLI participants in the prefrontal inferior region, the right area being much larger than the left, in contrast to symmetrical sizes in controls. The authors suggest that aberrant asymmetry is more likely due to reduction of left structures than to preservation of right structures. Gauger and colleagues (1997) also recently showed reduced size of the left side of the pars triangularis, making up the core of Broca's area, in children with SLI as compared with controls. This region is immediately anterior to the motor speech area and is related to language production. Lesions of this region in the left hemisphere typically result in dysfluent aphasia at the level of grammar and phonology. However, the area measured in this study is somewhat different from the frontal area measured in the study by Jernigan and colleagues (1991), being more limited and somewhat more posterior. In addition, SLI participants have been reported to have an atypical reversal of the normal (right being typically greater than left) asymmetry in the parietal superior temporal regions (Jernigan et al., 1991). Opposite anomalous asymmetries have also been reported in some severe cases. For example, Filipek and Kennedy (1991) found volumetric decrease of the right posterior temporal area, rather than the left area, in an MRI study of four adolescents with verbal auditory agnosia, characterized by the selective inability to understand spoken language despite preserved hearing and inner language.

Another example of atypical brain morphology that was found to be related to language impairment in adulthood was recently reported by Clark and Plante (1998). In an MRI study, an extra sulcus was identified in the inferior frontal gyrus in 68% of 19 adults with SLI as compared with 40% of controls. Although this is a significant difference, the incidence is relatively high for the control group. Interestingly, when the adults were classified according to family history for their SLI, no significant differences were found between parents with SLI family history and controls. Gyri and sulci atypicalities were also found by Kabani and colleagues (Kabani, MacDonald, Evans, & Gopnik, 1997; see also the erratum, Kabani, MacDonald, Evans, & Gopnik, 1998) in four adults in five families with familial language disorder. These adults showed generalized cortical atrophy, mostly in the anterior region as represented by narrow gyri, wide and deep sulci, and enlarged inter-hemispheric fissure. There were no comparable differences between children with SLI and control adults in this study. Due to the small number of participants, these initial findings can only be regarded as tentative. However, the authors suggest that familial SLI in adults may be associated with cortical atrophy.

Other structural differences identified in SLI as compared with control children, but not related to the asymmetries described earlier, include differences in the size of the corpus callosum (CC). The CC is the fiber tract that connects the two cerebral hemispheres and has been reported to be larger in 2.5- to 14-year-old children with developmental familial dysphasia (those who were school age were also dyslexic; Njiokiktjien, de Sonneville, & Vaal, 1994). Abnormalities often also occur in multiple brain areas and are not limited to well-known language areas. For example, a recent study reported a variety of different abnormalities in MRI scans in 34% of language-impaired children (12 out of 35) as compared with none in controls (Trauner, Wulfeck, Tallal, & Hesselink, 2000). Almost all of these anomalies were in white matter. These abnormalities included (in different children) left and right ventricular enlargement, central volume loss, areas of white matter hyperintensity, periventricular encephalomalacia, and asymmetry of the occipital lobes.

Some evidence suggests that the differences in brain organization and structure found in children with SLI may arise from cascading events in early brain development. For example, Clark and Plante (1998) argued that because the gyri, both in frontal and posterior areas, appear during the third trimester (Chi, Dooling, & Gilles, 1977a, 1977b) and are prenatally determined, the asymmetry findings suggest that altered prenatal development contributes to the expression of a developmental language disorder. This is in line with a similar notion by Galaburda and colleagues (1985) about the abnormal PT asymmetry findings for dyslexics. More recently, Njiokiktjien and colleagues (1994) suggested that the increased volume of the corpus callosum in some dysphasic children may be due to a disturbance in the neurodevelopmental mechanisms responsible for the establishment of cerebral dominance. One possible agent that might produce changes in brain asymmetry in individuals with SLI is increased testosterone levels in the developing brain, as has been suggested by Plante, Boliek, Binkiewicz, and Erly (1996).

In summary, neuroanatomical anomalies associated with SLI were most typically found in the perisylvian region, including atypical asymmetries, particularly in the posterior perisylvian area, usually considered to be a part of Wernicke's language area. Yet not all with altered brain morphology are language impaired; atypical asymmetries have also been found in individuals who show no evidence of language disorder (Jernigan et al., 1991). However, a subset of children with SLI show a normal asymmetric pattern (Plante, 1991) and have normal findings on MRI (Chiron et al., 1999). Opposite anomalous asymmetries (e.g., reduced right posterior area volume vs. typical left-hemispheric reduction in SLI) have also been reported in some severe cases (Filipek et al., 1991). In addition to abnormal asymmetries, children with SLI show differences in multiple brain areas. These kinds of findings speak to the notion that there is not a simple one-to-one correspondence between cortical structural differences and SLI, and that different brain regions may be selectively implicated in individuals with SLI.

DIFFERENCES IN THE LOCALIZATION OF BRAIN ACTIVITY

Hemodynamic Brain Imaging Techniques

Functional brain imaging techniques such as SPECT, PET, and fMRI[1] allow neural functioning to be linked to distinct brain areas, thus providing the means to go beyond mere structural abnormalities in SLI. These techniques have made it possible to image brain activation during ongoing mental operations including those related to language or phonological tasks. With current techniques, brain activation can be localized with high accuracy, reaching the precision of millimeters. The ongoing development of these techniques are also making them increasingly faster (see e.g., Kruggel & von Cramon, 1999), and some of them will soon be capable of revealing changes occurring second by second.

PET and SPECT studies take advantage of the increased neural activity reflected by changes in regional cerebral blood flow (rCBF). In PET, a small amount of water labeled with positron-emitting radioactive isotope (typically oxygen, ^{15}O) is administered to a participant during performance of a continuous task. The radioactive tracer accumulates in brain regions in direct proportion to the local blood flow, which increases relative to metabolic tissue activity. The increase in positron emission can be recorded accurately in three-dimensional space, and from this spatial distribution one can infer the location or source of increased neuronal activity. The temporal resolution (the precision of time scale within which brain processes can be measured), partly dependent on the kind of isotopes used (their half-lives) and partly on hemodynamic mechanisms of different brain areas, is typically on the order of tens of seconds (Banich, 1997;

---

[1]For methodological details and technique, see Conolly, Macovski, and Pauly (2000); for PET, see Frackowiak, Lenzi, Jones, and Heather (1980); Roland (1993); Posner and Raichle (1994); Budinger and VanBrocklin (2000); for fMRI, see Banich (1997); Kwong and Chesler (2000); for using these imaging techniques in the study of cognition, language, neuropsychology, and neuropathology, see Zatorre et al. (1996); Banich (1997); Drevets (1999); for developmental aspects, see Bookheimer and Dapretto (1996); Eden and Zeffiro (1997), see also Chiron et al. (1999); for reviews and critical discussion of using PET in language studies, see Demonet, Fiez, Paulesu, Petersen, and Zatorre (1996); Poeppel (1996); and for a review with fMRI, see Kent (1998).

Roland, 1993). PET has been popular in language-related studies with adults, but has only been used with children to a limited extent. More frequently used techniques in developmental studies include SPECT and older rCBF techniques (of which SPECT is an outgrowth). These are similar to PET, but use a smaller set of sensors instead of a donut-shaped ring of radiation detectors around the participant, rendering a poorer spatial resolution. These techniques also use different tracers with longer half-lives (e.g., xenon-133, iodine-123, and technetium-99), resulting in averaging of brain activity over longer time periods and thus generating less precise images. Because cognitive processes are so much faster than the temporal resolution of any of these techniques, paired comparisons of scans obtained during continuous performance tasks or during states related to contrasting cognitive processes are used. These images are superimposed and subtracted one from another to identify blood flow differences, which presumably reflect neuronal activity distinguishing between the experimental conditions or between active and passive (resting) states.

Functional magnetic resonance imaging (fMRI), a less invasive method of studying oxygen-consumption changes related to brain activation, takes advantage of the magnetic properties of the hemoglobin contained within red blood cells (see e.g., Banich, 1997; Kwong & Chesler, 2000). Hemoglobin occurs in two forms: *oxyhemoglobin*, which contains oxygen, and *deoxyhemoglobin*, which does not contain oxygen. These forms have different magnetic properties. Oxyhemoglobin interacts weakly with an applied magnetic field, whereas deoxyhemoglobin interacts strongly with the magnetic field. No contrast agents (such as gadolinium) are needed. The fMRI technique is sensitive primarily to postcapillary hemodynamics in the local microvascular bed of the gray matter. Active neural tissue requires more oxygen, and therefore there is an increase of cerebral blood flow into this area. The observed increased signal during activation reflects a decrease of deoxyhemoglobin content compared to rest state. Based on this relative change, fMRI creates a map of differences in regional blood flow that are coupled to local neuronal activity. Although fMRI is faster than PET, allowing at best single-plane imaging of 40 ms with echo-planar imaging techniques, its temporal resolution is still dependent on hemodynamics, and therefore a 4- to 10-sec lag in response is seen in fMRI signal changes as compared with fast neuronal changes. Also the time required for blood oxygen level changes may or may not be the same for all brain areas. A complicated issue in all PET and fMRI imaging studies is the definition of baseline—that is, to what contrasting task can the activation associated with the task of interest be compared. To appreciate the difficulty, consider, during an experimental reading task, the complexities involved in attempting to exclude (e.g., by using subtraction techniques) all those associated processes not specific to reading whose contribution may lead to erroneous conclusions. These issues are discussed in a comprehensive review of brain imaging studies of reading-related processes (Price, 1997). Similar difficulties are encountered in studies using complex language tasks. In the case of reading, for example, the images often show not less, but more activation in the brains of participants with reading problems as compared with controls. Overactivation may be associated with the necessity of using more processing capacity for a task whose execution is less automatic. As with PET, so far there are only few fMRI studies with children.

Brain Activity in Children with SLI

The functional imaging techniques have been widely used in language studies in adults and have confirmed, overall, what was already known of left-hemispheric language dominance from neuropsychological and lesion studies (Carr & Posner, 1995; Lukatela, Carello, Savic, & Turvey, 1986; Neville, Kutas, & Schmidt, 1982a, 1982b; Rugg, Kok, Barret, & Fischler, 1986; Zatorre et al., 1996). However, despite these data and their appeal for excellent localization of neural activation, the number of functional brain imaging studies with children with SLI is small. The studies reviewed in this chapter have mostly applied the rCBF techniques with xenon 133 inhalation and have assessed activity both during a rest-state and during language-related cognitive tasks. The blood flow differences between children with SLI and controls in rest-state measurements would reflect differences in baseline brain activity or nontask-related mental operations in brain regions of interest, in contrast to differences in cognitive processes measured during active tasks. The results from the few existing studies show some interesting parallels as well as some inconsistencies, which may be partly attributed to the heterogeneity in study populations.

In one of the first studies, Lou and colleagues (Lou, Henriksen, & Bruhn, 1984), using rCBF during rest-state, found brain regions, most often symmetrically, with focal cerebral hypoperfusion indicating low metabolic activity in all thirteen 6- to 15-year-old dysphasic children studied (11 of whom also had attention deficit disorder [ADD]). Only one dysphasic child showed a slight structural abnormality. Participants with verbal dyspraxia had lower activity in the anterior perisylvian regions (Broca's area), and one showed lower activity in posterior perisylvian areas. Children with phonologic-syntactic dysphasia showed hypoperfusion in both anterior and posterior perisylvian regions and an individual with verbal auditory agnosia (word-deafness) only posteriorly. Denays and colleagues (1989) also found hypoperfusion during rest-state in a SPECT study of 5- to 16-year-old dysphasic children. In two children with verbal dyspraxia, this occurred in the inferior frontal gyrus of the left hemisphere involving Broca's area. The left temporo-parietal region was implicated in nine participants with both comprehension and expression-phonologic syntactic disorder. In addition, lower blood flow in the middle and superior regions of the right frontal lobe was also reported.

In a later study by Lou, Henriksen, and Bruhn (1990), also using rest-state SPECT, the results of their previous study were only partially replicated most probably because the diagnostic groups were somewhat different. Asymmetric hypoperfusion (R > L) was found in the central perisylvian region in a group of four participants with decoding or lexical-semantic dysphasia and in the prefrontal area in three children with phonologic-syntactic dysphasia (but without any decoding or semantic difficulties). Recently, a reversed asymmetry (R > L), as compared with normal controls, was also found in eight 8- to 12-year-old boys with expressive dysphasia in sensorimotor and auditory brain areas by Chiron and colleagues (1999) during rest-state with the same technique. In this study, boys with Duchenne muscular dystrophy (with reading disorders, but normal speech) also showed a similar asymmetry in the same areas and in Broca's area. However, these findings seemed to be a result of higher levels of activation on the right, rather than from less activation in the left hemisphere as compared with controls.

A number of studies have not found such differences in children with SLI using rest-state SPECT. For example, Tzourio, Heim, Zilbovicius, Gerard, and Mazoyer (1994) did not find any hypoperfused areas in 8- to 10-year-old children with SLI (7 with expressive disorder, 7 with expressive-receptive dysphasia, and 6 with attention-deficit hyperactivity disorder [ADHD]). However, when comparing rCBF values in relation to the whole cortex CBF during an *active* language related task, decreased blood flow levels were found. The dysphasic children (using pooled groups as no significant differences emerged) showed decreased activation in the left inferior parietal region during a phonemic discrimination task as compared with ADHD children. However, no comparable differences were found during a simple nonverbal auditory listening task. Moreover, expressive and expressive-receptive groups had different left-to-right blood flow ratios for the given tasks: In the expressive group, left-hemispheric activation failed to increase during the nonverbal auditory task, whereas in the mixed group, this failure occurred during the phonemic task. Previously, Lou and colleagues (1984) found that object naming failed to produce increased blood flow in relevant cortical regions in dysphasic children during an active task.

Overall, the findings reviewed here seem to fit the general neuro-psychological view of language functions. Posterior perisylvian and temporo-parietal abnormalities could explain comprehension problems in children with receptive SLI or mixed language impairment. The fact that no hypoperfusion was found in these children in Broca's area suggests that congenital dysphasia with expressive problems might well be a consequence of impaired comprehension. Hypoperfusion in the region involving Broca's area would explain the difficulties seen in children with expressive language deficit. Abnormal blood flow has also been reported in frontal areas. It has been suggested that these abnormalities may be related to attentional problems, which have not, however, always been used as a diagnostic criterion for selecting clinical populations (i.e., some children with SLI are reported to have attentional disturbances without any diagnosis of ADHD; see e.g., Denays et al., 1989). For example, in the study by Lou and colleagues (1984) reported previously, low metabolic activity was found centrally in the frontal lobe in 11 out of 13 dysphasic children who were also diagnosed with ADD. The frontal hypoperfusion was taken to suggest reduced activity in the pathways passing through the central frontal lobe to reach the prefrontal cortex (thought to be involved in attention regulation).

The paucity of current hemodynamic studies with children with SLI, despite their popularity in language research in adult populations, is partly due to serious pragmatic problems of using such methodologies with children. The necessity of using a radioactive tracer for PET limits its use to clinical populations. Although radiation is not a problem for fMRI, a currently preferred technique in imaging language functions, there are other limitations that researchers are now attempting to overcome to make this method usable in developmental studies. Clinical fMRI scans usually involve sedating children, whereas cognitive language-related studies of brain activation imaging require alert and fully cooperative participants. In this respect, movement is also a major problem especially in clinical and younger child populations. Another major difficulty in applying fMRI techniques to the study of SLI populations is the level of sound (> 80 dB) produced by the magnet during the MRI scan, which severely limits its application in auditory studies.

Despite these limitations, fMRI has recently been extended to developmental studies. An example is the study by Hertz-Pannier and colleagues (1997), in which fMRI was used to assess language dominance in eleven 8- to 18-year-old right-handed participants with partial epilepsy during the performance of a word-generation task. Language dominance, as shown by fMRI, agreed with intracarotic amobarbital test (IAT in six participants) and electrostimulation mapping (ESM in 1 participant), showing left dominance of activation in six participants and bilateral language in one. Bilateral activation for auditory sentence comprehension, verb generation to line drawing, and mental rotation of alphanumeric stimuli were recently reported in six healthy 9- to 12-year-old children in another study using whole brain echo-planar fMRI (Booth et al., 1999). The patterns of activation seen were consistent with previous adult findings. One 12-year-old child with a left-hemisphere encephalomalacic lesion (as a sequellae of early strokes) showed evidence of homologous organization in the non-damaged hemisphere.

ELECTROCORTICAL PROCESSING DIFFERENCES

Event-Related Potentials (ERPs)

Although the brain imaging techniques measuring hemodynamic changes, described earlier, are accurate in localization of activation, they are limited in the imaging of fast electrical and chemical changes related to mental processes, which occur in the time frame of tens of milliseconds. Event-related potentials (ERPs) or evoked potentials (EP)[2] and magneto-encephalography (MEG) have a temporal resolution that allows measurement of these fast dynamic changes, allowing the sequence, timing, and stages of specific processes to be observed as they occur. ERP waves are thought to manifest specific brain responses that reflect physiological changes on which cognitive processes are based. Although the spatial localization with the ERP technique is still not as precise as with hemodynamic techniques, recent developments with increasing number of recording electrodes (in several laboratories, now up to 128 and in the future up to 256) has improved the spatial resolution. Further, utilizing current source density analyses and regional source or dipole modeling, it has become possible to estimate relatively accurately the locations of neural generators of scalp-recorded activity (see e.g., Scherg & Picton, 1990). However, until recently, source localization analyses have only rarely been applied to child and infant ERP data (see e.g., Dehaene-Lamberzt & Baillet, 1998). ERPs are stimulus-related voltage deflections of scalp-recorded electroencephalography (EEG), which is thought to be a result of brain electrical activation related to summated postsynaptic potentiation in vertically oriented cortical pyramidal neuron populations. ERPs are obtained by averaging numerous time-locked EEG epochs to a stimulus event (for cortical ERPs, typically from tens to more than a hundred), which makes it possible to clearly differentiate the response to the given stimulus (hence *event-related potential*) from spontaneous and random background EEG activity (see e.g., Regan, 1989). In the ERP technique, it is assumed that (a) the background EEG acts as noise for the ERP signal, (b)

---

[2]For general description and theoretical discussion on the ERP technique and different components, see Mendel (1980); Gevins and Cutillo (1986); Squires and Ollo (1986); Regan (1989); Coles et al. (1990); Näätänen (1992); Ritter and Ruchkin (1992); for development of ERPs, see Courchesne (1990); Friedman (1991); Thomas and Crow (1994).

the signal waveform is generated by a process that stays stationary from trial to trial, (c) the noise, background EEG, is produced by a stationary random process, and (d) the noise samples are uncorrelated from trial to trial (Regan, 1989).

The ERP waves, usually consisting of several negative and positive deflections, are classified into several components either according to the latencies of major deflections or cognitive processes. The latter components are sometimes derived, for example, by subtracting two deflections that are elicited by different but related stimulus events (e.g., example deviant and standard stimuli) from each other (see e.g., Kok, 1990; Näätänen, 1990, 1992; Näätänen & Picton, 1987; Wijker, Molenaar, & van der Molen, 1989). ERP components are characterized according to the following features: polarity of components (p = positive or n = negative), amplitude (magnitude of the deflection usually expressed in μV-units), latency (the elapsed time from the stimulus presentation usually expressed in ms-units), topography (distribution of voltage or electric fields on the scalp), or task parameters (Coles, Gratton, & Fabiani, 1990; Donchin, Karis, Bashore, & Coles, 1986; Donchin, Ritter, & McCallum, 1978; Gevins & Cutillo, 1986).

Early EP or ERP components (occurring before or around 100 ms), typically referred to as *exogenous* (or *sensory*) *components*, are immediate and obligatory responses of the physiological system to physical features of stimuli. For the most part, these components are much smaller than later responses and are referred to according to their source—for example, brain stem auditory evoked potentials (BAEP)—or latency—middle latency responses (MLR). These occur before higher cognitive processes have time to take place and, unlike later responses, are minimally affected by the manipulation of psychological variables if at all. Later endogenous ERP components are associated with the participant's task-related cognitive processes and are also dependent on other subjective factors, such as arousal (Hillyard, 1985; Näätänen, 1992; Squires & Ollo, 1986). The ERP components measuring auditory and speech processing, which have most consistently differentiated between SLI and normal groups, are N1 (belonging to the exogenous components), MMN (mismatch negativity), and P3. Of these, N1 and MMN do not require active attention to stimulus events to be generated (Lyytinen, Blomberg, & Näätänen, 1992; Näätänen, 1992). Therefore, these components are particularly suitable for studying automatic (preattentive) discrimination and perception processes in young participants and clinical populations (see e.g., Alho, Cheour, & von Suchodoletz, 1997; Cheour, Leppänen, & Kraus, 2000; Csepe, 1995). There are also ERP components that measure higher language functions—for example, early left anterior negativity thought to reflect early syntactic processes, a centroparietal negativity around 400 ms (N400) reflecting lexical-semantic integration processes, and a late centroparietal positivity (P600) thought to be related to secondary syntactic processes such as reanalysis and repair (for a review, see Friederici, 1997). Because there are no published studies, to our knowledge, of these components with SLI populations, they are not reviewed in this chapter (for an example of applying N400 in single-case studies with severely language-impaired individuals, see Connolly, D'Arcy, Newman, & Kemps, 2000).

Low-Level Auditory Processing

Brain Stem Auditory Evoked Potentials (BAEPs). BAEPs, generated by 1,000 to 2,000 short-click stimuli, consist of seven small components (designated as I–VII) and occur within 10 ms from the stimulus onset.[3] Although they are recorded through scalp electrodes, they reflect activation of the brainstem. Each component arises from structures at progressively higher levels of the brainstem. BAEPs are primarily used for clinical purposes in the diagnosis of the functionality of the peripheral auditory pathway; they are invariably elicited by an intact sensory system (Coles et al., 1990; Picton, Stapells, & Campbell, 1981; Picton, Taylor, Durieux-Smith, & Edwards, 1986) and have been found to be abnormal in subgroups of infants or children with neurological disorders and in neonatal populations at high risk for such disorders. These abnormalities can reflect hearing loss even when not consistent with audiometry findings and can result in language delay.

BAEP findings in language-impaired groups are somewhat inconsistent. Abnormal BAEPs have been most consistently found in children with severe language impairments, sometimes accompanied by abnormal EEGs. For example, Bö, Marklund, Hamsten, Persson, and Tonnquist-Uhlén (1992), in a study of children at a Swedish special school for children with serious speech problems, found abnormal BAEPs (classified as either borderline or pathological) in half of the 20 students evaluated. Eighteen of these also had either borderline or pathological EEG, and a significant correlation existed between the EEG and BAEP measures. However, BAEPs did not correlate to brain electric activity mapping of auditory N1, nor was there any consistent relationship between abnormal BAEPs and performance in various language-related psychological tests. More recently, Desai and colleagues (1997) found that abnormal neonatal BAEP significantly increased the probability of finding a receptive lan-

---

[3]For reviews on BAEPs, see Mendel (1980); Picton et al. (1981); Picton and Durieux-Smith (1988); Chiappa (1997); Malhotra (1997); on assessment of infants and children, see Guerit (1985); Kileny and Robertson (1985); Pettigrew, Henderson-Smart, and Edwards (1990); Stapells and Kurtzberg (1991).

guage delay during early childhood in infants treated before discharge with extracorporeal membrane oxygenation (ECMO) for severe and progressive respiratory failure.

The few existing BAEP findings in children with SLI without any neurologic background or peripheral hearing problems are more inconsistent. In one of the early studies, Mason and Mellor (1984) found reduced BAEP amplitudes in 9- to 12-year-old children with developmental expressive and mixed dysphasia in comparison with control children. They suggested that there may be abnormal functioning of the peripheral hearing mechanism despite normal hearing thresholds in audiometry. However, later on, Courchesne and Yeung-Courchesne (1988) and Grillon, Courchesne, and Akshoomoff (1989) did not find any consistent BAEP differences between children with receptive dysphasia and control children.

Middle Latency Responses (MLRs). MLRs are exogenous EPs that occur within a latency of about 50 ms and are thought to be generated in the afferent sensory pathways that transmit the signal to central processing systems (Coles et al., 1990; Loveless, 1983; Picton et al., 1981) and seem to partly arise from the primary auditory cortex (Musiek, Geurkink, Weider, & Donnelly, 1984; Squires & Ollo, 1986). As with BAEPs, results from the few existing MLR studies are also inconsistent, showing no systematic differences between children with language disorders and controls (Grillon et al., 1989; Mason & Mellor, 1984; see also Kraus, Smith, Reed, Stein, & Cartee, 1985).

Two studies using steady-state responses (SSR), belonging to cortical middle latency sensory components, report contradictory results. SSR are exogenous responses usually elicited by trains of relatively high-frequency stimuli resulting in periodic voltage oscillations (Coles et al., 1990).

In these studies, Stefanatos and colleagues (1989) and Tomblin and colleagues (1995) used frequency-modulated (FM) tones as stimuli. Difficulty discriminating these kinds of stimuli with fast modulation rates are thought to be related to problems that language-impaired children have in processing rapid changes and the temporal structure of auditory and speech elements (cf. Elliot, Hammer, & Scholl, 1989; Morgan, 1984; Tallal & Newcombe, 1978; Tallal & Piercy, 1973a, 1973b; Tallal, Stark, & Mellits, 1985; for reviews, see Tallal, 2000; Tallal & Curtiss, 1990; for recent findings in relation to dyslexia, see Witton et al., 1998). Stefanatos and colleagues (1989) observed abnormal SSR in six 11- to 16-year-old children with receptive dysphasia, in whom FM-tones, varying in frequency around a 1 kHz carrier, either failed to elicit a characteristic periodic response or in whom this response was missing. This seemed to suggest that children with SLI have a deficit in coding sensory information in central mechanisms subserving the cortical analysis of frequency transitions in temporally complex sounds, including speech. However, using a similar paradigm, Tomblin and colleagues (1995) did not find any SSR differences for FM tones among twelve 10-year-old children with mixed (both receptive and expressive) SLI and controls. Both control and SLI children showed typical averaged cortically evoked SSR in contrast to a flat response to an unmodulated 1 kHz steady tone. The authors interpreted their results as providing strong evidence against FM-evoked response serving as a phenotypic marker for SLI.

The conflicting results between the two studies may arise partly from differences in the depth of frequency modulation, which was ±100 Hz in Tomblin's study (Tomblin et al., 1995) and varied as ±20, ±60, and ±100 Hz in Stefanatos' study (Stefanatos et al., 1989; cf. Witton et al., 1998, in which study dyslexic were less sensitive to 2 Hz and 40 Hz frequency modulation, but not to 240 Hz FM). Another possible explanation for the conflicting results may be based on differences in participant groups. In the Stefanatos study, abnormal responses occurred in children with receptive dysphasia, whereas in Tomblin's study, differences were not found in children with mixed receptive-expressive language impairment. Tomblin et al. (1995) regarded the conflicting results to be solely due to population differences. They also claimed that the participants in the Stefanatos study (Stefanatos et al., 1989) were not pure SLI children, but children having Landau–Kleffner Syndrome, an acquired neurologic disorder with one of its characteristics being epileptic seizures. Tomblin et al. based their information on the unpublished dissertation by Stefanatos (1984); Stefanatos et al. (1989) did not report this information. Therefore, a possibility remains that, in the Stefanatos study, the children with receptive dysphasia had much more pervasive problems than the mixed SLI group in the Tomblin study (Tomblin et al., 1995).

N1.   Following MLRs, the first cortically generated auditory ERP is the exogenous N1–P2 complex, which is thought to reflect sensory processing in the auditory cortex and informing of the arrival of the auditory information to the central auditory system (Näätänen, 1988, 1990, 1992). The N1–P2 complex is elicited by transient aspects of stimulation (onsets as well as offsets in case of long-duration stimuli). It is also dependent on stimulus frequency, intensity, probability, and interstimulus interval (ISI; cf. Näätänen & Picton, 1987). N1–P2 reaches its peak negativity at about 100 ms and positivity at about 200 ms. N1 has been observed in school-age children, although developmental changes affect auditory N1 features, such as its latency, scalp distribution, and reliability with which it can be identified (see e.g., Ceponiene, Cheour, & Näätänen, 1998; Daruna et al., 1987; Johnson, 1989; Karhu et al., 1997; Martin et al., 1988; see also Leppänen, Laukkonen, & Lyytinen, 1992). For example, N1 latencies are typically longer in the younger age groups as compared with adults (e.g., Ladish & Polich, 1989).

N1 generated by speech and acoustic stimuli is often delayed and differentially lateralized in children with language impairment, showing either atypical asymmetry or reduction of amplitude at the hemisphere with the expected predominance (Dawson, Finley, Phillips, & Lewy, 1989; Jirsa & Clontz, 1990; Lincoln et al., 1995; Neville et al., 1993; Tonnquist-Uhlén, Borg, Persson, & Spens, 1996). For example, Dawson and his group (1989) found a reversed right-minus-left hemispheric index (R > L) of both N1 amplitude and latency for responses to a rarely presented target /da/-syllable in autistic and SLI children as compared with control children in whom L > R. In children with SLI, the N1 latency at the left hemisphere covaried with behavioral language measures—the longer the left-hemispheric latency, the poorer the language performance. The hemispheric N1 amplitude differences have also been found in studies using pure tones, in which one would not expect L–R asymmetry patterns to be in the same direction as with speech stimuli. For example, abnormal left-hemispheric dominance or reduced responses at the right hemisphere have been found in children with SLI (Mason & Mellor, 1984; Neville et al., 1993). In one study, Lincoln and colleagues (1995) showed, surprisingly, that the N1 amplitude in general was significantly larger in children with SLI.

At least two possible explanations for the N1 group differences exist. First, these differences may be explained, at least partly, by delayed maturation (e.g., Jirsa et al., 1990; Tonnquist-Uhlén et al., 1996). Yet the lack of an age-dependent decrease of the N1 latency in some children with SLI (see e.g., Tonnquist-Uhlén et al., 1996) suggests that the deficit may not result purely from maturational delay, but may also reflect a more persistent problem. Second, Lincoln and colleagues (1995) suggested that N1 differences, likely to reflect ineffective regulation of sensory input in children with SLI, may be due to abnormalities in serotonergic regulation of auditory cortex. There are also children with SLI or more severe LI in whom N1 differences or abnormalities, such as delayed N1 or missing T complex (Tonnquist-Uhlén, 1996a), are not found, which seems to suggest different pathophysiological causes for their language impairment.

Mismatch Negativity (MMN).   The first deflection following N1 that has received considerable attention in recent psychophysiological studies of language problems is called mismatch negativity (MMN; Näätänen, Gaillard, & Mäntysalo, 1978). For reviews, see Näätänen (1990, 1992, 1995); Lang et al. (1995); Näätänen and Alho (1997); Picton, Alain, Otten, Ritter, and Achim (2000); for development, see Csepe (1995), Cheour et al. (2000), and Kurtzberg et al. (1995). It is a response to infrequently presented rare and deviant auditory stimuli embedded in a stream of repeated auditory events. MMN is independent of stimulus features being sensitive to changes in, for example, pitch, duration, intensity, rise time, location, and even stimulus omissions. MMN has also been recorded for complex stimulus changes (Tervaniemi, Maury, & Näätänen, 1994) including speech signals (e.g., Näätänen et al., 1997). It is typically estimated from the difference wave computed by subtracting the response to repeated background stimuli from that to deviant stimuli. The resulting response, usually peaking at frontocentral areas about 200 ms from the point of stimulus difference, is thought to represent the brain's detection process of the deviation from the memory representation formed by preceding repeated stimuli. An MMN-like response seems to be identifiable in infancy (see e.g., Alho et al., 1990; Cheour-Luhtanen et al., 1995, 1996). However, maturational effects and experimental conditions under which MMN or corresponding infant/child response occurs in normal development still need to be mapped in more detail before the MMN paradigm can be applied as a clinical tool in developmental studies (see e.g., Cheour et al., 2000; Csepe, 1995; Kurtzberg, Vaughan, Kreuzer, & Fliegler, 1995; Leppänen, Eklund, & Lyytinen, 1997).

Few studies report differences in MMN amplitude in preschool and school-age children with SLI as compared with control children. In one of the first studies, Korpilahti and Lang (1994) found reduced MMN amplitude for frequency change in pure tones presented at a relatively rapid rate in fourteen 7- to 13-year-old dysphasic children (diagnosed in early childhood; for replications in children with the same as well as younger ages from 3–9 years, see Holopainen, Korpilahti, Juottonen, Lang, & Sillanpää, 1997, 1998; Korpilahti, 1995). Similar reduced MMN amplitude was also observed in a group of 5- to 8-year-old mentally retarded children with both low IQ (50–69) and poor linguistic skills (1.5 SD or more below normal range; Holopainen et al., 1998). These children did not differ in their responses from the dysphasic children. In their original study, Korpilahti and Lang (1994) also found a significantly reduced MMN to relatively large tone duration change (50 vs. 500 ms) in dysphasic children. No latency differences were found for deviant stimuli (either differing in frequency or duration) between the dysphasic and control groups. Interestingly, a prolonged latency was found in children with SLI for standard stimuli when presented in the context of the large duration change.

The reviewed MMN studies suggest that SLI is expressed at the preattentive level of acoustic information processing. The longer latency in children with SLI for repeated standard stimuli in one instance would seem to indicate, as already seen for N1 latency delays, differences in the obligatory response reflecting poorer sensitivity of the afferent system. MMN differences also seem to implicate a deficit related to the sensory memory functions in developmental language disorders and could reflect a more rapidly fading memory trace, as suggested by Korpilahti and Lang (1994).

Attention Modulated Discrimination—P3

Some differences have been reported, although inconsistently, in higher level processing reflected in the positive endogenous P3 (also referred to as P300), which is usually maximal at the parietal cortex peaking at 280 to 600 ms (Donchin & Coles, 1988; Donchin et al., 1984; Rösler et al., 1986; Sutton & Ruchkin, 1984). P3 is generated by target stimuli in oddball paradigms in all sensory modalities, and it has been related to several aspects of cognitive activity including attention, evaluation, or categorization of stimuli; time estimation; memory-related operations like recognition memory; updating of working memory; and context closure.

Smaller P3 amplitudes and prolonged latencies to pure tone target stimuli have been reported in 9- to 12-year-old children with central auditory processing disorder (with normal peripheral hearing) in comparison with control children (Jirsa, 1992; Jirsa & Clontz, 1990). However, failures to find P3 differences between SLI and control children also exist (Lincoln, Courchesne, Harms, & Allen, 1993; Neville et al., 1993). Interestingly, Courchesne and colleagues (1987) found an abnormal recovery cycle of P3 with rapid stimulus presentation rate in dysphasic children. They speculated that, because P3 can be observed even with short stimulus presentation intervals (down to 300 ms), P3 amplitude reduction in children with SLI suggests that these children have a deficit in processing rapidly delivered acoustic information. However, as Jirsa and Clontz (1990) pointed out, P3 is also elicited by tactile and visual stimulation, and hence the absence or delay of the auditory P3 cannot be attributed exclusively to the auditory system. It may also be due to a problem in the central processing system involved in coordinating all incoming sensory information. The fact that visual P3 has not been found to differ between dysphasic children and controls (see Courchesne et al., 1988) seems to suggest that possible P3 differences are related to the auditory modality. Lack of P3 differences between control and clinical participants may, therefore, be due to the insensitivity of stimuli to tap appropriate aspects of auditory processing. This possibility needs to be explored further in future studies.

Developmental ERPs in Studying Infants at Risk for Language Disorders

It is well established that SLI runs in families and infants born into families with affected parent/parents (and close relatives) are at an elevated risk for the disorder (Bishop & Edmundson, 1986; Bishop, North, &

Donlan, 1995; Choudhury & Benasich, in press; Lahey & Edwards, 1995; Neils & Aram, 1986; Tallal, Ross, & Curtiss, 1989; Tomblin, 1989, 1996; Tomblin & Buckwalter, 1998; van der Lely & Stollwerck, 1996). Data suggest that children from families with a history of SLI are approximately four times more likely to develop SLI as compared with children from control families. In a review of 18 family aggregation studies of language impairment, Stromswold (1998) found that the incidence of language impairment in families with a history of SLI ranged from 24% (Bishop et al., 1986) to 78% (van der Lely & Stollwerck, 1996; although this study also included individuals with reading problems), with an average rate of 46%. As a result of differences in selection criteria, the incidence of SLI in control families ranged from 3% (Bishop & Edmundson, 1986) to 46% (Tallal et al., 1989), with a mean rate of 18%. In addition to family aggregation studies, behavioral-genetics research has shown that SLI has a highly heritable component (for a review, see Leonard, 1998; for a review of the genetics of language and methodology, see Brzustowicz, 1996). These studies have reported that monozygotic twins show a higher concordance rate (range .70–.96) for language-based learning disorders as compared with dizygotic twins (range .46–.69; Bishop et al., 1995; Lewis & Thompson, 1992; Tomblin et al., 1998).

In the following section, we discuss the possibilities of using ERPs and behavioral measures together to study the processes that may, in part, underlie the development of SLI. The approach used in our laboratory allows us to address the issue of continuity of language-related problems from lower level processes to higher level dysfunction. Previously reviewed neuroimaging findings suggest that there are basic perceptual and processing constraints that could, in part, explain the etiology of SLI. Extensive research on speech perception and speech–sound representation with individuals with SLI suggests that these children differ from their peers in the ability to discriminate and process the basic components of speech (phonemes; for a review, see Tallal, 2000; Verhoeven & Segers, chap. 17, this volume; see also Studdert-Kennedy & Mody, 1995).

That acoustic rate processing deficits may subserve language impairment is supported by a series of studies that show that rapid rate auditory processing (RAP) thresholds of infants born into families with a history of language impairment is significantly longer than those of age-matched peers from control families (Benasich & Tallal, 1996, 2002). More important, RAP thresholds at 6 months were found to be predictive of later receptive and expressive language, such that infants with elevated thresholds were developing language more slowly than those with lower thresholds (Benasich, Spitz, Flax, & Tallal, 1997; Benasich & Tallal, 2002). Further, the differences in individual RAP thresholds were found to be the single best predictor of expressive and receptive language outcome at all subsequent ages, in both control children and children with a family history of language impairment.

Recently, Leppänen and colleagues (Guttorm, Leppänen, Richardson, & Lyytinen, 2001; Leppänen & Lyytinen, 1997; Leppänen, Pihko, Eklund, & Lyytinen, 1999; Leppänen et al., 2002; Pihko et al., 1999) have shown that ERPs to consonant–vowel syllables as well as vowel and consonant duration changes are different in infants at risk for familial dyslexia. Richardson and colleagues have also shown, in a behavioral study, that at-risk infants require a longer consonant duration (i.e., a longer silent gap) to respond to a pseudoword with a double consonant in a categorical fashion in a conditioned head-turn paradigm as compared with control infants (Richardson, 1998; Richardson, Leppänen, Leiwo, & Lyytinen, in press). In our current ongoing study at the Infancy Studies Laboratory at the Center for Molecular and Behavioral Neuroscience, Rutgers University, infants who have a sibling diagnosed as SLI are being followed in a prospective longitudinal study that allows examination of developmental changes and maturation of infant brain responses to rapidly changing auditory cues and their relations to behavioral performance (see Choudhury, Leppänen, & Benasich, 2002; for an illustration of measurement, see Fig. 4.2). Our preliminary analyses of infant data are promising, suggesting that infants between 6 and 24 months of age process pitch changes in stimuli (the

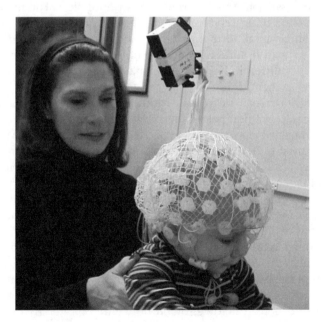

FIG. 4.2.   Photograph of a 6-month-old child seated on his mother's lap during an ERP testing session.

difference between the repeated [low-low] and changing [low-high] pairs) and that their ERPs, although different from adults (see Leppänen, Choudhury, Leevers, & Benasich, 2000), are affected by the presentation rate (the within-pair ISI) much like in adults (see Leppänen, Choudhury, Thomas, Jing, & Benasich, 2002). Our present findings suggest that the infant brain also processes rapidly occurring auditory changes (like the pitch change in the tone pair with 70 ms gap), which may be a critical ability to form accurate speech sound representations in the brain (acoustic changes in speech occur, though, even faster).

CONCLUSIONS AND DISCUSSION

Neuroimaging of language-impaired groups can provide critical insights as to the neural basis of such problems, and can thus help elucidate the etiology of SLI. Overall, findings from these diverse neuroimaging studies are, at best, fairly consistent. They provide converging evidence revealing differences between children with and without SLI both in the structure of the brain and its activation. Further, some relatively consistent differences are found in specific electrocortical measures, which reflect problems with auditory processing in this heterogeneous population. The most consistently implicated brain region that has been shown to either differ from controls or show an abnormal pattern in individuals with SLI is the area around the sylvian fissure. It should be noted, however, that in different studies slightly different brain regions may be involved due to variation in area measurement criteria.

Differences are seen in frontal, central, and posterior perisylvian regions. The central region below the sylvian fissure includes the auditory cortex. The posterior perisylvian areas, including the PT and Wernicke's area, are known to be important for phonological processing and receptive language (see e.g., Pennington, 1991). In anatomical studies, children with SLI often show an atypical asymmetry of the entire perisylvian area, although most frequently of the posterior regions (R > L in children with SLI and L > R in normal controls, or in some cases reduced volume is seen in the left region in children with SLI). Functional neuroimaging findings similarly show an atypical pattern of lower perisylvian activation during the rest-state in the left as compared with the right hemisphere, including the central perisylvian area. Deviations of the frontal perisylvian region, including most of Broca's area, involve reduced volume of the brain tissue on the left side as well as lower blood flow either bilaterally or in the left hemisphere during rest-state and active performance in children with SLI. Prefrontal and frontal cortex differences between language-impaired and control individuals have also been seen across some studies, but without such consistently altered asymmetry patterns.

Although no one-to-one mapping exists between abnormal brain region findings and diagnostic neuropsychological categories, such as receptive, expressive, or mixed SLI, a trend is evident especially in hemodynamic studies. For example, children with expressive SLI and dyspraxia have anomalies in Broca's area, whereas children with either mixed or receptive SLI and verbal agnosia show differences in the posterior regions. In addition, children with expressive problems also show atypical activation in the posterior areas. This is not surprising because it is possible that anomalies in these receptive areas may have contributed to their language problems. However, in many anatomical studies, children with SLI are often simply reported to be language impaired without further classification, making it difficult to draw any direct conclusions about implicated anatomical differences and subtypes of SLI. Furthermore, the currently reviewed findings do not provide the means to link anatomical anomalies in SLI to specific functional deviations because MRI findings are not typically reported in the functional imaging studies. Despite the lack of this direct link, recent studies suggest that linguistic skills are associated with brain anatomy, such as the morphological features of planum areas. For example, Morgan and Hynd (1998) posited that the leftward asymmetry of the length of the temporal bank of the PT confers linguistic advantages. Similarly, Dalby and collaborators (1998) found that the degree of left asymmetry in the temporal cortex correlated with both reading skills and skills in phonemic analysis of spoken language.

ERP differences between groups of children with and without SLI tap processing differences at a more dynamic level in the time frame of tens of milliseconds—the time frame of the sensory and cognitive processes in the neural networks. One of the earliest measured responses from the auditory pathway are typically BAEPs, which originate from the brainstem. However, the results from these studies are somewhat inconsistent. In a few cases, BAEP abnormalities exist in the severely language impaired with other problems (e.g., abnormal EEG or abnormal MRI findings). Even when found, however, BAEP abnormalities do not correlate to cortical N1 response or in any consistent way to performance in various language-related tests. Likewise, no consistent SLI-related findings exist for the MLR responses, originating either from thalamocortical pathways or in the primary auditory cortex. Therefore, possible auditory processing problems in SLI do not seem to arise from deviations in the signal transmission in the auditory pathway before or at the thalamic level.

N1–P2 ERP complex is the first cortical response following MLRs as the auditory information is further processed in primary auditory areas. Children with SLI differ from controls in both N1 amplitudes and latencies. N1 and the related T-complex latencies are consistently longer (i.e., N1 reaches peak amplitude later) in children with SLI. Because N1 is an exogenous sensory component related to afferent activation to transient aspects of stimuli, the prolonged latencies can be taken to reflect delayed or slower sensory processing. However, it is too premature to say whether the delayed N1 can be linked to the reported general timing deficits or to problems in processing rapid auditory changes (e.g., Tallal, 2000) because the nature of the neural mechanisms responsible for either phenomena is not yet well understood. Moreover, as in the case of BAEPs, delayed N1 and T-complex responses have also been found in severely language-impaired individuals with concomitant neurological problems (Tonnquist-Uhlén et al., 1996; Tonnquist-Uhlén, 1996a, 1996b).

N1 amplitudes in children with SLI have atypical asymmetry patterns in several studies in line with the reported hemodynamic findings. The left–right hemispheric index for speech sounds is opposite to that found in controls (in whom L > R). For pure tones, N1 amplitude is either reduced at the right hemisphere or shows a left-hemispheric dominance, contrary to typical right-hemispheric dominance in controls. Given that N1 reflects auditory afferent activation, these atypical asymmetries suggest that low-level auditory processing is also differently lateralized in children with SLI. Further, because N1 is generated in the auditory cortex, it is plausible to assume that these deviations in N1 amplitude asymmetry could be related to atypical anatomical asymmetries of the perisylvian area, especially in central regions, seen in children with SLI .

Group differences in the MMN response index a possible deficit further on in the processing stream in children with SLI. If MMN fails to be generated, it may be due to some problem in the auditory sensory memory and/or partly in auditory discrimination process based on the prior feature detection (e.g., the sharpness of tonotopic neural maps). The fact that children with SLI have reduced MMN amplitude for changes in pure tones (both pitch and duration) suggests that they have processing problems not only for speech and language elements, but also of other, more basic, acoustic information. However, it is likely that they would also have shown reduced MMN amplitude to changes in speech sounds had these been used as stimuli. In fact, a recent finding reported by Uwer and colleagues (Uwer, Albrecht, & von Suchodoletz, 1998) shows that children with SLI have an abnormal MMN to speech-related stimuli. Reduced MMN to speech sounds has also been shown in learning-disabled children (Kraus et al., 1996) and adults with dyslexia (Kujala et al., 2000).

There is evidence that the neurophysiological system that generates MMN can also be tuned in accordance with the typicality of speech sounds (Aaltonen et al., 1997) reflecting the magnet effect described by Kuhl (1991). Aaltonen and collaborators (1997) showed that there is individual variation in MMN for prototypes: Those who are poor in behavioral categorization show less MMN differences between prototype and nonprototype stimuli as compared with good categorizers, who show larger MMNs to nonprototypes. Therefore, the MMN differences in children with SLI can be taken to suggest that they are less efficient at laying down representations of speech signals, resulting in poorer speech sound prototypes (Kuhl, 1991). Deficits in forming speech sound representations can have cascading effects on the entire language-acquisition system. It is also known that long-term memory traces can, in turn, facilitate preattentive change-detection processes in a top–down fashion (Näätänen, 1992, 1999; Winkler et al., 1999). For example, Näätänen and colleagues (1997) showed that MMN is smaller to a deviation in a non-native speech sound as compared with that in a native speech sound (even when the magnitude of acoustic deviation was slightly larger for the non-native token). MMN seems to reflect such long-term effects related to the development of native speech sound categories well before children learn to speak (Cheour et al., 1998).

In addition to these relatively well-defined anatomical, hemodynamic, and brain response differences seen between language-impaired and control individuals, a host of other, less consistently reported, neurophysiological abnormalities have been shown in children with SLI. Across the reviewed studies, these include cortical atrophies, white matter abnormalities, abnormal corpus callosum size, and extra sulci. These various findings suggest that SLI may not be explained by any single deficit or precisely localized brain structure alone. This raises two possible issues, the first relating to the etiology of the biological/anatomical differences found in SLI and the second to the effect of the differential environmental input. Multiple brain structural and functional differences could be explained by multiple etiologies, which may accumulate in some cases. Because brain structures are formed, for the most part, during the prenatal period of neuronal migration, at least part of the structural anomalies in SLI could be due to disordered cell migration, resulting from genetic causes and/or biological insult during migration (Clark & Plante, 1998; Rosen, Press, Sherman, & Galaburda, 1992; see also Chi et al., 1977a, 1977b). For example, variation in the genetic basis for SLI could lead to multiple phenotypes. However, even if only one genetic variant exists, various prenatal and perinatal events may have differential cumulative effects on auditory perception and language development.

Although neuroimaging techniques have advanced our understanding of the origins and neural basis of SLI, the field is still relatively young, leaving us with a number of issues that need to be resolved. One tenacious problem is the inconsistent way in which children with SLI are diagnosed and classified. The interpretation of even the most consistent findings across studies, with regard to which brain areas or what brain processes might be involved in SLI, is complicated by this type of variability. Therefore, a more specific classification of phenotype is needed. We also need to go beyond the phenotype descriptions—affected by differences resulting, for example, from the way a child learns to cope with his/her difficulties—to understand how behavioral profiles or diagnostic categories relate to specific neural substrates. Converging evidence from different methodologies, including behavioral, neuroimaging, and genetic studies in the same participant groups, is necessary to develop a more comprehensive picture of the disorder (for an example of combining ERPs with fMRI, see Linden et al., 1999). Additionally, more complex transactional models (see Sameroff & Chandler, 1975) need to be developed to understand the contribution of both genetic and environmental effects across time on the development and expression of SLI.

Finally, before neuroimaging techniques, in general, can be regarded as a clinical tool for diagnostic classification, a number of factors need to be considered. For example, all functional imaging techniques, including ERPs, lack normative developmental data with common recording and analysis criteria, which would allow us to estimate deviations from the normal range. There is also considerable individual variation in ERPs, and test–retest reliability still needs to be improved. Further, not all individuals with SLI show neural anatomical anomalies or functional atypicalities despite the commonly accepted notion that SLI is based on brain-related problems (see Gilger & Kaplan, 2001). Most of the reviewed ERP measures have also been implicated in several other disorders (see e.g., Cheour et al., 1997; Dawson, Finley, Phillips, & Galpert, 1988; Dawson et al., 1989; Kujala et al., 2000; McAnally & Stein, 1997; cf. also Ohta, Uchiyama, Matsushima, & Toru, 1999). For example, Kraus and collaborators (1996) found that MMN to short duration spectral changes in the onset frequency of formant transition cues between syllables such as /da/ vs. /ga/ were reduced in learning-disabled children. That such a clear result was achieved is almost surprising because the selection of participants was not based specifically on diagnostic criteria of any specific language-related difficulty. Therefore, it is important to clarify whether distinct features of different ERP components (and other imaging measures) are specific to different disorders. Such profiles need to be linked with behavioral measures.

Studies of populations at risk for learning and language disorders could provide a means to screen and identify infants at risk for developmental language delays well before the diagnosis of the disorder. This would allow us to take advantage of current advancements in the field of neural plasticity and adaptive training. Evidence from a number of studies suggest that with well-directed training, one is able to improve both perceptual and language skills. Even a short-term training effect has been shown to generalize to new language contexts (Tremblay, Kraus, Carrell, & McGee, 1997). In one of the pioneering studies in this area, children with specific language-learning problems, who participated in specifically focused adaptive training, improved markedly in their ability to recognize brief and rapidly presented sound sequences with an associated enhancement of their language comprehension skills (Merzenich et al., 1996; Tallal et al., 1996). ERPs and other neuroimaging techniques could be utilized to identify children with poor auditory processing skills early in their development (see e.g., Molfese, 2000; Molfese & Molfese, 1985, 1997), so they could fully benefit from such remedial training programs. Some data already exist to support the idea that ERP measures are sensitive enough to detect changes in clinical status following a treatment program (Jirsa, 1992) or changes due to discrimination training of small acoustic contrasts (Kraus et al., 1995). The hope is emerging that, in the not so distant future, remediation efforts can also be guided by brain imaging results.

ACKNOWLEDGMENTS

This work is supported by the Human Frontier Science Program Organization, the Academy of Finland, Don and Linda Carter Foundation, and NICHD RO129419. The authors gratefully acknowledge the thoughtful comments of Jennifer Thomas, the technical assistance of Pirkko Leppänen and Jason Nawyn, as well as the help of Cecylia Chojnowski in ERP measurements. We also thank the families that participated in the study.

REFERENCES

Aaltonen, O., Eerola, O., Hellström, Å., Uusipaikka, E., Lang, A. H., & von Suchololetz, W. (1997). Perceptual magnet effect in the light of behavioral and psychophysiological data. *Journal of the Acoustical Society of America, 101*, 1090–1105.

Alho, K., Cheour, M., & von Suchodoletz, W. (1997). Auditory discrimination in infants as revealed by the mismatch negativity of the event-related brain potential. *Developmental Neuropsychology, 13*, 157–165.

Alho, K., Sainio, K., Sajaniemi, N., Reinikainen, K., Näätänen, R., & von Suchodoletz, W. (1990). Event-related brain potential of human newborns to pitch change of an acoustic stimulus. *Electroencephalography and Clinical Neurophysiology, 77*, 151–155.

Banich, M. T. (1997). *Neuropsychology: The neural bases of mental function*. Boston: Houghton-Mifflin.

Benasich, A. A., Spitz, R. V., Flax, J., & Tallal, P. (1997, April). *Early auditory temporal processing abilities and later language among children with a family history of language impairment*. Paper presented at the annual meeting of the Cognitive Neuroscience Society, Boston, MA.

Benasich, A. A., & Tallal, P. (1996). Auditory temporal processing thresholds, habituation and recognition memory over the first year of life. *Infant Behavior and Development, 19,* 339–357.

Benasich, A. A., & Tallal, P. (2002). Infant discrimination of rapid auditory cues: Links to family history and later language outcomes. *Behavioral Brain Research, 136,* 31–49.

Bishop, D. V. M., & Edmundson, A. (1986). Is otitis media a major cause of specific developmental language disorders? *British Journal of Disorders of Communication, 21,* 321–338.

Bishop, D. V. M., North, T., & Donlan, C. (1995). Genetic basis of specific language impairment: Evidence from a twin study. *Developmental Medicine and Child Neurology, 37,* 56–71.

Bookheimer, S. Y., & Dapretto, M. (1996). Functional neuroimaging of language in children: Current directions and future challenges. In R. W. Thatcher, G. R. Lyon, J. Rumsey, & N. Krasnegor (Eds.), *Developmental neuroimaging: Mapping the development of brain and behavior* (pp. 143–155). San Diego: Academic Press.

Booth, J. R., MacWhinney, B., Thulborn, K. R., Sacco, K., Voyvodic, J., & Feldman, H. M. (1999). Functional organization of activation patterns in children: Whole brain fMRI imaging during three different cognitive tasks. *Progress in Neuro-Psychopharmacology & Biological Psychiatry, 23,* 669–682.

Bö, O. O., Marklund, E., Hamsten, P. O., Persson, H. E., & Tonnquist-Uhlén, I. (1992). Relations between neurological aberrations and psychological dysfunctions in children with serious language problems. *Scandinavian Journal of Educational Research, 36,* 49–59.

Brzustowicz, L. (1996). Looking for language genes: Lessons from complex disorder studies. In M. L. Rice (Ed.), *Toward a genetics of language* (pp. 3–25). Mahwah, NJ: Lawrence Erlbaum Associates.

Budinger, T. F., & VanBrocklin, H. F. (2000). Positron-emission tomography (PET): Radiopharmaceuticals. In J. D. Bronzino (Ed.), *The biomedical engineering handbook* (2nd ed., pp. 67.1–67.7). Florida: CRC Press.

Carr, T. H., & Posner, M. I. (1995). The impact of learning to read on the functional anatomy of language processing. In B. Gelder (Ed.), *Speech and reading: A comparative approach* (pp. 267–301). Hove, England: Lawrence Erlbaum Associates.

Ceponiene, R., Cheour, M., & Näätänen, R. (1998). Interstimulus interval and auditory event-related potentials in children: Evidence for multiple generators. *Electroencephalography and Clinical Neurophysiology, 108,* 345–354.

Cheour, M., Ceponiene, R., Lehtokoski, A., Luuk, A., Allik, J., Alho, K., & Näätänen, R. (1998). Development of language-specific phoneme representations in the infant brain. *Nature Neuroscience, 1,* 351–353.

Cheour, M., Haapanen, M. L., Hukki, J., Ceponiene, R., Kurjenluoma, S., Alho, K., Tervaniemi, M., Ranta, R., & Näätänen, R. (1997). The first neurophysiological evidence for cognitive brain dysfunctions in CATCH children. *NeuroReport, 8,* 1785–1787.

Cheour, M., Leppänen, P. H. T., & Kraus, N. (2000). Mismatch negativity (MMN) as a tool for investigating auditory discrimination and sensory memory in infants and children. *Clinical Neurophysiology, 111,* 4–16.

Cheour-Luhtanen, M., Alho, K., Kujala, T., Sainio, K., Reinikainen, K., Renlund, M., Aaltonen, O., Eerola, O., & Näätänen, R. (1995). Mismatch negativity indicates vowel discrimination in newborns. *Hearing Research, 82,* 53–58.

Cheour-Luhtanen, M., Alho, K., Sainio, K., Rinne, T., Reinikainen, K., Pohjavuori, M., Renlund, M., Aaltonen, O., Eerola, O., & Näätänen, R. (1996). The ontogenetically earliest discriminative response of the human brain. *Psychophysiology, 33,* 478–481.

Chi, G. J., Dooling, E. G., & Gilles, F. H. (1977a). Gyral development of the human brain. *Annals of Neurology, 1,* 86–93.

Chi, G. J., Dooling, E. G., & Gilles, F. H. (1977b). Left-right asymmetries of the temporal speech areas of the human fetus. *Archives of Neurology, 34,* 346–348.

Chiappa, K. H. (1997). Brain stem auditory evoked potentials: Methodology. In K. H. Chiappa (Ed.), *Evoked potentials in clinical medicine* (3rd ed., pp. 157–197). Philadelphia: Lippincott-Raven.

Chiron, C., Pinton, F., Masure, M. C., Duvelleroy-Hommet, C., Leon, F., & Billard, C. (1999). Hemispheric specialization using SPECT and stimulation tasks in children with dysphasia and dystrophia. *Developmental Medicine & Child Neurology, 41,* 512–520.

Choudhury, N., & Benasich, A. A. (in press). A family aggregation study: The influence of family history and other risk factors on language development. *Journal of Speech, Language and Hearing Research.*

Choudhury, N., Leppänen, P. H. T., & Benasich, A. A. (2002, April). Assessing rapid auditory processing skills in family history and control infants: Evidence from converging assessments. *Journal of Cognitive Neuroscience, Suppl., Abstracts of Cognitive Neuroscience Society Annual Meeting 2002,* 40.

Clark, M. M., & Plante, E. (1998). Morphology of the inferior frontal gyrus in developmentally language-disordered adults. *Brain & Language, 61,* 288–303.

Coles, M. G. H., Gratton, G., & Fabiani, M. (1990). Event-related brain potentials. In J. T. Cacioppo & L. G. Tassinary (Eds.), *Principles of psychophysiology: Physical, social, and inferential elements* (pp. 413–455). Cambridge: Cambridge University Press.

Connolly, J. F., D'Arcy, R. C. N., Newman, R. L., & Kemps, R. (2000). The application of cognitive event-related brain potentials (ERPs) in language-impaired individuals: Review and case studies. *International Journal of Psychophysiology, 38,* 55–70.

Conolly, S., Macovski, A., & Pauly, P. (2000). Magnetic resonance imaging: Acquisition and processing. In J. D. Bronzino (Ed.), *The biomedical engineering handbook* (2nd ed., pp. 63.1–63.9). Florida: CRC Press.

Courchesne, E. (1990). Chronology of postnatal human brain development: Event-related potential, positron emission tomography, myelinogenesis, and synaptogenesis studies. In J. W. Rohrbaugh, R. Parasuraman, & R. Johnson, Jr. (Eds.), *Event-related brain potentials: Basic issues and applications* (pp. 210–241). New York: Oxford University Press.

Courchesne, E., Elmasian, R., & Yeung-Courchesne, R. (1987). Electrophysiological correlates of cognitive processing: P3b and Nc, basic, clinical, and developmental research. In A. M. Halliday (Ed.), *A textbook of clinical neurophysiology* (pp. 645–676). New York: Wiley.

Courchesne, E., & Plante, E. (1996). Measurement and analysis issues in neurodevelopmental magnetic resonance imaging. In R. W. Thatcher, G. R. Lyon, J. Rumsey, & N. Krasnegor (Eds.), *Developmental neuroimaging: Mapping the development of brain and behavior* (pp. 43–65). San Diego: Academic Press.

Courchesne, E., & Yeung-Courchesne, R. (1988). Event-related brain potentials. In M. Rutter, A. H. Tuma, & I. S. Lann (Eds.), *Assessment and diagnosis in child psychopathology* (pp. 264–299). New York: Guilford.

Csepe, V. (1995). On the origin and development of the mismatch negativity. *Ear and Hearing, 16,* 91–104.

Dalby, M. A., Elbro, C., & Stödkilde-Jörgensen, H. (1998). Temporal lobe asymmetry and dyslexia: An in vivo study using MRI. *Brain & Language, 62,* 51–69.

Damasio, H., & Damasio, A. R. (1989). *Lesion analysis in neuropsychology.* New York: Oxford University Press.

Daruna, J. H., & Rau, A. E. (1987). Development of the late components of auditory brain potentials from early childhood to adulthood. *Electroencephalography and Clinical Neurophysiology, 40*(Suppl.), 590–595.

Dawson, G., Finley, C., Phillips, S., & Galpert, L. (1988). Reduced P3 amplitude of the event-related brain potential: Its relationship to language ability in autism. *Journal of Autism and Developmental Disorders, 18,* 493–504.

Dawson, G., Finley, C., Phillips, S., & Lewy, A. (1989). A comparison of hemispheric asymmetries in speech-related brain potentials of autistic and dysphasic children. *Brain and Language, 37,* 26–41.

Dehaene-Lambertz, G., & Baillet, S. (1998). A phonological representation in the infant brain. *NeuroReport, 9,* 1885–1888.

Demonet, J. F., Fiez, J. A., Paulesu, E., Petersen, S. E., & Zatorre, R. J. (1996). PET studies of phonological processing: A critical reply to Poeppel. *Brain & Language, 55,* 352–379.

Denays, R., Tondeur, M., Foulon, M., Verstraeten, F., Ham, H., Piepsz, A., & Noel, P. (1989). Regional brain blood flow in congenital dysphasia: Studies with Technetium-99m HM-PAO SPECT. *The Journal of Nuclear Medicine, 30,* 1825–1829.

Desai, S., Kollros, P. R., Graziani, L. J., Streletz, L. J., Goodman, M., Stanley, C., Cullen, J., & Baumgart, S. (1997). Sensitivity and specificity of the neonatal brain-stem auditory evoked potential for hearing and language deficits in survivors of extracorporeal membrane oxygenation. *Journal of Pediatrics, 131,* 233–239.

Donchin, E., & Coles, M. G. H. (1988). Is the P300 component a manifestation of context updating? *Behavioral and Brain Sciences, 11,* 357–374.

Donchin, E., Heffley, E., Hillyard, S. A., Loveless, N., Maltzman, I., Öhman, A., Rösler, F., Ruchkin, D., & Siddle, D. (1984). Cognitive and event-related potentials: II. The orienting reflex and P300. *Annals of the New York Academy of Sciences, 425,* 35–57.

Donchin, E., Karis, D., Bashore, T. R., & Coles, M. G. H. (1986). Cognitive psychophysiology and human information processing. In M. G. H. Coles, E. Donchin, & S. Porges (Eds.), *Psychophysiology: Systems, processes, and applications* (pp. 244–267). New York: Guilford.

Donchin, E., Ritter, W., & McCallum, W. C. (1978). Cognitive psychophysiology: The endogenous components of the ERP. In E. Callaway, P. Tueting, & S. Koslow (Eds.), *Event-related potentials in man* (pp. 349–412). New York: Academic Press.

Drevets, W. C. (1999). Emerging neuroscience approaches to understanding cognition and psychopathology: Positron-emission tomography imaging. In C. R. Cloninger (Ed.), *Personality and psychopathology* (pp. 369–408). Washington, DC: American Psychiatric Press.

Eden, G. F., & Zeffiro, T. A. (1997). PET and fMRI in the detection of task-related brain activity: Implications for the study of brain development. In R. W. Thatcher, G. R. Lyon, J. Rumsey, & N. Krasnegor (Eds.), *Developmental neuroimaging: Mapping the development of brain and behavior* (pp. 77–90). San Diego: Academic Press.

Elliot, L. L., Hammer, M. A., & Scholl, M. E. (1989). Fine-grained auditory discrimination in normal children and children with language-learning problems. *Journal of Speech and Hearing Research, 32,* 112–119.

Filipek, P. A., & Kennedy, D. N. (1991). Magnetic resonance imaging: Its role in the developmental disorders. In D. D. Duane & D. B. Gray (Eds.), *The reading brain: The biological basis of dyslexia* (pp. 133–160). Parkton, MD: York.

Frackowiak, R. S. J., Lenzi, G. L., Jones, T., & Heather, J. D. (1980). Quantitative measurement of regional cerebral blood flow and oxygen metabolism in man using ^{15}O and positron emission tomography: Theory, procedure and normal values. *Journal of Computer Assisted Tomography, 4,* 727–736.

Friederici, A. D. (1997). Neurophysiological aspects of language processing. *Clinical Neuroscience, 4,* 64–72.

Friedman, D. (1991). The endogenous scalp-recorded brain potentials and their relationship to cognitive development. In J. R. Jennings & M. G. H. Coles (Eds.), *Handbook of cognitive psychophysiology: Central and autonomic nervous system approaches* (pp. 621–683). Chichester, England: Wiley.

Galaburda, A. M. (1991). Anatomy of dyslexia: Argument against phrenology. In D. D. Duane & D. B. Gray (Eds.), *The reading brain: The biological basis of dyslexia* (pp. 119–131). Parkton, MD: York.

Galaburda, A. M., Sherman, G. F., Rosen, G. D., Aboitiz, F., & Geschwind, N. (1985). Developmental dyslexia: Four consecutive patients with cortical anomalies. *Annals of Neurology, 18*, 222–234.

Gauger, L. M., Lombardino, L. J., & Leonard, C. M. (1997). Brain morphology in children with specific language impairment. *Journal of Speech & Hearing Research, 40*, 1272–1284.

Geschwind, N., & Levitsky, W. (1968). Human brain: Left-right asymmetries in temporal speech region. *Science, 161*, 186–187.

Gevins, A. S., & Cutillo, B. A. (1986). Signals of cognition. In F. H. Lopes da Silva, W. Storm van Leeuwen, & A. Remond (Eds.), *Clinical applications of computer analysis of EEG and other neurophysiological signals* (2nd ed., pp. 335–381). Amsterdam: Elsevier Science.

Gilger, J. W., & Kaplan, B. J. (2001). Atypical brain development: A conceptual framework for understanding developmental learning disabilities. *Developmental Neuropsychology, 20*, 465–481.

Grillon, C., Courchesne, E., & Akshoomoff, N. (1989). Brainstem and middle latency auditory evoked potentials in autism and developmental language disorder. *Journal of Autism & Developmental Disorders, 19*, 255–269.

Guerit, J. M. (1985). Applications of surface-recorded auditory evoked potentials for the early diagnosis of hearing loss in neonates and premature infants. *Acta Otolaryngologica, 421*(Suppl.), 68–76.

Guttorm, T. K., Leppänen, P. H. T., Richardson, U., & Lyytinen, H. (2001). Event-related potentials and consonant differentiation in newborns with familial risk for dyslexia. *Journal of Learning Disabilities, 34*, 534–544.

Hertz-Pannier, L., Gaillard, W. D., Mott, S. H., Cuednod, C. A., Bookheimer, S. Y., Weinstein, S., Conry, J., Papero, P. H., Schiff, S. J., LeBihan, D., & Theodore, W. H. (1997). Noninvasive assessment of language dominance in children and adolescents with functional MRI: A preliminary study. *Neurology, 48*, 1003–1012.

Hillyard, S. A. (1985). Electrophysiology of human selective attention. *Trends in Neurosciences, 8*, 400–405.

Holopainen, I. E., Korpilahti, P., Juottonen, K., Lang, H., & Sillanpää, M. (1997). Attenuated auditory event-related potential (Mismatch Negativity) in children with developmental dysphasia. *Neuropediatrics, 28*, 253–256.

Holopainen, I. E., Korpilahti, P., Juottonen, K., Lang, H., & Sillanpää, M. (1998). Abnormal frequency mismatch negativity in mentally retarded children and in children with developmental dysphasia. *Journal of Child Neurology, 13*, 178–183.

Humphreys, P., Kaufmann, W. E., & Galaburda, A. M. (1990). Developmental dyslexia in women: Neuropathological findings in three patients. *Annals of Neurology, 28*, 727–738.

Hynd, G. W., & Hiemenz, J. R. (1997). Dyslexia and gyral morphology variation. In M. Snowling & C. Hulme (Eds.), *Dyslexia: Biology, identification, and intervention* (pp. 38–58). London: Whurr.

Hynd, G. W., Marshall, R. M., & Semrud-Clikeman, M. (1991). Developmental dyslexia, neurolinguistic theory and deviations in brain morphology. *Reading and Writing, 3*, 345–362.

Hynd, G. W., Semrud-Clikeman, M., Lorys, A. R., Novey, E. S., & Eliopulos, D. (1990). Brain morphology in developmental dyslexia and attention deficit disorder/hyperactivity. *Archives of Neurology, 47*, 919–926.

Jancke, L., Schlaug, G., Huang, Y., & Steinmetz, H. (1994). Asymmetry of the planum temporale. *NeuroReport, 5*, 1161–1163.

Jernigan, T. L., Hesselink, J. R., Sowell, E., & Tallal, P. A. (1991). Cerebral structure on magnetic resonance imaging in language- and learning-impaired children. *Archives of Neurology, 48*, 539–545.

Jirsa, R. E. (1992). The clinical utility of the P3 AERP in children with auditory processing disorders. *Journal of Speech and Hearing Research, 35*, 903–912.

Jirsa, R. E., & Clontz, K. B. (1990). Long latency auditory event-related potentials from children with auditory processing disorders. *Ear and Hearing, 11,* 222–232.

Johnson, R. (1989). Developmental evidence for modality-dependent P300 generators: A normative study. *Psychophysiology, 26,* 651–667.

Kabani, N. J., MacDonald, D., Evans, A., & Gopnik, M. (1997). Neuroanatomical correlates of familial language impairment: A preliminary report. *Journal of Neurolinguistics, 10,* 203–214.

Kabani, N. J., MacDonald, D., Evans, A., & Gopnik, M. (1998). "Neuroanatomical correlates of familial language impairment: A preliminary report": Erratum. *Journal of Neurolinguistics, 11,* 329.

Karhu, J., Herrgård, E., Pääkkönen, A., Luoma, L., Airaksinen, E., & Partanen, J. (1997). Dual cerebral processing of elementary auditory input in children. *NeuroReport, 8,* 1327–1330.

Kent, R. D. (1998). Neuroimaging studies of brain activation for language, with an emphasis on functional magnetic resonance imaging: A review. *Folia Phoniatrica et Logopaedica, 50,* 291–304.

Kileny, P., & Robertson, C. M. (1985). Neurological aspects of infant hearing assessment. *Journal of Otolaryngology, 14,* 34–39.

Kok, A. (1990). Internal and external control: A two-factor model of amplitude change of event-related potentials. *Acta Psychologica, 74,* 203–236.

Korpilahti, P. (1995). Auditory discrimination and memory functions in SLI children: A comprehensive study with neurophysiological and behavioural methods. *Scandinavian Journal of Logopedics and Phoniatrics, 20,* 131–139.

Korpilahti, P., & Lang, H. A. (1994). Auditory ERP components and mismatch negativity in dysphasic children. *Electroencephalography and Clinical Neurophysiology, 91,* 256–264.

Kraus, N., McGee, T., Carrell, T. D., King, C., Tremblay, K., & Nicol, T. (1995). Central auditory system plasticity associated with speech discrimination training. *Journal of Cognitive Neuroscience, 7,* 25–32.

Kraus, N., McGee, T. J., Carrell, T. D., Zecker, S. G., Nicol, T. G., & Koch, D. B. (1996). Auditory neurophysiologic responses and discrimination deficits in children with learning problems. *Science, 273,* 971–973.

Kraus, N., Smith, D. I., Reed, N. L., Stein, L. K., & Cartee, C. (1985). Auditory middle latency responses in children: Effects of age and diagnostic category. *Electroencephalography and Clinical Neurophysiology, 62,* 343–351.

Kruggel, F., & von Cramon, D. Y. (1999). Temporal properties of the hemodynamic response in functional MRI. *Human Brain Mapping, 8,* 259–271.

Kuhl, P. K. (1991). Perception, cognition, and the ontogenetic and phylogenetic emergence of human speech. In S. E. Brauth, W. S. Hall, & R. J. Dooling (Eds.), *Plasticity of development* (pp. 73–106). Cambridge, MA: The MIT Press.

Kujala, T., Myllyviita, K., Tervaniemi, M., Alho, K., Kallio, J., & Näätänen, R. (2000). Basic auditory dysfunction in dyslexia as demonstrated by brain activity measures. *Psychophysiology, 37,* 262–266.

Kurtzberg, D., Vaughan, H. G., Jr., Kreuzer, J. A., & Fliegler, K. Z. (1995). Developmental studies and clinical application of mismatch negativity: Problems and prospects. *Ear and Hearing, 16,* 105–117.

Kwong, K. K., & Chesler, A. (2000). Magnetic resonance imaging: Functional MRI. In J. D. Bronzino (Ed.), *The biomedical engineering handbook* (2nd ed., pp. 63.22–63.31). Florida: CRC Press.

Ladish, C., & Polich, J. (1989). P300 and probability in children. *Journal of Experimental Child Psychology, 48,* 212–223.

Lahey, M., & Edwards, J. (1995). Specific language impairment: Preliminary investigation of factors associated with family history and with patterns of language performance. *Journal of Speech and Hearing Research, 38,* 643–657.

Lang, A. H., Eerola, O., Korpilahti, P., Holopainen, I., Salo, S., & Aaltonen, O. (1995). Practical issues in the clinical application of mismatch negativity. *Ear and Hearing, 16*, 118–130.

Larsen, J. P., Höien, T., Lundberg, I., & Ödegaard, H. (1990). MRI evaluation on the size and symmetry of the planum temporale in adolescents with developmental dyslexia. *Brain and Language, 39*, 289–301.

Leonard, C., Voeller, K. K. S., Lombardino, L. J., Morris, M. K., Hynd, G. W., Alexander, A. W., Andersen, H. G., Garofalakis, M., Honeyman, J. C., Mao, J., Agee, O. F., & Staab, E. V. (1993). Anomalous cerebral structure in dyslexia revealed with magnetic resonance imaging. *Archives of Neurology, 50*, 461–469.

Leonard, L. B. (1998). *Children with specific language impairment.* Cambridge, MA: The MIT Press.

Leppänen, P. H. T., Choudhury, N., Leevers, H. J., & Benasich, A. A. (2000). Brain event-related potentials to tone pairs are modulated by rate and attention. *Journal of Cognitive Neuroscience, Suppl., Abstracts of Cognitive Neuroscience Society Annual Meeting 2000*, 32.

Leppänen, P. H. T., Choudhury, N., Thomas, J., Jing, H., & Benasich, A. (2002, April). Brain event-related potentials index rapid auditory processing in adults and 24-month-old children. *Journal of Cognitive Neuroscience, Suppl., Abstracts of Cognitive Neuroscience Society Annual Meeting 2002*, 65.

Leppänen, P. H. T., Eklund, K. M., & Lyytinen, H. (1997). Event-related brain potentials to change in rapidly presented acoustic stimuli in newborns. *Developmental Neuropsychology, 13*, 175–204.

Leppänen, P. H. T., Laukkonen, K. M., & Lyytinen, H. (1992). Mismatch negativity in children and adults. *Abstracts of the 10th International Conference on Event-related Potentials of the Brain* (P90). Eger, Hungary.

Leppänen, P. H. T., & Lyytinen, H. (1997). Auditory event-related potentials in the study of developmental language-related disorders. *Audiology & Neuro-Otology, 2*, 308–340.

Leppänen, P. H. T., Pihko, E., Eklund, K. M., & Lyytinen, H. (1999). Cortical responses of infants with and without a genetic risk for dyslexia: II. Group effects. *NeuroReport, 10*, 969–973.

Leppänen, P. H. T., Richardson, U., Pihko, E., Eklund, K. M., Guttorm, T. K., Aro, M., & Lyytinen, H. (2002). Brain responses to changes in speech sound durations differ between infants with and without familial risk for dyslexia. *Developmental Neuropsychology, 22*, 407–422.

Lewis, B. A., & Thompson, L. A. (1992). A study of developmental speech and language disorders in twins. *Journal of Speech and Hearing Research, 35*, 1086–1094.

Lincoln, A. J., Courchesne, E., Harms, L., & Allen, M. H. (1993). Contextual probability evaluation in autistic, receptive developmental language disorder, and control children: Event-related brain potential evidence. *Journal of Autism & Developmental Disorders, 23*, 37–58.

Lincoln, A. J., Courchesne, E., Harms, L., & Allen, M. H. (1995). Sensory modulation of auditory stimuli in children with autism and receptive developmental language disorder: Event related brain potential evidence. *Journal of Autism & Developmental Disorders, 25*, 521–539.

Linden, D. E. J., Prvulovic, D., Formisano, E., Voellinger, M., Zanella, F. E., Goebel, R., & Dierks, T. (1999). The functional neuroanatomy of target detection: An fMRI study of visual and auditory oddball tasks. *Cerebral Cortex, 9*, 815–823.

Lou, H. C., Henriksen, L., & Bruhn, P. (1984). Focal cerebral hypo-perfusion in children with dysphasia and/or attention deficit disorder. *Archives of Neurology, 41*, 825–829.

Lou, H. C., Henriksen, L., & Bruhn, P. (1990). Focal cerebral dysfunction in developmental learning disabilities. *Lancet, 335*, 8–11.

Loveless, N. E. (1983). Event-related brain potentials and human performance. In A. Gale & J. A. Edwards (Eds.), *Physiological correlates of human behaviour: Basic issues* (1st ed., pp. 79–97). London: Academic Press.

Lukatela, G., Carello, C., Savic, M., & Turvey, M. T. (1986). Hemispheric asymmetries in phonological processing. *Neuropsychologia, 24*, 341–350.

Lyytinen, H., Blomberg, A. P., & Näätänen, R. (1992). Event-related potentials and autonomic responses to a change in unattended auditory stimuli. *Psychophysiology, 29*, 2–14.

Malhotra, A. (1997). *Auditory evoked responses in clinical practice.* New Delhi, India: Narosa.

Martin, L., Barajas, J. J., Fernandez, R., & Torres, E. (1988). Auditory event-related potentials in well-characterized groups of children. *Electroencephalography and Clinical Neurophysiology Evoked Potentials, 71*, 375–381.

Mason, S. M., & Mellor, D. H. (1984). Brain-stem, middle latency and late cortical evoked potentials in children with speech and language disorders. *Electroencephalography and Clinical Neurophysiology, 59*, 297–309.

McAnally, K. I., & Stein, J. F. (1997). Scalp potentials by amplitude-modulated tones in dyslexia. *Journal of Speech, Language, and Hearing Research, 40*, 939–945.

Mendel, M. I. (1980). Clinical use of primary cortical responses. *Audiology, 19*, 1–15.

Merzenich, M. M., Jenkins, W. M., Johnston, P., Schreiner, C., Miller, S. L., & Tallal, P. (1996). Temporal processing deficits of language-learning impaired children ameliorated by training. *Science, 271*, 77–81.

Molfese, D. L. (2000). Predicting dyslexia at 8 years of age using neonatal brain responses. *Brain and Language, 72*, 238–245.

Molfese, D. L., & Molfese, V. J. (1985). Electrophysiological indices of auditory discrimination in newborn infants: The bases for predicting later language development? *Infant Behavior and Development, 8*, 197–211.

Molfese, D. L., & Molfese, V. J. (1997). Discrimination of language skills at five years of age using event-related potentials recorded at birth. *Developmental Neuropsychology, 13*, 135–156.

Morgan, A. E., & Hynd, G. W. (1998). Dyslexia: Neurolinguistic ability and anatomical variation of the planum temporale. *Neuropsychology Review, 8*, 79–93.

Morgan, R. A. (1984). Auditory discrimination in speech-impaired and normal children as related to age. *British Journal of Disorders of Communication, 19*, 89–96.

Musiek, F. E., Geurkink, N. A., Weider, D. J., & Donnelly, K. (1984). Past, present, and future applications of the auditory middle latency response. *Laryngoscope, 94*, 1545–1553.

Näätänen, R. (1988). Implications of ERP data for psychological theories of attention: Special Issue. Event related potential investigations of cognition. *Biological Psychology, 26*, 117–163.

Näätänen, R. (1990). The role of attention in auditory information processing as revealed by event-related potentials and other brain measures of cognitive function. *Behavioral and Brain Sciences, 13*, 201–288.

Näätänen, R. (1992). *Attention and brain function.* Hillsdale, NJ: Lawrence Erlbaum Associates.

Näätänen, R. (1995). The mismatch negativity: A powerful tool for cognitive neuroscience. *Ear and Hearing, 16*, 6–18.

Näätänen, R. (1999). Phoneme representations of the human brain as reflected by event-related potentials. *Functional Neuroscience: Evoked Potentials and Magnetic Fields, 49*, 170–173.

Näätänen, R., & Alho, K. (1997). Mismatch negativity—the measure for central sound representation accuracy. *Audiology & Neuro-Otology, 2*, 341–353.

Näätänen, R., Gaillard, A. W. K., & Mäntysalo, S. (1978). Early selective-attention effect on evoked potential reinterpreted. *Acta Psychologica, 42*, 313–329.

Näätänen, R., Lehtokoski, A., Lennes, M., Cheour, M., Huotilainen, M., Iivonen, A., Vainio, M., Alku, P., Ilmoniemi, R. J., Luuk, A., Allik, J., Sinkkonen, J., & Alho, K. (1997). Language-specific phoneme representations revealed by electric and magnetic brain responses. *Nature, 385*, 432–433.

Näätänen, R., & Picton, T. W. (1987). The N1 wave of the human electric and magnetic response to sound: A review and an analysis of the component structure. *Psychophysiology, 24,* 375–425.

Neils, J., & Aram, D. M. (1986). Family history of children with developmental language disorders. *Perceptual and Motor Skills, 63,* 655–658.

Neville, H. J., Coffey, S. A., Holcomb, P. J., & Tallal, P. (1993). The neurobiology of sensory and language processing in language-impaired children. *Journal of Cognitive Neuroscience, 5,* 235–253.

Neville, H. J., Kutas, M., & Schmidt, A. (1982a). Event-related potential studies of cerebral specialization during reading: I. Studies of normal adults. *Brain and Language, 16,* 300–315.

Neville, H. J., Kutas, M., & Schmidt, A. (1982b). Event-related potential studies of cerebral specialization during reading: II. Studies of congenitally deaf adults. *Brain and Language, 16,* 316–337.

Njiokiktjien, C., de Sonneville, L., & Vaal, J. (1994). Callosal size in children with learning disabilities. *Behavioural Brain Research, 64,* 213–218.

Ohta, K., Uchiyama, M., Matsushima, E., & Toru, M. (1999). An event-related potential study in schizophrenia using Japanese sentences. *Schizophrenia Research, 40,* 159–170.

Pennington, B. F. (1991). *Diagnosing learning disorders: A neuropsychological framework.* New York: Guilford.

Pettigrew, A. G., Henderson-Smart, D. J., & Edwards, D. A. (1990). Evoked potentials and functional development of the auditory system. In M. Rowe & L. Aitkin (Eds.), *Information processing in mammalian auditory and tactile systems* (pp. 295–308). New York: Wiley-Liss.

Picton, T. W., Alain, C., Otten, L., Ritter, W., & Achim, A. (2000). Mismatch negativity: Different water in the same river. *Audiology and Neuro-Otology, 5,* 111–139.

Picton, T. W., & Durieux-Smith, A. (1988). Auditory evoked potentials in the assessment of hearing. *Neurologic Clinics, 6,* 791–808.

Picton, T. W., Stapells, D. R., & Campbell, K. B. (1981). Auditory evoked potentials from the human cochlea and brainstem. *Journal of Otolaryngology, 9,* 1–41.

Picton, T. W., Taylor, M. J., Durieux-Smith, A., & Edwards, C. G. (1986). Brainstem auditory evoked potentials in pediatrics. In M. J. Aminoff (Ed.), *Electrodiagnosis in clinical neurology* (2nd ed., pp. 505–534). New York: Churchill Livingstone.

Pihko, E., Leppänen, P. H. T., Eklund, K. M., Cheour, M., Guttorm, T. K., & Lyytinen, H. (1999). Cortical responses of infants with and without a genetic risk for dyslexia: I. Age effects. *NeuroReport, 10,* 901–905.

Plante, E. (1991). MRI findings in the parents and siblings of specifically language-impaired boys. *Brain & Language, 41,* 67–80.

Plante, E. (1996). Phenotypic variability in brain-behavior studies of specific language impairment. In M. L. Rice (Ed.), *Toward a genetics of language* (pp. 317–335). Mahwah, NJ: Lawrence Erlbaum Associates.

Plante, E., Boliek, C., Binkiewicz, A., & Erly, W. K. (1996). Elevated androgen, brain development and language/learning disabilities in children with congenital adrenal hyperplasia. *Developmental Medicine & Child Neurology, 38,* 423–437.

Plante, E., Swisher, L., Vance, R., & Rapcsak, S. (1991). MRI findings in boys with specific language impairment. *Brain & Language, 41,* 52–66.

Poeppel, D. (1996). A critical review of PET studies of phonological processing. *Brain & Language, 55,* 317–351.

Posner, M. I., & Raichle, M. E. (1994). *Images of mind.* New York: Scientific American Library.

Price, C. J. (1997). Functional anatomy of reading. In R. S. J. Frackowiak, K. J. Friston, C. D. Frith, R. J. Dolan, & J. C. Mazziotta (Eds.), *Human brain function* (pp. 301–328). San Diego: Academic Press.

Regan, D. (1989). *Human brain electrophysiology: Evoked potentials and evoked magnetic fields in science and medicine.* New York: Elsevier.

Richardson, U. (1998). *Familial dyslexia and sound duration in the quantity distinctions of Finnish infants and adults.* Doctoral dissertation, Studia Philologica Jyväskyläensia, University of Jyväskylä, Jyväskylä.

Richardson, U., Leppänen, P. H. T., Leiwo, M., & Lyytinen, H. (in press). Speech perception differs in infants at familial risk for dyslexia as early as six months of age. *Developmental Neuropsychology.*

Ritter, W., & Ruchkin, D. S. (1992). A review of event-related potential components discovered in the context of studying P3. *Annals of the New York Academy of Sciences, 658,* 1–32.

Roland, P. (1993). *Brain activation.* New York: Wiley.

Rosen, G. D., Press, D. M., Sherman, G. F., & Galaburda, A. M. (1992). The development of induced cerebrocortical migrogyria in the rat. *Journal of Neuropathology and Experimental Neurology, 51,* 601–611.

Rosen, G. D., Sherman, G. F., & Galaburda, A. M. (1993). Dyslexia and brain pathology: Experimental animal models. In A. M. Galaburda (Ed.), *Dyslexia and development: Neurobiological aspects of extra-ordinary brains* (pp. 89–111). Cambridge, MA: Harvard University Press.

Rösler, F., Sutton, S., Johnson, R., Jr., Mulder, G., Fabiani, M., Plooij-van Gorsel, E., & Roth, W. T. (1986). Endogenous ERP components and cognitive constructs. A review. *Electroencephalography and Clinical Neurophysiology, 38*(Suppl.), 51–92.

Rugg, M., Kok, A., Barret, G., & Fischler, I. (1986). ERPs associated with language and hemispheric specialization. A review. *Electroencephalography and Clinical Neurophysiology, 38*(Suppl.), 273–300.

Sameroff, A., & Chandler, M. J. (1975). Reproductive risk and the continuum of caretaking causality. In F. D. Horowitz (Ed.), *Review of child development research* (pp. 187–244). Chicago, IL: University of Chicago Press.

Scherg, M., & Picton, T. W. (1990). Brain electric source analysis of the mismatch negativity. In C. H. M. Brunia, A. W. K. Gaillard, & A. Kok (Eds.), *Psychophysiological brain research* (Vol. 1, pp. 94–98). The Netherlands: Tilburg University Press.

Schultz, R. T., Cho, N. K., Staib, L. H., Kier, L. E., Fletcher, J. M., Shaywitz, S. E., Shankweiler, D. P., Katz, L., Gore, J. C., Duncan, J. S., & Shaywitz, B. A. (1994). Brain morphology in normal and dyslexic children: The influence of sex and age. *Annals of Neurology, 35,* 732–742.

Squires, N. K., & Ollo, C. (1986). Human evoked potential techniques: Possible applications to neuropsychology. In H. J. Hannay (Ed.), *Experimental techniques in human neuropsychology* (pp. 386–418). New York: Oxford University Press.

Stapells, D. R., & Kurtzberg, D. (1991). Evoked potential assessment of auditory system integrity in infants. *Clinics in Perinatology, 18,* 497–518.

Stefanatos, G. A. (1984). *Nonverbal abilities in communication disorders.* Oxford, England: Oxford University Press.

Stefanatos, G. A., Green, G. G., & Ratcliff, G. G. (1989). Neurophysiological evidence of auditory channel anomalies in developmental dysphasia. *Archives of Neurology, 46,* 871–875.

Stromswold, K. (1998). Genetics of spoken language disorders. *Human Biology, 70,* 297–324.

Studdert-Kennedy, M., & Mody, M. (1995). Auditory temporal perception deficits in the reading-impaired: A critical review of the evidence. *Psychonomic Bulletin & Review, 2,* 508–514.

Sutton, S., & Ruchkin, D. S. (1984). The late positive complex: Advances and new problems. *Annals of the New York Academy of Sciences, 425,* 1–23.

Tallal, P. (2000). Experimental studies of language learning impairments: From research to remediation. In D. M. Bishop & L. B. Leonard (Eds.), *Speech and language impairments in children: Causes, characteristics, intervention, and outcome* (pp. 131–155). Philadelphia, PA: Psychology Press.

Tallal, P., & Curtiss, S. (1990). Neurological basis of developmental language disorders. In A. Rothenberger (Ed.), *Brain and behavior in child psychiatry* (pp. 205–213). Berlin: Springer-Verlag.

Tallal, P., Miller, S. L., Bedi, G., Byma, G., Wang, X., Nagarajan, S. S., Schreiner, C., Jenkins, W. M., & Merzenich, M. M. (1996). Language comprehension in language-learning impaired children improved with acoustically modified speech. *Science, 271*, 81–84.

Tallal, P., & Newcombe, F. (1978). Impairment of auditory perception and language comprehension in dysphasia. *Brain and Language, 5*, 13–24.

Tallal, P., & Piercy, M. (1973a). Defects of non-verbal auditory perception in children with developmental aphasia. *Nature, 241*, 468–469.

Tallal, P., & Piercy, M. (1973b). Developmental aphasia: Impaired rate of non-verbal processing as a function of sensory modality. *Neuropsychologia, 11*, 389–398.

Tallal, P., Ross, R., & Curtiss, S. (1989). Familial aggregation in specific language impairment. *Journal of Speech, Language and Hearing Disorders, 54*, 167–173.

Tallal, P., Stark, R. E., & Mellits, E. D. (1985a). Identification of language-impaired children on the basis of rapid perception and production skills. *Brain and Language, 25*, 314–322.

Tervaniemi, M., Maury, S., & Näätänen, R. (1994). Neural representations of abstract stimulus features in the human brain as reflected by the mismatch negativity. *NeuroReport, 5*, 844–846.

Thomas, D. J., & Crow, C. D. (1994). Development of evoked electrical brain activity in infancy. In G. Dawson (Ed.), *Human behavior and the developing brain* (pp. 207–231). New York: Guilford.

Tomblin, J. B. (1989). Familial concentration of developmental language impairment. *Journal of Speech and Hearing Disorders, 54*, 287–295.

Tomblin, J. B. (1996). Genetic and environmental contributions to the risk for specific language impairment. In M. L. Rice (Ed.), *Toward a genetics of language* (pp. 191–211). Mahwah, NJ: Lawrence Erlbaum Associates.

Tomblin, J. B., Abbas, P. J., Records, N. L., & Brenneman, L. M. (1995). Auditory evoked responses to frequency-modulated tones in children with specific language impairment. *Journal of Speech & Hearing Research, 38*, 387–392.

Tomblin, J. B., & Buckwalter, P. R. (1998). Heritability of poor language achievement among twins. *Journal of Speech, Language and Hearing Research, 41*, 188–199.

Tonnquist-Uhlén, I. (1996a). Topography of auditory evoked long-latency potentials in children with severe language impairment: The T complex. *Acta Otolaryngologica, 116*, 680–689.

Tonnquist-Uhlén, I. (1996b). Topography of auditory evoked cortical potentials in children with severe language impairment. *Scandinavian Audiology, 25*(Suppl.), 1–40.

Tonnquist-Uhlén, I., Borg, E., Persson, H. E., & Spens, K. E. (1996). Topography of auditory evoked cortical potentials in children with severe language impairment: The N1 component. *Electroencephalography and Clinical Neurophysiology, 100*, 250–260.

Trauner, D., Wulfeck, B., Tallal, P., & Hesselink, J. (2000). Neurological and MRI profiles of children with developmental language impairment. *Developmental Medicine & Child Neurology, 42*, 470–475.

Tremblay, K., Kraus, N., Carrell, T., & McGee, T. (1997). Central auditory system plasticity: Generalization to novel stimuli following listening training. *Journal of Acoustical Society of America, 102*, 3762–3773.

Tzourio, N., Heim, A., Zilbovicius, M., Gerard, C., & Mazoyer, B. M. (1994). Abnormal regional CBF response in left hemisphere of dysphasic children during a language task. *Pediatric Neurology, 10*, 20–26.

Uwer, R., Albrecht, R., & von Suchodoletz, W. (1998, October). *Mismatch negativity to speech stimuli in language impaired children*. Poster presented at the First International Workshop on Mismatch Negativity and Its Clinical Applications, Helsinki, Finland.

van der Lely, H. K. J., & Stollwerck, L. (1996). A grammatical specific language impairment in children: An autosomal dominant inheritance? *Brain and Language, 52*, 484–504.

Wijker, W., Molenaar, P. C. M., & van der Molen, M. W. (1989). Age-changes in scalp distribution of cognitive event-related potentials elicited in an oddball task. *Journal of Psychophysiology, 3*, 179–189.

Winkler, I., Kujala, T., Tiitinen, H., Sivonen, P., Alku, P., Lehtokoski, A., Czigler, I., Csepe, V., Ilmoniemi, R. J., & Näätänen, R. (1999). Brain responses reveal the learning of foreign language phonemes. *Psychophysiology, 36*, 638–642.

Witton, C., Talcott, J. B., Hansen, P. C., Richardson, A. J., Griffiths, T. D., Rees, A., Stein, J. F., & Green, G. G. R. (1998). Sensitivity to dynamic auditory and visual stimuli predicts nonword reading ability in both dyslexic and normal readers. *Current Biology, 8*, 791–797.

Zatorre, R. J., Meyer, E., Gjedde, A., & Evans, A. C. (1996). PET studies of phonetic processing of speech: Review, replication, and reanalysis. *Cerebral Cortex, 6*, 21–30.

5

Information Processing in Children With Specific Language Impairment

Ronald B. Gillam
LaVae M. Hoffman
University of Texas

This chapter reviews the research pertaining to various accounts of the relationship between cognition and language learning in children with specific language impairment (SLI). We explore the evidence for and against five hypotheses of the nature of information-processing difficulties experienced by children with SLI. First, attention problems may interfere with children's ability to select and concentrate on relevant stimuli in the environment. Second, children with SLI may have trouble perceiving speech. Third, children with SLI may have difficulty with the mental representation of speech (termed *phonological representation*). Fourth, children with SLI may present deficiencies in central executive functions. The final hypothesis we consider is that children with SLI have a generalized limitation in cognitive capacity that causes both information-processing problems and language learning problems. The evidence we review indicates that children with language impairments have information-processing systems that are simultaneously constrained by a variety of factors that lead to inadequate processing abilities.

LIMITATIONS IN ATTENTION

Attention involves at least two mechanisms: activation and focus (Cowan, 1995). Usually in language learning and use, individuals activate prior knowledge that is related to the information to which they are listening. Then they hold their activated knowledge in a state of readiness until it is needed for comprehending and responding.

Some mental activities occur without prior activation. Näätänen (1990) demonstrated this when he measured event-related brain potentials for sounds that differed from repeated tones. Näätänen's study demonstrated that individuals can focus on incoming information even when they are not consciously attending to it, suggesting there is a separation between activation and focus. If this is true, there could be independent limits in the persistence or capacity of attention activation and focus. Either of these limits (or both together) could affect the rate and course of language development.

There is widespread agreement that some children with language impairments exhibit general attention problems. Baker and Cantwell (1992) examined the concurrence of speech/language impairments in 65 children ages 6 to 15 years with attention deficit disorder (ADD). Seventy-eight percent of these children had speech articulation impairments, 58% had expressive language impairments, 34% had receptive language impairments, and 69% had language processing (auditory memory, discrimination, or association) impairments. These findings suggest some degree of overlap between attention deficits and language impairments.

There have been attempts to study the role of attention in language impairments more directly. Campbell and McNeil (1985) presented children with language impairments with one set of sentences at a slow rate of speed and a second set at a normal rate of speed. Children exhibited better comprehension of the normal rate sentences when they were presented after slowed sentences. Campbell and McNeil hypothesized that the attention deficits in children with language impairments were related to a limited capacity mechanism that could allocate spare attention to the normal sentence only when the first sentence was slowed.

Riddle (1992) employed a task in which preschoolers with SLI and age controls identified pictures of objects having the same name (e.g., two different looking shoes). A buzzer sounded during some of the picture identification trials. The children's task was to press a button as soon as they heard the buzzer. Although the children with SLI were highly accurate on the picture task, their responses to the buzzer were slower than those of the controls, suggesting poorer abilities to refocus attention.

Given these results, it is possible that the amount of stimulation that is necessary to be registered as awareness may be limited in children with SLI. That is, these children may need longer periods of sustained stimulation or repeated stimulation to trigger automatic attention-focusing mechanisms. Alternatively, children with SLI may exhibit a limited capacity for sustaining their focus of attention. That is, stimulation may trigger unconscious activation, and this activation may trigger focusing, but these children may not be able to allocate the specific attention resources needed to sustain their focus. Once focus is lost, it may not return until a certain level of stimulus activation is reached again. Whether children with language impairments have a diminished attention-triggering mechanism or a limited capacity for sustaining the focus of attention (or both), limitations in attention certainly could contribute to the language learning difficulties experienced by children with SLI.

LIMITATIONS IN SPEECH PERCEPTION

One of the oldest and widely studied hypotheses of language impairment is that speech-processing difficulties could disrupt the language development process. One of the best-known hypotheses of this type is Tallal's idea that difficulties processing the temporal properties of sound may underlie language learning impairments (Tallal, 1990; Tallal, Stark, & Mellits, 1985). For example, Tallal and Piercy (1973) found that children with SLI evidenced difficulty remembering sequences of rapidly presented tones. Similar results were obtained using computer-synthesized CV syllables (Tallal & Piercy, 1974). Interestingly, children with SLI who experienced difficulty remembering the order of syllables or words that were presented rapidly performed these tasks quite well when the interstimulus duration was increased (Tallal & Piercy, 1975; Tallal, Stark, Kallman, & Mellits, 1980). Tallal and her colleagues concluded that children with SLI have temporal processing problems, but their tasks really measured memory for sounds and syllables, not temporal processing or speech discrimination per se. What their results really indicate is that children with SLI make fewer errors indicating the order of two events when they are given more time to listen to the stimuli and formulate a response. It is not clear from these studies whether the problem with recalling rapidly presented tones and syllables involves perceiving the differences between sounds correctly (as Tallal and her colleagues assumed), rapidly creating well-specified mental representations of sound that include order information, and/or retrieving representations accurately when it is time to produce a motor response.

There is some evidence supporting Tallal's hypothesis that children with SLI have basic perceptual problems. Elliott, Hammer, and Scholl (1989) and Elliott and Hammer (1993) used an auditory discrimination task to determine the smallest acoustic differences among phonemic stimuli that could be discerned by children with SLI and their age-matched normal controls. The authors created synthesized CV stimuli that varied in voice onset time from 0 to 35 ms in 5-ms steps. For every trial, two syllables were presented sequentially with a 500-ms intersyllabic interval. Subjects were asked to judge whether syllables were the same or different.

In comparison with the age-matched controls, children in the SLI group required greater differences between the two-syllable presentations with respect to voice onset time to determine whether the syllables were different from each other. Like Tallal, Elliott and her colleagues hypothesized that fine-grained auditory discrimination may be related to their ability to learn language. Even if that is true, factor analysis revealed that auditory discrimination measures accounted for only 27% of the variance in language ability in 6- and 7-year-old children with SLI and only 16% of the variance in the language abilities of the age-matched controls.

Two studies using psychoacoustic protocols also support the notion of fine-grained auditory processing problems in children with SLI. Robin, Tomblin, Kearney, and Hug (1989) investigated the ability of children with SLI to identify nonspeech temporal information. Their stimuli were computer-generated square-wave pulses presented at 65 dB SPL. Each pattern consisted of six tones presented at 440 Hz separated by an interstimulus interval. Four of these intervals were equal in duration (termed the *long interstimulus intervals*) and one interval was shorter than the others (termed the *short interstimulus interval*). Subjects were asked to determine whether the two tones that were closer together than the rest were at the beginning or end of the pattern.

Starting with a pattern length of 2,020 ms, pattern length was decreased in 50% steps until an incorrect response was obtained. At that time, pattern length was increased in 50% steps until a correct response was obtained. This procedure was repeated three times to determine an average threshold over the four runs. Each subject performed this task on consecutive days for approximately 2 weeks.

Children with SLI failed to approach the performance of normal children who had one exposure to the task, although their performance improved significantly over repeated trials. Robin et al. (1989) concluded that children with SLI may have fundamental deficits in temporal processing. However, the authors noted that the children's performance on the processing tasks improved considerably with practice, suggesting that attention and learning mechanisms were also important contributing factors.

Wright et al. (1997) employed a backward masking paradigm to measure children's ability to detect a brief tone presented before two different masking noises. The children with SLI in their study had more difficulty than the normal controls with the backward masking task when the masking involved bandpass noise in which the tone and following noise had similar frequencies. They responded to the task much better in noise conditions in which the tone and following noise had different frequencies. Unlike Tallal, these authors concluded that children with SLI did not display a general deficit in the perception of rapidly presented sounds.

Rather, the children with SLI in this study appeared to present auditory perception difficulties with some temporal and spectral contexts, but not others.

Some children with SLI do not have difficulty with speech discrimination tasks. Sussman (1993) asked children with and without SLI to listen to a series of syllables whose starting formant frequencies were on a continuum from /ba/ to /da/. Children touched an "X" when they detected a change in the syllables. Next, children listened to the syllables again and touched a "B" if they thought the syllable was /ba/ and a "D" if they thought the syllable was /da/. Sussman found that children with SLI were as adept as their language and age-matched controls at discriminating changes in the CV syllables. However, these children presented unusual difficulties with the identification task using the same stimuli. In Sussman's study, responding meaningfully to sound was difficult for children with SLI, not perceiving differences between sounds. Sussman concluded that children with SLI have trouble forming phonological representations of acoustic information—a topic we consider in greater detail in the next section.

Some recent psychoacoustic evidence also raises doubt about the widespread presence of auditory perceptual problems in children with SLI. Bishop, Carlyon, Deeks, and Bishop (1999) presented backward masking, detection of frequency modulation, and pitch discrimination tasks to children with and without SLI. These authors administered the backward masking tasks five separate times. Bishop and her colleagues did not replicate the Wright et al. (1997) findings of unusual difficulties with backward masking on any of the five presentations of the task. However, performance on Tallal's Auditory Repetition task 2 years earlier was a good predictor of individual performance on the backward masking task. Clearly, there are some children with language impairments who have persistent difficulties with auditory tasks. However, such difficulties may have little to do with language development. Bishop et al. (1999) computed correlations between the backward masking results, language skills, nonword reading skills, and nonverbal intelligence. There was little relationship between performance on the backward masking task and the children's performance on language tests. However, nonverbal intelligence was significantly related to performance on the perception tasks, even when the affects of age and nonword reading skills were partialed out. These results suggest that backward masking tasks measure the mental abilities required to retain the relevant stimuli and perform the required responses as much or more than they measure the ability to perceive the temporal properties of the stimulus.

Helzer, Champlin, and Gillam (1996) used a masking-period paradigm task to evaluate the temporal resolution of children with SLI and their nonimpaired, age-matched peers. This paradigm enabled a measurement of children's ability to perceive nonspeech stimuli within three different masking conditions and two different signal frequencies. Eight children with SLI and eight, nonimpaired, age-matched peers completed a masking period pattern paradigm in which a signal (500 or 200 Hz) was measured with no competing noise, with continuous competing noise, with a short (40 ms) gap in the noise, or with a long (64 ms) gap in the noise. These authors used a trials-to-criteria procedure to account for practice effects, which have been shown to play a large role in responses to psychoacoustic tasks in studies by Robin et al. (1989) and Bishop et al. (1999).

Across frequencies and gap sizes, thresholds for children with SLI were quite similar to that of their nonimpaired, age-matched controls. Yet children with SLI required more trials to achieve the same threshold levels as their age-matched peers. This finding suggests that children in the SLI group responded inconsistently to the presentation of the tone across the masking conditions. Temporal processing mechanisms may not be unusual in children with SLI. However, the results of the trials to criteria measure suggest that attention, or lack thereof, may play an important role in perceptual functioning (see also Leppänen et al., chap. 4, this volume).

As a group, these investigations suggest that some children with SLI have persistent problems with auditory processing tasks. However, these problems do not appear to account for much of the variance in language development. Additionally, performance on auditory processing tasks appears to reflect a combination of general mental abilities, auditory perception, and task familiarity. Researchers and clinicians should be cautious about interpreting children's performance on most of the types of auditory processing tasks used in testing.

LIMITATIONS IN THE ADEQUACY OF PHONOLOGICAL REPRESENTATIONS

Another active line of investigation into information processing in children with language impairments centers on the role of phonological representation in working memory. Gathercole and Baddeley (1990, 1995) characterized language acquisition and processing as part of a working memory system consisting of separate mechanisms for verbal and visual information processing. Visual information is thought to be retained via the visuospatial sketchpad, whereas verbal information is processed in a phonological loop comprised of a phonological short-term store where speech input is encoded and a subvocal articulatory rehearsal process that serves to refresh speech material. According to Gathercole and Baddeley's working memory deficit hypothesis, children with language impairment have a reduced verbal working memory storage capacity. Further, these authors believe that phonological processing skills such as perception, encoding, or rehearsal may contribute to these children's language deficits (Gathercole & Baddeley, 1990).

According to this theory, children who have difficulties encoding phonological information should demonstrate unusual problems processing and remembering unmeaningful wordlike stimuli. Nonword repetition tasks have been used as measures of phonological working memory on the premise that recall of this type of stimuli should be independent of lexical knowledge, and therefore performance should reveal phonological processing efficiency rather than measuring vocabulary or semantic contributions to word retention. There is a consistently powerful and pervasive finding that children with language impairment recall less nonword information than their normally achieving peers (Kamhi et al., 1988) particularly when the task stimuli become polysyllabic (Edwards & Lahey, 1998; Montgomery, 1995).

Edwards and Lahey (1998) argued for caution in interpreting accuracy on nonword repetition tasks as a measure of phonological capacity. They proposed that reduced accuracy on these tasks could be indicative of processing aspects that require extra effort that may exceed processing capacity limitations. Poor performance may reflect effort rather than an inherently constrained working memory capacity or a specific phonological representation deficit. They stated,

> it is not that children with specific language impairment cannot form accurate phonological representations; rather it may be that some children with specific language impairment must work harder to form these representations than their peers, and in doing so they overload their system. (p. 305)

Edwards and Lahey (1998) suggested that "further research is also needed to examine how processing load might interact with the nature of phonological representations" (p. 304).

Gillam, Cowan, and Marler (1998) used a modality effect study to investigate processing load and phonological representation. If children with SLI had difficulty forming well-specified phonological representations, then recall should be better when items are presented visually and/or a pointing response is required. This is because an auditory stimulus usually results in a phonological code automatically, and a verbal response modality may encourage the participant to create the phonological code that is needed for the response. However, a visual stimulus leaves the phonological coding to the participant's discretion, especially when it is paired with a nonverbal response modality that does not necessitate such a code. Under the latter circumstances, it might be that normal children generally still form a phonological code adequate for recall, but that children with language impairment tend not to do so.

These possibilities were investigated with an experiment that involved immediate serial recall (working memory) of stimuli presented auditorally, visually, or audiovisually (Gillam, Cowan, & Marler, 1998). If children with SLI have a deficient or more rapidly decaying auditory memory trace, they should perform poorer than age-matched children on auditorally but not visually presented lists. If children with SLI have phonological encoding difficulties, they should perform poorer than age-matched children on the visual items. This is because printed input and pointing responses do not require phonological coding. If children with SLI have difficulties with speech production processes, they should perform more poorly than age-matched children in speaking rather than pointing conditions.

In a mixed design, Gillam et al. (1998) measured the digit recall of two groups of subjects (children with SLI and their age-matched controls) in six conditions that counterbalanced stimulus type (auditory, visual, and audiovisual) and response type (speaking or pointing). Sixteen children with SLI between the ages of 9 and 12 and 16 age-matched children recalled lists of digits presented in auditory, visual, and audiovisual (mixed) presentation modes.

Gillam and his colleagues found an auditory modality superiority in both groups. Despite that they controlled for capacity differences between groups by presenting the task at each child's short-term memory span, they found group differences between input and output modalities. The children in the SLI group showed especially poor performance when a visual stimulus was combined with a pointing response. They also found a general superiority of speaking responses in comparison with pointing responses in children with SLI. The children in the control group did not evidence this superiority.

These results are consistent with the idea that children with SLI have difficulties transforming and retaining well-specified mental phonological representations. If verbal codes are poorly created, retained, or used, one would expect reasonably good primacy and recency recall when auditorily presented stimuli are paired with spoken responses. Difficulties with recency recall and rapid conversion of visual input into phonological forms for rehearsal and then back into nonspeech (pointing) responses would also be expected. This is precisely the pattern of results that were demonstrated by the school-age children with SLI who participated in this investigation.

However, there are other possible explanations as well. For children with SLI, the increased mental processing required for recoding the phonological representation back into a visual form or simply the time required to perform a recoding operation may have interfered with retention of the initial phonological codes. As a result of extra mental processing and increased time, phonological representations, or any other type of representation for that matter, might have decayed such that they were not available for recall processes. It is also likely that children with SLI did not have the substantive long-term phonological representations and/or mental capacities needed to quickly rebuild decayed representations. Thus, they were more likely to forget the visually presented digits when a pointing response was required than when a speaking response was required.

If children with SLI do, in fact, have difficulties with phonological coding, what might be the nature of such a deficit? First, as suggested by Gathercole and Baddeley (1990), children with SLI may be limited in their capacity to form adequate phonological codes. That is, they may create incomplete or fuzzy phonological representations of spoken or written words. A second explanation might be that phonological coding deficiencies may involve limitations in the capacity to retain adequate representations across multiple processing conversions. Such phonological coding problems could be a consequence of phonologically specific processes or general difficulties with mental processing and retention of any type of information, including phonological stimuli.

Limitations in Central Executive Functions

There are other aspects of working memory besides phonological representation that may play a critical role in the development of language abilities and subsequent impairments. According to the Baddeley and Hitch (1974) model, there are three components of working memory. At the most basic level of information processing, there are two slave systems that are highly specialized for the processing and temporary storage of material within a particular domain. Verbally coded information is maintained by the phonological loop, whereas information that is spatial or visual is processed by the visuospatial sketchpad. The central executive component of working memory serves to coordinate the flow of information within working memory by encoding and retrieving information from both slave systems. Further, it activates and retrieves information from long-term memory and regulates the overall processing and storage of information. The central executive component of working memory is thought to be responsible for selective attention, coordination of performance on two or more separate tasks, and inhibition of disruptive effects of competing or irrelevant stimuli (Baddeley, 1996). As such it would appear to be the linchpin of processing between sensory stimuli and higher order cognitive processes and could, in fact, prove to be a critical bottleneck in the information-processing systems of children with language impairment.

Although the phonological loop component of working memory has been extensively studied, the central executive component has not. An investigation by Hale, Myerson, Rhee, Weiss, and Abrams (1996) revealed developmental differences in the efficiency of central executive function in typically developing children as measured by performance on dual-processing tasks. In their study, younger children were more influenced by nonspecific domain interference (deterioration in performance following presentation of a secondary task that is from a different domain than the primary task) than they are by domain-specific interference (deterioration in performance following presentation of a secondary task that is from the same domain as that of the primary task). There have been few investigations of possible constraints in central executive function in children with language impairments despite its potential significance for furthering our understanding of information-processing deficits and their relationships to language learning and use.

Hoffman and Gillam (in press) designed a study to explore the possibility of complex interactions among various information-processing factors, including central executive functions. Children were asked to repeat a series of visually presented digits or point to the locations of a series of Xs on grids. Sometimes they were also asked to complete secondary tasks requiring them to identify the color of the stimuli as they were presented using either a naming or pointing response. There were six conditions that crossed primary task (verbal or spatial) with secondary task (none, verbal, or spatial) under two rates of presentation (fast or slow). Forty-eight children (24 with SLI and 24 with normal language skills) between the ages of 8:0 and 10:11 years participated in the study.

The primary finding was a greater cross-modality effect for the control group than for the SLI group. In other words, children with SLI did not appear to benefit from the opportunity to disperse processing across modalities to the same extent that their age-matched peers did. This inability to effectively disperse processing across visual and spatial domains created a cumulative effect that resulted in inefficient and ineffective processing of visual information for the SLI group, particularly in conditions that included a spatial secondary task.

Analyses revealed that the processing difficulties related to phonological representation appeared to result from limitations in verbal storage capacity. There was no evidence to support a vulnerability in phonological representation under particularly taxing conditions as has been suggested by recent research. That is because children with SLI demonstrated greater difficulties when spatial rather than verbal responses were required.

This study brought to light a previously undocumented susceptibility on the part of children with SLI to nonspecific domain interference. That is, these children had difficulty processing secondary task information presented in the opposite domain of that of the primary tasks (i.e., a spatial secondary task paired with a verbal primary task). These results were interpreted as revealing group differences in central executive function in working memory.

The potential role of central executive function in language development can readily be hypothesized as follows. During the process of establishing semantic stores in long-term memory, all incoming stimuli could be conceived of as a continual sensory puzzle stream that requires analysis, coordination, and interpretation. Information that is spatial and visual in nature is processed by the visuospatial sketchpad component of working memory, whereas verbal/auditory information is processed by the phonological loop. The central executive component regulates the flow of information processing between these two slave systems as well as supporting the development of meaning by coordinating selective attention (which would also support the establishment of joint reference between child and caregiver) and the storage of information in long-term memory. Over time exposure to repetitive combinations of sensory stimuli would establish sensory patterns that could be recognized by the central executive as significant due to their consistency and frequency. In response, the central executive could regulate the long-term storage of this information so as to support the development of coherent phonological or imagistic representations in long-term memory, which would further support the development of cognitive schemata. Through the continual coordination of multidomain sensory information, regularity and meaningfulness are established within the long-term memory system, thereby creating cognitive representations. It is these representations that form the semantic network that is the basis of language development. In essence, adequate central executive function in working memory may be critical to the development of language in young children. In addition, the basic functions of the central executive component would appear to provide the bedrock foundation for the development of higher order metacognitive skills involved in self-regulation of learning tasks, such as attending selectively, inhibiting actions, restraining and delaying responses, planning, organizing, and maintaining and shifting set.

Limitations of General Cognitive Capacity

Johnston (1994) asserted that the critical mechanism underlying language development "is nothing more or less than the general information processing capabilities that constitute the mind" (p. 108), and that, by extension, deficits in language development should reflect and produce limitations in conceptual knowledge, reasoning patterns, and representational abilities. From this perspective, children with language impairments could be described as demonstrating cognition that is deficient in comparison to their age-matched peers, yet more advanced than their language-matched peers. Hence, cognition could not only be the initial cause of language deficits, but, through the subsequent inadequate ability to manipulate symbolism to support problem solving, could also be the recipient of the consequences of language deficits. This pattern of relationships should create a perpetual loop of processing difficulties.

If general cognitive limitations exist in children with language impairments, there should be evidence of these constraints in nonverbal cognitive processing in addition to their readily observable verbal difficulties. Johnston and Ellis Weismer (1983) provided support for this perspective in a study that contrasted mental rotation abilities of children with and without language deficits. They found that children with language deficits demonstrated longer response times when judging geometric shapes that had been rotated. Hence, the authors asserted that these children were more likely to use nonverbal imagistic strategies to complete the task than more efficient verbal mediation strategies. The children with language impairment were just as accurate in their final judgments as their age-matched peers, just slower. Johnston and Ellis Weismer concluded that children with language impairment presented cognitive deficits that resulted in slowed nonverbal functions.

The limited general capacity theory asserts that processing time and efficiency impact task performance, memory, and learning. Like Johnston and Ellis Weismer (1983), other authors have showed response times in children with and without language impairment (Kail, 1993, 1994; Kail & Hall, 1994; Kail & Park, 1994; Lahey & Edwards, 1996; Sininger, Klatzky, & Kirchner, 1989). Further, a growing body of evidence suggests that the rate of stimuli presentation influences language comprehension and learning. For example, Ellis Weismer (1996), and Ellis Weismer and Hesketh (1998) showed that increased rate of presentation is disproportionately detrimental to the acquisition of novel morpheme and lexical items in children with language impairments. However, the mechanisms by which such limitations might result in or contribute to language deficits have yet to be conclusively defined.

A research paradigm known as the *fan effect* has appealing properties as a measure of general activation and mental modeling. In this paradigm, participants learn a series of novel sentences and then perform a recognition recall task. Some of the training sentences share subjects, some share verb phrases, and some sentences are independent of all the others. The typical finding with adults is that sentences that share the most information yield the longest verification times (Cantor & Engle, 1993).

Gillam and Ellis Weismer (1997) administered a fan effect protocol to children with SLI, their age-matched peers, and their working memory-matched peers. Children memorized 12 target sentences that varied according to the amount of overlapping and nonoverlapping information. Later they listened to test sentences and were asked whether they had studied each one.

All students successfully learned the 12 sentences with minimal errors. Children in the SLI group were poorer than their age-matched peers, but similar to their memory-matched peers in verifying whether a sentence spoken by the examiner was one that they actually studied. Therefore, children with SLI performed the verification recognition task at a level consistent with their working memory ability.

When Gillam and Weismer analyzed response speed, they found that children in the SLI group responded significantly slower than children in both the age- and memory-matched groups. It appears that SLI children have lower activation rates for certain types of tasks and/or represent information in smaller units.

Overall, the results of this study suggest that all children retrieved information from a single mental model. Despite their unusually low phonological representation (as indicated by nonword spans that were significantly lower than their WM-matched peers), children with SLI performed much like their memory-matched peers on the training and verification tasks. Therefore, basic processes underlying capacity limitations (i.e., activation levels, representation units, scanning speed) may be more powerful for explaining language learning difficulties than phonological representation difficulties per se.

For trained sentences, children in the SLI group responded significantly slower than their age-matched controls. For foils, children in the SLI group were significantly slower than children in both the age- and memory-matched groups. These results suggest that children with SLI had lower activation rates for certain types of tasks and/or represented information in smaller units.

Evidence from a variety of studies suggests that children with SLI have generalized capacity limitations that disrupt language processing. Presently, it is not known whether these general capacity limitations reflect slower mental processing functions or different types of mental representation strategies.

SUMMARY

We have reviewed evidence supporting information-processing factors that are likely to constrain language processing in children with SLI. Children with language impairments may have limitations that affect attention, speech perception, adequacy of phonological representations, central executive functions, or general processing capacity. Regardless of what the primary or secondary limitation might be, it is likely that the language learning abilities of most children with language impairments are simultaneously constrained by multiple factors that affect information processing. Therefore, we question just how *specific* language impairments might be. Next, we turn our attention to the clinical implications of information-processing problems.

CLINICAL IMPLICATIONS

Many children who exhibit the characteristics of SLI present co-occurring language and information-processing problems. When assessing such children, speech-language pathologists should evaluate the psychological structures underlying language development (attention, perception, memory, and reasoning), children's use of language structures and functions in natural situations, and the level of their engagement in activities that involve communication (Gillam & Hoffman, 2001). In our opinion, one of the most ecologically valid ways to assess the psychological functions that support language development is through a process known as *dynamic assessment*. As we explain further in the next section, dynamic assessment is a test, teach, retest procedure in which clinicians observe children's information-processing and language skills while they are learning a new skill. When treating children with information-processing and language impairments, speech-language pathologists (SLPs) should focus primarily on social-interactive and academic uses of language in the types of communicative contexts the child routinely encounters. However, within the larger context of functional intervention, learners can benefit from a temporary focus on particular aspects of language or cognition (Gillam, McFadden, & van Kleeck, 1995; Montgomery, 1996). Some intervention procedures that benefit attention, perception, memory, and central executive processes are summarized in the section on intervention.

Dynamic Assessment

Dynamic assessment enables SLPs to observe psychological and linguistic functions and activities as children are engaged in language learning. Dynamic assessment usually begins with a testing phase in which the examiner administers a pretest. During a teaching phase, the examiner teaches one or two lessons designed to impact the child's performance on the pretest measure. Then in the posttest phase, examiners readminister the pretest.

Dynamic assessment yields data about language learning functions and language learning potential. Children's responses to the teaching phase of dynamic assessment provide important data about attention, perception, memory, and central executive functions during language learning. The amount and type of changes that result from intervention are an indication of the child's language learning potential.

Gillam, Peña, and Miller (1999) and Miller, Gillam, and Peña (2000) described an approach for the dynamic assessment of narratives. Clinicians begin by having children create stories as they look at wordless picture books. Then clinicians mediate some aspect of storytelling in two separate intervention sessions. After the mediation sessions, clinicians ask children to create a story about a second wordless picture book that contains the same number of pictures and the same story structure as the book used for the pretest.

Based on their analysis of the pretest story, clinicians select the goals for two mediation sessions. Clinicians should target aspects of narration that the child has some knowledge of in one of the mediation sessions. For example, if a child's story contained an incomplete episode, the clinician might decide to focus on teaching a missing element that would be required for a basic episode (initiating event, attempt, or consequence). During the second mediation session, clinicians should target an aspect of narration that the child did not demonstrate any knowledge of. For example, the clinician might focus on setting information if the child did not include any information about where the story occurred.

Clinicians administer a posttest after the two mediation sessions. Clinicians should consider the kinds of changes the child made, how much effort was required to accomplish these changes, and the type of the change observed. More specifically, clinicians should ask:

- Was the child able to form a more complete and/or more coherent story after mediation?
- How hard did the SLP have to work for the child to make positive changes?
- Did the child attend well and stay on task?
- Was the child's learning quick and efficient or slow and labored?

The answers to these questions are useful for determining whether a child's underlying information-processing abilities are sufficient to support language learning. Children who make rapid changes and are highly responsive to the mediation sessions rarely have information-processing problems or language impairments. When provided with instruction that focuses their attention on the necessary elements of narratives, these children are able to quickly and efficiently make changes. In contrast, children who need continued support and have a difficult time making even small changes are likely to have a language impairment. These children typically demonstrate low responsivity, require high examiner effort, and demonstrate few pre- to posttest changes.

As part of a complete assessment, clinicians should also assess children's participation in everyday activities; their level of involvement in social, educational, and prevocational experiences; and environmental factors that hinder or facilitate their functioning and participation. These areas are best assessed by interviewing children, parents, and teachers and observing children in their natural environments.

Intervention Suggestions

Because language and information processing are dynamically related, good language intervention is also good information-processing intervention (Peña & Gillam, 2001). We believe the primary focus of language intervention should concern form, meaning, and use interactions in pragmatically relevant contexts. For preschoolers, clinicians often use facilitative interactions that include imitation, modeling, focused stimulation (including milieu teaching), and growth-relevant recasts (see Leonard, 1998, for a summary of these techniques). These types of facilitative interactions can be used to teach a variety of intervention targets. For school-age children, many clinicians use book discussions as the primary context for intervention because this kind of talk commonly occurs in elementary-school classrooms. In this approach, activities that facilitate semantics, syntax, morphology, narration, and phonological awareness are centered on a common theme. Clinicians who believe that children need to learn language within natural contexts tend to use facilitative interactions (focused stimulation, modeling, recasting, and others) based on social and/or cognitive interactionist theories of language development and disorders. It may be useful for clinicians to provide children with occasional minilessons that focus more specifically on attention, perception, memory, or reasoning. Gillam (1997) suggested the following language intervention principles and activities.

Promote Attention. There are at least two attentional states that contribute to the client's encoding of the clinician's facilitative input. First, learners process information more quickly after they have preactivated relevant information in long-term memory. Second, encoding is enhanced when learners selectively attend to the most critical information.

Clinicians can mediate preparatory attention in school-age children by explaining what the goals of the session are and why they are important. When working with younger children, clinicians could influence preparatory attention by demonstrating the child's language targets three or four times within meaningful contexts.

Clinicians can mediate selective attention by making the intervention targets as salient as possible and by limiting distractions. For example, Ellis Weismer and Hesketh (1998) reported that children learned to produce novel words that clinicians had emphatically stressed better than novel words that had been produced with regular stress. These authors concluded that the emphatic stress helped direct the children's selective attention to new information to be learned. Increased selective attention appeared to influence children's encoding, recall, and reporting functions.

Speak Clearly and Slowly.   Speech perception and speed of cognitive processing contribute to encoding. As noted by Ellis Weismer (1996), clinicians who slow their rates of speech provide learners with more time for processing, encoding, storage, and retrieval.

Promote Phonological Coding.   Children with developmental language disorders frequently have difficulty with phonological aspects of encoding. Montgomery (1996) and Fazio (1996) suggested teaching children nursery rhymes to help them develop phonological coding skills. Similarly, Gillam and van Kleeck (1996) and van Kleeck, Gillam, and McFadden (1998) found that children who received rhyming and phonological awareness training improved considerably on a measure of phonological coding ability.

Training in listening skills might also promote more efficient and elaborate encoding. Recently, Tallal and her colleagues (1996) reported on a computer-assisted instruction program called *Fast Forword* that was designed to facilitate children's temporal processing abilities (see Verhoeven & Segers, chap. 17, this volume). At the present time, the authors' broad generalizations about the effectiveness of this intervention have yet to be empirically validated through careful experimentation and replication. Nonetheless, the efficacy data that have been reported (Tallal et al., 1996) appear promising. This intervention approach may be especially well suited to facilitating selective attention to sound, maintenance of attention (or prolonged concentration), and phonological coding. If this proves to be the case, programs like Fast Forword should have an indirect impact on language development when they are instituted as a temporary focus on auditory processing within a larger program of functional language intervention.

Plan Activities Around Topics or Concepts That Are Familiar to the Learner.   Increased prior knowledge enables learners to attend more carefully to new information, which leads to more elaborate encoding, increased storage, and a greater variety of retrieval cues. Clinicians who wish to teach new language forms or communicative functions should make optimal use of the learner's established scripts.

Help Learners Organize New Knowledge. Learners can remember much more information when they have organized their knowledge into meaningful chunks. For example, people struggle to recall 20 randomly presented letters, but they can easily remember 60 or 80 letters that are part of words that comprise sentences. Following the same logic, it makes sense to help learners organize new knowledge in ways that facilitate recall. For example, Montgomery (1996) suggested that practice with paraphrasing can help learners in the elementary grades use their own prior knowledge, vocabulary, and language structures to organize new information. Wynn-Dancy and Gillam (1997) described learning strategies that help adolescents organize and recall information from readings and lectures.

Provide Learners With Retention Cues. Clinicians need to build bridges between intervention targets and learners' knowledge and expectations. Clinician questions, summaries, drawings, and pictures can be internalized by learners as recall cues. Recall cues provided by clinicians, parents, or teachers can be powerful. In some studies, children who were given retention cues during a novel experience had greater recall than children who did not receive extra cues as much as a year after the experience.

CONCLUSIONS AND DISCUSSION

Research suggests that many children with SLI have problems in the areas of attention, speech perception, phonological representation, central executive functions, and/or general processing capacity. We believe there are dynamic relationships between these information-processing functions and language learning capabilities.

Clinicians should assess information-processing mechanisms that contribute to language learning. There are many standardized tests that claim to evaluate one or more information-processing functions. Most of them have questionable validity and reliability. It is our opinion that the best way to assess the information-processing abilities that affect language development is to carefully observe children as they are in the act of learning language. We summarized one approach known as dynamic assessment, in which examiners test a language skill, teach aspects of language that children do not know, and then retest to see how much the child profited from instruction.

Information processing is essential for language, and the development of more complex language increases the efficiency and capacity of information processing. As such, much of what happens in language intervention is also information-processing intervention. We have argued that the most effective language intervention is performed in contexts that are as similar as possible to children's everyday speaking experiences. However, at times, it may be wise for clinicians to focus on particular aspects of information processing within the larger context of pragmatically relevant therapy.

REFERENCES

Baddeley, A. (1996). Exploring the central executive. *Quarterly Journal of Experimental Psychology. A Human Experimental Psychology, 49*A(1), 5–28.

Baddeley, A. D., & Hitch, G. (1974). Working memory. In G. H. Bower (Ed.), *The psychology of learning and motivation* (Vol. 8, pp. 47–90). New York: Academic Press.

Baker, L., & Cantwell, D. P. (1992). Attention deficit impairment and speech/language impairments. *Comprehensive Mental Health Care, 2*(1), 3–16.

Bishop, D. V. M., Carlyon, R. P., Deeks, J. M., & Bishop, S. J. (1999). *Journal of Speech-Language-Hearing Research, 42,* 1295–1310.

Campbell, T. F., & McNeil, M. R. (1985). Effects of presentation rate and divided attention on auditory comprehension in children with an acquired language impairment. *Journal of Speech & Hearing Research, 28*(4), 513–520.

Cantor, J., & Engle, R. W. (1993). Working-memory capacity as long-term memory activation: An individual differences approach. *Journal of Experimental Psychology: Learning, Memory, and Cognition, 19,* 1101–1114.

Cowan, N. (1995). *Attention and memory: An integrated framework.* New York: Oxford University Press.

Edwards, J., & Lahey, M. (1998). Nonword repetitions of children with specific language impairment: Exploration of some explanations for their inaccuracies. *Applied Psycholinguistics, 19*(2), 279–309.

Elliott, L. L., & Hammer, M. A. (1993). Fine-grained auditory discrimination: Factor structures. *Journal of Speech & Hearing Research, 36*(2), 396–409.

Elliott, L. L., Hammer, M. A., & Scholl, M. E. (1989). Fine-grained discrimination: Factor structures. *Journal of Speech and Hearing Research, 36,* 112–119.

Ellis Weismer, S. (1996). Capacity limitations in working memory: The impact on lexical and morphological learning by children with language impairment. *Topics in Language Impairments, 17*(1), 33–44.

Ellis Weismer, S., & Hesketh, L. (1998). The impact of emphatic stress on novel word learning by children with specific language impairment. *Journal of Speech-Language-Hearing Research, 41,* 1444–1458.

Fazio, B. (1996). Serial memory in children with specific language impairment: Examining specific content areas for assessment and intervention. *Topics in Language Disorders, 17*(1), 58–71.

Gathercole, S. E., & Baddeley, A. D. (1990). Phonological memory deficits in language impaired children: Is there a causal connection? *Journal of Memory and Language, 29,* 336–360.

Gathercole, S. E., & Baddeley, A. D. (1995). Short-term memory may yet be deficient in children with language impairments: A comment on van der Lely & Howard (1993). *Journal of Speech & Hearing Research, 38*(2), 463–466.

Gillam, R. B. (1997). Putting memory to work in language intervention: Implications for practitioners. *Topics in Language Disorders, 18*(1), 72–79.

Gillam, R. B., Cowan, N., & Day, L. S. (1995). Sequential memory in children with and without language impairment. *Journal of Speech & Hearing Research, 38*(2), 393–402.

Gillam, R. B., Cowan, N., & Marler, J. A. (1998). Information processing by school-age children with specific language impairment: Evidence from a modality effect paradigm. *Journal of Speech Language & Hearing Research, 41*(4), 913–926.

Gillam, R. B., & Hoffman, L. M. (2001). Language assessment during childhood. In D. M. Ruscello (Ed.), *Tests and measurements in speech-language pathology* (pp. 77–117). Woburn, MA: Butterworth-Heinemann.

Gillam, R. B., McFadden, T. U., & van Kleeck, A. (1995). Improving the narrative abilities of children with language disorders: Whole language and language skills approaches. In M. Fey, J. Windsor, & J. Reichle (Eds.), *Communication intervention for school-age children* (pp. 145–182). Baltimore: Paul H. Brookes.

Gillam, R. B., Peña, E. D., & Miller, L. (1999). Dynamic assessment of narrative and expository discourse. *Topics in Language Disorders, 20*(1), 33–47.

Gillam, R. B., & van Kleeck, A. (1996). Phonological awareness training and short-term working memory: Clinical implications. *Topics in Language Disorders, 17*(1), 72–81.

Gillam, R. B., & Weismer, S. E. (1997, November). *Capacity limitations, activation, and working memory in specific language impairment.* Paper presented at the annual convention of the American Speech-Language-Hearing Association, Boston, MA.

Hale, S., Myerson, J., Rhee, S., H., Weiss, C. S., & Abrams, R. A. (1996). Selective interference with the maintenance of location information in working memory. *Neuropsychology, 10*, 228–240.

Helzer, J. R., Champlin, C. A., & Gillam, R. B. (1996). Auditory temporal resolution in specifically language-impaired and age-matched children. *Perceptual & Motor Skills, 83*(3, Pt 2), 1171–1181.

Hoffman, L. M., & Gillam, R. B. (in press). Verbal and spatial information processing constraints in children with language impairment. *Journal of Memory and Language.*

Johnston, J. (1994). Cognitive abilities of children with language impairment. In R. V. Watkins & M. L. Rice (Eds.), *Specific language impairments in children* (pp. 107–121). Baltimore, MD: Paul H. Brookes.

Johnston, J. R., & Ellis Weismer, S. (1983). Mental rotation abilities in language-impaired children. *Journal of Speech and Hearing Research, 26,* 397–403.

Kail, R. (1993). Processing time decreases globally at an exponential rate during childhood and adolescence. *Journal of Experimental Child Psychology, 56*(2), 254–265.

Kail, R. (1994). A method for studying the generalized slowing hypothesis in children with specific language impairment. *Journal of Speech & Hearing Research, 37*(2), 418–421.

Kail, R., & Hall, L. K. (1994). Processing speed, naming speed, and reading. *Developmental Psychology, 30*(6), 949–954.

Kail, R., & Park, Y. (1994). Processing time, articulation time, and memory span. *Journal of Experimental Child Psychology, 57*(2), 281–291.

Kamhi, A. G., Catts, H. W., Mauer, D., Apel, K., & Gentry, I. (1988). Phonological and spatial processing abilities in language- and reading-impaired children. *Journal of Speech & Hearing Disorders, 53*(3), 316–327.

Lahey, M., & Edwards, J. (1996). Why do children with specific language impairment name pictures more slowly than their peers? *Journal of Speech & Hearing Research, 39*(5), 1081–1098.

Leonard, L. B. (1998). *Children with specific language impairment.* Cambridge, MA: MIT Press.

Miller, L., Gillam, R. B., & Peña, E. (2000). *Dynamic assessment and intervention of children's narratives.* Austin, TX: Pro-Ed.

Montgomery, J. W. (1995). Sentence comprehension in children with specific language impairment: The role of phonological working memory. *Journal of Speech and Hearing Research, 38,* 187–199.

Montgomery, J. W. (1996). Sentence comprehension and working memory in children with specific language impairment. *Topics in Language Disorders, 17*(1), 19–32.

Näätänen, R. (1990). The role of attention in auditory information processing as revealed by event-related potentials and other brain measures of cognitive function. *Behavioral & Brain Sciences, 13*(2), 201–288.

Peña, E. D., & Gillam, R. B. (2001). Dynamic assessment of children referred for speech and language evaluations. In C. Lidz & J. Elliott (Eds.), *Dynamic assessment: Prevailing models and applications* (Vol. 6, pp. 543–576). Oxford: Elsevier Science Ltd.

Riddle, L. S. (1992). The attentional capacity of children with specific language impairment. *Dissertation Abstracts International, 53*(6-B).

Robin, D. A., Tomblin, J. B., Kearney, A., & Hug, L. N. (1989). Auditory temporal pattern learning in children with speech and language impairments. *Brain & Language, 36*(4), 604–613.

Sininger, Y. S., Klatzky, R. L., & Kirchner, D. M. (1989). Memory scanning speed in language-impaired children. *Journal of Speech & Hearing Research, 32*(2), 289–297.

Sussman, J. (1993). Perception of formant transition cues to place of articulation in children with language impairments. *Journal of Speech and Hearing Research, 36,* 1286–1299.

Tallal, P. (1990). Fine-grained discrimination deficits in language-learning impaired children are specific neither to the auditory modality nor to speech perception. *Journal of Speech & Hearing Research, 33*(3), 616–617.

Tallal, P., Miller, S. I., Bedi, G., Byma, G., Wang, X., Nagarajan, S. S., Schreiner, C., Jenkins, W. M., & Merzenich, M. M. (1996). Language comprehension in language-learning impaired children improved with acoustically modified speech. *Science, 271,* 81–84.

Tallal, P., & Piercy, M. (1973). Defects of nonverbal auditory perception in children with developmental aphasia. *Nature, 241,* 468–469.

Tallal, P., & Piercy, M. (1974). Developmental aphasia: Rate of auditory processing and selective impairment of consonant perception. *Neuropsychologia, 12*(11), 83–93.

Tallal, P., & Piercy, M. (1975). Developmental aphasia: The perception of brief vowels and extended stop consonants. *Neuropsychologia, 13*(1), 69–74.

Tallal, P., Stark, R. E., Kallman, C., & Mellits, D. (1980). Developmental dysphasia: Relation between acoustic processing deficits and verbal processing. *Neuropsychologia, 18*(3), 273–284.

Tallal, P., Stark, R. E., & Mellits, D. (1985). The relationship between auditory temporal analysis and receptive language development: Evidence from studies of developmental language impairment. *Neuropsychologia, 23*(4), 527–534.

van Kleeck, A., Gillam, R. B., & McFadden, T. (1998). Teaching rhyming and phonological awareness to preschool-aged children with language disorders. *American Journal of Speech-Language Pathology, 7,* 66–77.

Wright, B. A., Lombardino, L. J., King, W. M., Puranik, C. S., Leonard, C. M., & Merzenich, M. M. (1997). Deficits in auditory temporal and spectral resolution in language-impaired children. *Nature, 387,* 176–178.

Wynn-Dancy, M. L., & Gillam, R. B. (1997). Accessing long-term memory: Metacognitive strategies and strategic action in adolescents. *Topics in Language Disorders, 18*(1), 32–44.

6

Environmental Factors in Developmental Language Disorders

Sieneke Goorhuis-Brouwer
Francien Coster
Han Nakken
Henk lutje Spelberg
University of Groningen, The Netherlands

Language plays a crucial role in child development. That is, children's thinking, reasoning, and social competence develop via social interactions and functional communication with their parents (Bruner, 1977; Schaffer, 1996). Developmental language and behavior problems may, in turn, arise as a result of inadequate social interactions and communication during the preverbal period of socialization. This chapter considers the role and importance of adequate social interactions and communication in the ontogenesis of developmental language difficulties. It also examines how language development disorders may influence a child's socioemotional development, resulting in varying degrees of perceived and assessed challenging behavior.

A review of the literature on the presupposed relations between developmental language difficulties and the presence of problem behaviors results in three main areas of variability and sometimes discrepancy (Bishop & Mogford, 1989; Fletcher & Hall, 1992; Hart & Risley, 1999; Leonard, 1998). First of all, language disorders may be more or less specific. The original definition of specific language impairment (SLI) is based on exclusion criteria (Stark & Tallal, 1981). Social deprivation is one of the exclusion criteria (Bishop, 1997). The typology of nonspecific SLI, such as mental retardation, autistic spectrum disorders, and other multiply based language difficulties, is diverse and may thus affect social interactions and communication in different ways. Second, the children's age may span a broad range. It is clear from research that children's competence in managing interpersonal relationships is highly dependent on age (Schaffer,

TABLE 6.1
The Relation Between Language Disorders and Behavioral Problems
According to Parents, Teachers, Parents, and/or Teachers

| Author | SLI/ non-SLI | Method | Age (years) | Behavior Problems According to | | | n |
				Parents	Teachers	And/or	
Beitchman, Nair, Clegg, Ferguson, and Patel (1986)	non-SLI	CBCL Conners' TRS	5	32%	34%	55%	142
Cantwell and Baker (1987)	non-SLI	DSM	2–16			44%	600
Baker and Cantwell (1987)	non-SLI	DSM	7–21			60%	300
Silva, Williams, and McGee (1987)	non-SLI	Rutter-scales	7	28%	29%	46%	71
			9	56%	30%	49%	69
			11	21%	23%	33%	65
Tallal, Dukette, and Curtiss (1989)	SLI	CBCL	5	11%			81
Benasich, Curtiss, and Tallal (1993)	SLI	Conners'	9	32%			56
Goorhuis-Brouwer, Nakken, and van den Berg (1996)	SLI	CBCL	3–6	19%			21

1996). Third, the notion of socioemotional development is not always clearly defined. In most studies, problems in socioemotional development are described as *behavioral problems* according to interviews by parents and/or teachers or according to standardized tests—for instance, the Child Behavior Checklist (CBCL; Achenbach, 1991, 1993), the Conners' Teacher Rating Scale (Conners, 1969), the Conners' Parents Questionnaire (Conners, 1990), and the Rutter Parent and Teacher Scales (Rutter, Graham, & Yule, 1970). Occasionally, a psychiatric examination is used (DSM classification). Given the various language problems in question, the varying ages of the children and the different rating scales used to assess the behavior problems, the outcomes of these studies differ widely (see Table 6.1).

In children with SLI, behavioral problems are mostly evident at a relatively young age (Beitchman et al., 1986; Cantwell & Baker, 1987); in children with SLI, the problems are initially difficult to detect and seem to increase in quantity and severity with age (Benasich et al., 1993). Only some of the children with SLI develop behavioral problems, however—about 60%, according to the literature (Baker & Cantwell, 1987). In addition, the judgments of parents and teachers can differ (Beitchman et al., 1986; Silva et al., 1987). Research findings indicate that developmental language difficulties and behavioral problems can go together, but that more factors than just language difficulties must be considered to explain this relationship.

In the remainder of this chapter, empirical data on the amount of behavioral problems in children with language impairment is discussed. The children in these studies were selected according to Stark and Tallal's (1981) definition of SLI. This means that the children were healthy, showed normal hearing, had normal nonverbal intelligence, and experienced no social deprivation. Before going into the main study, a series of pilot studies is reviewed. To arrive at a better understanding of the complex relations between childhood language impairment and the socioemotional development of children, three pilot studies were conducted with children at three different age levels:

- Preschool (1–3 years)
- Kindergarten (3–6 years)
- Elementary and secondary school (6–15 years)

THREE PILOT STUDIES

Preschool Children

In this study (Goorhuis-Brouwer, 1988), we compared the behavior of 46 SLI children with the behavior of 32 normal language acquiring (NLA) children. The SLI children were ages 24 to 29 months (mean: 32 months), and the NLA children were ages 22 to 46 months (mean: 34 months). The children's language behavior was assessed with the revised version of the Reynell Language Developmental Scales (Reynell, 1974). The children's social behavior was assessed using the questionnaire *Behavior and Language Development in Two- and Three-Year Olds* (Swets-Gronert & Kohnstamm, 1986). In addition, the parents were asked about their impressions of the child and the childrearing task in an open-ended interview.

The results of the *Behavior and Language Development in Two- and Three-Year Olds* questionnaire showed the only difference between the group of SLI children and the group of NLA children to concern the category *adaptation*. The SLI children were less open in their contact with other children than the NLA children were (Mann Whitney, two-tailed $p = .04$, $z = -2.06$). The results for the SLI children were quite similar to those for the NLA children in the categories of *mood* (i.e., pleasure), *tempers*, and *sleeping rhythm*. According to these data, thus, the group of SLI children did not show overt behavioral problems. However, the results of the parental interview show the group of SLI children to be perceived as more self-oriented, less socializing, and less enterprising than the group of NLA children (see Table 6.2). In other words, the data from the parental interviews show these preschool children to be clearly perceived as having

TABLE 6.2

Behavior of Two- and Three-Year-Old Children According
to Parents of Children With Language Problems (n = 46)
and Age-Adequate Speaking Children (n = 32)

Described Behavior	Children With SLI		Children With NLA		χ^2	Sign. (df = 1)
	n	100%	n	100%		
Normal	8	18%	8	25%	.670	.413
Cheerful, enterprising	3	6%	13	41%	13.461	.000*
Withdrawn	13	28%	3	9%	4.128	.042**
Excited, restless	18	40%	8	25%	1.696	.193
Quick to irritate	3	6%	0	0%	—	—
No information	1	2%	0	0%	—	—

*χ^2 significant, $p < .01$.
**χ^2 significant, $p < .05$.

TABLE 6.3

Easiness of Childrearing Practice According to Parents of Children
With SLI (n = 46) and Children With NLA (n = 32)

Childrearing Practice	Children With SLI		Children With NLA		χ^2	Sign. (df = 1)
	n	100%	n	100%		
Easy	31	67%	17	53%	1.623	.203
Sometimes difficult	5	11%	15	47%	12.832	.000*
Often difficult	9	20%	0	0%	7.078	.008*
No information	1	2%	0	0%	—	—

*χ^2 significant ($p < .01$).

overt behavioral problems. The data derived from the parental interviews also show the task of childrearing for the group of SLI children to be perceived as more difficult than the task of childrearing for the group of NLA children (see Table 6.3).

Kindergarten Children

In this study, the behavior of 21 SLI children ages 3 to 6 years was assessed using the CBCL (Achenbach, 1991). Similar to the previous study, the parents of the children were also asked about their impressions of the children and the childrearing task.

According to the CBCL, 19% of the SLI children showed challenging behaviors (see Table 6.4), which does not differ significantly from the 10%

TABLE 6.4
Behavior of Kindergarten Children With
SLI According to the CBCL ($n = 21$)

Behavior According to CBCL	n	100%
Normal score	14	67%
Borderline score	3	14%
Clinical score	4	19%

observed for the norm group for the checklist. However, the results of the parental interview show 76% of the parents to experience problems with their SLI kindergartner. Only 24% of the SLI kindergartners were described as normal and cheerful, moreover.

A discrepancy thus exists between the actual behavior observed for SLI children and the problems experienced by the parents of such children. As can be seen when the results for the SLI preschoolers are compared with those for the SLI kindergartners, moreover, the discrepancy has only increased for the SLI kindergarten children.

Elementary and Secondary School Children

In this study, the behavior of eight SLI children ages 6 to 15 years attending a school for children with speech and hearing disorders in The Netherlands was examined. When the children were admitted to the school, their language development lagged an average of 1 year behind the language development of other children with the same chronological age. We compared the teachers' perceptions of the children's behavior, as reported in an open interview, with actual measures of the children's behavior using the Teacher's Report Form (TRF), which is the teacher's version of the CBCL (Eleveld et al., 1994). All eight of the children showed socio-emotional problems in the opinions of their teachers: social withdrawal (reported twice), aggression (reported three times), or both (reported three times; see Table 6.5).

The TRF results reveal clinically critical scores for externalizing and/or internalizing behavior problems for six of the children. One child performed at a borderline level for both scales, and one child could not pass the test (missing data). The interview data thus support the TRF findings: No differences are found in the amount of perceived problem behaviors and the amount of objectively observed behavior problems for this group of older SLI children.

TABLE 6.5
Behavioral Problems in Elementary and Middle-School Children With
SLI According to Teachers, Following TRF or Interview

| | | According to TRF | | | |
Sex	Age (years)	Score Internalizing Scale	Score Externalizing Scale	Behavioral Problems	According to Interview
Boy	7	60+	73++	Externalizing	Externalizing
Girl	12	65++	60+	Both	Both
Girl	12	65++	65++	Both	Both
Girl	15	71++	64++	Both	Both
Boy	8	53	82++	Externalizing	Externalizing
Boy	10	62+	56+	Borderline	Externalizing
Boy	6	75++	50	Internalizing	Internalizing
Boy	8	—	—	—	Internalizing

+ borderline score; ++ clinical score.

Conclusions and Discussion

The findings of the pilot studies indicate a gradually increasing match between the level of behavior problems experienced by parents or teachers and the amount of formally observed behavior problems as the age of the SLI children studied here increased. For the group of SLI children 6 years of age or older, the level of experienced problem behaviors reported by the teachers clearly matches the objectively collected data on the occurrence of problem behaviors for the same children. Prior to the age of 6, however, little congruence exists between parental reports of problem behavior and objective measures of the occurrence of challenging behavior.

On the basis of these pilot results, it is hypothesized that the actual amount of problem behavior increases with age due, in part, to the changing reactions of parents to the occurrence of overt challenging behaviors on the part of an SLI child. In other words, the persisting level of problem behavior in combination with severe language difficulties appear to negatively influence the reciprocity, fluency, intelligibility, and meaningfulness of the social interactions and communication of SLI children with their parents, teachers, and peers (see Fig. 6.1).

On the basis of the foregoing results and hypothesis, further research was undertaken on the behavior problems perceived and observed for a larger group of 8-, 10-, and 12-year-old SLI children. The main hypothesis to be tested was that the amount of problem behavior actually observed for the SLI children would increase as a result of growing social interaction and communication problems with parents and teachers and thus with the age of the children. An inability to verbally communicate emotions was hypothesized to be a critical component of the increased behavior problems displayed by the SLI children.

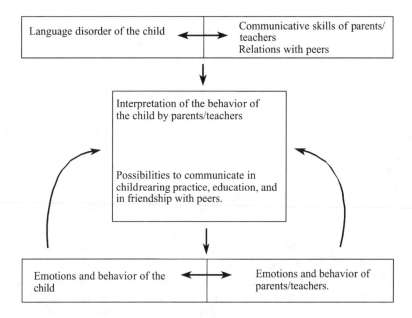

FIG. 6.1. Supposed relations of factors influencing behavior in SLI children.

THE MAIN STUDY

Method

The subjects for the present study were selected from five schools for language- and hearing-impaired children throughout The Netherlands. The children studied here were referred to the schools for specific speech and language problems. Their language production and/or language comprehension lagged at least 1 year behind their chronological age at the time of entering the school. The total group of 154 identified SLI children included 107 boys and 47 girls (see Table 6.6).

For the 154 children, 139 parents completed the CBCL (90%) and 150 teachers completed the TRF (97%). *Both* the parents and teachers completed the relevant questionnaires for 136 of the children (88%).

The CBCL and TRF are standardized questionnaires used to assess the occurrence of emotional and behavioral problems for children between the ages of 4 and 18 years, and both questionnaires consist of 118 items. The questionnaires involve three broad-band scales: a Total Behavior scale, an Internalizing Behavior scale, and an Externalizing Behavior scale. In addition, eight narrow-band profiles can be calculated: (a) withdrawal, (b) somatic complaints, (c) anxious/depressed behavior, (d) social prob-

TABLE 6.6
Children With SLI Attending Schools for the Speech
and Hearing Impaired ($n = 154$)

Group	Sex		
	Boys	Girls	Total
Age			
8	51	23	74
10	39	16	55
12	17	8	25
Language problem			
Language production	44	22	66
Language production as well as language comprehension	63	25	88

lems, (e) thought problems, (f) attention problems, (g) delinquent behavior, and (h) aggressive behavior.

The score on the Total Behavior scale involves all 118 items and thus all eight of the narrow-band profiles. The score on the Internalizing Behavior scale consists of the items constituting the narrow-band profiles of social withdrawal, anxious/depressed behavior, and somatic complaints. The score on the Externalizing Behavior scale consists of the items constituting the narrow-band profiles of delinquent behavior and aggressive behavior.

For each subject, a T-score based on the normal population can be assigned for each behavioral scale. According to Achenbach, T-scores of 64 or above fall within the clinically abnormal range. These T-scores fit the 10% of the reference group. An SLI child was considered behaviorally disturbed when the T-score for at least one of the three broad-band scales for the CBCL or TRF fell within the clinical range (Verhulst et al., 1996, 1997).

Results

Behavior According to Parental Ratings. When the 139 CBCL forms completed by mostly mothers were analyzed, the scores for 44 of the 139 children were found to fall within the clinical range (32%). The distribution of the problem behaviors displayed by the children across the three broad-band scales is presented in Table 6.7. Of the 44 SLI children showing problem behaviors, 33 had problems on the Total Behavior scale (A+C+E+D), 33 had internalizing problem behaviors (B+C+F), and 23 had externalizing problem behaviors (D+E+F).

Of the 139 children with SLI, 24% scored within the clinical range on the Total Behavior scale, 24% on the Internalizing Behavior scale, and 17%

TABLE 6.7
Behavior Problems in Children With SLI
According to the CBCL (n = 139)

Codes	Behavioral Problems	n
A	Total behavior	2
B	Total and internalizing behavior	11
C	Total and externalizing behavior	6
D	Total and internalizing and externalizing behavior	14
E	Internalizing behavior	8
F	Externalizing behavior	3
	Total	44

TABLE 6.8
Observed Percentages of Behavior Problems Within the Sample
(n = 139) Compared to Expected Percentages

Broad-Band Scales CBCL	Behavioral Problems		χ^2	Sign. (df = 1)
	Observed	Expected		
Total	24%	10%	29.161	.000*
Internalizing	24%	10%	29.161	.000*
Externalizing	17%	10%	6.629	.010**

*χ^2 significant (p < .01).
**χ^2 significant (p < .05).

on the Externalizing Behavior scale. A chi-square goodness-of-fit test comparing the observed and expected frequencies of problem behavior for the SLI sample studied here showed a significant difference for the Total Behavior scale and the Internalizing Behavior scale ($p \leq .01$). The expected frequencies were based on the 10% norm from the CBCL manual (see Table 6.8).

Behavior According to Teacher Ratings. When the 150 TRF completed by the teachers were analyzed, 50 of the SLI children were found to score within the clinical range and thus display problem behaviors (see Table 6.9). Of the 50 SLI children showing behavior problems, 31 had problems on the Total Behavior scale (A+C+E+F), 38 on the Internalizing Behavior scale (B+C+F), and 21 on the Externalizing Behavior scale (D+E+F). Of the 150 SLI children assessed using the TRF, 21% scored within the clinical range on the Total Behavior scale, 25% on the Internalizing Behavior scale, and 14% on the Externalizing Behavior scale. According to a chi-square goodness-of-fit test, the observed and expected

TABLE 6.9
Behavior Problems in Children With SLI According to TRF ($n = 150$)

Codes	Behavioral Problem	n
A	Total behavior	3
B	Total and internalizing behavior	11
C	Total and externalizing behavior	5
D	Total and internalizing and externalizing behavior	12
E	Internalizing behavior	15
F	Externalizing behavior	4
	Total	50

TABLE 6.10
Observed Percentages of Behavioral Problems Within
the Sample ($n = 150$) Compared to Expected Percentages

Broad-Band Scales TRF	Behavioral Problems		χ^2	Sign. (df = 1)
	Observed	Expected		
Total	20%	10%	18.963	.000*
Internalizing	25%	10%	39.185	.000*
Externalizing	14%	10%	2.667	.102

*χ^2 significant ($p < .01$).

frequencies of problem behavior for the SLI sample studied here differed significantly for the Total Behavior scale and Internalizing Behavior scales ($p \leq .01$; see Table 6.10).

Behavior According to Parents and Teachers. As already mentioned, the ratings provided by *both* the parents and teachers for 136 of the SLI children are available. Comparison of the CBCL and TRF ratings showed 66 children (49%) to be rated within the clinical range by the parents, teachers, or both. The parents found 41 of the 136 children to be behaviorally disturbed (30%), and the teachers found 47 of the 136 children to be behaviorally disturbed (34%). However, the ratings of the parents and teachers showed agreement on the occurrence of behavioral problems for only 22 of the 136 children (16%; see Table 6.11).

TABLE 6.11
Behavior According to CBCL and TRF ($n = 136$)

Scale	CBCL Normal	CBCL Clinically	Total
TRF normal	52%	14%	66%
TRF clinically	18%	16%	34%
Total	70%	30%	100%

Conclusions

The present study of older SLI children shows the presence of SLIs to increase the risk of problematic behavior: 49% of the SLI children between the ages of 8 and 12 years were judged as having behavior problems by their parents, teachers, or both. The problems do not stem primarily from language problems because the parents and teachers only agree on the occurrence of behavior problems for 16% of the children. Either the parents (30%) or teachers (34%) may encounter problems in their interactions with the children in question, but they do not both encounter problems with the children in every case. The lack of correspondence in the two questionnaires suggests that the behavioral problems displayed by the SLI children depend on the conversational situation and people with whom they interact, rather than simply insufficient language skill.

Both the parents and teachers reported problems on mainly the Total Behavior scale (24% and 20%, respectively) and the Internalizing Behavior scale (24% and 25%, respectively). Relatively few problems are reported with respect to the Externalizing Behavior scale.

GENERAL CONCLUSIONS AND DISCUSSION

The results of the foregoing study, together with the results of the pilot studies reported earlier, provide support for the hypothesis that the incidence of problem behavior tends to increase as SLI children get older. Objective measures of the behavior of SLI preschool children showed no differences in their profiles or the incidence of behavior problems when compared to NLA preschool children. In the group of 8- to 12-year-old SLI children, 49% were judged as having clinically significant behavior problems by their parents, teachers, or both.

The hypothesis that the development of the behavior problems is due in part to the poor quality of the social interactions and communication with others also receives affirmative support. The growth of the behavioral problems is *not* due to only the language impairment experienced by the children, but also the—often emotional—impact of the disorder on the parents of the children, teachers, and SLI children. For even young children with SLI, many of the parents perceived the childrearing task as particularly difficult. In light of the fact that not all children with SLI develop behavioral problems, it can therefore be asserted that styles of childrearing practice and educational instruction clearly influence the behavioral development of children and SLI children in particular.

The results of the four studies discussed previously show the behavioral problems demonstrated by children with a SLI—whether younger or older—to be largely internalizing. The group of young SLI children are described by their parents and teachers as more withdrawn and less enterprising than other children. The group of older SLI children score mainly within the clinical ranges on the Internalizing Behavior scales from both the CBCL and TRF. The consistency of these findings are rather surprising as children can express feelings of incompetence or frustration in any number of ways depending on their personality and temperament—by either withdrawing from contact with others or reacting in an aggressive manner (Thomas & Chess, 1980, 1982). Apparently, the impact of the language difficulties encountered by SLI children is a more powerful determinant of their behavior than their individual temperament.

ACKNOWLEDGMENTS

This research was supported by STINAFO and the Heinsius Houbolt Foundation; it is part of the research program *Communication through Hearing and Speech* in the ENT Department at the University Hospital, Groningen. The research program is also part of the Sensory Systems Group at the Groningen Graduate School for Behavioral and Cognitive Neurosciences (BCN).

REFERENCES

Achenbach, T. M. (1991). *Manual for the Child Behavior Checklist 4–18 and 1991 Profiles.* Burlington: University of Vermont Department of Psychiatry.

Achenbach, T. M. (1993). *How to use syndromes and profile types derived from the CBCL, TRF and YSR.* Burlington: University of Vermont Department of Psychiatry.

Baker, L., & Cantwell, D. P. (1987). A prospective psychiatric follow-up of children with speech/language disorders. *Journal of the American Academy of Child Adolescence Psychiatry, 26*(4), 546–553.

Beitchman, J. H., Hood, J., Rochon, J., & Peterson, M. (1989). Empirical classification of speech/language impairment in children: II. Behavioral characteristics. *Journal of the American Academy of Child Adolescence Psychiatry, 28*(1), 118–123.

Beitchman, J. H., Nair, R., Clegg, M., Patel, P. G., Ferguson, B., Pressman, E., & Smith, A. (1986). Prevalence of speech and language disorders in 5-year-old kindergarten children in the Ottawa-Carleton region. *Journal of Speech and Hearing Disorders, 51*, 98–110.

Benasich, A. A., Curtiss, S., & Tallal, P. (1993). Language, learning and behavioral disturbances in childhood: A longitudinal perspective. *Journal of the American Academy of Child Adolescence Psychiatry, 32*(3), 585–594.

Bishop, D. V. M. (1997). *Uncommon understanding. Development and disorders of language comprehension in children.* Cambridge: Psychology Press.

Bishop, D. V. M., & Mogford, K. (1989). *Language development in exceptional circumstances.* Edinburgh: Churchill Livingstone.

Bruner, J. S. (1977). Early social interaction and language acquisition. In H. R. Schaffer (Ed.), *Studies in mother–infant interaction* (pp. 271–289). New York: Academic Press.

Cantwell, D. P., & Baker, L. (1987). Prevalence and type of psychiatric disorders in three speech and language groups. *Journal of Communication Disorders, 20,* 151–160.

Conners, C. K. (1969). A teacher rating scale for use in drug studies with children. *American Journal of Psychiatry, 126,* 152–156.

Conners, C. K. (1990). *Conners' Rating Scales Manual.* North Tonawanda, NY: Multi-Health Systems.

Eleveld, J., Nakken, H., & Goorhuis-Brouwer, S. M. (1994). Taal en sociale problemen, Onderzoek naar sociaal-emotionele problemen bij specifiek taalgestoorde kinderen (Language and social problems, investigation of problem behavior in SLI children). *Tijdschrift voor Orthopedagogiek, 33,* 550–556.

Fletcher, P., & Hall, D. (1992). *Specific speech and language disorders in children: Correlates, characteristics and outcomes.* London: Whurr.

Goorhuis-Brouwer, S. M. (1988). *Gesprekspartners? Taalontwikkelingsstoornissen als pedagogisch probleem, een verkenning (Partners in communication? Language disorders as a child-rearing problem).* Utrecht: Elsevier/De Tijdstroom.

Goorhuis-Brouwer, S. M., Nakken, H., & van der Berg, H. (1996). De relatie tussen specifieke taalstoornissen, gedrag van het kind en beleving van de ouders (The relation between specific language impairment, child behavior and parental experiences). *Tijdschrift voor Orthopedagogiek, 35,* 352–360.

Hart, B., & Risley, T. R. (1999). *The social world of children learning to talk.* Baltimore: Paul Brookes.

Leonard, L. B. (1998). *Children with specific language impairment.* Cambridge, MA: MIT Press.

Reynell, J. K. (1974). *Manual for the Reynell Developmental Language Scales* (rev. ed.). Windsor, England: The NFER, Nelson Publishing Company.

Rutter, M., Graham, P., & Yule, W. (1970). *A neuropsychiatric study in childhood.* Philadelphia: Lippincott.

Schaffer, H. R. (1967). *Social development.* Oxford: Basil Blackwell.

Silva, P. A., Williams, S., & McGee, R. (1987). A longitudinal study of children with developmental language delay at age three: Later intelligence, reading and behavior problems. *Developmental Medicine and Child Neurology, 27,* 630–640.

Stark, R. E., & Tallal, P. (1981). Selection of children with specific language deficits. *Journal of Speech and Hearing Research, 46*(2), 114–122.

Swets-Gronert, F. A., & Kohnstam, G. A. (1986). *Vragenlijst Gedrag en Taalontwikkeling 2 en 3 jarigen (Questionnaire on behavior and language development in two and three year olds).* Lisse: Swets & Zeitlinger.

Tallal, P., Dukette, D., & Curtiss, S. (1989). Behavioral/emotional profiles of preschool language-impaired children. *Developmental Psychopathology, 1,* 51–67.

Thomas, A., & Chess, S. (1980). *The dynamics of psychological development.* New York: Brunner/Mazel.

Thomas, A., Chess, S., & Korn, S. J. (1982). The reality of difficult temperament. *Merrill Palmer Quarterly, 28,* 1–20.

II

TYPOLOGY

7

Speech Output Disorders

Ben Maassen
University of Nijmegen, The Netherlands

The jury is still out on whether speech output or articulation disorders form part of the diagnostic entity *specific language impairment*. According to Rapin and Allen (1987), developmental apraxia of speech (their term: *verbal dyspraxia*) forms one cluster in the classification of SLI. They seem to apply the label SLI to all children who attend language units provided they have no other major developmental problems than in the domain of verbal communication skills. In contrast, De Jong (1999) tended to reserve the label SLI for the subgroup of grammatical SLI. The grammatical sub-type of SLI is characterized by lacking or inadequate use of morphological and subject–verb agreement rules. Because of this ambiguity, and because speech disorders comprise a separate diagnostic entity, the acronym SLI is used in the sense of speech-language impairment. In the present study, the speech output of a rather heterogeneous group of children with speech-language impairment, receiving special education, is compared to children with unambiguous speech output disorders: dysartria and developmental apraxia of speech (DAS).

THEORETICAL BACKGROUND

Modeling Speech Output Processes

The speech production model that is used as a reference in the studies presented here is the model of Levelt (1989). This model comprises routines for phonological encoding and articulation, covering the processes that start with word form retrieval and find their conclusion in the production of the acoustic speech output. This part of Levelt's blueprint for the speaker was developed as a model for normal speech production, and its empirical domain consists of reaction time data in a wide variety of tasks (e.g., picture naming, lexical decision, phoneme detection) and different paradigms (e.g., priming). Although the model was not developed for pathological speech, the model may be used to help derive symptoms or symptom clusters in speech pathology. Dodd (1996), Dodd and Mc-Gormack (1996), and Ozanne (1996) developed more global stage models of speech production as a framework for the categorization of symptoms in speech pathology. These global stage models allow for the assignment of speech symptoms to a particular stage—at least that is what the models claim—without explicit description of the mechanisms operating at each stage. The Levelt model is more detailed in that it goes beyond a mere enumeration of stages and gives explicit accounts of the subprocesses. Of particular interest for the studies presented in this chapter is that the Levelt model, which can be characterized as a slots-and-fillers model, is explicit about the role of the syllable in speech. First, routines at the segmental spellout level produce a string of syllables, each spelled out in terms of syllable constituents: *onsets*, *rimes*, *nuclei*, and *codas*. The output is a labeled string of segments. Second, at the phonetic spellout level, syllable plans for strings of segments are retrieved, specifying the articulatory gestures to be executed. It is hypothesized that the normal speech production system comprises a syllabary consisting of stored patterns of frequently used phonetic plans for syllables. When executed, the result is a sequence of articulatory gestures over time.

In contrast, the models originating from speech pathology studies are much less explicit with respect to the speech production processes, but more explicit as regards the symptoms that can be observed in the different pathologies. However, the hypothesized relationships between the observed symptoms in different speech disorders and the suggested stages from which these symptoms originate according to the models remain to be established. The present study is an attempt to bridge the gap between existing models and clinical diagnoses.

Speech Output Disorders

In the studies presented next, developmental apraxia of speech (DAS) is compared to dysarthria, other articulation disorders, among which those due to phonological delay, and normal speech. There is much dispute about whether DAS exists as an identifiable syndrome—to be more precise, in a relatively pure form with specific etiological, medical, developmental, and psychological conditions. Although there is much less controversy about the speech symptoms typical for DAS, the interpretation of these symptoms in terms of the underlying disorder or underlying process they reflect is still much debated. One of the reasons that DAS has attracted so much attention in the literature is that there have always been outspoken theories or hypotheses regarding the underlying deficit. Focus has shifted from a linguistic perspective, as expressed in the term *developmental verbal dyspraxia* (DVD), to the more recent speech-motor view, as expressed in the term *developmental apraxia of speech* (DAS; Hall, Jordan, & Robin, 1993). However, in all views, there is consensus that DAS is a disorder, which, in Levelt's model, can be localized somewhere between word form retrieval and articulation. In her explanation of speech output in so-called *functional articulation disorders*, Bishop maintained that the child is "lacking the ability to convert an abstract phonological representation into a set of motor commands to the articulators" (Bishop, 1992, p. 5). Ozanne (1996) classified these disorders as developmental verbal apraxia, which comprises three subtypes: speech with inconsistent deviant errors due to a phonological planning deficit, articulatory dyspraxia due to a deficit in phonetic program assembly, and a speech motor programming disorder. In previous studies, we argued along a similar line. The only way to clear up the controversy about the diagnosis DAS is to define this disorder in line with Bishop as a deficit in phonology–motor conversion ability (Maassen, Thoonen, & Wit, 1991; Thoonen, 1998; Thoonen, Maassen, Gabreëls, & Schreuder, 1994; Thoonen, Maassen, Gabreëls, Schreuder, & de Swart, 1997). Whether this is too broad a definition and whether identifiable subtypes can be distinguished remains to be established. For the time being, we use this broad, model-oriented definition as our working definition.

How to Assess Speech Output Disorders?

In a review article on the assessment of speech output disorders, Kent, Miolo, and Bloedel (1994) pointed out that the available clinical procedures are deficient with respect to a quantitative evaluation of the severity of involvement. They argued that the measurement of intelligibility, which is the "functional common denominator of verbal behavior" (Kent, Miolo, & Bloedel, 1994, p. 81), would yield the desired quantitative estimate. The problem is that intelligibility not only depends on the quality of the speech output, but also, among other factors, on the familiarity of the listener with both the speech pathology of the speaker and with the speaker him or herself, on the linguistic and extralinguistic context, and on transient speaker variables. The solution they propose is to implement in clinical practice standardized evaluation methods that have so far only been used in research settings and also to focus on a particular output process (lexical, phonological, motoric). Five categories of procedures that each solves part of the problem can be distinguished. The first group comprises procedures that emphasize phonetic contrast analyses. Typically, the child to be tested is requested to vocalize one of the words from a series of words with minimal contrast (e.g., *tea–key, my–might, feel–fill–fall–fell*). A normal, adult listener evaluates the production by marking the word the child has articulated in a multiple-choice task. Apart from a quantitative measure of intelligibility, represented by the percentage of correctly identified words, this particular procedure yields an identification of the phonetic contrasts the child is able to articulate. The focus is on speech motor control in dysarthric patients.

The second category consists of phonological process analyses. For these analyses, a representative sample of speech is collected on the basis of which an inventory is made of normal phonological processes (typical for developmental delay) and unusual phonological processes (signaling pathology). Not so much the number of phonological processes the child employs, but rather, and more important, the type of processes used, the consistency with which they are used, and the occurrence of unusual processes will give an adequate account of intelligibility. For Dutch, the phonological process analysis by Beers (1995) has been made suitable for use in a clinical setting.

The last three categories yield a measure of degree of involvement without specific reference to a particular deficit. They comprise (a) procedures that emphasize word identification (e.g., the Communication Efficiency Ratio; Yorkston & Beukelman, 1981) to identify speakers who are intelligible only at a low speech rate; (b) the index Percentage Consonants Correct (PCC), defined as the total number of consonants correctly uttered divided by the total number of intended consonants (Shriberg & Kwiatkowski, 1982a, 1982b, 1982c); and (c) scaling methods for specific articulatory or speech qualities.

Apart from a quantitative measure of intelligibility, the first two procedures in particular yield an analytical assessment of why the speech intelligibility of a particular child is reduced—that is, in which aspects their speech output is deviant. In many cases, the latter information can serve as a starting point for the formulation of therapeutic targets. Also these evaluation procedures yield an objective description of speech symptoms, which is needed to establish the differential diagnosis of the speech disorder. However, they do not permit any conclusions regarding the underlying deficits or etiology of the speech disorder. To make these methods more suitable as diagnostic instruments, they need to be elaborated. In particular, to allow for a differential diagnosis, the validation of speech symptoms against clear cases is needed as well as a quantification of symptoms in the form of a speech profile to establish an index of severity.

To summarize, the information that one should be able to derive from an articulation test should comprise the following aspects:

1. An identification of the underlying deficits. An analysis of the cognitive architecture of the speech production mechanism in a particular child is essential to further our understanding of types of speech disorders, their etiology and developmental history, and issues such as interactions between subprocesses and comorbidity.

2. A differential diagnosis (i.e., a classification of the disorder in speech-pathological, medical, developmental, or etiological terms). Relevant information can be obtained from a comparison of the symptomatology with well-documented syndromes or clear cases.

3. Quantification of speech symptoms to assess degree of involvement. Generally, clinical reports of articulation problems are qualitative and descriptive in nature. The only quantitative information usually reported is an estimate of developmental delay (expressed in months behind chronological age). Rarely do the reports provide any quantitative indexes of the degree of phonological, articulatory, or motor involvement, or of overall intelligibility. It is exactly this quantitative information that could contribute greatly to the much-needed improvement of therapeutic guidelines especially because most children being referred for treatment are not clear cases, but exhibit a mixture or multitude of diverse symptoms.

DESIGN OF THE PRESENT STUDY

In the present study, the speech performance of carefully selected children with DAS and spastic dysarthria was compared with the performance of children with normal speech and also with that of larger groups of children with speech-language impairment (SLI). The aim of this study was to contribute to the development of an articulation test as described in the introduction. Part of the results has been published in Maassen, Thoonen, and Boers (1997).

Participants

For the selection of children with DAS and dysarthria, the following criteria were employed. The criteria for DAS were derived from Hall, Jordan, and Robin (1993) and previously used in Thoonen et al. (1994). The most important inclusion criteria for DAS were the presence of multiple articulation errors, episodes of low intelligibility, difficulty with complex sound sequences and groping, inconsistent speech output, resistance to therapy, normal hearing, normal performance IQ, and normal receptive language;

criteria for exclusion were dysarthria and/or structural problems. The criteria for dysarthria were derived from Darley, Aronson, and Brown (1975) and previously used in Wit, Maassen, Gabreëls, and Thoonen (1993). The most important criteria for dysarthria were quadriplegia due to cerebral palsy, slow speech rate, imprecise consonant production, hypernasality, and low and monotonous pitch.

Two studies were performed. In Study 1, children with DAS ages 6 to 8 were compared with age-matched children with normal language acquisition (NLA) and dysarthria. In Study 2, a larger group of slightly younger children with DAS were compared with normal children and children with SLI. The latter group of children attended a special school for the speech-and-language impaired primarily because of expressive speech and language problems. Hearing loss, mental retardation, neurological involvement, severe language comprehension disorders, and a diagnosis of DAS were used as exclusion criteria for this group. The studies were conducted a few years apart; there were slight differences in the speech material and elicitation procedure used in the two studies. The groups of children participating in each of the two studies are characterized in Table 7.1.

Particularly in Study 2, it became obvious that, following these strict selection criteria, DAS rarely occurs as an isolated disorder. Sixty-four children were referred by speech pathologists with the diagnosis DAS. By means of anamnestic information (questionnaire filled out by both teacher and parents) and a pretest (articulation test plus diadochokinetic task and word- and pseudoword repetition) evaluated by independent assessors, 28 of these children were diagnosed with suspected DAS. These children were administered an articulation test, a language comprehension test, and a neuropsychological examination. It turned out that of these 28 children, 7 children showed a delay of more than 1 standard deviation in language comprehension or intelligence, 1 child had hearing loss, 1 child

TABLE 7.1
Characteristics of Children Participating in Study 1 and Study 2

Diagnosis	Study 1		Study 2	
	n	Age	n	Age
DAS	11	6;3–7;9	18	4;11–6;10
DysA	9	6;4–10;3		
SLI			23	4;6–7;0
NLA	11	6;0–8;3	29	4;9–6;10

Note. DAS: Developmental Apraxia of Speech; DysA: (Spastic) dysarthria due to cerebral palsy; SLI: Speech Language Impairment; NLA: Normal Language Acquisition; n: number of children; Age: age range, expressed in years;months.

experienced fluency problems, and 1 child exhibited rather severe concentration problems. Consequently, of the originally referred 64 children, 18 could be classified as pure DAS (i.e., DAS without comorbidity). This is not to say that the speech production of the remaining 10 children with suspected DAS was not for a major part characterized by apraxic symptoms. However, these children did not pass the strict admission criteria for this study.

Tasks and Materials

All children were requested to produce words and pseudowords. In Study 1, the words and pseudowords were elicited by imitation (experimenter speaks the word or pseudoword and the child imitates). In Study 2, the words were first elicited by means of picture naming, supported by sentence completion, immediately followed by imitation. For standardization purposes, only the imitations were analyzed.

For the maximum performance tasks (MPTs), children were requested to imitate the monosyllabic sequences *papa..*, *tata..*, and *kaka..* and the multisyllabic sequence *patakapataka..* as fast as possible. (The quality of the vowel /a/ was not important; in fact, the vowel tended to be slightly neutralized.) After instruction and three practice trials, at least three attempts per sequence were elicited. Performance was evaluated by measuring the number of syllables per second of the fastest attempt. Because some children had difficulty with the multisyllabic sequence, the number of extra trials (after the practice trials) needed to produce a correct sequence was an additional assessment parameter (Thoonen, Maassen, Wit, Gabreëls, & Schreuder, 1996). MPTs are generally considered to yield valid data for dysarthria or more generally motor speech involvement (Netsell, 1982).

Analysis Procedure

The word and pseudoword imitations were broadly phonetically transcribed, followed by a quantitative analysis by means of the LIPP program (Oller, 1991). The advantage of transcription analysis with LIPP is that, once data have been typed in, frequency counts can be easily obtained, features can be isolated, and analyses related to context (anticipations, perseverations, transpositions) can be conducted (Thoonen et al., 1994).

The utterances from the MPTs were analyzed with the help of Kay-CSL. Onsets of all syllables were marked by interactive inspection of the acoustic signal. By means of a semi-automatic procedure (a macro within CSL), the repetition rates and standard deviations were calculated from these marks.

RESULTS

Word and Pseudoword Imitation

In Table 7.2, main error types are compared for children with dysarthria and DAS and children with normal language acquisition (NLA; Study 1). Children with DAS produced the highest error frequencies, followed by children with dysarthria and NLA. After correction for total error rate by calculating proportions, dysarthric children scored highest on distortions. In Table 7.3, consonant substitutions are divided into substitutions by place of articulation, manner of articulation, and voicing. Children with dysarthria produced relatively many voicing errors, whereas DAS children produced relatively many place substitutions.

Because the DAS diagnosis is particularly controversial, the next step in the analysis comprised a search for typical apraxic symptoms often reported in the literature. First, an in-depth comparison was made between the DAS and NLA children of Study 1. Retention percentages were calculated by dividing the number of substitutions that were correct with respect to a particular feature or feature value (but incorrect with respect to another feature or feature value) by the total number of substitutions (Thoonen et al., 1994). The results of the DAS and NLA children, presented in Table 7.4a

TABLE 7.2

Main Error Types Produced by Children With DysA and DAS as Compared With Children With Normal Speech, Expressed in Percentages Relative to the Number of Consonants in the Material (Study 1); For Each Error Type Its Proportion (Relative to the Sum of Error Types) Is Given Between Brackets

Error Type	NLA	DysA	DAS
Substitutions	11.8 (.67)	29.1 (.48)	57.2 (.58)
Omissions	3.8 (.21)	13.6 (.22)	24.3 (.24)
Distortions	2.2 (.12)	17.9 (.30)	18.2 (.18)

TABLE 7.3

Substitutions by Feature: Place of Articulation, Manner of Articulation, and Voicing as Percentages of the Total Number of Consonant Substitutions (Study 1)

Feature	DysA	DAS
Place	33%	58%
Manner	27%	43%
Voicing	60%	41%
Total	120%	132%

Note. Total percentages are higher than 100 because of multiple feature errors.

show striking similarities with respect to the feature place of articulation as well as the distinct feature values (labial, alveolar, dorsal). The slightly lower percentage of place retention of the DAS children as compared to the NLA children may be a genuine effect because a similar but larger difference was found between the SLI and DAS children of Study 2 presented in Table 7.4b. (The differences in overall percentages between Studies 1 and 2 may be the result of differences in speech material.) This needs to be further established in future research. The similarities across subject groups for manner of articulation (feature values: plosive, fricative, nasal, semivowel) and voicing (voice, voiceless) were even more striking in both studies (data not presented; see Thoonen et al., 1994).

The substitutions of Study 1 were also analyzed with respect to context. It turned out that the percentage of syntagmatic (as compared with para-

TABLE 7.4
Confusion Matrixes of Place-of-Articulation Substitutions
in Study 1 (Table 7.4a) and Study 2 (Table 7.4b)

Group					
Table 7.4a					
DAS (Study 1)					Mean
	Labial	Alveolar	Dorsal	Retention	Retention
Labial	**82**	31	16	64%	
Alveolar	36	**116**	40	60%	54%
Dorsal	17	32	**6**	11%	
NLA (Study 1)					Mean
	Labial	Alveolar	Dorsal	Retention	Retention
Labial	**43**	13	3	73%	
Alveolar	6	**28**	8	67%	59%
Dorsal	2	8	**1**	9%	
Table 7.4b					
DAS (Study 2)					Mean
	Labial	Alveolar	Dorsal	Retention	Retention
Labial	**113**	62	38	53%	
Alveolar	104	**91**	55	36%	38%
Dorsal	37	72	**22**	16%	
SLI (Study 2)					Mean
	Labial	Alveolar	Dorsal	Retention	Retention
Labial	**118**	26	19	72%	
Alveolar	32	**75**	52	47%	57%
Dorsal	10	19	**18**	38%	

Note. The tables present confusion matrixes of place-of-articulation substitutions. Only those substitutions are presented that are either correct (labial-labial, etc. on the diagonal) or incorrect (off-diagonal) with respect to place of articulation. For each particular place, dividing the correct cell by the number of targets yields a percentage of retention of that place.

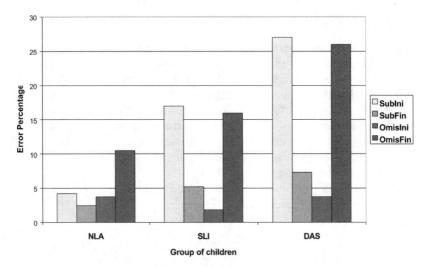

FIG. 7.1.   Error patterns across syllable-initial and syllable-final position
are similar for the two pathological groups and the control children with
normal speech.

   *SubIni, SubFin: consonant substitutions in syllable-initial position and sylla-
ble-final position, respectively; OmisIni, OmisFin: consonant omissions in syllable-initial position and syllable-final position, respectively; DAS = Developmental
Apraxia of Speech; SLI = Speech-Language Impairment; NLA = Normal Language
Acquisition.*

digmatic) substitutions was similar—not significantly different—for DAS
(64%) and NLA children (59%).

   Finally, similar distributions of substitutions and omissions over syllable-initial and syllable-final position were found across the DAS, SLI, and
NLA children of Study 2. The results are presented in Fig. 7.1. All three
groups produced more substitutions in syllable-initial position and more
omissions in syllable-final position.

Conclusions Imitation Task

In these extensive comparisons of error profiles of DAS, SLI, dysarthria,
and NLA children, we first found large quantitative differences between
groups: DAS children produced the highest error frequencies, followed
by SLI and dysarthria, and NLA children. Dysarthric children can be distinguished on the basis of the high proportion of distortions. There is a
tendency for DAS children to produce a relatively high frequency of
place-of-articulation errors. The remaining comparisons, particularly with
respect to context, syllable position, and feature value, revealed striking
similarities between groups.

Maximum Performance Tasks (MPT)

In Fig. 7.2, maximum repetition rates of DAS, dysarthria, SLI, and NLA children are presented (both Study 1 and Study 2). Overall, the children with dysarthria produced the slowest repetition rates. DAS children were similar to SLI children with respect to the monosyllabic sequences; both groups were slightly slower than NLA children. Also both the DAS and SLI children had difficulty producing the multisyllabic sequence (7 children out of 23 and 11 out of 23 being successful in these sequences, respectively). If they were able to produce this sequence, they needed more time to produce it.

Subgroups of SLI

The similarities in relative error frequencies and repetition rates between DAS and SLI children suggest similarities in the underlying deficit. Perhaps some SLI children also have speech problems of a dyspraxic nature. In an attempt to establish whether this was indeed the case, the SLI children were divided into two groups: (a) SLI children who could produce *pataka..* five

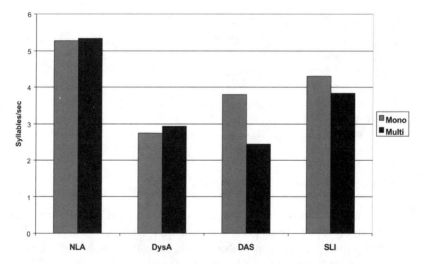

FIG. 7.2. Maximum repetition rate of monosyllabic sequences (*papa.., tata.., kaka..*) and multisyllabic sequences (*pataka..*) for the three pathological groups and the control children with normal speech. *Note:* 22 of 25 NLA children correctly produced the multisyllabic sequence, as compared with 8 of 9 dysarthric children, 7 of 23 children with DAS, and 11 of 23 children with SLI.

DysA = (spastic) dysarthria; DAS = Developmental Apraxia of Speech; SLI = Speech-Language Impairment; NLA = Normal Language Acquisition.

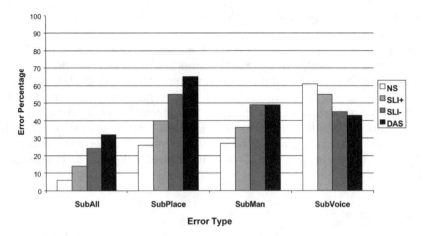

FIG. 7.3. The error profiles of children with SLI who failed on multisyllabic repetition (SLI-, $n = 12$) are more similar to the DAS profiles than the profiles of the SLI children who were successful on multisyllabic repetition (SLI+, $n = 11$).

SubAll: total percentage of substitutions in the nonword repetition task (as compared to target consonants); SubPlace: percentage of place-of-articulation substitutions (as compared to substitutions); SubMan: percentage of manner substitutions; SubVoic: percentage of voicing substitutions.

times in succession (SLI+ children: $n = 11$), and (b) SLI children who could not produce *pataka..* five times in succession (SLI– children: $n = 12$). Results (Fig. 7.3) show that the error percentages for the SLI– children—those who were not able to produce *pataka..*—showed far more similarities to the DAS profile than the error percentages produced by the SLI+ group. From these results, it can provisionally be concluded that among the SLI children about 50% exhibited clear dyspraxic characteristics.

CONCLUSIONS AND DISCUSSION

In summary, children with spastic dysarthria produced slower speech, with relatively many distortions and voicing errors. Children with developmental apraxia of speech (DAS) had difficulty producing alternating sequences of syllables and produced the highest error rates with a tendency toward a relatively high frequency of errors of place of articulation. A striking result was the similarities in the error profiles of DAS and normally speaking (NLA) children. The performance of children with speech language impairment (SLI) was in between those of the NLA and DAS groups. The division of the SLI children into two groups on the basis of their multisyllabic maximum repetition rate performance showed that the error profiles of those SLI children who were not able to produce rapid sequences of *pataka*.. showed more similarities with the profiles of the children with DAS than with those of the other group of children with SLI, who were able to produce the multisyllabic sequence.

One of the goals of this study was to devise a more sophisticated test to assess articulation, and the latter result indicates that the test procedure used in the present study provides more refined measures in that a clear delineation of the underlying processing deficit was established. The combination of poor performance on multisyllabic sequences and a high substitution rate as an index of dyspraxia, together with similarities in error profile as far as syllable structure is concerned, suggests that the underlying problem in DAS is related to speech segments or articulatory movements rather than word or syllable structures. In Levelt's model, two subprocesses can be considered as the underlying deficit in DAS. The first is the subprocess segmental spellout, in which phonemes are inserted into a syllabic slot. A deficit in this subprocess might be characteristic of the type of children who have problems with generating the phonological plan or template—a group termed the *inconsistent deviant* by Ozanne (1996). The hypothesized deficits for this subprocess are: (a) an inability to assemble the plan, (b) the resulting template is incorrect or underspecified, (c) the template cannot be accessed, or (d) the structure of the template is influenced by the linguistic load.

The second subprocess is phonetic spellout, in which syllables are transformed into speech movements. A deficit would lead to articulatory dyspraxia (Ozanne, 1996) due to the inability to assemble the phonetic program or due to an incorrect or underspecified program. Typical symptoms are groping behavior, different performance on voluntary versus involuntary tasks, and inconsistency. It is not yet clear whether the present finding that children with DAS produce relatively many place of articulation errors as compared with manner of articulation and voicing errors helps distinguish between the two types of deficiency. Currently, a project is carried out, in which the role of the syllabary in the development and persistence of DAS is studied by means of acoustic analyses with the specific aim to identify the phonetic symptoms of the disorder. Preliminary results indicate that the speech output of children with DAS show different and more variable coarticulation patterns consisting of decreased intrasyllabic coarticulation and increased intersyllabic coarticulation as compared with the normal speech of 5-year-olds (Boers, Maassen, & van der Meulen, 1998; Nijland, Maassen, & van der Meulen, 1999).

As far as the second research question, that of the differential diagnosis, is concerned, clear differences in the speech profiles of children with dysarthria and DAS were found. Children with dysarthria produced a relatively high number of distortion errors and errors of voicing, whereas children with DAS not only had difficulty producing alternating sequences of syllables, they also produced the highest error rates with relatively many errors of place of articulation. In a series of studies, Shriberg, Aram, and Kwiatkowski (1997a, 1997b, 1997c) tried to determine a diagnostic marker for DAS. Conversational data indicate that a deficit in phrasal stress was the only linguistic variable that statistically differentiated half of the children with suspected DAS—as Shriberg et al. called this speech disorder—from age-matched children with speech delays of unknown origin. They concluded that, on the basis of inappropriate stress, a particular subtype of DAS can be identified. Furthermore, no differences with respect to other error targets or error types could be found between children with suspected DAS exhibiting inappropriate stress as compared with children with suspected DAS who used appropriate stress or children with speech-language delays. In our study, we did find a particular combination of features that might indicate DAS—namely, poor performance on the multisyllabic repetition task combined with a high proportion of place-of-articulation substitutions. It is not to be expected that pathological groups can be identified on the basis of single measures alone, and therefore further analyses are needed to find specific error profiles.

As Thoonen (1998) concluded on the basis of a series of studies involving children with DAS, in clinical practice, the typical speech characteristics of DAS are only rarely found in isolation. First, there is the issue of *comorbidity*. Most children with dyspraxic speech characteristics also have other deficiencies in their speech and language development, possibly combined with cognitive and motoric problems. Furthermore, there is the issue of *diagnostic entity*. There is still no consensus for which group of speech disordered children the term DAS must be reserved. Should the diagnosis of DAS be restricted to children having pure symptoms (i.e., with a high degree of involvement but without comorbidity)? Can other children with speech and language disorders also be said to be suffering from DAS to a certain extent? Thoonen took the latter standpoint. Apart from the 1 to 2 per 1,000 children with pure DAS, there are many other children who have dyspraxic involvement, show dyspraxic speech characteristics, and, during a particular stage in their speech and language development, will profit from a therapeutic approach based on remediation of dyspraxia. In clinical practice, most children with articulation disorders show a mixture of problems. Assessing the degree of involvement of dysarthria, apraxia, or delay yields guidelines for an individualized, goal-directed speech therapy program. The assessment procedures presented in this chapter contribute to the establishment of such a quantitative speech profile.

REFERENCES

Beers, M. (1995). *The phonology of normally developing and language-impaired children*. Unpublished doctoral dissertation, University of Amsterdam, The Netherlands.

Bishop, D. V. M. (1992). The underlying nature of specific language impairment. *Journal of Child Psychology and Psychiatry, 33*, 3–66.

Boers, I., Maassen, B., & van der Meulen, S. (1998). Phonological encoding processes in children with developmental apraxia of speech. In W. Ziegler & K. Deger (Eds.), *Clinical phonetics and linguistics* (pp. 131–138). London: Whurr.

Darley, F. L., Aronson, A. E., & Brown, J. R. (1975). *Motor speech disorders*. Philadelphia/London/Toronto: W.B. Saunders.

Dodd, B. (1996). Children with speech disorders. In B. Dodd (Ed.), *Differential diagnosis & treatment of children with speech disorders* (pp. 1–20). London: Whurr.

Dodd, B., & McGormack, P. (1996). A model of speech processing for differential diagnosis of phonological disorders. In B. Dodd (Ed.), *Differential diagnosis & treatment of children with speech disorders* (pp. 65–90). London: Whurr.

Hall, P. K., Jordan, L. S., & Robin, D. A. (1993). *Developmental apraxia of speech*. Austin, TX: Pro-ed.

De Jong, J. (1999). *Specific language impairment in Dutch: Inflectional morphology and argument structure*. Unpublished doctoral dissertation, University of Groningen.

Kent, R. D., Miolo, G., & Bloedel, S. (1994). The intelligibility of children's speech: A review of evaluation procedures. *American Journal of Speech-Language Pathology, 3*(2), 81–95.

Levelt, W. J. M. (1989). *Speaking: From intention to articulation*. Cambridge, MA: Bradford Books/MIT Press.

Maassen, B., Thoonen, G., & Boers, I. (1997). Quantitative assessment of dysarthria and developmental apraxia of speech. In W. Hulstijn, H. F. M. Peters, & P. H. H. M. van Lieshout (Eds.), *Speech production: Motor control, brain research and fluency disorders* (pp. 611–620). Amsterdam: Elsevier Science.

Maassen, B., Thoonen, G., & Wit, J. (1991). Toward assessment of articulo-motoric processing capacities in children. In H. F. M. Peters, W. Hulstijn, & C. W. Starkweather (Eds.), *Speech motor control and stuttering* (pp. 461–469). Amsterdam: Excerpta Medica.

Netsell, R. (1982). Speech motor control and selected neurologic disorders. In S. Grillner et al. (Eds.), *Speech motor control* (pp. 247–261). New York: Pergamon.

Nijland, L., Maassen, B., & van der Meulen, Sj. (1999, August 1–7). Use of syllables by children with developmental apraxia of speech. *Proceedings of the 14th International Congress of Phonetic Sciences*, San Francisco, CA.

Oller, D. K. (1991). *Logical international phonetics program V 1.40 (LIPP)*. Miami, FL: Intelligent Hearing Systems.

Ozanne, A. (1996). The search for developmental verbal dyspraxia. In B. Dodd (Ed.), *Differential diagnosis & treatment of children with speech disorders* (pp. 91–110). London: Whurr.

Rapin, I., & Allen, D. A. (1987). Developmental dysphasia and autism in preschool children: Characteristics and subtypes. In J. Martin, P. Fletcher, P. Grunwell, & D. Haall (Eds.), *Proceedings of the First International Symposium on Specific Speech and Language Disorders in Children* (pp. 20–35). London: AFASIC.

Shriberg, L. D., Aram, D. M., & Kwiatkowski, J. (1997a). Developmental apraxia of speech: I. Descriptive and theoretical perspectives. *Journal of Speech and Hearing Research, 40*, 273–285.

Shriberg, L. D., Aram, D. M., & Kwiatkowski, J. (1997b). Developmental apraxia of speech: II. Toward a diagnostic marker. *Journal of Speech and Hearing Research, 40*, 286–312.

Shriberg, L. D., Aram, D. M., & Kwiatkowski, J. (1997c). Developmental apraxia of speech: III. A subtype marked by inappropriate stress. *Journal of Speech and Hearing Research, 40,* 313–337.

Shriberg, L. D., & Kwiatkowski, J. (1982a). Phonogical disorders: I. A diagnostic classification system. *Journal of Speech, and Hearing Disorders, 47,* 226–241.

Shriberg, L. D., & Kwiatkowski, J. (1982b). Phonogical disorders: II. A conceptual framework for management. *Journal of Speech, and Hearing Disorders, 47,* 242–256.

Shriberg, L. D., & Kwiatkowski, J. (1982c). Phonogical disorders: III. A procedure for assessing severity of involvement. *Journal of Speech, and Hearing Disorders, 47,* 256–270.

Thoonen, G. (1998). *Developmental apraxia of speech in children. Assessment of speech characteristics.* Unpublished master's thesis, University of Nijmegen.

Thoonen, G., Maassen, B., Gabreëls, F., & Schreuder, R. (1994). Feature analysis of singleton consonant errors in developmental verbal dyspraxia (DVD). *Journal of Speech and Hearing Research, 37,* 1424–1440.

Thoonen, G., Maassen, B., Gabreëls, F., Schreuder, R., & de Swart, B. (1997). Towards a standardised assessment procedure for developmental apraxia of speech. *European Journal of Disorders of Communication, 32,* 37–60.

Thoonen, G., Maassen, B., Wit, J., Gabreëls, F., & Schreuder, R. (1996). The integrated use of maximum performance tasks in differential diagnostic evaluations among children with motor speech disorders. *Clinical Linguistics & Phonetics, 10,* 311–336.

Wit, J., Maassen, B., Gabreëls, G., & Thoonen, G. (1993). Maximum performance tests in children with developmental spastic dysarthria. *Journal of Speech and Hearing Research, 36,* 452–460.

Yorkston, K. M., & Beukelman, D. R. (1981). Communication efficiency of dysarthric speakers as measured by sentence intelligibility and speaking rate. *Journal of Speech and Hearing Disorders, 46,* 296–301.

8

Central Auditory Processing

Jack Katz
University of Kansas Medical Center

Kim Tillery
State University College of New York at Fredonia

Central auditory processing (CAP) tends to be a confusing topic for many professionals and for the public. In part, people have difficulty understanding what CAP is because CAP disorder (CAPD) (a) can express itself in many ways, (b) is associated with many disorders, and (c) is evaluated by a variety of tests that often show little resemblance to one another. This chapter's purpose is to clarify what CAP is and to show how to divide the problem into its component parts. In this way, CAP is not only more understandable, but also quite predictable, and this knowledge gives us the ability to better remediate the auditory and related difficulties. When we take into account the large proportion of the central nervous system (CNS) devoted to auditory and auditory-related functions, it not surprising that so many academic and communicative problems are associated with CAPD (see also Leppänen et al., chap. 4, this volume).

In 1994, the American Speech-Language and Hearing Association (ASHA) convened a task force to develop a definition of CAPD. The report published in 1996 indicated that CAPD consists of preconscious events resulting in the inability to discriminate auditory patterns, localize sound, and understand speech with competing or degraded stimuli.

We define CAP as *what we do with what we hear*. Thus, CAPD is not a hearing problem (although it often resembles one), but rather what the CNS does to make what we hear most valuable and efficient. Hearing loss is closely associated with the peripheral auditory system (e.g., the middle ear and cochlea), whereas CAPD is primarily associated with the central auditory nervous system (CANS).

CAPD is frequently thought of as a listening disorder because individuals who may have entirely normal hearing are not able to use what they hear effectively. This may be because the person misunderstands or is confused by what was heard, missed the auditory information because of competing background noise, and/or forgets what was said. Just as in the case of a hearing loss, the individual is generally aided by watching the speaker's face and also by clear speech that is spoken more slowly. These and other characteristics of CAPD are quite comprehendible when we study the components of the disorder.

BREADTH OF THE PROBLEM

Critics of CAPD tried to defame our activities by suggesting that we see CAPD every place we look. Unfortunately, their argument has some merit. It is indeed difficult to look far without encountering CAPD and with good reason.

CAP is based on the functions of the auditory brain and brainstem. These encompass pathways, nuclei, and centers from the lower pons of the brainstem and the cerebellar vermis to major portions of the cerebrum. A significant problem—whether of genetic origin (including chemical or hormonal imbalance), deprivation (e.g., otitis media), or other adventitious causes (e.g., anoxia, lead poisoning, skull trauma)—could affect the development or function of this intricate system. Each portion of the system serves an important purpose and therefore would require, at a minimum, compensations to fill the breach. Although compensations are vital for most of us with CAPD, we should recognize that they are generally not as good as the typical approach and take more time and effort.

There are no definitive population statistics on the incidence of CAPD. General estimates of CAPD are found to vary between 5% and 10% of school children. However, based on a large sample of learning disabled children seen, Katz estimated a prevalence of about 20% in a middle-class school system 30 years ago when testing was less refined than today and the demands on children were far less. Kindergarten children in the United States are now taught to read and spell, whereas when the first author was in school reading and spelling were taught in the second grade. Thus, the current literacy demands on children are greater, and so they are referred for special care at an earlier age than in previous years. Children from families in low socioeconomic conditions have been found to display more CAP difficulties than in middle-class families. Therefore, prevalence of CAP needs to take into account the various regions and populations.

With such a high incidence of CAPD in the general population, what is the likelihood that the incidence is any less among individuals with mental retardation, attention deficit hyperactivity disorder (ADHD), cerebral palsy, autism, aphasia, or other CNS conditions? Other groups that are at risk for CAPD include schizophrenic (Green & Kotenko, 1980) and fragile-X cases, as well as incarcerated youth (Katz, Fanning, & Singer, 1988).

For each group there appears to be good reasons why they might have CAPD (e.g., some type of brain involvement, environmental factors, high incidence of otitis media), whereas other groups behave as if they have CAPD and are benefited by therapy directed toward this type of auditory problem. For example, we have used CAP techniques, most successfully, with hearing-impaired individuals, those who have cochlear implants, and individuals who have tenacious foreign dialect problems. These techniques are discussed in the section on therapeutic intervention.

CAP TEST BATTERY

In the past 30 years, audiologists have used a variety of tests to assess CAP performance. The audiologist has an important role in determining the types of auditory dysfunction based on academic behavior and test performance. Therefore, generally three CAP tests are administered, which provide a great deal of detailed and clinically useful information, affording the clinician the opportunity to recommend appropriate treatment.

In addition to behavioral tests, electrophysiological measures may be recommended (Jerger & Musiek, 2000). Because of the lack of norms for CAP cases using electrophysiological measures and the added time and expense, without adding necessary information for typical CAP evaluations, they are not included in this discussion.

Staggered Spondaic Word (SSW) Test

The SSW, a dichotic test, contains items that are made up of two spondaic (equal stressed) words with a staggered onset presented at 50 dB above threshold for each ear. The last syllable of the first spondee and the first syllable of the second spondee are presented simultaneously in opposite ears. The remaining two monosyllabic words are presented in isolation to opposite ears. The individual must repeat the words heard in each ear. Test scores are compared to age-appropriate norms (Katz, 1998). This 40-item test is scored for the number of errors in each listening condition: right noncompeting, right competing, left competing, and left noncompeting. Below-normal scores may indicate dysfunctions in selective listening, rapid decoding, binaural integration, and/or sequencing (Katz & Smith, 1991).

An important element that aids in understanding the individual's struggle on this test is to record qualitative findings. These consist of delays, quick responses, repetition of the carrier phrase, combining or repeating previously heard information, and difficulty in proficiently saying the response. Other signs that show aberrant behavior on the SSW test include reversals, order effects, ear effects, and Type A patterns. These important indicators provide considerable support for the CAP categories that are impaired.

Phonemic Synthesis (PS) Test

The PS test (Katz & Harmon, 1981) assesses a sound blending skill. The child must recognize the individual sounds presented one at a time, put them together, and respond with the blended monosyllabic word (e.g., *sh* and *e* = *she*). The diotic presentation of the PS is 50 dB above threshold for each ear. Test norms are available by age or grade level. Below normal scores may indicate difficulty in speech-sound discrimination, memory, and/or blending, as well as sequencing ability (Katz & Smith, 1991). For preschool children, there is a PS Picture (PS-P) test (Katz & Harmon-Fletcher, 1993) that may be administered. As in the case of the PS test, it provides both quantitative and qualitative information for this underserved population.

Speech-in-Noise Test

The Speech-in-Noise test is a monotic procedure in which 25 single-syllable recorded words are presented at a level of 40 dB above threshold, with speech-spectrum noise presented 5 dB below the level of the speech for each ear. The purpose of this test is to examine the person's ability to process speech in the presence of noise. A difference score is computed by subtracting the noise score from a standard word-recognition score in quiet. Comparisons are made to age norms, but in general those whose noise scores fall more than 20% below the quiet score are usually found to have a speech-in-noise problem.

Disorders Associated with CAPD

The study of CAP began in the 1960s when professionals finally realized the presence and importance of learning disabilities (Kass & Myklebust, 1969). Because sensory disorders were specifically excluded from the definition, perceptual and integration disorders were studied (Katz & Illmer,

1972). Since that time, children with learning problems have been the focus of CAP diagnosis and management.

The most common academic difficulty associated with CAP is reading. However, poor spelling and difficulty in foreign language learning are also common struggles. General problems in the classroom associated with CAPD involve not following directions (in some cases, the directions are misunderstood; in other situations, simply forgotten or not carried out in the proper order), difficulty understanding in noise, and the child may be easily distracted.

Those who are speech-language impaired are also high risk for CAPD. These individuals generally have articulation problems. In an early study, it was noted that /r/ and /l/ were common difficulties and intradental /s/ was *not* associated with a phonemic type of CAPD. Receptive and expressive language difficulties have also been linked to CAP (Katz, 1983). When the CAP problems are addressed, it was often found that CAP and learning as well as communicative difficulties improve.

In recent years, the relationship between CAPD and attention deficit hyperactivity disorder (ADHD) has been questioned due to the similar behaviors seen in these two disorders (Keller, 1992; Moss & Sheiffele, 1994). Symptoms of inattention, distractibility, poor listening skills, and excessive activity occur quite frequently among children in both these disorders. Child psychologists and other mental health professionals must bear in mind that behaviors seen as *hyper* may not be hyperactivity. Speech pathologists and audiologists must be aware that *poor listening* may not be CAPD, and proper differential diagnosis may only occur when these professionals work together (Keller, 1998).

When a child is referred to the clinic for a CAP evaluation and exhibits a profile suggesting an attention deficit, our testing must accommodate the child's poor attentive ability and hyperactivity. The CAP test battery should be administered in a manner that controls for fatigue, attention, and the child's ADHD behaviors (Tillery, 1998). In the United States, children with ADHD receive a multimodal treatment approach: counseling and tutorial services, behavior modification, and the prescription of a CNS stimulant medication.

For the past 15 years, there has been controversy as to the effects of CNS stimulant medication on auditory processing abilities of those with ADHD. The 1996 ASHA consensus statement on CAPD encouraged research in this area: What are the effects of a CNS stimulant medication on auditory processing abilities? Tillery, Katz, and Keller (2000) found no effect on the auditory processing abilities of 32 children diagnosed with both ADHD and CAPD. This was the first double-blind, placebo-controlled study that investigated the effects of a commonly prescribed CNS stimulant in the United States, methylphenidate (Ritalin[TM]), on auditory processing test performance of the three CAP tests discussed in our test battery (SSW, PS, and Speech-in-Noise). However, test performance on the Auditory Continuous Performance Test was found to significantly improve in the medicated condition versus the placebo condition (p = .0004). Therefore, children with ADHD who benefit from medication should receive the CAP test battery while medicated.

Our study also found that at least 50% of children with ADHD also have CAPD, particularly in the TFM and Organization (ORG) categories. This was not surprising because of the many behavioral similarities of these CAP categories and those seen in ADHD. For example, those with ORG CAPD and those with ADHD tend to be disorganized and manifest more reversals than normal (Tillery, 1999). Obviously the advent of the CAP categories allow us to better provide remedial services to those with both ADHD and CAPD.

Besides those with ADHD, the auditory processing abilities of the mentally challenged also deserve attention. Hadaway (1969) studied central auditory disorder in a residential facility for mentally retarded adults. Although there was a significant correlation between IQ and SSW test results (r = 0.37), it accounted for only a small portion of the variance. Mean word recognition scores were not significantly depressed, but not surprisingly SSW performance was generally very poor. What is of great importance is that a small number of cases among those with moderate and severe mental retardation had essentially normal SSW scores. Thus, it appears that the SSW test (and likely other CAP tests—e.g., speech-in-noise), which simply requires an echo response, does not exceed the cognitive abilities of the group despite greatly impaired language functions. Further evidence that the results are a reflection of central auditory disorder and not intellect or language abilities is the pattern of errors seen on the test. SSW results for two residents are shown in Fig. 8.1. It is obvious that the patterns are completely different, with the right-competing condition being severely affected in one case (60 IQ) and the other with the poorest condition in the left-competing condition. If cognition or language vocabulary were important factors, a lack of response or pretty much a flat (and very poor) response across the four conditions would have been found. Support for the presence of CAPD in many individuals with low IQs (30s–60s) was when they were given CAP therapy we found considerable improvement in speech, communication abilities, and reading.

CAP CATEGORY SYSTEM

This category system is based on information from patients with CNS lesions, which helped us understand the relationship of damage to regions of the brain and the signs found on a central auditory test. The Staggered

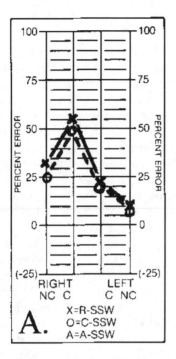

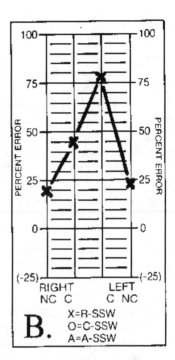

FIG. 8.1. SSW test results for two residents of an institution for the mentally retarded (Hadaway, 1969). (A) Results for a 26-year-old man with a 60 IQ. (B) Results for a 35-year-old woman with a 44 IQ. The data are shown for percent of error, both Raw (X) and Corrected scores (correction reduces the Raw score because of word recognition errors). Subject B had no correction because word recognition was 100% in each ear. The test results, even in cases with mental retardation, can indicate the types of CAPD the person has. The SSW results are *not* consistent with insufficient cognitive or language functions because the pattern of errors are so specific and not simply random errors or random responses.

Spondaic Word (SSW) test is a dichotic (true binaural) procedure developed to identify lesions of the brain and brainstem (Katz, 1962). The SSW has been used to gather data on a great many patients with localized CNS and peripheral hearing disorders. Over a period of 20 years, a map of the brain's vital auditory areas was constructed. This included most of the temporal and frontal lobes as well as parts of the parietal and a small section of the occipital lobe. In addition, auditory regions were noted in the brainstem and cerebellum. Not surprisingly, many areas associated with audition, speech-language, and learning were found not only to be associated with poor SSW performance, but, more important, different test signs were found for different regions of the brain. This provided the underlying assumptions of the category system (Katz & Smith, 1991).

Decoding (DEC) Category

A breakdown of the auditory message at the phonemic level is the basis of
the most common category of CAPD—decoding. Besides discrimination
errors, poor decoding ability is also manifested by difficulty in manipulating sounds, resulting in poor ability to blend sounds together. Such errors
may reflect the child's faulty mental concepts of the sounds, resulting in
poor reading, spelling, and word finding abilities and difficulty in understanding accurately what is said. A decoding sign is significant errors on
the right-competing measure of the SSW test associated with the phonemic area of the left posterior temporal region (Katz, 1992). This area is responsible for receptive language functions, thus giving rise to the poor receptive language skills commonly associated with clients who are poor
decoders. The SSW signs used initially to establish the DEC category were
those that identified the posterior temporal region—more specifically,
area 22 of Brodmann. A small portion of the parietal lobe adjacent to this
also seems to be associated with auditory decoding. Luria (1966) considered the posterior temporal area to be the phonemic region. Indeed the
majority of skills listed in Table 8.1 are associated with limited phonemic
or temporal integration abilities. It is also likely that most of the functions
ascribed to phonological awareness involve this same region. Baru and
Karaseva (1972) pointed out that lesions in this region are associated with
temporal resolution difficulties. That is, much longer signals are required
when there is damage to this region, even when the signals are simple
puretones. Recent studies (e.g., Tallal et al., 1996) make clear that such difficulties in the processing of brief, rapidly changing auditory information
can indeed be reduced by implementing an intervention program in
which acoustic stimuli are lengthened and intensified (for a further discussion of this hypothesis, see Verhoeven & Segers, chap. 17, this volume).

Tolerance-Fading Memory (TFM) Category

It was the signs of frontal and anterior temporal involvement that developed into the second most common type of CAPD—the TFM category. A
small region of the parietal lobe (postcentral gyrus) may also be associated
with TFM. Prior to this research, we did not appreciate the close relationship between short-term memory limitations and speech-in-noise difficulty. That is, the ability to listen in noise does not seem to incorporate
similar functions as those needed for short-term memory. However, it
soon became apparent that these two functions are closely related.

This association is perhaps best understood anatomically because both
are considered primarily anterior cerebral skills. For example, we know
that the hippocampus (a vital memory center) is in the anterior temporal

TABLE 8.1
The Auditory Problems and the Functional Characteristics That Are Associated
With the Four CAP Categories (Katz & Smith, 1991; Katz, 1992)

CAP Category	Underlying Auditory Problem	Associated Academic and Communicative Problems
Decoding (DEC)	Not able to quickly and accurately analyze speech. Often associated with poor processing at the phonemic level and auditory confusions when teacher gives instructions.	Difficulties in phonics, oral reading accuracy, spelling, speech articulation (especially /r/ and /l/), and receptive language.
Tolerance-Fading Memory (TFM)	A combination of two factors, difficulty understanding under moderately noisy conditions and also poor short-term memory.	Difficulties with reading comprehension, expressive language (generally both oral and written), and poor handwriting.
Integration (INT)	Inability to combine knowledge, generally associated with bridging the right and left hemispheres easily/effectively.	This is associated with the most severe learning problems. Reading and spelling are the paramount difficulties. Generally, characteristics of very poor DEC and/or very poor TFM are seen in these cases. Often writing ability is profoundly affected. Some individuals have exceedingly long delays in responding.
Organization (ORG)	Difficulty maintaining proper sequence and organizing oneself. This requires considerable effort to monitor everyday activities and thus reduces one's capacity to handle other important functions.	This problem is not strongly associated with any specific learning problem, but its presence makes any other CAPD much more difficult to deal with and compensate for. Spelling reversals and difficulty in delivering an organized argument are thought to be associated problems. It might also have a place in explaining aspects of cluttering.

region and other memory functions reside in the frontal lobes. However, significant speech-in-noise (cocktail party effect) problems are also associated with the anterior temporal region (Efron et al., 1983). Our data also indicate that speech-in-noise is connected with the anterior temporal and frontal regions. Thus, if one of these skills is affected, there is a good chance that nearby regions will be involved as well.

When studying those with relatively pure TFM problems, we were not surprised that they tended to have quick responses on the SSW and PS tests, but it was not at all expected that reading comprehension would be linked to TFM. In retrospect, this makes good sense. The task used to measure reading comprehension is to have the child read a paragraph and then relate the contents or answer questions about what was just read. Clearly, the element of short-term memory plays an important role in this task. Although pure TFM cases understand the individual spoken sounds and words when reading, they have great difficulty in retaining the information, resulting in poor reading comprehension.

An individual who exhibits a TFM problem will have difficulty remembering lengthy statements or multistep commands. For instance, the teacher may state, "Take out your math book and turn to page ten. Do problems 1–5, then on page 12 do problems 1–8." In such a case, the child with TFM will forget the initial directions. To cope with this auditory memory difficulty, the same child may respond quickly or even answer before the question is completed. Quicker than normal responses assist in reducing the memory task, but sometimes result in errors at the ends of SSW items. Other TFM signs include some that are not strictly auditory—for example, tongue twisters (having difficulty saying things other than due to an articulation problem—e.g., *chee chain* for *key chain* or saying *b-boy*) and poor handwriting are not listening problems, but are associated anatomically with TFM: the premotor (motor planning region) of the frontal lobes.

Besides the poor auditory memory, poor speech-in-noise ability is also characteristic of a TFM problem. Children with speech-in-noise problems have great difficulty understanding the auditory message in the presence of background noise because they cannot ignore the competing noise. They appear just as attentive to the background noise as to the primary speech message.

To understand why poor auditory memory and speech-in-noise abilities are usually seen together, consider the involved anatomical regions. Broca's area (inferior frontal region) is associated with expressive language, and both motor programming of articulatory movements and writing functions are regulated by the premotor area of the frontal lobes. These functions are in close proximity to speech-in-noise functions (Efron et al., 1983).

Organization Category

Although Decoding and TFM types of CAPD are seen in isolation or with each other, the Organization category is not usually seen by itself. The main identifying characteristic of an Organization CAP category is significant reversals on the SSW, Phonemic Synthesis, or any other tests in which corrupted sequencing is noted. Usually, this is a person who has difficulty with sequential information and is disorganized at home or in school. It has been suggested that the pre- and postcentral gyri and anterior temporal areas are responsible for these auditory behaviors (Katz, 1992; Luria, 1966).

These individuals when free of other CAPDs have relatively little associated academic or communication difficulties. However, sequencing is critical in copying numbers, spelling, typing, as well as writing a composition or relating a story. Although the problem is a subtle one, the efforts one uses to monitor this difficulty are often great. Because these errors can happen at any time, the individual must expand considerable mental resources to be sure they do not reverse and then also monitor their output (written or oral) to be sure it was delivered correctly. Thus, when it occurs in combination with DEC or TFM, it reduces one's capacity for compensating for other deficits.

Integration

This fourth category of CAP—Integration—is less well understood than TFM or DEC. These individuals often have difficulty integrating auditory and visual information and require a long delay to provide the correct response. The test sign seen in this group is the Type A pattern on the SSW (showing a specific relationship in the pattern of errors and usually an error peak in left competing condition). This sign is associated with poor interhemispheric function, resulting in several types of Integration difficulty (Katz & Brandner, 2002). These types generally differ in the constellation of CAP test failures and may be associated with posterior versus anterior corpus callosum malfunctions (Katz, Avellanosa, & Aguilar-Markulis, 1980).

The posterior corpus callosum region is associated with auditory, visual skills, and auditory–visual integration as well as Integration plus DEC. Because reading is heavily dependent on both vision and audition, as well as integrating these functions, the connection of the Type A with severe reading–spelling difficulties is logical. The posterior corpus callosum also transports phonemic decoding information. Thus, it is not surprising that, in those with posterior corpus callosum dysfunction, poor phonemic decoding is almost always present.

Involvement of the anterior corpus callosum generally combines INT and the TFM type of CAPD, because this region is in close proximity to the frontal cortical region deep and just above the anterior temporal lobe. The characteristics of these Integration cases are Type A pattern on the SSW and speech-in-noise and memory difficulty, similar to the TFM cases.

Integration and Decoding. Classic characteristics of Integration and Decoding difficulties include poor phonemic awareness, severe reading–spelling problems, and (extraordinarily) poor handwriting, which are all

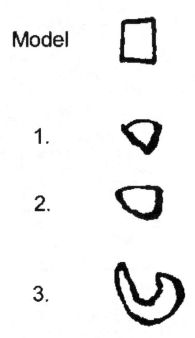

FIG. 8.2. Drawing sample for a 7-year-old girl who was classified as having Integration and Decoding CAPD. She was given a square as a model (at the top) and asked to copy it below. She was not satisfied with her first attempt (#1) and tried again (#2). The third attempt clearly showed that she was not able to perceive normally and/or represent what she saw in a reasonably accurate manner (#3).

related to poor auditory-visual integration, decoding, or visual perceptual difficulties. Test scores in phonemic synthesis are depressed, similar to the poor decoder, but generally more severe, with qualitative struggles such as quiet rehearsals and nonfused and extreme delays in responding. However, unlike the poor decoder, this group may have normal speech-in-noise ability and have their major discrepancy in the left competing condition of the SSW. Other behaviors noted in this group include difficulty reproducing certain geometric forms (see Fig. 8.2) and better cursive writing than printing.

Integration and TFM.   Individuals in this Integration group tend to resemble the behaviors of TFM group and usually have less difficulty in academics than the group with DEC problems. Common behaviors in this group include poor speech-in-noise ability, weak short-term memory characteristics, and may appear to be malingering on audiometric tests because they respond better to fainter speech than tonal stimuli (Katz, 1992; Tillery, 1998).

AN ILLUSTRATIVE CASE

Jaclyn, a 10-year-old, 5th-grade girl was referred for a CAP evaluation because of her weakness in short-term memory and phonics as reported by her remedial reading teachers. Although Jaclyn has normal intelligence, her achievement in reading, spelling, and math are only at the 3rd-grade level despite remedial services. She has difficulty in oral reading, reading comprehension, spelling, and math. She struggles learning to pronounce long words, responds slowly to questions, does not like loud music or sounds, is easily distracted, and displays poor organizational skills. Her medical history includes chronic otitis media starting at 4 months of age and continuing to 3 months before the CAP evaluation. Jaclyn's mother reports that she herself had learning difficulties when she was a child.

Jaclyn was extremely pleasant, cooperative, and polite. Testing indicated normal hearing and middle ear pressure, as well as normal middle ear reflexes to loud sounds. Thus, she has sufficient hearing function to perform normally on the CAP battery. Three CAP tests from the Central Test Battery-CD (Katz, 1998) were administered to Jaclyn: SSW, Phonemic Synthesis, and speech-in-noise tests.

Table 8.2 shows the test results and age-based norms. Jaclyn's test results reveal that she has both DEC and TFM characteristics. Of the 11 positive signs on the battery, 7 were DEC, 3 TFM, and 1 simply an indication of CAPD, not specific to a category. These results support our informal assessment that DEC was the primary category of dysfunction (although initially based on the schools concern, TFM appeared to be their major consideration).

The only potential area of CAP difficulty mentioned by Jaclyn's parents and teachers that was not supported by our tests was the reported organization problem. This may be because the SSW and PS tests missed picking up reversals or perhaps the disorganization does not have an auditory basis. It should be noted that DEC and TFM are commonly seen together because they are adjacent regions in the brain. However, when a person has both characteristics, the problem is more than the sum of the two parts be-

TABLE 8.2
Test Results and Age-Based Norms

	SSW	RC	LC	LNC	Tot	Ord	X	TTW	PS	Quant	NF	SN	R-dif	L-dif
Jaclyn		9	11	3	24	−4	4	3		16	2		24	24
Norm		2	5	1	10	−2	0	1		21	0		21	22

RC = right competing, LC = left competing, LNC = left noncompeting, Tot = total, Ord = order effect, X = delay, TTW = tongue twister, Quant = quantitative, NF = nonfused, R-dif = right difference score, L-dif = left difference score.

cause they interact negatively on one another. Poor decoders need more time to compensate for their problem. Unfortunately, those with TFM have below-normal memory spans and therefore cannot provide the added time needed. If they respond quickly and take a chance without fully understanding what was heard, they will have a high percentage of errors. If they wait to better process the speech (as Jaclyn generally does), it increases the likelihood that she will forget the message altogether. This is why Jaclyn's teachers are so concerned about her memory because it looks worse than it actually is as a result of the decoding difficulty.

The following recommendations were made (see specific procedures in the therapy section of this chapter):

1. Decoding therapy to improve her understanding of speech sounds. This should aid her in following lectures and instructions, as well as the ability to sound out words (with additional assistance from the reading specialist).

2. Speech-in-noise desensitization should aid her in two ways: She should become more tolerant of loud sounds and understand speech in the presence of background noise.

3. Memory work should address both rote skills and teaching Jaclyn to use visualization and chunking to assist with her weak memory ability.

4. Ordinarily an auditory trainer is not our standard recommendation. However, in this case, Jaclyn has two significant problems that are more than the sum of the parts, in which each problem will benefit from the use of this device. However, the deciding factors were that Jaclyn's academic class instruction is a large traditional class and she is a cooperative and motivated child (and not yet a teenager), so that she is more likely to take advantage of the benefits that the auditory trainer offers. We expect Jaclyn to show good progress, with noticeable improvement within 4 to 6 weeks after the initiation of therapy.

MANAGEMENT PROCEDURES FOR CAPD

For Decoding Problems

An example of the frustration that an individual with a CAPD may have is as follows: Imagine a geography class in which a speaker informs the audience that the discussion will be about the state of New York. The person with a CAPD will automatically try to re-auditorize this information and be confident that the subject will be understood because he lives in New York. Then, without warning, the speaker changes the subject to Bolivia. The individual with a decoding type of CAPD will be thinking, "Did I hear this word correctly?" By the time this individual finally realizes that he did hear *Bolivia*, he has missed all of the important facts about Bolivia. It is common for these children to fall behind and make guesses to catch up. Sometimes they are right and sometimes woefully wrong.

Such confusions cause the child to not understand the exact message and exhibit weak vocabulary. In these cases, we have found that remedial efforts should concentrate on increasing the client's phonemic awareness. In English-speaking countries, the Phonemic Synthesis Training (Katz & Harmon, 1981) program is an excellent intervention strategy often implemented. This training provides numerous opportunities for the client to discriminate, remember, and blend sounds at a slow and reinforced pace. Other intervention techniques may involve specific tasks to increase the discrimination ability of vowel sounds and rhyming abilities (Tillery, 1998). All of these assist the child with spelling and reading difficulties. Strong visual memory skills may assist those with this type of CAP dysfunction by permitting them to supplement their understanding.

For Tolerance-Fading Memory Problems

One remedial strategy for the child with a TFM problem is speech-in-noise desensitization therapy. This therapy provides the child words from one tape recorder while another tape recorder delivers background noise. The child should be allowed to progressively increase the noise intensity as long as he or she does reasonably well at the current noise level. When difficulty is encountered at a level, the noise is eliminated and the initial procedures are followed again. The short-term purpose is to increase correct identification of words at increasing levels of noise. The long-term goal of this therapy is to decrease the person's sensitivity to extraneous stimuli and teach him or her to focus on the message while disregarding the noise.

Other speech-in-noise strategies are to teach the child how to improve the listening environment especially when it is noisy. Role-playing with children will help them advocate effectively for themselves to improve the signal-to-noise ratio. They should be encouraged to ask the speaker to talk louder, repeat the information, and utilize visual cues. The child should be encouraged to ask for repeated directions at school and to sit closer to the teacher. Therapy can also take the form of lip-reading exercises to assist the child in receiving the auditory message when in a noisy listening environment.

Another common recommendation for the individual who displays a significant speech-in-noise problem is using an auditory trainer. Such a device improves the signal-to-noise ratio, the clarity of the speaker's voice, and allows the child to hear the message when the teacher turns toward the chalkboard. Using such a device not only improves the child's understanding and attention to the verbal message, but increases the listener's eye contact with the speaker (Blake, Field, Foster, Platt, & Wertz, 1991).

For Organization Problems

Although we are still learning much about this category, there are several recommendations that may provide assistance to individuals with this type of CAPD. Therapy activities that involve sequencing and list making greatly enhance organizational skills. Even the use of a homework note-book can assist the child who fails to do homework assignments because of disorganization.

For Integration Problems

Specific remedial work can be directed to each type of Integration CAPD. These include following multistep directions and noise desensitization therapy for those with TFM and strengthening phonemic awareness for those with DEC problems. For the phonemic awareness portion, sound blending is a useful approach, and both the Phonemic Synthesis Training and the LIPS (Lindamood, 1996) training programs are successful types of intervention. Also a visual-rhyming therapy, which involves the client rhyming a specific word to the written sounds on a chart, coordinates the visual and auditory modalities (Ferre, 1998). These types of therapy may assist with the poor integration of audition and vision that is seen in these groups.

CONCLUDING REMARKS

CAP is closely associated with important communicative and academic skills. Often without addressing the underlying CAP factors, progress in therapy is slow and difficult. Our experience with therapy shows that CAP skills can be improved readily, especially decoding skills. Along with improved auditory functions, we see improvement in the presenting speech-language and learning problems, or at a minimum they are more amenable to standard interventions. This chapter has presented a CAP category system that will aid the reader in differentiating the various sub-types and to have some ideas of how to remediate the problem. Some management approaches were mentioned to aid each of the types of prob-lems. With respect to clinical practice, an important consideration is to what extent central processing problems relate to a general information-processing deficit. Tallal (2000) presented an overview of studies that provide evidence for problems children with SLI have in processing rapid changes and the temporal structure of auditory and visual cues. For these and other clinical aspects of CAP problems, see Part III of this volume.

REFERENCES

American Speech-Language and Hearing Association. (1996). Task Force on Central Auditory Processing Consensus Development. Central auditory processing: Current status of research and implications for clinical practice. *American Journal of Audiology, 5,* 41–54.

Baru, A., & Karaseva, T. (1972). *The brain and hearing: Hearing disturbances associated with local brain lesions.* New York: New York Consultants Bureau.

Blake, R., Field, B., Foster, C., Platt, F., & Wertz, P. (1991). Effect of FM auditory trainers on attending behaviors of learning disabled children. *Language, Speech and Hearing Services in Schools, 22,* 111–114.

Efron, R., Crandall, P., Koss, P., Divenyl, P., & Yund, E. (1983). Central auditory processing: III. The cocktail party effect and temporal lobectomy. *Brain & Language, 19,* 254–263.

Ferre, J. (1998). The M^3 model for treating central auditory processing disorders. In G. Masters, N. Stecker, & J. Katz (Eds.), *Central auditory processing disorders: Mostly management* (pp. 103–116). Boston: Allyn & Bacon.

Green, P., & Kotenko, V. (1980). Superior speech comprehension in schizophrenics under monaural versus binaural listening conditions. *Journal of Abnormal Psychology, 89,* 339–408.

Hadaway, S. (1969). *An investigation of the relationship between measured intelligence and performance on the staggered spondaic word test.* Unpublished master's thesis, Oklahoma State University.

Jerger, J., & Musiek, F. (2000). Report of the consensus conference on the diagnosis of auditory processing disorders in school-age children. *Journal of American Academy of Audiology, 11, 9,* 467–474.

Kass, C., & Myklebust, H. (1969). Learning disability, an educational definition. *Journal of Learning Disabilities, 2,* 38–40.

Katz, J. (1962). The use of staggered spondaic words for assessing the integrity of the central auditory system. *Journal of Auditory Research, 2,* 327–337.

Katz, J. (1983). Phonemic synthesis. In E. Lasky & J. Katz (Eds.), *Central auditory processing disorders: Problems of speech, language, and learning* (pp. 269–296). Baltimore, MD: University Park Press.

Katz, J. (1992). Classification of auditory processing disorders. In J. Katz, N. Stecker, & D. Henderson (Eds.), *Central auditory processing: A transdisciplinary view* (pp. 81–93). Mosby Year Book: St. Louis, MO.

Katz, J. (1998). *Central Test Battery-CD.* Vancouver, WA: Precision Acoustics.

Katz, J., Alvellanosa, & Aguilar, M. (1980). *The use of the SSW, CES, and PICA tests to examine performance in patients with corpus callosum tumors.* Presented at American Speech-Language-Hearing Association Convention, Detroit, MI.

Katz, J., & Brandner, S. (2002). Integration-8 Analysis. *SSW Reports, 24*(1), 2–6.

Katz, J., Fanning, J., & Singer, S. (1988). *Unusual central auditory processing functions in incarcerated youths.* Presented at New York State Speech-Language-Hearing Association Meeting, Buffalo, NY.

Katz, J., & Harmon, C. (1981). Phonemic synthesis: Testing and training. In R. Keith (Ed.), *Central auditory and language disorders in children* (pp. 145–159). Houston, TX: College-Hill Press.

Katz, J., & Harmon-Fletcher, C. (1993). *Tester's manual: Phonemic synthesis picture test.* Vancouver, WA: Precision Acoustics.

Katz, J., & Illmer, R. (1972). Auditory perception in children with learning disabilities. In J. Katz (Ed.), *Handbook of clinical audiology* (pp. 540–563). Baltimore, MD: Williams & Wilkins.

Katz, J., & Smith, P. (1991). A ten minute look at the CNS through the ears: Using the SSW test. In R. Zappula et al. (Eds.), *Windows on the brain: Neuropsychologies technical frontiers. Annals NY Acad Science, 620,* 233–251.

Keller, W. (1992). Auditory processing disorder or attention deficit disorder? In J. Katz, N. Stecker, & D. Henderson (Eds.), *Central auditory processing: Transdisciplinary view* (pp. 107–114). St. Louis, MO: Mosby.

Keller, W. (1998). The relationship between attention deficit hyperactivity disorder, central auditory processing disorders, and specific learning disorders. In G. Masters, N. Stecker, & J. Katz (Eds.), *Central auditory processing disorders: Mostly management* (pp. 33–48). Boston: Allyn & Bacon.

Lindamood, P., & Lindamood, P. (1996). *Lindamood Phonological Sequencing* (LiPS) *program.* San Luis Obispo, CA: Gander.

Luria, A. (1966). *Higher cortical functions in man.* New York: Basic Books.

Moss, W. L., & Sheiffele, W. A. (1994). Can we differentially diagnose an attention deficit disorder without hyperactivity from a central auditory processing disorder? *Child Psychiatry and Human Development, 25*(2), 85–96.

Tallal, P. (2000). Experimental studies of language learning impairments: From research to remediation. In D. M. Bishop & L. B. Leonard (Eds.), *Speech and language impairments in children: Causes, characteristics, intervention and outcome* (pp. 131–155). Philadelphia, PA: Psychology Press.

Tallal, P., Miller, S. L., Bedi, G., Byma, G., Wang, X., Nagarajan, S. S., Schreiner, C., Jenkins, W. M., & Merzenich, M. M. (1996). Language comprehension in language-learning impaired children improved with acoustically modified speech. *Science, 271,* 81–84.

Tillery, K. L. (1998). Central auditory processing assessment and therapeutic strategies for children with attention deficit hyperactivity disorder. In G. Masters, N. Stecker, & J. Katz (Eds.), *Central auditory processing disorders: Mostly management* (pp. 175–194). Boston: Allyn & Bacon.

Tillery, K. L. (1999). Reversals, reversals, reversals: Differentiating information for CAPD, LD and ADHD. *SSW Reports, 21*(2), 1–6.

Tillery, K. L., Katz, J., & Keller, W. (2000). Effects of methylphenidate (Ritalin) on auditory performance in children with attention and auditory processing disorders. *Journal of Speech, Language and Hearing Research, 43,* 893–901.

9

Lexical Deficits in Specific Language Impairment

Laurence B. Leonard
Patricia Deevy
Purdue University

In this chapter, we examine the lexical abilities of children with specific language impairment (SLI). These children exhibit a significant deficit in language ability, yet show no evidence of obvious neurological impairment or significant limitations in nonverbal intellectual functioning. In addition, the hearing of these children is within normal limits, and they provide no indication of serious emotional difficulties.

In recent years, the grammatical limitations of children with SLI have received the greatest investigative attention (see reviews by Bishop, 1997; Leonard, 1998). However, many of these children also experience difficulty in learning, understanding, and using words. According to the clinical classification system developed by Rapin and Allen (1983), one subtype of SLI can be characterized as a lexical-semantic subtype. In a study by Korkman and Häkkinen-Rihu (1994), one subgroup of children with SLI seemed to perform especially poorly on naming tasks. Although other studies have not been successful in identifying a subgroup whose problems are limited to lexical difficulties (e.g., Aram & Nation, 1975; Wilson & Risucci, 1986; Wolfus, Moscovitch, & Kinsbourne, 1980), the literature makes it clear that many children with SLI have lexical problems along with difficulties in other areas of language. These lexical limitations are the focus of this chapter.

THE IMPORTANCE OF THE LEXICON

Problems with the lexicon can cause several types of difficulties for children with language learning limitations. Most obviously, if children fail to acquire particular words, their ability to express the corresponding meanings is restricted, and communication could suffer. Likewise, these children's understanding of what others say is likely to be significantly reduced if the words in the message are beyond the children's grasp. Such lexical restrictions could hinder these children's reading abilities as well given that unknown words place added demands on the children's decoding skills.

Lexical limitations can also have an adverse effect on sentence structure. For example, if children do not discern that the meaning of, say, *put* requires specification of the new location of a transferred object, ungrammatical sentences can result (e.g., *I put the ball*). Likewise, if children fail to see the common properties shared by, say, *give* and *throw*, they may have difficulty recognizing that alternative sentence structures for one of these verbs (e.g., *Let's give the ball to Mary; Let's give Mary the ball*) are applicable as well to the other verb (e.g., *Let's throw the ball to Mary; Let's throw Mary the ball*).

Finally, lexical deficits might be detrimental to the acquisition of grammatical morphology. For example, the co-occurrence of nouns and function words such as *the*, and the co-occurrence of verbs and inflections such as *-ing*, probably facilitate children's learning of the specific functions of these grammatical morphemes. However, if children have difficulty determining the meanings expressed by the nouns and verbs, their use of these words as a cue to the functions of the grammatical morphemes will necessarily be postponed, causing a delay in grammatical morpheme acquisition.

EARLY LEXICAL MILESTONES AND PATTERNS OF USE

SLI is a disorder manifest from the outset of development; children given this clinical description do not begin to acquire language normally and then incur neurological damage or disease that disrupts language functioning. Rather, from the earliest point at which it is possible to record language milestones, children with SLI appear to lag behind typically developing children. Early case studies suggest that first words emerge no sooner than age 1;6, and can emerge as late as age 5;0 (Bender, 1940; Morley, Court, Miller, & Garside, 1955; Nice, 1925; Weeks, 1974; Werner, 1945). In a comparative study employing parental report, Trauner, Wulfeck, Tallal, and Hesselink (1995) found that children with SLI reportedly acquired their first words at an average age of 1;11, whereas their typically developing peers appeared to reach this milestone at an average age of only 0;11.

Even after first words are acquired by children with SLI, the number of different words produced by these children appears to be smaller than expected. Using a well-developed and validated parent report measure, Thal, O'Hanlon, Clemmons, and Fralin (1999) found that children with SLI produced an average of approximately 17 different words at age 2;2— a number more characteristic of children age 1;4. For children with SLI somewhat older, ranging in age from 3;2 to 4;1, approximately 426 words were used. Although this number seems rather large, it is comparable to the number produced by typically developing children age 2;3 using the same measure. (For evidence that mothers of children with SLI provide accurate estimates of their children's lexicons, see Evans & Wodar, 1997.) Clarke and Leonard (1996) inquired whether 3-year-olds with SLI whose speech was limited to one-word utterances would show comparable limitations in lexical comprehension. They found that these children's comprehension abilities were also below age level.

Some investigators have compared children with SLI and normally developing peers in terms of the lexical diversity reflected in their spontaneous speech. Leonard, Miller, and Gerber (1999) found that the number of different words used in a 100-utterance sample was smaller for children with SLI than for same-age peers through the age range of 3;1 to 6;11. Similar results were reported in a study by Watkins, Kelly, Harbers, and Hollis (1995) involving children with SLI with a narrower age range of approximately 4;6 to 5;6. A mean of 111 different words was reported in the 100-utterance speech samples of the children with SLI, whereas an average of 160 different words was noted in the speech samples of the age controls. Watkins et al. also included a group of younger normally developing children (mean age 3;3) whose mean lengths of utterance (MLUs) were similar to those of the children with SLI. The number of different words used by these children proved similar to the number used by the children with SLI.

Of course the number of different words used and ages at which they are acquired can only provide part of the picture of the early lexical skills of children with SLI. Several studies have examined the nature of the words acquired by these children, as well as the manner in which they are applied to referents. It appears that children with SLI acquire the same types of words as younger normally developing children during the early stages of lexical development. For example, for both groups, names of objects, substances, and animals collectively constitute approximately 55% of words used (Leonard, Camarata, Rowan, & Chapman, 1982). As seems to be the case for younger normally developing children, individual differences can be seen in the population of children with SLI. The lexicons of some of these children can be characterized as biased toward object names, whereas the words used by other children have a stronger social orientation, with relatively frequent use of interaction words such as *hi* and *thank you* (Weiss, Leonard, Rowan, & Chapman, 1983). Like young typically developing children, children with SLI sometimes extend words to inappropriate exemplars that are both perceptually and functionally similar to the appropriate referent (e.g., using *spoon* to refer to forks as well as spoons; Chapman, Leonard, Rowan, & Weiss, 1983). Even exotic errors such as *brooming* and *barefeeting* (Weeks, 1975) have, on close inspection, a sensible basis (cf. *hammering*, *skating*). Errors in which words from one class (e.g., verbs) are used for words from another class are quite rare (Rice & Bode, 1993).

EXPERIMENTAL STUDIES OF LEXICAL ABILITY

Although descriptive studies of children's lexical use can be quite informative, greater insight into the nature of the children's difficulties often requires the use of experimental studies. Studies of this type began to appear in the 1980s and represent the bulk of lexical studies in the current literature. Experimental studies have dealt with lexical learning, naming, recall, and other types of lexical processing abilities. To facilitate the presentation of the findings from these studies, we provide a brief overview of some common assumptions made about lexical processing in general.

Lexical Processing: Some Assumptions

Experimental studies of lexical ability have examined lexical learning, lexical comprehension, and lexical production. It is not clear that there are any models of lexical processing so comprehensive as to account for all three of these types of lexical skills to an adequate degree. In fact, it is likely that operations involved in some of these types of skills are not involved in others. Accordingly, we limit our assumptions to those that seem applicable in general ways to all three areas. To avoid an excess of terminology, we apply terms more common to the language production literature (e.g., Bock & Levelt, 1994), to learning and comprehension as well.

We assume that by the time typically developing children demonstrate rapid growth in their lexicons between the ages of approximately 1;6 and 2;6, the acquisition of each lexical item is multifaceted. Certainly an important part of the information about each lexical item is its meaning, sometimes referred to as the *lexical concept*. The lexical concept does not appear in an individual's lexical system as a segregated entity. Rather, most if not all concepts will be linked to related concepts. Thus, the lexical concept *car* might have links to concepts such as *truck*, *wheels*, and so on.

As the child develops and has more experience with the world and with language, the network of associations for each lexical concept becomes more elaborate. Thus, for older children, concepts such as *vehicle*, *steering wheel*, and *Ford* might be linked with *car*. In addition, many of these links between lexical concepts become stronger over time because they often co-occur in the child's experience.

Lexical concepts do not constitute everything known about a word. The grammatical properties of a word are also acquired. For example, in addition to semantic information for *car*, there is information that *car* is a noun. In a language such as Italian, the grammatical gender of the word is also represented. For example, *macchina*—the Italian equivalent of *car*—is a feminine noun. In the case of an action word such as *drive*, the grammatical information includes the fact that the word is a verb, that it requires a direct object, and so on. The representation of a word at this grammatical level is often referred to as the *lemma*. Just as lexical concepts can be associated, so, too, can lemmas. For example, two lemmas may be related by their shared link to a noun node or grammatical gender node. As is true for lexical concepts, lemmas become more elaborate, and associated links become stronger as the child gains experience with a word and its linguistic contexts.

Finally, the representation of a word at the level at which it has phonological form is called the *lexeme*. Here the morphological and phonological shape of the word is available. Thus, *car* is represented as a monomorphemic form with the segments /k/, /a/, and /r/. Because the segmental composition of a word is represented at the lexeme level, there are links between lexemes sharing segmental content (e.g., between *car* and *card*).

We assume that in comprehension the listener's perception of a word activates a lexeme, followed by activation of the lemma and the lexical concept. In production, activation proceeds from the lexical concept (once the speaker's message is conceptually prepared) to the lemma, then to the lexeme. As noted earlier, we do not assume that comprehension and production involve precisely the same processes. However, it seems safe to conclude that comprehension must begin with the phonetic form of the word and progress toward meaning, whereas production begins with an intended meaning and progresses toward generation of the phonetic form of the word. We assume as well that the more frequent the occasion to hear or produce the word, the stronger the links become. Put differently, each encounter with the word leads to an increase in the resting activation level of its lexical concept, lemma, and lexeme.

A body of systematic research on lexical processing in adults has provided us with a good understanding of how these three levels function. For example, when adults are asked to name a picture and the picture (e.g., of a cow) is immediately preceded by a word (e.g., *farm*) semantically related to the name of the picture, the response time for naming the picture becomes faster. It is assumed in this case that the preceding word—the prime—activated associated lexical concepts, including the one appropriate for the following picture. Thus, the name of the target picture was more readily accessible than if prior activation had not taken place.

An example of lemmas at work can be seen in studies of tip-of-the-tongue phenomena. For example, in languages with grammatical gender, speakers unable to retrieve the appropriate lexeme can often report—at levels well above chance—the grammatical gender of the word for which they are searching.

Conversely, evidence of the lexeme level can be seen when a speaker is unable to retrieve the required word, but can accurately report details of the word's phonological form, such as whether it is a long word or a word that begins with a consonant cluster. It also appears to be the case that the often noted finding of faster picture-naming times for frequently occurring words than for infrequently occurring words can be attributed to the frequency of the lexemes, rather than the lexical concepts or lemmas (e.g., Jescheniak & Levelt, 1994). Because frequently occurring lexemes have strong links to their lexical concepts, they can be accessed more readily when called for in a picture.

Studies of Lexical Learning

Some of the earliest experimental studies of the lexical abilities of children with SLI were studies of 3-year-olds' lexical learning. In these studies, the children participated in play sessions during which the experimenter produced novel words to refer to novel referents. Following this exposure period, the children's comprehension and production of these words were tested (Leonard, Schwartz, Allen, Swanson, & Loeb, 1989; Leonard et al., 1982; Leonard, Schwartz, Swanson, & Loeb, 1987; Schwartz, 1988; Schwartz, Leonard, Messick, & Chapman, 1987). In these studies, each word was presented several times per play session, for up to 10 sessions (depending on the study), prior to testing. The performance of the children with SLI was compared with that of younger typically developing children with similar lexical sizes and utterance lengths. In most respects, the children with SLI were found to perform at levels similar to those seen for the younger comparison group. For both groups, comprehension proved better than production. However, the children with SLI showed a somewhat reduced tendency to extend newly learned object names to appropriate but previously unnamed exemplars during the comprehension task.

Given that the lexical diversity of preschoolers with SLI is lower than age expectations, the prior findings are surprising. One might have predicted generally poorer performance by the children with SLI on the assumption that, if they have smaller lexicons, they probably require more exposure to each word than do their normally developing peers before a lexical concept–lexeme association is developed. Of course had age controls been the comparison group, differences might have been observed.

Dollaghan (1987) employed age controls along with children with SLI in a study of fast mapping ability. *Fast mapping* refers to the ability to form an initial association between a word and its referent with only one or two exposures of the word. Dollaghan found that a group of 4- to 5-year-old children with SLI were as capable as same-age peers in their ability to associate the novel word *koob* with an unfamiliar object in a comprehension task. In production, however, the children with SLI performed below the level of their agemates. The group differences for production but not comprehension suggest that, for the children with SLI, the segmental details of the lexeme were weakly or incompletely represented. The segmental information in the lexeme may have been sufficient to distinguish the word from (phonologically distant) alternatives (e.g., *fork*). However, for production, a stronger or more complete lexeme than these children possessed was probably required.

Subsequent studies altered the fast mapping paradigm by employing a greater number of exposures of each word, ranging from 3 to 10, and several different words, rather than only one. In these investigations, children with SLI generally performed below the level of age controls (Rice, Buhr, & Nemeth, 1990; Rice, Buhr, & Oetting, 1992; Rice Oetting, Marquis, Bode, & Pae, 1994). In a study by Kiernan and Gray (1998), intervention activities were used to teach new lexical items to a group of age-matched normally developing peers as well as to a group of children with SLI. They found that the children with SLI learned to produce fewer words than their agemates. Those children who performed especially poorly in production nevertheless demonstrated comprehension of the great majority of the words they failed to produce.

There is evidence that the manner in which new words are presented can influence lexical learning. For example, when new words are presented as bare stems in sentence-final position (Leonard et al., 1982), they seem to pose less difficulty for children with SLI than when they appear in inflected form in a variety of sentence contexts (Haynes, 1982). Adding a pause before the novel word at the end of the sentence does not appear especially facilitative (Rice et al., 1992), whereas for both control children and children with SLI alike presenting new words with emphatic stress appears to be helpful (Ellis Weismer & Hesketh, 1998). When words are presented at a rapid rate, the performance of children with SLI seems to fall below that of normally developing children, especially when learning is assessed through production (Ellis Weismer & Hesketh, 1993, 1996).

Such findings suggest that children with SLI may require an atypically large number of exposures to a new word before the lexeme is adequately represented. The quality of these exposures is also important. These children seem to require a more ideal input, one in which new words are made salient through stress, sentence position, slow rate of pronunciation, and/or the absence of accompanying inflection.

LEXICAL ABILITIES ON NAMING TASKS

Accuracy

For some time, it has been known that children with SLI are less accurate in naming pictures even when the words required are those that the children appear to comprehend (Rubin & Liberman, 1983; Wiig, Semel, & Nystrom, 1982). These word-finding problems were often attributed to difficulties of word retrieval. That is, it was assumed that the children with SLI had adequate knowledge of the words, but employed inefficient or inappropriate retrieval strategies relative to their typically developing peers. However, a body of evidence suggests that these naming limitations are more likely to be due to limitations in the degree of knowledge that the children with SLI possessed about each word (see Kail & Leonard, 1986; McGregor & Leonard, 1995). Placed within the general framework employed in this chapter, the lexical networks of the children with SLI could be described as less elaborate than those of their same-age peers. Each lexical concept, lemma, and lexeme has fewer and weaker links. This does not mean that retrieval is not affected. However, the problem is not one of retrieval per se; retrieval is less successful because, in a less elaborate network with weaker associations, activation of the to-be-retrieved item is not as strong. This situation can be likened to that of adults' performance on picture-naming tasks that require access of frequently and infrequently occurring words. On occasion, naming errors will surface for the latter, although the adults will know the appropriate name. Because the lexeme–lexical concept link is not as strong for these words, retrieval is simply more difficult. However, if the problem were one of retrieval only, errors would be more evenly distributed across frequently and infrequently occurring names. Given the less elaborate and weaker lexical networks of children with SLI, it might be fair to say that words of intermediate frequency are, functionally speaking, like words of low frequency in typical children.

McGregor and Windsor (1996) examined the issue of word retrieval in children with SLI by employing a priming task. The children named pictures in one of two conditions. In one condition, the examiner provided the child with a prime sentence that contained information semantically related to the picture to be named. For example, for the target picture for *cane*, the examiner said, "This man likes to go walking." In the remaining condition, no prime was provided before the children named the picture. McGregor and Windsor reasoned that if the difficulties of children with SLI were principally one of retrieval, their performance should approximate that of age controls in the prime condition because in this condition the children are provided with a retrieval aide. Within the framework adopted here, related lexical concepts will have been activated by the prime, and this activation should spread to the lexical concept required for the target picture. Relative to age controls, the children with SLI committed a higher percentage of naming errors. Both groups of children benefited from the primes; naming errors were lower in the priming condition. In addition, there was overt evidence that the lexical information in the preceding primes was playing a role in the children's naming. Both groups were more likely to use a compound noun in their naming response in the prime condition than in the nonprime condition. Thus, a production such as *walking stick* instead of *cane* was more likely if the prime "This man likes to go walking" preceded the naming attempt. This suggests that activation at the lemma level influenced the word choice for the target. However, there was no evidence that the limitations of the children with SLI centered on retrieval; their performance in the prime condition remained well below that of their same-age peers even in the prime condition.

Early descriptions of the naming errors of children with SLI included errors bearing a semantic relation to the target word, as in *shirt* for *pants*, as well as errors in which the word produced was phonologically similar to the target word, such as producing *tangerine* for *tambourine*. The former appear to be glitches at either the lexical concept level or in the link between the lexical concept and the lemma. Phonologically similar errors, in contrast, probably occur in the link between the lemma and lexeme. Semantically related errors appear to be the more frequent of the two (Fried-Oken, 1984; Rubin & Liberman, 1983). This was confirmed in a more recent study by McGregor (1997). Using three different tasks, McGregor observed a higher frequency of semantically related errors than phonologically related errors in the responses of both children with SLI and age controls. Not surprisingly, the children with SLI committed a higher number of naming errors overall.

Evidence obtained by Lahey and Edwards (1999) raises the possibility that the degree of errors with a semantic basis is related to the specific profile of SLI exhibited by the child. They noted that semantic errors were more likely to be committed by children with both receptive and expressive language deficits than by a group of children whose problems were restricted to expressive language. However, both groups were less accurate in their naming than were a group of typically developing children of the same age. In retrospect, the finding that semantic errors were more likely from the group with receptive difficulties does not seem surprising. If comprehension is limited in this group, their lexical networks are likely to be less elaborate, leaving ample room for retrieval of mere semantic approximations to the target.

Faust, Dimitrovsky, and Davidi (1997) explored the tip-of-the-tongue phenomenon in children with SLI and a group of age controls. The children participated in a picture-naming task; when they failed to name a picture, they were asked whether they felt they knew its name but were simply unable to recall it at the moment. If the children responded in the affirmative, they were then asked to provide partial information. The children with SLI not only committed a greater number of naming errors, but were also more likely to provide partial information that was phonologically inaccurate. Furthermore, the children with SLI were more likely than the age controls to fail to recognize the appropriate word on a recognition task when they had reported that they knew the word but were unable to retrieve it at the moment. These findings indicate that the word-finding deficits of children with SLI may be even more serious than their lower accuracy suggests. Even when typically developing children fail to name a picture, they appear to have more accurate information about the word at the lemma and lexeme levels, and a more accurate sense of their knowledge of the word, than do children with SLI.

Response Time

Accuracy is not the only metric of word finding. Response time can also serve as an excellent gauge of children's naming abilities. Here it is assumed that words named more slowly have fewer and weaker links in the network and, consequently, a lower resting activation level.

Findings of slower response times in (accurate) picture naming by children with SLI than by age controls are a long-time fixture in the literature, dating back at least to Anderson (1965). Representative studies include Wiig, Semel, and Nystrom (1982), Ceci (1983), Leonard, Nippold, Kail, and Hale (1983), Kail and Leonard (1986), Katz, Curtiss, and Tallal (1992), Lahey and Edwards (1996), Windsor and Hwang (1999b), and Miller, Kail, Leonard, and Tomblin (2001). Some investigators have reported that slower picture naming holds only for children with SLI who have both expressive and receptive language deficits (Lahey & Edwards, 1996). However, others have found that children with SLI whose deficits are limited to expressive language also show significant, although less dramatic, slowing (Windsor & Hwang, 1999b).

Intervention

There have been several attempts to assist children's word finding through intervention. The design of some of these studies has also led to greater understanding of some of the variables that might be operative. McGregor and Leonard (1989) compared the effectiveness of three kinds of activities—one aimed to improve the children's degree of semantic and phonological knowledge of each word (the elaboration method), another designed to provide the children with strategies of word retrieval without providing new information about the words to be retrieved, and the last included activities to assist both elaboration and retrieval. Words that were taught in the combined elaboration and retrieval condition were more likely to be acquired and retained by the children with SLI participating in the study. Similar results have been reported by Wright (1993; see also Casby, 1992). Wing (1990) also reported success with word-finding intervention. One group of children received semantically based information, whereas the other group focused on phonologically based retrieval strategies. The phonologically oriented approach proved more effective. Unfortunately, because the two approaches differed in the degree to which they involved elaboration versus retrieval activities, the precise basis for the children's gains is not clear.

McGregor (1994) pointed out that a higher frequency of semantic errors than phonological errors may not always be due to breakdowns at the level of semantic representation. For example, in the general framework adopted here, once the picture is identified, activation proceeds from lexical concept and lemma to lexeme. However, if the segmental information of the lexeme is too weak for reliable retrieval, instead of selecting a phonologically similar lexeme, the child might retrieve the lexeme of a lemma and lexical concept that received some degree of activation through its semantic similarity to the target. Thus, a semantically related word was produced, but the source of difficulty was phonological in nature. McGregor tested this assumption by providing a strictly phonologically based intervention program to children with SLI. She found that the procedures not only reduced the children's phonologically based errors, but also their semantic errors.

OTHER LEXICAL PROCESSING ABILITIES

Other lexical abilities of children with SLI have been examined using processing tasks (e.g., Kail & Leonard, 1986; Miller et al., 2001; Sininger, Klatsky, & Kirchner, 1989). One of the most frequently used tasks is that of lexical decision. In this type of task, children must judge whether a phonetic string is a real word; thus, the task involves identifying those strings that have direct links to lemmas. Response time as well as accuracy are measured. On both types of measures, children with SLI perform more poorly than age controls (Edwards & Lahey, 1996; Windsor & Hwang, 1999a).

Word monitoring tasks have also been employed in research on SLI. Children are asked to listen for a particular word in a sentence or word list and respond (typically with a button press) as soon as the word is heard. Montgomery and his colleagues have made considerable use of this task (Montgomery & Leonard, 1998; Montgomery, Scudder, & Moore, 1990; Stark & Montgomery, 1995). Children with SLI show slower response times than age controls on this task, but in most respects show the same pattern of responding as a function of condition. For example, like same-age peers, children with SLI have faster response times when a sentence context is provided rather than a list of unrelated words. The later the target word appears in a sentence, the faster the response time, suggesting again that children with SLI are able to take advantage of grammatical and semantic context. It is reasonable to assume that as grammatical and semantic context is provided there is activation of links to the target word at the lemma level.

Dollaghan (1998) made use of a gating procedure to examine the word recognition abilities of children with SLI. Children heard successively longer portions of words (120 ms, 180 ms, 240 ms, etc.), and at each point they were to guess the word they believed was presented. When the stimuli consisted of familiar words, the children with SLI did not differ from age controls in the point at which they successfully identified the words. For unfamiliar words, in contrast, the children with SLI required more of the stimulus than did their same-age peers before they showed accurate identification. The findings for familiar words were replicated in a recent investigation by Montgomery (1999). Dollaghan's findings for unfamiliar words are consistent with other results discussed earlier in suggesting that children with SLI need more exposures to a word to develop an adequate representation at the level of the lexeme.

Word recall tasks also have provided data suggesting that the lexical skills of children with SLI are somewhat weak. Lists of familiar words are recalled less well by children with SLI than by same-age peers (Kirchner & Klatsky, 1985; Kushnir & Blake, 1996; Sommers, Kozarevich, & Michaels, 1994). Performance improves if the words in the list can be grouped into categories (e.g., vehicles, clothing)—that is, if they are likely to be directly or indirectly linked at the lexical concept level—although children with SLI do not perform as well as age controls in the same condition (Kail, Hale, Leonard, & Nippold, 1984). When children listen to sentences and must remember the last word in the sentence, the recall of children with

SLI falls below that of typically developing children of the same age (Ellis Weismer, Evans, & Hesketh, 1999). The same is true in tasks where children listen to stories and attempt to recall a word in the story that immediately followed a probe word (Kail & Leonard, 1986). Although children with SLI recall fewer words than same-age peers on such a task, they resemble their peers in recalling more words if the number of intervening words between the target word and the recall prompt is small.

Some word recall studies have included tasks in which two types of word lists are used—one containing phonologically similar words, the other containing phonologically distant words. In these studies, children with SLI recall fewer words than control children on both kinds of lists (although see van der Lely & Howard, 1993). However, they resemble the control children in having greater difficulty with the lists of phonologically similar words (e.g., Gathercole & Baddeley, 1990, 1993; James, van Steenbrugge, & Chiveralls, 1994). This type of list is likely to be more problematic because, during presentation of the items on the list, the lexemes of other lemmas are likely to receive some degree of activation due to the significant degree of shared segmental material.

Children with SLI have also participated in free recall tasks in which they are asked to generate as many items from a category (e.g., animals) that come to mind. Children with SLI have been found to generate fewer items per category than age controls, and the items generated reflect fewer subcategories (e.g., pets, animals of the jungle; Kail & Leonard, 1986). However, the organization of their responses, as defined by the order in which items are listed and the pauses between items from different subcategories, suggests that children with SLI and age controls share similar retrieval processes. McGregor and Waxman (1995) have also reported similar semantic organization in children with SLI and control children. These findings suggest that the lexical networks of children with SLI might be sparse relative to those of their peers, but they involve the same kinds of links within and between levels.

DO VERBS CONSTITUTE AN AREA OF SPECIAL DIFFICULTY FOR CHILDREN WITH SLI?

In many Germanic languages, children with SLI seem to have serious difficulty with verb morphology pertaining to tense and agreement (e.g., de Jong, chap. 11, this volume; Rice & Wexler, 1996). This has prompted investigators to ask whether the difficulty might also involve the verbs. That is, children with SLI might find notions of tense and agreement difficult because the kinds of words requiring them are also difficult for them. Alternatively, if children with SLI do not grasp the grammatical function of inflections and auxiliary verbs that mark tense and agreement, they might be unable to use these forms as a cue that a new word is a verb. As a result, their acquisition of verbs will lag behind their acquisition of other types of words.

Studies of the early stages of lexical development do not provide an indication that verbs are differentially problematic. Action words—many of which can be characterized as verbs—seem to be represented in the early speech of children with SLI to the same extent as in younger normally developing children with lexicons of similar size (Leonard, Camarata, Rowan, & Chapman, 1982). Furthermore, experimental studies of these children at the single-word utterance level suggest they are able to acquire at least novel intransitive verbs as quickly as younger controls (Leonard, Schwartz et al., 1982).

However, there are indications that verbs are disproportionately problematic for children with SLI once these children reach the point of using multiword utterances. These verb difficulties can be seen in both production and comprehension.

Perhaps the first study of production that revealed verb deficits was the investigation by Fletcher and Peters (1984). These researchers found that one of the variables that served to distinguish preschoolers with SLI from age controls in a discriminant function analysis was verb type frequency. Higher frequencies for verbs were seen in the speech of the age controls. Watkins, Rice, and Moltz (1993) found that preschoolers with SLI used a more limited variety of verbs than MLU controls as well as age controls. The particular measure used—verb type-token ratio—has not produced group differences in subsequent studies (Grela & Leonard, 1997). However, related measures of verb diversity have revealed differences. For example, Leonard, Miller, and Gerber (1999) found fewer verb types in 100-utterance speech samples of children with SLI than in comparable samples obtained from normally developing children in the same age range. In a longitudinal study of three children with SLI and their younger, normally developing siblings, Jones and Conti-Ramsden (1997) noted that the number of verb tokens used by each normal sibling was greater than the number used by the child with SLI, particularly in the later sessions. However, the two children in each pair did not differ in the number of verb types used.

The particular verbs used by children with SLI during the preschool period seem to resemble those used by their normally developing peers. Watkins et al. (1993) found that the verbs used with high frequency by children with SLI (e.g., *go, get, put, want,* and the main verb *do*) were also among the most frequently used by the MLU and age controls in their study. Rice and Bode (1993) also observed that children with SLI made frequent use of these same verbs. In a study requiring children to describe scenes shown in a video program, Kelly (1997) found that both children with SLI and control children relied heavily on the same, frequently occurring verbs. However, the children with SLI committed a greater number of semantic errors in verb use. Loeb, Pye, Redmond, and Richardson (1996) administered a set of verb elicitation probes and found that children with SLI were less accurate than age controls. Differences appeared to be greatest for verbs of low frequency of occurrence.

Some of the experimental studies of lexical learning discussed earlier also contained evidence of verb difficulty. For example, Rice et al. (1994) discovered that even when children with SLI showed evidence of acquiring new action names after 10 exposures, these gains were not retained. Kelly and Rice (1994) obtained evidence suggestive of differences in the way children with SLI and same-age peers interpret new verbs. Both types of children were shown two videorecorded actions simultaneously via split screen and heard a novel verb in a neutral sentence. One of the screens illustrated a change-of-state verb, the other a motion verb. The children selected the screen they felt most closely corresponded to the sentence. Although the normally developing children showed a clear preference for a change-of-state interpretation, the children with SLI showed no preference.

Most studies of verb use and comprehension have been directed at preschoolers. However, Oetting, Rice, and Swank (1995) studied a group of school-age children with SLI and their same-age peers in a task requiring the learning of new object words and action words. The differences between the two groups—favoring the typically developing children—was considerably greater for action words.

It appears then that children with SLI might have greater difficulty with verbs than with other types of lexical items and are more likely to differ from normally developing peers in this area of the lexicon. There are several possible sources of difficulty. For example, because verbs tend to appear in sentence-medial position rather than sentence-final position and are subject to a wider variety of inflections than are nouns, children with SLI might be slower or more erratic in recognizing instances of new verb stems. This would lead to a protracted rate of building and strengthening the segmental content of these lexemes.

However, verbs also differ from nouns in that their lexical concepts and lemmas contain information about the kinds of logical arguments and grammatical functions (e.g., subject, direct object), respectively, that must accompany the verb. It seems possible that this additional complexity slows the pace at which children with SLI acquire and strengthen verbs in their lexicons. Of course it could also be the case that these children are slow to acquire some of this accompanying information. It is to this topic that we now turn.

DO VERB DEFICITS CAUSE COLLATERAL DAMAGE?

By their nature, verbs are grammatical. The meaning of a verb (e.g., *put*) constrains syntactic structure, for example, by dictating the number of arguments that must be included. In addition, if children note similarities between the meanings of two verbs, they may be in a position to extend the use of a syntactic construction that is appropriate for one verb, to the other verb (e.g., noting parallels between *send* and *give* and concluding that *send* can be used in *Let's send Mary the money* as well as in *Let's send the money to Mary*). To be sure, the child must have some knowledge of hierarchical syntactic structure and how grammatical functions such as subject and direct object are associated with positions in this structure. Nevertheless, one cannot discount the role played by the verbs in these difficulties because information stored with the verb determines which arguments must be expressed and how they are expressed in the syntactic structure. In the framework used in this chapter, in fact, some of this syntactic information is considered to be bound up with the verb at the lemma level. Several verb-related grammatical weaknesses are discussed here.

Watkins and Rice (1991) discovered a discrepancy in the ability of children with SLI to use two types of phonetically identical morphemes. They found that these children performed as well as MLU controls in their use of forms such as *in*, *on*, and *over* when these served as prepositions (as in *Jump over the table*). However, the children with SLI were less proficient than these younger controls in using these forms as verb particles (as in *Push over the table*). Because particles can alter the meaning of the associated verb, it seems plausible that this interaction contributed to the children's difficulty.

Several studies have examined the use of obligatory arguments by children with SLI. Compared with same-age peers, children with SLI seem more likely to omit arguments that should be obligated given the verbs produced (e.g., Fletcher, 1991; Roberts, Rescorla, & Borneman, 1994). King and Fletcher (1993) found no differences between children with SLI and younger MLU controls in argument structure errors. However, they noted that the control children's difficulties were confined to particular verbs, whereas errors of the children with SLI occurred with a wide variety of verbs.

Grela and Leonard (1997) examined the use of arguments as a function of the type of verb used. They observed that children with SLI were more likely than MLU controls to omit subject arguments, especially when unaccusative intransitive verbs such as *fall* were used. With such verbs, the subject of the sentence is typically assigned to the semantic role of theme (the person or thing moved by the action expressed by the verb). In most instances, themes are postverbal and expressed as direct objects.

Grela and Leonard speculated that the children with SLI might have been delayed in their recognition that themes can sometimes be placed in preverbal position. Faced with this confusion, the children might have opted to omit the subject. To the extent that arguments are dictated by the verb, any difficulties seen in children's argument use might be attributed to limitations in verb knowledge. Unlike arguments, adjuncts are substantive elements of a sentence not grammatically obligated by the verb. For example, in the sentence *We washed the car in the street*, the adjunct *in the street* adds a type of information that is not required by *wash*. Children with SLI appear to make less use of adjuncts than age controls (e.g., Wren, 1980) and resemble instead typically developing children matched on other measures of language (e.g., Fletcher & Garman, 1988; Johnston & Kamhi, 1984).

Findings of adjunct difficulties certainly suggest that limitations are not caused by the verb, which in turn raises the possibility that even argument structure problems are not verb-based. However, there are indications that the failure to use adjuncts need not be independent of children's knowledge of verbs. For example, Fletcher and Garman (1988) observed that the children with SLI in their study were much less likely than younger controls to recognize that grammatical utterances such as *We left* were quite incomplete in particular contexts. For example, a temporal specification such as *last Saturday* might have been required. This difficulty could certainly be caused by pragmatic limitations. However, we cannot rule out the possibility that the children with SLI had less knowledge of the meanings that each verb entailed.

Ingham, Fletcher, Schelletter, and Sinka (1998) examined children's use of resultative verb phrases—constituents that function like arguments, but are not obligated by the verb. For example, in the sentence *The boy rolled the ball under the porch*, the phrase *under the porch* behaves like an argument. This is apparent when one compares the grammatical construction *The boy wrote the letter at school and the girl did so at home* with the ungrammatical construction *The boy rolled the ball under the porch and the girl did so under the car*. Yet it is equally clear that the verb *roll* does not require a third argument (hence, *The boy rolled the ball* is grammatical). Ingham et al. found that children with SLI were less likely than both age controls and younger vocabulary-matched controls to include these types of verb phrases in their sentences. Errors included sentences such as *Sweep a tree* for a man sweeping leaves under a bush and *The little boy blow a gate* for a boy blowing a balloon over a fence.

Insight into another type of verb-related difficulty comes from research on children's ability to use syntactic information to determine the appropriate argument structure of a verb. As reported by van der Lely (1994), if children with SLI hear a new word (e.g., *tiv*) produced in isolation in the context of a new action being performed with familiar characters and objects, they can construct an appropriate sentence to describe the event (e.g., *The cow tivs the pig to the farmhouse*). On such a task, children with SLI seem as capable as younger controls. However, when the children hear a new word in a sentence without benefit of visual information (e.g., *The car zafs the train to the truck*), they have more difficulty than the control children in demonstrating its meaning by acting out the sentence. Performance is substantially better if the children had already seen the new verb acted out with another set of props. O'Hara and Johnston (1997) obtained nearly identical findings using a similar procedure.

In studies employing procedures different from those cited earlier, children with SLI appear to have less difficulty in deriving the verb's meaning from its syntactic frame. For example, Hoff-Ginsberg, Kelly, and Buhr (1996) observed that children with SLI often modified their interpretation of familiar verbs on hearing them in novel syntactic frames (e.g., *The lion falls the camel*). In a study by Kouri, Lewis, and Schlosser (1992), children with SLI proved able to use syntactic information to decide whether a verb was causal.

More recently, Oetting (1999) sought to determine not only how well children with SLI could use argument structure to determine a verb's meaning, but also how well these children retained this meaning. The children observed videorecorded action scenes and heard alternative constructions such as *Look, the monkey is kibbing* or *Look, the bear is kibbing the monkey*. On this and a related task, the children with SLI scored as high as language comprehension control children in determining the meaning of the new word (e.g., describing the first example as meaning "eating" and the second example as "feeding"). However, when the children's retention of the verbs' meanings was assessed by asking them to identify the meanings after the story had been completed, the children with SLI were less accurate than the control children.

Loeb, Pye, Richardson, and Redmond (1998) examined the use of causative alternations by children with SLI. The children were tested both in their ability to alternate from an intransitive to a transitive version of the same verb (e.g., from *The toothpick broke* to *You broke the toothpick*) and in their ability to produce an intransitive following a transitive (e.g., from *You dropped the ball* to *The ball dropped*). Fixed transitive (e.g., *throw*) and intransitive (e.g., *dance*) verbs were also included to determine whether the children would overgeneralize causative alternations by producing sentences such as *You danced them* or, instead, use appropriate periphrastic constructions (e.g., *You made them dance*) or passives (e.g., *The ball was thrown*). The children with SLI were as successful as age controls in using alternation with appropriate causative verbs. However, for other verbs, their responses were less mature. They were more likely to avoid passive and periphrastic constructions and instead substitute verbs, or even use an adjective in place of a verb. For example, instead of using *The ball was thrown*, some of the children with SLI produced *The ball fell*; instead of *The floor was swept*, they produced *The floor is clean*. Some degree of overregularization of the causative alternation was also seen in the responses of the children with SLI (e.g., *You swam her*). Such responses were also seen in the typically developing children. These findings led Loeb et al. to conclude that the children with SLI had adequate knowledge of causative alternation, but were less proficient in using other syntactic means of expressing causal notions when the particular verb did not lend itself to alternation. In a study employing videotaped events by King, Schelletter, Sinka, Fletcher, and Ingham (1995), a group of children with SLI showed a tendency to rely on one argument order (e.g., *She's loading the bricks onto the truck*) even when the events in the video promoted a change in order (as in *She's loading the truck with bricks*). In this respect, the children with SLI resembled younger control children matched according to vocabulary test score.

The findings do not clearly implicate a single source of verb-related problems. Some of the problems could be due to strictly lexical limitations such as incomplete information in the verb's lemma or lexical concept. For example, difficulties with verb particles and obligatory arguments could reflect deficiencies in the lexical concepts or lemmas of these words, which lead to incorrectly formulated sentences. Oetting's (1999) finding of poor retention of verb meanings also implicates lexical limitations. Here it appears that key information about the logical arguments and grammatical functions relevant for the verb were not of sufficient strength in the lexical networks of the children with SLI to be called on when needed.

Yet other difficulties noted in this literature seem to be more likely due to syntactic limitations separate from the lexicon. The resultative verb phrase findings suggest a difficulty with the syntactic expression of complex argumentlike relations, which are not necessarily supported by stored lexical knowledge. The findings of van der Lely (1994) may be a clearer example of syntactic difficulties. When the children with SLI in that study succeeded in producing an appropriate sentence with a new verb to describe an observed event (as in the prior example, *The cow tivs the pig to the farmhouse*), they demonstrated an ability to use nonlinguistic input to encode appropriate information about logical arguments and their semantic roles into a new lexical representation, specifically at the levels of the lexical concept and lemma. However, their difficulty in acting out sentences such as *The car zafs the train to the truck* when they had never seen the action performed before suggests that they have difficulty encoding the same kind of information in a representation's lexical concept or lemma on the basis of syntactic information alone. The findings of Loeb et al. (1998) and King et al. (1995) also suggest greater difficulties with syntax than with the lexicon. In these studies, the children with SLI attempted to express the appropriate notions (e.g., causative and locative notions), but seemed to be restricted in their syntactic means of doing so.

SUMMARY AND INTERPRETATION

Children with SLI are late to acquire their early words and slow to add new words thereafter. At any point in time, their lexicons are less diverse than those of same-age peers. To acquire new words at a typical rate, they appear to require an optimal input, not only in terms of frequency of exposure, but in quality of exposure as well. Although the lexical limitations of children with SLI cover a broad range of lexical types, verbs are clearly among the weakest. These children's difficulties with verbs seem to be accompanied by verb-related problems with syntax.

Examination of the nature of the children's lexical limitations suggests that the children's lexical networks are organized in a generally appropriate manner at the lexical concept, lemma, and lexeme levels. However, these networks are relatively sparse, and resting activation levels of the entries and the links among entries are relatively weak. The sparse network has implications for grammar as well as for the lexicon. For example, incomplete or weakly represented information at the lemma level can lead to sentences with missing constituents.

In the years since the Rapin and Allen (1983) proposal of a lexical-semantic subtype of SLI, there has been little evidence pointing to a distinct subgroup with problems restricted to the lexical area. However, in hindsight, this should not be surprising. Given the findings reviewed here, it is clear that lexical limitations—especially those pertaining to verbs—will cause problems for syntax as well.

Nevertheless, a close look at the children's verb-related difficulties suggests that lexical limitations can only be part of the problem. Independent difficulties with syntax seem to exist alongside lexical limitations. An important goal of future research will be to identify with greater precision those problems that have a strictly lexical, or syntactic basis, and those that are caused by the joint effects of both of these areas.

REFERENCES

Anderson, J. (1965). Initiatory delay in congenital aphasoid conditions. *Cerebral Palsy Journal*, 26, 9–12.

Aram, D., & Nation, J. (1975). Patterns of language behavior in children with developmental language disorders. *Journal of Speech and Hearing Research, 18*, 229–241.

Bender, J. (1940). A case of delayed speech. *Journal of Speech Disorders, 5,* 363.

Bishop, D. (1997). *Uncommon understanding: Development and disorders of language comprehension in children.* Hove, UK: Psychology Press.

Bock, K., & Levelt, W. (1994). Language production: Grammatical encoding. In M. Gernsbacher (Ed.), *Handbook of psycholinguistics* (pp. 945–984). San Diego: Academic Press.

Casby, M. (1992). An intervention approach for naming problems in children. *American Journal of Speech-Language Pathology, 1,* 35–42.

Ceci, S. (1983). Automatic and purposive semantic processing characteristics of normal and language/learning-disabled children. *Developmental Psychology, 19,* 427–439.

Chapman, K., Leonard, L., Rowan, L., & Weiss, A. (1983). Inappropriate word extensions in the speech of young language-disordered children. *Journal of Speech and Hearing Disorders, 48,* 55–62.

Clarke, M., & Leonard, L. (1996). Lexical comprehension and grammatical deficits in children with specific language impairment. *Journal of Communication Disorders, 29,* 95–105.

Dollaghan, C. (1987). Fast mapping in normal and language-impaired children. *Journal of Speech and Hearing Disorders, 52,* 218–222.

Dollaghan, C. (1998). Spoken word recognition in children with specific language impairment. *Applied Psycholinguistics, 19,* 193–207.

Edwards, J., & Lahey, M. (1996). Auditory lexical decisions of children with specific language impairment. *Journal of Speech and Hearing Research, 39,* 1263–1273.

Ellis Weismer, S., Evans, J., & Hesketh, L. (1999). An examination of verbal working memory capacity in children with specific language impairment. *Journal of Speech, Language, and Hearing Research, 42,* 1249–1260.

Ellis Weismer, S., & Hesketh, L. (1993). The influence of prosodic and gestural cues on novel word acquisition by children with specific language impairment. *Journal of Speech and Hearing Research, 36,* 1013–1025.

Ellis Weismer, S., & Hesketh, L. (1996). Lexical learning by children with specific language impairment: Effects of linguistic input presented at varying speaking rates. *Journal of Speech and Hearing Research, 39,* 177–190.

Ellis Weismer, S., & Hesketh, L. (1998). The impact of emphatic stress on novel word learning by children with specific language impairment. *Journal of Speech, Language, and Hearing Research, 41,* 1444–1458.

Evans, M. A., & Wodar, S. (1997). Maternal sensitivity to vocabulary development in specific language-impaired and language-normal preschoolers. *Applied Psycholinguistics, 18,* 243–256.

Faust, M., Dimitrovsky, L., & Davidi, S. (1997). Naming difficulties in language-disabled children: Preliminary findings with the application of the tip-of-the-tongue paradigm. *Journal of Speech, Language, and Hearing Research, 40,* 1026–1036.

Fletcher, P. (1991). Evidence from syntax for language impairment. In J. Miller (Ed.), *Research on child language disorders* (pp. 169–187). Austin, TX: Pro-Ed.

Fletcher, P., & Garman, M. (1988). Normal language development and language impairment: Syntax and beyond. *Clinical Linguistics and Phonetics, 2,* 97–113.

Fletcher, P., & Peters, J. (1984). Characterizing language impairment in children: An exploratory study. *Language Testing, 1,* 33–49.

Fried-Oken, M. (1984). *The development of naming skills in normal and language deficient children.* Unpublished doctoral dissertation, Boston University.

Gathercole, S., & Baddeley, A. (1990). Phonological memory deficits in language disordered children: Is there a causal connection? *Journal of Memory and Language, 29,* 336–360.

Gathercole, S., & Baddeley, A. (1993). *Working memory and language.* Hillsdale, NJ: Lawrence Erlbaum Associates.

Grela, B., & Leonard, L. (1997). The use of subject arguments by children with specific language impairment. *Clinical Linguistics and Phonetics, 11,* 443–453.

Haynes, C. (1982). *Vocabulary acquisition problems in language disordered children.* Master's thesis, Guys Hospital Medical School, University of London.

Hoff-Ginsberg, E., Kelly, D., & Buhr, J. (1996). Syntactic bootstrapping by children with SLI: Implications for a theory of specific language impairment. *Proceedings of the 20th Annual Boston University Conference on Language Development, Volume 1* (pp. 328–339). Somerville, MA: Cascadilla Press.

Ingham, R., Fletcher, P., Schelletter, C., & Sinka, I. (1998). Resultative VPs and specific language impairment. *Language Acquisition, 7,* 87–111.

James, D., van Steenbrugge, W., & Chiveralls, K. (1994). Underlying deficits in language-disordered children with central auditory processing difficulties. *Applied Psycholinguistics, 15,* 311–328.

Jescheniak, J., & Levelt, W. (1994). Word frequency effects in speech production: Retrieval of syntactic information and of phonological form. *Journal of Experimental Psychology: Language, Memory, and Cognition, 20,* 824–843.

Johnston, J., & Kamhi, A. (1984). Syntactic and semantic aspects of the utterances of language-impaired children. The same can be less. *Merrill-Palmer Quarterly, 30,* 65–85.

Jones, M., & Conti-Ramsden, G. (1997). A comparison of verb use in children with SLI and their younger siblings. *First Language, 17,* 165–193.

Kail, R., Hale, C., Leonard, L., & Nippold, M. (1984). Lexical storage and retrieval in language-impaired children. *Applied Psycholinguistics, 5,* 37–49.

Kail, R., & Leonard, L. (1986). Word-finding abilities in language-impaired children. *ASHA Monographs, 25.*

Katz, W., Curtiss, S., & Tallal, P. (1992). Rapid automatized naming and gesture by normal and language-impaired children. *Brain and Language, 43,* 623–641.

Kelly, D. (1997). Patterns in verb use by preschoolers with normal language and specific language impairment. *Applied Psycholinguistics, 18,* 199–218.

Kelly, D., & Rice, M. (1994). Preferences for verb interpretation in children with specific language impairment. *Journal of Speech and Hearing Research, 37,* 182–192.

Kiernan, B., & Gray, S. (1998). Word learning in a supported-learning context by preschool children with specific language impairment. *Journal of Speech, Language, and Hearing Research, 41,* 161–171.

King, G., & Fletcher, P. (1993). Grammatical problems in school-age children with specific language impairment. *Clinical Linguistics and Phonetics, 7,* 339–352.

King, G., Schelletter, I., Sinka, I., Fletcher, P., & Ingham, R. (1995). Are English-speaking SLI children with morpho-syntactic deficits impaired in their use of locative-contact and causative alternating verbs? *Reading Working Papers in Linguistics, 2,* 45–65.

Kirchner, D., & Klatsky, R. (1985). Verbal rehearsal and memory in language-disordered children. *Journal of Speech and Hearing Research, 28,* 556–565.

Korkman, M., & Häkkinen-Rihu, P. (1994). A new classification of developmental language disorders. *Brain and Language, 47,* 96–116.

Kouri, T., Lewis, M., & Schlosser, M. (1992). *Children's action word comprehension as a function of syntactic context.* Paper presented at the Convention of the American Speech-Language-Hearing Association, San Antonio, TX.

Kushnir, C., & Blake, J. (1996). The nature of the cognitive deficit in specific language impairment. *First Language, 16,* 21–40.

Lahey, M., & Edwards, J. (1996). Why do children with specific language impairment name pictures more slowly than their peers? *Journal of Speech and Hearing Research, 39,* 1081–1098.

Lahey, M., & Edwards, J. (1999). Naming errors of children with specific language impairment. *Journal of Speech, Language, and Hearing Research, 42,* 195–205.

Leonard, L. (1998). *Children with specific language impairment.* Cambridge, MA: MIT Press.

Leonard, L., Camarata, S., Rowan, L., & Chapman, K. (1982). The communicative functions of lexical usage by language impaired children. *Applied Psycholinguistics, 3*, 109–125.

Leonard, L., Miller, C., & Gerber, E. (1999). Grammatical morphology and the lexicon in children with specific language impairment. *Journal of Speech, Language, and Hearing Research, 42*, 678–689.

Leonard, L., Nippold, M., Kail, R., & Hale, C. (1983). Picture naming in language-impaired children. *Journal of Speech and Hearing Research, 26*, 609–615.

Leonard, L., Schwartz, R., Allen, G., Swanson, L., & Loeb, D. (1989). Unusual phonological behavior and the avoidance of homonymy in children. *Journal of Speech and Hearing Research, 32*, 583–590.

Leonard, L., Schwartz, R., Chapman, K., Rowan, L., Prelock, P., Terrell, B., Weiss, A., & Messick, C. (1982). Early lexical acquisition in children with specific language impairment. *Journal of Speech and Hearing Research, 25*, 554–564.

Leonard, L., Schwartz, R., Swanson, L., & Loeb, D. (1987). Some conditions that promote unusual phonological behavior in children. *Clinical Linguistics and Phonetics, 1*, 23–34.

Loeb, D. F., Pye, C., Redmond, S., & Richardson, L. (1996). Eliciting verbs from children with specific language impairment. *American Journal of Speech-Language Pathology, 5*, 17–30.

Loeb, D. F., Pye, C., Richardson, L., & Redmond, S. (1998). Causative alternations of children with specific language impairment. *Journal of Speech, Language, and Hearing Research, 41*, 1103–1114.

McGregor, K. (1994). Use of phonological information in a word-finding treatment for children. *Journal of Speech and Hearing Research, 37*, 1381–1393.

McGregor, K. (1997). The nature of word-finding errors of preschoolers with and without word-finding deficits. *Journal of Speech, Language, and Hearing Research, 40*, 1232–1244.

McGregor, K., & Leonard, L. (1989). Facilitating word-finding skills of language-impaired children. *Journal of Speech and Hearing Disorders, 54*, 141–147.

McGregor, K., & Leonard, L. (1995). Intervention for word-finding deficits in children. In M. Fey, J. Windsor, & S. Warren (Eds.), *Language intervention: Preschool through the elementary years* (pp. 85–105). Baltimore: Paul H. Brookes.

McGregor, K., & Waxman, S. (1995). *Multiple level naming abilities of children with word-finding deficits*. Paper presented at the Boston University Conference on Language Development, Boston.

McGregor, K., & Windsor, J. (1996). Effects of priming on the naming accuracy of preschoolers with word-finding deficits. *Journal of Speech and Hearing Research, 39*, 1048–1058.

Miller, C., Kail, R., Leonard, L., & Tomblin, J. B. (2001). Speed of processing in children with specific language impairment. *Journal of Speech, Language, and Hearing Research, 44*, 416–433.

Montgomery, J. (1999). Recognition of gated words by children with language impairment: An examination of lexical mapping. *Journal of Speech, Language, and Hearing Research, 42*, 735–743.

Montgomery, J., & Leonard, L. (1998). Real-time inflectional processing by children with specific language impairment: Effects of phonetic substance. *Journal of Speech, Language, and Hearing Research, 41*, 1432–1443.

Montgomery, J., Scudder, R., & Moore, C. (1990). Language-impaired children's real-time comprehension of spoken language. *Applied Psycholinguistics, 11*, 273–290.

Morley, M., Court, D., Miller, H., & Garside, R. (1955). Delayed speech and developmental aphasia. *British Medical Journal, 2*, 463–467.

Nice, M. (1925). A child who would not talk. *Pedagogical Seminary, 32*, 105–144.

Oetting, J. (1999). Children with SLI use argument structure cues to learn verbs. *Journal of Speech, Language, and Hearing Research, 42*, 1261–1274.

Oetting, J., Rice, M., & Swank, L. (1995). Quick incidental learning (QUIL) of words by school-age children with and without SLI. *Journal of Speech and Hearing Research, 38*, 434–445.

O'Hara, M., & Johnston, J. (1997). Syntactic bootstrapping in children with specific language impairment. *European Journal of Disorders of Communication, 32,* 189–205.

Rapin, I., & Allen, D. (1983). Developmental language disorders: Nosologic considerations. In U. Kirk (Ed.), *Neuropsychology of language, reading, and spelling* (pp. 155–184). New York: Academic Press.

Rice, M., & Bode, J. (1993). GAPS in the lexicon of children with specific language impairment. *First Language, 13,* 113–132.

Rice, M., Buhr, J., & Nemeth, M. (1990). Fast mapping word-learning abilities of language-delayed preschoolers. *Journal of Speech and Hearing Disorders, 55,* 33–42.

Rice, M., Buhr, J., & Oetting, J. (1992). Specific-language-impaired children's quick incidental learning of words: The effect of a pause. *Journal of Speech and Hearing Research, 35,* 1040–1048.

Rice, M., Oetting, J., Marquis, J., Bode, J., & Pae, S. (1994). Frequency of input effects on word comprehension of children with specific language impairment. *Journal of Speech and Hearing Research, 37,* 106–122.

Rice, M., & Wexler, K. (1996). Toward tense as a clinical marker of specific language impairment in English-speaking children. *Journal of Speech and Hearing Research, 39,* 1239–1257.

Roberts, J., Rescorla, L., & Borneman, A. (1994). *Morphosyntactic characteristics of early language errors: An examination of specific expressive language delay.* Poster presented at the Symposium on Research in Child Language Disorders, University of Wisconsin, Madison.

Rubin, H., & Liberman, I. (1983). Exploring the oral and written language errors made by language disabled children. *Annals of Dyslexia, 33,* 111–120.

Schwartz, R. (1988). Early action word acquisition in normal and language-impaired children. *Applied Psycholinguistics, 9,* 111–122.

Schwartz, R., Leonard, L., Messick, C., & Chapman, K. (1987). The acquisition of object names in children with specific language impairment: Action context and word extension. *Applied Psycholinguistics, 8,* 233–244.

Sininger, Y., Klatsky, R., & Kirchner, D. (1989). Memory-scanning speed in language-disordered children. *Journal of Speech and Hearing Research, 32,* 289–297.

Sommers, R., Kozarevich, M., & Michaels, C. (1994). Word skills of children normal and impaired in communication skills and measures of language and speech development. *Journal of Communication Disorders, 25,* 3–22.

Stark, R., & Montgomery, J. (1995). Sentence processing in language-impaired children under conditions of filtering and time compression. *Applied Psycholinguistics, 16,* 137–154.

Thal, D., O'Hanlon, L., Clemmons, M., & Fralin, L. (1999). Validity of a parent report measure of vocabulary and syntax for preschool children with language impairment. *Journal of Speech, Language, and Hearing Research, 42,* 482–496.

Trauner, D., Wulfeck, B., Tallal, P., & Hesselink, J. (1995). *Neurologic and MRI profiles of language impaired children* (Technical Report CND-9513). Center for Research in Language, University of California at San Diego.

van der Lely, H. (1994). Canonical linking rules: Forward versus reverse linking in normally developing and specifically language-impaired children. *Cognition, 51,* 29–72.

van der Lely, H., & Howard, D. (1993). Children with specific language impairment: Linguistic impairment or short-term memory deficit? *Journal of Speech and Hearing Research, 36,* 1193–1207.

Watkins, R., Kelly, D., Harbers, H., & Hollis, W. (1995). Measuring children's lexical diversity: Differentiating typical and impaired language learners. *Journal of Speech and Hearing Research, 38,* 1349–1355.

Watkins, R., & Rice, M. (1991). Verb particle and preposition acquisition in language-impaired preschoolers. *Journal of Speech and Hearing Research, 34,* 1130–1141.

Watkins, R., Rice, M., & Moltz, C. (1993). Verb use by language-impaired and normally developing children. *First Language*, *13*, 133–144.

Weeks, T. (1974). *The slow speech development of a bright child*. Lexington, MA: D.C. Heath.

Weeks, T. (1975). The use of nonverbal communication by a slow speech developer. *Word*, *27*, 460–472.

Weiss, A., Leonard, L., Rowan, L., & Chapman, K. (1983). Linguistic and non-linguistic features of style in normal and language-impaired children. *Journal of Speech and Hearing Disorders*, *48*, 154–164.

Werner, L. (1945). Treatment of a child with delayed speech. *Journal of Speech Disorders*, *10*, 329–334.

Wiig, E., Semel, E., & Nystrom, L. (1982). Comparison of rapid naming abilities in language-learning-disabled and academically achieving eight-year-olds. *Language, Speech, and Hearing Services in Schools*, *13*, 11–23.

Wilson, B., & Risucci, D. (1986). A model for clinical-quantitative classification: Generation I. Application to language-disordered preschool children. *Brain and Language*, *27*, 281–309.

Windsor, J., & Hwang, M. (1999a). Children's auditory lexical decisions: A limited processing capacity account of language impairment. *Journal of Speech, Language, and Hearing Research*, *42*, 990–1002.

Windsor, J., & Hwang, M. (1999b). Testing the generalized slowing hypothesis in specific language impairment. *Journal of Speech, Language, and Hearing Research*, *42*, 1205–1218.

Wing, C. (1990). A preliminary investigation of generalization to untrained words following two treatments of children's word-finding problems. *Language, Speech, and Hearing Services in Schools*, *21*, 151–156.

Wolfus, B., Moscovitch, M., & Kinsbourne, M. (1980). Subgroups of developmental language impairment. *Brain and Language*, *10*, 152–171.

Wren, C. (1980). Identifying patterns of syntactic disorder in six-year-old children. *Proceedings from the Symposium on Research in Child Language Disorders*, *1*, 113–123. Madison, WI: University of Wisconsin.

Wright, S. (1993). Teaching word-finding strategies to severely language-impaired children. *European Journal of Disorders of Communication*, *28*, 165–175.

10

Morphological Disorders

Dorit Ravid
Ronit Levie
Galit Avivi Ben-Zvi
Tel Aviv University

The present chapter considers knowledge of the morphological class of adjectives in Hebrew-speaking SLI compared with NLA school children. We argue that the domain of derivational morphology is particularly appropriate for the investigation of linguistic disorders in SLI school children because knowledge of obligatory grammatical morphology is so well established and automatic in this age period that it would not serve as a good diagnostic. Derivational morphology, in contrast, is a semiproductive, rich, and complex system, and it demonstrates sufficient semantic and structural diversity to constitute an appropriate diagnostic tool for elementary school age. The category of Hebrew adjectives was selected because it is noncanonical in a number of senses, on the one hand, whereas it maps a variety of meanings onto various types of Hebrew morphological structure, on the other hand.

We focus on derivational adjective formation in SLI and NLA school-age children with the view to contribute to the debate on the nature of language disorders in children. One view holds that this is a developmental delay relative to children without language disorders. Another view holds that the linguistic system in SLI children is essentially different and deviant from normal development patterns (Leonard, Bortolini, Caselli, McGregor, & Sabbadini, 1992). This chapter shows that SLI school children have serious problems in processing the internal structure of Hebrew adjectives and in using morphological cues in both comprehension and production.

LANGUAGE DEVELOPMENT AT SCHOOL AGE

This chapter focuses on morphological knowledge in normal language acquiring (NLA) and specific language impaired (SLI) children who attend
elementary school. It is well accepted by now that natural language development runs its course over a long and protracted period until adolescence and beyond, and that during the school years it interacts intensively
with the acquisition of literacy (Berman & Ravid, 1999; Nippold, 1998).
Language acquisition during the school years (termed *later language development*) takes place at every linguistic level—lexical, grammatical, and
pragmatic—and is accompanied by increasing metalinguistic awareness,
abstractization, and explicitation of linguistic representation (Karmiloff-
Smith, 1992; Scholnick, Nelson, Gelman, & Miller, 1999). Concomitantly,
perception of nonliteral linguistic functions such as figurative language,
linguistic ambiguity, sarcasm, irony, and language puns emerges and
consolidates during the school-age and adolescent years (Ashkenazi &
Ravid, 1998; Nippold, 1998).

By elementary school, children have acquired a large and varied vocabulary with complex hierarchical lexical and morphological connections
(Anglin, 1993; Olson & Astington, 1986). Morphological and syntactic
knowledge is well established beyond the level of the simple clause. By
the end of elementary school, children are able, at the one extreme, to tell
well-formed narratives; at the other extreme, they are familiar with most
morphophonological variants of words and morphemes in their language
(Berman & Slobin, 1994; Ravid, 1995). Growing familiarity with written
language both as a notational system and discourse style contributes to increasing linguistic literacy during the school years, side by side with the
acquisition of new, less canonical structures typical of written language
(Levin, Ravid, & Rappaport, 2001; Ravid & Avidor, 1998; Ravid & Tolchinsky, 2002).

Focusing on the population of the current study, Israeli school children
formally relate words by their morphological structure, productively use
semantic and structural options in morphology, and show awareness of
basic morphological components such as roots and suffixes. By third and
fourth grade, NLA Israeli children have already mastered reading and
writing skills, can tell well-formed narratives, and are well on the way to
correct Hebrew spelling—a skill that involves phonological and morphological representation and processing (Berman & Ravid, 1999; Berman &
Slobin, 1994; Ravid, 2001). They have been exposed to a variety of texts including Biblical Hebrew since second grade and have been learning English, sometimes also French or Arabic, since third grade.

Language in school children is thus different from preschool linguistic
knowledge, and a critical distinguishing factor is the acquisition of liter-

acy. This has not escaped the notice of language disorders researchers, as summed up in a number of recent publications that have looked at the relationship between language disorders and literacy (Catts, Fey, Zhang, & Tomblin, 1999; Catts & Kamhi, 1999). SLI children's ability to acquire new words, a critical factor in later language development, is impaired, and they demonstrate difficulty with productive application of morphological knowledge (Nagy, Anderson, Scommer, Scott, & Stellmen, 1989). Accordingly, problems in school-related abilities such as persistent spelling errors and dropping morphological suffixes in writing are reported. Although similar to their age-matched NLA peers in oral judgment, SLI children demonstrate more difficulties in spontaneous writing (Rubin, Kantor, & Macnab, 1990). The majority of SLI children are thus at a very high risk for learning disability in elementary school, initially with learning to read and later on in situations requiring complex language skills (Paul, 1995; Weiss, 1997).

In this chapter, we examine the ability to comprehend and produce Hebrew adjectives in SLI school children compared with NLA children of the same age, and with younger NLA language-matched children. In this age group, it is possible to examine morphological knowledge beyond the obligatory inflectional systems, which are mastered early on, and to look for more subtle differences in formal and semantic mapping, which can supply further clues on the nature of SLI.

MORPHOLOGICAL PROCESSING

There are a number of reasons for selecting derivational word formation as the main focus of this study. One relates to the central role of the lexicon in acquisition and language disorders. Studies have pointed out a host of lexical processing problems in SLI children, such as (a) taking more time in tasks of lexical retrieval and fast mapping, (b) a reduced tendency to extend new object names to unnamed members of the same category, (c) a need for phonologically and syntactically clearer and more transparent lexical input than NLA children, and (d) inefficient use of sentence and discourse structure in identifying the meaning of unfamiliar words (Stone & Connel, 1993; Leonard & Deevy, chap. 9, this volume). Studies have also identified morphological analysis difficulties in SLI children, a reduced ability to manipulate morphemes and generalize morpheme meaning, and resulting problems in word learning, especially under explicit experimental conditions (Swisher, Restrepo, Plante, & Lowell, 1995; Swisher & Snow, 1994). In addition, metalinguistic problems have been detected in language-disordered children at a number of levels that interact and affect each other, resulting in some cases in communicative impairment (Bishop, 2000; Rubin, 1988; Swisher et al., 1995). The immense importance of lexical development in school children, which underlies almost every other linguistic achievement (Berman & Ravid, 1999), directs our attention to words and their structure.

The focus on Hebrew relates to the growing body of evidence of typological considerations in language learning. Recent cross-linguistic research has demonstrated the powerful impact of target-language typology on the process of acquisition in a range of domains, revealing that early on children are sensitive to the typological imperatives of their language (Berman, 1986). Findings of research in different domains such as speech perception, spatial relations, word-class acquisition, word formation, narrative development, and learning to spell converge to show that early on children are attuned to the language-particular way of encoding form-meaning relationships in their language (Bowerman, 1996; Clark & Berman, 1984; Gathercole, 1997; Gillis & Ravid, 2000; Jucszyk, 1997). In each case reported, how children encode form-meaning relations accords with how this is done by adult speakers of the same target language, rather than by children of the same age in other languages. Hebrew, a highly synthetic Semitic language, challenges its speakers with a rich and complex morphological system.

Interestingly, comparative studies of inflectional morphology in languages with varying degrees of syntheticity suggest that language-impaired children learning morphologically rich languages such as Hebrew or Italian fare on the whole better than English-speaking SLI children, learning a language with a sparse morphology (Dromi, Leonard, & Shteiman, 1993; Leonard et al., 1992; Rom & Leonard, 1990). It seems that children growing up in highly synthetic languages featuring a variety of salient, stressed morphemes find inflectional morphology tasks easier than children growing up in languages with impoverished inflection. Word formation in a highly synthetic language such as Hebrew seems like a promising domain of investigation in SLI and NLA children. Morphological difficulties constitute the core of a complex disorder, or a complex of disorders, which calls for description, assessment, and explanation at more than a single level (Bishop, chap. 13, this volume) and for which derivational morphology is suggested to be a diagnostic tool.

SLI, especially in school children who are already fairly proficient in both oral and written facets of their native tongue, calls for an assessment tool that demands elaborate knowledge related to lexicon size as well as to a grasp of network relations between words with the same lexical substance or belonging to the same ontological category. The unpredictable, nonobligatory, semantically opaque nature of derivational morphology contributes to this challenge. Derivational morphology provides a useful, although to date largely untapped, source for examining linguistic command in SLI. Word formation is a domain that requires complex, integrated knowledge of the interrelation among lexical convention, semantic content, and formal structure. As such it is an area where knowledge continues to develop well into school age and is related to literacy.

To date, most studies on derivational morphology in SLI English-speaking children have been conducted on school children because rich derivational structures in English mostly require components beyond its (mostly) monomorphemic Germanic core lexicon, and are therefore acquired later. These studies have found that SLI children are insensitive to derivational relationships (Moats & Smith, 1992), storing words in isolated rather than network forms (Carlisle, 1988). They also have difficulty applying morphological rules to unfamiliar words, and they demonstrate a reduced ability for organizing and accessing words through morphological relations (Freyd & Baron, 1982; Nagy et al., 1989).

In a recent study, Ravid, Avivi Ben-Zvi, and Levie (1999) reported on comprehension and production of novel Hebrew nouns in SLI and age- and language-matched NLA school children. The nominal categories tested ranged from agent, instrument, and place to collective, abstract, and action nominals. The comprehension task tested children's ability to analyze a novel noun into its components, which were extant morphemes in Hebrew—roots, stems, patterns, and suffixes. The production task tested children's ability to produce novel nouns from verbs and other nouns. There was no difference among the study groups on the comprehension task, which required the ability to relate words through their roots or stems. However, the SLI group was consistently worse than the age- and language-matched controls on the production task, which required relating words through their patterns and suffixes. This suggests that SLI children are able to manipulate roots and stems, morphemes conveying lexically encodable information; but they find it harder to manipulate patterns and suffixes, morphemes with a categorizing function that require a higher order linguistic capacity for analyzing and extending morphological knowledge. The SLI group also showed a deviant pattern on classifying nouns semantically and was not able to make maximal use of the whole possible array of root-and-pattern structures in production.

The novel noun study indicated that derivational nominal morphology is a sufficiently sensitive tool for characterizing language knowledge in typically and nontypically developing Israeli school children. The study discussed in this chapter examines knowledge of adjectives in this population.

REPRESENTING ADJECTIVES

The three well-known content-word (or *open class*) categories in the world's languages are nouns, verbs, and adjectives. These categories differ in their degree of universality and prototypicality as defined by a number of criteria. Semantically, a lexical category is characterized by the concepts it refers to and, syntactically, by the syntactic functions it fulfills. It has also been proposed that lexical categories have discourse roles, and that the prototypical status of category members depends to what extent they introduce participants or events into the discourse (Hopper & Thompson, 1984). Finally, a lexical class may also have language-specific morphological characteristics. Typical members of the *class* of lexical categories fulfill these requirements. Thus, the two basic lexical categories that participate in making up a language either onto- or phylogenetically are nouns and verbs. Although these two categories contain more and less typical members (e.g., concrete vs. abstract nouns, dynamic vs. state verbs), they are both primary lexical classes in the sense of referring to the basic lexical notions of objects and events, and implementing primary syntactic functions such as arguments and predicates (Schachter, 1985). In both English and Hebrew, nouns and verbs are rather easy to characterize in uniform grammatical and structural terms such as morphosyntactic behavior (e.g., nouns take possession markers and verbs decline in tenses).

Adjectives constitute a third content-word class, which is less primary in a number of senses. From a pragmatic point of view, Thompson (1988) showed that adjectives have differential discourse functions in spontaneous conversation, together with nouns and verbs. Semantically, adjectives denote attributes or properties of nouns—that is, they serve in a secondary function to a primary class. Syntactically, adjectives fulfill two functions, again, in relation to nouns: Predicative adjectives have the function of predicate heads (e.g., *Mary is smart*), and attributive adjectives have the function of NP modifiers (e.g., *the smart student*). In both cases, the adjective denotes a property attributed to a noun—either the subject of the sentence or the NP head (Ferris, 1993).

In classical linguistic terms, nouns are those terms that refer, describe, or designate objects in some way, whereas adjectives characterize them (Lyons, 1966). This is reflected in the fact that, in many languages, adjectives agree with the noun they modify in number, gender, and in many others also in additional values such as definiteness or case (e.g., French, Latin, Hebrew). In his survey of linguistic universals, Greenberg (1966) noted that in all languages where the adjective follows the noun, it expresses all the inflectional classes marked by the noun, even in cases where the noun may lack overt expression of one or all of them. This implies that nouns have a fixed form independent of any modifier they receive, whereas adjectives presuppose a noun and adjust their form to correspond to its inflection (Markman, 1989).

The secondary nature of adjectives is expressed typologically in the fact that many languages lack an open-class category of adjectives. In some languages, this is a closed-class system expressing mainly dimensions, color, age, and value. Others such as Biblical Hebrew lack an adjective class altogether (Gesenius, 1910). In such cases, adjectival meanings are expressed by (mainly abstract) nouns (e.g., in Hausa) and (again, mainly) relativized stative verbs (e.g., Bemba and Mandarin Chinese; Dixon, 1977; Schachter, 1985).

In psycholinguistic terms, the representation of adjectives in the mental lexicon is less richly structured and more arbitrary than that of nouns. Working within a categorization framework, Markman (1989) presented evidence that people expect nouns but not adjectives to refer to concepts that have considerably enduring and permanent inferential depth; that provide fundamental, essential information about the object and its identity; that are more readily placed in a taxonomy; and that are difficult to combine with richly structured categories. Adjectives, in contrast, are less dense in meaning, have a less correlated structure than nouns, and are more prone to adjusting not only their form but also their meaning according to the modified noun. Compare, for example, *good person–good knife, large house–large mouse*, and, even more dramatically, *criminal act–criminal lawyer* (Bolinger, 1967). Comparing the two lexical categories, Markman claimed that frequently used nouns tend to convey richer, stronger, and more stereotyped information than do common, frequently used adjectives. Adjectives point to arbitrary categories—where a single property might be the defining characteristic implying a contrast between members of the same noun category and specifying subdivisions within a richer category along many different dimensions. It seems that adjectives presuppose nouns in some way, whereas nouns do not presuppose adjectives.

Another facet of the representation of adjectives versus nouns is the different ways the two lexical classes function in the way people organize and retrieve information in memory. Markman (1989) presented evidence from studies of paired associate learning and semantic memory in English that suggest nouns may have some privileged status in memory, allowing more accurate, quicker access to information, and being more effective as memory cues than adjectives and verbs. For example, nouns are better retrieval cues than adjectives, and when nouns precede adjectives, N-A pairs are learned better despite the word order mismatch in English.

The essential difference between the lexical classes of nouns and adjectives emerges early on in development. Gelman and Markman (1985) reported an experimental study of noun and adjective interpretation in young children (ages 2;6–3;6) who were asked to "find the ball" or to "find the red one." When asked to interpret adjectives, children tended to focus on a contrast between members of the same object category, but nouns prompted children to select the more distinctive exemplar of the category.

Diary studies and surveys of natural language acquisition show that adjectives appear later in child speech than do nouns and verbs (Casseli,

Bates, Casadio, & Fenson, 1995; Rice, 1990; Sommers, Kozarevich, & Michaels, 1994). They also constitute a low-frequency class when compared with other content words in children's early lexicons in various languages (Dromi, 1987; Marvin, Beukelman, & Bilyeu, 1994; Ravid & Nir, 2000; Valian, 1986). Nevertheless, after an early phase of acquiring predominantly common nouns, children come to acquire larger numbers of verbs and adjectives as well (Barret, 1995). Ninio (1988) claimed that the emergence of abstract predicative categories such as verbs and adjectives in child language follows the emergence of hierarchical syntax involving the insight of creating higher order complex units. According to Berman (1988), adjectives enter the child's repertoire relatively later than do verbs and nouns because they share features with both and are therefore less prototypical than verbs and nouns. Thus, it takes time for children to integrate semantic, syntactic, and morphological cues to make the necessary distinctions between nouns and verbs, on the one hand, and adjectives, on the other.

Given this background, it is clear that adjectives constitute a non-canonical lexical class across languages, that their representation is less robust than that of nouns, and that they nevertheless have clearly defined semantic, syntactic, and discourse characteristics. This category is thus a promising candidate for a study of later language development during the school years.

THE CASE OF HEBREW

Hebrew adjectives are interesting both as a language-specific example of this category, but even more so because of their diverse morphological structures in Hebrew.

Hebrew morphology makes use of two major types of word formation devices: root-and-pattern Semitic forms, alongside with concatenated, linear structures. Thus, it permits testing contrasts not found in non-Semitic languages (Bolozky, 1997).

All Hebrew verbs and most nouns and adjectives contain a tri- or quadriconsonantal core, the Semitic *root*, which carries the main lexical substance of the word. This structural core appears discontinuously in the word because it is interdigitated by vowels provided by the complementary vocalic structure of the *pattern*. The combination of root and pattern into a word is termed *nonlinear affixation*. It is illustrated in Table 10.1 in a set of words related by the consonantal skeleton constituting root *k-l-t take in, absorb*. Patterns have classificatory functions indicating features of syntactico-semantic nominal and verbal classes. The seven verbal patterns are termed *binyanim* (literally, buildings), and they indicate transitivity values. For example, *kalat* absorbed is a transitive verb, whereas *hiklit* re-

TABLE 10.1
Nonlinear Structure in Hebrew:
Words Related by the root *k-l-t* take in, absorb

Verb	Gloss	Pattern	Pattern Meaning
kalat	Absorbed	CaCaC	Basic verb
niklat	Was absorbed	niCCaC	Passive verb
hiklit	Recorded	hiCCiC	Causative verb
huklat	Was recorded	huCCaC	Passive verb

Noun	Gloss	Pattern	Pattern Meaning
klita	Absorption	CCiCa	Action nominal
haklata	Recording	haCCaCa	Action nominal
kélet	Input	CéCeC	Abstract noun
taklit	Record	taCCiC	Derived nominal
maklet	Receiver	maCCeC	Instrument noun
miklat	Shelter	miCCaC	Place noun
koltan	Receptor	CoCCan	Agent noun
kalit	Absorbable	CaCiC	Potential attribute adjective

corded is causative and *huklat* was recorded is its passive counterpart. Nominal patterns, a few dozen in number, indicate ontological categories (Clark, 1993) such as agent, instrument, place, and abstract nominal. For example, *CoCCan* is an agent pattern (cf. *tsolelan* submariner), whereas *maCCeC* indicates instruments (cf. *mavreg* screwdriver).

In addition to root-and-pattern structures, the Hebrew lexicon contains concatenated or *linear* stem-and-suffix forms (e.g., *mal'ax-i* angel-ic, *amin-ut* trustworthi-ness). Table 10.2 illustrates linear structures in derivation.

The components of linear formation are more analytic than those of nonlinear forms. Unlike Semitic roots, which are unpronounceable, discontinuous entities, Hebrew stems contain vowels and are almost always words in their own right. The concatenated stem-and-suffix form marks the boundaries of discernibly distinct entities (e.g., *kos-it, lamdan-ut*), and the stem is usually an identifiable, independent, pronounceable lexical unit.

TABLE 10.2
Linear Structure in Hebrew

Derived Word	Gloss	Stem and Derivational Suffix	Stem and Suffix Meaning
mada'an	Scientist	mada-an	Science-agent
pa'oton	Nursery school	pa'ot-on	Toddler-collective
kosit	Wine glass	kos-it	Glass-diminutive
ma'afiya	Bakery	ma'afe-iya	Baked product-place
lamdanut	Scholarship	lamdan-ut	Scholar-abstract

Hebrew adjectives constitute a recently evolved lexical class because Biblical Hebrew, although highly synthetic, did not have a morphological class of adjectives (Gai, 1995; Gesenius, 1910). Primary property notions such as *tov* good, *ra* bad were mainly expressed by present-tense (*benoni*) participial verb forms that shared many features with nouns. At the same time, Biblical Hebrew had a small class of nouns denoting ethnic origin with the suffix -*i* (e.g., *Yevusi* belonging to the nation of *Yevus*). These constitute the roots of present-day adjectival derivation in Hebrew.

Modern Hebrew, which is about 100 years old, has three[1] structural classes of adjectives: The most basic both semantically and structurally is an essentially closed class of primary *CVC* adjectives originating in Biblical present-tense verbs (e.g., *xam* hot, *tov* good). These adjectives are *morphologically simplex* because, despite their verbal origin, they are monomorphemic as well as monosyllabic, having lexicalized into a single unit. They also designate basic semantic relations such as good, bad, hot, and cold (Ravid & Nir, 2000). As a result, they are early acquisitions. This study, which focuses on morphologically complex adjectives in Hebrew, does not include basic *CVC* adjectives.

A second structural class of adjectives takes a nonlinear root-and-pattern form. Except for a class of color terms, which is inherently adjectival (e.g., *kaxol* blue, *sagol* purple), these are always structures appropriated from either verbal or nominal patterns. For example, *mahir* fast and *axil* edible take the agentive noun pattern *CaCiC* (cf. *pakid* clerk), whereas *mafxid* scary and *mesukan* dangerous use present-tense *maCCiC* and *meCuCaC* verbal patterns, some of which are depicted in Table 10.1. The semantic content of these classes varies across structural categories and designates a range of general and specific properties, attributes, and states. Times of acquisition also vary in accordance with the semantic content of the adjective class. For example, color terms are acquired and conjugated correctly early despite their structural complexity (Ravid, 1995), whereas resultative adjectives emerge and consolidate between the ages of 4 and 6 (Berman, 1994).

The current study contains three types of root-and-pattern adjectives: a category of resultative adjectives, sharing their patterns with present-tense verbs (patterns *CaCuC*, *meCuCaC*, *muCCaC*) and two nominal-pattern attributive adjective types: *CaCCan* agentive-attributive and *CaCiC* potential-attribute adjectives.

The third and most productive class of adjectives in Modern Hebrew is a late historical development deriving from those Biblical ethnic nouns that evolved in Medieval Hebrew into a full-fledged class of denominal

---

[1]A fourth class of diminutives is not included in this study. Please see Ravid (1998) for some discussion.

adjectives (e.g., *xashmal-i* electr-ic, *tsibur-i* publ-ic). Structurally, denominal adjectives are simpler than the root-and-pattern class because they involve linear formation of a nominal stem and the addition of the adjectival suffix *-i*. However, they are typical of higher register, written Hebrew, such as literary prose, journalistic, and expository texts, and their meaning is quite complex (Berman & Ravid, 1999; Ravid & Shlesinger, 1987). Apart from lexicalized forms such as *xagigi* festive and the original Biblical ethnic-attributive meaning (e.g., *dati* religious, *rusi* Russian), they are completely absent from child-directed speech. Denominal *i*-suffixed adjectives are the last type of adjectives to emerge in Hebrew child language around age 6, and they do not emerge in text production before high school (Berman & Ravid, 1999; Levin et al., 2001; Ravid & Nir, 2000; Zilberbuch, 1998). Denominal adjectives constitute another adjective category tested in this study.

This array of possible nonlinear versus linear morphological structures, coupled with the variety of semantic types encoded in them, makes Hebrew adjectives a promising class to focus on in the examination of NLA versus SLI language in elementary school.

THE HEBREW ADJECTIVE STUDY

In this study, we examined the ability to comprehend and produce Hebrew adjectives in SLI school children compared with NLA children of the same age, and with younger NLA language-matched children.

Research Questions

Given the problematic nature of the adjective category, we were interested in SLI and NLA school children's ability to comprehend and produce Hebrew adjectives in the structural classes described earlier. Specifically, we were interested in finding out whether the two populations follow similar or distinct paths in analyzing adjectives.

Subjects

The test group consisted of 14 SLI children (9 boys, 5 girls) ages 8;7 to 10;3. They were all third and fourth graders who had been diagnosed at the municipal speech services clinic by a speech pathologist. All of them had taken tests indicating a discrepancy of at least 15 points between their verbal and nonverbal abilities. There were two NLA control groups: The age-matched controls were 14 NLA children (9 boys, 5 girls) ages 8;3 to 10;3 with no language or other problems. They were matched one to one to the

SLI subjects by chronological age +/− 4 months and by SES (high, middle, low). There was also a NLA language-matched control group of 14 children (9 boys, 5 girls) ages 6;4 to 8;3. This group was matched one to one to the SLI subjects by language level (+/− 6 months) using a subset of the ITPA test that examines completion of auditory analogies (which is the only normed tool in Hebrew for this age bracket, up to 10 years of age) and by SES. All the study children were native monolingual speakers of Hebrew with normal hearing and no other disorders.

Experimental Tasks

The adjective test consisted of two tasks: comprehension and production, each containing 13 items in three adjective categories. Two of them had nonlinear root-and-pattern structure: resultative adjectives (employing verbal patterns) and attributive adjectives (employing nominal patterns). A third category of denominal *i*-suffixed adjectives had linear stem-and-suffix structure. The comprehension task preceded the production task to serve as a facilitator. It introduced the child to thinking about the components of adjectives, their structure, and semantics so that by the time he or she got to the production part it was no longer an unfamiliar task. The final form of the adjective test was decided on after a pilot test. Before the construction of the tests, elementary school teachers were consulted about the words selected so as to make sure they were all known to school children. Internal consistency of both tests was computed and found to be α (Kronbach) 0.8. The appendix lists the two parts of the adjective test.

Comprehension

The comprehension task tested children's ability to analyze 13 adjectives into their morphological components—roots, stems, patterns, and suffixes—by interpreting a set of given adjective stimuli. The child was told that the investigator had some hidden pictures (used as incentives) and that he or she would be asked a question and then would both look at the pictures (see the Appendix for a full set of the instructions). Then the child was presented with an adjective embedded in a sentential context and asked to explain its meaning, which entailed using a related noun or verb. For example: "I have a picture here showing a glass with some juice, and a picture of some *spilled* juice (*mits shafux* juice spilled). What happened here?" The expected response to this resultative adjective was: *shafxu oto* (they) spilled,Pl it, an impersonal active verb form from the same root and in the appropriate verb pattern (see the Appendix for more examples and a full list of the comprehension task items). The accompanying picture was *not* shown and was only revealed after the item was completed.

The *comprehension* responses were scored on a scale of 1 to 4. A score of 1 was assigned to *no response* and responses such as *don't know*. A score of 2 was assigned to a semantically, but not morphologically, appropriate response (e.g. *ko'éset* is angry,Fm instead of *mit'atsbénet* becomes annoyed) as a response to the stimuli *atsbanit* nervous, annoyed. A score of 3 was assigned to a partial, although morphologically appropriate, response, where one structural element—stem or root, suffix, or pattern—was absent. For example, the laughy boy (*tsaxkan*) *matsxik harbe* makes (you) laugh a lot instead of *tsoxek harbe* laughs a lot, where the verb pattern used is the inappropriate causative instead of the desired simple active pattern. A score of 4 was assigned to a fully correct response.

Production

The production task tested children's ability to produce 13 adjectives from randomly presented verb and noun stimuli. The child was told that the investigator had some more hidden pictures, that he or she would be asked a question, and then would both look at the appropriate picture (see the Appendix for a full set of the instructions). The child was then presented with a sentence containing a verb or noun and asked to derive an adjective from it. For example: "I have a picture here of a hand that got *stuck* in *glue* (*nidbeka be-dévek*). What can we say now about the hand that has got glue on it?" This sentence contained the requested root *d-b-k* in the two stimuli *stuck* and *glue*. The response could be something like "*hi dvika* it (is) sticky"—an attributive adjective in the nominal *CaCiC* pattern with the same root (see the Appendix for more examples and a full list of the comprehension task items). The picture again was produced only *after* the child had given the response.

The *production* responses were scored on a 1 to 7 scale. A score of 1 was assigned to *no response* and responses such as *don't know*. A score of 2 was assigned to a repetition response. A score of 3 was assigned to analytic rather than morphological expression (e.g. can kill somebody for *arsi* venomous). A score of 4 was assigned to a semantically, but not morphologically, appropriate response (e.g., *paxdan* coward for *xamkan* slippery) as a response to the stimuli *xomek* slips away. A score of 5 was assigned to a partial response with the requested root, but from another lexical category (e.g., *bniya* building for *banuy* built) as a response to *banu oto* (they) built Acc-it from root *b-n-y*. A score of 6 was assigned to an unconventional adjective (e.g., *pruka* [*CaCuC* pattern] for *meforéket* [*meCuCaC* pattern] taken apart) as a response to *perku ota* (they) took it apart. A score of 7 was assigned to a fully correct response.

Predictions

No differences were predicted among the test and control groups on comprehension because the task requirement was minimal: The semantic content of the categorial element, which is the most difficult to identify (i.e., the pattern or suffix), was provided in the question, and the child was requested only to provide the same lexical substance (root or stem) by a verb or noun related in structure to the given form. Root and stem functions are present in children as young as 5 (Ravid & Malenky, 2001). This prediction also stemmed from the results of the nonce nouns test (Ravid et al., 1999).

For the production task, two alternative scenarios were hypothesized: the SLI group would fare as well as the young language-matched controls, supporting a delayed development model, or it would do worse than them, supporting the deviant development model.

A hierarchy of difficulty on the adjectival categories, suggested by evidence from acquisition, was predicted: All groups were expected to find easiest the resultative category, which is acquired in late preschool years (Berman, 1994). The next category on this scale of difficulty was predicted to be attributive adjectives, containing two subcategories: *CaCCan* nominal-pattern items, a structural category that is semantically close to agent and instrument nouns and is acquired early on by Hebrew speakers (Clark & Berman, 1984; Ravid et al., 1999); and a more difficult *CaCiC* category that also shares its pattern with nouns, yet is less accessible to children because it contains potential-attribute *-able* adjectives. Last on this hierarchy should come denominal *i*-suffixed adjectives, which are completely absent in preschool language as well as from everyday speech (Berman & Ravid, 1999; Levin et al., 2001).

RESULTS

A one-way Pearson test between the comprehension and production tasks showed a positive correlation ($N = 42$, $p < 0.001$, $r = .64$), indicating that success on comprehension and production was correlated.

Comprehension

Table 10.3 presents the mean scores of correct responses on the comprehension task by the three study groups. A one-way ANOVA showed an effect of group [$F(2,39) = 15.51$, $p < .001$] counter to our prediction. A

TABLE 10.3
Mean Scores (on a Scale of 1–4) and Standard Deviations
on the Comprehension Task by Study Group

Study Group →	SLI		Language Matched		Age Matched	
General Results	Mean	SD	Mean	SD	Mean	SD
Comprehension: Scale 1–4	3.57	0.21	3.82	0.16	3.9	0.11

Scheffé procedure showed this effect to derive from a difference between the study SLI group, on the one hand, and the two control groups, which did not differ from each other, on the other hand.

Production

General Results. Table 10.4 presents the general mean scores of correct responses on the production task by the three study groups. A one-way ANOVA showed an effect of group [$F(2,39) = 18.98$, $p < .001$] as predicted. A post hoc Scheffé procedure showed this effect to derive from a difference between the SLI group and the language-matched younger controls, on the one hand, and the age-matched older controls, on the other hand.

Category Analysis. Table 10.4 also presents the mean scores of correct responses on the production task by adjectival category: resultative adjectives (e.g., *muxba* hidden), attributive adjectives (e.g., *navranit* pokey,Fm), and denominal adjectives (e.g., *kalbi* canine). A two-way ANOVA on study group (3) X morphological category (3) showed an effect for group [$F(2,39) = 17.16$, $p < .001$] and for morphological category [$F(2,78) = 38.59$, $p < .001$]. To detect the source of the differences t tests were conducted be-

TABLE 10.4
Mean Scores (on a Scale of 1–7) and Standard Deviations on the
Production Task by Study Group and Morphological Category

Study Group →	SLI		Language Matched		Age Matched	
Adjective Category	Mean	SD	Mean	SD	Mean	SD
General results	4.81	0.79	5.4	0.68	6.31	0.42
Resultative	5.34	1.21	6.17	0.63	6.86	0.19
Attributive	4.22	0.62	4.60	1.08	5.89	0.74
Denominal	4.52	1.27	4.88	0.8	5.78	0.86

tween each two morphological categories (significance at the .05 level). These showed that the category of resultative adjectives differed significantly from the other morphological categories and was easier for all study groups as predicted. The attributive and denominal adjectives did not differ counter to our prediction.

Focusing on the three adjectival categories, one-way ANOVAs were carried out on each of adjectival categories by group.

Resultative Adjectives. A significant effect was found for group [F(2,39) = 12.59, $p < .001$], which the Scheffé procedure showed to derive from a difference between the two control groups, on the one hand, and the SLI group, on the other hand.

Attributive Adjectives. A significant effect was found for group [F(2,39) = 15.28, $p < .001$], which the Scheffé procedure showed to derive from a difference between the older age-matched control group, on the one hand, and the younger language-matched control group and SLI group, which did not differ from each other, on the other hand.

Denominal i-Suffixed Adjectives. A significant effect was found for group [F(2,39) = 5.91, $p < .001$], which the Scheffé procedure showed to derive from a difference between the older age-matched control group, on the one hand, and the SLI group, which did not differ from the younger language-matched control, on the other hand.

CONCLUSIONS AND DISCUSSION

This study investigated knowledge of Hebrew adjectival categories in three study groups: a group of SLI school children, and two NLA control groups matched one-to-one to the study group by language level (a younger group) and by age (same age as the SLI). The results do not clearly support either the model of deviant or of delayed development in SLI children. These results, however, justify the choice of derivational morphology, and specifically of the category of adjectives, to assess the language of SLI, allowing an in-depth look into the nature of the differences between them and normally developing children.

Comprehension Versus Production

One surprising result, which had not been anticipated, was the difference between the SLI and control groups on comprehension. Although all groups did quite well on this task, the control groups, even the younger language-matched group, almost reached ceiling, whereas the SLI did more poorly. The nonce noun test (Ravid et al., 1999) was not sensitive enough to discern such differences. The greater difficulty experienced by the SLI on the adjective test may have derived from the noncanonical, semantically, and structurally diverse category of adjectives. This may have been exacerbated by the fact that the comprehension task required the analysis of extant adjectives into their morphological components. Specifically, correct responses consisted of morphologically appropriate nouns and verbs with specific patterns related to the stimulus adjective by root. Thus, although comprehension responses involved nouns and verbs rather than adjectives, the required analysis may have proved too difficult for the SLI school children, especially on the more difficult categories of attributive and denominal adjectives. This result reflects a weaker processing capacity for linguistic information, difficulty in using sentence structure for the analysis of word meaning, and a reduced ability of perceiving derivational relations among words (Carlisle, 1988; Moats & Smith, 1992; Swisher et al., 1995).

On the production task, the scenario providing support for the deviant development model may be indicated. Almost all production results point to a reduced morphological ability in the SLI group: They scored lowest of the three study groups, whereas both control groups did better. However, this rather extreme scenario may not be necessary to explain these results. Although the SLI children were older than the language-matched group, and therefore officially had more schooling, it can be assumed that their level of linguistic literacy was not as advanced (Ravid & Tolchinsky, 2002). SLI interferes with the acquisition of reading and writing skills so that children from this group were less familiar with written language. This means they had had less exposure to written texts and fewer opportunities to write, and therefore were less likely to learn new words from the written language, which constitutes the main source for new vocabulary in elementary school (Anglin, 1993; Rubin et al., 1990).

Moreover, this linguistic disorder is characterized by problems in phonological and morphological processing: SLI children are not sensitive to derivational information conveyed by words, they tend to remember words as separate, discrete units rather than members of networks and hierarchies, and they find morphological generalization especially difficult. In addition, they have difficulties in storing and retrieving linguistic information based on derivational relations. These considerations would explain why the SLI group found it difficult to interpret and create lexically linked words (Swisher & Snow, 1994). However, note that no interaction was found between study group and morphological category: The SLI group did not exhibit deviant patterning in their morphological knowledge. Like the control groups, they found resultatives to be easier than both attributive and denominal adjectives.

Morphological Strategies

Two production strategies were found to be especially prevalent in the responses of the SLI group as compared with the two control groups. These were designated earlier as *analytic expression* and *semantic response*, respectively, on the production scale. Analytic responses made use of periphrastic or syntactic means of expression. These were syntactic responses such as *ha-pérax ibed máyim* the-flower lost water for *meyubash* dried or *sharvul ad la-katef* sleeve up to-the-shoulder for *mufshal* turned up. Semantic responses were retrieved extant words, which were semantically close to the required form (e.g., *atsits* potted plant for *ets gamadi* tree dwarf-like = dwarf-like tree, *sharvul katsar* sleeve short = short sleeve for *mufshal* turned up, *pérax navul* flower dead = dead flower for *meyubash* dried). These two nonmorphological strategies—retrieval of familiar forms from the stored mental lexicon and syntactic expression—reflect morphological processing problems in SLI and were not as widely used by the younger language-matched group. They point at difficulties in performing meta-linguistic derivational analyses in an online experimental situation and a failure to identify shared morphemes, which would facilitate establishing connections between words from the same morphological family.

However, a third, morphological strategy *was* shared by the SLI and their language-matched peers. This was unconventional adjective, which also appeared on the production scale. In such responses, the root was correct and the semantic content appropriate, but the resulting combination was an unconventional form. Such unconventional adjectives typically arose from the application of an incorrect resultative pattern to the correct root (e.g., *nexba* [*niCCaC* pattern] for correct *xavuy* [*CaCuC*] hidden or *muvne* [*muCCaC*] for correct *banuy* [*CaCuC*] built). This strategy is well known from both naturalistic and experimental Hebrew child language data and is characteristic of spontaneous expression in preschoolers (Berman, 1994). Thus, it indicates juvenile, less well-developed morphological skills, rather than deviant strategies in the SLI group.

Morphological Categories

This study provided a window on typical and atypical acquisition of later-emerging adjectival constructions in Hebrew. The results of this study are uniform in placing resultative adjectives as a much earlier acquired form in both populations than other adjectival classes, supporting previous findings (Berman, 1994). In both SLI and NLA populations, resultative adjectives scored higher than the other morphological categories, although the control groups have almost perfect scores while the SLI lag behind. From a structural point of view, resultatives are not harder than other root-and-pattern forms that children acquiring Semitic languages manip-ulate from early on (Berman, 1985; Ravid & Farah, 1999). They occur in early child speech from the first as lexicalized forms such as *meluxlax* dirty, but they emerge productively only in preschool age (4–6) not only due to their passive, resultative semantics, but also simply because they belong to the semiproductive, semantically opaque, and unpredictable derivational system, which does not consolidate before school age (Berman, 1995).

The fact that *i*-suffixed denominal adjectives did not differ significantly from attributive adjectives was not predicted. Both categories were more difficult than the resultatives for all populations, demonstrating the inter-face of semantic and structural factors in the acquisition of a complex mor-phological system.

The nonlinear root-and-pattern attributives could be expected to be more difficult than the linear stem-and-suffix denominals: Root-and-pattern (nonlinear) morphology is more abstract and difficult to process than the linear attachment of suffixes onto stems. Each of the components of the nonlinear template occurs at a different representational tier or plane (Anderson, 1992), which makes them less accessible to speakers than linear segments. However, because all verbs and most other catego-ries in Hebrew are constructed of roots and patterns, there should be no reason that school children should have trouble with them. Moreover, *i*-suffixed denominals may undergo radical stem changes as in *kélev/kalbi* dog/canine (cf. English *five/fifth*), which are known to pose structural dif-ficulties to young learners (Jones, 1991; Levin et al., 2001; Ravid, 1995).

Semantics seems to be a more weighty factor in this case. The attribu-tive category that we tested consisted of two structural constructions: One was *CaCCan* adjectives (e.g., *xamkan* slippery), an early emerging attribu-tive-agentive class that is immensely productive and occurs frequently in both child and child-directed speech (Clark & Berman, 1984). The second was *CaCiC* potential-property adjectives, whose semantics is comparable to the English *-able* category (e.g., *axil* edible). The option of encoding a *po-tential* attribute morphologically is not available to preschoolers and is typical mostly of formal, written Hebrew. The combination of the two at-tributive adjective categories with the easier and more difficult semantics resulted in similar scores to those of the denominal category.

Focusing on denominals, it is not the formal addition of the suffix *-i* to the noun base and the consequent morphophonological stem changes that make it so difficult. These same morphophonological stem changes as in *kélev/kalbi* dog/canine occur across the board in all types of nominal oper-ations in Hebrew, both inflectional and derivational, some of which (such as noun plurals, noun feminines, noun possessives, and noun com-pounds) are acquired early on. Children have plenty of opportunities to learn the rules and intricacies of the system from early childhood, although radical, idiosyncratic stem changes are difficult even for school children (Levin et al., 2001; Ravid, 1995).

Denominal adjectives are semantically complex entities. A construction such as *venomous* has the general meaning of "A with the property of N." However, the appropriate property of the base noun carried over to the derived adjective is not always predictable, as in other cases of denominal derivation (Aronoff, 1980; Clark & Clark, 1979). To create a denominal adjective, the base N has to be dissolved into its component semantic properties so as to select the specific property to be carried over to the derived adjective. Like potential-attribute *CaCiC* adjectives, denominals are typical of formal, written Hebrew and occur almost only in expository texts (Ravid & Shlesinger, 1987). Although Hebrew speakers are exposed to such texts in school and school-related activities, they do not use them productively before the end of high school (Berman & Ravid, 1999; Zilberbuch, 1998). Certainly the younger language-matched and SLI groups have had fewer opportunities to encounter such forms and are less able to process them.

In general, what makes morphological forms in a synthetic language like Hebrew hard or easy in acquisition does not seem to be solely structural, formal factors, but rather their combination with semantic factors together with processing factors such as transparency and saliency of form and meaning.

HOW SPECIFIC ARE MORPHOLOGICAL DISORDERS?

In this chapter, we examined morphological abilities in Hebrew-speaking school children with SLI compared with their NLA age- and language-matched peers. We focused on adjectives, a structurally rich and semantically diverse noncanonical lexical category, which made it possible to investigate both formal and semantic facets of morphological knowledge. Examination of adjective comprehension and production suggests that, in this domain, morphological knowledge is patterned in a similar way in both SLI and NLA school children. However, the SLI lagged behind both control groups, indicating serious problems in processing the internal structure of adjectives and in using morphological cues in both comprehension and production.

This study highlights the importance of derivational morphology in testing linguistic abilities in school children and in particular language-disordered populations. Berman and Ravid (1999) identified lexicon size and diversity as crucial in later language development in morphology, syntax, and text production. According to Anglin (1993), processes of morphological analysis and generalization underlie lexical expansion in children, and at least half of the words in a child's lexicon are acquired through morphological form-to-meaning mapping. Future studies of specific derivational domains can further determine the boundaries of lexical and morphological limitations of children with SLI growing up in a highly synthetic language.

REFERENCES

Anderson, S. R. (1992). *A-morphous morphology*. New York: Cambridge University Press.

Anglin, J. M. (1993). Vocabulary development: A morphological analysis. *Monographs of the Society for Research in Child Development, 58*, 10.

Aronoff, M. (1980). Contextuals. *Language, 56*, 744–758.

Ashkenazi, O., & Ravid, D. (1998). Children's understanding of linguistic humor: An aspect of metalinguistic awareness. *Current Psychology of Cognition, 17*, 367–387.

Barrett, M. (1995). Early lexical development. In P. Fletcher & B. MacWhinney (Eds.), *The handbook of child language* (pp. 362–392). Oxford: Blackwell.

Berman, R. A. (1985). Acquisition of Hebrew. In D. I. Slobin (Ed.), *The crosslinguistic study of language acquisition* (Vol. I, pp. 255–371). Hillsdale, NJ: Lawrence Erlbaum Associates.

Berman, R. A. (1986). A step-by-step model of language acquisition. In I. Levin (Ed.), *Stage and structure: Reopening the debate* (pp. 191–219). Norwood, NJ: Ablex.

Berman, R. A. (1988). Word-class distinctions in developing grammars. In Y. Levy, I. M. Schlesinger, & M. D. S. Braine (Eds.), *Categories and processes in language acquisition*. Hillsdale, NJ: Lawrence Erlbaum Associates.

Berman, R. A. (1994). Formal, lexical, and semantic factors in the acquisition of Hebrew resultative participles. *Berkeley Linguistic Society, 20*, 82–92.

Berman, R. A. (1995). Word-formation as evidence. In D. McLaughlin & S. McEwen (Eds.), *Proceedings of the 19th Annual Boston University Conference on Language Development* (Vol. I, pp. 82–95). Somerville, MA: Cascadilla.

Berman, R. A., & Ravid, D. (1999). *The oral/literate continuum: Developmental perspectives*. Final report submitted to the Israel Science Foundation, Tel Aviv University.

Berman, R. A., & Slobin, D. I. (1994). *Relating events in narrative: A crosslinguistic developmental study*. Hillsdale, NJ: Lawrence Erlbaum Associates.

Bishop, D. V. M. (2000). Pragmatic language impairment: A correlate of SLI, a distinct subgroup, or part of the autistic continuum? In D. V. M. Bishop & L. B. Leonard (Eds.), *Speech and language impairments in children: Causes, characteristics, intervention and outcome*. Hove, UK: Psychology Press.

Bolinger, D. (1967). Adjectives in English: Attribution and predication. *Lingua, 18*, 1–34.

Bolozky, S. (1997). Israeli Hebrew phonology. In A. S. Kaye (Ed.), *Phonologies of Asia and Africa* (pp. 287–311). New York: Eisenbrauns.

Bowerman, M. (1996). Learning how to structure space for language: A crosslinguistic perspective. In P. Bloom, M. Peterson, L. Nadel, & M. Garrett (Eds.), *Language and space*. Cambridge, MA: MIT Press.

Carlisle, J. F. (1988). Knowledge of derivational morphology and spelling ability in fourth, sixth and eighth graders. *Applied Psycholinguistics, 9*, 247–266.

Casseli, M. C., Bates, E., Casadio, P., & Fenson, J. (1995). A cross-linguistic study of early lexical development. *Cognitive Development, 10*, 159–199.

Catts, H. W., Fey, M. E., Zhang, X., & Tomblin, J. B. (1999). Language basis of reading and reading disabilities; evidence from a longitudinal investigation. *Science Studies of Reading, 3*, 331–361.

Catts, H. W., & Kamhi, A. G. (Eds.). (1999). *Language and reading disabilities.* Needham Heights, MA: Allyn & Bacon.

Clark, E. V. (1993). *The lexicon in acquisition.* Cambridge: Cambridge University Press.

Clark, E. V., & Berman, R. A. (1984). Structure and use in the acquisition of word-formation. *Language, 60*, 542–590.

Clark, E. V., & Clark, H. H. (1979). When nouns surface as verbs. *Language, 55*, 767–811.

Dixon, R. M. W. (1977). *A grammar of Yidin.* Cambridge: Cambridge University Press.

Dromi, E. (1987). *Early lexical development.* Cambridge: Cambridge University Press.

Dromi, E., Leonard, L. B., & Shteiman, M. (1993). The grammatical morphology of Hebrew-speaking children with specific language impairment: Some competing hypotheses. *Journal of Speech and Hearing Research, 36*, 760–771.

Ferris, C. (1993). *The meaning of syntax: A study in the adjectives of English.* Longman: London.

Freyd, P., & Baron, J. (1982). Individual differences in acquisition of derivational morphology. *Journal of Verbal Learning and Verbal Behavior, 21*, 282–295.

Gai, A. (1995). The category "adjective" in Semitic languages. *Journal of Semitic Studies, 1*, 1–9.

Gathercole, V. C. (1997). Word meaning biases, or language-specific effects? Evidence from English, Spanish, and Korean. *First Language, 17*, 31–56.

Gelman, S. A., & Markman, E. M. (1985). Implicit contrast in adjectives vs. nouns: Implications for word-learning in preschoolers. *Journal of Child Language, 12*, 125–143.

Gesenius. (1910). *Gesenius' Hebrew Grammar* (E. Kautzsch, Ed., A. E. Cowley Rev.). Oxford: Clarendon.

Gillis, S., & Ravid, D. (2001). Typological differentiation in the development of orthographic systems: Evidence from Hebrew and Dutch. In I. Barriere, G. Morgan, S. Chiat, & B. Woll (Eds.), *Child Language Seminar Proceedings* (pp. 182–189). London: City University.

Greenberg, J. H. (1966). Language universals. In T. A. Sebeok (Ed.), *Current trends in linguistics: Vol. 3. Theoretical foundations* (pp. 61–112). The Hague: Mouton.

Hopper, P., & Thompson, S. (1984). The discourse basis for lexical categories in universal grammar. *Language, 60*, 703–752.

Jones, K. N. (1991). Development of morphophonemic segments in children's mental representations of words. *Applied Psycholinguistics, 12*, 217–239.

Jucszyk, P. W. (1997). *The discovery of spoken language.* Cambridge, MA: Bradford Books.

Karmiloff-Smith, A. (1992). *Beyond modularity: A developmental perspective of cognitive science.* Cambridge, MA: MIT Press.

Leonard, L. B., Bortolini, V., Caselli, M. C., McGregor, K. K., & Sabbadini, L. (1992). Morphological deficits in children with specific language impairment: The status of features in the underlying grammar. *Language Acquisition, 2*, 151–179.

Levin, I., Ravid, D., & Rappaport, S. (2001). Morphology and spelling among Hebrew-speaking children: From kindergarten to first grade. *Journal of Child Language, 28*, 741–769.

Lyons, J. (1966). Towards a notional theory of the parts of speech. *Journal of Linguistics, 79*, 1–13.

Markman, E. M. (1989). *Categorization and naming in children: Problems of induction.* Cambridge, MA: The MIT Press.

Marvin, C. A., Beukelman, D. R., & Bilyeu, D. (1994). Vocabulary-use patterns in preschool children: Effects of context and time sampling. *Augmentative and Alternative Communication, 10*, 224–237.

Moats, L. C., & Smith, C. (1992). Derivational morphology: Why it should be included in language assessment and instruction. *Language, Speech and Hearing Services in Schools, 23*, 312–319.

Nagy, W. E., Anderson, R. C., Scommer, M., Scott, J. A., & Stellmen, A. C. (1989). *Reading Research Quarterly, 24*, 262–283.

Ninio, A. (1988). On formal grammatical categories in early child language. In Y. Levy, I. M. Schlesinger, & M. D. S. Braine (Eds.), *Categories and processes in language acquisition.* Hillsdale, NJ: Lawrence Erlbaum Associates.

Nippold, M. A. (1998). *Later language development: The school-age and adolescent years.* Austin, TX: PRO-ED.

Olson, D. R., & Astington, J. W. (1986). Children's acquisition of metalinguistic and metacognitive verbs. In W. Demopoulos & A. Marras (Eds.), *Language learning and concept acquisition: Foundational issues* (pp. 184–199). Norwood, NJ: Ablex.

Paul, R. (1995). *Language disorders from infancy through adolescence: Assessment and intervention.* St. Louis: Mosby.

Ravid, D. (1995). *Language change in child and adult Hebrew: A psycholinguistic perspective.* New York: Oxford University Press.

Ravid, D. (1998). Diminutive *-i* in early child Hebrew: An initial analysis. In S. Gillis (Ed.), *Studies in the acquisition of number and diminutive marking* (pp. 149–174). Antwerp: Antwerp University Press.

Ravid, D. (2001). Learning to spell in Hebrew: Phonological and morphological factors. *Reading and Writing, 14*, 459–485.

Ravid, D., & Avidor, A. (1998). Acquisition of derived nominals in Hebrew: Developmental and linguistic principles. *Journal of Child Language, 25*, 229–266.

Ravid, D., Avivi Ben-Zvi, G., & Levie, R. (1999). Derivational morphology in SLI children: Structure and semantics of Hebrew nouns. In M. Perkins & S. Howard (Eds.), *New directions in language development and disorders* (pp. 39–49). New York: Plenum.

Ravid, D., & Farah, R. (1999). Learning about noun plurals in early Palestinian Arabic. *First Language, 19*, 187–206.

Ravid, D., & Malenky, A. (2001). Awareness of linear and nonlinear morphology in Hebrew: A developmental study. *First Language, 21*, 25–56.

Ravid, D., & Nir, M. (2000). On the development of the category of adjective in Hebrew. In M. Beers, B. van den Bogaerde, G. Bol, J. de Jong, & C. Rooijmans (Eds.), *From sound to sentence: Studies on first language acquisition* (pp. 113–124). Groningen: Center for Language and Cognition.

Ravid, D., & Shlesinger, Y. (1987). Classification of denominal *i*-suffixed adjectives. *Hebrew Linguistics, 25*, 59–70. [in Hebrew]

Ravid, D., & Tolchinsky, L. (2002). Developing linguistic literacy: A comprehensive model. *Journal of Child Language, 29*, 419–448.

Rice, M. L. (1990). Preschoolers' QUIL: Quick incidental learning of words. In G. Contini-Ramsden & C. Snow (Eds.), *Children's language* (Vol. 7). Hillsdale, NJ: Lawrence Erlbaum Associates.

Rom, A., & Leonard, L. B. (1990). Interpreting deficits in grammatical morphology in specifically language-impaired children: Preliminary evidence from Hebrew. *Clinical Linguistics and Phonetics, 4*, 93–105.

Rubin, H. (1988). Morphological knowledge and early writing ability. *Language and Speech, 31*, 337–355.

Rubin, H. M., Kantor, & Macnab, J. (1990). Grammatical awareness in the spoken and written language of language-disabled children. *Canadian Journal of Psychology, 44*, 483–500.

Schachter, P. (1985). Parts-of-speech systems. In T. Shopen (Ed.), *Language typology and syntactic description: Vol. I. Clause structure* (pp. 3–61). Cambridge: Cambridge University Press.

Scholnick, E. K., Nelson, K., Gelman, S. A., & Miller, P. H. (Eds.). (1999). *Conceptual development: Piaget's legacy.* Mahwah, NJ: Lawrence Erlbaum Associates.

Sommers, R. K., Kozarevich, M., & Michaels, C. (1994). Word skills of children normal and impaired in communication skills and measures of language and speech development. *Journal of Communications Disorders, 27,* 223–240.

Stone, C. A., & Connell, P. J. (1993). Induction of a visual symbolic rule in children with specific language impairment. *Journal of Speech and Hearing Research, 36,* 599–608.

Swisher, L., Restrepo, M. A., Plante, E., & Lowell, S. (1995). Effect of implicit and explicit "rule" presentation on bound-morpheme generalization in specific language impairment. *Journal of Speech and Hearing Research, 38,* 168–173.

Swisher, L., & Snow, D. (1994). Learning and generalization components of morphological acquisition in children with SLI: Is there a functional relation? *Journal of Speech and Hearing Research, 37,* 1406–1413.

Thompson, S. A. (1988). A discourse approach to the cross-linguistic category adjective. In *Universals.* Oxford: Oxford University Press.

Valian, V. (1986). Syntactic categories in the speech of young children. *Developmental Psychology, 22,* 562–579.

Weiss, A. L. (1997). Planning language intervention for young children. In D. K. Bernstein & E. Tiegerman-Farber (Eds.), *Language and communication disorders in children* (pp. 272–323). Boston: Allyn & Bacon.

Zilberbuch, S. (1998). *Two types of compounds in spoken and written biographical and descriptive texts of school children, highschoolers and adults, compared with encyclopedic texts.* Unpublished master's thesis, School of Education, Tel Aviv University. [in Hebrew]

APPENDIX (*NOTE.* HEBREW WORD ORDER WITHIN THE NP IS N-A)

I *Comprehension*

I have a pack of pictures here. I will ask you some questions, and then we will look at the pictures together.
Sample questions:

1. I have a picture here of a baby, and a diaper, and a picture of *tinoket mexutélet* diapered,Fm baby,Fm (root *x-t-l*, pattern *meCuCaC*). What's happened to her?

Possible response: *xitlu ota* (they) diapered,Pl Acc-her (root *x-t-l*, pattern *CiCeC*).

2. I have a picture here of *béged raxits washable* garment (root *r-x-c*, pattern *CaCiC*). If we want to, what can we do to it?

Possible response: *li-rxots oto* to-wash Acc-it (root *r-x-c*, pattern *li-CCoC*).

3. I have a picture here of a boy with *halixa barvazit* duck-like,Fm walking,Fm. What is duck-like walking?

Possible response: *halixa shel barvaz* walking of (a) duck = duck-like walking.

Comprehension Test Items

1) Resultative adjectives
   CaCuC pattern   *shafux* spilled
                         atufa wrapped up,Fm
   meCuCaC pattern   *menusar* sawn
                         mexutélet diapered,Fm
   muCCaC pattern   *muram* elevated
                         mushxal threaded

2) Attributive adjectives
   CaCCan pattern   *tsaxkan* laughy
                         atsbanit nervous,Fm
   CaCiC pattern   *ra'il* poisonous
                         raxits washable

3) Denominal adjectives
                         tinoki babyish
                         xorpi wintry
                         barvazit duck-like

II *Production*

I have another pack of pictures here. I will ask you some more questions, and then we will look at the pictures together.
Sample questions:

1. I have a picture here of a chain that *perku ota* (they have) *taken*,PL *it apart* (root *p-r-k*, pattern *CiCeC*). What can be said now about the chain that (they have) taken apart?

Possible response: *hi meforéket* it (is) taken apart,Fm (root *p-r-k*, pattern *meCuCaC*).

2. I have a picture here of something that *efshar le-exol* possible to-eat (root *'-x-l*, pattern *li-CCoC*), for example, ice-cream; and something that is impossible to eat, like a shoe. What can you say about something that's possible to eat?

Possible response: *ze axil* it's edible (root *'-x-l*, pattern *CaCiC*).

3. I have a picture here of a snake with *éres* venom (root *'-r-s*, pattern *CéCeC*). What can you say about a snake that has venom?

Possible response: *hu arsi* it's venomous (root *'-r-s*, adjectival suffix *-i*).

Production Test Items

1) Resultative adjectives
   CaCuC pattern   *tsavua* painted
                        banuy built
   meCuCaC pattern   *meyubash* dried
                        meforéket taken apart,Fm
   muCCaC pattern   *mufshal* turned up
                        muxba hidden
2) Attributive adjectives
   CaCCan pattern   *xamkan* slippery
                        navranit pokey,Fm
   CaCiC pattern   *axil* edible
                        dvika sticky,Fm
3) Denominal adjectives
                        arsi venomous
                        gamadi dwarf-like
                        kalbi canine

Grammatical Impairment: An Overview and a Sketch of Dutch

Jan de Jong
University of Utrecht

A casual inspection of the recent literature on specific language impairment (SLI) in children suggests that these children's core difficulties are exclusively in the area of grammatical morphology. This impression is misleading. Although no classification of SLI is universally accepted, the subgroup from which subjects in studies on SLI are most often recruited shows grammatical symptoms often accompanied by phonological symptoms—they belong to the so-called *phonological-syntactic subtype*. Although this subtype harbors the largest number of language-impaired children, it is not the only one—there are various subtypes of SLI, although some are more common than others (Conti-Ramsden et al., 1997; Haynes & Naidoo, 1991; Rapin & Allen, 1983).

Although SLI is heterogeneous, difficulties with grammatical morphology are indeed seen as a hallmark of SLI. This was shown recently in a report from a workshop that aimed to define a phenotype for SLI at large. In this report, Tager-Flusberg and Cooper (1999) named two measures that are promising in their capacity to determine whether a child has SLI. One is nonword repetition, and the other is the child's ability to mark finiteness on the verb. This observation echoes previous suggestions that impaired inflectional morphology is a clinical marker of SLI (Rice & Wexler, 1996).

There is another reason—besides its status as a key symptom—that SLI children's poor handling of grammatical morphology receives much scientific attention. This has to do with the theoretical issues raised by the morphological symptoms. Mastery of grammatical morphemes appeals to grammatical knowledge per se, but also to processing at various levels (phonological, paradigmatic, syntactic), both in the receptive and productive modalities. Because of this mix of contributing factors, grammatical morphology is at the heart of the debate on the nature of SLI.

In this chapter, I pinpoint the morphosyntactic symptoms of SLI and briefly review the explanations advanced for this condition. In the past decade, descriptions of SLI have moved beyond their original focus on English-speaking children. I illustrate this by including references to studies on other languages and by adding results from a study on grammatical morphology in Dutch SLI. These results are taken as a test for current theories that aim to account for morphosyntactic deficits in SLI.

GRAMMATICAL SYMPTOMS OF SLI

Over the last decades, evidence has accumulated showing that SLI is not a disorder that causes global language deficits: Within grammar not every aspect is affected to a similar degree.

Until the 1960s, the common practice in establishing characteristics of language disorder was to compare language-impaired children with normally developing children of the same chronological age. Such comparisons resulted in a list of linguistic (sub)modules in which the delay was significant. For example, Menyuk (1964) showed that, if accounted for in terms of—in the Chomskyan terminology of the time—phrase structure rules and transformations, language-impaired children had a grammar that was qualitatively different from that of normal controls. The range of grammatical rules that could be inferred from their verbal output was smaller than among their nonimpaired chronological age peers. However, it is quite plausible that these grammars, due to the language delay, resembled the grammars available to the normal children when they were younger. This made Menyuk's claim of a *qualitative* difference between the two groups questionable.

Morehead and Ingram (1973) adopted a methodology that allows the researcher to abstract away from known language delay and identify characteristics that are associated more closely with SLI—characteristics that show as weaknesses in an already established pattern of delay. The tool that they relied on was a matching procedure of a different kind. Brown (1973) showed that children's mean length of utterance (MLU)—especially when it is measured in morphemes rather than words—is an index of the development of their productive morphosyntax in the initial stages (the correlation is less stable once mean length exceeds four morphemes). Morehead and Ingram used this measure to recruit a group of normal children whose general language proficiency in terms of output constraints was comparable to that of their SLI subjects. The rationale is that this use of MLU leads to the verification of a language age in the impaired children that can be matched to the control children's chronological age (the assumption is that language age equals chronological age in normals). Like Menyuk (1964), Morehead and Ingram wrote grammars for their subjects and compared these grammars across groups. They found that the grammars of children with SLI and controls—again described by the range of phrase structure rules and transformations that were evidenced by their output—were virtually identical. The only measure on which the groups differed was the diversity of the construction types their grammars generated. The set of construction types that were the outcome of the SLI children's grammars was more restricted.

Morehead and Ingram's matching on MLU resulted in the disappearance of apparent group differences, in sharp contrast to the clinical picture that Menyuk's data had suggested. In subsequent studies, however, the MLU matching procedure has led to the identification of grammatical features and rules that *do* raise difficulties for language-impaired children (e.g., Johnston & Schery, 1976; Leonard et al., 1992; Steckol & Leonard, 1979). The implication was that any differences that remain when groups with similar MLU values are compared can be seen as departures from an even profile of delay—that is, they point to specific symptoms of SLI.

Research that adopted the MLU matching procedure has generated a list of grammatical symptoms. Reviewing the literature, Fletcher and Ingham (1995) listed the affected categories mentioned most often for SLI in English-speaking children. Items that are vulnerable in children with SLI include: plural -*s*, third-person singular -*s*, past tense -*ed*, auxiliary verb *be*, determiners *the* and *a*, infinitive particle *to*, and case marking on pronouns. Not all of these items are equally vulnerable. In particular, it appears that, for language-impaired children, verbal morphology is more severely affected than nominal morphology.

Originally, the diagnostic profile of SLI was largely determined by the symptoms that English-speaking children present. As can be seen from the items just quoted, these symptoms by necessity are described in terms of the English grammar (for the inflectional paradigm, case marking, and structural composition of the verb phrase). By now, however, symptoms of SLI have been described in several languages, and the symptoms have been proved not to be identical even when corrections are made that accommodate for the paradigm of the targeted language.

These cross-linguistic differences can be described in two interdependent ways. Where languages differ structurally, this leads first of all to descriptive differences in the characterization of symptoms. However, typological differences also have implications for the processing strategies that work for children.

One example of the relevance of typology can be found in morphology. Inflectional paradigms (Pinker, 1984) differ, for instance, in the number of features that are morphologically encoded. For example, in Swedish and Norwegian, subject–verb agreement is not encoded in the verb form. In contrast, tense is. Person is not marked on plural forms of the English or Dutch verb. In French, it is. Even without considering the symptoms as they actually occur, it can be predicted that their native language in part determines the problem space with which language-impaired children are faced.

Slobin (1973) formulated a set of principles that concern the processing of language. One of the Operating Principles that Slobin (1973) formulated for the language-learning child is to pay attention to the end of words because grammatical affixes can guide the child to the correct interpretation of the sentence structure. Clearly this particular principle is more useful if the target language is consistent in its grammatical marking of syntactic relations (like subject–verb agreement). If affixes are not a reliable cue, word order may be more informative (Bates & MacWhinney, 1987; cf. Chiat, 2001).

SLI IN ENGLISH AND OTHER LANGUAGES

It is useful to discuss some findings on SLI in some non-English languages before considering explanatory accounts of (grammatical) SLI. These data are crucial because a true explanation of grammatical impairment should encompass the symptoms that SLI entails in each and every language. An explanation that fails to do this is a descriptive generalization that merely holds for the languages it covers.

A valid explanation should predict the similarities and discrepancies between the language behavior of SLI children from different language backgrounds. This is a highly challenging task because SLI at first sight has a different appearance depending on what the child's native tongue is. As Leonard (1998) put it, based on a review of studies of SLI across languages: "if there is a universal feature of SLI, apart from generally slow and poor language learning, it is well hidden" (p. 117).

Clearly, typological differences between languages determine the make-up of the disorder. For example, subject–verb agreement (as well as other types of agreement) has proved to be a major obstacle for German-speaking children with SLI (Clahsen, 1989, 1992). In Swedish, these difficulties are absent by definition because there is no subject–verb agreement in the Swedish language. Instead, SLI in Swedish involves word order errors: Children with SLI do not consistently apply the inverted word order in obligatory contexts—that is, in sentences with a topicalized element (Hansson, 1998).

In turn, such word order errors are not found in English (topicalization in English does not trigger the inversion of subject and verb).

Another example of how language type may influence the symptoms of SLI concerns the inflectional paradigm (the different inflectional affixes that a verb can take) of the target language. A typical finding in English-speaking children with SLI is that their morphological marking of verbs is inconsistent. Errors take the form of omission; there are frequent unmarked verb forms in their verbal output (Bedore & Leonard, 1998; Fletcher & Peters, 1984). Substitution, however, is rare in English, but bear in mind there is not much room for substitution within the rather sparse inflectional paradigm of that language.

Nevertheless, it has been found that children speaking languages other than English may substitute erroneous morphemes for correct ones instead of (or in addition to) omitting a requisite morpheme. In Norwegian, only tense is marked on the verb. Bjerkan (1999) found that language-impaired children substitute present tense forms for past tense forms, rather than omitting the inflectional morpheme. de Jong (1999) found similar errors and also substitutions in the number dimension. It must be added that the studies by Bjerkan and de Jong included impaired children between 6 and 8 or 9 years of age. Grammatical morphology is often studied in younger (preschool) children. The frequent occurrence of substitutions in Dutch-speaking children with SLI may therefore be an artifact of subject selection: There may be an earlier stage in which omission is the predominant error. For instance, an (extended) optional infinitive stage (during which nonmarking is prevalent) may occur with younger children. This does not detract from the point made here (i.e., that substitution errors do occur in some languages and hardly ever in others; I refer specifically to the lack of agreement errors during the optional infinitive stage in English-speaking children as claimed by Rice & Wexler, 1996). Consequently, the errors found within the relatively poor verbal paradigm that English-speaking children with SLI must learn may not be representative of SLI at large.

Finally, Italian presents an interesting picture. Italian has an inflectional paradigm that is rich (in that every verb form is marked for person and number) and filled with highly salient surface forms. The morphemes are syllabic and allow for lengthening. Leonard and his collaborators (Leonard et al., 1987, 1988) demonstrated that these characteristics correlate with more consistent morphological marking by children with this language background. To return to Slobin's (1973) Operating Principle: Taking word endings as a cue proves to be useful in Italian. The morphemes are informative on syntactical relationships (and thus on semantic constellations) and are more easily processed than, for instance, English morphemes (which are segmental and prone to deletion).

It is clear from this section that typology and processing are associated—they represent different ways of looking at the same phenomena, either as description or interpretation. Typology and differential processing strategies together obscure our vision of *universal* features of SLI. In the following section, I review some theories that have nevertheless attempted to trace a pattern in the linguistic symptoms of SLI.

LINGUISTIC EXPLANATIONS FOR THE GRAMMATICAL SYMPTOMS OF SLI

Even at first glance, the symptoms outlined by Fletcher and Ingham (1995) suggest that morphosyntactic disorder does not happen across the board.

First of all, there is dissociation between the morphology on nouns and verbs. Nouns are not as problematic to children with SLI as verbs are. The common denominator of the majority of symptoms is that they can be found in the area of functional categories. Functional categories include, roughly, verbal inflections, determiners, and complementizers. Determiners have not drawn as much attention as verb morphology, but the production of determiners does lag behind that in normally developing language learners (Eyer & Leonard, 1995). In general, however, linguistic explanations have centered on the verb. It has been shown that difficulties with the inflectional system can persist over a longer period of time (Rice, Wexler, & Hershberger, 1998) and therefore continue to invite inspection. Explanations have often started from characteristics of the verb form (its morphology and phonology) and the syntactic relations in which the verb features. The authors who advance explanations of this kind attempt to identify the linguistic constellations involved in the symptom pattern and thus to improve diagnosis (Clahsen, 1992).

In this section, I briefly describe the most widely discussed theories—past and present.

Explanation 1: The Nonsaliency of Inflectional Markings Adds to Their Vulnerability in Language-Impaired Children

In a range of studies by Leonard and his colleagues (e.g., Leonard et al., 1987, 1988), comparisons are drawn between English-speaking and language-impaired children with a different language background. Some other languages—like Italian and Hebrew—have grammatical morphemes that are highly salient and/or are part of a rich inflectional paradigm. *Rich* in this context means that every cell in the paradigm is filled by a different morpheme. The poverty of English, in contrast, is reflected by its high degree of syncretism. The unmarked form *move*, for instance, is homonymous to the first- and second-person present singular as well as to the forms that fill the plural cells.

The revelation in the studies by Leonard and his co-authors was that children with SLI who learn, for instance, Italian are more consistent in their production of grammatical morphemes than English-speaking children are. Leonard proposed two complementary explanations of this cross-linguistic difference.

One is that children can benefit from the richness of the inflectional system that they acquire (and children who learn a language that is not so rich cannot—therefore an explanation along these lines of SLI is called the *sparse morphology hypothesis*; Leonard et al., 1987).

The other is that children are in a better position to learn grammatical morphemes when the relevant morphemes have a high degree of saliency. This explanation is called the *surface hypothesis*. The explanation is a morphophonological one: It predicts that weak surface characteristics pose problems in a specific (morphological) context. If the morpheme represents an abstract feature (like agreement) and is phonologically weak, the difficulty increases.

The surface explanation (Leonard, 1989) accounts for cross-linguistic differences. English morphemes -*s* and -*ed* (note that, in terms of processing, we should transcribe the latter morpheme as phoneme /-*d*/) are prototypical examples of morphemes that have weak surface properties: They are nonsyllabic and consequently by definition unstressed. Italian morphemes, in contrast, are highly salient. Depending on the verb class, the third-person singular inflection is -*a* or -*e* (*canta*, s/he sings; *vende*, s/he sells; the Italian forms exemplify the pro-drop nature of Italian: the pronominal subject is omitted). These inflections are syllabic and, by virtue of being vowels, can be lengthened.

Explanation 2: Children With SLI Do Not Control Subject–Verb Agreement Relationships

German shows several instances of agreement relationships: not only between grammatical subject and verb, but also between determiner and noun and adjective and noun (gender marking). Clahsen (1989, 1992) hypothesized that the common feature of grammatical symptoms of SLI is that they reveal a lack of insight in the agreement relationship. His German SLI subjects used infinitival forms or zero-affixation instead of verb forms that agreed with subject features. Surveying the literature, he proposed that this is not just true for German. English-speaking children's difficulties with inflection can also be explained by a missing agreement hypothesis. The frequent omission of inflectional markers by English-speaking SLI children flags, in Clahsen's view, an absence of agreement marking, not of tense marking.

Explanation 3: The Developmental Stage in Which Finiteness Is Marked on Verbs Optionally Is Protracted in Language-Impaired Children

Wexler (1994) proposed a stage in normal development during which typically developing children fail to acknowledge that verbs in main clauses must be marked for tense features. The optionality expresses itself as the temporary coexistence of verb forms marked for tense and unmarked verb forms whereas the verb root may be the same. Under this account, it is assumed that once children mark tense they mark agreement correctly as well. Rice and Wexler (1996) found evidence of an extension of this stage in children with SLI—an extended optional infinitive stage.

Explanation 4: Language-Impaired Children Lack Knowledge of the Abstract Features That Must Be Grammatically Encoded

Gopnik (1990) advanced the most radical explanation of grammatical symptoms of SLI, in the sense that she claimed a serious hiatus in the children's linguistic knowledge. According to her *missing feature account*, features like number, person, tense, and many more are conspicuously absent from the grammars of language-impaired children. This would predict that no system underlies their grammatical morphology. Correct forms would only surface by chance or would be rote learned and then stored in memory. In a revised version of this theory, Gopnik and Crago (1991) sought the locus of the deficit in the *rules* that map the features onto grammatical morphemes—those rules would be unavailable to SLI children. This idea derived from Pinker's dual-route model of the normal acquisition of past-tense morphology (cf. Pinker, 1999). According to this model, past-tense formation of regular and irregular verbs is qualitatively different: Whereas irregular forms are recruited from associative memory, regular forms are the outcome of an abstract rule. Extrapolating this idea to SLI, children with SLI would not be impaired in their accessing of irregular forms (their associative memory, in this view, is claimed to be intact), but would be unable to apply the linguistic rule for (regular) past-tense formation.

LINGUISTIC THEORIES: SOME EVIDENCE TO THE CONTRARY

The explanations discussed so far serve as hypotheses about the locus of the grammatical deficit in SLI. These hypotheses are continuously tested. They have moved researchers to present evidence that refutes one or more of these explanations. Two examples of the kind of evidence that has been advanced may illustrate this.

An intriguing phenomenon is that the same children who mark tense and/or agreement features inconsistently may produce overgeneralizations in past-tense verb forms (Leonard, 1994). If one assumes that these children cannot refer back to symbolic rules for verb morphology, such novel forms should not be found because they are primary evidence of hypotheses formed by the child on the nature of an abstract (past-tense) rule. Overregularizations, after all, cannot be learned from the input. Consequently, such data flatly contradict the claim that children with SLI have no access to linguistic rules.

Another piece of evidence that is hard to explain under some accounts concerns rote learning. The assumption of a rule deficit in children with SLI leads researchers to believe that (correct) forms are learned in a lexical way, item by item. Under this premise, frequency effects would influence the learning of selected items. Miller and Leonard (1998) tested this hypothesis by exploring whether morphological marking was restricted to a small number of verb types. They found no such pattern, which contradicts rote learning of inflected verb forms.

THE DUTCH STUDY

In the following sections, I return to the theories summarized earlier. Data are presented from a language—Dutch—in which the symptoms of SLI have so far not been studied in depth. For that reason, Dutch data have not featured in the debate on the current set of linguistic explanations.

Research Questions

The research question in the study was: What are the characteristics of tense and agreement marking in Dutch children with SLI? The background of this question is that language type influences symptoms of language disorder, and symptoms cannot be derived in full from what occurs in different languages. A second question is whether predictions that follow from prevailing linguistic theories on SLI are proved to be valid. Each of the explanations argues that some symptoms will occur and others will not. To that end, data on inflectional morphology in Dutch children with SLI are analyzed to monitor which predictions hold true.

Before discussing the grammatical symptoms of SLI in Dutch, a description of the verb system is required. On the one hand, the nature of the inflectional paradigm (the features that are marked, the relative richness or poverty of the paradigm) is highly relevant. On the other hand, verbal morphology in Dutch is strongly associated with the position of the verb in the sentence structure, and this correlation must be outlined.

Typology

Table 11.1 shows the (regular) inflectional paradigm of the Dutch verb presented next to the English paradigm. The juxtaposition of these paradigms clarifies the relative problem space for the language-impaired children in each of the two languages. Each paradigm allows for a number of potential errors that a child—whether normally developing or language disordered—can make.

The brackets that accompany the /n/ in the cells for plural marking indicate that this consonant is prone to omission in word-final position. In the past-tense paradigm, this reduction renders the plural form homonymous to the singular form. This is true for colloquial speech of adults as well, so the reduction is part of the child's input. The infinitive form is identical to the present-tense plural form and allows for a similar consonant deletion.

The table demonstrates that Dutch has a somewhat richer morphology than English. English present tense, save for the third-person singular, is zero-marked. This helps explain why inflectional errors in English SLI almost exclusively concern omissions. As we see underneath, within the Dutch paradigm substitutions can and do occur.

TABLE 11.1
Inflectional Paradigms for Dutch and English

Tense	English	Dutch
Present-tense singular		
First person	-0	-0
Second person	-0	-t (-0 in inverted order)
Third person	-s	-t
Present-tense plural		
First person	-0	-e(n)
Second person	-0	-e(n)
Third person	-0	-e(n)
Past tense		
Past-tense singular	-ed	-te/-de
Past-tense plural	-ed	-te(n)/-de(n)

The second point to be made about the Dutch verb system is that word order is correlated with the form of the verb. Dutch, like German, is a verb-second language. The infinitive is restricted to clause-final position and, in nonelliptical adult Dutch, must be premodified by an auxiliary verb in the second position that is reserved for the finite verb.

Acquisition

This correlation of verb form and verb position is learned stepwise in the acquisition of Dutch. The production of the infinitive verb in base-generated position (utterance final) is the starting point of children's verb use. In fact, the early association of infinitive and final position has contributed to the interpretation of Dutch as an SOV (subject–object–verb) language. Wijnen (2000; Wijnen & Verrips, 1998) has drawn up a developmental order for the acquisition of verbal morphology in Dutch. The main parameters of this order are finiteness, verb position, and verb class. The developmental stages are different from the stages known for English. In particular, the optional infinitive stage has a different context in Dutch. The intermediate lexical-finite stage and the co-occurrence of an auxiliary and a lexical infinitive are not found to a similar extent in English (Wexler, 1994). These differences are strongly related to the form-position correlation that Dutch demonstrates. The order described by Wijnen is highly relevant to the explanations advanced by linguists for grammatical SLI. In particular, it puts the optional infinitive stage in a different perspective. I return to this developmental context when I discuss the patterns found in the Dutch data to be reviewed later. The stages described by Wijnen are the following. The examples are quoted verbatim from Wijnen and Verrips (1998).

1. *Infinitival stage*
   The child uses verbs in the infinitival form only (during this stage, nonfiniteness is obligatory)

   ik zelf doen
   I-myself -do
   I want to do it myself

2. *Lexical-finite stage*
   The child marks a subset of verbs for finiteness, whereas other verbs remain infinitival. Typically, there is no overlap between the items in the two verb sets. The finite subset consists primarily of modal auxiliaries (*kan*, can), copula *is* and some state or nondynamic verbs (*zit*, sit[s]).

Peter kan bij
Peter-can-it-by
Peter can reach it

3. *Optional infinitive stage*
The child now marks more verbs for finiteness. In addition, lexical verbs are premodified by auxiliaries (most often the pleonastic verb *gaan* [go]). The optionality concerns:
a. root infinitives
b. finite forms and Aux + Vinf combinations.
At this stage, there *is* overlap between (a) and (b): the same lexical verbs can occur in either form.

doe je ook handje geven
do-you-also-hand-give
are you shaking hands too?

Method

The research to be reported here was part of the present author's doctoral dissertation (de Jong, 1999). The original study dealt with inflectional morphology and verb argument structure. For the topic of this chapter, the task that addressed verb inflection is most relevant. After all, each of the linguistic theories on SLI that were summarized earlier starts from the error patterns that characterize the verb phrase in SLI. The error pattern found for Dutch is used as a litmus test for the cross-linguistic validity of such explanations. It is screened for evidence that is incompatible with the predictions that are the outcome of the accounts.

Subjects

Dutch children with SLI ($n = 35$) were recruited from three schools for language-impaired children (in the Netherlands, special schools cater to these children). The language-impaired children were on average 7;8 years old (see Table 11.1). The children were matched to normally developing children by their chronological ages. To ensure that the markers of language impairment also distinguished children with SLI from the children they are habitually compared with in SLI research, the comparison was extended to include an additional control group of children who are 2 years younger ($n = 20$). Matching by MLU was disfavored because it would be highly circular with respect to verb morphology. Therefore, it was decided to adopt a more random composition of the younger control group. Nevertheless, the age difference with the younger group resembles that of MLU-matched control groups reported in the literature (Table 11.2). Because these children were not formally matched by a language

TABLE 11.2
Age of Subjects

	Children With SLI (n = 35)	Younger ND children (n = 20)	ND Chronological Age matches (n = 35)
Chronological age	93.4 (11.9)	59.6 (7.4)	91.4 (13.8)

Note. ND = normally developing.

measure, they are referred to as *younger children*, rather than *language age matches*, although they perform a similar role in the discussion.

Task Description

Because past-tense morphology is considered a prototypical measure of abstract rule learning, a task was selected in which the use of past-tense forms was encouraged. Narrative episodes were elicited by showing a video film to each child individually. A 5-minute animation film (*Pingu and Pinga at home*) was shown to the children three times in a single session. First the child watched the film without verbal input from the researcher. The second time the researcher read a prepared narrative to accompany the videotape. The story was read in the present tense. Because regular verbs are less frequent than irregular verbs and require additional elicitation, the majority of the verbs selected for the narrative were regular verbs. Finally, the film was divided into 16 short episodes. After each episode, the tape was paused and the child was asked to tell the researcher what happened. By phrasing the question in the past tense, the child was encouraged to adopt the past tense as well. The children's responses were audiotaped, transcribed, and analyzed for inflectional errors.

Results

I start by pointing out the error patterns that were particularly visible in the data gathered from the task described earlier.

First of all, the past-tense forms that were targeted were not supplied consistently. The SLI children sometimes switched to the historical present when recounting the narrative. When they did adopt a past narrative mode, they failed to mark past tense consistently on the verb (Table 11.3). To analyze the errors, past-tense contexts were established by selecting the utterances that contained a past adverbial. The children with SLI filled fewer contexts for past-tense forms than either the age matches or younger children [SLI < Chronological age peers (p = .0000; Z = −6.1823)].

Errors took three forms: Past-tense markings were omitted (zero marking) or substituted by present-tense affixes (or, if the verb was irregular

TABLE 11.3
Realization of Three Morphemes in Obligatory Context:
Present-Tense -t, Plural Marker -en, and Past-Tense Marking
(Overt or Fusional; means, standard deviations in brackets)

Present-Tense Marker -t	Children With SLI (n = 31)	Younger ND Children (n = 15)	CA Matches (n = 16)
Percentage of use of -t marker for third person in obligatory context	0.61 (0.34)	0.87 (0.28)	0.89 (0.27)
Plural marker -en	Children with SLI (n = 35)	Younger ND children (n = 20)	CA matches (n = 35)
Percentage of use of -en marker for third person in obligatory context	0.69 (0.30)	0.95 (0.13)	0.97 (0.05)
Past-tense form	Children with SLI (n = 29)	Younger ND children (n = 20)	CA matches (n = 35)
Percentage of use of past tense form in obligatory context	0.77 (0.26)	0.98 (0.04)	0.99 (0.00)

and its form consequently fusional, the present-tense *form* was substituted) or the verb form was infinitival.

Due to the narrative mode chosen by several children, many present-tense forms were found among the data. It became clear during the analysis that, apart from past-tense errors, there are three other types of errors (all *agreement* errors related to the encoding of person and number features) that overwhelmingly appear to mark morphosyntactic deficit in Dutch—differences between the SLI group and either group of normally developing children were highly significant. However, this is not to say that the errors are exclusive to SLI. They are found in normally developing children as well, although at an earlier age (de Haan, 1996).

The first error concerns the omission of an inflectional marker. Because of the perspective of the narrative (the child recounted a story about a third party), this applied for the omission of the third-person marker (most often in the singular form -t, but sometimes also in the plural -en). An example is:

(1) *die gooi 'm in de lucht*
    die gooit 'm in de lucht
    that+one throw (*unmarked verb form*) him (*pronominal clitic*) in the air

The third-person marker -t was omitted more often in obligatory contexts by the children with SLI than by either control group (SLI < Younger children, p = .0000; Z = –4.2563; SLI < Chronological age peers, p = .0012; Z = –3.2397; SLI < Younger children, p = 0.0037; Z = –2.9040).

The second type involves a misrepresentation of the number feature on the verb. In nearly all instances, this implies the production of a singular verb form with a plural subject.

(2) *dat doet altijd mijn vade [vader] en moeë [moeder]*
    dat doen altijd mijn vader en moeder
    that does (*singular third person*) always my father and mother

Realization of the *-en* marker in the obligatory, plural context was less consistent among the language-impaired children than among the normals (SLI < Chronological age peers, p = .0000; Z = – 4.8199; SLI < Younger children, p = .0001; Z = – 3.8446).

The third error type is closely connected to the form-position correlation that is characteristic of Dutch. Here the verb remains uninflected but true to the correlation rationale and fills the base, utterance-final position. The first example has a plural subject—note that the infinitival form of the verb is homonymous to the—correct—plural form; the verb position, in contrast, suggests an infinitival interpretation.

(3) *hun allemaal rommel maken*
    hun maken allemaal rommel
    they all+sort+of rubbish make

(4) *en dan mama papa wakker maken*
    en dan maakt mama papa wakker
    and then mother father wake

The extent to which obligatory markers were supplied is listed in Table 11.3. Production in obligatory context clarifies, on the one hand, the group differences between children with SLI and controls. On the other hand, the numbers also illustrate that language-impaired children are inconsistent in morphological marking (while making errors, they do not consistently omit the marker).

In the table, one can observe some discrepancies in the composition of the groups. The reason for this is that more control children followed the cue to use past tense. By preferring past tense, obligatory contexts for present tense were absent in their output. Some children with SLI, however, produced no utterances that necessitated a past-tense form and therefore are excluded from Table 11.3. Plural contexts occurred in present- and past-tense contexts. Consequently, all children feature in the table. Because the numbers of subjects differ, mean age differs as well. Be-

TABLE 11.4
Use of Nonelliptical Infinitives (Means; Standard Deviations)

Children with SLI (n = 35)	Younger ND Children (n = 20)	CA Matches (n = 35)
2.85 (5.36)	0.10 (0.31)	0.03 (0.17)

SLI > Chronological age peers (p = .0000; Z = –5.2839). SLI > Younger children (p = .0001; Z = –3.8769).

cause this difference was only marginal, the recalculated ages are not represented.

The third type of agreement error—the infinitival form—cannot simply be interpreted as the absence of a suffix and does not allow for an obligatory context analysis. Instead, its key property is that the inflectional marker is maintained in a main clause and precludes the marking of finiteness. The position of the verb, however, is compatible with the nonfinite form. The SLI children produced significantly more instances of these errors than either control group (Table 11.4).

Although traditionally children's morphosyntactic proficiency is measured by realization of a grammatical morpheme in an obligatory context, this analysis obscures one element that must not go unmentioned. Although inflectional errors in English feature omissions, a significant number of errors in the Dutch data concern substitutions. This is true for past-tense marking (substitution by present tense) and number marking (singular for plural). This should be noted in view of the absence of substitution errors in most SLI corpora from studies on English. In Table 11.3, nonuse in obligatory context is either omission of the marker or substitution of the marker (substitutions of -t by -en were rare and ambiguous; the ambiguity derives from the homophony of infinitive and plural and from a verb position that could not convincingly be labeled either *final* or *second*). Omissions and substitutions are collapsed in the nonuse totals.

CONCLUSIONS

Taking into consideration the error patterns found in Dutch grammatical SLI, how well are they explained by the current range of linguistic explanations? As a starting point, let us take the four error types (including errors in past-tense marking) and consider whether they are compatible with the linguistic accounts.

First of all, the omission of the marker for third-person -t is predicted by theories that locate the deficit in the linguistic rule system, either by pointing out that the child is not aware of the grammatical features to be encoded on the verb or of the linguistic rules that implement them. According to these accounts, nonmarking is expected. The marker, -t, is nonsyllabic and qualifies as a nonsalient morpheme. Consequently, it is prone to omission if we follow the surface account. The missing agreement hypothesis predicts zero affixation as well (Clahsen, 1992). The single hypothesis that cannot account for this symptom is the extended optional infinitive hypothesis. This hypothesis claims that children oscillate between root infinitives and finite forms. The proviso, however, is that a finite form is correctly inflected for person and number features (Rice & Wexler, 1996). I propose that errors of this type exemplify finite forms. The position of the verb warrants this interpretation: Finite verbs in Dutch are in second position. The distribution of the zero-marked form closely matches that of forms that are properly marked. However, if it is accepted that these forms are finite, they must be considered to violate agreement constraints.

The substitution of the plural marker -en by singular marker -t is compatible with theories that anticipate a nonconsistent marking pattern (due to the fact that either features or rules are not part of the child's grammar). It must be added, however, that this error deviates from the omission pattern commonly associated with the accounts involved. Clahsen (1992) only mentioned zero affixation and infinitive use as symptoms of agreement difficulties. However, substitutions of singular forms can be explained as well by arguing that the child fails to recognize agreement features: Clahsen et al. (1997) referred to similar errors. In that sense, this symptom can be reconciled with the missing agreement explanation. When substitution concerns the overt morphemes (rather than irregular verb forms), the errors provide a challenge for the surface explanation. After all it is hard to account for the fact that a syllabic morpheme is substituted by a single consonant (even if we consider the fact that the plural morpheme does not receive stress). Again, under the extended optional infinitive explanation, this is an error not expected to appear to a significant extent.

The third error—the use of an infinitival verb form in its base final position (note that this error violates tense as well as agreement conditions)—can be said to reflect an inability to mark finiteness. In this way, it is predicted by all explanations that view SLI as a knowledge problem. In addition, the fact that the nonsalient inflectional markers are not inserted adds credibility to the surface account.

Although at first glance this symptom is convincing evidence for the extended optional infinitive explanation, it is necessary to observe the language-specific context. The developmental order outlined by Wijnen (2000) and listed earlier contains two stages in which infinitives feature: infinitival and optional. A first question, of course, is what the equivalent stage is in Dutch to which we should compare the OI stage in English children. As for the Dutch infinitival period, the infinitive is obligatory at this stage, so optionality is a misnomer. In the lexical-finite stage, there is no overlap between finite and infinitive verb sets and therefore no true optionality. The optional infinitive stage in Dutch, as conceived by Wijnen, leaves Dutch children with an option—the auxiliary plus verb combinations—that is far less prominent in English. As such it clouds the cross-linguistic comparison where an optional infinitive stage is concerned.

I should add that, if a child produces instances of an infinitive, it is not possible, in analyzing an individual utterance, to identify it as an expression of either the infinitival or optional infinitive stage. After all, within the (Dutch) optional infinitive stage it is still possible to hypothesize that a child produces infinitives without expressing the auxiliary that premodifies it. Interestingly, in the present data set, utterance-final infinitives were found in the context of a topicalized adverb; to repeat an example quoted before (minus the conjunction *en*): *dan mama papa wakker maken*. Movement of the topic (*dan*) is justified by fronting of the finite verb. Such topicalizations can be interpreted as evidence that there is an underlying auxiliary not overtly expressed by the child (cf. Boser et al., 1992; Poeppel & Wexler, 1993). If so, the infinitive is not the (optional) alternative to the finite verb, but part of a verb phrase with an auxiliary node. In that sense, it is evidence contra the extended optional infinitive stage (for a more elaborate discussion of this point, see de Jong, 2002).

Many of the past-tense expressions did not contain a finite lexical verb because the past-tense form of a pleonastic auxiliary (*gaan*, go) preceded the lexical infinitive. Together with instances in which the auxiliary was dropped after a topic, this argues for the validity of a stage in which combinations of an auxiliary and a lexical verb feature prominently.

Finally, how are the past-tense errors best explained? Explanations that argue for rule or feature deficits can cope with problems in tense marking. The past-tense affix, unlike the present-tense (singular) affix, is not consonantal, but the syllabic morpheme is not stressed, potentially inviting omission. An explanation that does not foresee serious past-tense problems is Clahsen's missing agreement account. Clahsen (1992) acknowledged these difficulties, but suggested the difficulties are less severe than those that affect marking of person and number. In one respect, the findings by Clahsen et al. (1997) are mirrored in the present study: Past tense was marked more consistently than person and number. Still it should be noted that there was a highly significant difference with the control groups for past-tense marking. I suggest that tense as well as agreement errors require explanation. Although the optional infinitive account explicitly underexposes agreement errors, the missing agreement account runs the risk of doing the same with respect to (past) tense marking.

Theories that propose a grammar in which linguistic rules are absent face another problematic finding that relates to past tense. In the present data set, several instances were found of the most explicit evidence of rule learning—that is, overgeneralization of the regular past-tense paradigm to irregular verbs. The SLI children's production of overregularizations did not differ from that of either control group. This apparent contradiction—omission of past-tense morphemes next to production of overgeneralizations—was noted by Leonard (1994) first. Overgeneralizations convincingly argue against a paradigmatic deficit.

IMPLICATIONS FOR CROSS-LINGUISTIC RESEARCH

Cross-linguistic comparisons have different implications for different explanations of SLI. Accounts that assume that part of the linguistic knowledge is not accessible to language-impaired children ultimately predict a universal set of symptoms. Restrictions only apply where typology interferes with the overt symptoms. A language that has no person or number agreement between subject and verb makes an SLI child immune to overt difficulties in that area. At the same time, this puts restrictions on the generality of a theory that claims the locus of the deficit is in agreement. Accounts that refer to processing problems must spell out the extent to which a child's native language can promote or prevent the occurrence of specific linguistic symptoms.

Whether the perspective is on representation or processing, it is important to consider the linguistic context that a language offers. This is true for typology. It also holds for the developmental order reported for the language under review.

In the present chapter, evidence has shown that explanations for grammatical symptoms of SLI currently in vogue reveal some myopia that derives from the language background that inspired them. The literature focuses predominantly on omission as the main way in which impairment shows itself. Also the focus on languages that are not verb second has led to a premature equalization of finiteness and agreement in verb forms (Clahsen's work on German has made significant contributions in highlighting the nature of SLI in a verb-second language). The only way to broaden the view of SLI (an impairment, after all, that is not language specific) is to add data from language backgrounds that allow for a different perspective.

ACKNOWLEDGMENT

The author would like to thank Paul Fletcher, Frank Wijnen and the editors of this volume for their helpful comments.

REFERENCES

Bates, E., & MacWhinney, B. (1987). Competition, variation, and language learning. In B. MacWhinney (Ed.), *Mechanisms of language acquisition* (pp. 157–193). Hillsdale, NJ: Lawrence Erlbaum Associates.

Bedore, L. M., & Leonard, L. B. (1998). Specific language impairment and grammatical morphology: A discriminant function analysis. *Journal of Speech, Language and Hearing Research, 41*, 1185–1192.

Bjerkan, K. M. (1999). *Verbal morphology in specifically language impaired children: Evidence from Norwegian.* Unpublished doctoral dissertation, University of Oslo.

Boser, K., Lust, B., Santelmann, L., & Whitman, J. (1992). The syntax of V-2 in early child German grammar: The Strong Continuity Hypothesis. *Proceedings of the Northeast Linguistic Society, 22.*

Brown, R. (1973). *A first language. The early stages.* Cambridge, MA: Harvard University Press.

Chiat, S. (2001). Mapping theories of developmental language impairment: Premises, predictions and evidence. *Language and Cognitive Processes, 16*, 113–142.

Clahsen, H. (1989). The grammatical characterisation of developmental dysphasia. *Linguistics, 27*, 897–920.

Clahsen, H. (1992). Linguistic perspectives on specific language impairment. *Theorie des Lexikons. Arbeiten des Sonderforschungsbereichs 282.* Düsseldorf: Universität Düsseldorf.

Clahsen, H., Bartke, S., & Göllner, S. (1997). Formal features of impaired grammars: A comparison of English and German SLI children. *Journal of Neurolinguistics, 10*, 151–171.

Conti-Ramsden, G., Crutchley, A., & Botting, N. (1997). The extent to which psychometric tests differentiate subgroups of children with SLI. *Journal of Speech, Language and Hearing Research, 40*, 765–777.

Eyer, J., & Leonard, L. B. (1995). Functional categories and specific language impairment: A case study. *Language Acquisition, 4*, 177–203.

Fletcher, P., & Ingham, R. (1995). Grammatical impairment. In P. Fletcher & B. MacWhinney (Eds.), *The handbook of child language* (pp. 603–622). Oxford: Blackwell.

Fletcher, P., & Peters, J. (1984). Characterising language impairment in children: An exploratory study. *Language Testing, 1*, 33–49.

Gopnik, M. (1990). Feature blindness: A case study. *Language Acquisition, 1*, 139–164.

Gopnik, M., & Crago, M. (1991). Familial aggregation of a developmental language disorder. *Cognition, 39*, 1–50.

Haan, A. de (1996). *De verwerving van morfologische finietheid in het Nederlands* (The acquisition of morphological finiteness in Dutch). Unpublished master's thesis, University of Groningen.

Hansson, K. (1998). *Specific language impairment in Swedish. Grammar and interaction.* Unpublished doctoral dissertation, Lund University.

Haynes, C., & Naidoo, S. (1991). *Children with specific speech and language impairment.* Oxford: Mac Keith Press.

Johnston, J. R., & Schery, T. K. (1976). The use of grammatical morphemes by children with communication disorders. In D. M. Morehead & A. E. Morehead (Eds.), *Normal and deficient child language* (pp. 233–259). Baltimore: University Park Press.

Jong, J. de (1999). *Specific language impairment in Dutch: Inflectional morphology and argument structure.* Unpublished doctoral dissertation, University of Groningen.

Jong, J. de (2002). Specific language impairment and linguistic explanation. In Y. Levy & J. Schaeffer (Eds.), *Language competence across populations: Towards a definition of specific language impairment.* Hove: Lawrence Erlbaum Associates.

Leonard, L. B. (1989). Language learnability and specific language impairment in children. *Applied Psycholinguistics, 10*, 179–202.

Leonard, L. B. (1994). Some problems facing accounts of morphological deficits in children with specific language impairment. In R. V. Watkins & M. L. Rice (Eds.), *Specific language impairments in children* (pp. 91–105). Baltimore, MA: Brookes.

Leonard, L. B. (1998). *Children with specific language impairment.* Cambridge, MA: MIT Press.

Leonard, L. B., Bortolini, U., Caselli, M. C., McGregor, K. K., & Sabbadini, L. (1992). Morphological deficits in children with specific language impairment: The status of features in the underlying grammar. *Language Acquisition, 2,* 151–180.

Leonard, L. B., Sabbadini, L., Leonard, J., & Volterra, V. (1987). Specific language impairment in children: A cross-linguistic study. *Brain and Language, 32,* 233–252.

Leonard, L. B., Sabbadini, L., Volterra, V., & Leonard, J. S. (1988). Some influences on the grammar of English- and Italian-speaking children with specific language impairment. *Applied Psycholinguistics, 9,* 39–57.

Menyuk, P. (1964). Comparison of grammar of children with functionally deviant and normal speech. *Journal of Speech and Hearing Research, 7,* 109–121.

Miller, C. A., & Leonard, L. B. (1998). Deficits in finite verb morphology: Some assumptions in recent accounts of specific language impairment. *Journal of Speech, Language and Hearing Research, 41,* 701–707.

Pinker, S. (1984). *Language learnability and language development.* Cambridge, MA: Harvard University Press.

Pinker, S. (1999). *Words and rules. The ingredients of language.* London: Weidenfeld & Nicolson.

Poeppel, D., & Wexler, K. (1993). The full competence hypothesis of clausal structure in early German. *Language, 69,* 1–33.

Rapin, I., & Allen, D. A. (1983). Developmental language disorders: Nosological considerations. In U. Kirk (Ed.), *Neuropsychology of language, reading and spelling* (pp. 155–180). New York: Academic Press.

Rice, M. L., & Wexler, K. (1996). Toward tense as a clinical marker of specific language impairment in English-speaking children. *Journal of Speech and Hearing Research, 39,* 1239–1257.

Rice, M. L., Wexler, K., & Hershberger, S. (1998). Tense over time: The longitudinal course of tense acquisition in children with specific language impairment. *Journal of Speech and Hearing Research, 41,* 1412–1431.

Slobin, D. (1973). Cognitive prerequisites for the development of grammar. In C. A. Ferguson & D. Slobin (Eds.), *Studies of child language development* (pp. 175–208). New York: Holt, Rinehart & Winston.

Steckol, K., & Leonard, L. (1979). The use of grammatical morphemes by normal and language impaired children. *Journal of Communication Disorders, 12,* 291–302.

Tager-Flusberg, H., & Cooper, J. (1999). Present and future possibilities for defining a phenotype for specific language impairment. *Journal of Speech, Language and Hearing Research, 42,* 1261–1274.

Wexler, K. (1994). Optional infinitives, head movement and the economy of derivations. In D. Lightfoot & N. Hornstein (Eds.), *Verb movement* (pp. 305–382). Cambridge: Cambridge University Press.

Wijnen, F. (2000). Input, intake and syntactic development. In M. Beers, B. van de Bogaerde, G. Bol, J. de Jong, & C. Rooijmans (Eds.), *From sound to sentence—studies on first language acquisition* (pp. 163–186). Groningen: Centre for Language and Cognition.

Wijnen, F., & Verrips, M. (1998). The acquisition of Dutch syntax. In S. Gillis & A. De Houwer (Eds.), *The acquisition of Dutch* (pp. 223–299). Amsterdam: John Benjamins.

Pragmatic Disability in Children With Specific Language Impairments

Hans van Balkom
Ludo Verhoeven
Nijmegen University

Pragmatics can be studied from two perspectives: as a relatively isolated component of language or as an integral part of all aspects of language. In general, *pragmatics* is defined as the study of the communicative use of language. As a consequence, pragmatic language disorders encompass significant problems with the communicative use of language. The classification of pragmatic disability thus applies to children who have problems with the recognition and application of the social rules for language and discourse. These children often have difficulties at school, making friends, and taking part in everyday conversations. The problems are quite diffuse, difficult to assess, and hard to define. In the present chapter, we therefore limit our discussion to the issue of pragmatic disability in children with specific language impairments (SLI). We define *pragmatic disability* as an inability to select and match a suitable linguistic form to the most appropriate and effective communicative function. The main problem for many children with SLI, then, is adequate acquisition of appropriate form–function linkages.

Two different theoretical approaches have shaped the study of pragmatic language disorders to date. The first is based on the theoretical assumption that pragmatics constitutes a separate level of linguistic analysis, analogous to the phonology, syntax, morphology, and semantics of language. McTear and Conti-Ramsden (1992) referred to this approach as the "pragmatics-as-separate" view, and Craig (1995) described it as "the modular competence-based approach" or "modular approach."

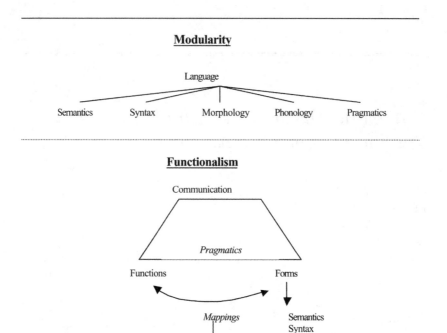

FIG. 12.1.   Modular approach versus functionalist approach (Craig, 1995, p. 625)

The second approach views pragmatics as an interactive and competitive system of language regulation aimed at attaining the "best fit" between language structure and language use. Along these lines, Craig (1995) discussed the competition model of language, its acquisition, and concomitant disorders and the functionalist performance-based approach or functionalist approach to language concerned with form–function mappings (see Fig. 12.1).

THE MODULAR APPROACH

The modular approach is the most traditional and widely adopted approach to the pragmatics of language. Pragmatic rules exist parallel to the rules of the other linguistic systems. The emphasis within this approach is therefore on distinguishing the different rule systems and particularly the semantic versus pragmatic rules of language.

The modular approach has also been adopted in the majority of studies related to pragmatic disability. In essence, a child with a primary pragmatic disability shows an intact or less impaired ability to apply the semantic, phonological, syntactic, and morphological rules of a language with significant difficulties in the domains of communicative interaction and discourse rules. Many of the relevant studies discuss the presence (or absence) of particular communicative functions extensively. Most studies do not focus on the mastery of the underlying rules or mechanisms and do not discuss plausible clarifications for difficulties with communicative functions while showing no problems with language structure. Inspection of the literature on children's language disabilities thus reveals little or no evidence for such a pure modular approach. In fact SLI children rarely show pragmatic disabilities independent of lexical or structural disabilities (Bishop & Leonard, 2000; Craig, 1995; Bishop, chap. 13, this volume). In general, modular-based studies have shown children with SLI to *not* use significantly fewer or a deviant range of linguistic functions or communicative acts when compared with children with normally developing language: They all initiate, respond, comment, request, demand, and clarify. Children with SLI appear to have difficulties with the formulation of speech acts rather than the completeness of their speech act repertoire (McTear & Conti-Ramsden, 1992; van Balkom, 1991). SLI children do not present separate or specific pragmatic problems, but simply formulate various pragmatic functions in linguistically atypical ways (Craig, 1995; Leonard, 1986).

Other studies with a focus on such aspects of language as discourse, subsequences,[1] presuppositions, turn taking, topic-theme management, narratives, and the use of verbal and nonverbal acts reveal a similar pattern of results. Children with SLI show some knowledge of the conversational structure and communicative functions of language and understand the need to make coherent ties between the subcomponents of language to establish a cohesive whole. Once again, however, SLI children are found to depend on a fairly limited, ineffective, and sometimes erroneous set of linguistic forms (Conti-Ramsden, 1988; Liles, 1985; McTear & Conti-Ramsden, 1992; van Balkom, 1991). In examinations of how SLI children respond to requests and comments, they have also been found to establish less cohesive links with the prior utterances of their conversational partners and react semantically inappropriately more often than their agemates with normally developing language (Bishop & Leonard, 2000; Brinton & Fujiki, 1982; Fey & Leonard, 1983; Lasky & Klopp, 1982; Leinonen, Letts, & Rae Smith, 2000; McTear & Conti-Ramsden, 1992; van

---

[1]Subsequences are stretches or units of discourse on which the conversational partners mutually agree with respect to the purpose and current topic (Wells, 1985).

Balkom, 1991; Watkins, 1998). In all of the studies and reviews involving comparison to MLU-matched (younger) normal language-acquiring children, the SLI children have been found to show responses with not only significantly less varied, but also poorer quality linguistic structures.

Considered as a whole, the research based on a modular approach to language and language disorders fails to reveal specific pragmatic deficits. In fact, children with SLI are found to have intact pragmatic knowledge. The children respond with and spontaneously use a wide range of communicative acts and functions, but often do this in linguistically atypical and/or inappropriate ways (van Balkom, 1991; Watkins, 1998). Viewed from a modular perspective, thus, there is actually no need for a separate pragmatic theory of SLI.

THE FUNCTIONALIST APPROACH
AND COMPETITION MODEL

Rather than conceptualizing pragmatics as an independent system of rules operating parallel to a number of other linguistic systems and rules, pragmatics can be conceptualized as an intermediate system of rules for linking linguistic forms to discourse functions. Pragmatic knowledge thus encompasses a specific set of form–function markers for specifying the dependencies between linguistic forms and communicative functions. Pragmatic knowledge concerns the achievement of communicative effectiveness. McTear and Conti-Ramsden (1992) described pragmatics as "relating language form and language use." These views are less modular in nature and view the various linguistic systems as interrelated, competitive, and working together to establish the most effective communication.

Craig (1995) described this functionalist approach to language in terms of a competition model in which pragmatic knowledge operates on and via other linguistic rule systems to establish the best contextual fit among structure, meaning, and function. Discourse functions and situational context directly influence the selection and use of specific linguistic forms for both acquisition and everyday communication. Effective communication is thus the result of a highly complex level of reasoning and fine tuning to establish the best fit of form–function mapping, involving conventional knowledge of the interdependencies among various linguistic systems, socioemotional cues, and cognitive processes. Ineffective communication can reflect breakdowns in the encoding of particular functions, selection of specific forms, or the match between the two. Pragmatic disability is then conceptualized as a mismatch between form and function due to insufficient knowledge of the rules needed to weigh and fine tune form–function mappings.

Adoption of a functionalist approach implies major changes in the manner in which we study pragmatic ability and disability. The focus is now on children's knowledge of communicative functions, linguistic forms, and the ways of linking the two. To demonstrate pragmatic disability, studies of SLI children's ability to match forms to functions in relation to their knowledge of the relevant linguistic structures and communicative functions are needed. For example, children with SLI may be found to use a wide and appropriate range of communicative functions, but with a highly restricted and thus redundant set of linguistic forms or encounter problems with the establishment of discourse cohesion due to poor mastery of the rules for encoding specific functions.

Adoption of a functionalist approach may thus lead to the identification of pragmatic disability in cases of SLI when the definition is expanded to include the rules for linking specific forms and functions (marking interdependencies). Of particular research interest, then, are such topics as: discourse coherence; topic–theme management across turns; conversational fit across turns and speakers; appropriateness of the form, meaning, and function of verbal and nonverbal acts across turn sequences and speakers; and methods to demonstrate knowledge of the linguistic features used to link spoken and written discourse and/or narratives. Just why some SLI children show specific difficulties with the form–function mappings needed to communicate effectively should also be examined. The explanation may lie in subtle cognitive and/or specific information-processing deficits that degrade the quality and quantity of linguistic input. An alternative explanation may lie in sequential processing difficulties and the malfunctioning of short-term verbal memory (for extended discussion, see Leinonen et al., 2000). Difficulties with word finding may be due to an underspecified lexicon characterized by an underspecified associative network of meaning relations as a result of central auditory processing disorders (see Katz & Tillery, this volume) or attention deficits and poor phonological awareness (see Leonard & Deevy, this volume). Functionalist approaches to the study of pragmatic disability are thus thought provoking and have the potential to clarify some of the problems SLI children have been found to have with form-function mappings (Bishop, 2000, chap. 13, this volume; Craig, 1995; van Balkom, 1991).

PRAGMATIC DISABILITY AND SLI

Children with SLI show significant difficulties in mastering language without any clear etiology. The diagnosis of SLI is typically one of exclusion (Stark & Tallal, 1981). The general typology of SLI is that the children show difficulties with the acquisition of specific—structural—aspects of language: namely, the morphology, syntax, and/or phonology. The status of pragmatic knowledge within this disorder remains unclear. Pragmatics is often viewed as the conversational analogue to the phonology, morphology, syntax, and semantics of language. Pragmatic problems in the form of observable communication and discourse difficulties may be the result of word-finding problems, difficulties with the formulation of grammatically correct and intelligible utterances, or significant comprehension problems. However, for a subgroup of children with SLI, the pragmatics of the language appear to be the problem. This has been found to be particularly the case for children who have made rapid progress with regard to structural linguistic difficulties after a period of early language intervention and remediation. These children have been found to speak in sufficiently long and grammatically correct/complex sentences, but the utterances are inappropriately positioned in conversations (Bishop, 1992; Bishop & Leonard, 2000; Leinonen et al., 2000; Rapin, 1996; van Balkom, 1991). In interactions with peers, parents, and teachers, these children show clear difficulties keeping track of the line of discourse. The study of the pragmatic knowledge of children with an SLI is thus at the interface of language structure and language use and thereby presents us with a means of examining the relation of pragmatics (i.e., language use) to the different aspects of language (i.e., language structure) more generally.

The term *pragmatic disability* provides a neutral and collective label for all difficulties using language. Several other terms are commonly used in the literature, including: semantic-pragmatic disorder, fluent language disorders, and pragmatic (language) impairment. However, we do not see pragmatic difficulties as an impairment or disorder, but as a disability in keeping with the "International Classification of Impairments, Disability and Handicap" (ICIDH) published by the World Health Organization (2000). Incoherent discourse, tangential speech, problems with word finding, poor social interaction, limited conversational skills, and minimal narrative skills are often noted as characteristics of pragmatic disability (Bishop, 2000; Leinonen et al., 2000; McTear & Conti-Ramsden, 1992; Prutting & Kirchner, 1987; van Balkom, 1991; Watkins, 1998). The term *semantic-pragmatic disorder* (SPD) is used most frequently, but found to be rather unsatisfactory when viewed from a functionalist perspective (Bishop, chap. 13, this volume; Bishop & Leonard, 2000; Craig, 1995). In a clinical account of SLI, Rapin (1996) and Rapin and Allen (1983) distinguished various subtypes of language development disorders, including those with problems mainly in the areas of phonology and syntax or so-called *phonologic-syntactic disorders* (PSD) and the areas of language content and language use or so-called *semantic-pragmatic disorders* (SPD).

Based on a review of the literature and increased evidence from clinical practice, Bishop (2000, chap. 13, this volume) has shown the pairing of semantic and pragmatic to obscure the differences between the predominantly lexical aspects of language and the actual use aspects of language in context, including the structure of discourse and conversation. In addition to this, clinical evidence suggests that the classification *pragmatic disability* does not apply exclusively to children with SLI. Pragmatic disability frequently co-occurs with autistic spectrum disorders (ASD), Asperger's syndrome, William's syndrome, pervasive diagnostic disorders not otherwise specified (PDDNOS), and attention deficit hyperactivity disorders (ADHD; Bishop & Leonard, 2000; Leinonen et al., 2000; O'Hare et al., 1998). Whether such a pragmatic disability is the result of a specific underlying disorder or the result and/or part of a complex of linguistic deficits is not as yet clear. The term SLI resembles the term *autistic spectrum disorders* and can also be denoted as a *spectrum disorder*.

THE PRESENT STUDY

For purposes of the present study, we reinterpret—from a functionalist perspective—some of the data from a longitudinal study of the discourse coherence in conversations of SLI and normally developing children with their parents (van Balkom, 1991). The SLI children are expected to show greater difficulties with form–function mappings than predicted by their level of structural linguistic knowledge. That is, despite age-appropriate performance on measures of vocabulary, morphology, and syntax, the SLI children are expected to have problems with the pragmatics of language operationalized in terms of conversational coherence.

The reinterpretation of the former results were guided by three main research questions:

- How can the pragmatic abilities of SLI children be characterized?
- What are the relations between the grammatical and pragmatic abilities of the SLI children and the normal language acquiring (NLA) children in conversations with their primary caregivers?
- What is the role of parental input in the conversations of the SLI and NLA children with their primary caregivers?

Design of the Study

Longitudinal data were collected between 1987 and 1991 in the Netherlands and concerned the conversational abilities of specific language impaired (SLI) and normal language acquiring (NLA) toddlers in interaction with their parents (van Balkom, 1991). Eighteen parent–child dyads participated in a series of nine semistructured play sessions. The sessions took place at 2-month intervals during 18 months for each parent–child pair. The aim of the study was to characterize the caregivers' and children's communicative behaviors particularly with respect to (a) their conversational roles, (b) ability to create and maintain a connected or coherent discourse, and (c) the adjustment or nonadjustment of the parents' speech to the child's syntactic and pragmatic development.

Definition of Discourse Coherence

Discourse coherence was defined, for both the previous and present studies, as a property of the participants' activities and something that is established during the interpretation and production of discourse to facilitate the flow of information. We use the term *discourse* to refer to any sequence or combination of verbal and nonverbal acts in a conversational context. Conversation or spoken discourse is jointly produced by parent and child with a specific intention on an act-by-act basis. Discourse coherence is maintained by specific acts on the parts of the conversational partners. Discourse coherence is an integral part of language use and at the interface of structural-linguistic and pragmatic knowledge.

Aspects of Discourse Coherence Studied

The aspects of discourse coherence specifically investigated in both the previous and present studies were turn taking, parental input or child-adjusted register, conversational topic and theme management, the frequency and variety of communication acts, and the frequency and variety of communication breakdowns and conversational repairs. The verbal and nonverbal performance data of the children while conversing with one of the parents during a number of free-play sessions at the Speech and Hearing Center Hoensbroeck were analyzed.

Subjects

For the original longitudinal study of 18 months, the SLI and NLA children were matched according to chronological age. The ages of the children at the beginning of study ranged from 2;6 to 3;0 (with an average of 2;11 for the SLI group and 2;10 for the NLA group). At the end of the study, the chronological ages varied from 4;1 to 4;10 (with an average of 4;7 for the SLI group and 4;6 for the NLA group). The SLI children were selected according to Stark and Tallal's (1981) exclusion criteria. At the start of the original study, the SLI group showed language production delays ranging from 10 to 20 months with an average MLU of 1.62 (range of 1.02–2.57, $SD = .47$). The average MLU-equivalent language-production age for the SLI children was 1;6. All of the SLI children demonstrated se-

TABLE 12.1
Subject Information at Start of Study

(1)	(2)	(3)	(4)	(5)	(6)	(7)
1	Linda (SLI)	F	3;1	−6	2.25	43%
2	Saskia (SLI)	F	2;10	0	1.35	68%
3	Rianne (SLI)	F	2;9	−4	1.56	41%
4	Davy (SLI)	M	3;0	−3	1.56	41%
5	Lisette (SLI)	F	3;1	0	1.97	67%
6	Geronimo (SLI)	M	2;7	0	1.02	87%
7	Marcel (SLI)	M	3;1	0	2.30	40%
8	Bjorn (SLI)	M	3;2	−1	1.79	47%
9	Sebastian (SLI)	M	2;10	−9	1.13	72%
10	Johny (SLI)	M	3;2	−8	2.57	65%
11	Christiaan (SLI)	M	3;2	?	1.61	47%
12	Remco (SLI)	M	3;0	0	1.59	52%
13	Rachel (NLA)	F	2;6	+14	2.89	37%
14	Bram (NLA)	M	3;0	+3	4.04	32%
15	Tim (NLA)	M	2;8	+36	4.02	40%
16	Michel (NLA)	M	3;0	+18	3.04	37%
17	Rosanna (NLA)	F	3;0	+26	3.07	33%
18	Chantalle (NLA)	F	3;1	+13	4.66	24%
Mean SLI			**2;11**	**−3**	**1.62**	**57%**
Mean NLA			**2;10**	**+18**	**3.62**	**34%**

(1) Parent–child dyad
(2) Name of child: SLI = specific language impaired and NLA = normal language acquiring
(3) Sex: F = Female and M = Male
(4) Chronological age (year; month)
(5) Language comprehension delay: "?" = not possible to test; "0" = no delay; "−" = delay; "+" = above normal
(6) MLU in syllables
(7) Percentage of child's verbal acts (utterances) that could not be analyzed

vere morphosyntactic difficulties in their spontaneous language production (analysis based on GRAMAT; Bol & Kuiken, 1989).

At the start of the study, the SLI group showed an underdeveloped active vocabulary according to the Reynell Developmental Language Scales (RDLS) and had a language comprehension delay that ranged from 0 to 9 months. All of the NLA children showed age-appropriate or superior levels of language development when selected for study (see Table 12.1).

Data Collection

Twelve SLI child–parent dyads and six NLA child–parent dyads participated in the longitudinal study of 18 months for each child–parent pair. The selection of the SLI children was made according to the aforementioned exclusion criteria. Formal tests on language production and language comprehension were administered at the beginning and end of the study. In addition, the parents had to meet the following requirements: Dutch as their first language or Dutch as their official language with a regional dialect as the first language, no history of hearing impairments, no history of language or literacy difficulties, no incidence of learning disorders, and a complete family constitution. The parents were informed that the focus of the study was on the child's language development.

The free-play sessions lasted 30 minutes and were held at the Speech and Hearing Center Hoensbroeck, which provided for standardized and thus comparable play materials and situations across all dyads and sessions. The free-play sessions were videotaped from behind a one-way mirror. A microphone (type Sennheiser ME 20) was positioned in the play room, and an additional audiorecorder (type Philips D 9610) connected to the same type of microphone was positioned out of sight. The video camera (type color Philips VK 4002) was connected to a UMATIC color recorder (type JVC CR 6650E) and color monitor (type BARCO CR 2032), and all were situated in the adjacent observation room and thus out of sight for the parents and children.

A random 5-minute sample was selected from each session in the longitudinal study for transcription and analysis; the first 5 minutes of a session were always excluded from such selection (see Ochs, 1979; Wells, 1985). An extensive protocol for interactional analyses was followed for transcription and further analysis. The transcription included all verbal and nonverbal acts on the parts of the parent and child with any additional contextual information and paraphrasing when needed (based on Ochs, 1979; Schachter, 1979; for further details on the transcription and analysis protocol, see van Balkom, 1991). Formal test scores on language production and comprehension, together with the qualitative data from the syntactic and pragmatic analyses of the selected 5-minute samples, form the results of the original study.

Data Analysis

The analyses involved only the grammar of the child's verbal acts and the pragmatics of the verbal and nonverbal acts of both the child and parent. The grammatical analysis was based on GRAMAT (Bol & Kuiken, 1989). The pragmatic analyses involved a protocol designed specifically for this purpose and based on Wells, Montgommery, and MacLure (1979) and Wells (1985). A set of hypotheses with regard to discourse coherence was then formulated for the previous and present study based on an extensive review of the literature by van Balkom (1991).

TABLE 12.2
Interjudge Reliability Scores for Pragmatic Analyses

Pragmatic Analysis Category	Cohen's Kappa	Confidence Limits (95%)
Mutual utterance relations (verbal and nonverbal) - initiations, responses, comments	0.72	0.67–0.75
Simultaneous relations (verbal and nonverbal) - overlaps, parallel talk	0.89	0.86–0.92
Correctness of interaction (verbal and nonverbal) - content and use correct or incorrect	0.95	0.92–0.96
Direction and relation of verbal and nonverbal acts - partner, self, other	0.89	0.86–0.91
Feedback (verbal and nonverbal) - backchannels, clarification requests	0.78	0.75–0.81
Imitations (verbal and nonverbal) - acts of partner, acts of self	0.98	0.97–0.99
Elaborations of previous act (verbal and nonverbal) - suppletion, correction	0.96	0.95–0.98
Topic organization (verbal and nonverbal) - introduction, continuation, closing	0.98	0.97–0.99
Communicative functions (verbal and nonverbal) - Controls, tutorials, representationals	0.65	0.60–0.72
Total Pragmatic Reliability Score	**0.78**	**0.74–0.83**

The statistical analyses included intrareliability and interreliability correlations for all of the coding categories (Cohen's Kappa 0.78 at 95% confidence interval) based on analyses of 12% of the total material by two independent coders.

The results of the syntactic and pragmatic analyses were compared with the test scores for language production and comprehension administered at the beginning and end of the original study (Table 12.2).

RESULTS

Verbal Acts, Nonverbal Acts, and Communicative Functions

In the original study, the SLI children were found to use significantly more nonverbal acts and nonverbal initiations across all sessions than the NLA children. The SLI children appeared to be active initiators. However, they realized most of the initiations via nonverbal behavior. According to the results presented in Table 12.3, the SLI group used significantly more nonverbal initiations than the NLA group. The SLI children used nonverbal initiations predominantly to initiate or restart play activities. Their

TABLE 12.3
Verbal and Nonverbal Acts, Communicative
Functions, and Communication Breakdowns

	Session Effect		
	SLI	NLA	Group
	Sign of F	Sign of F	Sign of F
Effect	(df 88/df 8)	(df 40/df 8)	(df 16/df 1)
Verbal and nonverbal acts			
Verbal, nonverbal acts of parents	—	—	0.300
Verbal, nonverbal acts of children	—	—	**0.036***
Verbal acts of parents	0.547	0.432	0.978
Verbal acts of children	0.346	0.557	0.111
MLU verbal acts of parents	0.117	0.665	0.115
MLU verbal acts of children	**0.000***	**0.032***	**0.001***
Nonverbal acts of parents	0.320	0.945	0.110
Nonverbal acts of children	**0.049***	0.890	**0.036***
Verbal and nonverbal initiations			
Initiations by parents	**0.000***	0.949	0.050
Reintroductions by parents	**0.000***	0.160	**0.038***
Expansions by parents	**0.000***	0.956	0.090
Nonverbal initiations by children	**0.041***	0.997	**0.021***
Communicative functions			
Information requests by parents	**0.001***	0.665	0.115
Backchannels by parents	**0.000***	0.641	0.462
Backchannels by children	0.691	0.306	**0.019***
Controls by parents	0.187	0.062	0.488
Controls by children	**0.049***	0.259	0.253
Expressives by parents	0.123	0.526	0.654
Expressives by children	**0.014***	0.0182	0.096
Representationals by parents	0.053	0.112	0.419
Representationals by children	**0.008****	**0.049***	0.523
Tutorials by parents	0.518	0.627	0.177
Tutorials by children	0.361	0.325	0.223
Procedurals by parents	**0.000***	0.139	0.665
Procedurals by children	**0.000***	0.247	0.615
Communication breakdowns			
Clarification requests by parents	**0.000***	0.213	**0.011***
Corrections by parents	**0.000***	0.745	**0.011***
Faulty responses by parents	0.913	0.217	**0.023***
Faulty initiations by parents	**0.000***	**0.016***	**0.012***
Faulty initiations by children	**0.000***	0.216	0.285
Self-repetitions by parents	**0.000***	0.612	**0.002****

*$p = .05$.
**$p = .01$.
***$p = .001$.

nonverbal initiations were not aimed at or related to the parents and did not contribute to the flow of conversation.

The SLI and NLA children did not differ in the frequency or variety of communication acts used. The use of controls (i.e., requests, wants, demands, rejections, refusals) decreased significantly from Session 1 to 9 for the SLI children. The SLI children used significantly more expressives (i.e., acts that express feelings/emotions or attitudes), representationals (i.e., acts for the meaningful exchange of information), and procedurals (i.e., acts intended to control the conversational flow, modality, and attention) at the end of the study than at the beginning (see Table 12.3). The parents of the SLI children used significantly more information requests and procedurals at the end of the study when compared with the beginning. The NLA children and their parents only showed significant increases in the use of representationals during the course of the study.

Grammatical and Pragmatic Disabilities

By the end of the longitudinal study, all of the SLI children achieved age-appropriate scores on the formal language comprehension and language production tests administered at the beginning and end of the original study (van Balkom, 1991). The age-appropriate language production data should nevertheless be interpreted with caution because the data only represent information on clearly intelligible utterances that could thus be analyzed for grammatical correctness. Of the SLI language production data, at least 45% could not be analyzed or judged; of the NLA language production data, some 34% could not be analyzed due to ellipsis, self-repetition, ambiguity, echolalia, imitation, or unintelligibility. The label *age appropriate* thus applies to 55% of the SLI data and 66% of the NLA data at the end of the original study.

Although the SLI children were found to use more grammatically correct utterances at the end of the study, the incidence of poorly constructed linguistic utterances remained high with a significant difference in the MLUs for the SLI versus NLA children as a result. Dysfluencies, together with poorly constructed utterances, also produced more misunderstandings and disruptions in the conversation flow for the SLI children than for the NLA children.

The results show a clear and significant increase in the use of clarification requests, procedurals, backchannels (an attention getting device), corrections, and reinitiations (or reintroductions) by the parents of the SLI children as the study progressed. These indicate attempts to redirect the child's largely self-directed and self-related intentions and play behaviors toward a more shared and mutual focus (see Table 12.3).

Compared with the parents of the NLA children, the parents of the SLI children used significantly more clarification requests, corrections, self-repetitions, reinitiations, and acts in which they attempt to regain the child's attention or redirect the child's attention away from the child. These parental strategies are mainly meant to (re)establish mutual interaction or encourage coherent discourse via the use of so-called *faulty initiations* and *faulty responses* (see Table 12.3). Faulty initiations and faulty responses are intended to disrupt the ongoing (mostly self-directed) activities of the interlocutor or, in this case, child. Other than these differences, the parents of the SLI children do not differ from the parents of the NLA children; the complexity of their linguistic input, as measured by MLU, does not differ (Table 12.3).

As already noted, the age appropriateness of the SLI data on the formal tests of language comprehension and production at the end of the study suggest that the SLI children ultimately display normal linguistic skills. However, when considered in connection with the aforementioned pragmatic performance data, the overall picture becomes less favorable and more diffuse. A lack of conversational cohesiveness and mutual involvement in the discourse appears to be associated with thin grammatical competence and performance of the SLI children even when the latter have improved. In other words, at the end of the study, the SLI children still showed a number of difficulties with form–function mapping, however masked by proficient and age-appropriate test scores. The results from the original study (formal test scores on language comprehension and language production together with pragmatic performance data), however, were based on a modular approach to pragmatic disability and cannot be taken as direct evidence for difficulties with the form–function mappings among SLI children. To gather more explicit support for the functional approach, a quick inspection and reanalysis of data from the original study is needed, explicitly focusing on form–function mappings. If the results of these reanalyses prove interesting enough, more extensive follow-up study is justified. The subset of data analyzed again concerns discourse coherence and any problems encountered with the establishment of connected discourse.

IDENTIFICATION OF HIGH-
AND LOW-PERFORMING SLI CHILDREN
FOR SUPPLEMENTAL ANALYSES

To examine the form–function mappings produced by the SLI children in greater detail, the data from Sessions 8 and 9 (toward the end of the longitudinal study) were selected to analyze the performance of a relatively low-functioning group of children and the performance of a relatively high-functioning group of children. Despite generally significant gains by the end of the longitudinal study, that is, the group of 12 SLI children could be divided into two distinct subgroups at the end of the study (Sessions 8 and 9) based on marked differences in their language performance data (MLU and percentage of utterances that could not be grammatically analyzed). The group of low-functioning SLI children was defined on the basis of an MLU lower than 2.5 (i.e., the group mean for all of the SLI children in Sessions 8 and 9) and an incidence of nonanalyzable utterances in a sample due to unintelligibility, repetition, or ambiguity larger than 48% (i.e., the mean group percentage for Sessions 8 and 9). In addition, the low-functioning SLI group showed poor syntactic skills, performed at a maximum linguistic clause level of I or II (i.e., single- to three-word utterances), and demonstrated a high incidence of ellipsis and imitation of adult utterances (i.e., more than five utterances in a sample or the entire group mean for Sessions 8 and 9). The remaining SLI children constituted the group of so-called *high-functioning* SLI children. This procedure nicely and unexpectedly produced two subgroups of six SLI children each (see Table 12.4).

DIFFICULTIES WITH FORM–FUNCTION MAPPING

Based on a functionalist approach to pragmatic disability, SLI children with particularly low-performance scores for pragmatic abilities (relative to the SLI group means) can be expected to also score relatively low on grammatical abilities (also relative to the SLI group means). Conversely, SLI children with particularly high-performance scores for pragmatic abilities (relative to the SLI group means) can be expected to also perform relatively better on grammatical abilities (relative to the SLI group means).

The set of variables selected for the supplemental analyses pertain to the creation of discourse coherence and the connectedness of discourse. Appendix 1 specifies definitions of the categories used in the supplemental form-function analysis. In Table 12.4, the results of the reanalysis of the data gathered at the end of the longitudinal study (namely, during Sessions 8 and 9) are presented. Four form-related variables were used to divide the SLI group into low versus high functioning. Five variables related to discourse coherence were used to measure the impact of particular form–function mapping difficulties on the flow of conversation. Connectedness or discourse cohesion is often realized via the use of anaphoric reference, colexical reference, ellipsis, imitation, expansion, and contingent queries. Breakdowns in communication (i.e., misunderstandings, ambiguities, unintelligibility, or overuse of self-directed speech) and in-

TABLE 12.4

Results of Supplemental Form–Function Mapping Analyses for Low- Versus High-Functioning SLI Children (Means for Sessions 8 and 9)

SLI "low" MLU < 2.5	MLU	Form-Related Categories			Co-lexical Reference, Elaboration	Incorrect Acts	Discourse Coherence Categories (Form–Function Mapping Relations)		
		No Analysis Possible	Clause Level	Ellipsis, Imitation			Control, Procedural, Tutorial Acts	Calls for Attention, Reintros	Breakdowns
Linda	2.04	48%	I+II	6	72	71	65	17	70
Saskia	2.10	52%	II-I	7	64	60	70	22	60
Rianne	2.00	47%	I+II	11	63	67	126	30	90
Geronimo	1.68	67%	II+I	8	62	53	50	25	115
Sebastiaan	2.00	61%	I+II	7	60	51	50	20	82
Christiaan	2.15	50%	I+II	12	34	51	96	20	112
MEAN	2.00	54.17%	n.a.	8.50	59.17	58.83	76.2	22.33	88.17
SD	.17	8.04%	n.a.	2.43	13.00	8.64	29.7	4.59	22.15

SLI "high" MLU > 2.5		Form-Related Categories					Discourse Coherence Categories (Form–Function Mapping Relations)		
Davy	3.41	7%	IV+III	5	178	12	34	5	65
Lisette	3.32	48%	IV+III	5	120	26	32	5	38
Marcel	4.21	41%	V+IV	4	103	30	41	10	42
Bjorn	3.12	38%	III+II	6	107	21	33	12	50
Johny	3.18	43%	III+II	4	121	20	19	10	52
Remco	3.62	39%	III+II	3	113	24	50	10	53
MEAN	3.48	41.00%	n.a.	4.50	123.67	22.17	34.83	8.67	50.00
SD	.40	4.05%	n.a.	1.05	27.54	6.15	10.30	2.94	9.44

n.a. = not applicable.

correct acts or turns clearly distort the flow of conversation and establishment of discourse coherence. To prevent such distortions, speakers may use such speech or communication acts as controls, attention-getting devices, procedurals (i.e., clarification requests), or tutorials (i.e., cues, frames, and scripts for conversation or narrative).

More generally, a discourse situation without mutual involvement in the exchange of information or intentions does not produce a conversation or discourse. To establish or reestablish discourse coherence, thus, the flow of conversation can be either created or corrected by explicitly reintroducing a topic or elaborating on an ongoing topic or activity (reinitiations and elaborations).

In light of the previous considerations, it was expected that the low-functioning SLI group would have significantly more problems with the creation of coherent discourse and thus show significantly more communication breakdowns and incorrect moves (turns) than the high-functioning SLI group. More important, the discourse difficulties can be expected to stem from underlying problems with the linking of a suitable form to the desired or required communicative function. Indications of such problems may be significantly lower figures for referential language use (i.e., limited use of co-lexical reference and elaboration) and a significantly higher incidence of ellipsis and imitation among the low-functioning group relative to the high-functioning group. Compared with the parents of the high-functioning SLI children, moreover, the parents of the low-functioning SLI children can be expected to use significantly more repair strategies and thus a greater number of controls, procedurals, tutorials, calls for attention, and reinitiations.

In Table 12.4, an overview of the figures for the two groups of SLI children is presented. The results of an independent samples *t* test are presented in Table 12.5 and show all of the differences between SLI low- and SLI high-functioning children to be highly significant. Finally, the results presented in Table 12.6 show the SLI low and SLI high children to still differ significantly from each other when the categories of form and discourse coherence are considered together.

CONCLUSIONS AND DISCUSSION

The main differences between the conversations of the parents with SLI children and the conversations of parents with NLA children in the original study is that the SLI conversations lack conversational fit. The SLI conversations miss fluency and integration of themes and topics. There is a general lack of connectivity across turns, topics, themes, and speakers for the SLI dyads. The high incidence of communication breakdowns and pa-

TABLE 12.5
Means, Standard Deviations, and Differences Between High- Versus
Low-SLI Groups for Various Form and Form–Function Categories

Category of Analysis	SLI Group	M	SD	Range	t	Df
MLU	SLI High	3.48	.40	3.12–4.21	8.38**	10
	SLI Low	2.00	.17	1.68–2.15		
Analysis not possible	SLI High	41.00	4.05	37–48	–3.58**	10
	SLI Low	54.17	8.04	47–67		
Ellipsis and imitation	SLI High	4.50	1.05	3–6	–3.70**	10
	SLI Low	8.50	2.43	6–12		
Co-lexical reference	SLI High	123.67	27.54	103–178	5.19**	10
and elaboration	SLI Low	59.17	13.00	34–72		
Incorrect acts and	SLI High	22.17	6.15	12–30	–8.47**	10
turns	SLI Low	58.83	8.64	51–71		
Controls, procedurals,	SLI High	34.83	10.30	19–50	–3.22**	10
and tutorials	SLI Low	76.17	29.69	50–126		
Calls for attention	SLI High	8.67	2.94	5–12	–6.14**	10
and reintroductions	SLI Low	22.33	4.59	17–30		
Communication	SLI High	50.00	9.44	38–65	–3.88**	10
breakdowns	SLI Low	88.17	22.15	60–115		

*$p < .05$.
**$p < .01$.

TABLE 12.6
Results of ANOVAs Comparing Low- Versus High-SLI Groups
for Various Categories of Form and Form–Function Categories

Category of Analysis	F	Significance of F
MLU	70.147	.000**
Analysis not possible	12.847	.005**
Ellipsis and imitation	13.714	.004**
Co-lexical reference and elaboration	26.920	.000**
Incorrect acts and turns	71.810	.000**
Controls, procedurals, and tutorials	10.375	.009**
Calls for attention and reintroductions	37.691	.000**
Communication breakdowns	15.075	.003**

*$p < .05$.
**$p < .01$.

rental repairs in the conversations with the SLI children was particularly striking. During the course of the longitudinal study (Sessions 1–9), both the quality and quantity of the verbal input provided by the parents of the SLI children declined and was less adjusted and connected to the child's verbal and nonverbal activities. The detection of functional differences via formal testing based on predominantly modular approaches remains difficult. The present data generally underscore the assumption that the SLI children lack the appropriate linguistic tools and capacities to create fluent, connected, and coherent discourse. This lack, in turn, gives the parents or caregivers of SLI children little to go by, which may explain the observed decrease of verbal acts, increase of maladjusted input register, increase of calls for attention and reinitiations, and increase of repairs and requests for clarification (see Table 12.4). The thin linguistic competence and performance skills of the SLI children and scanty linguistic input provided by their parents may impede the process of learning how to relate specific communicative intentions to suitable and efficient linguistic forms. The parent and SLI child appear to be caught in a vicious circle or downward spiral.

In the following, an attempt is made to answer the three research questions formulated earlier on the basis of the results of the present study.

How Can the Pragmatic Abilities of SLI Children Be Characterized?

We can start by observing that all of the SLI children in the present study showed a varied and appropriate range of communicative functions and therefore did not differ from the NLA children. However, the SLI children showed a clear tendency to overuse atypical or canonical sets of linguistic forms as evidenced by a significantly higher incidence of ellipsis, imitations, and self-repetitions when compared with the NLA children. By the end of the study, the SLI children's structural language production and language comprehension (as measured by formal language tests and the results of the reanalyses) reached age-appropriate or nearly age-appropriate levels. The richness and variation of their linguistic knowledge and performance capacities remained too frail, however, to provide a substratum for sufficient pragmatic functioning. The competition model tries to explain how pragmatic knowledge operates on and via more structural meaning relations, morphosyntactic rule systems (e.g., co-lexical and anaphoric reference, agreement relations), and social rules for language use. A lack of experiential language learning due to an impoverished conversational setting and an underdeveloped network of meaning associations to compete may explain why the group of linguistically low-functioning SLI children had more difficulties with the establishment and maintenance of discourse coherence than the group of high-functioning SLI children. The latter group shows a more extensive and detailed system of linguistic rules enabling them to select from and map a relatively greater number of linguistic forms onto the relevant communicative functions.

What Are the Relations Between the Grammatical
and Pragmatic Abilities of the SLI Children
and NLA Children in Conversations
With Their Primary Caregiver?

Viewed from a functionalist approach, the SLI children were expected to demonstrate more severe difficulties with the effective matching of linguistic forms to communicative functions than predicted by their level of grammatical and lexical knowledge alone. On the basis of this expectation, we predicted that the six SLI children with a higher level of morphosyntactic functioning would perform significantly better with regard to effective form–function mapping than the six SLI children with a lower level of morphosyntactic functioning. Effective form–function mapping was operationalized within the context of the present study as sufficiently connected or coherent discourse. The results clearly show significant differences between the two groups of SLI children and thus confirm our predictions. The parents and many SLI children appear to get caught in a downward spiral of mutual deprivation and mutual neglect or conversational segregation that ultimately result in increased language and learning difficulties in the end.

Reexamination of a subset of the longitudinal data from a clearly functionalist perspective provided further support for the hypothesis that the SLI children studied here encountered difficulties with the form–function mappings needed for adequate pragmatic functioning as a result of insufficient morphosyntactic knowledge and linguistic skills. The results presented here also suggest that the conversations between the NLA children and their parents are more balanced than the conversations between the SLI children and their parents (or primary caregivers). That is, the conversations with the NLA children show a more equal distribution of both verbal and nonverbal acts across the participants. In addition, the conversations with the NLA children show greater involvement of both the parent and child.

What Is the Role of Parental Input in the Conversations
of the SLI and NLA Children With Their
Primary Caregivers?

In early childhood, narratives and clearly connected discourse constitute the cradle for the acquisition of language and later development of literacy. The aforementioned comparison of the patterns of discourse for SLI versus NLA children with their parents or primary caregivers points to an impoverished conversational context with few anchors for the children's language development and pragmatic functioning in cases of SLI. In addition to clear linguistic difficulties, the SLI children appear to miss the scaffolding effects of functionally cohesive and well-structured conversations with their parents or primary caregivers. Such a lack of experiential learning and concomitant knowledge clearly hinders the SLI children in their weighting and fine tuning of appropriate form–function mappings. Such problems may also, then, contribute to the observed differences in the cohesiveness of the conversations between the parents of the SLI children and the parents of the NLA children. Nearly empty and clearly unbalanced parent–child interactions do not provide sufficient opportunities for the identification of suitable form–function mappings.

Although it is difficult to find concrete evidence for the existence of a specifically pragmatic disability among children with SLI, the results produced here—on the basis of a reexamination of modular-based data from a functionalist perspective—appear to be quite promising. Obviously more in-depth studies are still needed in our quest to understand the exact nature of pragmatic disability.

REFERENCES

Balkom, H., van (1991). *The communication of language impaired children*. A study of discourse coherence in conversations of Specific Language Impaired and Normal Language Acquiring children with their caregivers. Lisse/Amsterdam: Swets & Zeitlinger.

Bishop, D. (1992). The underlying nature of specific language impairment. *Journal of Child Psychology and Psychiatry, 33,* 1–64.

Bishop, D., & Leonard, L. (2000). *Speech and language impairments in children. Causes, characteristics, intervention and outcome*. Hove, UK: Psychology Press.

Bishop, D. V. M. (2000). Pragmatic language impairment: A correlate of SLI, a distinct subgroup, or part of the autistic continuum? In D. V. M. Bishop & L. B. Leonard (Eds.), *Speech and language impairments in children. Causes, characteristics, intervention and outcome* (pp. 99–113). Hove, UK: Psychology Press.

Bol, G., & Kuiken, F. (1989). Handleiding GRAMAT. Een methode voor het diagnostiseren en kwalificeren van taalontwikkelingsstoornissen *(Gramat Manual. A method to diagnose and qualify developmental language disorders)*. Nijmegen: Berkhout.

Brinton, B., & Fujiki, M. (1982). The development of topic manipulation skills in discourse. *Journal of Speech and Hearing Research, 27,* 350–358.

Conti-Ramsden, G. (1988). Mothers in dialogue with language-impaired children. *Topics in Language Disorders, 5,* 58–68.

Craig, H. K. (1995). Pragmatic impairments. In P. Fletcher & B. MacWhinney (Eds.), *The handbook of child language* (pp. 623–640). Oxford: Basil Blackwell.

Fey, M., & Leonard, L. (1983). Pragmatic skills of children with specific language impairments. In T. Gallagher & C. Prutting (Eds.), *Pragmatic assessment and intervention issues in language* (pp. 65–82). San Diego: College Hill Press.

Lasky, E., & Klopp, K. (1982). Parent–child interactions in normal and language disordered children. *Journal of Speech and Hearing Disorders, 47,* 7–18.

Leinonen, E., Letts, C., & Rae Smith, B. (2000). *Children's pragmatic communication difficulties*. London: Whurr.

Leonard, L. (1986). Conversational replies of children with specific language impairment. *Journal of Speech and Hearing Disorders, 37,* 427–446.

Liles, B. (1985). Cohesion in the narratives of normal and language disordered children. *Journal of Speech and Hearing Research, 28,* 123–133.

McTear, M. F., & Conti-Ramsden, G. (1992). *Pragmatic disability in children.* London: Whurr.

Ochs, E. (1979). Transcription as theory. In E. Ochs & B. B. Schieffelin (Eds.), *Developmental pragmatics* (pp. 3–25). New York: Academic Press.

O'Hare, A. E., Quew, R., & Aitken, K. (1998). The identification of autism in children referred to a tertiary speech and language clinic and the implications for service delivery. *Autism, 2,* 171–180.

Prutting, C. A., & Kirchner, D. M. (1987). A clinical appraisal of the pragmatic aspects of language. *Journal of Speech and Hearing Disorders, 52,* 105–119.

Rapin, I. (1996). Developmental language disorders: A clinical update. *Journal of Child Psychology and Psychiatry, 37,* 643–655.

Rapin, I., & Allen. (1983). Developmental language disorders: Nosologic considerations. In U. Kirk (Ed.), *Neuropsychology of language, reading and spelling* (pp. 155–184). New York: Academic Press.

Schachter, F. F. (1979). *Everyday mother talk to toddlers. Early intervention.* New York: Academic Press.

Stark, R. E., & Tallal, P. (1981). Selection of children with specific language deficits. *Journal of Speech and Hearing Research, 46*(2), 114–122.

Watkins, R. V. (1998). The linguistic profile of S.I.: Implications for accounts of language acquisition. In L. B. Adamson & M. A. Romski (Eds.), *Communication and language acquisition. Discoveries from atypical development* (pp. 161–185). Baltimore: Paul Brookes.

Wells, G. (1985). *Language development in the preschool years. Language at home and at school 2.* Cambridge: Cambridge University Press.

Wells, G., Montgommery, M., & MacLure, M. (1979). Adult-child discourse: Outline of a model of analysis. *Journal of Pragmatics, 3,* 337–380.

World Health Organization. (2000). ICD-10: *Classification of mental and behavioral disorders.* Geneva: Author.

APPENDIX 1

Definitions of categories used in suppletional form–function mapping analyses:

1. **MLU:** Mean Length of Utterance: measured in syllables.
2. **Analysis not possible:** Verbal utterances of SLI children that cannot be analyzed due to ellipsis, unintelligibility, ambiguity, self-repetition, imitation of adult-utterance, or exclamation.
3. **Clause level at the end of the study:** Sentence structure. Presented are the clause levels in which *most* (>60%) of the utterances are classified.
4. **Ellipsis:** Regular deletion of one or more sentence constituents that is redundant with a prior message.

5. **Imitation:** An utterance by the child was considered to be imitative of an adult model utterance if the child repeated all or part of a preceding adult utterance, and did not change the model utterance in any way except to leave something out.

6. **Co-lexical reference:** The use of alternative words or phrases to refer to earlier introduced words or circumscriptions.

7. **Anaphoric references:** Anaphoric reference means that something in one message refers back to something in a prior message or is a shared reference between conversational events (e.g., *it* is used instead of a noun).

8. **Reinitations:** Initiations that are repeated in order to (re)gain attention, stress an intention, get a more satisfactory response, or improve the quality of pronunciation.

9. **Elaborations:** Initiations that elaborate on a current conversational theme.

10. **Incorrect acts:** Verbal and nonverbal acts that are structural and/or functional incorrect within the conversational flow. Incorrect acts do not contribute to connected discourse; they cause disruptions and communication breakdowns.

11. **Controls, procedurals, tutorials:** Communication acts used by caregivers to (re)establish coherent discourse. *Control Acts:* Acts that control the sequencing and intentional content of a conversation. *Procedural Acts:* Acts connected with the channel of communication rather than with its content. Acts explicitly meant to (re-)initiate, end, or rectify a communication dysfluency. *Tutorial Acts:* Interaction in which one of the participants deliberately adopts didactic role.

12. **Calls for attention:** A specific "procedural" communication act used by the caregiver to (re)gain the child's attention.

13. **Re-introduction of theme (Reintro):** Initiations that reintroduce a conversational theme, mostly to regain attention or get a more satisfactory answer.

14. **Communication breakdowns:** Erroneous acts that mostly lead to requests and attempts to repair (e.g., contrastive functional relations of simultaneous verbal and nonverbal acts, consecutive initiations of the two partners with different communicative intentions).

III

ASSESSMENT AND INTERVENTION

13

Specific Language Impairment: Diagnostic Dilemmas

Dorothy V. M. Bishop
Oxford University

In general terms, *specific language impairment* (SLI) is easy to define: It is diagnosed when a child fails to make normal progress in language learning for no obvious reason. In practice, however, this simple characterization is deceptive. Deciding who should or should not be regarded as having SLI can be fiendishly difficult. In this chapter, I discuss three issues that arise when defining diagnostic criteria for SLI: (a) the question of whether there should be a substantial discrepancy between IQ and language level, (b) comorbidity with and differentiation from other developmental disorders, and (c) heterogeneity of developmental language impairment. Experts differ in their recommendations as to how these issues should be addressed. My own view is that much of the controversy arises because people are looking for a single diagnostic solution to a range of different problems.

IS A SINGLE DEFINITION FEASIBLE?

We first need to consider the purpose to which we put our diagnostic definition. When we do so, we find that the optimal way to define SLI varies according to the context. Many of the early attempts to formulate diagnostic criteria for SLI were made by researchers whose goal was either to discover the underlying cognitive basis of SLI or to characterize the linguistic deficits of the disorder. In this kind of study, it is important to adopt stringent criteria. One wants to select the purest cases so as to study the correlates of language impairment without any confound caused by comorbid conditions, low IQ, and so on. Typically, one would look for children whose language level was substantially below both chronological age and nonverbal ability and who had normal hearing. Furthermore, one would want to exclude children with additional disorders, such as attention deficit hyperactivity disorder (ADHD). Medical or environmental factors that might possibly influence language development, such as a history of seizures or otitis media or a bilingual or impoverished home background, might also be used as exclusionary criteria. However, if we import these stringent research criteria into clinical contexts, we immediately run into problems because such pure cases of impairment are not the norm. In reality, there is substantial comorbidity with other developmental disorders, and the same pattern of linguistic impairment may be seen in children with low or high nonverbal IQ. If we insist that only pure cases receive a diagnosis of SLI, and access to the intervention that such a diagnosis brings, then many children with language problems will be excluded. I argue here that an insistence on stringent discrepancy and exclusionary criteria has no rational justification in clinical and educational contexts.

One reason that stringent research definitions have gone unchallenged for so long is because they appear to conform to our notions of good scientific practice. In science, it is usually far better to err on the side of rigor than to be too lax. Suppose we screen 100 children for a research study and find that only 20 of them meet our diagnostic criteria, but by adopting less rigorous criteria we might include 50 children. Most researchers would conclude that the loss of statistical power is a small price to pay for the increased purity of the sample. To include additional children with less clear-cut impairments could just introduce noise and dilute the effects of interest. In a field where there is typically wide heterogeneity even in carefully selected samples, an exclusive approach to diagnosis is often seen as essential. Although it has been known for many years that research definitions exclude many children who are thought, on clinical grounds, to have SLI (Stark & Tallal, 1981), this has been seen as a problem for clinicians to resolve. Awareness that stringent definitions may have scientific as well as clinical drawbacks only began to dawn on researchers when research on genetics of SLI got underway. In these studies, one is interested in how far genetic relatedness can predict who will and will not have a language disorder. Thus, the critical thing is correct classification of individuals as affected or not affected. Suppose we have a pedigree study, where we assess first-degree relatives of children with SLI. We have to classify a father who reports that he did not have speech-language therapy as a child, but was slow to start to talk and subsequently had literacy difficulties. We then directly assess his language abilities and find vocabulary is in the normal range. We do not have the luxury of excluding marginal cases: We must decide whether to regard such a person as affected or unaffected. If we settle on the wrong definition of the phenotype, we run the risk of obtaining misleading results about heritability of SLI. This is not just a fictional example: The famous three-generation K family who shows a classic autosomal dominant pattern of inheritance includes some language-impaired individuals whose nonverbal ability is below average (Vargha-Khadem, Watkins, Alcock, Fletcher, & Passingham, 1995). Longitudinal studies confirm that affected individuals may compensate for their problems, so that their underlying difficulties are only evident by taking a history or using specific tests (e.g., Bishop, North, & Donlan, 1996; Lewis & Freebairn, 1992; Tomblin, Freese, & Records, 1992). Thus, for this kind of study, we need tests that are sensitive to residual problems in compensated cases. Typically tests that do best at discriminating compensated from unaffected individuals tend to be ones that minimize the role of learned knowledge and use nonsense materials.

Can these etiological studies show the way forward to a better definition for clinical purposes? Unfortunately, the answer is no. Suppose we were to use a test such as nonword repetition to identify cases of SLI. The characteristic that makes such a definition so useful for etiological studies—its sensitivity to residual problems—makes it unsuitable in clinical contexts. The last thing that clinicians need is to be swamped with affected individuals who have compensated for their underlying difficulties to the extent that they are coping well with everyday language demands. A crucial part of any sensible clinical definition of SLI must be that the language problem interferes significantly with communication in everyday life.

In summary, there is no single correct way to define SLI. For many kinds of research studies, it is sensible to adopt a stringent definition to study the correlates of the disorder in its purest form. For genetic studies, however, we want a definition of the phenotype that gives a coherent pattern of results, and it is important to avoid underdiagnosing SLI. For clinical purposes, the goal is to identify children whose language impairments affect everyday functioning, and we need to classify together children who will benefit from similar kinds of intervention. In recognizing these different uses to which definitions are put, some of the thorny diagnostic issues become more tractable.

These different goals of diagnosis of SLI relate quite closely to the distinctions drawn by the World Health Organization (1980) in their Classification of Impairment, Disability and Handicap (see Table 13.1). This classification distinguishes different levels of description that can be used when identifying the consequences of disease: organic (impairment), functional (disability), and social (handicap) aspects. SLI can be used to illustrate these distinctions. If we find that a child has limitations

TABLE 13.1
Definitions of Impairment, Disability, and Handicap
(World Health Organization, 1980)

Variable	Definition
• Impairment	Abnormality at the level of organ or system functioning: This includes psychologic, physiologic, or anatomic abnormalities.
• Disability	Restriction or loss at the functional level. Inability to carry out activities that most humans can do.
• Handicap	Social disadvantage arising from impairment: This depends on the social environment as well as the level of impairment and disability.

of auditory perception (e.g., Tallal, Miller, & Fitch, 1995), phonological short-term memory (e.g., Gathercole & Baddeley, 1990), or a major delay in acquiring a component of grammatical knowledge (e.g., Rice & Wexler, 1996), these would be examples of impairments. Although we do not know the biological basis of such difficulties, we assume that they reflect an underlying neurodevelopmental abnormality. Tests that assess how well the child can use and understand language in the home or classroom, without attempting to pinpoint specific underlying processes, would be regarded as measures of disability. Thus, we may find that the child cannot understand complex sentences that contain more than one clause. Such a problem could reflect an impairment in auditory processing, phonological short-term memory, or grammatical knowledge. However, when we consider disability, we are less concerned with underlying processes, but rather are focusing on whether the child's communicative functioning is adequate. It is possible for a person to have an impairment that does not lead to disability. Thus, a bright person with limited phonological short-term memory may develop strategies to compensate for the impairment and show normal understanding and sentence production. *Handicap* refers to the social consequences of impairment and disability and is influenced by the environment. Suppose we have a child who has major impairments in auditory processing that lead to functional difficulties in comprehending speech in noise. The extent to which this causes handicap depends on whether the child is in a large, noisy classroom or taught in a small group with little background noise. Consider the theory of Rice, Wexler, and Cleave (1995), which proposes that the fundamental problem in SLI is delayed maturation of a grammatical module that specifies how verb tense is marked. Whether such an underlying impairment results in disability and handicap would depend on the language being learned. A child with such an impairment will have obvious language problems if learning English, but will have no overt difficulties if learning a language such as Chinese, which uses no tense inflections.

At the clinical level, our primary interest is in identifying disability and exploring how to minimize any handicap resulting from disability. For basic research studies, however, we are usually much more interested in underlying impairment.

The three-fold distinction among impairment, disability, and handicap is not watertight and has come under some criticism (e.g., Thuriaux, 1995). In the context of language problems, where we lack biological indicators of underlying disease, the boundary between impairment and disability can become blurred because, in effect, we use functional measures to evaluate impairment. Nevertheless, it can be helpful to draw a line between measures that are intended to pinpoint specific component processes that influence language functioning and those that act as more global indicators of the ability to use and understand language in more realistic contexts.

USE OF IQ DISCREPANCY CRITERIA

Traditionally, the diagnosis of SLI is made only if there is a substantial discrepancy between language level and nonverbal IQ. This is a clear case of a criterion that may serve a purpose in research studies concerned with cognitive and linguistic correlates of SLI, but which is of questionable validity in other contexts. For instance, when arguing that SLI is associated with deficits of auditory processing, symbolic functioning, or specific syntactic knowledge, one wants to control for general intellectual level using a nonverbal IQ test. Selecting children whose poor language is discrepant with average nonverbal ability is an effective control procedure.

However, for genetic studies, there is evidence that it is overrestrictive to insist that a child has a substantial discrepancy between verbal and nonverbal ability. In my own work, I have found that MZ twins show good concordance for language impairment, but poor concordance for language-IQ discrepancy (Bishop, 1994). Furthermore, although twin studies give high indexes of heritability for language impairment, the discrepancy between language level and nonverbal IQ does not show significant heritability (Bishop, North, & Donlan, 1995). This is perhaps not so surprising when we consider that discrepancy scores are notoriously unreliable. It is a mathematical fact that a difference score between two measures will be less reliable than either of the measures on which it is based. Cole and his colleagues demonstrated the practical consequences of this; the IQ-language discrepancy is sufficiently unreliable that many children change category from one test occasion to another (Cole, Dale, & Mills, 1990, 1992; Cole, Mills, & Kelley, 1994; Cole, Schwartz, Notari, Dale, & Mills, 1995).

This has led to a trend for abandoning discrepancy criteria. For instance, it is noteworthy that in a large U.S. epidemiological study by Tomblin and colleagues (Tomblin, 1996; Tomblin et al., 1997), SLI was defined in terms of having poor language skills in the context of a nonverbal IQ above 85 (1 *SD* below the mean). The definition of language impairment corresponded to a cutoff on a composite language battery of –1.14 *SD*. This definition would include some children whose language and nonverbal IQ are not substantially different: In the most extreme case, the child might have a language standard score of 82 and a nonverbal score of 85.

Should this worry us? It depends on one's underlying model of language impairment. Imagine that SLI is caused by some factor X that depresses verbal abilities so that the distribution of verbal scores is shifted down by 1 *SD* for those who have factor X. Assuming factor X has no effect on nonverbal abilities, we would find that among children with factor X the proportion with large verbal–nonverbal discrepancies will be increased relative to the general population. However, the distribution of nonverbal ability would be the same as for the general population so that some children would be expected to have nonverbal abilities at the lower end of the normal range. In short, we might argue that having poor language does not protect a child from having a low nonverbal IQ.

Despite such considerations, most people are understandably nervous about abandoning discrepancy scores. There is real concern that this will open the floodgates to hordes of children whose low language test scores arise from a range of heterogeneous etiologies. In research contexts, this could lead to a dilution of effects of interest. In clinical contexts, services might be overwhelmed by inclusion of large numbers of children whose language difficulties are part of a broader developmental delay. So what is the answer?

On the basis of what I have argued so far, you may not be surprised to hear me say that it depends. If one's interest is in studying the genetics of SLI, the way forward is to look for a reliable measure of the underlying impairment. Bishop et al. (1996) argued that a test of nonword repetition provided an excellent behavioral marker for genetic studies because, as well as showing high heritability, the test revealed underlying deficits in people whose overt language difficulties had resolved. Furthermore, this measure shows weak or nonsignificant correlations with nonverbal IQ (Bishop et al., 1996), maternal education (Coleman et al., 1999), or ethnic background (Campbell, Dollaghan, Needleman, & Janosky, 1997). Furthermore, in those with mental handicap, low IQ is not necessarily a barrier to developing good phonological short-term memory: Individuals with Williams syndrome do well on nonword repetition despite poor performance on other cognitive tests (Karmiloff-Smith et al., 1997). Quite simply, if one uses a measure like this, IQ becomes irrelevant because there is no indication that IQ level exerts any important effect on task performance.

USE OF QUALITATIVE MARKERS FOR SLI

Another approach to identifying language impairment is to move away from IQ-discrepancy measures and look instead at qualitative aspects of language functioning. Many people suspect that there is something distinctive about the nature of the language problems in children typically recognized as cases of SLI as opposed to those with common or garden low-language levels. If this is right, then we have a way forward by looking for indicators that identify children who have a qualitatively distinct deficit. This may mean rethinking how we use standardized language tests in diagnosis. The advantages of standardized tests are well known. They allow us to quantify the severity of impairment in relation to a peer group using instruments shown to have acceptable reliability. However, most standardized tests are not well suited for identifying qualitative abnormalities. Typically, they are designed so as to yield a normal distribution of scores, rather than to divide a population into an impaired and unimpaired subgroup. Suppose, however, that what distinguishes SLI from normality is an inability to carry out certain grammatical operations that are normally mastered by 5 years of age. Such a model predicts that most children above age 5 will perform at ceiling on measures of the grammatical skill, and that failure on such a test is a marker for SLI. In other words, we would not expect to find a normal distribution, but rather a bimodal one. Rice (2000) argued that her extended optional infinitive test acts in just this way. Research on this measure is still at an early stage, but it has considerable promise and provides a nice illustration of the different types of measure that are required if one's underlying model of disorder is qualitative rather than quantitative.

Should we substitute measures such as nonword repetition or extended optional infinitive tests for conventional language assessments in clinical contexts? Once again, it depends. The point that makes nonword repetition a useful test for genetics studies—its sensitivity to residual deficits—makes it of questionable utility as a clinical diagnostic test. Quite simply, many children who do poorly on nonword repetition tests do not have major problems on formal language tests and may be coping well in everyday life. In relation to Table 13.1, we may say that they have an impairment but not a disability. The picture would seem rather different for extended optional infinitives because, if a child has problems using and understanding these constructions, this is likely to have an impact on everyday communication and thus entails disability and probable handicap.

Indeed, Rice has shown that this measure has good sensitivity and specificity in discriminating children who, on clinical grounds, are deemed language impaired from those who are typically developing.

In the final analysis, the important fact to bear in mind is that a clinical diagnosis should identify children who will benefit from specific forms of intervention and educational placement and whose difficulties with communication interfere with everyday life and academic achievement. There is already good evidence that conventional psychometric tests do not always succeed in identifying those children who attract clinical and parental concern (Dunn, Flax, Sliwinski, & Aram, 1996). Furthermore, IQ-discrepancy indexes are, on the one hand, unreliable and, on the other hand, exclude a substantial proportion of children who are thought, on clinical grounds, to have specific language impairments. What is needed are improved measures of underlying impairment that mesh better with clinical impressions of disability. I expect that as we develop such measures, we will find that the debate about IQ discrepancies becomes irrelevant.

Comorbidity With and Differentiation From Other Developmental Disorders

Comorbidity between developmental disorders is so widespread that the child with a truly specific disorder is the exception rather than the rule. There is ample evidence that children with SLI have high rates of ADHD (Beitchman, Brownlie, & Wilson, 1996), developmental coordination disorder (Powell & Bishop, 1992), literacy problems (Bishop & Adams, 1990), and impairments of social interaction (Brinton & Fujiki, 1993). Any attempt at specifying diagnostic criteria must grapple with this issue.

Once again, we have a situation where the research focus on pure cases has had a negative impact on clinical practice by leading to restrictive diagnostic criteria that exclude a substantial proportion of children. In seeking to arrive at a single diagnostic label, clinicians are discouraged from considering the whole spectrum of impairments that one typically sees. My experience is that there are many children where the particular diagnostic label that a child receives is more a function of the specialist who makes the diagnosis than of the characteristics of the child. The same child might receive a label of SLI from a speech-language pathologist, dyslexia from a school psychologist, ADHD from a pediatrician, PDDNOS from a child psychiatrist, right-hemisphere learning disability from a neuropsychologist, and developmental coordination disorder from a physical therapist.

I do not think the answer is to lump all disorders together, as tended to be the case in the past with concepts such as minimal brain dysfunction. However, it would seem important to stress the importance of multidisciplinary assessment of a child presenting with communication difficulties, many of whom will have associated difficulties in nonlinguistic domains. Elsewhere (Bishop, 2000) I argued that a dimensional approach to the classification of developmental disorders may be more appropriate than the categorical approach inherited from those working in the tradition of the medical model. On this view, the distinction between SLI and autistic disorder is not a sharp divide. Certainly, there are many children whose differential diagnosis is quite unambiguous: These would correspond to textbook cases of SLI or autistic disorder. However, there are others who have social and pragmatic impairments that go beyond what one would expect to see in SLI, yet whose difficulties are not as severe or pervasive as is typically seen in autistic disorder. I have used the term *pragmatic language impairment* to refer to these cases. The model could be made even more complex by incorporating the domains of attention and motor skill. A multidimensional model appears to do a better job in capturing clinical reality than a diagnostic system with sharp divisions between discrete disorders. However, we cannot afford to simply abandon the diagnostic labels even if we recognize that they are artificial abstractions. Quite simply, a label provides a shorthand description of a child's problems that provides access to appropriate services. Certainly, in the United Kingdom, it can make a tremendous difference to the intervention and educational provision that is offered whether a child receives a diagnosis of SLI or autistic disorder.

If we turn back from clinical to research questions, the comorbidity that we see poses the question as to whether we should alter our diagnostic boundaries. Comorbidity can arise for many different reasons (Caron & Rutter, 1991). It could be that a common genetic defect leads to diverse behavioral outcomes, perhaps by affecting adjacent brain areas. It might be that environmental risk factors for one disorder raise the likelihood of the other being present. One disorder, such as language impairment, could lead to another (e.g. social impairment; see Rice, Sell, & Hadley, 1991). The plausibility of these different lines of explanation varies from one case to another. For instance, it is easy to see how language difficulties might lead to reading problems, but harder to postulate a causal route from language difficulties to motor clumsiness. As yet, we have little understanding of the origins of comorbidity with language disorders, but genetic studies may lead to a way forward because they can help us discover whether co-occurring disorders have common etiological origins (cf. Stevenson, Pennington, Gilger, DeFries, & Gillis, 1993). Although comorbidity is widespread, one can find cases of relatively pure disorder, and these may be the optimal cases to use for certain types of research study where one wants to study the correlates of language difficulties in the absence of confounding factors. The critical point to remember, however, is that such children are not representative of SLI in the general population, and the nature and origins of their problems could be quite different.

Heterogeneity of SLI

There is little agreement on how to subclassify SLI. As a field develops, the basis of classification tends to move from superficial observable characteristics to underlying processes. In the case of SLI, we would ultimately hope to identify subtypes based on etiology and underlying cognitive mechanisms, but as yet the field is not sufficiently advanced for this to be possible. In general, therefore, classifications tend to be based on the linguistic characterization of the language impairment. Bishop (1998) argued that attempts to derive categories by using cluster analysis with test data have been largely unsuccessful probably because the available tests do not cover aspects of communication that are important, such as pragmatics. More agreement has been achieved by those adopting a clinical approach, such as Rapin and Allen (1983), and those who combine test data with more impressionistic qualitative data, as exemplified by Conti-Ramsden, Crutchley, and Botting (1997) and Botting and Conti-Ramsden, chap. 1, this volume).

I close by briefly describing some subtypes of developmental speech and language impairment about which there is at least some broad agreement among clinicians.

TYPICAL SLI

A large percentage of research on SLI focuses on children who have disproportionate problems with grammatical development. In English, this is manifested in frequent omission of grammatical endings, such as past tense -ed or third-person singular -s. Such errors are, of course, also seen in normally developing young children, but in SLI they persist well beyond the normal age, and the grammatical difficulties do seem out of proportion with other linguistic problems. Leonard (1997) provided a masterly overview of the literature on such disorders, taking into account the manifestations in languages other than English. He also reviewed the wide range of theories of underlying impairment that have been proposed to account for this pattern of language development. First, there are theories that postulate a low-level auditory perceptual impairment as the primary cause of the language difficulties (Tallal & Piercy, 1973). According to this view, which is reviewed in detail by Bishop (1997), children have difficulty in perceiving oral language at the rate at which it is normally produced, and this leads to slow and distorted acquisition of phonology and syntax. This contrasts sharply with theories that argue for impairment of innate brain modules specialized for processing grammar (e.g., Gopnik & Crago, 1991). Yet another group of researchers proposed limitations in processing capacity and/or working memory as the fundamental problem in such children (Gathercole & Baddeley, 1990; Joanisse & Seidenberg, 1998; Leonard, 1997).

It can be difficult to disentangle these theories because they make many of the same predictions (Bishop, 1997). On the grounds of parsimony, researchers in this area tend to look for a single underlying cause that might explain all cases of grammatical impairment in children, but it is of course possible that different explanations apply in different cases. It is unfortunate that many studies report only group data when testing a specific hypothesis without indicating how typical findings are for group members. Often, however, there can be quite substantial variation from child to child. For instance, Bishop et al. (1999) found that children with SLI did more poorly than a control group on a test of auditory perception based on Tallal's theory. However, they did not show the expected rate-specific deficit, and the effect size was relatively modest. This meant that there were many children with SLI who were not impaired in auditory processing and many controls who were. A subsequent study by Bishop, Carlyon, Deeks, and Bishop (1999) on a subset of these children considered whether the variable results simply reflected poor reliability of the auditory test. Eleven children with SLI were compared with 11 matched controls on a range of auditory psychophysical tasks, with repeat administration over a period of several months. On a test of auditory backward masking, there was reasonable test–retest reliability although practice led to improvements in scores for all children with repeat testing. However, there was substantial individual variation in both control and SLI groups, and in this relatively small sample there was no significant difference between them. The conclusion from this study was that auditory deficit was neither necessary nor sufficient to cause SLI, but we suggested that it might be a risk factor that assumed importance when it occurred in a child who had a genetic predisposition to SLI.

Although grammatical difficulties are one of the most noticeable and common manifestations of SLI (e.g., Conti-Ramsden et al., 1997), one should beware of assuming that all children with grammatical problems are the same. Phonological difficulties appear to be a common, but not universal, correlate (Rapin & Allen, 1983). The existence of children who have severe problems in understanding grammar in the context of superior nonverbal ability, good pragmatics and phonology, and normal auditory processing is of considerable theoretical interest in demonstrating the potential independence of grammar from other aspects of cognition (Van der Lely, 1997). However, such children appear to be the exception rather than the rule (Bishop, Bright, James, Bishop, & van der Lely, 2000). More commonly, one sees children whose grammatical difficulties co-occur with major problems in semantics and some limitations of nonverbal ability.

SEVERE RECEPTIVE LANGUAGE DISORDER

Although one can usually find comprehension problems in children with grammatical difficulties, these are typically less obvious and severe than their expressive difficulties (e.g., Bishop, 1979). Much rarer are those children who have such severe problems in understanding language that they are initially thought to be deaf. This is sometimes referred to as a childhood manifestation of verbal auditory agnosia (Rapin, Mattis, & Rowan, 1977). Much of the research on these children consists of single case studies because they are so rare. Some of these studies have demonstrated impairment of nonverbal auditory processing in such children (e.g., Rosen, van der Lely, & Dry, 1997; Stefanatos, Green, & Ratcliff, 1989). This is one subtype of language impairment that is associated with a distinctive etiology—that of acquired epileptic aphasia or Landau–Kleffner syndrome (see Deonna, 2000, for a review). Typically, the child starts out developing language normally, but regresses in the preschool years, losing language comprehension and expression over a period that may range from a few days to several months. Although an epileptic etiology underlies this disorder, this can be difficult to demonstrate because often the seizures are nocturnal and may only be evident when a sleep EEG is carried out. Deonna (2000) raised the interesting speculation that a similar etiological process may be implicated in some cases of milder SLI, although he noted that studies looking for elevated rates of EEG abnormalities in children with SLI have not yielded consistent findings.

DEVELOPMENTAL VERBAL DYSPRAXIA

Developmental verbal dyspraxia is possibly one of the most controversial of all the subtypes of SLI. Some authorities deny its existence. Others accept that a clinical picture resembling dyspraxia may be seen, but query whether the label is an appropriate one. Even those who use the term do so in rather different ways. In adult neurology, *dyspraxia* refers to difficulty in programming movements that cannot be explained in terms of muscle weakness or sensory loss. Typically, the patient is able to imitate individual movements or speech sounds, but has great difficulty producing longer sequences. In developmental cases, one also sees children whose intelligibility declines markedly when they attempt complex utterances compared with when they are producing individual sounds or syllables. Some authorities argue that a diagnosis of dyspraxia is most appropriate when the child also has evidence of difficulty imitating nonspeech oral movements. Others maintain that the programming impairment can be specific to speech production, and that the most critical diagnostic feature is inconsistency of speech sound production from one occasion to another.

Although the term *dyspraxia* suggests a pure output disorder, systematic studies of phonological processing in children with a diagnosis of dyspraxia indicates that many—perhaps all—of these children have difficulty doing tasks that involve mentally manipulating speech sounds, such as classic phonological awareness tasks (Stackhouse, 1992). Therefore, their difficulties may have more to do with problems in forming segmental phonological representations than with programming motor output. In contrast to children with speech disorders arising from physical or neurological impairment of the articulators, those with verbal dyspraxia typically have major literacy problems, and receptive language levels may be poor on tests of vocabulary and grammar (Stackhouse, 1982; see also Bishop, 1985). Such findings suggest that the label of *dyspraxia* may be inappropriate in suggesting a circumscribed motor programming problem.

PRAGMATIC LANGUAGE IMPAIRMENT

The traditional view of SLI is of a child with normal sociability whose communication is limited only by difficulties in mastering the structural aspects of language (i.e., phonology and syntax). However, there is a substantial literature indicating an elevated level of difficulties in the social use of language in this population (see van Balkom & Verhoeven, chap. 12, this volume). Bishop (2000) reviewed this work and concluded that, although some social communication problems in SLI could be secondary consequences of difficulties in formulating intelligible utterances or comprehending what others were saying, others were less easy to explain this way. This is particularly true in the case where the child with early language delay goes on to make rapid progress in mastering phonology and grammar and starts to speak in long and complex sentences, but uses utterances inappropriately. Such children may offer tangential answers to questions, lack coherence in conversation or narrative speech, and appear overliteral in their comprehension. In the past, I adopted the terminology based on the nosology of Rapin and Allen (1983), referring to these children as cases of *semantic-pragmatic disorder*, but there is little evidence that semantic and pragmatic difficulties tend to co-occur, and I now prefer the term *pragmatic language impairment*. One might expect a child with language difficulties to compensate by developing a rich repertoire of nonverbal communication, but in these cases of pragmatic language impairment, that is not typically seen (Bishop, Chan, Adams, Hartley, & Weir, 2000). A critical question is whether such children should be regarded as part of the autistic continuum, rather than classified with SLI. They certainly share a number of features with high-functioning autistic children and would in most cases meet the admittedly rather vague diagnostic criteria for Pervasive Developmental Disorder Not Otherwise Specified (PDDNOS; see American Psychological Association, 1994). In our current state of knowledge, I regard it as premature to conclude that all children with PLI should be placed on the autistic spectrum. Some of these children do have clear autistic features, but others do not (Bishop, 1998). The diagnostic overlap with the category of ADHD is also of interest. Incoherent, tangential speech is often remarked on as a correlate of that disorder, with poor social interaction and limited narrative and conversational skills (Tannock, Fine, Heintz, & Schachar, 1995; Tannock, Purvis, & Schachar, 1993). For clinicians, the message seems to be that one should be alert to the possibility that a child's communicative difficulties might extend beyond language structure to encompass social use of language and nonverbal communication. Most formal language assessments are not sensitive to these problems, and so one should not assume that they are absent just because they do not show up on a test. Where the child does have pragmatic problems, a multidisciplinary assessment is warranted to consider whether a diagnosis of ADHD or autistic spectrum disorder (PDDNOS) would be appropriate. It can be particularly difficult to find appropriate educational placements for such children. Schools for children with autism tend to focus more on the needs of those of low IQ, who may need much more focus on structured activities and behavior control. Schools for those with language difficulties may, however, be less well prepared to deal with the nonverbal and social impairments, which become increasingly important as children grow older.

CONCLUDING COMMENT

Specific language impairment poses enormous challenges for both clinicians and researchers. The existence of children with communication problems is not in doubt. There is little consensus about diagnostic criteria, diagnostic boundaries, or subclassification. The principal message of this chapter is that we have to consider the purpose of diagnosis and match our methods to our goals, rather than look for a single gold standard to apply in all situations. The pure, clear-cut categories described in textbooks bear little relation to clinical reality.

I have deliberately emphasized the challenges that lie ahead for those of us working with SLI because I believe that only by confronting them and analyzing the reasons for diagnostic difficulties can we resolve them. However, it would be wrong to give the impression that the problems are insuperable. Just over the past decade, we have seen enormous advances in our understanding of SLI on many fronts. We now know considerably more than we did 10 years ago about the causes of SLI (e.g., Bishop, 2001), the nature of linguistic difficulties (Leonard, 1997), epidemiology (Tomblin et al., 1997), and comorbidity (e.g., Beitchman et al., 1996). We know just how common SLI is, and we also know just how serious it is, in terms of putting the child at risk for later problems, both academic and psychiatric (e.g., Beitchman et al., 1996; Snowling, Bishop, & Stothard, 2000). Fortunately, we are also starting to see many more scientific studies of intervention that allow us to identify the characteristics of successful interventions (see chaps. 14–18, this volume).

REFERENCES

American Psychological Association. (1994). *Publication manual of the American Psychological Association* (4th ed.). Washington, DC: Author.

Beitchman, J. H., Brownlie, E. B., & Wilson, B. (1996). Linguistic impairment and psychiatric disorder: Pathways to outcome. In J. Beitchman, N. J. Cohen, M. M. Konstantareas, & R. Tannock (Eds.), *Language, learning and behavior disorders: Developmental, biological and clinical perspectives* (pp. 493–514). New York: Cambridge University Press.

Bishop, D. V. M. (1979). Comprehension in developmental language disorders. *Developmental Medicine and Child Neurology, 21,* 225–238.

Bishop, D. V. M. (1985). Spelling ability in congenital dysarthria: Evidence against articulatory coding in translating between graphemes and phonemes. *Cognitive Neuropsychology, 2,* 229–251.

Bishop, D. V. M. (1994). Is specific language impairment a valid diagnostic category? Genetic and psycholinguistic evidence. *Philosophical Transactions of the Royal Society, Series B, 346,* 105–111.

Bishop, D. V. M. (1997). *Uncommon understanding: Development and disorders of language comprehension in children.* Hove: Psychology Press.

Bishop, D. V. M. (1998). Development of the children's communication checklist (CCC): A method for assessing qualitative aspects of communicative impairment in children. *Journal of Child Psychology and Psychiatry, 39,* 879–891.

Bishop, D. V. M. (2000). Pragmatic language impairment: A correlate of SLI, a distinct subgroup, or part of the autistic continuum? In D. V. M. Bishop & L. B. Leonard (Eds.), *Speech and language impairments in children: Causes, characteristics, intervention and outcome.* Hove, UK: Psychology Press.

Bishop, D. V. M. (2001). Genetic and environmental risks for specific language impairment in children. *Philosophical Transactions of the Royal Society: Series B, 356,* 369–380.

Bishop, D. V. M., & Adams, C. (1990). A prospective study of the relationship between specific language impairment, phonological disorders and reading retardation. *Journal of Child Psychology and Psychiatry, 31,* 1027–1050.

Bishop, D. V. M., Bishop, S. J., Bright, P., James, C., Delaney, T., & Tallal, P. (1999). Different origin of auditory and phonological processing problems in children with language impairment: Evidence from a twin study. *Journal of Speech, Language and Hearing Research, 42,* 155–168.

Bishop, D. V. M., Bright, P., James, C., Bishop, S. J., & van der Lely, H. K. J. (2000). Grammatical SLI: A distinct subtype of developmental language impairment? *Applied Psycholinguistics, 21,* 159–181.

Bishop, D. V. M., Carlyon, R. P., Deeks, J. M., & Bishop, S. J. (1999). Auditory temporal processing impairment: Neither necessary nor sufficient for causing language impairment in children. *Journal of Speech, Language and Hearing Research, 42,* 1295–1310.

Bishop, D. V. M., Chan, J., Adams, C., Hartley, J., & Weir, F. (2000). Evidence of disproportionate pragmatic difficulties in a subset of children with specific language impairment. *Development and Psychopathology, 12,* 177–199.

Bishop, D. V. M., North, T., & Donlan, C. (1995). Genetic basis of specific language impairment: Evidence from a twin study. *Developmental Medicine and Child Neurology, 37,* 56–71.

Bishop, D. V. M., North, T., & Donlan, C. (1996). Nonword repetition as a behavioural marker for inherited language impairment: Evidence from a twin study. *Journal of Child Psychology and Psychiatry, 37,* 391–403.

Brinton, B., & Fujiki, M. (1993). Language, social skills, and socioemotional behavior. *Language, Speech and Hearing Services in Schools, 24,* 194–198.

Campbell, T., Dollaghan, C., Needleman, H., & Janosky, J. (1997). Reducing bias in language assessment: Processing-dependent measures. *Journal of Speech, Language and Hearing Research, 40,* 519–525.

Caron, C., & Rutter, M. (1991). Comorbidity in child psychopathology: Concepts, issues and research strategies. *Journal of Child Psychology and Psychiatry, 32,* 1063–1080.

Cole, K. N., Dale, P. S., & Mills, P. E. (1990). Defining language delay in young children by cognitive referencing: Are we saying more than we know? *Applied Psycholinguistics, 11,* 291–302.

Cole, K. N., Dale, P. S., & Mills, P. E. (1992). Stability of the intelligence quotient—language quotient relation: Is discrepancy modeling based on a myth? *American Journal on Mental Retardation, 97,* 131–143.

Cole, K. N., Mills, P. E., & Kelley, D. (1994). Agreement of assessment profiles used in cognitive referencing. *Language, Speech and Hearing Services in Schools, 25,* 25–31.

Cole, K. N., Schwartz, I. S., Notari, A. R., Dale, P. S., & Mills, P. E. (1995). Examination of the stability of two methods of defining specific language impairment. *Applied Psycholinguistics, 16,* 103–123.

Coleman, C. E., McMillin, A. C., Szwarc, L. K., Williams, M. J., Kaufhold, S. M., Kriniske, L. M., & Dollaghan, C. A. (1999). *Maternal education and the nonword repetition task.* Poster presented at the Symposium for Research on Child Language Disorders, Madison, WI.

Conti-Ramsden, G., Crutchley, A., & Botting, N. (1997). The extent to which psychometric tests differentiate subgroups of children with SLI. *Journal of Speech, Language and Hearing Research, 40,* 765–777.

Deonna, T. (2000). Acquired epileptic aphasia (AEA) or Landau–Kleffner syndrome: From childhood to adulthood. In D. V. M. Bishop & L. B. Leonard (Eds.), *Speech and language impairments in children: Causes, characteristics, intervention and outcome* (pp. 261–272). Hove, UK: Psychology Press.

Dunn, M., Flax, J., Sliwinski, M., & Aram, D. (1996). The use of spontaneous language measures as criteria for identifying children with specific language impairment: An attempt to reconcile clinical and research findings. *Journal of Speech and Hearing Research, 39,* 643–654.

Gathercole, S. E., & Baddeley, A. D. (1990). Phonological memory deficits in language disordered children: Is there a causal connection? *Journal of Memory and Language, 29,* 336–360.

Gopnik, M., & Crago, M. (1991). Familial aggregation of a developmental language disorder. *Cognition, 39,* 1–50.

Joanisse, M. F., & Seidenberg, M. S. (1998). Specific language impairment: A deficit in grammar or processing? *Trends in Cognitive Sciences, 2,* 240–247.

Karmiloff-Smith, A., Grant, J., Berthoud, I., Davies, M., Howlin, P., & Udwin, O. (1997). Language and Williams syndrome: How intact is "intact"? *Child Development, 68,* 246–262.

Leonard, L. B. (1997). *Children with specific language impairment.* Cambridge, MA: MIT Press.

Lewis, B., & Freebairn, L. (1992). Residual effects of preschool phonology disorders in grade school, adolescence, and adulthood. *Journal of Speech and Hearing Research, 35*, 819–831.

Powell, R., & Bishop, D. V. M. (1992). Clumsiness and perceptual problems in children with specific language impairment. *Developmental Medicine and Child Neurology, 34*, 755–765.

Rapin, I., & Allen, D. (1983). Developmental language disorders: Nosologic considerations. In U. Kirk (Ed.), *Neuropsychology of language, reading, and spelling* (pp. 155–184). New York: Academic Press.

Rapin, I., Mattis, S., & Rowan, A. J. (1977). Verbal auditory agnosia in children. *Developmental Medicine and Child Neurology, 19*, 192–207.

Rice, M. L. (2000). Grammatical symptoms of specific language impairment. In D. V. M. Bishop & L. B. Leonard (Eds.), *Speech and language impairments in children: Causes, characteristics, intervention and outcome* (pp. 17–34). Hove, UK: Psychology Press.

Rice, M. L., Sell, M. A., & Hadley, P. A. (1991). Social interactions of speech and language impaired children. *Journal of Speech and Hearing Research, 34*, 1299–1307.

Rice, M. L., & Wexler, K. (1996). Toward tense as a clinical marker of specific language impairment in English-speaking children. *Journal of Speech and Hearing Research, 39*, 1239–1257.

Rice, M. L., Wexler, K., & Cleave, P. L. (1995). Specific language impairment as a period of extended optional infinitive. *Journal of Speech and Hearing Research, 38*, 850–863.

Rosen, S., Van der Lely, H., & Dry, S. (1997). Speech and nonspeech auditory abilities in two children with disordered language. UCL Department of Phonetics. *Work in Progress, 10*, 186–198.

Snowling, M., Bishop, D. V. M., & Stothard, S. E. (2000). Is preschool language impairment a risk factor for dyslexia in adolescence? *Journal of Child Psychology and Psychiatry, 41*, 587–600.

Stackhouse, J. (1982). An investigation of reading and spelling performance in speech disordered children. *British Journal of Disorders of Communication, 17*, 53–60.

Stackhouse, J. (1992). Developmental verbal dyspraxia: I. A review and critique. *European Journal of Disorders of Communication, 27*, 19–34.

Stark, R. E., & Tallal, P. (1981). Selection of children with specific language deficits. *Journal of Speech and Hearing Disorders, 46*, 114–122.

Stefanatos, G. A., Green, G. G. R., & Ratcliff, G. G. (1989). Neurophysiological evidence of auditory channel anomalies in developmental dysphasia. *Archives of Neurology, 46*, 871–875.

Stevenson, J., Pennington, B. F., Gilger, J. W., DeFries, J. C., & Gillis, J. J. (1993). Hyperactivity and spelling disability: Testing for shared genetic aetiology. *Journal of Child Psychology and Psychiatry, 34*, 1137–1152.

Tallal, P., Miller, S., & Fitch, R. H. (1995). Neurobiological basis of speech: A case for the preeminence of temporal processing. *Irish Journal of Psychology, 16*, 194–219.

Tallal, P., & Piercy, M. (1973). Developmental aphasia: Impaired rate of non-verbal processing as a function of sensory modality. *Neuropsychologia, 11*, 389–398.

Tannock, R., Fine, J., Heintz, T., & Schachar, R. J. (1995). A linguistic approach detects stimulant effects in two children with attention-deficit hyperactivity disorder. *Journal of Child and Adolescent Psychopharmacology, 5*, 177–189.

Tannock, R., Purvis, K., & Schachar, R. (1993). Narrative abilities in children with attention deficit hyperactivity disorder and normal peers. *Journal of Abnormal Child Psychology, 21*, 103–117.

Thuriaux, M. C. (1995). The ICIDH: Evolution, status, and prospects. *Disability and Rehabilitation, 17*, 112–118.

Tomblin, J. B. (1996). Genetic and environmental contributions to the risk for specific language impairment. In M. L. Rice (Ed.), *Toward a genetics of language* (pp. 191–211). Mahwah, NJ: Lawrence Erlbaum Associates.

Tomblin, J. B., Freese, P. R., & Records, N. L. (1992). Diagnosing specific language impairment in adults for the purpose of pedigree analysis. *Journal of Speech and Hearing Research, 35*, 832–843.

Tomblin, J. B., Records, N., Buckwalter, P., Zhang, X., Smith, E., & O'Brien, M. (1997). Prevalence of specific language impairment in kindergarten children. *Journal of Speech and Hearing Research, 40*, 1245–1260.

van der Lely, H. K. J. (1997). Language and cognitive development in a grammatical SLI boy: Modularity and innateness. *Journal of Neurolinguistics, 10*, 75–107.

Vargha-Khadem, F., Watkins, K., Alcock, K., Fletcher, P., & Passingham, R. (1995). Praxic and nonverbal cognitive deficits in a large family with a genetically transmitted speech and language disorder. *Proceedings of the National Academy of Sciences, 92*, 930–933.

World Health Organization. (1980). *International classification of impairments, disabilities, and handicaps.* Geneva: Author.

14

A Dynamic Systems Approach to Diagnostic Measurement of SLI

Paul van Geert
University of Groningen

A dynamic system is a structure of interacting forces. *Structure* refers to a relatively stable form of order and coherence of the properties of the system at issue. An interacting force is any variable that can affect—and can be affected by—some other variable. An important and maybe also the most interesting property of dynamic systems—at least of an important subclass that is worth studying—is that such systems of interacting forces show a spontaneous increase in structure and order. This spontaneous increase in structure (order, size, complexity, coherence, etc.) is the consequence of a consumption of energy that flows through the structure of interacting components (e.g., in the case of a plant, solar light, nutrients, etc.). The technical name of this spontaneous increase in order is *self-organization*.

In this chapter, a dynamic systems approach to SLI assessment is presented. First of all, the notion of self-organization in normal and defective language development is explained. In addition, a dynamic systems approach to SLI is proposed, starting from iterative models of long-term change. The dynamics of interacting growth processes within developmental language disorders is also explored. The chapter ends with implications for diagnostic measurement of SLI. Both the nature of psychological variables and the approach to diagnostic measurement in terms of a variable-by-characteristicness approach are reviewed from a dynamic systems perspective.

SELF-ORGANIZATION IN LANGUAGE

Dynamic Causes of Defective Language Development

In the late 1950s, Chomsky laid the foundations for a nativist approach to language and language development. He showed that the available linguistic input—the language heard or perceived by a language learner—in fact underdetermined the linguistic competence to be constructed on the basis of this input. Chomsky implicitly relied on the entropic principle, according to which higher order structure cannot spontaneously result from lower order structure. The notion of underdetermination in addition to the—most probably implicit—axiom of entropy led to the assumption that language cannot be learned from an external input unless the core knowledge that specifies linguistic competence is already present. Because the core knowledge is not in the external input, it must be present in the learner—that is, it must consist of some innate core of knowledge (or acquisition principles).

The dynamic systems view on language development agrees with the nativist view that the structure constituting a person's linguistic competence—whatever that structure might be—is not as such present in the environment and is not acquired by mere transmission. However, the dynamic systems approach does not adhere to the view that the principle of entropy applies to the level of organization characteristic of such highly organized systems as language learners in their environments. The principle of self-organization, which governs most of the organic world, allows for a spontaneous emergence of higher out of lower order. That is, even if the linguistic input underdetermines linguistic competence, linguistic competence—as higher order structure—can still emerge as a result of a self-organizational process.

The nativist view that the internal conditions of language development take the form of internal (genetic) instructions, representations or categories that fully specify the basic contents and forms of the outcomes of development, is closely linked with the assumption that those internal conditions are the ultimate causes of those outcomes. In this respect, a theoretically interesting possibility is that the causes of defective development lie in defective internal conditions, such as lacking or defective specifications of the contents, categories, and rules that constitute universal grammar. Because those conditions are assumed to be represented in the form of specific genetic codes, it makes sense to look for genetic deficits as the ultimate causes of defective language development. Specific language impairment (SLI) is such an interesting condition because it appears that the causes should not be sought in a defective unpacking machinery or a defective linguistic environment. If viewed under the entropic assumption—claiming that order and structure do not arise spontaneously—the causes of SLI should be sought in defective internal specifications of those components of language that cannot be transmitted from the outside.

The causal model advocated by the dynamic systems approach is entirely different, however. Every step in a self-organizing process is as ultimate a step as any other. Every step creates the conditions under which the next step is made possible. However, with every step, new conditions are created not in any way directly implied by the previous step. It is possible—at least theoretically possible—that children who demonstrate SLI suffer from a highly specific genetic defect. However, the link between the genetic defect and condition of impairment is not direct. A dynamic systems model follows a cascading-causes model. That is, Condition A creates Condition B, B creates C, and so forth. During each step, environmental inputs are assimilated in ways that are specific to the properties of the assimilating state (A, B, C, etc.).

Modeling Iterative Developmental Processes

The difference between the nativist and dynamic systems model basically refers to the distinction between additive and iterative processes. In an additive process, the outcome is the result of components that come from some external source and have been added to the outcome state. The developmental or acquisition theory associated with an additive model explains how the process of addition occurs, the order in which the components are added, and so forth. The classical learning theoretical approach to language as well as the generative approach that relies on innate components are examples of an additive approach. The generative, nativist approach localizes the fundamental components of language in the genetic makeup of the organism. It views the genetic conditions of language, and of grammar in particular, as representationally specific conditions. For instance, specific (sets of) genes may code for specific grammatical rules, categories, or basic principles. It is clear that any defect in such genetic conditions will lead to representationally specific language impairments in subjects who suffer from that defect (see e.g., Gopnik et al., 1996; Gopnik 1999a, 1999b; van der Lely, 1994, 1997a, 1997b, 1998; van der Lely & Stollwerck, 1996, 1997). The genetic, generative approach looks for the conditional components in representationally specific primary causes (e.g., genes coding for a specific universal grammar). An alternative view, which also approaches the problem of impairment from a basically additive angle of incidence, is the approach of cognitive neuroscience (see e.g., Bishop, 1997, for a discussion). The conditional components are not representational, but functional. That is, specific neural components perform specific linguistic functions. If the neural component is either lacking or damaged, the function it embodies is similarly affected.

Another way of characterizing the additive approach is by referring to its componential nature. That is, language skill consists of various components. The components are true in the sense that they are based on highly specific internal modules and components of such modules. The modules can be specified in different ways. One is to specify the function a module fulfills in terms of representational processes (e.g., a module that produces syntactic representations based on a set of specific rules). Another approach is to specify a module by its neurophysiological place and function. If a module is lacking or otherwise impaired, the corresponding component does not occur in the subject's competence. It may eventually occur in performance, at least to a certain, functional extent, if the subject has seen fit to achieve some or other form of compensation (see e.g., Bishop, chap. 12, this volume). Thus, to understand why a specific person's language performance has certain properties (or not), one has to study the underlying components directly linked to those defective properties.

The second type of process—iteration—lies at the heart of dynamic systems and developmental approaches. In an iterative process, the input to any successive process state is the preceding process state (in addition to inputs from its environment). To understand why a person is characterized by a specific form of impairment, for instance, one has to reconstruct the iterative process that has led to the current impairment condition. Needless to say, an additive approach is considerably easier to pursue than an iterative, developmental approach. In the developmental approach, most of the information needed to reconstruct the impaired developmental process lies in the past and can be retrieved only incompletely. The problem is that from a developmental view, the search for causes of an impairment condition is an ex post facto endeavor (if a person has the impairment, one can look backward for the eventual causes; only if one carries out large-scale follow-up studies in sufficiently large populations is it possible to trace deviant developmental trajectories in a prospective way).

One of the major findings of dynamic systems theory is that iterative processes may spontaneously lead to states of (dynamic) equilibrium— the so-called *attractor states*. They are the states of increased order that characterize self-organization. The notion of attractor state has considerable implications for the study of development. Let us assume there exists an arbitrarily complicated iterative process that operates on a current state of language development and produces some future (succeeding) state of language development. During the actual developmental process, the succeeding state is different from the preceding one in that it is more complex, better consolidated, or whatever. After a while, however, the iterative process tends to produce an output state (i.e., a level of language performance) that is similar to the input state (the preceding level of language performance; note that *similar* implies within a specific range of stationary fluctuations). This self-reproductive state is the attractor of the process. It is a (semi-)stable state, the stability of which depends on the total set of current conditions (internal and external). If the conditions change (e.g., a person is equipped with a hearing aid or is given specific training), the attractor state may change. Whether it changes depends on its stability and on the strength or magnitude of the alterations brought about in the system. The question one may ask at this point is: What are the implications of a dynamic systems view for the study, explanation, and eventual treatment of an impairment condition such as SLI?

A DYNAMIC SYSTEMS APPROACH TO SLI

One of the advantages of the dynamic systems approach is that it allows one to formally model complex phenomena with the aid of categories or variables that are inherently fuzzy (van Geert, 1991, 1994, 1998a, 1998b). Let us begin with identifying a few of those categories and variables that could be used to build a simple dynamic systems model of potentially impaired language development. The literature focuses on grammatical limitations in SLI children—for instance, limitations in inflectional morphology. The first variable in the model is the child's grammatical ability (G). In the current volume, Leonard and Deevy argue that SLI children also experience problems in learning, understanding, and using words. Lexical ability (L) is thus introduced as the second variable in the model. It is obvious that neither grammar nor the lexicon is acquired if there is no input of grammatical and lexical information: A general input function I is the third variable in the model. However, a language learner is always limited in the amount of input he or she can take per unit time. There are limitations of attention, auditory acuity, time, working memory, and so forth. That is, there exists a parameter a that specifies the accessibility of the input for a specific language learner, such that the input accessed by a learner is aI/dt (a certain amount of input over a time interval dt). In the extreme case, a is zero. For instance, a deaf child has no access to auditory linguistic input. A similar case may occur under the assumption of specific innate conditions or modularity. For instance, if we assume that a child needs an innate category N to access grammatical information about nouns or nounhood and assume that this innate category is lacking (e.g., as a consequence of a genetic deficit), the a-parameter for the input of nouns, I_N is 0. Similarly, if the processing of linguistic information depends on a neurologically specified cognitive module, any impairment in that module negatively affects the processing of the input to which that module gives access.

Linear Versus Iterative Models of Long-Term Change

There exists a fundamental distinction between linear componential and dynamic models. Let us assume that a thorough investigation of grammatical and lexical ability in a specific population has shown that m % of the variance of the abilities at issue is explained by a factor M (e.g., a genetically prespecified module, whatever that may be), n % by a neurological factor N, o % by some other factor O, and so forth. A linear componential model predicts the level of a subject S's grammatical ability G_S as a sum

$$G_S = G_o + mM_S + nN_S + oO_S \ldots + \chi$$
for G_o an intercept variable and χ an error. (Eq. 1)

A dynamic model, in contrast, specifies G (or any other variable for that matter) as a time-dependent function of itself and other factors. Let us say we take an arbitrarily short time span dt for which we can specify the change in G (grammatical ability) or L (lexical ability). Let us simply assume that the change is a function of the input I and the access parameter a

$$G_{t + dt} = G_t + aI_{dt} \qquad\qquad (\text{Eq. 2})$$

This model is a simple linear increase model: It says that the increase in G (or L for that matter) is a function of the current input. We can now add a simple decrease function (which depends on forgetting, decay, interference, etc.). If the increase and decrease functions vary randomly and are about equal in size (stochastically), they will *not* average each other out, but instead lead to an interesting dynamic pattern that we call a *random walk*:

$$G_{t + dt} = G_t + aI_{dt} - D_{dt} \qquad\qquad (\text{Eq. 3})$$

It is important to note that this model is inherently developmental in that its successive state depends on its preceding state and some form of input. It is this developmental character—or, more precisely, the iterative character—that makes this particular process look different from a simple linear juxtaposition of random influences that would cancel each other out.

Under normal circumstances, we would not expect the decay factor to outweigh the increase factor. On balance, the increase is greater than the decay. If the decay were bigger than the increase, G (or any other factor for that matter) would decline toward 0 after some time, which would boil down to a permanent loss of linguistic ability. However, if, on average, the increase and decay are similar (more precisely, are statistically of the same magnitude), G would run into the random walk pattern initiated earlier. Although they are simple, random walk models possess interesting, nonintuitive, dynamic properties. For instance, they can show long-term fluctuations that are apparently determined by long-term systematic influences, but in reality are caused by unsystematic short-term fluctuations. The short-term fluctuations would cancel each other out if they were treated in a linear, additive way. The fact that they feature in an iterative, developmental process, however, explains why they can produce particular long-term patterns.

There exists an interesting form of acquired aphasia, the Landau–Kleffner syndrome, that might involve a random walk-like process of change. Landau–Kleffner syndrome (LKS) is a rare, childhood neurological disorder characterized by the sudden or gradual development of aphasia. It usually occurs in children between the ages of 4 and 8. These children develop normally and then lose the ability to understand others and to speak. The aphasia often—but certainly not always—occurs after seizures. Some affected children may have a permanent severe language disorder, whereas others may regain much of their language abilities (although it may take months or years). In some cases, remissions and relapse may occur. van de Sandt-Koenderman et al. (1984) described a case that showed repetitive recovery and breakdown of linguistic productivity. This pattern of inexplicable loss and recovery is reminiscent of a random walk pattern provided the maintenance (or increase) and decay parameters are about equal. Figure 14.1 presents an idealized picture of a random walk dichotomized in normal and aphasic periods.

Let us assume that the seizures—or any other physiological disorder—affect the condition of the increase/maintenance and decay functions in the brain to such an extent that the magnitudes of both are about equal, statistically speaking. The probability that such statistical equality occurs is quite small, of course, but it is consistent with the fact that the syndrome occurs very infrequently. Given such statistical equality, the iterative system described in Equation 3 describes a random walk. By way of caution, I should add that the present random walk explanation of the Landau–Kleffner syndrome is given for no other reason than to illustrate the dynamic systems approach. The point of this illustration is that an extremely simple dynamic (i.e., iterative) process is capable of producing the type of decay and recovery that is typical of this particular syndrome without having to resort to explanatory forces that are external to the process.

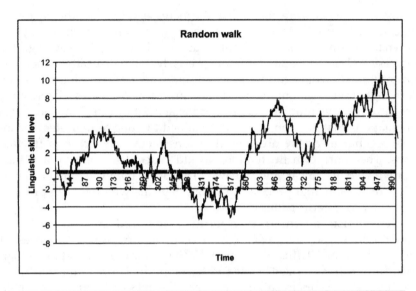

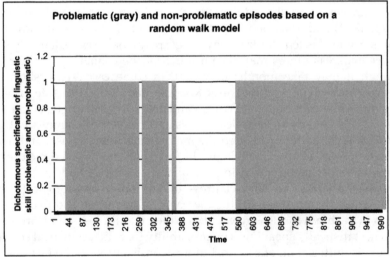

FIG. 14.1.   A random walk pattern (top) is based on an iterative process in which each step adds a completely randomized, small increase or decrease. If the iterative principle applies to linguistic skill, the skill level would show slow long-term oscillations. If the 0 level is treated as arbitrary boundary, the resulting pattern shows an arbitrary succession of problematic and nonproblematic episodes, somewhat reminiscent of the Landau–Kleffner syndrome.

The Dynamics of Interacting Growth Processes

The simple constant increases and decreases as shown in Equations 2 and 3 are not the only type of process that occurs with change and development. It is more likely that a simple constant increase, depending on some external factor, is the exception rather than the rule. A more realistic assumption is that the development of language—a grammar G, the lexicon L—is an instance of a growth process (among others). A fundamental feature of growth processes is that the rate of growth is a constant. The rate of growth is the ratio between any two successive levels of the grower. For instance, the ratio between L (assume that L represents the level of lexical development) at Time 2 and L at Time 1 should be similar to that between Time 6 and Time 5 (or any other successive time periods for that matter). From the observation of the constant rate of growth follows the elementary growth equation

$$dL/dt = RL \qquad\qquad (Eq. 4)$$

Equation 4 specifies exponential growth: As time passes, L becomes bigger and bigger (and eventually becomes *very* big). In the real world, however, growth depends on available means that are always limited: the growth resources. For instance, as the lexicon increases, it becomes increasingly difficult to find new words (the more words one knows, the smaller the number of unknown words heard during, for instance, an arbitrary hour of conversation). That is, R is supposed to decrease as L increases. This principle can be expressed mathematically in the following way:

$$dL/dt = (r - aL)L \qquad\qquad (Eq. 5)$$

Equation 5 is the logistic growth equation, which specifies growth as a phenomenon of increase that depends on the amount of available resources. Those resources are a function of all factors and variables that contribute, positively or negatively, to the growth of L (or G for that matter). Part of the resources is external (e.g., the quality and magnitude of the language input) and part is internal (e.g., the quality of the nervous system and sensory organs).

In the case of language, an important set of internal resources consists of the grower's conspecifics. For instance, lexical growth is most likely positively affected by the child's grammatical knowledge because that knowledge may help the child better understand linguistic input needed for the learning of new word meanings. A similar relationship holds in the opposite direction. If children have a good representation of the meaning of various words, it makes it easier for them to acquire the grammatical morphology associated with these words (Leonard & Deevy, this volume; see also Bishop, 1997, for comparable examples). The relationship between conspecific growers may become quite complicated. For instance, it is likely that the onset of grammar requires a minimal lexical mass (L as a precursor condition to G; see e.g., Jones & Conti-Ramsden, 1997; Marchman & Bates, 1994). The initial growth of grammar may temporarily decrease the rate of lexical growth, for instance, because both growers compete for limited attention resources. After the first grammatical discoveries have become consolidated, grammatical knowledge may be used to enhance the process of lexical acquisition (van Geert, 1991; see Robinson & Mervis, 1998, for an empirical demonstration of these changing relationships). That is, lexical and grammatical abilities not only affect one another over time, but also the nature of the relationships between them changes as a consequence of their respective growth levels. These patterns of mutual, changing relationships are characteristic of developmental processes and may explain phenomena such as the existence of various forms of development (linear, S-shaped, stepwise, U-shaped, etc.) and the nonlinearity of many of the developmental trajectories. Because these principles are basic to development in general, there is no reason that they should not apply to the development of impairment and disorder (see also Bishop, 1997).

Growth Models and SLI

Elsewhere I have argued that models based on resource-dependent growth processes provide good approximations of many kinds of developmental processes, in particular those that can be specified in terms of an increase (or decrease) in a capacity, skill, knowledge base, and so on (van Geert, 1991, 1993, 1994, 1995). The question is, however, what can we do with dynamic growth models in the context of language impairment? Ideally, it should be possible to come up with models of actual impaired developmental processes similar to those that have been formulated for normal or unimpaired development. The problem is that, in contrast with unimpaired development, hardly any longitudinal databases exist that are suited for a model-building exercise (an exception is Cipriani et al., 1998). However, dynamic models can play an interesting role in the theoretical phase of research projects: They can be used to explore the possibilities and properties of our theoretical models. The point is that the models we work with in developmental psychology are usually considerably more complicated than we think. The complicated character does not necessarily lie in the models, but in the fact that the models mostly refer to iterative processes. To find out what the models predict, given different conditions (e.g., in terms of individual and environmental properties of a developmental process), we usually resort to a simple linear extrapolation. This is fine with models that are inherently linear, but the procedure breaks down if the process is nonlinear or iterative. Let me give an example of how dynamic modeling can be used to help us understand the properties of our models.

Assume we have a simple theory that says that lexical and syntactic development are related. That is, lexical growth affects syntactic growth and vice versa. The way this happens can take many forms. Suffice it to say that we specify both lexical and syntactic growth in the form of two simple quantitative variables that represent the level of lexical and syntactic ability. Those levels can be defined in various ways that are not of primary concern to the present demonstration. I now introduce an impairment condition that consists of some deep phonological problem in the processing of phonological information (see e.g., Benasich & Tallal, 1996; Curtiss et al., 1992; Merzenich et al., 1996; Tallal et al., 1993, 1995, 1996). Let us assume that this phonological impairment obliges the child to invest considerably more attention and effort in listening to linguistic signals than would normally be expected. As a result, the processing of lexical and syntactic information are no longer mutually supporting functions, but become mutually competing functions. They compete for the scarce resource of attention (working memory, etc.). What should we expect of this process in terms of possible developmental outcomes? The obvious answer is that the outcome depends on how much one variable (lexicon or syntax) competes with the other. However, a simple simulation of this process with the aid of a coupled dynamic growth model shows an unexpected interaction between the amount of competition and the rate of growth of the variables. Note that in our model there is no inherent, prespecified relationship between the impairment condition and rate of growth (empirically speaking, it is likely that such a relationship exists; what is important now, however, is that for any degree of competition there can still be a wide variation between individuals in the growth rates of the affected variables). It turns out that the growth rate of the variables is a crucial factor in determining either whether the variables will both grow toward a reasonable level (which is lower than the level that would be expected without the impairment, however) or whether one variable will actually completely suppress the other. Figure 14.2 shows what happens under conditions of two different growth rates and identical competition conditions.

It goes without saying that this model is not intended as an illustration of a real language developmental process. Real developmental processes are not deterministic (whereas the model is). In addition, in reality, it is highly unlikely that a variable (either the lexicon or syntax) is completely

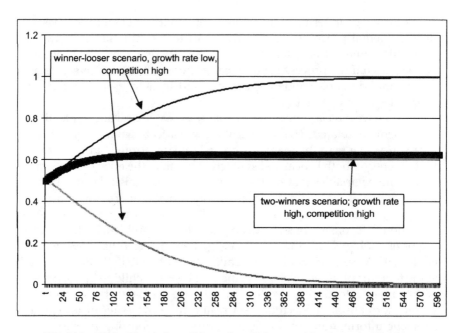

FIG. 14.2.   Under identical conditions of mutual competition (e.g., a competition for attention resources), two growers (e.g., lexical and syntactic skills) will show qualitatively different growth patterns dependent on the magnitude of the growth rate (the relative increase per unit time). If the growth rate is low and the competition is high, one grower (e.g., lexical knowledge) will completely suppress the growth of the other (e.g., syntactic skill). If the growth rates are high and the competition is high, both growers will move toward a similar, intermediate level.

suppressed by another one. The reason is that the lexical and syntactic abilities feed on more resources than only syntax or only the lexicon. The point of this model simulation is that it gives us some unexpected information about the behavior of competing growth variables—namely, that the effect of the competition parameters crucially depends on the growth rate in a way that introduces an interesting nonlinearity in the process. However, knowing that competition models tend to bifurcate into two qualitatively different outcomes (both competitors either find an equilibrium at some intermediate value or one wins and takes all and the other looses everything) is not enough. We should try to find out what the model predicts under more realistic assumptions.

    The more realistic assumptions are the following. First, we assume that the variables have both a lower and an upper limit, the levels of which depend on the available resources (environmental help, effort, intelligence, seriousness of the impairment, etc.). Second, we assume that both the growth rates and amount of competition between the variables vary between individuals. Third, we assume that all the variations in parameters and conditions are normally distributed across our subjects. We can build these assumptions into our dynamic model and simulate the outcome of—for instance—1,000 cases. Each case represents a possible but different combination of parameters, which are made to vary in accordance with our assumptions. The result of this simulation is that the end levels of (simulated) development follow a bimodal distribution (see Fig. 14.3). The modes overlap to a considerable extent. The correlation between the simulated levels (lexicon and syntax) is −.72.

The fact that we find a bimodal distribution for each variable separately is not trivial. Given that all the parameters vary according to a normal distribution, we should have expected that the outcomes of each variable separately are similarly normally and unimodally distributed. In view of the competitive relationship, we also should have expected that the correlation between the variables is negative, which is indeed corroborated by the simulation (see the correlation of −.72). From the simulation, we can conclude that a slightly bimodal distribution in a variable is like a fingerprint of a competitive relationship, provided a comparable bimodal distribution is also found in the competing variable. Again this model is not primarily intended as an empirical model of language acquisition. Its function is to calculate what should be expected, in terms of empirical distributions in a population, if specific assumptions are true. If the assumptions are based on a reasonable theory of impaired language acquisition—for instance, the assumption that due to some deeper eventually phono-

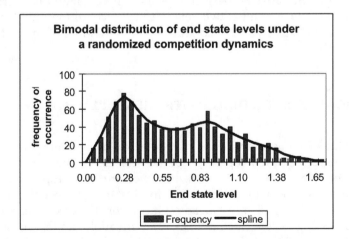

FIG. 14.3.   Under more realistic assumptions, a competition dynamics between two variables (see also Fig. 14.2) leads to a bimodal distribution of the attractor levels of the variables involved (the figure presents only one of the two variables).

logical impairment a competitive relationship is established where normally a supportive relationship should be found—the resulting model can be used to predict empirical distributions.

Given that SLI is indeed the manifestation of an ongoing developmental process described by dynamic interactions of the type introduced in this chapter, we should expect that SLI shows all the properties of a highly dynamic phenomenon. For instance, we should expect that the form and nature of SLI changes across the developmental process, with earlier manifestations differing from later ones (see e.g., Bishop, 1994, 1997). We should also expect a considerable intra-individual variation in the nature of the symptoms assuming that the symptoms are the products of developmental processes governed by many interacting forces instead of the direct manifestation of some inherent and stable impairment condition. This expectation is supported by the observation that even if SLI runs in families and seems genetically (co-)determined, its manifestation in family members and even in twins (both MZ and DZ) can be widely varying (Bishop, 1994; Bishop et al., 1995; Lewis, 1990, 1992; Lewis & Thompson, 1992, Lewis & Freebairn, 1997). An interesting finding from a twin study by Bishop, North, and Donlan (1995) might provide an illustration of the competition dynamics described earlier in this section. The authors found that in discordant twins (where one was characterized as having SLI, the other not) the non-SLI twin nevertheless displayed evidence of problematic language development. More interesting, however, is the observation that the non-SLI twins obtained significantly lower scores on nonverbal IQ than their SLI-affected peer. It appears as if verbal and nonverbal aspects enter into a competitive relationship if conditions for language learning are relatively impaired and thus require more of the child's resources.

IMPLICATIONS FOR DIAGNOSTIC MEASUREMENT

One of the major assumptions of psychological measurement is that people have specific psychological properties that can be measured with appropriate instruments—tests. Tests, however, are error prone. They measure a psychological property—take, for instance, a specific linguistic ability in a child—with a certain amount of error. The error is usually due to confounding factors, such as (lack of) motivation, limitations of working memory, and so forth. A test hardly, if ever, addresses only the variable it is supposed to measure. The error-laden nature of measurement explains why repeated tests rarely produce identical measurements.

The Nature of Psychological Variables

According to dynamic systems theory, in particular the approach advocated by Thelen and Smith (1994), it is incorrect to say that people *have* specific psychological properties, that they *have* such-and-such knowledge, and so forth. Psychological properties come about in the ongoing interaction between the person and environment. The interaction consists of an online mutual cospecification of properties, affordances, and capacities, both of the person and environment. Of course one can say that a person has a certain capacity to act in such-and-such way given a particular context. Attributing this capacity, however, is different from saying that somewhere inside the person there is some particular action-producing engine that prescribes and prespecifies what should be done and that has some definite, measurable quality. A person's psychological properties and capacities, therefore, are as much a property of the person him or herself as of that person's characteristic contexts and environments. This view on the nature of psychological properties has particular consequences for the issue of diagnostic measurement. If it is true, it defies the conception of a specific, measurable property that a test can address with a certain amount of measurement error, however.

This dynamic view on the nature of psychological variables on the relatively short time scale of action (and test administration for that matter) is supplemented with a developmental view on the nature of psychological properties. Whatever a person does or can do is to a considerable extent the product of a past but still ongoing developmental process. In this chapter, I have discussed the iterative nature of developmental process (i.e., processes that continuously transform the nature of the properties on which they operate). Stability (i.e., the fact that some properties or characteristics last for a considerable time, if not throughout life) is the product of a dynamic process that continuously creates stability. This is not just a vague philosophical or literary way to put otherwise trivial things in an extraordinary manner. Dynamic systems theory can give a highly specific definition of what it means for a system to (re-)produce its own equilibrium or stability.

The field of diagnostic research has to cope with the dynamic—developmental and contextual—nature of psychological properties and categories all the time. For instance, the observed impairments (e.g., SLI) are often highly sensitive to contextual variation. In addition, diagnostic categories are only rarely present in pure form. There is often a considerable incidence of co-morbidity, but also of compensation and compensatory strategies (Bishop, 1992, 2000). The diagnostic picture that describes a particular person is often made of a combination of symptoms that belong to various categories. Moreover, from a clinical point of view, the problem is not so much to focus on the exact nature of the diagnostic category that should be attributed to a person, but to ask oneself what can be done about the problem or impairment (Law, chap. 18, this volume).

Measuring by Variables and Characteristicness

Both from the viewpoint of dynamic systems and clinical diagnosis it is worthwhile to explore an alternative way to measure and specify a person's psychological properties. Although this issue far extends the scope of the present chapter, I nevertheless try to discuss a few important viewpoints. Let me begin with a dynamic model of development that I have explored fairly recently and that aimed to describe general developmental mechanisms (see van Geert, 1998a, 1998b). In this model, a person's developmental level (or whatever variable that matters for the problem in question) was conceived of as a person-and-context specific range. Take for instance a child's morphosyntactic capacity and assume we have a test to measure it. The test is like a ruler along which the child's morphosyntactic capacity is measured. The child will obtain a mark on the ruler, and this mark will be seen as an error-laden estimation of the child's real mark. However, we can step aside the question of whether the child has a real value on this ruler. We say that the child has a certain *range of characteristic values* on this ruler. Those values are characteristic in the sense that they also reckon with the characteristic contexts in which this particular child uses his or her morphosyntactic ability, whatever exactly the latter may be. In fact, we now measure the child's morphosyntactic ability (or whatever else we wish to diagnose) with *two* rulers. One specifies different degrees of morphosyntactic capacity, and the other specifies different degrees of characteristicness (see Fig. 14.4).

Figure 14.4 shows that a score of 12, 13, and so on is highly characteristic of this particular child (with a degree of characteristicness of 1), whereas a score of 10 is only moderately (somewhere around .5) characteristic. Note that with this particular way of scoring, we can explicitly account for contextual dependency and variation. For any context, we can specify—a test condition, normal communication, communication under stress, and so forth—and in principle estimate how the child would perform relative to the measurement ruler (again in the form of a range with varying degrees of characteristicness). All these contexts can then be combined into a range that is in fact the range depicted in Fig. 14.4 (for the technical details, see van Geert, 1997, 2000). Working with ranges specified in terms of degrees of characteristicness has several diagnostic advantages. For instance, it is likely that children with language problems are characterized by a broader range—that is, by more variability—than chil-

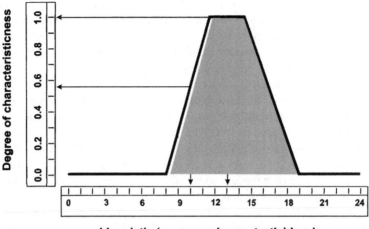

FIG. 14.4. Instead of assigning one (unknown) true level on a variable (e.g., morphosyntactic level), it is more realistic to assign a range of levels to a person. Whereas the horizontal axis specifies the variable measured (morphosyntactic level), the vertical axis specifies the degree of characteristicness. For instance, a score of 10 has a degree of characteristicness of about 0.5, whereas a score of 13 has a degree of characteristicness of 1 (maximal).

dren without problems (e.g., studies on motor impairment have shown a comparable association between impairment and range of variability; see Visser et al., 1998; Volman & Geuze, 1998). This variability should not be seen as noise or error variance. Rather, a characteristic feature of a some-what problematic line of development might be that such development leads to higher vulnerability or sensitivity to contexts.

If psychological variables such as a child's morphosyntactic ability are specified in terms of a characteristic range that depends among others on the dynamics of the variable at issue, we should expect to find rather considerable variation between repeated measures in the same child. Test–retest variation is the rule rather than the exception. It occurs, for instance, with measures of the discrepancy between verbal and nonverbal capacities that lead to (unwanted) variations in the attribution of the SLI category based on repeated testing (Cole et al., 1992, 1995). This form of intra-individual instability is usually attributed to measurement error. However, if abilities are viewed as ranges—which they should be in view of their inherent dynamic and context- (co-)specified properties—the amount of intra-individual variability found in repeated testing provides relevant information about the nature of the variable under scrutiny (Alibali, 1999; de Weerth et al., 1999; Granott, 1998; Kuhn et al., 1995;

Lautrey, 1993; Lautrey & Caroff, 1996; Rittle-Johnson & Siegler, 1999; Siegler, 1994; Thelen, 1990; van Geert, 1997). Of course the adoption of a developmental range concept does not rule out the existence of measurement error, but it does provide a different view on the issue. For instance, if one wants to generalize from a test score to daily performance, one expects a mapping of the test score onto a range of levels within which daily performance varies. The question of how broad this range is could eventually be asked in a more reliable way if one would know a little more about the spontaneous variations in the test scores. Formulated in this way, the problem of the test score is not one of measurement error. It is a problem of a—relative—lack of information given the problem of estimating a range of daily performance. A comparable problem is the use of parent or teacher questionnaires as a means to diagnose a child's linguistic problems. It is clear that the questionnaire reflects the dynamics of reflection (on the behavior and development of their children) in parents or teachers. Test–retest stabilities of questionnaires are sometimes surprisingly small (see e.g., Luteyn, 2000). This variation could be the result of enhanced parental reflection and observation due to the first questionnaire administration or any other sources of variability in the adult's perception and interpretation of the child's behavior. However, it is equally likely that at least part of the variability in the parents' and teachers' answers is due to the fact that the behavior at issue is variable. This does not necessarily mean that variations in the answers on the questionnaire reliably reflect variations in the target behavior. However, a better understanding of how educators form and change their minds about their children's variable, flexible, and adaptive behavior could eventually lead to a more adequate interpretation of the meaning of questionnaire results that goes beyond the notion of measurement error.

Finally, it should be noted that an approach to diagnostic measurement in terms of a variable-by-characteristicness approach could solve some of the categorization problems that often arise in the context of developmental impairments. For instance, SLI is related—but not necessarily similar—to communicative problems, whereas communicative problems are related—and again not necessarily similar—to pervasive developmental disorders such as autism (Bishop, 1998). The distinction between categories is an all-or-none matter and is often based on standardized diagnostic decisions that do not necessarily correspond with clinical intuitions and practical applications. The fact that diagnostic categories (SLI, PDD-NOS, autism, mental retardation, etc.) must be treated as exclusive classes is basically a problem of binary logic: Something is true of a person or it is not true. However, in modal logic, predicates can be true or, more precisely, can be applicable to or characteristic of something to various degrees. Comparable to stating that a particular test score has a degree of characteristicness of either 1, 0.5, or 0, one can say that a diagnostic category (e.g., SLI) is characteristic of a specific person to a degree of approximately 0.5 (or 1, 0.75, or 0 for that matter; van Geert, 2002). This approach makes it possible to characterize a child by various diagnostic categories that apply with distinct degrees of characteristicness (e.g., SLI and PDD-NOS, SLI and borderline mental retardation, etc.). Note that this way of diagnosis can be as quantitative and precise as standard categorical approaches, meanwhile retaining a reference to the fact that diagnostic categories are inherently fuzzy and dynamic.

Finally, it is important to note that the fact that levels and patterns of performance are characterized by ranges of varying width has potentially important consequences for a theory of the dynamics of development (van Geert, 1998a, 1998b). For instance, an increase in variability in performance may indicate a developmental jump not only because it is the consequence of a destabilization of the skills and knowledge that will undergo a transition, but also because the increased variability offers increased opportunities to experiment with new linguistic formats and communicative contexts (see Savelsbergh et al., 1999, for examples from various developmental fields).

REFERENCES

Alibali, M. W. (1999). How children change their minds: Strategy change can be gradual or abrupt. *Developmental Psychology, 35*, 127–145.

Benasich, A. A., & Tallal, P. (1996). Auditory temporal processing thresholds, habituation, and recognition memory over the 1st year. *Infant Behavior and Development, 19*, 339–357.

Bishop, D. V. M. (1992). The underlying nature of specific language impairment. *Journal of Child Psychology and Psychiatry and Allied Disciplines, 33*, 3–66.

Bishop, D. V. M. (1994). Is specific language impairment a valid diagnostic category? Genetic and psycholinguistic evidence. *Philosophical Transactions of the Royal Society London B, 346*, 105–111.

Bishop, D. V. M. (1997). Cognitive neuropsychology and developmental disorders: Uncomfortable bedfellows. *Quarterly Journal of Experimental Psychology: Human Experimental Psychology, 50A*, 899–923.

Bishop, D. V. M. (1998). Development of the Children's Communication Checklist (CCC): A method for assessing qualitative aspects of communicative impairment in children. *Journal of Child Psychology and Psychiatry and Allied Disciplines, 39*, 879–891.

Bishop, D. V. M., North, T., & Donlan, C. (1995). Genetic basis of specific language impairment: Evidence from a twin study. *Developmental Medicine and Child Neurology, 37*, 56–71.

Cipriani, P., Bottari, P., Chilosi, A. M., & Pfanner, L. (1998). A longitudinal perspective on the study of specific language impairment: The long term follow-up of an Italian child. *International Journal of Language and Communication Disorders, 33*, 245–280.

Cole, K. N., Dale, P. S., & Mills, P. E. (1992). Stability of the intelligence quotient language quotient relation: Is discrepancy modeling based on a myth? *American Journal on Mental Retardation, 97*, 131–143.

Cole, K. N., Schwartz, I. S., Notari, A. R., & Dale, P. S. (1995). Examination of the stability of two methods of defining specific language impairment. *Applied Psycholinguistics, 16,* 103–123.

Curtiss, S., Katz, W., & Tallal, P. (1992). Delay versus deviance in the language acquisition of language-impaired children. *Journal of Speech and Hearing Research, 35,* 373–383.

de Weerth, C., van Geert, P., & Hoijtink, H. (1999). Intraindividual variability in infant behavior. *Developmental Psychology, 35,* 1102–1112.

Gopnik, M. (1999a). Some evidence for impaired grammars. In R. Jackendoff & P. Bloom (Eds.), *Language, logic, and concepts: Essays in memory of John Macnamara* (pp. 263–283). Cambridge, MA: MIT Press.

Gopnik, M. (1999b). Familial language impairment: More English evidence. *Folia Phoniatrica et Logopaedica, 51,* 5–19.

Gopnik, M., Dalalakis, J., Fukuda, S. E., Fukuda, S., & Kehayia, E. (1996). Genetic language impairment: Unruly grammars. In W. G. Runciman & J. M. Smith (Eds.), *Evolution of social behaviour patterns in primates and man* (pp. 223–249). Oxford, England: Oxford University Press.

Granott, N. (1998). Unit of analysis in transit: From the individual's knowledge to the ensemble process. *Mind, Culture, and Activity, 5,* 42–66.

Jones, M., & Conti-Ramsden, G. (1997). A comparison of verb use in children with SLI and their younger siblings. *First Language, 17,* 165–193.

Kuhn, D., Garcia-Mila, M., Zohar, A., & Andersen, C. (1995). Strategies of knowledge acquisition. *Monographs of the Society for Research in Child Development, 60,* 128.

Lautrey, J. (1993). Structure and variability: A plea for a pluralistic approach to cognitive development. In R. Case & W. Edelstein (Eds.), *The new structuralism in cognitive development: Theory and research on individual pathways* (pp. 101–114). Basel, Switzerland: Karger.

Lautrey, J., & Caroff, X. (1996). Variability and cognitive development. *Polish Quarterly of Developmental Psychology, 2,* 71–89.

Lewis, B. A. (1990). Familial phonological disorders: Four pedigrees. *Journal of Speech and Hearing Disorders, 55,* 160–170.

Lewis, B. A. (1992). Pedigree analysis of children with phonology disorders. *Journal of Learning Disabilities, 25,* 586–597.

Lewis, B. A., & Freebairn, L. (1997). Subgrouping children with familial phonologic disorders. *Journal of Communication Disorders, 30,* 385–402.

Lewis, B. A., & Thompson, L. A. (1992). A study of developmental speech and language disorders in twins. *Journal of Speech and Hearing Research, 35,* 1086–1094.

Luteyn, E. (2000). *The development of the Children's Social Behaviour Questionnaire.* Unpublished doctoral dissertation, Groningen.

Marchman, V. A., & Bates, E. (1994). Continuity in lexical and morphological development: A test of the critical mass hypothesis. *Journal of Child Language, 21,* 339–366.

Merzenich, M. M., Jenkins, W. M., Johnston, P., Schreiner, C., Miller, S. L., & Tallal, P. (1996). Temporal processing deficits of language-learning impaired children ameliorated by training. *Science, 271,* 77–81.

Rittle-Johnson, B., & Siegler, R. S. (1999). Learning to spell: Variability, choice, and change in children's strategy use. *Child Development, 70,* 332–348.

Robinson, B. F., & Mervis, C. B. (1998). Disentangling early language development: Modeling lexical and grammatical acquisition using and extension of case-study methodology. *Developmental Psychology, 34,* 363–375.

Savelsbergh, G., van der Maas, H., & van Geert, P. (1999). *Non-linear developmental processes.* Amsterdam: Royal Netherlands Academy of Arts and Sciences.

Siegler, R. S. (1994). Cognitive variability: A key to understanding cognitive development. *Current Directions in Psychological Science, 3,* 1–5.

Tallal, P., Miller, S., Bedi, G., Wang, X., & Nagarajan, S. S. (1996). Language comprehension in language-learning impaired children improved with acoustically modified speech. *Science, 271,* 81–84.

Tallal, P., Miller, S., & Fitch, R. H. (1993). Neurobiological basis of speech: A case for the preeminence of temporal processing. In P. Tallal & A. M. Galaburda (Eds.), *Temporal information processing in the nervous system: Special reference to dyslexia and dysphasia* (pp. 27–47). New York: New York Academy of Sciences.

Tallal, P., Miller, S., & Fitch, R. H. (1995). Neurobiological basis of speech: A case for the preeminence of temporal processing. *Irish Journal of Psychology, 16,* 194–219.

Thelen, E. (1990). Dynamical systems and the generation of individual differences. In J. Colombo & J. W. Fagen (Eds.), *Individual differences in infancy: Reliability, stability, prediction* (pp. 19–43). Hillsdale, NJ: Lawrence Erlbaum Associates.

Thelen, E., & Smith, L. B. (1994). *A dynamic systems approach to the development of cognition and action.* Cambridge, MA: Bradford Books/MIT Press.

van de Sandt-Koenderman, W. M. E., Smit, I. A. C., van Dongen, H. R., & van Hest, J. B. C. (1984). A case of acquired aphasia and convulsive disorder: Some linguistic aspects of recovery and breakdown. *Brain and Language, 21,* 174–183.

van der Lely, H. K. J. (1994). Canonical linking rules: Forward versus reverse linking in normally developing and specifically language-impaired children. *Cognition, 51,* 29–72.

van der Lely, H. K. J. (1997a). Language and cognitive development in a grammatical SLI boy: Modularity and innateness. *Journal of Neurolinguistics, 10,* 75–107.

van der Lely, H. K. J. (1997b). Narrative discourse in grammatical specific language impaired children: A modular language deficit? *Journal of Child Language, 24,* 221–256.

van der Lely, H. K. J. (1998). SLI in children: Movement, economy, and deficits in the computational-syntactic system. *Language Acquisition: A Journal of Developmental Linguistics, 7,* 161–192.

van der Lely, H. K. J., & Stollwerck, L. (1996). A grammatical specific language impairment in children: An autosomal dominant inheritance? *Brain and Language, 52,* 484–504.

van der Lely, H. K. J., & Stollwerck, L. (1997). Binding theory and grammatical specific language impairment in children. *Cognition, 62,* 245–290.

van Geert, P. (1991). A dynamic systems model of cognitive and language growth. *Psychological Review, 98,* 3–53.

van Geert, P. (1993). A dynamic systems model of cognitive growth: Competition and support under limited resource conditions. In L. B. Smith & E. Thelen (Eds.), *A dynamic systems approach to development: Applications* (pp. 265–331). Cambridge, MA: MIT Press.

van Geert, P. (1994). *Dynamic systems of development: Change between complexity and chaos.* London, England: Harvester Wheatsheaf.

van Geert, P. (1995). Growth dynamics in development. In R. F. Port & T. van Gelder (Eds.), *Mind as motion: Explorations in the dynamics of cognition* (pp. 313–337). Cambridge, MA: MIT Press.

van Geert, P. (1997). Variability and fluctuation: A dynamic view. In E. Amsel & K. A. Renninger (Eds.), *Change and development: Issues of theory, method, and application* (pp. 193–212). Mahwah, NJ: Lawrence Erlbaum Associates.

van Geert, P. (1998a). A dynamic systems model of basic developmental mechanisms: Piaget, Vygotsky, and beyond. *Psychological Review, 105,* 634–677.

van Geert, P. (1998b). Dynamic modeling of cognitive and language development: From growth processes to sudden jumps and multimodality. In K. M. Newell & P. C. M. Molenaar (Eds.), *Applications of nonlinear dynamics to developmental process modeling* (pp. 129–160). Mahwah, NJ: Lawrence Erlbaum Associates.

van Geert, P. (2002). Developmental dynamics, intentional action and fuzzy sets. In N. Granott & J. Parziale (Eds.), *Microdevelopment: Transition processes in development and learning* (pp. 319–343). Cambridge, England: Cambridge University Press.

Visser, J., Geuze, R. H., & Kalverboer, A. F. (1998). The relationship between physical growth, the level of activity and the development of motor skills in adolescence: Differences between children with DCD and controls. *Human Movement Science, 17*, 573–608.

Volman, M. C., & Geuze, R. H. (1998). Relative phase stability of bimanual and visuomanual rhythmic coordination patterns in children with a developmental coordination disorder. *Human Movement Science, 17*, 541–572.

15

Early Detection of Developmental Language Disorders

Hanneke de Ridder
Heleen van der Stege
Dutch Foundation for the Deaf and Hard of Hearing Child (NSDSK)

About 5% of all young children encounter language delays relative to their peers (Reep, de Koning, de Ridder-Sluiter, van der Lem, & van der Maas, 1990; Law et al., 1998). Law's review of the literature on screening for speech and language delays shows such delays to pose serious problems for both the child and the social environment. Additional difficulties are sometimes involved such as hearing loss, cognitive delay, general health problems, and behavioral problems. In addition, early speech and language difficulties can slow not only the socioemotional development of children, but also their school success and emergent literacy in particular. A number of the reading and learning problems encountered in early school years are outlined by Beitchman et al. (1996a). The incidence of challenging or problem behavior is discussed by these and other authors (Baker & Cantwell, 1982; Beitchman et al., 1996b; Benasich, Curtiss, & Tallal, 1993; Goorhuis-Brouwer et al., chap. 6, this volume). Finally, Law (1998) reported some positive effects of therapy programs and tailor-made intervention programs in particular, but also observed that the limited number of efficacy studies published to date does not warrant the introduction of national screening programs.

The focus of the present chapter is on the early detection of developmental language disorders. After a discussion on the problems in detecting children's language disorders at an early age, a report is given on the development and validation of a screening instrument for the early detection of language disorders of children in the Netherlands. The chapter ends with a perspective on the close relationship among the detection, diagnosis, and remediation of early language disorders.

DIFFICULTIES DETECTING ATYPICAL FACTORS IN EARLY LANGUAGE DEVELOPMENT

Child development is a dynamic process and obviously depends on a variety of factors that may differentially influence the developmental process and produce a high degree of both inter- and intrapersonal variation. A relatively high number of the those children diagnosed early as language disordered appear to recover without any intervention at all (Hall, 1999). For about 50% of the children diagnosed as language disordered, however, the problems tend to persist and negatively influence their socioemotional, communicative, cognitive, and/or early literacy development (Paul et al., 1991; Paul & Smith, 1993; Rescorla, Hadicke-Wiley, & Escarce, 1993). Early detection followed by early intervention could probably have helped these children.

Enderby and Emerson (1996) noted the many difficulties associated with the definition and identification of those factors that appear to put children at risk for severe developmental language problems during early childhood. The variability of normal language development and related behavior makes it difficult to distinguish atypical from typical development. Nevertheless, severe language disorders do not resolve themselves spontaneously, can lead to a range of later difficulties, and should thus be identified as early as possible.

A high percentage of the parents with young children between 0 and 4 years of age visit the public health centers in the Netherlands. This offers an excellent opportunity to screen the children for a variety of risk factors including those related to language difficulties. Each newborn child and his or her parents are invited to visit the public health center on a regular basis during the first 4 years of life. In the first year of their lives, about 95% of the children are brought to a public health center in the Netherlands by their parents. In the period thereafter, the percentage is about 85%. The health care for these young children in the Netherlands between the ages of 0 and 4 years involves a variety of activities including vaccinations, monitoring of growth, medical examinations for the early detection of various risk factors (i.e., screening for phenylketonuria and congenital hypothyroidism (PKU, CHT), screening for visual or hearing impairments), and health education with regard to the somatic, psychosocial, and pedagogical aspects of early child development.

In the 1990s, child health care practitioners called for the development of a simple and clearly validated screening instrument for the detection of those factors that put children at high risk for the development of language and communication disorders. The discrimination of children with abnormal language development from those with normal language development during the regularly planned but very brief visits of about 10 minutes to the public health centers was experienced as very difficult.

DEVELOPMENT OF A SCREENING INSTRUMENT

A screening instrument for the early detection of those factors placing children at a high risk for the development of language problems or the *VTO* (Dutch *Vroegtijdige Onderkenning*) *language screening instrument* was developed in 1990 at the request of the National Committee on the Early Detection of Developmental Disorders in the Netherlands. This committee considered improvement of the early detection and potential prevention of developmental language disorders to be important and thus stimulated the development of a standardized method for monitoring the early communicative development of children between the ages of 0 and 3 years as well. The screening instrument developed to test the early communicative behavior of children was based on the assumption that the precursors to the development of language disorders may already be present at a very early age and thus visible in the early communicative interactions between children and parents (Locke, 1994).

The topic of this chapter is thus the development and validation of the VTO screening instrument with a focus on the detection of factors placing children at a high risk for developmental language difficulties. The VTO screening instrument has also been examined in a number of implementation and follow-up studies (de Ridder-Sluiter, 1990; de Ridder-Sluiter & van der Lem, 1995) and also in an extensive cost-effectiveness outcome study (de Koning et al., 2000).

THE PRESENT STUDY

A first functional requirement to be met during the development of the VTO screening instrument was that it fit into the daily routine of the practitioners working at a public health center. The examination of children for risk factors relevant to the development of communication and language disorders had to be integrated into the regular series of visits at 1, 2, 3, 6, 9, 12, 15, 18, 24, and 30 months of age. This did not mean that the screening for communication and language difficulties took place during *every* visit.

The VTO screening instrument involves 10 measurements. In the present study, different measurements were administered at 12, 15, and 18 months of age (de Ridder-Sluiter & van der Lem, 1995) and also at the age of 24 months (de Koning et al., 2000). The examination time per visit was less than 5 minutes. Because there is so little time available per visit, most of the questions are addressed to the parents. To attain the most reliable answers from the parents as possible, considerable attention was paid to the construction and formulation of the questions. This means that the instrument has been standardized and questions should be stated literally. In Box A, an overview of the screening questions used with 15-month-old children is presented. Of course the instrument is easy to use and score, and the training for such purposes encompassed two or three short sessions.

Content Validity

The aim of the VTO screening instrument is to detect risk factors for delayed communicative development in Dutch children between the ages of 0 and 3 years. The instrument should be administered at 10 points in time. During almost all of the examinations, questions about the child's production of language, comprehension of language, and the flow of conversation or play between the parent and child are posed. These three aspects of language and communication are critical to the communicative interactions between a young child and his or her parents (Bates, 1976; Bruner, 1983). Strong affective interactions between mother and child are known to occur both before and after birth. Parents typically communicate with their young children using verbal utterances supported by nonverbal behaviors, whereas the young child typically communicates using various nonverbal behaviors or cues. Either parent or child may initiate the interaction. As the child grows older, he or she will increasingly take the initiative using verbal utterances. Obviously the characteristics of the communicative situation and conversational partners play an important role in learning to communicate. During the course of early communicative development, a number of critical skills can be discerned, and the VTO screening instrument is based on these skills. Critical information about the level of communicative development for a child is gathered by assessing the production and comprehension of various nonverbal and verbal acts along with the quality of the language input provided by the parents and the ways in which the parent and child organize the communicative interaction.

The assessment of particular communicative skills occurs at a time when it can be theoretically assumed that the skills should be performed at a 90% level of satisfaction. The relevant landmarks are based on a long line of research concerned with the identification of early communicative milestones (Bates & Marchman, 1988; Bloom & Lahey, 1978; Brown, 1973; Bruner, 1983; Dale, 1976; Landau, 1977; McShane, 1980; Miller & Chomsky, 1963; Rutter & Bax, 1972; Rutter & Martin, 1972; Schaerlakens, 1980; Schaerlakens & Gillis, 1987; Schlesinger, 1971; Slobin, 1970; Tulkin & Kagan, 1972).

The intelligibility of the questions addressing the different communicative milestones was found to be satisfactory for health care practitioners. However, this does not mean that the questions were easy for the parents to understand. During the construction of the screening instrument, parents were asked to provide their opinions about the intelligibility of the questions and just what they thought was intended. This information was then used to modify the first version of the VTO screening instrument and improve the content validity of the instrument (see Box A). The following recommendations were thus formulated on the basis of the parental interviews:

• Parents give more reliable answers when the topic of the question is introduced in a short sentence. For example, the following sentence was used to introduce a question about the child's language comprehension: "The next question is about how your child understands spoken language."

• Parents find consideration of a specific time and/or setting in conjunction with a question about the behavior of their child to be helpful. For example, *"When you consider last week*, did you notice that Kevin understood what you meant when you said 'We are going to eat'?"

• The VTO screening instrument uses sets of hierarchical, interrelated questions to follow up on negative responses. When parents say their child does not communicate or show them that he or she wants to eat, for example, the interviewer should continue with such with questions as: "Did you ever notice that your son or daughter is making sounds? What kinds of sounds did he or she make and when? How did you respond?"

• Specific linguistic terms such as *babbling* should be avoided to prevent misunderstandings and ambiguities. With regard to the term *babbling*, for example, some of the parents thought that the term meant the sounds that children make around 2 months of age. Others thought the term meant the incorrect pronunciation of words.

Construct Validity

In the present study, it was expected that 90% of all children would perform satisfactorily on the groups of questions related to the different topics covered by the VTO screening instrument. To verify this assumption, a study was conducted at 61 public health centers in the Netherlands: 894

Box A: Questions From the VTO Screening Instrument for Children 15 Months of Age

Words

Let's talk about the sounds or words of for *Kevin*. When you consider last week, what does *Kevin* call animals? What does *Kevin* call various people in his environment? What does *Kevin* call different toys? What does *Kevin* call eating or drinking?

Answers to the above four questions are categorized as follows:
- ❏ child uses words
- ❏ child uses generalizations (e.g., *daddy* for all people)
- ❏ child makes sounds or uses sound-a-like words
- ❏ child does not say anything

With regard to the last category, the practitioner continues and asks the parent: Have you ever heard *Kevin* make sounds? What kinds of sounds does *Kevin* make?

Understanding words

This question deals with understanding language. When you consider last week, did you notice that *Kevin* understood what you meant when you said any of the following? *We are going out. We are going to eat. Where is the ball? Put the doll in the bed. Pick up your spoon. Give the doll something to eat.*

The answers to the six questions are categorized as "yes" or "no."

Making yourself clear

This question deals with how your child makes himself clear. When you consider last week, how does *Kevin* make himself clear when he wants something to eat or drink? How does *Kevin* make himself clear when he needs your help?

Answers to the two questions are categorized as follows:
- ❏ child uses words
- ❏ child points at something and makes sounds
- ❏ child calls parent
- ❏ child picks up object (e.g., a bottle)
- ❏ child makes sounds
- ❏ child yells or whines
- ❏ child cries
- ❏ child points at something without making any sound
- ❏ child does not do anything

(Box continues)

**Box A: Questions From the VTO Screening
Instrument for Children 15 Months of Age
*(Continued)***

Playing

This question deals with playing together. When you consider last week, how often did you and your child play together?
☐ never
☐ sometimes
☐ often

What is the preferred activity for playing together?

How does *Kevin* make it clear that he wants to play with you?
☐ uses words
☐ challenges parent
☐ pulls parent
☐ points at toys
☐ picks up toys
☐ looks at toys
☐ does not do anything

Does *Kevin* like to play on his own?
☐ yes, what does he like to play?
☐ no

---

children brought to a public health center between the ages of 0 and 3 years were randomly selected for inclusion in the study. In Table 15.1, an overview of the information on the subjects is presented.

Two semilongitudinal sets of data were then collected. The first set of data was collected at bimonthly intervals across a period of 1 year and thus in six sessions (Version 1). The second set of data was collected every 3 months across a period of 2 years and thus in eight sessions (Version 2). In Table 15.2, an overview of the communicative skills assessed by the VTO screening instrument is presented. Two slightly different versions of the instrument have been developed. The second version is shorter than the first and consists of fewer open questions. Two slightly different versions of the instrument, which took less than 5 minutes to administer, were used. The child health care practitioners were briefly trained to become more confident with the use of the VTO screening instrument. More than half of the questions were found to meet the 90% norm for both versions of the instrument. The p values for all of the questions pertaining to a particular topic at a particular age are presented in Table 15.2.

For each topic mentioned in Table 15.2, a frequency distribution for the different responses is can be charted. In Figs. 15.1 and 15.2, for example,

TABLE 15.1
Overview of Subjects

	Group	Measurement	Number of Children
Version 1	1	1, 2, 3, and 6 months	146
	2	6, 9, and 12 months	145
	3	12, 15, and 18 months	154
	4	24 and 30 months	147
			$n = 592$
Version 2	1	1, 2, and 3 months	45
	2	3 and 6 months	41
	3	6 and 9 months	32
	4	9 and 12 months	30
	5	12 and 15 months	29
	6	15 and 18 months	39
	7	24 months	49
	8	30 months	37
			$n = 302$

TABLE 15.2
Topics Addressed by the VTO Screening Instrument at Different Ages

Examination Moment	Topics Addressed	Version 1 (p)	Version 2 (p)
1 month (0–7 weeks)	• Parent tries to get child's attention	.99	.86
	• Periods of crying (how long?)	.81	.61
	• Openness to comfort	.95	.91
2 months (8–12 weeks)	• Smiling at parent	.98	.97
	• Periods of crying (how long?)	.75	.80
	• Openness to comfort	.95	.94
3 months (13–21 weeks)	• Smiling at parent	1.00	.95
	• "Conversations"/uttering sounds to parent	.96	.99
	• Periods of crying (how long?)	.87	.89
	• Openness to comfort	.88	.84
6 months (21–35 weeks)	• Reactions to calls	.96	.95
	• Different sorts of sounds made by the child	.84	.92
	• Playing together	.99	.89
	• Different sorts of crying (how long?)	.92	.95
	• Openness to comfort	.90	.90
9 months (35–47 weeks)	• Different sorts of sounds made by the child	.91	.90
	• Recognition of different people	.91	.98
	• Reactions to language/listens to language	.89	.86
12 months (48–60 weeks)	• How child makes clear that he or she wants to be picked up, eat, play, or refuse something	.90	.95
	• Playing together	.83	.75
	• Reactions to language	.90	.84

(Continued)

TABLE 15.2
(Continued)

Examination Moment	Topics Addressed	Version 1 *(p)*	Version 2 *(p)*
15 months (14–17 months)	• Words (animals, people, toys, food and drinks)	.71	.80
	• Understanding language (going out, eating, where is the ball, doll in the bed, pick up spoon, give the doll something to eat)	.92	.81
	• How child makes clear that he or she wants to eat/drink or needs help	.83	.87
	• Playing together: how often, preference for playing, making clear that he or she wants to play together or alone	—	.87
18 months (17–23 months)	• Words (people, food and drinks, toys)	.92	.94
	• Playing together: how often, preference for playing, making clear that he or she wants to play together or alone	.95	.89
	• Go pick up three objects: sock, spoon, cube (child question)	.80	.75
24 months (23–29 months)	• Words (people, food and drinks, toys)	.93	.92
	• Playing together: how often, preference for playing, making clear that he or she wants to play together or alone	.98	.94
	• Point to body parts of doll: eyes, mouth, belly, foot, hair, hand (child question)	.92	.91
30 months (29–35 months)	• Use of two- and three-word sentences when child wants to go out, wants to draw attention to something	.80	.89
	• Playing together: how often, preference for playing, making clear that he or she wants to play together or alone	—	.89
	• Pointing to pictures in book: car, house, banana, chair, eggs, shoe (child question)	.96	.92

the children's language production is represented. That is, an overview of the children's ability to express their intentions—namely, that they want something to eat or to drink—is presented for the sessions in which this topic is addressed—namely, at 12, 15, 18, 24, and 30 months of age.

Inspection of Figs. 15.1 and 15.2 shows a transition to occur at around the age of 18 months from nonverbal to verbal attempts at communication. This finding is in keeping with our already established knowledge of the development of children's language production (Schaerlakens & Gillis, 1987). Around the age of 18 months, almost all children start to verbally express themselves using either isolated words or prototypical sentences. The small percentage of children who do not start to speak around this age also remains relatively stable until the age of 24 to 30 months of age. For Version

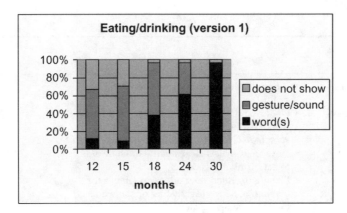

FIG. 15.1.   Frequencies of answers to: "How does your child make clear that he or she wants something to eat or drink?" (Version 1, n = 301).

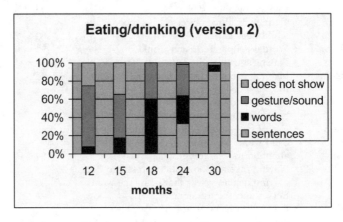

FIG. 15.2.   Frequencies of answers to: "How does your child make clear that he or she wants something to eat or drink?" (Version 2, n = 177).

1 of the screening instrument, the scores simply reflect verbal output (i.e., a word or prototypical sentence). For Version 2 of the screening instrument, the scoring was modified and now allowed us to distinguish between the use of isolated words versus prototypical sentences that become more clearly formulated between the ages of 24 and 30 months.

Discriminating Power

To determine whether language production, language comprehension, and communicative interaction appear to be independent at this young age, a nonmetric multidimensional analysis (PRINCALS) was conducted.

PRINCALS is a type of principal components analysis appropriate for nominal or ordinal data (Gifi, 1983). PRINCALS is used to determine whether an underlying structure connecting the different items in a test exists. No structure was found to characterize the production, comprehension, or interaction aspects of the communication of the group of children 0 to 6 months of age (Fig. 15.3). A PRINCALS solution is provided for the different aspects of communication at the ages of 3 months (black circles) and 6 months (open circles). The responses regarding language production are reflected by dark lines, responses regarding comprehension by interrupted lines, and responses regarding interaction by dotted lines. The eigenvalues for the solutions were 0.19 and 0.15. The proportion variance explained was 0.34.

More structure was found as the children became older. At the age of 9 months, the language comprehension aspect emerges as a cohesive underlying structure. At the age of 12 months, the language production aspect emerges as a cohesive structure and the interaction aspect to a lesser extent. At the age of 24 months (see Fig. 15.4) and 30 months (see Fig. 15.5), clearly independent structures are detected for language production (dark lines) and language comprehension (interrupted lines).

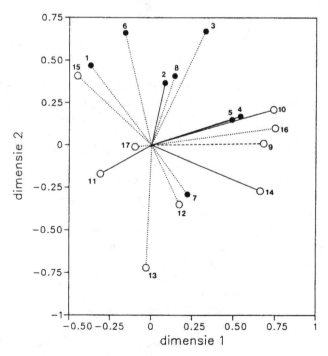

FIG. 15.3. Princals solution for different aspects of communication at 3 months (black circles) and 6 months (open circles; $n = 32$).

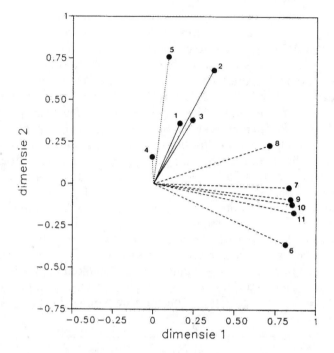

FIG. 15.4.   PRINCALS solution for different aspects of communication at 24 months (n = 49).

The eigenvalues for Fig. 15.4 were 0.39 and 0.14. The proportion variance explained was 0.54. The eigenvalues for Fig. 15.5 were 0.30 and 0.25. The proportion variance explained was 0.55. In contrast to the production and comprehension aspects of communication, the interaction aspect does not appear to form a clear underlying structure. Thus, the data reflect the basic theoretical subdivision between the comprehension and production of language. At the older ages of 24 to 30 months, it is thus possible to identify children with comprehension problems versus expression problems (de Ridder-Sluiter, 1990).

Based on the PRINCALS solutions for the different populations, the present manner of scoring has been validated. The most relevant questions contribute to the scoring (one point or zero points). This means that the questions in the instrument that satisfy the 90% norm are the questions in the PRINCALS solutions with a distance from more than 0.5 from zero. These questions account for between 53% and 64% of the variance in the responses (de Ridder-Sluiter, 1990). For each child, all of the scores are added up. The cut-off score for the instrument lies between the low and high estimation of the language disorder prevalence in the country (e.g., about 5%).

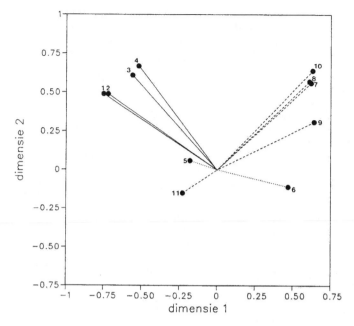

FIG. 15.5. PRINCALS solution for different aspects of communication at 30 months (n = 37).

Predictive Validity

With regard to the predictive validity of the instrument, we expect the measures of language production, language comprehension, and communicative interaction to correlate highly with linguistic proficiency later in development. A follow-up study was therefore carried out 1 year and 3 years after original examination using the VTO screening instrument. The follow-up study included 93 children (1;3 to 5;9 years of age) scoring either low, medium, or high at initial screening. Positive correlations were expected to be found between the results attained using the VTO screening instrument and later language measures and either no correlations or negative correlations between the results attained using the VTO screening instrument and later nonlanguage measures such as difficult behavior or crying. The results are based on those children with scores available on all of the relevant instruments (n = 50). Due to the differences in the ages of the children at follow-up, the follow-up measures were not suitable for use with all of the children. In Table 15.3, the results regarding the predictive validity of the VTO screening instrument are summarized.

On the one hand, a significant positive correlation with the same language concepts measured by different instruments at 1 and 3 years of follow-up was observed. The correlation with the widely used Reynell test of

TABLE 15.3
Predictive Validity: Correlations of Different
Language and Behavior Scales

Scale	VTO	R	ST	LC	NC	CD
Reynell (comprehension scale)	+0.48**					
ST (spontaneous language)	+0.34*	+0.32				
Language and behavior scale (2–3 years)	+0.36*	*	+0.40*			
LC (language)	−0.26	+0.18	*	−0.34*		
NC (noncompliance)	+0.03	−0.06	−0.14	+0.02	+0.41**	
CD (crying and difficult behavior)		+0.14	−0.12			
	+0.18			+0.49*	−0.24	−0.03
LT (language test for 3–6 years of age)		+0.07	+0.30*	*		

VTO: Early detection of developmental language disorder
R: Reynell Test (comprehension scale) (Reynell, 1974)
ST: Spontaneous use of language (analyzed by two raters)
Language and behavior scale for 2 and 3 years of age (Swets-Gronert, 1986)
LC: Language competence
NC: Noncompliance
CD: Crying and difficult behavior
LT: Language test for 3 to 6 years of age (Gerritsen, 1988)

language comprehension was particularly high. On the other hand, very low or negative correlations with measures of noncompliance and crying at 1 and 3 years of follow-up were observed. Taken together, these results show the scores on the VTO screening instrument to correlate with the scores on other language instruments measures a few years later, but not with the scores on nonlanguage tests a few years later.

CONCLUSIONS AND DISCUSSION

The VTO language-screening instrument appears to be sufficiently simple, clearly useful, and empirically valid. The instrument is suitable for use in public health centers to measure the language development of very young children. When the instrument is used two or three times across a period of 3 to 6 months, it can distinguish those children at risk for the development of severe language problems.

Some Limitations

In the development of a screening instrument, it is necessary to answer some methodological questions regard the acceptable number of false positives and false negatives. A few small implementation studies have been carried out for this purpose (de Ridder & van der Lem, 1995). The results show a detection percentage of 5% with a percentage of false positives of about 10%. Further research is needed to study the incidence of false negatives.

The number of false negatives and the sensitivity of the VTO screening instrument has nevertheless been recently estimated in the Dutch cost-effectiveness study with 10,331 children (de Koning et al., 2003). To date, however, randomized controlled studies are still scarce. More evidence is thus needed before it can be decided whether national screening for language disorders at public health centers is merited.

Another limitation is the Dutch language. In this study, a Dutch-speaking sample of children and their parents were studied. Particularly in the four big cities in the Netherlands, however, the number of immigrant parents with young children is rather large and on the increase. To use the VTO screening instrument to identify minority children at risk for a language disorder, thus, substantial adjustments will have to be made or another instrument developed.

From Screening to Diagnostics to Intervention: Some Problems

A screening instrument provides a distinction between normally developing children and children at risk. Children at risk for language problems need multidisciplinary diagnostics to indicate the types of disorders involved. The children's hearing, speech, language, intelligence, and parent–child interactions are generally tested at the Speech and Hearing Centers located throughout the Netherlands. In 1998, these centers were also authorized to carry out the diagnostic examination of the group of very young children at risk for the development of language difficulties. However, for some parents, the step into the diagnostic center is hard for them to take. It also appears that the *early* detection of the risk in particular gives some parents less reason for worry; in several studies involving the use of the VTO screening instrument, about 20% of the parents simply refused to go to the Speech and Hearing Centers for further diagnostic testing after initial detection of a risk. The most common reason mentioned by the parents was no perception of a problem or no motivation. The no-show of parents is a factor that clearly complicates the screening and monitoring of young children's development. The distribution of information on the importance of the early detection of language problems and the so-called critical period for language development is thus an important component of early detection.

What to Do After Having Diagnosed a Developmental Language Problem?

What to do after the diagnosis of a developmental language problem? Developmental language difficulties are complex and multidimensional. The task of assessing a child for developmental language disorders is therefore not easy. Just how certain language disorders connect to other difficulties and how these difficulties interact with various environmental factors is still not clear. Should the language problem be classified as a pure production or comprehension deficit or is it a combination of both? Is the language problem a matter of developmental delay and will the child therefore catch up gradually and more or less spontaneously or is something else going on? In many cases, exactly what has caused the language disorder remains unclear and what the best treatment may be is also unclear. There is a paucity of data on the efficacy of various intervention programs and those factors that appear to be critical for the success of a particular treatment method, which makes it difficult to argue for the selection of one therapy program over another (Law, 1997; Whitehurst & Fischel, 1994). Most recently, Law (1997) concluded that young children with predominantly expressive language deficits may benefit more from child-oriented therapy programs, whereas young children with primarily language comprehension difficulties and concomitant communication problems may benefit more from indirect parent- or family-oriented therapy programs.

An increased number of more extensive empirical studies with clearly randomized subject selection and a carefully controlled research design are needed to determine the most effective and best fitting therapy for a particular language disorder. The development of a reliable method for the screening, identification, and monitoring of developmental language difficulties is definitely a step in the right direction. The VTO screening instrument developed in the Netherlands makes it possible to detect those factors placing children at risk for the development of language problems on a large-scale, possibly national, basis. This information then allows us to monitor the further development of those children at risk or not at risk for the development of language disorders.

REFERENCES

Baker, L., & Cantwell, D. P. (1982). Developmental, social and behavioral characteristics of speech and language disordered children. *Child Psychiatry and Human Development, 12,* 195–206.

Bates, E. (1976). Pragmatics and sociolinguistics in child language. In D. M. Morehead & E. A. Morehead (Eds.), *Normal and deficient child language* (pp. 247–307). Baltimore: University Park Press.

Bates, E., & Marchman, V. A. (1988). What is and is not universal in language acquisition. In F. Plum (Ed.), *Language, communication and the brain* (pp. 19–38). New York: Raven.

Beitchman, J. H., Wilson, B., Brownlie E. B., Walters, H., Inglis, A., & Lancee, W. (1996b). Long-term consistency in speech/language profiles: II. Behavioral, emotional, and social outcomes. *Journal of the American Academy of Child & Adolescent Psychiatry, 35*(6), 815–825.

Beitchman, J. H., Wilson, B., Brownlie, E. B., Walters, H., & Lancee, W. (1996a). Long-term consistency in speech/language profiles: I. Developmental and academic outcomes. *Journal of the American Academy of Child & Adolescent Psychiatry, 35*(6), 804–814.

Benasich, A. A., Curtiss, S., & Tallal, P. (1993). Language, learning, and behavioral disturbances in childhood: A longitudinal perspective. *Journal of the American Academy of Child and Adolescent Psychiatry, 32*(3), 585–594.

Bloom, L., & Lahey, S. M. (1978). *Language development and language disorders.* New York: Wiley.

Brown, R. (1973). *A first language: The early stages.* Cambridge: Harvard University Press.

Bruner, J. (1983). *Child's talk, learning to use language.* Oxford: Oxford University Press.

Dale, P. S. (1976). *Language development: Structure and function.* New York: Holt, Rinehart & Winston.

Enderby, P., & Emerson, J. (1996). Speech and language therapy: Does it work? *British Medical Journal, 312,* 1665–1668.

Gerritsen, F. M. E. (1988). *VTO-taalscreening 3- tot 6 jarigen [Language screening in three to six-years old].* Lisse: Swets & Zeitlinger.

Gifi, A. (1983). *Princals user's guide.* Leiden: Department of data theory, University of Leiden.

Hall, D. M. B. (1999). *Health for all children.* Oxford: Oxford University Press.

Koning, H. J. de, Ridder-Sluiter, J. G. de, Agt, H. M. E. van, Stege, H. van der, Korfage, I. J., Polder, J. J., Reep-van den Bergh, C. M. M., Lem, G. J. van der, & Maas, P. J. van der (2000). *Vroegtijdige onderkenning van taalontwikkelingsstoornissen 0–3 jaar; Een gerandomiseerd onderzoek naar de effecten, kosten en mogelijkheden van toepassing van het VTO-taal signaleringsinstrument (Costs and effects of screening for language disorders in preschool children with the VTO-screeninginstrument; a randomised controlled screening trial).* Rotterdam/Amsterdam: iMGZ/NDSDK.

Koning, H. J. de, Ridder-Sluiter, J. G. de, Agt, H. M. E. van, Stege, H. van der, Reep-van den Bergh, C. M. M., Lem, G. J. van der, & Maas, P. J. van der (2003). *Effects of screening for language disorders in preschool children; a randomised controlled screening trial comprising 10,331 children.*

Landau, R. (1977). Spontaneous and elicited smiles and vocalisations of infants in four Israeli environments. *Developmental Psychology, 13,* 389–400.

Law, J. (Ed.). (1997). Evaluating intervention for language impaired children: A review of the literature. *European Journal of Disorders of Communication, 32,* 1–14.

Law, J., Boyle, J., Harris, F., Harkness, A., & Nye, C. (1998). Screening for speech and language delay: A systematic review of the literature. *Health Technology Assessment, 2*(9).

Locke, J. L. (1994). Gradual emergence of developmental language disorders. *Journal of Speech and Hearing Research, 37,* 608–616.

McShane, J. (1980). *Learning to talk.* London: Cambridge University Press.

Miller, G. A., & Chomsky, N. (1963). Finitary models of language users. In R. D. Luce, R. R. Bush, & E. Galanter (Eds.), *Handbook of mathematical psychology* (Vol. 2, pp. 419–491). New York: Wiley.

Paul, R., & Smith, R. L. (1993). Narrative skills in 4-year-olds with normal, impaired and late-developing language. *Journal of Speech and Hearing Research, 36*(3), 592–598.

Paul, R., Spangle-Looney, S., & Dahm, P. S. (1991). Communication and socialization skills at ages 2 and 3 in "late-talking" young children. *Journal of Speech and Hearing Research, 34*, 858–865.

Reep-van den Bergh, C. M. M., Koning, H. J. de, Ridder-Sluiter, J. G. de, Lem, G. J. van der, & Maas, P. J. van der (1998). Prevalentie van taalontwikkelingsstoornissen bij kinderen [The prevalence of child language disorders]. *Tijdschrift voor de gezondheidswetenschappen, 76,* 311–317.

Rescorla, L., Hadicke-Wiley, M., & Escarce, E. (1993). Epidemiological investigation of expressive language delay at two: Special issue. Language development in special populations. *First Language, 13*(37, Pt 1), 5–22.

Reynell, J. K. (1974). *Manual for the Reynell Developmental language scales* (rev. ed.). Windsor: N.F.E.R. Publishing Company.

Ridder-Sluiter, J. G. de (1990). *Vroegtijdige onderkenning van communicatieve ontwikkelingsstoornissen [Early detection of delays and deviations in the communicative development in children].* Leiden: Academisch proefschrift.

Ridder-Sluiter, J. G. de, & Lem G. J. van der (1995). Vroegtijdige onderkenning van communicatieve ontwikkelingsstoornissen [Early detection of delays and deviations in the communicative development in children]. *Stem-, spraak- en taalpathologie, 2,* 103–114.

Rutter, M., & Bax, M. (1972). The normal development of speech and language. In M. Rutter & J. A. M. Martin (Eds.), *The child with delayed speech* (pp. 1–13). London: Heinemann.

Rutter, M., & Martin, J. A. M. (1972). *The child with delayed speech.* London: Heinemann.

Schaerlakens, A. M. (1980). *De taalontwikkeling van het kind: Een oriëntatie in het Nederlandstalig onderzoek [The development of child language: an orientation on Dutch research].* Groningen: Wolters-Noordhoff.

Schaerlakens, A. M., & Gillis, S. (1987). *De taalverwerving van het kind [Child language acquisition].* Groningen: Wolters-Noordhoff.

Schlesinger, J. M. (1971). Production of utterances and language acquisition. In D. I. Slobin (Ed.), *The ontogenesis of grammar: A theoretical symposium* (pp. 63–101). New York: Academic Press.

Slobin, D. I. (1970). Universals of grammatical development in children. In G. B. Floris D'Arcais & W. J. M. Levelt (Eds.), *Advances in psycholinguistics* (pp. 174–186). Amsterdam: North Holland.

Swets-Gronert, F. (1986). *Temperament, taalcompetentie en gedragsproblemen van jonge kinderen [Temperament, linguistic competence and problem behavior in children].* Lisse: Swets & Zeitlinger.

Tulkin, S., & Kagan, J. (1972). Mother–child interaction in the first years of life. *Child Development, 43,* 31–41.

Whitehurst, G., & Fischel, J. E. (1994). Early developmental language delay: What, if anything, should the clinician do about it? *Journal of Child and Psychiatry, 35*(4), 613–648.

16

Early Intervention for Young Children With Language Impairments

Steven F. Warren
University of Kansas

Paul J. Yoder
Vanderbilt University

It is inevitable that we will eventually possess the means to reliably identify many, perhaps most, young children who are at risk for developing language impairments. As chaotic as our efforts may seem at times, we are making steady progress in our knowledge of early development. Breakthroughs in genetics and neuroscience may further accelerate the pace of progress. Meanwhile we are developing a more sophisticated understanding of environmental effects and risk factors. As more and more young children participate in preschool and child-care programs, the age at which children are identified with language impairments will continue to drop.

If you accept the basic premise of the prior paragraph—that with improvements in our knowledge base the age of identification will continue to drop—then the importance of the following question is clear: Will we then be able to reliably prescribe and implement effective early interventions capable of minimizing the long-term effects of the child's impairment or even of curing the child? To some extent, the ultimate value and validity of the child language intervention field demands that we eventually achieve a positive answer to this question.

The purpose of this chapter is to provide a progress report on our efforts to create effective early intervention approaches for children identified early in life with a language impairment. We first describe what we believe to be the emerging developmental model of early communication and language intervention. We describe the basic framework for this model and then summarize the research that supports it. Then we discuss various challenges ahead and what we believe to be some of the most fruitful areas for future research.

Research on methods to enhance and remediate the communication and language development of children identified with early delays and impairments has been ongoing since the early 1960s. Scores of studies have been conducted over this time period, the vast majority aimed at testing various procedures or intervention packages with relatively small numbers of children for limited periods of time. This technology-building period is gradually receding, and the framework of a developmental model of early communication and language intervention is emerging. This model supports the use of different intervention procedures at different points in a child's development.

FOUNDATIONS OF THE DEVELOPMENTAL INTERVENTION MODEL

There are two basic premises of the developmental model of communication and language intervention. First, the rate and quality of language input that a child receives is viewed as crucially important to their optimal development. Second, the most effective intervention protocol depends on the child's developmental level and the nature of the intervention goal. On the surface, these statements sound simplistically self-evident, but each premise encapsulates much of what has been learned about early language development and intervention across three decades of research. Consequently, some discussion of the meaning and interpretation of each is in order.

RATE AND QUALITY OF LANGUAGE INPUT MATTERS

This premise is important because of the possibility that inadequate input might cause or contribute to language delay and, conversely, that enhanced input (i.e., language intervention) might have a stimulating or remedial effect on development. Since the 1970s, proponents of the social interactionist perspective of language development (e.g., Bruner, 1975; Gallaway & Richards, 1994; Nelson, 1989; Snow, 1984; Tomasello, 1992) have been building the case that adults can play an important role in children's language acquisition. They noted that from birth onward children are exposed to an ocean of language. Hour after waking hour, day after day, month after month, the child encounters the natural curriculum provided by exposure to his native language. Furthermore, the millions of words and sentences that children experience are not just undifferentiated sounds. Much of this curriculum is specifically adjusted and fine tuned (Bruner, 1975; Sokolov, 1993) to the child's language comprehension level. A wide range of teaching devices have been detected in common use by adults including expansions, models, contingent imitations, growth recasts, use of concrete, simplified vocabulary, slower rate of articulation, use of higher pitch and exaggerated intonation, a focus on objects and events to which the child is attending, and so on (Hoff-Ginsburg, 1986; Menyuk, 1988; Nelson, 1991; Snow, Perlmann, & Nathan, 1987; van Kleeck, 1994). These adjustments, termed *parentese* or *motherese*, appear to aid the acquisition of linguistic and communicative competence. The rate at which adults talk to children (Hart & Risley, 1995; Huttenlocher et al., 1991), the rate at which children talk (e.g., Hart & Risley, 1980, 1995; Nelson, 1973), and the responsiveness of parents to their child's communication attempts (Yoder & Warren, 1998) have all been shown to correlate with faster acquisition of various components (e.g., vocabulary growth) of language acquisition.

Strong counterarguments have been put forth that language input is a relatively unimportant variable. These arguments have largely been based on the fact that most children ultimately acquire language competence (i.e., adult syntax) irrespective of their circumstances or the nature of the input they received as children (Pinker, 1994). However, such arguments may miss the point at least for children who are at risk for mental retardation and developmental disabilities. There is clear evidence that language input can affect the rate and quality of language development for both typical and atypically developing children. Moreover, development can be enhanced for at least some critical components of the language system (e.g., vocabulary) via modifications in input. Finally, optimal input may have a far greater effect on the ultimate language development of children with developmental disabilities than on typically developing children (Snow, 1994). The questions then, from the perspective of language intervention researchers, is not "does input matter?" but rather how can it be made to matter the most?

HOW INPUT IS PROVIDED MATTERS TOO

Once the premise that input matters is accepted, we can examine the second premise: The most effective form of intervention depends on the developmental level of the child as well as temperament issues in some cases (e.g., autism). The first premise has been accepted as an article of faith by interventionists for decades. This second premise is a more recent addition and its importance is only beginning to emerge as a result of studies of the relative treatment effectiveness of different intervention protocols. The mere fact that such studies are now being conducted is evidence of the field's movement beyond the initial technology building stage.

Twenty-five years ago, language intervention approaches were developed almost independent of any concern about how they might best match up to different phases in the child's development or different characteristics of the language skills to be mastered (e.g., pragmatics vs. syntactic rules). However, as an increasing array of approaches and techniques have become available, families of techniques have emerged that vary along a small number of important dimensions. Some of the key variables include whether the procedure is based on following the child's attentional lead, whether specific or general goals are targeted, whether elicited imitation prompts are used, whether growth recasts are used, and so on. We briefly review the support for three of the primary families of techniques that have emerged from the research. These are the responsive interaction approach, milieu teaching, and direct instruction. We have selected these intervention approaches because they differ from one another in theoretically important ways that exemplify how different approaches can have differential effectiveness along the developmental continuum.

Responsive Interaction

Many terms are used to describe the responsive interaction approach in the literature, including the interactive model (Tannock & Girolametto, 1992) and the conversational model (MacDonald, 1985). This approach is widely used in parent training throughout North America. Its major immediate goals are to increase the child's social communication skills and facilitate grammar by enhancing the quality of interaction between the adult and child. Interaction is usually initiated and controlled by the child. Adults follow the child's attentional lead and respond contingently to the child's behavior in a manner that is congruent with the child's immediate interest. Modeling, recasting, and expansions of the child's communication attempts are encouraged (Nelson, 1989), whereas the use of directives (e.g., elicited imitation, mands, testing questions) is discouraged because it is assumed they will disrupt the flow of interaction and the child's attentional engagement (Harris et al., 1986). Thorough descriptions of the responsive interaction approach can be found in Nelson (1989) and Wilcox and Shannon (1998).

Responsive interaction approaches are particularly well suited for facilitating the acquisition of higher level morphological and syntactic skills that can be made salient through growth recasts (e.g., Baker & Nelson, 1984; Camarata, Nelson, & Camarata, 1994; Fey, Cleave, Long, & Hughes, 1993). A growth recast is a specific expansion or modification of a child's immediately preceding utterance in which new syntactic or semantic information is added. Theoretically, the temporal proximity and semantic overlap of the recast and the child's utterance aids the child in making comparisons between his or her own utterance and the recast. Such comparisons may make differences between the two utterances salient. If this comparison is made at a time when the child is ready to acquire the new semantic or grammatical structure (Nelson, 1989), or if the child notices this difference repeatedly in similar linguistic contexts (Camarata, 1995), the child should acquire the structure. Finally, responsive interaction approaches are relatively easy to learn and can be used virtually anywhere and at anytime.

Several recent studies have found that responsive interaction approaches are more effective than milieu teaching (discussed later) with children who have a mean length of utterance (MLU) above 2.5, but less effective than milieu teaching with children who have an MLU under 2.0 (the treatments are nonsignificantly different between MLU 2.0–2.5; Yoder et al., 1995). Children with MLUs above 2.5 likely have the attentional and memory resources necessary to efficiently learn from recasts that require them to compare their own utterance with the following adult utterance (Yoder et al., 1995).

The relative ineffectiveness of the responsive interaction approach below MLU 2.0 may be due to the avoidance of elicited production prompts (e.g., elicited imitation, test questions, etc.). During this period of development, these types of prompts may be significant contributors to language acquisition at least in children with developmental delays. Imitation seems to be a particularly powerful learning strategy at this point in development (Speidel & Nelson, 1989). Also a growing body of literature demonstrates that the use of directives (as opposed to the redirectives like "look here") in the context of joint-attention routines (interactions in which both the child and adult focus their attention on the same action or activity) aids learning and social engagement in both typically and atypically developing children (McCathren, Warren, & Yoder, 1995). Finally, test questions about the child's attentional focus (e.g., What is that? What are you doing?) may aid children in verbally participating in activities while giving adults a window into the child's thoughts that allow them to construct teaching episodes about the child's focus of attention (Yoder et al., 1994a, 1994b).

Milieu Teaching

Milieu teaching subsumes several specific techniques including incidental teaching (e.g., Hart & Risley, 1980), the mand-model procedure (Warren, McQuarter, & Rogers-Warren, 1984), and time delay (e.g., Halle, Marshall, & Spradlin, 1979). These procedures share several common features including: (a) teaching follows the child's attentional lead; (b) child production can be prompted indirectly through environmental arrangement or directly through explicit prompts as necessary; (c) natural consequences are used; (d) specific skills are targeted (e.g., vocabulary growth; two term semantic relations; prelinguistic communication functions); and (e) teaching episodes are embedded in ongoing interaction. Responsive interaction and milieu teaching approaches are similar in many ways, but vary substantially on one important dimension. Responsive interaction emphasizes the use of growth recasts to teach new responses, whereas milieu teaching uses elicited prompts for the initial productions of target forms and/or functions. In a typical interaction, the adult's decision to elicit a more complete response from the child (e.g., with a mand) is incompatible with expanding what the child said; you can do one or the other, but not both simultaneously. For example, the child might initiate the word *push* to which the adult might respond, "Push what?" in milieu teaching (an elaborative question) or "push car" (an expansion) in responsive interaction.

Fey (1986) categorized milieu teaching as a *hybrid* intervention approach representing a selective blend of techniques long used by behavior analysts (e.g., elicited imitation) with other techniques (e.g., basing teaching on the child's attentional lead), a technique with roots in the Vygotskian influenced mother–child interaction literature (Bruner, 1975). Thorough descriptions of milieu teaching approaches can be found in Warren and Kaiser (1988) and Warren (1991).

As noted, milieu teaching interventions seem to be particularly effective in teaching prelinguistic communication functions (Warren & Yoder, 1998), basic vocabulary, and initial two- and three-term semantic relationships (e.g., agent–action–object) to children with MLUs under 2.0 (Kaiser, Yoder, & Keetz, 1992; Wilcox, Kouri, & Caswell, 1991). This is probably due to the constraints in children's attentional and memory resources at this point in development, which make elicited production techniques relatively more effective when combined with the conversational scaffolds that are part of milieu teaching (e.g., modeling, time delay). Like responsive interaction techniques, milieu teaching can be embedded into routines at home (e.g., Kaiser, 1993), activity-based preschool curriculum models (e.g., Bricker, Pretti-Frontczak, & McComas, 1998), and book-reading formats (e.g., Whitehurst et al., 1989), and it can be intensively applied in contexts that support a high degree of social interaction (e.g., game playing routines) or spread episodically across the day (Hart, 1985).

Although children at risk for more severe developmental disabilities and language impairments often show clear delays in critical foundational communication skills during their first year of life (see McCathren, Warren, & Yoder, 1996, for a review), research on prelinguistic communication intervention is relatively recent phenomena. There are less than a dozen published studies of prelinguistic communication intervention with young children at present. Nevertheless, the research is quite promising. In our initial explorations of the effects of prelinguistic milieu teaching (Warren, Yoder, Gazdag, Kim, & Jones, 1993; Yoder, Warren, Kim, & Gazdag, 1994), we demonstrated that increases in the frequency and clarity of prelinguistic requesting covaried with substantial increases in linguistic mapping by parents and teachers. We then conducted an experimental longitudinal analysis in which 58 young children with delays in prelinguistic communication were randomly assigned to one of two treatments: prelinguistic milieu teaching (PMT) or a modified responsive interaction approach. Our results indicate that PMT was more effective with children whose mothers showed slightly above average maternal responsivity prior to the intervention, whereas the modified responsive interaction intervention was relatively more effective with children whose mothers were very unresponsive to them prior to treatment (Yoder & Warren, 1998, 1999a, 1999b). Wilcox and Shannon (1998) also reported that an adapted version of responsive interaction that is similar to prelinguistic milieu teaching has some positive effects.

Milieu procedures have three main limitations. First, they may represent a relatively inefficient means of facilitating grammatical development because it is more difficult to find mands (questions that prompt a specific response in an ongoing interaction) on the fly that elicit a specific grammatical rule. Second, milieu procedures attempt to elicit production of specific sentences and phrases, thus possibly drawing the child's attention to the example phrases, rather than the underlying rule that is the real target of the intervention. Third, fluid and effective use of these procedures may be difficult to maintain at home or in the classroom (Roberts, Bailey, & Nychka, 1991).

Direct Teaching

Direct teaching, sometimes referred to as *didactic instruction*, has a long history as a language intervention approach (e.g., see Schiefelbusch & Lloyd, 1974). It is typically characterized by the use of specific prompts and reinforcement, rapid massed trial instruction, frequent direct assessment of learning, and use of task analysis to break targeted skills down into small, easily learned parts (e.g., Guess, Sailor, & Baer, 1974). In contrast to responsive interaction and milieu teaching, direct teaching is adult directed, and the specific content of teaching is carefully prespecified. It is assumed that child engagement will be maintained by well-organized instructional materials, rapid pacing, and immediate, contingent feedback (Klinder & Carnine, 1991). Well-developed curricula, most notably the

DISTAR Language Program (Englemann & Osborn, 1976), have been widely utilized in schools to teach higher level language skills at the early childhood and elementary school levels. Carefully prescribed programs have also been developed for children with moderate to severe levels of mental retardation (e.g., Guess et al., 1974).

Direct teaching has some clear strengths. With language instruction, it can be used ensure those specific skills and concepts that are difficult to teach conversationally are actually taught and learned by children with mental retardation. Indeed the more abstract and specific the skill, the more effective direct instruction may be (Cole, 1995; Connell, 1987). Research has indicated that direct instruction is relatively more effective than milieu teaching (Yoder, Kaiser, & Alpert, 1991) and more effective than mediated instruction (an approach that is similar to responsive interaction; Cole & Dale, 1986; Cole, Dale, & Mills, 1991) particularly with relatively higher functioning children. The results of these studies run counter to the conventional wisdom that children who are more severely retarded benefit more from greater amounts of structure and children who are high functioning are more equipped to learn from interactive, child-directed instruction (Snow, 1984). It may be because highly structured and scripted interventions are difficult for lower functioning children because they are less able to follow the adult's lead (Cole, 1995), whereas milieu teaching approaches are easier for them to learn from because they are based on following the child's lead.

An impressive amount of research has supported the efficacy of direct teaching with children with developmental delays or mild levels of mental retardation and MLUs above 2.5 (Klinder & Carnine, 1991; White, 1988). Yet direct teaching is not likely to be effective in most circumstances at the prelinguistic or early language levels because it requires attentional resources and other cognitive skills (e.g., ability to learn from a decontextualized format), which developmentally young children typically have not yet acquired. Indeed Yoder et al. (1991) found that milieu teaching was more effective than direct instruction for teaching early vocabulary. Furthermore, direct instruction is likely to be of little use for teaching pragmatic skills, and its inherent emphasis on structure and form may impede generalization of learning if it is not supplemented by activities designed to make newly taught skills meaningful for children (Spradlin & Siegel, 1982).

AN OPTIMAL CONTINUUM OF INTERVENTION APPROACHES

Our intention in this brief review has been to trace the outlines of an emerging model of communication and language intervention that is based on what types of input are optimally effective at different points in development. This model posits that no single approach or family of techniques (e.g., milieu teaching) is appropriate for the wide range of skills that develop as the child progresses from initial prelinguistic communication to sophisticated linguistic development and reading. Instead a continuum of specific approaches is likely to be optimal, particularly when applied against the backdrop of an environment populated with highly responsive adults who continually engage the child in positive, stimulating forms of social interaction (Warren & Yoder, 1997). This continuum favors specific approaches during prelinguistic and early language development that utilize elicited production prompts, models, and contingent input techniques intended to foster initial receptive and productive vocabulary development and two- and three-term semantic relationships. As the child's MLU exceeds 2.0, emphases should switch from elicited production techniques to techniques like growth recasts that require a child to compare their utterance and the adults recast of it. Finally, as the child's syntactic skills advance and their language becomes increasingly decontextualized and abstract, direct teaching techniques may also be utilized to facilitate the acquisition of specific forms. Such direct teaching techniques might be used in combination with responsive interaction techniques.

At the most general level, only two strategies exist for facilitating communication and language acquisition from initial prelinguistic development to linguistic competence: (a) attempt to directly teach communication and language skills, and (b) teach adults (e.g., parents and teachers) who interact frequently with the child to be highly responsive to the child's communication attempts whenever possible and use relatively simple techniques like linguistic mapping and recasting to help strengthen the child's skills. The emerging model of communication and language intervention posits that continuous exposure to highly responsive adults is necessary, but frequently not sufficient by itself, to ensure an optimal outcome. However, when high levels of adult responsivity are combined with the appropriate specific intervention strategy (e.g., milieu teaching or direct instruction), an optimal outcome for a given child should result in terms of their communication and language development. This assertion must remain a working hypothesis until it can be confirmed or modified by additional research.

FUTURE RESEARCH DIRECTIONS

Can we reliably prescribe and implement effective early intervention programs capable of minimizing the long-term effects of a young child's language impairment? The development of optimally effective communication and language intervention approaches has proceeded steadily for the past three decades, but there is clearly a great deal of work left to be done before we can confidently answer this question in the affirmative.

Much of the emphasis during the past 30 years has been on the design and evaluation of specific techniques and procedures. This initial technology-building period has relied on studies with limited numbers of subjects and of short duration. With the exception of interventions targeted on the prelinguistic period of development, the field is clearly nearing the end of this phase in its evolution. If additional progress is to be made, researchers must turn their efforts toward conducting comparative, longitudinal intervention studies that (unfortunately) are usually complicated, lengthy, and relatively expensive to conduct. A relatively small number of well-executed studies of this nature could lead to the refinement and confirmation of the emerging model of intervention framed previously.

To determine the ultimate effectiveness of each component of the emerging developmental model requires answers to a range of questions concerning the relative efficacy between different treatments (Is Treatment A more effective than Treatment B at this point in development?) and between a given treatment and the developmental and temperamental characteristics of the learner (e.g., young children with expressive language impairments versus those with receptive and expressive impairments) and the instructional context (home vs. classroom vs. clinic). Genetic differences have been almost totally ignored in intervention and efficacy treatment studies to date, yet it is likely that characteristics associated with specific genetic conditions (e.g., Prader–Willi syndrome, fragile X syndrome) will interact with various intervention approaches to influence their effectiveness (Hodapp & Fidler, 1999). More cross-sectional studies (e.g., Cole et. al., 1991) are needed that effectively untangle developmental level from individual subject differences to allow us to truly understand the sources of variance in treatment outcome studies.

Research is particularly needed on the effects of more comprehensive interventions that integrate various components previously studied in limited contexts and shown to be effective. An obvious characteristic of most intervention studies reported in the literature is their relatively narrow focus. For example, most early intervention studies emphasize expressive skills, whereas comprehension, despite its fundamental importance, has been rarely studied as an outcome. Furthermore, virtually no studies have attempted to achieve what many believe to be the crucial basic goal for young children with language impairments—preparation to meet the written language and social demands of elementary school (Fey, Catts, & Larrivee, 1995). This requires that language intervention be linked to emergent literacy skills as well as general social competence.

Studies on general efficacy questions are daunting methodologically and financially, yet there is no denying their potential value. At the least for communication and language intervention research to generate important new knowledge in the future, investigators need to move beyond simple main effects analyses aimed at showing that more is better or earlier is better. These are not trivial questions. A more sophisticated knowledge of how intervention can interact with the forces of the natural environment and the child's own emerging abilities may be achieved by pursuing theory-driven aptitude by treatment interactions. These types of analyses can lead to more precise, elegant interventions that are truly cost-effective for young children and societies with limited resources.

It is obvious that the further development of increasingly effective early intervention approaches will require the participation of highly trained scientists and the provision of substantial resources. Longitudinal intervention studies that utilize random assignment and maintain a high degree of treatment fidelity simply cannot be done without these supports.

The good news is that the field has now reached the point in its evolution where such studies are likely to yield highly valuable information. Important questions await such efforts. For example, we may presume that interventions starting earlier in development and continuing longer afford greater benefits to the participants than ones that start later. However, there is little direct empirical support for this premise. The same holds true for program intensity: We presume it is an important variable in determining outcomes, yet there is less empirical support for this premise than some may realize. Generating clear, unambiguous answers to these questions is an important task for the future.

The eventual development of highly effective intervention approaches does not mean that such treatments are routinely available to those children and families who would benefit the most from them. The inadequate implementation of optimally effective treatments and practices will surely continue to be a major challenge for the field of child language intervention just as it is in many other human endeavors. Nevertheless, the task for the moment is to complete the development of those optimally effective practices.

ACKNOWLEDGMENTS

Support for the preparation of this manuscript and for the authors' research was provided by grants from the National Institute of Child Health and Human Development (R01 HD27594) and the Office of Special Education Programs of the U.S. Department of Education (H023C20152). However, the opinions expressed are solely those of the authors.

REFERENCES

Baker, N., & Nelson, K. (1984). Recasting and related conversational techniques for triggering syntactic advances by young children. *First Language, 5,* 3–22.

Bricker, D., Pretti-Frontczak, K., & McComas, N. (1998). *An activity-based approach to early intervention* (2nd ed.). Baltimore: Brookes.

Bruner, J. S. (1975). The ontogenesis of speech acts. *Journal of Child Language, 2,* 1–19.

Camarata, S. C. (1995). A rational for naturalistic speech intelligibility interaction. In M. Fey, J. Windsor, & S. Warren (Eds.), *Language interaction: Preschool through elementary years* (pp. 63–84). Baltimore: Brookes.

Camarata, S. C., Nelson, K., & Camarata, M. (1994). Comparison of conversational-recasting and imitative procedures for training grammatical structures in children with specific language impairment. *Journal of Speech and Hearing Research, 37,* 1414–1423.

Cole, K. N. (1995). Curriculum models and language facilitation in the preschool years. In M. Fey, J. Windsor, & S. Warren (Eds.), *Language intervention: Preschool through the elementary years* (pp. 39–62). Baltimore: Brookes.

Cole, K. N., & Dale, P. S. (1986). Direct language instruction and interactive language instruction with language delayed preschool children: A comparison study. *Journal of Speech and Hearing Research, 29,* 206–217.

Cole, K. N., Dale, P. S., & Mills, P. E. (1991). Individual differences in language delayed children's responses to direct and interactive preschool instruction. *Topics in Early Childhood Special Education 11,* 99–124.

Connell, P. J. (1987). An effect of modeling and imitation teaching procedures on children with and without specific language impairment. *Journal of Speech and Hearing Research, 30,* 105–113.

Englemann, S., & Osborn, J. (1976). *DISTAR language.* Chicago: Science Research Associates.

Fey, M. (1986). *Language intervention with young children.* San Diego: College-Hill Press.

Fey, M., Catts, H. W., & Larrivee, L. S. (1995). Preparing preschoolers for the academic and social challenges of school. In M. Fey, J. Windsor, & S. Warren (Eds.), *Language intervention: Preschool through elementary years* (pp. 3–38). Baltimore: Brookes.

Fey, M., Cleave, P., Long, S., & Hughes, D. (1993). Two approaches to the facilitation of grammar in language-impaired children: An experimental evaluation. *Journal of Speech and Hearing Research, 36,* 141–157.

Gallaway, C., & Richards, B. J. (1994). *Input and interaction in language acquisition.* Cambridge, England: Cambridge University Press.

Guess, D., Sailor, W., & Baer, D. M. (1974). To teach language to retarded children. In R. L. Schiefelbusch & L. L. Lloyd (Eds.), *Language perspectives: Acquisition, retardation, intervention* (pp. 477–516). Baltimore: University Park Press.

Halle, J. W., Marshall, A., & Spradlin, J. E. (1979). Time delay: A technique to increase language use and facilitate generalization in retarded children. *Journal of Applied Behavior Analysis, 12,* 431–439.

Harris, M., Jones, D., Brookes, S., & Grant, J. (1986). Relations between the non-verbal context of maternal speech and rate of language development. *British Journal of Developmental Psychology, 4,* 261–268.

Hart, B. (1985). Naturalistic language training techniques. In S. F. Warren & A. Rogers-Warren (Eds.), *Teaching functional language* (pp. 63–88). Austin: PRO-ED.

Hart, B., & Risley, T. R. (1980). In vivo language training: Unanticipated and general effects. *Journal of Applied Behavior Analysis, 12,* 407–432.

Hart, B., & Risley, T. R. (1995). *Meaningful differences in the everyday experiences of young American children.* Baltimore: Brookes.

Hodapp, R. M., & Fidler, D. J. (1999). Special education and genetics: Connections for the 21st century. *Journal of Special Education, 33,* 130–137.

Hoff-Ginsburg, E. (1986). Function and structure in maternal speech: Their relation to the child's development of syntax. *Developmental Psychology, 22*(2), 155–163.

Huttenlocher, J., Haight, W., Bryk, A., Seltzer, M., & Lyons, T. (1991). Early vocabulary growth: Relation to language input and gender. *Developmental Psychology, 27*(2), 236–248.

Kaiser, A. (1993). Parent-implemented language intervention: An environmental system perspective. In A. Kaiser & D. Gray (Eds.), *Enhancing children's communication: Research foundations for intervention* (pp. 63–84). Baltimore: Brookes.

Kaiser, A., Yoder, P., & Keetz, A. (1992). Evaluating milieu teaching. In S. F. Warren & J. Reichle (Eds.), *Causes and effects in communication and language intervention* (pp. 9–47). Baltimore: Brookes.

Klinder, D., & Carnine, D. (1991). Direct instruction: What it is and what it is becoming. *Journal of Behavioral Education, 1,* 193–213.

MacDonald, J. (1985). Language through conversation: A model for intervention with language delayed persons. In S. F. Warren & A. Rogers-Warren (Eds.), *Teaching functional language* (pp. 89–122). Austin: PRO-ED.

McCathren, R. B., Warren, S. F., & Yoder, P. J. (1996). Prelinguistic predictors of later language development. In K. Cole, P. Dale, & D. Thal (Eds.), *Assessment of communication and language* (pp. 57–76). Baltimore: Brookes.

McCathren, R. B., Yoder, P. J., & Warren, S. (1995). The role of directives in early language intervention. *Journal of Early Intervention, 19*(2), 91–101.

Menyuk, P. (1988). *Language development: Knowledge and use.* Glenview, IL: Scott, Foresman.

Nelson, K. (1973). Structure and strategy in learning to talk. *Monographs of the Society for Research in Child Development, 38*(1-2, Serial No. 149).

Nelson, K. E. (1989). Strategies for first language teaching. In M. Rice & R. L. Schiefelbusch (Eds.), *The teachability of language* (pp. 263–310). Baltimore: Brookes.

Nelson, K. E. (1991). On differentiated language-learning models and differentiated interventions. In N. A. Krasnegor, D. M. Rumbaugh, R. L. Schiefelbusch, & M. Studdert-Kennedy (Eds.), *Biological and behavioral determinants of language development* (pp. 319–428). Hillsdale, NJ: Lawrence Erlbaum Associates.

Pinker, S. (1994). *The language instinct.* New York: Morrow.

Roberts, J. E., Bailey, D. B., & Nychka, H. B. (1991). Teachers' use of strategies to facilitate the communication of preschool children with disabilities. *Journal of Early Intervention, 15,* 358–376.

Schiefelbusch, R. L., & Lloyd, L. L. (1974). *Language perspectives: Acquisition, retardation, intervention.* Baltimore: University Park Press.

Snow, C. (1984). Parent–child interaction and the development of communicative ability. In R. L. Schiefelbusch & J. Pickar (Eds.), *The acquisition of communicative competence* (pp. 69–108). Baltimore, MD: University Park Press.

Snow, C. (1994). Beginning from baby talk: Twenty years of research on input in interaction. In C. Gallaway & B. J. Richards (Eds.), *Input and interaction in language acquisition* (pp. 1–12). Cambridge, England: Cambridge University Press.

Snow, C. E., Perlmann, R., & Nathan, D. (1987). Why routines are different: Toward a multiple factors model of the relation between input and language acquisition. In K. E. Nelson & A. van Kleeck (Eds.), *Child language* (Vol. 16, pp. 65–97). Hillsdale, NJ: Lawrence Erlbaum Associates.

Sokolov, J. L. (1993). A local contingency analysis of the fine-tuning hypothesis. *Developmental Psychology, 29*(6), 1008–1023.

Speidel, G. E., & Nelson, K. E. (1989). A fresh look at imitation in language learning. In G. E. Speidel & K. E. Nelson (Eds.), *The many faces of imitation in language learning* (pp. 1–21). New York: Springer-Verlag.

Spradlin, J. E., & Siegel, G. M. (1982). Language training in natural and clinical environments. *Journal of Speech and Hearing Disorders, 47*, 2–6.

Tannock, R., & Girolametto, L. (1992). Reassessing parent-focused language intervention programs. In S. F. Warren & J. Reichle (Eds.), *Causes and effects in communication and language intervention* (pp. 49–80). Baltimore: Brooks.

Tomasello, M. (1992). *First verbs.* Cambridge, England: Cambridge University Press.

van Kleeck, A. (1994). Potential cultural bias in training parents as conversational partners with their children who have delays in language development. *American Journal of Speech-Language Pathology, 31*, 67–78.

Warren, S. F. (1991). Enhancing communication and language development with milieu teaching procedures. In E. Cipani (Ed.), *A guide for developing language competence in preschool children with severe and moderate handicaps* (pp. 68–93). Springfield, IL: Charles C. Thomas.

Warren, S. F., & Kaiser, A. P. (1988). Research in early language intervention. In S. I. Odom & M. A. Karnes (Eds.), *Early intervention for infants and children with handicaps: An empirical base* (pp. 84–108). Baltimore: Brookes.

Warren, S. F., McQuarter, R. J., & Rogers-Warren, A. (1984). The effects of mands and models on the speech of unresponsive language delayed preschool children. *Journal of Speech and Hearing Disorders, 49*, 42–52.

Warren, S. F., & Yoder, P. J. (1997). A developmental model of early communication and language intervention. *Mental Retardation and Developmental Disabilities Research Reviews, 3*, 358–362.

Warren, S. F., & Yoder, P. J. (1998). Facilitating the transition to intentional communication. In A. M. Wetherby, S. F. Warren, & J. Reichle (Eds.), *Transitions in prelinguistic communication* (pp. 365–384). Baltimore: Brookes.

Warren, S. F., Yoder, P. J., Gazdag, G. E., Kim, K., & Jones, H. A. (1993). Facilitating prelinguistic communication skills in young children with developmental delay. *Journal of Speech and Hearing Research, 36*, 83–97.

White, W. A. T. (1988). A meta-analysis of effects of direct instruction in special education. *Education and Treatment of Children, 11*, 364–374.

Whitehurst, G. J., Falco, F. L., Fischel, J. E., Lonigan, C., Valdez-Menchaca, M. C., DeBaryshe, B. D., & Caulfield, M. B. (1989). Accelerating language development through picture book reading. *Developmental Psychology, 24*, 552–559.

Wilcox, M. J., Kouri, T., & Caswell, S. (1991). Early language intervention: A comparison of classroom and individual treatment. *American Journal of Speech-Language Pathology, 1*, 49–62.

Wilcox, M. J., & Shannon, M. S. (1998). Facilitating the transition from prelingusitic to linguistic communication. In A. Wetherby, S. Warren, & J. Reichle (Eds.), *Transitions in prelinguistic communication* (pp. 385–416). Baltimore: Brookes.

Yoder, P. J., Davies, B., Bishop, K., & Munson, L. (1994). Effect of adult continuing wh-questions on conversational participation in children with developmental disabilities. *Journal of Speech and Hearing Research, 37*, 193–204.

Yoder, P. J., Kaiser, A., & Alpert, C. (1991). An exploratory study of the interaction between language teaching methods and child characteristics. *Journal of Speech and Hearing Research, 34*, 155–167.

Yoder, P. J., Kaiser, A. P., Goldstein, H., Alpert, C., Mousetis, L., Kaczmarek, L., & Fischer, R. (1995). An exploratory comparison of milieu teaching and responsive interaction in classroom applications. *Journal of Early Intervention, 19*(3), 218–242.

Yoder, P. J., & Warren, S. F. (1998). Maternal responsivity predicts the extent to which prelinguistic intervention facilitates generalized intentional communication. *Journal of Speech, Language, and Hearing Research, 41,* 1207–1219.

Yoder, P. J., & Warren, S. F. (1999a). Maternal responsivity mediates the relationship between prelinguistic intentional communication and later language. *Journal of Early Intervention, 22,* 126–136.

Yoder, P. J., & Warren, S. F. (1999b). Self-initiated proto-declaratives and proto-imperatives can be facilitated in prelinguistic children with developmental disabilities. *Journal of Early Intervention, 22,* 205–216.

Yoder, P. J., Warren, S. F., Kim, K., & Gazdag, G. E. (1994). Facilitating prelinguistic communication skills in young children with developmental delay: II. Systematic replication and extension. *Journal of Speech and Hearing Research, 37,* 841–851.

17

Benefits of Speech Manipulation for Children With Language Disorders

Ludo Verhoeven
Eliane Segers
University of Nijmegen

The relationship of auditory processing problems to language learning problems is well established (see chaps. 4 and 8, this volume; Tallal, 2000). It is generally believed that language impairment is strongly related to difficulties in the temporal processing of both auditory and visual information. It is hypothesized that children with SLI differ from their peers in the ability to discriminate and process the basic components of speech, and that such speech discrimination problems are related to difficulties in the processing of brief sensory cues or rapidly changing sequential information. Such temporal processing deficit is even thought of as a biological marker of language disorders given that such deficits appear to emerge as early as the first year of life (see Benasich & Tallal, 1996). From an etiological point of view, temporal processing deficits are assigned to incomplete mental representations of phonetic information due to inherited inferior learning systems or speech and/or visual reception problems, which are associated with a limited use of the temporal information available in acoustic and visual stimuli (Merzenich et al., 1993; Merzenich & Jenkins, 1995). It is assumed that limitations in the segmentation and integration of temporal information may lead to neurological changes affecting language development.

The claim that deficits in the ability to process temporal information may be the cause of language impairment has important implications for remediation. In recent research, an attempt has been made to develop speech modification algorithms to evoke critical language learning processes. The main idea of such algorithms has been to remodel the brain of the child in such a way that rapid temporal changes in sounds are better perceived. The basic assumption is that training engages brain plasticity mechanisms, which leads to changes in the cortex. Through multiple training experiences, new neural groups can be formed and further extended. Empirical evidence for this assumption came from brain studies among adult monkeys before and after they were trained to process rapidly successive acoustic or tactile stimuli (Jenkins et al., 1990; Merzenich & Jenkins, 1995; Merzenich et al., 1996). As a consequence of intensive practice following strict behavioral training procedures, neural connections in the brains of these monkeys could be reshaped. With practice individual acoustic or tactile events could be represented neurologically with greater clarity and with sharper time distinction. As a result, the progressively trained brain could correctly identify or distinguish between successive events that it was receiving at ever-increasing rates. From these studies, it was concluded that defective acoustic signal segmentation and integration effects may be the result of early receptive learning progressions in individuals with impairments, and that a particular form of training may drive progressive improvements in the brain representations of rapidly successive inputs in individuals with learning impairments. This train of thinking has led the foundation for development of the so-called *Fast ForWord* program (Merzenich et al., 1996). This computer-based program contains a series of games in which phonemes that were found to be difficult for children with language impairment are being lengthened and intensified. In these games, the discrimination of tones with decreasing interstimulus intervals is also being practiced.

In the present chapter, the research on speech manipulation for children with language impairment is reviewed. We restrict ourselves to research conducted on the impact of formant transitions and their manipulation in the speech perception of children and adults with language/speech problems. Searching through PsychINFO on keywords as: formant transition, speech manipulation, transition length, varying duration, categorical perception, and searching through reference lists, we found several articles concerning this subject. The start of this line of research can be put at the articles of Tallal and Piercy in 1974 and 1975. The two articles describe a series of experiments with a subject group of 12 children who enter a special school for aphasic children and 12 control children. The former 12 children have a diagnosis of developmental aphasia, but no other problems on hearing or intelligence. In a first experiment (1974), the researchers show how the aphasic children have no problems in discriminating vocals. In consonant–vowel stimuli however, when there is a short formant transition, the aphasic group shows more problems than the control group. In a second experiment (1975), it is shown that this same group of aphasic children performs as well as the control group when the formant transition is set longer. In later studies, Tallal and colleagues have reconfirmed how dysphasics have problems discriminating CVs containing stop consonants, which have a fast formant transition. These studies are described in the following section, along with articles that used a continuum to prove the difference in speech perception between children with or without language/speech problems. In the next section, we describe research that has followed the article from 1975. Several scientists have done research on the lengthening of fast formant transitions and the effects this can have on people with language/speech problems. In the follow-up section, we describe research on the effects of intensive training with manipulated speech. There are only two studies that compare a training and a control group on such effects. In the final discussion section, we describe the gaps in this line of research and the questions that remain to be answered.

THE DIFFICULTY OF FAST FORMANT TRANSITIONS

With respect to the claim that individuals with language impairment have difficulty in processing brief, rapidly successive acoustic cues in verbal stimuli, a distinction can be made between studies focusing on the discrimination of CV segments containing a stop consonant and studies using a continuum instead of end-point discrimination. The difference between these two types of studies is described by Thibodeau and Sussman (1979) as phonemic versus phonetic discrimination:

> Phonemic discrimination tests require a child to decide whether pairs of auditory stimuli are alike or different, to make correct/incorrect judgements regarding the accuracy of production of auditory stimuli in association with a picture, or to identify a picture from a group that corresponds to a heard auditory stimulus. Tokens from this type of tests are exemplars from a phonetic category. Phonetic discrimination on the other hand allows for investigation of differences in the perception of subtle allophonic variations upon which phonemic boundaries are established. Stimuli are systematically varied along an acoustic continuum. (p. 376)

Only a few studies have investigated the difficulty language impaired individuals have in discriminating CVs containing a stop consonant. Table 17.1 gives an overview of these studies.

The results of these studies generally show how language and reading impaired individuals have problems in discriminating synthetic speech stimuli containing a stop consonant followed by a vowel. However, the studies differ in subject population, method, and data analysis. The study by Tallal and Piercy (1974) consisted of two identification experiments:

TABLE 17.1
Overview of Studies on the Difficulty Children With Developmental Language
Disorders Have in Discriminating CVs Containing a Stop Consonant

Year	Authors	Subject Group	Speech Material	Conclusion
1974	Tallal & Piercy	12 aphasic children 12 controls ages 6.9–9.3	/bɑ/–/dɑ/; formant transition 43 msec	Aphasics have more problems than controls
1980a	Tallal, Stark, Kallmann, & Mellits	35 developmental dysphasics 38 controls average age: 6.8	/bɑ/–/dɑ/ as in Tallal and Piercy (1974) Synthetic copies of natural utterances /bɑ/–/be/ /bi/– /dae/, /dɛ/–/di/; formant transition varying naturally	Dysphasics have more problems than controls
1981	Tallal & Stark	same as above	/bɑ/–/dɑ/, /dɑ/– /tɑ/, /ɛ/–/ae/, /dɑb/–/daeb/, /sɑ/–/stɑ/, /sɑ/– /ʃɑ/	Dysphasics have more problems than controls in /bɑ/–/dɑ/, /dɑ/ –/tɑ/ and also /sɑ/–/ʃɑ/.
1989	Reed	23 reading disabled 23 normals average age: 8;11	/ba/–/da/, /ɛ/– /æ/	Reading disabled have problems in /ba/–/da/ as opposed to controls.
1992	Leonard, McGregor, & Allen	8 SLI, 8 normals. 4;6 tot 5;7 jaar	/ba/–/da/, /dab/ –/dæb/, /i/–/u/, /dab-i-ba/–/dab-u-ba/, /das/– /daʃ/	SLIs have more problems than controls except in /dab/–/dæb/ and /i/–/u/.

The subject had to push one button if he or she heard Syllable 1 and the
other if he or she heard Syllable 2. In a discrimination task in the same
study, the subjects had to push one button if the two presented items were
the *same* and the other button if the items were different. The criterion
used in this study was that subjects have to have 20 correct answers out of
24 in a series of maximum 48 trials. The aphasics differ from the normal
controls, for example, in the same–different task because 2 out of 12 subjects did not reach this criterion, whereas all controls did. This difference
was significant as measured by a Likelihood Ratio Test ($p < .01$). Notice
that we do not know how many errors the subjects made and to what extent the groups differ on this variable.

Tallal, Stark, Kallman, and Mellits (1980a) did not use a same–different
task, only the identification task as is described in the previous experi-

ment. This time the difference between language delayed and controls is established by the number of errors they made (*t* test). The language delayed made significantly more errors.

Tallal and Stark (1981) used a new sort of task: a change/no change task where children did not have to make a same/different judgment. Children had to click on a button when they heard a target word (e.g., /ba/) in a series (of, e.g., /da/). The criterion was also changed: Subjects now had to have 12 out of 16 correct answers in 48 trials at maximum. This time a Mann–Whitney *U* test was used to show the difference between the groups. Tallal and Stark pointed out that the developmental dysphasics made significantly more errors than the controls.

Reed (1989) used several tasks: One is the same as used by Tallal et al. (1980a). A *t* test showed the difference in the number of mistakes made by reading disabled and controls to be significant. She also used a task in which subjects have to point at one of two pictures when hearing a word; again the difference in the number of errors between the two groups turned out to be significant.

Leonard et al. (1992) used the same task as Tallal and Stark (1981). The criterion measure was 12 out of 16 correct answers, with a maximum of 48 trials. The difference between the two groups was demonstrated by means of a new measure: the number of errors made in the first 16 trials. This was not measured for the /ba/–/da/ contrast, where it was only said that 6 out of the 8 regular subjects and 2 out of 8 SLIs did not reach the criterion measure.

Reed (1989) also described two experiments in which she used a continuum. Reading disabled individuals showed a difference in the curve in their answering behavior as opposed to the controls at the /ba/–/da/ continuum. In a /bap–/dap/ continuum, the reading-disabled group showed a large effect of lexical status near the category boundary contrary to the control group.

Further studies exploring the difficulty of fast formant transitions using a continuum (phonetic discrimination) are listed in Table 17.2. These studies do not exclusively investigate the difference of fast formant transitions, which are responsible for place of articulation. Also Voice Onset Time is sometimes the changing variable. Subjects in most of these studies have less severe oral or written language problems. They are often labeled as *dyslexics, poor readers,* or *having learning problems.* In most studies, small differences have been found between the population studied and the control group. The subjects showed more variability in their answers and more uncertainty in their discrimination. However, in the vast majority of cases, they were able to discriminate the endpoints of the continuum—a task that the subjects in the studies listed in Table 17.1 had more problems with.

TABLE 17.2

Studies Investigating the Difference in Speech Perception Between Speech/Language Disordered Subjects and Controls Using a Speech Continuum

Year	Authors	Subjects	Speech Stimuli	Results
1979	Thibodeau & Sussman	17 communication disordered (7;0) 12 controls (6;11)	/ba/–/pa/ 21 step continuum (VOT)	No significant effects; greater variability in the communication disordered group.
1980	Brandt & Rosen	12 reading disabled 4 normal reading 10.5 years	/da/–/ta/ 11 step continuum (VOT) /ba/–/da/–/ga/ 14 step continuum	No differences found
1981	Godfrey et al.	17 dyslexics 16 controls age: 7;3–15;1	/ba/–/da/ and /da/–/ga/ 8 step continua	Difference between groups
1987	Werker & Tees	14 reading problems (2 years behind) (8–14) 14 controls (8–13)	/ba/–/da/ 8 step continuum	Difference between groups
1988	Elliot & Hammer	21 normal (7;0) 21 learning problems (7;2)	/ba/–/pa/ 8 step and /ba/–/da/–/ga/ 13 step continua	Difference between groups at VOT, not place of articulation
1988	De Weirdt	Study 1: 48 first graders, analysis 25 left study 2: 11 high achievers 11 low achievers 11 moderate dyslexic 11 severe dyslexic Study 3 18 good readers 18 poor readers	Studies 1, 2 & 3: /pʌ/–/tʌ 10 step continuum In Study 3, it was found that same/different judgment. Generates about the same results as speech repetition.	Study 1: Results of Godfrey et al. are "not replicated very convincingly" (p. 171) Study 2: Differences in discrimination, not identification Study 3: Differences in discrimination
1989	Elliot, Hammer, & Scholl	Younger group: 77 regular, 61 learning problems (6- and 7-year-olds) older group 66 regular, 90 learning problems (8- to 11-year-olds)	/ba/–/pa/ 8 step and /ba/–/da/–/ga/ 13 step continua	Differences between learning and age groups

Year	Authors	Subjects	Stimuli	Results
1992	Steffens, Eilers, Gross-Glenn, & Jallad	18 adult dyslexics 18 adult normal readers 11 5/6-year-olds language impaired 10 controls (age = 4;3)	/a/–/ə/, /ba/–/da/ and /sta/–/sa/ 11 step continua	Differences between groups
1993	Sussman		/ba/–/da/ 7 step continuum	Differences in identification, not discrimination with age-matched controls from former study (Sussman, 1993b)
1997	Irausquin	17 poor readers (11;11) 17 chronological age matched controls (11;11) 17 reading age matched controls (8;4)	Study 1 /da/–/ba/ (place of articulation) and /da/–/ta/ (VOT) 9 step continua NATURAL speech Study 2 phonetically similar pseudowords (e.g., buto-duto)	Study 1 difference between poor readers and controls on place of articulation discrimination accuracy. Study 2 no differences except for reaction time: poor readers are slower at making different judgments, CA in making same judgments.
1997	Groenen	Study 1 8 developmental dyslexia (8;8) 12 age matched controls Reading matched controls (7;0) Study 2 10 children articulation problems (9;0) 10 controls (9;1) 10 adolescents articulation problems (14;11) 10 adults (36;2) Study 3 17 apraxia (8;9) 16 controls (8;0)	Study 1 /bak/–/dak/ 7 step continuum /bak/–/pak/ 8 step continuum Study 2 /pak/–/tak/ 7 step continuum Study 3 /bak/–/dak/ synthesized and resynthesized 7 step continua	Study 1 identification, dyslexics perform as well as RA, worse than CA discrimination: dyslexics differ from both controls. Study 2 difference between adolescents and adult controls and between children articulation problems and both controls. Study 3 difference between groups
1997	Manis et al.	25 dyslexics grade (4–10 years) 25 age matched controls 24 reading age matched controls	/bath/–/path/ 13 step continuum	Difference between controls and dyslexics, especially phonemic awareness group

Brandt and Rosen (1980) found no differences between the two groups of subjects. However, Godfrey et al. (1981) argued the authors would have found differences if they had used a more appropriate analysis.

In all studies, synthetic speech was used except for the one by Irau-squin (1997), who is also the first to take reaction time into consideration. Groenen (1997) used both synthesized and resynthesized speech. The number of steps in the continua of the studies varied and also may have influenced the results along with the different analysis techniques being used.

The overall conclusion by Manis et al. provides a good summary: "the differences are real, but small and therefore hard to detect" (p. 214). They also pointed out that some of the differences found in all of these studies can be attributable to intrinsic differences in attention levels.

THE BENEFITS OF SPEECH MANIPULATION

The 1975 study by Tallal and Piercy showed how the performance of the dysphasic children on the repetition task can be dramatically improved when lengthening the formant transition. They found that if fast formant transitions in stimuli like /ba/ were stretched, the results of the language-impaired children greatly improved (Tallal & Piercy, 1975). Studies concerning manipulating speech to improve results of people with language/speech problems are listed in Table 17.3. One can notice that the subject samples in these studies are more in line with the ones from Table 17.1.

For this domain, the results are far from conclusive. Tallal and Piercy (1975) showed that if fast formant transitions in stimuli were stretched, the auditory discrimination results of the language-impaired children greatly improved. In this experiment, the duration of the formant transition within the syllables ba and da was extended from 40 to 80 msec, whereas the duration of the following vowel representation was reduced from 210 to 170 msec. By extending the brief intrasyllabic cues within the speech waveform in a similar way, Frumkin and Rapin (1980) and Alexander and Frost (1982) also showed a significant improvement in auditory discrimination of subgroups of language-impaired children. Stark and Heinz (1996) applied a Klatt synthesis extending the formant transition in /ba/ and /da/ from 30 to 80 msec, and found a positive effect for children with expressive and receptive language problems. In the study by Tallal et al. (1980b), a combined effect of an acceleration of syllables and a decrease in interstimulus intervals was found for the group dysphasics. In the study by Tallal, Stark, and Mellits (1985), there was a tendency that the length of transitions varied with the difficulty level for dysphasics. However, the statistical procedure being followed in this study can be ques-

TABLE 17.3

Studies on Manipulating Speech to Improve Results of People With Language/Speech Problems

Year	Authors	Subjects	Speech Stimuli	Results
1975	Tallal & Piercy	as in Tallal and Piercy (1974) 12 aphasic children 12 controls age 6;9–9;3	ba–da; formant transition extended from 40 to 80 msec	Positive effects
1980	Frumkin & Rapin	20 dysphasic children 9 control children average age 9;7	ba–da and /a/–/u/ Synthetic speech, Haskins Lab. CV: 2nd and 3rd formant 40 msec or 80 msec; total length 250 msec V: 40, 80 or 250 msec.	Positive effects for subgroup
1980b	Tallal, Stark, Kallman, & Mellits	14 developmental aphasics 23 normally developing age 5–9	ba–da as in Tallal and Piercy (1974). Synthetic copies of natural utterances /ba/–/be/, /bi/–/dae/, /de/–/di/; formant transition varying naturally	Results aphasics dependent on syllable speed and ISI time
1982	Alexander & Frost	24 children from special education, language/speech problems age: 7;2–11;7	/ba/–/da/ as in Tallal and Piercy (1974). Formant transitions: 80, 70, 60 and 40 msec.	Positive effects
1984	Blumstein, Tartter, Nigro, & Statlender	1) 22 adults (16 aphasics, 6 controls) 2) 18 aphasics, 5 controls	1) 2 synthetic /ba/–/da/–/ga/ continua. 2) 12 CV's /da/–/ga/ from two continua exp 1, the same four but with formant transition 65 and 85 msec.	No effects
1985	Riedel & Studdert-Kennedy	12 adult aphasics. average age 55	ba–da as in Tallal and Piercy (1974). Formant transition 30 and 82 msec.	No effects
1985	Tallal, Stark, & Mellits	Subgroup of Tallal, Stark, Kallmann, and Mellits (1980) and Tallal and Stark (1981) 26 developmental dysphasics	Same as Tallal and Stark 1981	Unclear
1996	Stark & Heinz	11 children with expressive problems 21 children with expressive and receptive problems 22 controls age 6–10	ba–da Klatt synthesis. Formant transition 30 to 80 msec. in steps of 10.	Positive effect for children with expressive and receptive problems
1999	Bradlow et al.	32 children with learning problems 72 controls age 6–16	two /da/–/ga/ continua 40 msec and 80 msec formant transition Control: /ba/–/wa/	No effects

tioned (cf. Elliot, Hammer, & Scholl, 1989). No significant effects were reported in the studies by Blumstein et al. (1984), Riedel and Studdert-Kennedy (1985), and Bradlow et al. (1999), all exploring the effects of the extension of patterns such as /ba/, /da/, and /ga/ on their auditory discrimination.

COMPUTER-ASSISTED TRAINING
WITH SPEECH MANIPULATION

Given the positive effects of training studies with animals showing that sensory processing skills could be sharpened by intensive practice, an intervention program for children with SLI was developed by Tallal, Merzenich, and colleagues. The program consisted of computer games using acoustically modified speech signals in which the duration of the speech signal was prolonged and the transitional elements were amplified. The speech manipulation used in this study is different from what was previously tested in experiments. Instead of lengthening the formant transition, a speech modification algorithm was used, which slowed down the complete speech signal and amplified fast transitional elements up to 20dB. Details of the speech modification algorithm were described by Nagarajan et al. (1998).

In a study by Tallal et al. (1996), the effects of this program were examined (see Table 17.4). Other training studies (e.g., Merzenich et al., 1996), which did not include a control group that got the same training without manipulated speech, were left out of this survey because they do not prove the benefits of speech manipulation. In the training study displayed in Table 17.4, 11 children with SLI were exposed to the program, whereas a group of 11 control children with SLI received a similar training using unmodified speech signals. Following a 4-week period of training, the children in the experimental group gained an average effect 18 to 24 months on standardized tests for language comprehension. However, as Bishop (1997) and Rice (1997) proposed, other than temporal processing, aspects in the games under consideration might have explained the gains in the experimental condition, such as direct clinician-to-client interaction or additional listening homework.

The promising results of this pilot study encouraged the development of a computer-based intervention program called *Fast ForWord* (Scientific Learning Corporation, 1999). The creation of this computer program was guided by several neuropsychological principles. First of all, the program needed to be adaptive, being attuned to the individual learner, increasing in difficulty as the child progresses, and maintaining motivational and behavioral control. Second, the training exercise designs were based on the

TABLE 17.4
Training Study Concerning Speech Manipulation
and Children With Language/Speech Problems

Year	Authors	Subjects	Speech Material	Results
1996	Tallal et al.	22 SLI Average age 7;4	Computer games with or without speech manipulation	Positive effects

presupposed magnitude and deficits in acoustic signal reception for the individual child. Exercises started with nonspeech stimuli or acoustically modified speech stimuli. Gradually the stimuli changed until, at the highest game level, the child was operating with normal speech or making accurate acoustic distinctions about the rapidly successive or dynamically changing sounds. Third, the program was hierarchically built up in that trained acoustic and speech processing abilities were transferred to higher level speech and language contexts, enforcing generalizations to real-world speech and language comprehension. Finally, in the program explicit training in syntax and morphology was also provided using acoustically modified speech.

The Fast ForWord program consists of seven computer games: (a) focusing at processing and temporal sequencing skills, (b) phonemic sound change discrimination, (c) phoneme identification, (d) matching nonsense syllables that differ by a single phoneme, (e) recognition of words differing by a single phoneme, (f) syntax and listening comprehension, and (g) higher level language skills. Each game consists of five levels. The first level incorporates digitally manipulated stimuli in which the duration and intensity of certain phonemic or transition elements is increased. Each successive game level reduces the parameters by which the signals are modified until the level of natural speech is reached. One hundred minutes of play over five different games is programmed for each day. The child's performance is continuously monitored by the program. The suggested criterion for finishing the program is a performance level of 80% correct on five of the seven games. With the recommended pace of 5 days per week, the program is usually completed within 6 weeks.

Several large-scale field effect studies on the Fast ForWord program have been conducted by Tallal, Merzenich, and associates. Statistically significant gains in receptive and productive language scores have been reported in presentations (e.g., Tallal & Merzenich, 1997). However, the gains in norm-referenced test scores being reported turned out not to be unusually large in comparison to the gains in other intervention studies (see Law, chap. 18, this volume). A problem is that no reports on training effects have been published yet in scientific journals. Several critical comments can be made with regard to the studies being reported. The most serious flaws include the inadequacy of subject selection, the absence of no-treatment control groups, and the lack of control of assessment procedures (no standard errors of measurements have been reported so that regression-to-the-mean effects cannot be excluded).

We found one more article that described a training study in which manipulated speech was used. Habib et al. (1999) trained six French dyslexic children with acoustically modified speech, and a control group received the same training with unmodified speech. Both training exercises and pre- and posttraining tests were created with words and nonwords according to difficulties inherent to the French language. The manipulated speech group outperformed the normal group on posttests. The researchers claim to have used the same speech modification as in the Fast ForWord program. However, they described that they first amplify "unstable portions" in the speech signal and then they slow it by a constant factor (p. 144). We should remind the reader that the algorithm described by Nagarajan et al. (1998) takes these steps in a different order by slowing down speech first and then enhancing fast transitional elements.

CONCLUSIONS AND DISCUSSION

From the present review, several conclusions can be made. Research on the discrimination of speech segments convincingly shows that children with language impairment have a reduced capacity for processing rapidly successive information. Additional support for the hypothesis that acoustic rate processing deficits underlie language impairment comes from a series of studies showing that rapid auditory processing thresholds of infants at risk for language impairment are significantly longer than those of peers from control families (Benasich & Spitz, 1998; Benasich & Tallal, 1996, 1998).

With respect to the benefits of speech manipulation, the results are less pronounced. Positive effects have been reported in about half of the studies being conducted. The lengthening of fast formant transitions seems to foster speech discrimination only in children with speech/language problems and probably a subgroup of the children: the ones with both expressive and receptive problems (Stark & Heinz, 1996). The manipulation seems unhelpful for children with the more vague label of *learning problems*. However, only one study was published on this subject. Children in this study had a large age range, so maybe an effect can only be found in younger children. Adult aphasics do not seem to benefit from speech manipulation.

In training, an extensive program is probably necessary to show improvements because the brain has to be retrained. However, so far there is no direct evidence that an extensive training program such as Fast ForWord training alters brain morphology in children with SLI. Although the design of the training can be seen as highly challenging, its effectiveness still has to be showed. A problem is that the Fast ForWord program has a lot more to offer than manipulated speech. Also the training study conducted is not in line with the previously described research. In the training, the whole speech signal is stretched, not only the fast formant transitions. They are amplified up to 20dB following the neurological study by Merzenich et al. on monkeys. The study reported by Habib et al. (1999) followed still another algorithm. More research is necessary on this front to overcome the methodological shortcomings of the studies conducted so far.

In conclusion, the hypothesis that a temporal processing constraint affects the development of normal phonological processing and grammatical morphology, leading to oral language and in many cases also literacy deficits, can be seen as a strong one (see also Bishop, 1997; Leonard, 1998; Tallal, 2000). There is clear evidence that individuals with language impairment in many cases have deficits in processing brief, rapidly successive acoustic cues in nonverbal stimuli. However, several limitations of a more generalized temporal processing deficit theory can be summed up. First of all, it should be mentioned that the experimental evidence for problems in processing rapid changes in speech was derived from studies in which synthetic speech was used as input variable. Segers and Verhoeven (2002) found differences between SLI kindergartners and controls on an auditory discrimination task when using natural speech. However, no effects of speech manipulation were found. Segers and Verhoeven (2000) also found that—with SLI kindergartners—speech manipulation in natural speech produced no extra effects after a short training. They also found that in synthetic speech both lengthening of the complete speech signal and lengthening of the fast formant transition had a positive effect on discrimination. This contradicts Leonard's hypothesis (Leonard, McGregor, & Allen, 1992) that the difficulty for SLI children is the fast formant transition relative to the rest of the speech signal. However, the positive effect of enhancing the speech signal never appeared in any well-designed experimental study.

Second, contaminating variables may explain the variation in temporal processing abilities in children with language impairment. In many cases, information-processing disabilities in children related to attention, memory, or executive functions coincide with language impairment (see Gillam & Hoffman, chap. 5, this volume). For instance, Stark and Montgomery (1995) showed that attention problems may lead to poorer performance on speeded auditory tasks. To exclude such contaminating factors in experiments, control measures need to be taken with great care.

Furthermore, the temporal deficit hypothesis presupposes a causal relationship between temporal processing problems and SLI, whereas most empirical studies follow a correlational design leaving the problem of causality unresolved. In Tallal's bottom–up approach, it is claimed that rapid and transient processing skills are mandatory for normal language development to take place. An alternate top–down approach was forwarded by Bishop (1992) suggesting that poor performance on auditory tests may also be the consequence of a defective language-learning system. Because children with language impairment are unfamiliar with stimulus words being presented, their performance on auditory processing tasks may be relatively low. Bishop et al. (1999a, 1999b) investigated auditory processing skills in twins, including children with language impairment and control children, following a longitudinal design. No auditory measure demonstrated significant differences between the language impaired and control groups. Their performance turned out to be influenced more by nonverbal skills than language ability. From these studies, it was concluded that low-level auditory temporal processing deficits are neither necessary nor sufficient for causing language impairment in children. Instead, auditory processing was regarded to be a moderating variable, which exerts an effect on language development only in children who are already at genetic risk for LI. Higher level phonological processing deficits may be the central cause of children's language and literacy problems (cf. Brady, 1997). In a series of studies by Studdert-Kennedy and his colleagues, it was found that frequency and amplitude characteristics of speech sounds instead of temporal perception were crucial for building adequate phonological representations. They claimed that perceptual deficits can be identified in children with language and literacy problems when these children are presented with synthetic speech, but not when they are presented with nonverbal auditory signals that have acoustic properties similar to the speech stimuli (Mody, Studdert-Kennedy, & Brady, 1997). With respect to literacy problems, they found that poor readers did not differ from a control group in discriminating nonverbal stimuli no matter how long the interstimulus interval. On the basis of these findings, they concluded that language-based dysfunction of these children was due to phonological problems and not so much to auditory perceptual problems.

From the present research evidence, it can tentatively be concluded that neither bottom–up nor top–down models have proved to be fully satisfactory. Given that both basic acoustic processing and higher level linguistic processing can make significant contributions to language development, interactive models, which take both sources of information into account, can be seen as more realistic. Neuroimaging studies may be better suited to address the issue of continuity of language-related problems from lower processes to higher level dysfunction. Earlier neuroimaging findings suggest that there are at least basic perceptual and processing constraints that partly explain the etiology of SLI (see Leppanen et al., chap. 4, this volume). However, so far no attempt has been made to study brain functioning by means of ERPs in infants at risk for language impairment.

Intervention studies such as the one of Fast ForWord can be seen as promising and highly relevant from a clinical point of view (see also Veale, 1999). Further research on the early identification and remediation of language impairment along this track seems to be mandatory. To start interventions during the critical early periods of language development, we are in need of prospective longitudinal studies examining developmental changes and maturation of infant brain responses to rapidly changing auditory cues and their relations to behavioral performance. From such studies, the development of reliable and valid measurement techniques for the early identification of children at risk for later language impairment could also be advanced.

REFERENCES

Alexander, D. W., & Frost, B. P. (1982). Decelerated synthesized speech as a means of shaping speed of auditory processing of children with delayed language. *Perceptual and Motor Skills, 55,* 783–792.

Benasich, A. A., & Spitz, R. V. (1998). Insights from infants: Temporal processing abilities and genetics contribute to language impairment. In K. Whitmore, H. Hart, & G. Williams (Eds.), *A neurodevelopmental approach to specific language disorders* (pp. 191–209). London: MacKeith.

Benasich, A. A., & Tallal, P. (1996). Auditory temporal processing thresholds, habituation, and recognition memory over the first year. *Infant Behavior and Development, 19,* 339–357.

Benasich, A. A., & Tallal, P. (1998). Infant processing of auditory temporal information: Links to family history and later language outcome. *Society for Neuroscience Abstract, 24,* 819.

Bishop, D. V. (1992). The underlying nature of specific language impairment. *Journal of Child Language Psychology & Psychiatry, 33,* 3–66.

Bishop, D. V. (1997). *Uncommon understanding: Development and disorders of language comprehension in children.* Cambridge, England: Psychology Press.

Bishop, D. V. M., Bishop, S. J., Bright, P., James, C., Delaney, T., & Tallal, P. (1999a). Different origin of auditory and phonological processing problems in children with language impairment: Evidence from a twin study. *Journal of Speech, Language and Hearing Research, 37,* 155–168.

Bishop, D. V. M., Carlyon, R. P., Deeks, J. M., & Bishop, S. J. (1999b). Auditory temporal processing: Neither necessary nor sufficient for causing language impairment in children. *Journal of Speech, Language and Hearing Research, 42,* 1295–1310.

Blumstein, S. E., Tartter, V. C., Nigro, G., & Statlender, S. (1984). Acoustic cues for the perception of place of articulation in aphasia. *Brain and Language, 22,* 128–149.

Bradlow, A. R., Kraus, N., Nicol, T. G., McGee, T. J., Cunningham, J., Zecker, S. G., & Carrell, T. D. (1999). *Journal of the Acoustic Society of America, 106*(4), 2086–2096.

Brady, S. (1997). Ability to encode phonological representations: An underlying difficulty of poor readers. In B. Blachman (Ed.), *Foundations of reading acquisition and dyslexia* (pp. 21–47). Mahwah, NJ: Lawrence Erlbaum Associates.

Brandt, J., & Rosen, J. J. (1980). Auditory phonemic perception in dyslexia: Categorical identification and discrimination of stop consonants. *Brain and Language, 9*, 324–337.

De Weirdt, W. (1988). Speech perception and frequency discrimination in good and poor readers. *Applied Psycholinguistics, 9*, 163–183.

Elliot, L. L., & Hammer, M. A. (1988). Longitudinal changes in auditory discrimination in normal children and children with language-learning problems. *Journal of Speech and Hearing Disorders, 53*, 467–474.

Elliot, L. L., Hammer, M. A., & Scholl, M. E. (1989). Fine grained auditory discrimination in normal children and children with language-learning problems. *Journal of Speech and Hearing Research, 32*, 112–119.

Frumkin, B., & Rapin, I. (1980). Perception of vowels and consonant-vowels of varying duration in language impaired children. *Neuropsychologica, 18*, 443–454.

Gillam, R. B. (1999). Computer-assisted language intervention using Fast ForWord: Theoretical and empirical considerations for decision-making. *Language, Speech, and Hearing Services in Schools, 30*, 363–370.

Godfrey, J. J., Syrdal-Lasky, A. K., Millay, K. K., & Knox, C. M. (1981). Performance of dyslexic children on speech perception tests. *Journal of Experimental Child Psychology, 32*, 401–424.

Groenen, P. (1997). *Central auditory processing disorders.* Unpublished doctoral dissertation, University of Nijmegen, The Netherlands.

Habib, M., Espesser, R., Rey, V., Giraud, K., Bruas, P., & Gres, C. (1999). Training dyslexics with acoustically modified speech: Evidence of improved phonological performance. *Brain and Cognition, 40*, 143–146.

Irausquin, R. (1997). *Quality and use of phonological representations in poor and normal readers.* Unpublished doctoral dissertation, University of Tilburg, The Netherlands.

Jenkins, W. M., Merzenich, M. M., Ochs, M. T., Allard, T., & Guic, R. E. (1990). Functional reorganization of primary somatosensory cotex in adult owl monkeys after behaviourally controlled tactile stimulation. *Journal of Neurophysiology, 63*, 82–104.

Law, J. (in press). The teachability of language impaired children. In L. Verhoeven & H. van Balkom (Eds.), *Classification of developmental language disorders.* Mahwah, NJ: Lawrence Erlbaum Associates.

Leonard, L. B. (1998). *Children with specific language impairment.* Cambridge, MA: MIT Press.

Leonard, L. B., McGregor, K. K., & Allen, G. D. (1992). Grammatical morphology and speech perception in children with specific language impairment. *Journal of Speech and Hearing Research, 25*, 1076–1085.

Leppänen, P. H. T., Choudhury, N., Benasich, A. A., & Lyytinen, H. (in press). Neuropsychological aspects of language impairment. In L. Verhoeven & H. van Balkom (Eds.), *Classification of developmental language disorders.* Mahwah, NJ: Lawrence Erlbaum Associates.

Manis, F. R., McBride-Chang, C., Seidenberg, M. S., Keating, P., Doi, L. M., Munson, B., & Petersen, A. (1997). Are speech perception deficits associated with developmental dyslexia? *Journal of Experimental Child Psychology, 66*, 211–215.

Merzenich, M. M., & Jenkins, W. M. (1995). Cortical plasticity, learning and learning dysfunction. In B. Julesz & I. Kovacs (Eds.), *Maturational windows and adult cortical plasticity* (pp. 247–272). New York: Addison-Wesley.

Merzenich, M. M., Jenkins, W. M., Johnston, P., Schreiner, C., Miller, S. L., & Tallal, P. (1996). Temporal processing deficits of language-learning impaired children ameliorated by training. *Science, 271*(5245), 77–81.

Merzenich, M. M., Schreiner, C., Jenkins, W. M., & Wang, X. (1993). Neural mechanisms underlying temporal integration, segmentation, and input sequence representation: Some implications for the origin of learning disabilities. *Annals of the New York Academy of Sciences, 682*, 1–21.

Mody, M., Studdert-Kennedy, M., & Brady, S. (1997). Speech perception deficits in poor readers: Auditory processing or phonological coding? *Journal of Experimental Psychology, 64,* 199–231.

Nagarajan, S. S., Wang, X., Merzenich, M. M., Schreiner, C. E., Johnston, P., Jenkins, W. M., Miller, S., & Tallal, P. (1998). Speech modification algorithms used for training language learning-impaired children. *IEEE Transactions on Rehabilitation Engineering, 6*(3).

Reed, M. A. (1989). Speech perception and the discrimination of brief auditory cues in reading disabled children. *Journal of Experimental Child Psychology, 48,* 270–292.

Rice, M. (1997). Evaluating new training programs for language impairment. *ASHA, 29,* 12–13.

Riedel, K., & Studdert-Kennedy, M. (1985). Extending formant transitions may not improve aphasics perception of stop consonant place of articulation. *Brain and Language, 24,* 223–232.

Scientific Learning Corporation. (1999). *Fast ForWord* (computer software). Berkeley, CA: Author.

Segers, E., & Verhoeven, L. (2000, July). *Enhancing metalinguistic awareness in specific language impaired kindergartners by use of a computer program.* Poster presented at the seventh annual meeting of the Society for the Scientific Study of Reading, Stockholm.

Segers, E., & Verhoeven, L. (2002). Does speech manipulation make word discrimination easier? In L. Verhoeven, C. Elbro, & P. Reitsma (Eds.), *Precursors of functional literacy* (pp. 109–118). Amsterdam/Philadelphia: John Benjamins.

Stark, R. E., & Heinz, J. M. (1996). Perception of stop consonants in children with expressive and receptive-expressive language impairments. *Journal of Speech and Hearing Research, 39,* 676–686.

Stark, R. E., & Montgomery, J. (1995). Sentence processing in language impaired children under conditions of filtering and time compression. *Applied Psycholinguistics, 16,* 337–353.

Steffens, M. L., Eilers, R. E., Gross-Glenn, K., & Jallad, B. (1992). Speech perception in adult subjects with familial dyslexia. *Journal of Speech and Hearing Research, 35,* 192–200.

Sussman, J. E. (1993a). Perception of formant transition cues to place of articulation in children with language impairments. *Journal of Speech and Hearing Research, 36,* 1286–1299.

Sussman, J. E. (1993b). Auditory processing in children's speech perception: Results of selective adaptation and discrimination tasks. *Journal of Speech and Hearing Research, 36,* 380–395.

Tallal, P. (2000). Experimental studies of language learning impairments: From research to remediation. In D. V. M. Bishop & L. B. Leonard (Eds.), *Speech and language impairments in children: Causes, characteristics, intervention and outcome* (pp. 131–155). Hove, United Kingdom: Psychology Press.

Tallal, P., & Merzenich, M. M. (1997). *Fast ForWord training for children with language impairment. National field test results.* Paper presented at the 1997 annual meeting of the American Speech-Language-Hearing Association, Boston, MA.

Tallal, P., Miller, S. L., Bedi, G., Myma, G., Wang, X., Nagarajan, S. S., Schreiner, C., Jenkins, W. M., & Merzenich, M. M. (1996). Language comprehension in language-learning impaired children improved with acoustically modified speech. *Science, 271,* 81–84.

Tallal, P., & Piercy, M. (1974). Developmental aphasia: Rate of auditory processing and selective impairment of consonant perception. *Neuropsychologica, 12*(1), 83–93.

Tallal, P., & Piercy, M. (1975). Developmental aphasia: The perception of brief vowels and extended stop consonants. *Neuropsychologica 13*(1), 69–74.

Tallal, P., & Stark, R. E. (1981). Speech acoustic-cue discrimination abilities of normally developing and language-impaired children. *JASA, 69*(2), 568–574.

Tallal, P., Stark, R. E., Kallman, C., & Mellits, D. (1980a). Perceptual constancy for phonemic categories: A developmental study with normal and language impaired children. *Applied Psycholinguistics, 1,* 49–64.

Tallal, P., Stark, R. E., Kallman, C., & Mellits, D. (1980b). Developmental dysphasia: Relation between acoustic processing deficits and verbal processing. *Neuropsychologica, 18*, 273–284.

Tallal, P., Stark, R. E., & Mellits, D. (1985). The relationship between auditory temporal analysis and receptive language development: Evidence from studies of developmental language disorder. *Neuropsychologica, 23*(4), 527–534.

Thibodeau, L. M., & Sussman, H. M. (1979). Performance on a test of categorical perception of speech in normal and communication disordered children. *Journal of Phonetics, 7*, 375–391.

Veale, T. K. (1999). Targeting temporal processing deficits through Fast ForWord: Language therapy with a new twist. *Language, Speech, and Hearing Services in Schools, 30*, 353–362.

Werker, J. F., & Tees, R. C. (1987). Speech perception in severely disabled and average reading children. *Canadian Journal of Psychology, 41*, 48–61.

18

The Close Association Between Classification and Intervention for Children With Primary Language Impairments

James Law
City University, London

It is quite clear that it is possible to identify a group of children for whom language and communication abilities are somehow different from their other skills. We have the discrepancy scores on a range of standardized measures to prove it. We have made a differential diagnosis that the child does not have a secondary language difficulty,[1] and therefore we feel secure in concluding that we have identified a primary speech and/or language impairment, even a specific language impairment (SLI). There is something so intrinsically appealing about the concept of a discrete language difficulty that many authors have overlooked that the defining of language impairment is at best an imprecise art that is highly dependent on measurement of constructs about which we still know so little. One of the main diagnostic/classificatory challenges is the need to distinguish between permanent and transient manifestations of the condition in the earlier years. There remains a cognitive dissonance for many authors who freely accept that SLI is neither specific nor an impairment (Leonard, 1987) yet feel compelled to continue using the terminology because it has some notional clinical validity.

The argument put forward in this chapter is that it is necessary to move beyond narrow paradigmatic constructions of (specific) language impair-

---

[1]A primary language impairment is one for which there is no obvious cause. A secondary language impairment is one that can be explained in terms of another condition experienced by the child—cerebral palsy, autism, hearing loss.

ment driven by often rather vague theory toward a more pragmatically driven approach, which has the child and his or her disabilities as its focus. Classification is inextricably linked to the recognition of there being differentiated and effective treatments for the conditions identified. Once it is possible to get a clear picture of the construct from the child's point of view, the issue of what we can do about improving the lot of the child moves into the spotlight, and we can creatively use our best efforts in intervention rather than in arid circular discussions, which often arise out of our attempts to define SLI. Worse, we settle for classification systems of convenience that do not bear close scrutiny. As it stands, intervention is often given low prominence in our understanding of the issues involved. For many researchers, it is seen as an add on. For some this may be because they feel they know that intervention works. It has even been suggested that we can move beyond primary effects (which we can take for granted) to concentrate our attentions on secondary effects (McLean & Woods Cripe, 1997). For others it may be that the concept of modularity may leave little room for the possibility of measuring the effects of environmental modification (Pinker, 1994). This is a position that would have made little sense to one of the great students of learning disabilities, Lev Vygotsky. He argued that pedagogy is the main application of psychology, much as medicine is of the biological sciences and politics of the social sciences, because "man proves the truth of his thoughts only by application" (Vygotsky, 1993, p. 55).

Is there a reasonable case for extending this functional approach to intervention to the classification process? If we have identified an intervention that consistently matches up with a behavioral profile, and even in the future a genotype, perhaps we are moving toward a useful model of classification. Some work has recently been published using this framework in the closely related field of reading disabilities. Vellutino and colleagues (1996) took their daily tutoring for reading impaired first graders as a first-cut diagnostic to discriminate between reading difficulties caused by reading deficits and those caused by experiential deficits. The majority of reading delays resolved with one term's input. Those that did not resolve were distinguished by poor phonological skills, but not by poor visual, syntactic, or semantic skills. As a result of the intervention, proportions with reading impairment fell from 9% to 3% or 1.5% depending on whether the 15th or the 30th percentile cutoff was adopted. The authors concluded,

> To render a diagnosis of specific reading disability in the absence of early and labour intensive remedial reading that has been tailored to the child's individual needs is, at best, a hazardous and dubious exercise, given all the stereotypes attached to this diagnosis. One can increase the probability of

validating the diagnosis if one combines impressions and outcomes derived from early individualised remediation with the results from relevant psychological and educational testing in evaluating the etiology of a child's difficulties in learning to read. (p. 632)

Hence, it is reasonable to examine the case for using intervention as the first-step diagnostic of language impairments to separate transient and persistent problems. Is it possible to define interventions sufficiently clearly to say that we know that if we do this with a given set of children exhibiting a given set of behaviors that we can affect change in such and such a way? It is true that the margin for error is probably greater than it is for the application of pharmaceutical interventions, but the same phenomenon exists. If a recognized intervention is able to produce a predictable effect, we are beginning to triangulate intervention and description, and this is likely to lead to a more useful classification system than we have at the moment.

How far does our present knowledge help us in this functional approach to classification? The first stage is to summarize what we know about the effects of intervention. The first study to do this suggested that intervention had different effects on different elements of language (Nye, Foster, & Seaman 1987). They suggested that it was possible to predict effect sizes of 0.65 for intervention aimed at remediating semantics and 1.4 for syntactic disabilities. By contrast, the few studies that have addressed pragmatics suggested that intervention was not useful (ES = .005). Pragmatic skills are also the most difficult to measure and the area where classification and diagnosis have proved most problematic. Such attempts to synthesize are, by their nature, complex to carry out and, in the developmental speech and language literature, few and far between. The important point to take from this is that if we know enough about the condition to treat it in a predictable manner, we probably know enough to classify it.

THE EFFECTS OF INTERVENTION: A META-ANALYSIS

The evidence in the present chapter is taken from a systematic review of the literature carried out for the Health Technology Assessment program of the National Health Service in Britain (Law, Boyle, Harris, Harkness, & Nye, 1998). The review was set up to evaluate the evidence for and against the use of mass or universal screening for speech and language delay in Britain. It is important to note that a systematic review is different from a more traditional narrative review insofar as the process of the selection of material to be reviewed is entirely transparent. The authors specify a time period, the methods of searching the literature, the methodological, and

other criteria for including and excluding studies. The intention is to minimize the risk of bias by making the process of the selection of papers explicit. Subsequent reviewers can either replicate or modify the study in
specific ways to address different issues. The systematic review is becoming the foundation stone of health policy in Britain.

To address the issue of whether universal screening is feasible, four domains of literature were identified and searched—prevalence, natural history, intervention, and screening. All four have a bearing on whether
screening could be introduced. For example, any screening program relies
on an understanding of the target prevalence. It must also be predictive in
the sense that it must be known that those identified by any screening
process will continue to have difficulties unless they receive intervention.
It is difficult to introduce screening for a noisy condition because the false
positive rate is likely to be very high. Intervention is also a central cam-
paign in any plank to introduce screening. Put simply, there is no point in
identifying unless there is good evidence that you can do something about
it. The duty of care changes in universal screening from one of voluntary
self-referral to active identification. In the first scenario, it can reasonably
be assumed that client and therapist share the risk for diagnosis. In the
second, the service is making a strong claim for the impact of the identification process. Finally, screening obviously requires a screening test or
identification procedure, and the systematic review drew these together.
The outcome of this review, at least insofar as it affects screening, is not
the subject of this chapter, except the conclusion reached was that there
were too many gaps in the available data set to warrant universal screening. The focus here is the set of intervention data.

The Identification of the Data Set

Published, unpublished, and grey literature from January 1967 to May
1997 was searched for relevant studies. Searches were carried out on
the six databases that Cros and DiallIndex searches indicated were most
relevant for this subject area—namely, CINAHL (Cumulative Index of
Nursing and Allied Health), Embase, ERIC (Educational Resources International Clearing House), LLBA (Linguistics and Language Behaviour
Abstracts), Medline, and PsycLIT. Two databases dealing with unpublished literature (SIGLE and Boston Spa Conferences) were also checked.
In addition, bibliographies from compilation volumes and articles retrieved
and Internet sources were checked, key journals were hand searched, and
calls for information were made to professional organizations, institu-
tions, and authors. Full details of the literature retrieval process may be
found in Law et al. (1998).

In all, 9,983 relevant papers were identified from 1967 to 1997, and of these 48 studies met the inclusion criteria for study design for intervention; 22 of the studies were group designs (randomized control trials and quasi-experimental designs) and 26 were single-subject experimental designs. It is the group design studies that have been selected in the present chapter to shed light on the issue of classification. The papers are cited in Appendix A.

Well-designed, randomized control trials (RCTs) provide the strongest and most widely recognized evidence for treatment efficacy (Crombie & Davies, 1996). Quasi-experimental designs, often a result of real-world constraints resulting in the nonrandom assignment of subjects to treatment or control conditions, provide a further source of evidence that can be cross-validated with the results from RCTs. However, the high spontaneous remission rates for speech and language delays in the preschool period, particularly for children with specific expressive delays, where some 60% of cases at 2 to 3 years may resolve without treatment (Rescorla & Schwartz, 1990; Thal & Tobias, 1992; see also Law, Boyle, Harris, Harkness, & Nye, 2000, for a review) pose particular problems for attempts to determine the effectiveness of treatment/intervention on primary speech or language delay in children up to 7 years of age. In view of the effects of maturation, a decision was taken to include only group design studies with an untreated control group.

Overall Results

Reviews of the literature (e.g., Guralnick, 1988; Law, 1997; McLean & Woods Cripe, 1997; Olswang & Bain, 1991; Snyder McLean & McLean, 1987; Zwart, 1997) identify a number of key variables that should be considered when the effects of intervention are being evaluated. These include child variables (age, gender, social class, nature of presenting difficulties) and program variables (e.g., area[s] of language treated; direct or indirect treatment by the clinician; model of intervention; intensity and duration of treatment), as well as the role of parents or caregivers.

A separate fixed-effects meta-analysis (Rosenthal, 1994) was carried out for each component areas of language for which data are available (i.e., articulation/phonology, expressive language [including syntax, semantics, and vocabulary], receptive language [including comprehension and vocabulary], and auditory discrimination/listening skills/phoneme awareness). This circumvents many of the problems of combining effect sizes across multiple measures of different dependent variables and ensures independence of measures (Lipsey, 1994; Rosenthal, 1984). Separate analyses were carried out for norm- and criterion-referenced measures because Nye, Foster, and Seaman (1987) found that the latter generated higher effect sizes. Different treatments were analyzed separately, but similar multiple criterion-referenced measures from one treatment within a given domain were averaged to yield a single combined measure (Rosenthal, 1994). Effect sizes from the RCT/quasi-experimental designs were analyzed following the procedures recommended by Hedges and Olkin (1985) for weighted analysis of variance (ANOVA).

The analysis of treatment outcomes was further explored using effect sizes. Table 18.1 provides a summary of the number of reported effect sizes by study design. The effect sizes for the different language areas are reported in Table 18.2. Figure 18.1 provides a plot of average effect sizes from each language domain (with 95% confidence intervals), revealing statistically significant effects for intervention for problems in articulation/phonology, expressive language, and receptive language. Due to the presence of confounding factors (i.e., variables such as age, gender, language area, intervention approach, and study design, which vary with each other so that the results ostensibly due to one variable could be due to another), the only comparison possible across studies was of direct ver-

TABLE 18.1
Summary of Number of Effect Sizes of Included Studies-by-Study Design

Design	Total No. of Subjects	Mean CA (Age Range)	Treatment Characteristics	No. of Effect Sizes
RCT	250	42 months (23–70 months)	Direct treatment by clinician: median 9 hours per child, in 21 half-hour sessions over 4 months	10
			Indirect treatment by clinician (e.g., parent-administered): median 17 hours per child of clinician time, in 10 ninety-minute sessions (usually group sessions) over 5 months	50
Quasi-Experimental	368	39 months 8–98 months*	Direct treatment by clinician: median 14 hours, in 21 forty-minute sessions over 5 months	23
			Indirect treatment (e.g., parent-administered): median 19.5 hours of clinician time, in 11 ninety-minute sessions (usually group sessions) over 4–5 months	26

*Three of Wilcox and Leonard's (1978) sample (N = 24) were aged between 7 years and 8 years 2 months. It was decided to include them rather than discard the study.

TABLE 18.2
Summary of Effect Sizes (*d*) by Language Area

Area of Language	No. of Effect Sizes	Average d	95% Confidence Interval
Articulation phonology	29	+0.35*	+0.10/+0.60
Expressive language	57	+1.07*	+0.85/+1.29
Receptive language	7	+1.09*	+0.44/+1.74
Auditory discrimination	14	+0.23	−0.10/+0.56

*Statistically significant results ($p < .05$).

sus indirect treatment. Unfortunately, it was not feasible given the rigorous way in which data were combined in the present data set to replicate the level of analysis carried out by Nye and colleagues (1987).

The overall results reveal statistically significant treatment outcomes ($p < .05$ or better) for 9 of the 10 RCT studies across the three areas of language despite the relatively small numbers of subjects involved. The two direct comparisons found parent-administered treatment to be as effective as direct treatment by the clinician (Fey et al., 1993; Gibbard, 1994), and both of the studies evaluating outcomes from the Hanen parent-training program yielded significant results (Girolametto et al., 1995, 1996). In addition, there was evidence of a two-way transfer of training in syntax to

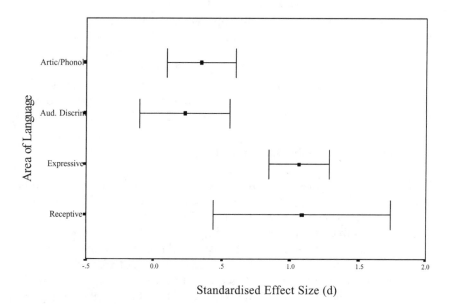

FIG. 18.1. Mean effect sizes from each language domain (with 95% confidence intervals) based on 109 effect sizes.

phonology and vice versa (Methany & Panagos, 1978), although one short-term intensive parent-administered program failed to show any effects of generalization from auditory training to improved articulation (Shelton et al., 1978, Study 1). However, only one of the studies (Lancaster, 1991) provided any information about normalization of subjects following treatment: Six of the subjects in her treatment groups in total showed some degree of normalization of their posttest scores.

As in the case of the RCTs, the results from studies utilizing quasi-experimental designs reveal statistically significant treatment outcomes (p < .05 or better) for 10 of the 12 studies, with substantial treatment effects in a further two that did not report any statistical analysis. Significant outcomes were observed in all six of the areas of language in which intervention took place. As before, the only nonsignificant finding was that of Shelton et al. (1978, Study 2), where the authors again found that auditory training did not generalize to improvements in the target sound production of children with problems in articulation and phonology. Parent-administered treatment was effective in three of four cases and, where a direct comparison was possible, resulted in outcomes that did not differ from those of direct treatment.

Treatment for Disorders of Articulation and Phonology

Four RCT and two quasi-experimental designs yielded 18 standardized effect sizes for outcomes following intervention for problems in articulation and/or phonology (see Table 18.2). Table 18.3 provides a summary of the results from both norm-referenced outcome measures and criterion-referenced measures. However, further evidence is provided by studies using criterion-referenced measures. Effect sizes are available from seven studies (four RCTs and three quasi-experimental designs), and the direct/indirect treatment variable is not confounded with study design.

Treatment for Expressive Language Disorders

Six RCT and eight quasi-experimental designs yielded outcomes for intervention in expressive language. The results are summarized in Table 18.2. The data indicate a strong statistically significant treatment effect, indicating that the subjects on average made progress of around one standard deviation on norm-referenced tests. For a child scoring at the 5th percentile on a standardized test with a standard deviation of 15, progress of the order of one standard deviation as a result of intervention would represent a shift to the 25th percentile (i.e., to within the normal range).

The results from the analysis of the effect sizes based on the criterion-referenced scores reveal a similar picture, with no difference between the

TABLE 18.3
Summary of Effect Sizes by Language Area and by Direct/Indirect Treatment

	Norm-Referenced Measures (and 95% Confidence Intervals)				Criterion-Referenced Measures (and 95% Confidence Intervals)			
	N	Direct	N	Indirect	N	Direct	N	Indirect
Articulation/ phonology	2	+1.11* (+.46/+1.77)	2	0.20 (−0.44/+0.83)	3	+0.94* (+0.37/+1.52)	4	−0.02 (−0.52/+0.47)
Expressive	5	+0.65* (+.23/+1.10)	9	+1.08* (+0.83/+1.34)	4	+1.11* (+0.58/+1.63)	5	+1.16* (+0.75/+1.56)
Receptive	2	−0.02 (−0.66/+0.63)	5	+1.43* (+1.09/+1.77)	N/A	N/A	N/A	N/A

N refers to the number of studies which contributed an effect size.
*Statistically significant results ($p < .05$).

two groups [Qb(1) = 0.021, p = .88). Although there is no significant difference between the two groups in terms of effect size for interventions in expressive language, the overall results indicate that indirect parent-administered treatment is at least as effective as direct clinical treatment in this area.

Treatment for Receptive Language Disorders

Two RCTs and four quasi-experimental designs yielded effect sizes for the effects of intervention on receptive language outcome measures. The results (see Table 18.2) indicate a significant difference between indirect and direct treatment, with indirect treatment resulting in highly significant effects of almost one-and-a-half standard deviations. However, caution is again required on account of the small number of studies and because of the marked heterogeneity in the sample of indirect treatment studies. Furthermore, one would need to be careful in assuming that these children had primary receptive difficulties. In fact these data came from studies where the primary difficulty was an expressive or expressive/receptive difficulty.

Treatment for Disorders Associated With Difficulties in Auditory Discrimination, Listening, and Phoneme Awareness

Three quasi-experimental studies were carried out in the broad area of auditory discrimination/listening skills (Table 18.2). The two studies of parent-administered training in listening skills did not produce successful outcomes (Shelton et al., 1978, Studies 1 and 2), but the subjects who participated in the Warrick et al. (1993) phoneme training program made significant gains (d = +0.81, p < .05).

Direct Versus Indirect Treatment

One of the most interesting axes through the data was the relative effects of direct and indirect intervention[2] (see Table 18.3). The results reveal the effectiveness of direct and indirect treatment approaches for expressive language and receptive language across both norm- and criterion-referenced measures. However, only direct treatment was effective in the case of articulation/phonology, although the small number of studies in this area and the use of nonstandard treatment approaches in the indirect treatment condition should be noted.

---

[2]*Direct* refers to intervention provided directly to the child by the speech and language therapist. *Indirect* refers to intervention provided by the parent under the guidance of the speech and language therapist. In the studies reviewed here, it does not mean intervention provided by a teacher or learning support staff.

CONCLUSIONS AND DISCUSSION

Although these findings provide overall support for the effectiveness of intervention, the relatively small number of studies should be noted, particularly in the case of direct treatment for articulation/phonology and receptive language problems. Despite this the effect sizes are impressive. Recall that an effect size of 1.00 on a norm-referenced test represents a level of progress equivalent to that from the 5th to the 25th percentile—a considerable degree of normalization.

The results from the controlled studies here are comparable to those reported by Nye, Foster, and Seaman (1987) when reviewing a larger number of studies across a wider range of study design and study quality. Nye et al. found an average effect size of +1.42 from 23 effect sizes for outcomes in syntax and an average effect size of +0.65 for comprehension from 13 effect sizes. Shonkoff and Hauser-Cram (1987) also reported an average effect size of +1.17 for language outcomes from 31 studies of intervention with disabled children.

However, the findings are somewhat higher than the estimates reported by Casto and Mastropieri (1986; an average effect size of +0.67 for language in a meta-analysis of the outcomes from 37 early intervention programs for a broad range of handicapped preschool children) and by Arnold, Myette, and Casto (1986; an average effect size of +0.59 from 30 studies). However, these latter results are difficult to interpret because: (a) effect sizes are based on a wide range of measures, including IQ; and (b) factors such as severity of the handicapping condition are confounded with the type of intervention program and factors such as the age of the child. The results from the meta-analysis carried out on posttest scores from the reviewed studies confirm that intervention can be effective for problems in articulation/phonology, expressive language, and receptive language. The inclusion criteria for the review were stringent. As a result, there were too few studies to synthesize the findings from treatment of problems in auditory discrimination and phoneme awareness, but a training program in the latter area generalized to progress in reading with gains that were evident a year later (Warrick et al., 1993).

The strongest and most consistent evidence for effectiveness comes from the intervention studies in expressive language as the higher number of studies involved in the analysis adds to the reliability and generality of the findings. Overall, 10 of the studies with RCT/quasi-experimental designs involved children with specific expressive language delays, 7 involved children with specific articulation/phonological problems, and only 5 involved children with mixed receptive/expressive delay. Although the original studies report significant gains in these areas, it was not possible to compare the outcomes directly across subgroups because of the small number of subjects and the presence of confounding variables. In addition, behavior difficulties in particular appeared to be underspecified in the present sample. Only Girolametto et al. (1995) reported a reduction in acting-out behavior in a small experimental group of eight children following language intervention.

It would be reasonable, given the care with which the authors of these studies sought to reduce bias, to suggest that these findings are pointing toward a real understanding about the malleability of children's language development. If this is the case, what does it tell us about language development in young children—that it is apparently so malleable given appropriately structured input, but not with the type of stimulation which children normally receive? Is it that the children are really learning new language skills, that the trajectory of their language learning is changing? If this is the case, what does this tell us about more formalistic, modular accounts of the language learning process? It is difficult to be clear about this at this stage, but it may be that the language learning process is insufficiently canalized in these children (Locke, 1993) and it is the source of their difficulties, which effectively creates opportunities for change in the language-impaired child that has begun to recede in the child with normally developing language. If this is the case, it might be reasonable to expect there to be qualitative differences in their psycholinguistic systems after intervention. The common practice of using standardized procedures as outcome measures in the studies cited makes this difficult to establish. Alternatively it may be that the intervention process does not teach them language skills at all, but simply re-orientates the child to the language system to which he or she is exposed and that reorientation effectively provides a kick start to the language learning process, changing the child's developmental trajectory. If this is the case, one might expect changes for these children to be long term. Finally, it is possible that this relatively small amount of input simply teaches the child short-term skills that make it possible to respond effectively to standardized tests of language. If so then one might expect changes to fade with time. Given the lack of careful follow-up data from most of these intervention studies, it is difficult to be clear which explanation best fits the data at this stage.

These studies do not directly address the issue of the diagnosis and classification of language impairment, and any extrapolations must be treated with care. However, there does appear to be a good case for representing our current understanding of intervention related to expressive language difficulties as a first-step diagnostic of the type postulated by Vellutino and colleagues (1996) in relation to reading disabilities. The relatively high effect sizes together with the relatively narrow variance in the results suggests that intervention is consistently targeting the correct skills. The same case could be made for the use of direct speech and language intervention for phonological disabilities. The case for defining a receptive language disorder in this way is more complex because the intervention studies that report gains in this area do so for children who were, for the most part, identified because they also had expressive language difficulties. They were not, in the main, children with severe expressive/receptive difficulties, and the results should not be taken to mean that receptive difficulties can be as easily treated as expressive difficulties. Similarly the lack of data related to intervention for pragmatic disorders would suggest that we are a long way from defining what we mean by this term.

The result of this analysis is a bottom–up, pragmatically driven model of classification. Inevitably it is full of gaps because it is so dependent on the development of a relevant good quality intervention literature. Gradually this is emerging, and every new paper will shed light on areas not covered here. Every new intervention will potentially target new subcategories of language disability and over time treatment and description will coalesce. There is a case for building intervention in as part of the triangulation of case definition. As new conditions are identified, it should be possible to establish whether they are truly new in the sense that they warrant a new intervention or whether they are marginal modifications of what we know already. The dearth of data about pragmatic and receptive language impairments suggests we are a long way from defining this group of conditions.

Could the intervention-focused approach do away with other models of classification? Probably not because, in the final analysis, broad-band interventions combining more than one feature are likely to be the most effective for the greatest number of children. The breadth that provides the range of effectiveness also makes the mapping of intervention onto condition imprecise. Perhaps it is more appropriate to see intervention as the first step, effectively a dynamic assessment that places children in a small number of clinical groups on the basis of their response to intervention. Increasingly sophisticated ways to measure language development have led to increasingly subtle subdivisions of language disorders. Which approach provides the most information about the children? Ostensibly the more subtle levels of classification do just this. However, it is those same methods of providing fine cuts within the language system that are likely to prove most changeable across time. As new methods of assessment arise and old techniques become obsolete, the more refined systems of classification will change. By contrast, effects from intervention may provide a more consistent model of classification. Broad approaches to intervention—for example, milieu treatments incorporating direct and indirect methods—can consistently be shown to impact on language learning for children with particular types of difficulties.

Finally, of course, the nirvana of classification is the linking of phenotype and genotype. It is tempting to assume that it will be possible to identify specific subclassifications of language impairment with genotypic manifestations. The limited evidence that we have to date in this area suggests that, although the level of genetic involvement in language impairment may be high, the same probably does not go for the level of genetic specificity. In the end, there may be relatively crude genetic markers that may be able to disambiguate speech disorders from grammatical disorders from pragmatic disorders. If this proves true, it may be that the rather broad clinical groupings arising out of the intervention studies reported here will have long-term validity as clinical and diagnostic constructs. It may be recognized that the refinements that those involved in classification seek may appear more context dependent than the results of intervention studies.

The weakness of this type of analysis is that there are many children about whom we effectively know little because we have little idea of how to intervene to help them. This is true, but it does reflect the current state of science in this area. I would argue that it is better to put it this way than to impose the latest, somewhat arbitrary, classification system and convey an undue level of certainty about the condition to parents and educationalists. It is better to say we are not sure than claim we *are* on the basis of tentative data and then risk parents being bamboozled by different certainties from different professionals.

I would argue that the analysis that I am presenting, although retrospective by its nature, is forward looking in that it identifies the gaps that need to be filled in our understanding. Without an attempt to identify those gaps, we are in danger of reinventing the wheel all the time, restricting ourselves to specific research paradigms.

ACKNOWLEDGMENTS

The research reported in this chapter was supported by a grant from the National Health Service Centre for Review Dissemination, University of York, United Kingdom. Particular thanks go to Jim Boyle from the Department of Psychology, University of Strathclyde, for the meta-analysis presented here and for the many discussions related to it. Thanks also go to Christopher Norris, Dr. Bill Cheyne, and Tony Gurney for their assistance.

REFERENCES

Almost, D., & Rosenbaum, P. (1998). Effectiveness of speech intervention for phonological disorders: A randomized controlled trial. *Developmental Medicine and Child Neurology, 40*, 319–352.

Arnold, K. S., Myette, B. M., & Casto, G. (1986). Relationships of language intervention efficacy to certain subject characteristics in mentally retarded preschool children: A meta-analysis. *Education and Training of the Mentally Retarded*, 108–116.

Casto, G., & Mastropieri, M. A. (1986). The effectiveness of early intervention programs: A metanalysis. *Exceptional Children, 52*, 417–424.

Conant, S., Budoff, M., Hecht, B., & Morse, R. (1984). Language intervention: A pragmatic approach. *Journal of Autism and Developmental Disorders, 14*(3), 301–317.

Crombie, I. K., & Davies, H. T. O. (1996). *Research in health care: Design, conduct and interpretation of health services research*. Chichester: Wiley.

Fey, M. E., Cleave, P. L., Long, S. H., & Hughes, D. L. (1993). Two approaches to the facilitation of grammar in children with language impairment: An experimental evaluation. *Journal of Speech and Hearing Research, 36*, 141–157.

Fey, M. E., Cleave, P. L., Ravida, A. I., Long, S. H., Dejmal, A. E., & Easton, D. L. (1994). Effects of grammar facilitation on the phonological performance of children with speech and language impairments. *Journal of Speech and Hearing Research, 37*, 594–607.

Gibbard, D. (1994). Parental-based intervention with pre-school language-delayed children. *European Journal of Disorders of Communication, 29*(2), 131–150. (Study 1 and Study 2)

Girolametto, L., Pearce, P. S., & Weitzman, E. (1995). The effects of focused stimulation for promoting vocabulary in young children with delays: A pilot study. *Journal of Children's Communication Development, 17*(2), 39–49.

Girolametto, L., Pearce, P. S., & Weitzman, E. (1996). Interactive focused stimulation for toddlers with expressive vocabulary delays. *Journal of Speech and Hearing Research, 39*(6), 1274–1283.

Guralnick, M. J. (1988). Efficacy in early childhood intervention programs. In S. J. Odom & M. B. Karnes (Eds.), *Early intervention for infants and children with handicaps*. Baltimore, MD: Paul H. Brookes.

Hedges, L. V., & Olkin, I. (1985). *Statistical methods for meta-analysis*. London: Academic Press.

Lancaster, G. (1991). *The effectiveness of parent administered input training for children with phonological training for children with phonological disorders*. Unpublished master's thesis, City University, London, England.

Law, J. (1997). Evaluating intervention for language impaired children: A review of the literature. *European Journal of Disorders of Communication, 32*, 1–14.

Law, J., Boyle, J., Harris, F., & Harkness, A. (1998). Screening for speech and language delay: A systematic review of the literature. *Health Technology Assessment, 2*(9), 1–184.

Law, J., Boyle, J., Harris, F., Harkness, A., & Nye, C. (2000). The relationship between the natural history and prevalence of primary speech and language delays: Findings from a systematic review of the literature. *International Journal of Language and Communication Disorders, 35*(2), 165–188.

Leonard, L. (1987). Is specific language impairment a useful construct? In S. Rosenberg (Ed.), *Advances in applied psycholinguistics* (Vol. 1, pp. 1–30). Cambridge, England: Cambridge University Press.

Lipsey, M. W. (1994). Identifying potentially interesting variables and analysis opportunities. In H. Cooper & L. Hedges (Eds.), *Handbook of research synthesis*. London: Russell Sage Foundation.

Locke, J. (1993). *The child's path to spoken language*. London: Harvard Medical Press.

Matheny, N., & Panagos, J. M. (1978). Comparing the effects of articulation and syntax programs on syntax and articulation improvement. *Language, Speech and Hearing Services in Schools, 9*, 57–61.

McDade, A., & McCartan, P. A. (1996). *"Partnership with parents": A pilot study*. Unpublished manuscript.

McLean, L. K., & Woods Cripe, J, W. (1997). The effectiveness of early intervention for children with communication disorders. In M. J. Guralnick (Ed.), *The effectiveness of early intervention*. Baltimore, MD: Paul H. Brookes.

Nye, C., Foster, S. H., & Seaman, D. (1987). Effectiveness of language intervention with the language/learning disabled. *Journal of Speech and Hearing Disorders, 52*, 348–357.

Olswang, L. B., & Bain, B. A. (1991). Intervention issues for toddlers with specific language impairment. *Topics in Language Disorders, 11*(4), 69–86.

Pinker, S. (1994). *The language instinct: The new science of language and mind.* Harmondsworth: Penguin.

Reid, J., Donaldson, M. L., Howell, J., Dean, E. C., & Grieve, R. (1996). The effectiveness of therapy for child phonological disorder: The Metaphon Approach. In M. Aldridge (Ed.), *Child language* (pp. 165–175). Clevedon Avon: Multilingual Matters.

Rescorla, L., & Schwartz, E. (1990). Outcome of toddlers with specific language delay. *Applied Psycholinguistics, 11*(4), 393–407.

Rosenthal, R. (1994). Parametric measures of effect size. In H. Cooper & L. Hedges (Eds.), *Handbook of research synthesis.* London: Russell Sage Foundation.

Schwartz, R. G., Chapman, K., Terrell, B. Y., Prelock, P., & Rowan, L. (1985). Facilitating word combination in language-impaired children through discourse structure. *Journal of Speech and Hearing Disorders, 50*, 31–39.

Shelton, R. L., Johnson, A. F., Ruscello, D. M., & Arndt, W. B. (1978). Assessment of parent-administered listening training for preschool children with articulation deficits. *Journal of Speech and Hearing Disorders, 43*(2), 242–254. (Study 1 and Study 2)

Snyder-McLean, L., & McLean, J. (1987). Children with language and communication disorders. In M. J. Guralnick & F. C. Bennett (Eds.), *The effectiveness of early intervention.* New York: Academic Press.

Stevenson, P., Bax, M., & Stevenson, J. (1982). The evaluation of home-based speech therapy for language delayed preschool children in an inner city area. *British Journal of Disorders of Communication, 17*(3), 141–148.

Thal, D. J., & Tobias, S. (1992). Communicative gestures in children with delayed onset of oral expressive vocabulary. *Journal of Speech and Hearing Research, 35*, 1281–1289.

Vellutino, F. R., Scanlon, D. M., Sipay, E. R., Small, S. G., Chen, R., Pratt, A., & Denckla, M. B. (1996). Cognitive profiles of difficult-to-remediate and readily remediated poor readers: Early intervention as a vehicle for distinguishing between cognitive and experiental deficits as basic causes of specific reading disability. *Educational Psychology, 4*, 601–638.

Ward, S. (1984). *Validation of a treatment method.* 2nd Conference of the Comite Permanente de Liaison des Othophonistes-Logopedes del'UE [CPLOL], Antwerp. (Group 1 and Group 2)

Zwart, E. W. (1997). *Effectiveness of language intervention with language impaired children: A literature review.* The Institute of Phoniatrics, Utrecht University.

APPENDIX A

Group Design Studies ($N = 22^3$) Included in the Systematic Review

1. Almost, D., & Rosenbaum, P. (1998). Effectiveness of speech intervention for phonological disorders: A randomized controlled trial. *Developmental Medicine and Child Neurology, 40*, 319–352.

2. Conant, S., Budoff, M., Hecht, B., & Morse, R. (1984). Language intervention: A pragmatic approach. *Journal of Autism and Developmental Disorders, 14*(3), 301–317.

---

[3]Three studies include two data sets each (Gibbard, Shelton, and Ward).

3. Fey, M. E., Cleave, P. L., Long, S. H., & Hughes, D. L. (1993). Two approaches to the facilitation of grammar in children with language impairment: An experimental evaluation. *Journal of Speech and Hearing Research, 36*, 141–157.

4. Fey, M. E., Cleave, P. L., Ravida, A. I., Long, S. H., Dejmal, A. E., & Easton, D. L. (1994). Effects of grammar facilitation on the phonological performance of children with speech and language impairments. *Journal of Speech and Hearing Research, 37*, 594–607.

5. Gibbard, D. (1994). Parental-based intervention with pre-school language-delayed children. *European Journal of Disorders of Communication, 29*(2), 131–150. (Studies 1 and 2)

6. Girolametto, L., Pearce, P. S., & Weitzman, E. (1995). The effects of focused stimulation for promoting vocabulary in young children with delays: A pilot study. *Journal of Children's Communication Development, 17*(2), 39–49.

7. Girolametto, L., Pearce, P. S., & Weitzman, E. (1996). Interactive focused stimulation for toddlers with expressive vocabulary delays. *Journal of Speech and Hearing Research, 39*(6), 1274–1283.

8. Lancaster, G. (1991). *The effectiveness of parent administered input training for children with phonological training for children with phonological disorders.* Unpublished master's thesis, City University, London, United Kingdom.

9. Matheny, N., & Panagos, J. M. (1978). Comparing the effects of articulation and syntax programs on syntax and articulation improvement. *Language, Speech and Hearing Services in Schools, 9*, 57–61.

10. McDade, A., & McCartan, P. A. (1996). *"Partnership with parents": A pilot study.* Unpublished manuscript.

11. Reid, J., Donaldson, M. L., Howell, J., Dean, E. C., & Grieve, R. (1996). The effectiveness of therapy for child phonological disorder: The metaphon approach. In M. Aldridge (Ed.), *Child language* (pp. 165–175). Clevedon Avon: Multilingual Matters.

12. Schwartz, R. G., Chapman, K., Terrell, B. Y., Prelock, P., & Rowan, L. (1985). Facilitating word combination in language-impaired children through discourse structure. *Journal of Speech and Hearing Disorders, 50*, 31–39.

13. Shelton, R. L., Johnson, A. F., Ruscello, D. M., & Arndt, W. B. (1978). Assessment of parent-administered listening training for preschool children with articulation deficits. *Journal of Speech and Hearing Disorders, 43*(2), 242–254. (Studies 1 and 2)

14. Stevenson, P., Bax, M., & Stevenson, J. (1982). The evaluation of home-based speech therapy for language delayed preschool children in an inner city area. *British Journal of Disorders of Communication, 17*(3), 141–148.

15. Ward, S. (1984). *Validation of a treatment method.* Second Conference of the Comite Permanente de Liaison des Othophonistes-Logopedes del'UE [CPLOL], Antwerp. (Groups 1 and 2)

16. Warrick, N., Rubin, H., & Rowe-Walsh, S. (1993). Phoneme awareness in language-delayed children: Comparative studies and intervention. *Annals of Dyslexia, 43*, 153–173.

17. Whitehurst, G. J., Fischel, J. E., Lonigan, C. J., Valdez-Menchaca, M. C., Arnold, D. S., & Smith, M. (1991). Treatment or early expressive language delay: If, when, and how. *Topics in Language Dis.orders, 11*(4), 55–68.

18. Wilcox, M. J., & Leonard, L. B. (1978). Experimental acquisition of Wh-questions in language-disordered children. *Journal of Speech and Hearing Research, 21*, 220–239.

19. Zwitman, D. H., & Sonderman, J. C. (1979). A syntax program designed to present base linguistic structures to language-disordered children. *Journal of Communication Disorders, 12*(4), 323–335.

Author Index

Subject Index

A

Abstract features, 268
Accuracy, 216–218, 223
Acoustic information, 117, 122
Acoustic rate processing, 118
Activation, 137–138, 213–214
Activation rates, 149
Adaptive resonance theory, *see* ARTPHONE model
ADD, *see* Attention deficit disorder
Additive approach, 330
ADHD, *see* Attention deficit hyperactivity disorder
Adjectives
  Hebrew
    characterization, 242
    properties and derivation, 244
    study, 245–248
    representing, 239–242
Adjuncts, 225
Age
  developmental language disorders, 12, 159–160, 164
  Dutch study of language impairment, 273

morpheme substitution in Norwegian, 265
morphological errors in story telling, 45, 47
pragmatic disabilities, 295, 296
tags question task, 51, 54
Agnosia, 103
Agreement errors, 274–276, 277, *see also* Errors
American Speech, Language, and Hearing Association (ASHA), 191
Analysis of variation (ANOVA), 248, 249, 406
Analytic expression, 252
ANOVA, *see* Analysis of variance
Aphasia, 103, 333, 384–385, *see also* Landau–Kleffner syndrome
Argument structure, 224–225, 226
Articulation, 187, 195, 408, 409
Articulation errors, 187, *see also* Errors
Articulatory dyspraxia, 187
ARTPHONE model, 72, 73–74, 75, 77–83
ASHA, *see* American Speech, Language, and Hearing Association
Assessment, 3, 12–13, 177–179
At-risk children, *see* Children, at-risk
At-risk infants, *see* Infants, at-risk